The Original San Francisco

GIANTS

The Giants of '58

by Steve Bitker

SP
SPORTS
PUBLISHING
INC.

www.SportsPublishingInc.com

Interior design: Michelle R. Dressen
Production Coordinator: Kenneth J. O'Brien
Cover design: Julie L. Denzer and Kenneth J. O'Brien

Front cover photo courtesy of the San Francisco Giants
Back cover photo courtesy of the San Francisco History Center,
San Francisco Public Library
Ticket stub photo courtesy of Steve Bitker

ISBN: 1-58261-335-4

Sports Publishing Inc.
www.SportsPublishingInc.com

Printed in the United States.

To Mom and Dad, for taking me to Seals Stadium when I was five . . .
And to the '58 Giants, for cementing a relationship with the national pastime.

Table of Contents

Foreword vii

Acknowledgments x

Introduction xi

PART ONE: The Move to San Francisco, Seals Stadium and The 1958 Pennant Race 1

TOPPS PRESENTS: THE '58 SF GIANTS 47

PART TWO: The Ballplayers 51

Bill Rigney (manager) 51
Felipe Alou 66
Hank Sauer 77
Jim Davenport 83
Mike McCormick 87
Orlando Cepeda 101
Ruben Gomez 107
Valmy Thomas 115
Whitey Lockman 118
Leon Wagner 124
Willie Kirkland 133
Ed Bressoud 146
Stu Miller 155
Paul Giel 161
Al Worthington 167
Daryl Spencer 170
Marv Grissom 180
Willie Mays 183
Pete Burnside 199
Bob Speake 202
Dom Zanni 205
Ray Crone 207
Joe Shipley 209
Jim Constable 210
Bill White 212
John Antonelli 218
Jackie Brandt 225
Don Johnson 228
Jim King 232
Don Taussig 234
Ramon Monzant 235
Nick Testa 237
Andre Rodgers 239
Bob Schmidt 239
John Fitzgerald 240
Herman Franks (coach) 240
Wes Westrum (coach) 242

In Memory Of:

Ray Jablonski 246
Danny O'Connell 246
Curt Barclay 247
Gordon Jones 247
Jim Finigan 248
Salty Parker (coach) 248

PART THREE: Behind the Scenes 249

Bob Stevens 249
Lon Simmons 254
Mike Murphy 260
Roy McKercher 263

Epilogue 267

Bibliography 269

Appendix A 271

Appendix B 274

Appendix C 276

Appendix D 286

Team Photo 300

Endorsements 300

FOREWORD
by Peter Magowan

I remember the opening of the Giants' 1958 season as if it were yesterday. I was 16 at the time, a sophomore at Groton School in Groton, Massachusetts. I had just finished baseball practice and I went up to my room and tried to catch Les Keiter's reconstructed broadcast of the game. It was difficult to hear, through all the static, as I was trying to pick up the New York station. But for almost three hours I listened to that game, and no one could have been more pleased with the outcome–an 8-0 shutout–than me.

I had been a Giants fan since June 1950. My father took my brother and me to my first game–a night game at the venerable Polo Grounds–against the Phillies. The moment I saw the field for the first time I was hooked. I must have gone to at least 10 games that first year, and then a lot more in 1951. And what I didn't see I listened to. What a team to fall in love with! The Giants of 1950 were getting better. They got hot at the end and finished third, and expectations were high for 1951. We had Alvin Dark and Eddie Stanky up the middle, Whitey Lockman at first; the great Monte Irvin in left; a good hitter, Don Mueller, in right; and a tremendous clutch hitter, Bobby Thomson, in center. Wes Westrum was a fine defensive catcher and the pitching staff was strong, too: Sal Maglie, Larry Jansen, Jim Hearn, Dave Koslo.

And then in mid-May we brought up Willie Mays. I remember going to a night game in late June. Like thousands of other fans I got there early, just to see Willie. He was in deep center field, throwing balls to third base. Dark was at the bag, and he held out his glove knee-high over the bag. And Willie threw about 10 in a row–from about 400 feet away–that landed on one bounce right in Alvin's glove. He never had to move the glove!

I'm sure everybody knows about that 1951 season. How the Giants got off to a terrible start, at one point losing 11 in a row. How Willie went 0-for-12 before getting his first hit, a mammoth home run against Warren Spahn. How the Giants found themselves 13 1/2 games out on August 11th. And how they managed to catch their hated rivals, the Dodgers, on the last day of the season, forcing a three-game series to decide the pennant. Ah, the hated Dodgers. One of the greatest teams ever put together: Campanella, Hodges, Robinson, Reese, Cox, Pafko, Snider, Furillo. Don Newcombe and Carl Erskine and Preacher Roe. How great they were–and how I *despised* them. What *despair* to lose to them. And what *joy* to beat them.

Well, you all know the outcome of that series. The Giants won the first game, 3-1. The crucial hit was a home run by Bobby Thomson. They lost the next game, 10-0. Then the decider. How I *wished* I could have been there. But I was in school that gray Wednesday. The Giants were losing, 4-1, in the bottom of the ninth. I was in study class–a nine-year-old fifth-grader who absolutely could not concentrate on his homework. Our class had persuaded the teacher to let us listen to the game. Half of us were Giants fans and the other half were for the Dodgers. So there were cheers and groans on every pitch.

Dark led off with a single, just past Gil Hodges' glove. Mueller followed with another single, again just past Hodges, who would have gloved it *easily* if he had not held Dark close to the bag. Then our best clutch hitter, Irvin, was up. We were *crazed* with hope. But Irvin popped out. *Groans*. Then Lockman doubled, scoring Dark and sending Mueller to third. *Delay*. Mueller was hurt and had to be carried off the field. The exhausted Newcombe was removed and Ralph Branca came in. Bobby Thomson at the plate, Willie Mays on deck. I knew they would walk Thomson, since he had hit Branca well all year, and first base was open. And why not put the pressure on the rookie? But they pitched to him. A single would tie it. Strike one. And then the next pitch, and we all know what happened. In the immortal words of Russ Hodges:

"It's a long drive, it's gonna be, I believe—the Giants win the pennant! The Giants win the pennant! The Giants win the pennant! The Giants win the pennant! Bobby Thomson hit it into the lower deck of the left field stands. The Giants win the pennant, and they're going crazy! They're going crazy! Heeeeeeeeeeoooooooooo!!!"

They say that everybody has a moment in life when he can remember every last detail–see every part of it as if it were a photograph, when no moment is ever forgotten. For most people I know it is President Kennedy's death. For me it is "the shot heard 'round the world." Maybe it is a little strange for the deciding moment in your life to occur when you are nine years old. But I have never been able to trade that moment for any other.

I came home later that day. And then my father walked through the door, a big smile on his face. "Guess where I've been?" he asked. And somehow I just knew. He said, "I went to the game with three others from work. And the other three all left at the beginning of the bottom of the ninth. You remember this, Peter, as long as you live. It's never over till it's over." It's a lesson I've never forgotten. Then he asked, "Would you like to go to the World Series tomorrow?" I had never missed a day of school in my life. I just could not believe this invitation. My first World Series–and the *Giants* in it. We would be playing the most famous team in baseball, the New York Yankees. Well, the next day somehow came. The only pitcher we had who wasn't worn out was Dave Koslo. He was the last guy anybody expected to pitch. But pitch he did–magnificently–and we beat the Yanks, 5-1. Monte Irvin stole home. Dark hit a home run. And I was there.

We lost the series, but after beating the Dodgers the way we did, that was OK. We finished second to the Dodgers in 1952. Willie was in the army then, and Irvin was hurt. We were just lousy in '53. The hated Dodgers won again. Before the '54 season we traded my favorite ballplayer, Bobby Thomson, to the Braves for Johnny Antonelli. And best of all, Willie was now back from the Army. We beat the Dodgers and won the pennant. Now we had Davey Williams at second and Hank Thompson at third, but it was still basically the team I had fallen in love with that June night in 1950. And it was still the same great, hated Dodger team. And then we surprised everybody and beat the Indians, who had won 111 games (more than any other club in the history of baseball) in the series. We didn't just beat them–we swept them in four straight. The Giants were the *World Champions*. They haven't been since.

In most of those years in the late 1940s and early 1950s, if you were the champion of New York you were the champion of baseball. The Dodgers won the National League in 1947, '49, '52, '53 and '55. They finished second by two games in 1950, and by one in '51. The Giants won in 1951 and '54. The Yankees won in 1947, '49, '50, '51, '52, '53 and '55. So, *two of the three* New York teams played each other in the World Series in 1947, '49, '51, '52, '53 and '55. What a time for a kid who loved baseball to live in New York. You could get to any one of the three ballparks for a 10-cent subway ride.

Well, just three years after that World Series triumph–the second-best moment in my young life–the Giants were *gone*. So were the Dodgers. New York now had only one team. I just could not believe it. How could anybody take my Giants away from me? To think that the saddest day would come so soon after the happiest–I had a lot of difficulty in dealing with this loss. I was inconsolable. Life seemed so sad and unfair. But then a miracle happened. My father was suddenly given a new job opportunity. Our family was going to leave New York, where I had lived my entire life. We were going to San Francisco, of all places. Which is *exactly* where the Giants were going, too.

So on that April 1958 day, when I came off the practice field to turn on my radio, my Giants were still accessible to me. A New York radio station would be recreating every one of their games. And I was going to listen to every one that I could–until school got out. Then I would be able to *see* them. The second game that year was a night game. The games came in much clearer at night. Because of the time difference it didn't come on the air until 11:30. Our "lights out" policy at school was 10 p.m. Somehow I had to try to stay awake until 11:30. Then the game would go on until about 2 a.m., and naturally I would listen until the end because, as my father had taught me, the game is never over till it's over.

One nice May day I got another good lesson on the wisdom of that credo. The Giants were trailing the Pirates, 11-1, in the bottom of the ninth. We scored nine runs and loaded the bases, before Don Taussig popped up to end the game. *Never over till it's over*. I would say that to my friends, all of whom knew about my crazy love affair with my Giants.

They were, by now, a very different team from the one I had grown up with. No more

Dark, Thomson, Maglie, Irvin, Mueller, Westrum, Jansen, Hearn, Koslo. We still had other connections to our glorious New York past. The uniforms had hardly changed at all–*SF* on the hat instead of *NY*. And our manager was still Bill Rigney. We still had Ruben Gomez and Antonelli and Lockman, though he was now on his last legs. And, of course, we still had Willie–not only the best player in the game but, many would say, the best player the game ever had. And we had surrounded him with maybe the greatest combination of quantity and quality rookies ever assembled. Four were in our regular lineup: Jim Davenport, Bob Schmidt, Orlando Cepeda and Willie Kirkland. And before 1959 was over we had three more: Felipe Alou, Leon Wagner and Willie McCovey. The Giants were young and exciting. And I was able to be a part of it–first through my radio, and then later, when school was out, at Seals Stadium.

I've already talked a bit about the radio. It was my most important possession. I concealed it very well. And no one knew my secret. I couldn't afford to tell anybody because radios were not allowed at Groton. It was a small transistor. It fit very nicely under my pillow at night. I hid it in the pillow case. I spent my allowance on batteries. I said before that Les Keiter would recreate the games from New York. When I heard that first game [in '58] I thought it was a live broadcast. I groaned when I heard the sharp crack of the bat–Snider was up with men on base. Then relieved (though surprised) that the Duke had hit what was described as a weak tap back to the pitcher. No tap had ever sounded like that. Then Daryl Spencer came up. *Crack*! Les Keiter then described the first home run ever hit at Seals Stadium, and then came the first of Cepeda's 379. Well, that sure sounded like a home run. But after a while I caught on–the games were not being broadcast live. But that didn't make them any less real to me.

It seemed school would never get out in 1958. Finally June 15 came and I hopped on the first plane I could. It stopped in Chicago and a Catholic priest got on and sat next to me. I was in the midst of my *Sporting News* when he said, "That's my favorite magazine," and pulled out of his briefcase his copy of the very same issue. We became good friends (he was, of course, a Cubs fan).

I spent many happy days that summer at Seals Stadium. What a *jewel* of a ballpark. How much closer we could sit to the field than at the Polo Grounds. Everything was different–the city, the small ballpark, so many of the players. I have so many memories of those players: Valmy Thomas, Andre Rodgers, Ed Bressoud, Ray Jablonski, Jackie Brandt, and yet everything was the same as well. Russ Hodges was still the announcer, just as he had been in New York. Willie's cap would still fly off his head as he ran down yet another fly ball that no one else could get to. I was watching the Giants, watching the Giants play the hated Dodgers. I was doing what I most wanted to do.

I still am.

Peter A. Magowan
President and Managing General Partner
San Francisco Giants
San Francisco, California

ACKNOWLEDGMENTS

As anyone who has ever endeavored to write a book well knows, it is simply not possible without the invaluable assistance of many, many people.

My mother told me repeatedly, dating back to my high school years, that I had a book in me to write, that someday I would do it. Neither one of us knew what it would be about until the fall of 1993 when I sat down to breakfast with a friend and fellow would-be author Tim Liotta, who was working on a book of his own at the time about the late, great Brooklyn Dodger, Pete Reiser. Tim was truly inspiring, and as I told him how I fantasized writing a book about the '58 Giants, he sparked me to take on the project myself. He knew I had a passion for it and helped convince me that I could do it, that it had my name written all over it. Tim, you'll never realize how important your inspiration was. Thank you.

I'm particularly thankful to Mike Pearson of Sports Publishing Inc., who believed enough in my project to invest in it. Mike not only knows the publishing world, he's an old-time baseball buff who knows his '58 Giants. Special thanks also to Michelle Dressen, Lisa Peretz and Julie Denzer with Sports Publishing Inc. for working so closely with the manuscript and treating it (and me) with loving care and attention.

Peter Magowan, Pat Gallagher, Rebecca Nerland, Bob Rose, Dave Craig, Mike Sadek, Luis Rosa, Luis Torres and Jim Moorhead of the San Francisco Giants all provided logistical help and support. So did Doreen Alves of the Oakland Athletics. Dick Dobbins, the incomparable collector of Giants memorabilia, graciously opened the doors of his collection for me to peruse, and use. Thanks also to Missy Mikulecky with the Giants, John Curley and Gary Fong of the *San Francisco Chronicle*, Pat Akre with the San Francisco Public Library, and Darci Harrington from the National Baseball Hall of Fame Library in Cooperstown with assistance in securing vintage photographs.

Without the help of Katy Feeney, Victor Reichman and, again, Pat Gallagher, three of these interviews in particular may not have been possible. Thank you to Jim Gates and Tim Wiles at the National Baseball Hall of Fame Library who made me feel like a most welcome and valuable visitor and couldn't have been more helpful. Thanks also to Marty Lurie, Tom Stern, Bill Arnold, Lowell Cohn, Cynthia Wilbur, Rick Wilbur, Don Perata, Rich Muschell, and Len Hail. Each of you provided something special in the way of much-appreciated assistance.

Of course, a most sincere and heartfelt thanks to those members of the 1958 San Francisco Giants who took the time and trouble to sit down with me and open up their hearts and minds on the subject of baseball *and* on their lives in general. Needless to say, without your contributions, without your willingness to spend a half hour, an hour, often two and three hours with me, at absolutely no charge (aside from one notable exception), this project never would have gotten off the ground. Thank you all again, to Bill Rigney, Ruben Gomez, Valmy Thomas, Felipe Alou, Ed Bressoud, Orlando Cepeda, Jim Davenport, Willie Kirkland, Whitey Lockman, Willie Mays, Hank Sauer, Mike McCormick, Leon Wagner, Stu Miller, Daryl Spencer, Paul Giel, Marv Grissom, Al Worthington, Bill White, Pete Burnside, Bob Speake, Dom Zanni, Ray Crone, Jim Constable, Joe Shipley, Don Johnson, Jim King, Don Taussig, Jackie Brandt, John Antonelli, Ramon Monzant, Nick Testa, Herman Franks and Wes Westrum. And to Lon Simmons, Bob Stevens, Mike Murphy and Roy McKercher.

Finally, a million thanks to my next-door neighbor Bill Tom, who took me by the hand, introduced me to my first home computer, answered all my naive questions, answered many of them again and again, and basically turned a computer-illiterate person into a functioning semi-literate. Without you, Bill, I know not where I'd be right now. But I do know I wouldn't be nearly as far along as I am. Your generosity and patience will never be forgotten.

And last but not least, to my devoted wife Alice, and my loving daughters Mei-Ling and Janelle, whose support never wavered, I say thank you so much. With love.

Alameda, California

INTRODUCTION

 **IN 1958, DWIGHT EISENHOWER** was President of the United States, Richard Nixon was Vice-President and John Kennedy was a popular young Senator from Massachusetts. The National Aeronautics and Space Administration was established, as was the Federal Aviation Administration. The 12-year-old Tokyo Tsushin Kogyo Kabushiki Kaisha changed its name to Sony Corporation. Jimmy Stewart starred in Alfred Hitchcock's thriller *Vertigo* (filmed largely in San Francisco) and Jimmy Swaggart became a full-time preacher. Lawrence Harvey Zeigler (Larry King) was hired by a Miami radio station to host a four-hour morning show broadcast from a local restaurant, where he conducted impromptu interviews with both celebrities and diners. And in Bay City, Michigan, was born Madonna Louise Veronica Ciccone—now known the world over, simply, as Madonna.

The Bridge over the River Kwai was the top grossing film of 1958, a year that also featured box office winners *Peyton Place, Sayonara* and *South Pacific,* among others. Yet *Gigi* took Best Picture honors at the Academy Awards. *Gunsmoke* was the top-rated television show, followed by *Wagon Train* and *Have Gun Will Travel.* The top-rated song in '58 was *At the Hop,* by Danny & the Juniors. The best-selling fiction book was *Doctor Zhivago,* by Boris Pasternak. The top-selling non-fiction title was *Kids Say the Darnedest Things,* by Art Linkletter. And the Edsel became a full-fledged debacle and automotive laughingstock, only to be resuscitated decades later as a work of art. OK, that's debatable. But at least we can say it was resuscitated decades later as a priceless collectible.

Gaylord Perry, the first pitcher to win the Cy Young award in both the National and American Leagues, signed his first professional contract in 1958, with the San Francisco Giants. Ernie Banks won the first of his unprecedented back to back Most Valuable Player awards, and the Yankees won the World Series in seven games over the Milwaukee Braves. And Roy Campanella's

stellar career with the Dodgers came to a tragic end with a paralyzing car accident.

Bill Russell of the Boston Celtics won the first of his five Most Valuable Player awards in 1958, and the St. Louis Hawks won their first and only National Basketball Association title, in six games over the Boston Celtics. Arnold Palmer won the first of his four Masters championships at Augusta, Georgia, and Althea Gibson won both the Wimbledon and U.S. Open singles titles for the second straight year. The Baltimore Colts won the first overtime championship game in National Football League history, 23-17, over the New York Giants, on a short touchdown run by Alan Ameche, and Bear Bryant coached the first of his 25 straight winning seasons at the University of Alabama. The Montreal Canadians won their third consecutive National Hockey League Stanley Cup, in six games over the Boston Bruins, and Sugar Ray Robinson regained his middleweight boxing championship.

Unfortunately, the only one of these historic events I can recall is the Colts' overtime win over the Giants. I remember watching it on the black-and-white Zenith in our family room, about 30 miles down the road from San Francisco. After all, I was just 5 years old in 1958. However, I *vividly* remember the *original* San Francisco Giants—the Giants of '58.

My mother always told me as a child that if I devoted as much time, interest and energy to my schoolwork as I did to collecting and studying baseball cards and magazines, playing baseball, watching the Giants and reading about them in the morning paper, I would have straight A's. Years later, she would say that if I had applied myself to my schoolwork with the same sort of zest I did to baseball, I could have gone to the university of my choice and would probably be a lawyer or doctor today. Instead, I graduated from the University of California, at Berkeley, with a B average, and make a living as a sportscaster, play-by-play announcer and free-lance writer. I doubt I'll ever be rich, but I do enjoy my work.

My wife always tells me that if I would devote as much time, interest and energy to studying the business world as I do to sports, our family would be a whole lot better off financially. I have no doubt that she's right. However, as I am invariably quick to point out to her, it is with our family finances in mind that I watch all these games nowadays, because I have to pay the mortgage.

I remember my introduction to the wonderful game of baseball as if it were yesterday. Okay, I'm guilty of hyperbole. I remember it as if it were just a few years ago. That's the truth. My mother took my older brother and me to the local toy store in Woodside (near Stanford University), and bought us one shining pack each of baseball cards. They were a thing of beauty to my impressionable eyes—each pack of 10 cards, wrapped in cellophane, with the top card shining through. I picked the pack with Early Wynn of the White Sox on top, because his face was printed on a yellow background and yellow was my favorite color. Little did I realize then that my very first card would turn out to be an eventual Hall of Famer, a five-time 20-game winner with 300 wins.

Shortly thereafter, my parents took my brother and me to our first big league game, at Seals Stadium, near downtown San Francisco. Unfortunately, Seals was torn down after the '59 season because the Giants were moving a few miles down the freeway to Candlestick Park. Trading Seals for Candlestick should go down as the worst deal in San Francisco Giants history, although many would insist it was the Orlando Cepeda-for-Ray Sadecki trade in 1966. I would disagree, though. Sadecki pitched 23 complete games, with eight shutouts and a 2.80 earned run average, in his first two full seasons with the Giants. But Candlestick has been a colossal blunder from its inception, something few if any would argue with. Fans and players continue to pay for that mistake to this day.

My own personal memories of Seals Stadium are brief, but vivid. I remember walking into an auditorium-like building, holding my dad's hand tightly as we made our way through the dark and crowded corridor, before exiting through an open door to our right and seeing the most beautiful park I'd ever seen. Hell, it was the most beautiful *sight* I had ever seen, covered with glistening green grass and bright white bases, basking in sunshine. It was intimate, it was elegant, it was *regal* in my eyes, and now I was watching the same ballplayers on those cards I collected, performing in their clean white flannels. When I wasn't glued to the action on the field I was transfixed by the Hamm's Brewery's flashing mug high behind the stands in back of home plate. The glass would gradually fill with beer to its foam-covered top, flash on and off three times, then start all over again. That alone could keep this 5-year-old's attention, whenever there was a break on the diamond. Years later, I would discover that I wasn't the only one transfixed. The late Don Drysdale said he didn't remember much about losing the first big league game in West Coast history, but he did remember looking up at the big Hamm's beer glass on the brewery, and watching it fill up again and again. Drysdale said he was intrigued by it, and said after getting knocked out early in that historic opener, he could have *used* a cold beer out there.

When the games at Seals Stadium ended, the center field scoreboard would open magically, and fans were allowed to walk down to the field and across the grass out to the parking lot

Hamm's Brewery glass was memorable backdrop for fans and players alike at Seals Stadium. (SF Chronicle)

and the surrounding streets of the neighborhood. There were times, of course, when my folks parked closer to home plate than center field, but they understood the thrill their kids always got walking across their field of dreams, even if it occasionally meant doubling back on 16th Street, beyond the right field bleachers, to get to our car.

It's ironic that with more than 20 years of failed attempts to get a new ballpark built for the Giants, ideally near downtown, the Giants actually *had* a downtown ballpark their first two seasons in San Francisco. Talk to the guys who played both at Seals and at Candlestick and, almost to a man, they'll tell you that moving to Candlestick was a mistake, that Seals should have been enlarged and the Giants should have stayed right where they were, at 16th and Bryant Streets. San Francisco baseball legend Lefty O'Doul lamented the destruction of Seals, saying what a crime it was to tear down the most beautiful little ballpark in America. Few actively supported his argument then. Few would argue with it now.

The 1958 San Francisco Giants won 80 ballgames and lost 74, finishing third in the National League standings, 12 games behind the champion Milwaukee Braves. So why write a book about these guys? Why write a book about a team that nobody ever confused with the *The Boys of Summer*? Well, first and foremost because these guys are the *original* San Francisco Giants, the guys who brought big league ball to San Francisco. The '58 Giants were supposed to finish in the second division of the National League but, in fact, were in first place as late as July 30, something of a surprise, since they finished a distant sixth each of the previous two seasons. But that was when they were the *New York* Giants. And that's why this '58 Giants club is something very special. It was *San Francisco*.

I decided to write this book as, above all, a tribute to the men who introduced major league baseball to the San Francisco Bay Area. There are hundreds of thousands of men and women today who were children in 1958, who had never seen a big league ballgame until they saw the '58 Giants at Seals Stadium. For so many of them–for *us*–the players who made up the '58 Giants will always be special, perhaps even a bit larger than life. For those of us who have held this game close to our hearts ever since 1958, the *original* San Francisco Giants will forever be magical in a sort of way that not even the 1962 National League cham-

pion Giants were, because the '58 Giants were *first*. And fans all over the Bay Area responded accordingly. Despite a seating capacity of under 23,000, Seals Stadium drew 1,272,625 fans in 1958, nearly doubling the Giants draw the year before in the Polo Grounds in New York.

Leonard Koppett called this the *Golden Age*, the earliest days of a fan's awareness, when the names and events on the field are indelible, and grow more golden with the passage of time. Bart Giamatti said that much of what we love later in sport is what it recalls to us about ourselves at our earliest—memories of a time when all that would be better was before us, as a hope, and that the hope was fastened to a game.

I know that I never forgot the players who made up the 1958 Giants. I followed them throughout their major league careers, even when they were traded elsewhere, even when they played in other countries. Ruben Gomez, for example, pitched marvelously for many years in the Mexican League and in Puerto Rico, long after he shut out the Dodgers, 8-0, in the first big league game ever played on the West Coast. Willie Kirkland became a folk hero in Osaka, Japan, when he played for the Hanshin Tigers, learning to speak excellent Japanese in the process (virtually unheard of for American players), long after he started that first game as a rookie right fielder for the Giants. Daryl Spencer became a legend in Japan with the Hankyu Braves, also long after he started at shortstop in the '58 Giants opener. Leon Wagner became a great home run hitter in the American League. Bill White became a great player with St. Louis, and later became National League president. Stu Miller and Al Worthington became outstanding relief pitchers in the American League. The list goes on and on.

These men were my heroes as a child. I memorized their vital statistics on the backs of my baseball cards, and when I wasn't at the ballpark itself I was listening to the games on the radio, many times as I lay in bed at night, eyes closed, *seeing* every play before me, as Russ Hodges or Lon Simmons called it. As I got older, as *all* of us got older, this hero-worship of the players appropriately faded, even as our love of the game itself continued to grow. In subsequent years that love has been sorely tested, by labor issues primarily, but also by expansion, realignment, second-place teams going to the playoffs, domed stadiums, artificial surfaces, network television influence (*night* World Series games), and overall greed by the two sides that somehow managed to force the first cancellation of the fall classic in 90 years. I found myself wishing that I could go back in time to the innocence of my childhood when these ballplayers seemed larger than life, when baseball was unquestionably the national pastime, when Topps cards were the *only* cards, when nobody cared about the monetary value of those cards, and when the baseball winter meetings—and all the trade talk that surrounded them—got as much or more coverage in the local papers than the NBA, NHL and NFL combined. Yet through it all the game itself remains relatively pure, largely unchanged from the game we fell in love with as kids. To the degree that we can watch a game and, at the same time, divorce ourselves from the financially based and power-driven decisions off the field that trouble us, we can still enjoy it with nearly the same innocence and passion we did as kids. The game itself continues to survive, despite the efforts of so many within the game to destroy it.

Author Steve Bitker (R), at age six, with older brother Alan, outside Woodside, California home in 1959. (Steve Bitker)

As the years have gone by, I often wondered what happened to many of the men who made up the 1958 Giants. Some of them are easy to find, easy to keep tabs on. Willie Mays, Orlando Cepeda and Jim Davenport continue to work for the Giants, maintaining a relatively high profile. Felipe Alou continues to manage the Montreal Expos. But what about the rest? Some disappeared completely from the public eye after their playing careers ended. How has life treated them over the years? What significance do their baseball careers hold in their lives today? What memories from those careers stand out for them today, 30-50 years later? And what memories from that magical season in 1958, if any in particular, stand out?

I decided to find out. With the help of the Giants Community Relations staff in particular, I started with addresses and phone numbers, some not surprisingly outdated, in an effort to contact these former players. And I planned a working vacation with my wife Alice to the Caribbean to jump-start the effort. First, I contacted Valmy Thomas on St. Croix, in the U.S. Virgin Islands. Then, with the assistance of the Giants' then-Latin American scouting director, Luis Rosa, in Puerto Rico, I tracked down Ruben Gomez in San Juan. Not only did both of them agree to be interviewed for this book, but they couldn't have been more warm and gracious in the process. My project was under way.

Ruben Gomez offered to come to our hotel in San Juan, saying he could meet with me for an hour or two, before his scheduled golf game. He never played golf that day, sitting with me instead for well over three hours, regaling me with tale after tale from his colorful baseball career, and then insisting on hosting Alice and me for a beer at one of his favorite nearby pubs that evening. He also joined me for coffee the next day, before I left for the Dominican Republic, and insisted I play golf with him during my next visit to San Juan. And he proudly pointed to his 28-inch waistline that hasn't changed since he threw his patented screwball.

Valmy Thomas insisted on picking us up at the airport on St. Croix and showing us some of his beloved island. Several hours later we had seen virtually the entire island, learned some of its history, joined him for lunch at an off-the-beaten-track restaurant in Christianstedt, and realized that he is one of St. Croix's most prominent citizens, only incidentally because he played major league ball long ago. Everywhere we went, people called out to him, from small children to older residents. And it was clear that his work on the island, in education and recreation affairs, and in broadcasting, explained his renown at least as much as, if not more than, his baseball career of so many years back.

My project was underway. I had interviewed the Giants' starting battery, Gomez and Thomas, from their first game in San Francisco. Each interview made me look forward to the next one.

Felipe Alou showed, from his sheer presence, why he has long been one of the most respected men in baseball, a statesman for the game if you will. He speaks honestly and passionately, and from the heart. He is also strikingly handsome—a testament to the fountain of youth, in a sense. This man continues to be in superb physical condition.

During the subsequent months, I endeavored to contact every surviving member of the '58 Giants. With rare exceptions—only two, in fact, who steadfastly declined to return phone calls—everybody was willing to sit down and talk with me. Willie Mays invited me into his home for two hours, and couldn't have been more gracious. Willie Kirkland invited me into his home for three hours, sharing memory after memory after memory. One question would lead to a lengthy series of recollections, and that would lead the interview in a different direction, and so on and so on. The result was that I got a lot more from him on his days in the minor leagues and in Japan than I did on his days with the '58 Giants. And that was *fine*. Memories of a season 40 years gone will invariably be more vivid for some than for others. What I found, though, is that there *are* vivid baseball memories for every one of these ballplayers. Those memories are not always with the Giants, and not always from '58. And sometimes they are. Again, this book is about the '58 Giants—the memories and lives of the members of the '58 Giants—but not simply about the '58 season.

Ed Bressoud, retired and golfing several times a week, still cares deeply about the game he once played. He speaks articulately and passionately about it. Orlando Cepeda continues to approach life with the same enthusiasm he did as a ballplayer. Jim Davenport speaks with modesty and dignity, never wavering in his sincerity. Whitey Lockman brings the '51 playoff with the Dodgers back to life with his recollec-

tions. Hank Sauer and Marv Grissom, both over 80, continue to play golf. And both can occasionally boast about shooting their age on the links.

Daryl Spencer brings scrapbooks of his career to the interview, to rekindle his memories. Frankly, listening to Spencer talk about his career, I'm not sure the scrapbooks are necessary reminders. He still thinks of himself as a Giant, *and* still reacts with anguish at the mere mention of the '62 playoff, because he was a *Dodger* that season. Those scrapbooks, by the way, include box scores from every game he played, in Japan, in the majors *and* in high school.

Leon Wagner tells baseball stories with the same playful zeal he brought to the ballpark as a player. Paul Giel, an All-America back at The University of Minnesota before his professional baseball career started, and a longtime athletic director at Minnesota after it ended, brings a most impressive and varied athletic resume to the table. And he's an absolute gentleman to boot. So are Mike McCormick, at 19 the youngest of the '58 Giants, *and* Pete Burnside, who speaks with a self-deprecating humor about his career on the mound. Did you know he's a Dartmouth man?

Stu Miller, the diminutive change-up artist who baffled the likes of Frank Howard with regularity, looks you in the eye and says *his* change-up was the greatest in the history of the game. There's not a hint of boasting in his voice, nor in the expression on his face. He's telling you this matter-of-factly, because you've asked about his change-up. Al Worthington speaks quietly and softly, until you bring up the most important year of his life, 1958, when he became a born-again Christian. Then, the conviction in his voice, and the passion behind his message come through.

Bill White was an *original* San Francisco Giant, something many Giants fans are not even aware of. He hit 22 homers as a rookie with the New York Giants in '56, spent nearly two years in the army, then rejoined the Giants in August of '58, only to learn that his first base job had been taken away by another rookie, named Cepeda. He spent the rest of his career with St. Louis and Philadelphia, but came back to bat for the Giants in a very big way in the fall of 1992 when, as National League president, he helped keep the team in San Francisco, instead of it moving to Tampa Bay. Bill White always spoke the truth, as he saw it and felt it, and carried himself with a quiet dignity. He still does.

So does Johnny Antonelli. Here's a guy who won 35 games for the Giants in '58 and '59, absolutely loves the city of San Francisco to this day, and yet still shakes his head at the memory of being blasted by San Francisco sportswriters for having the temerity to criticize the weather conditions at Seals Stadium, historically not a friendly ballpark for left-handed pitchers. For those who wonder why Antonelli's brilliant career ended suddenly at age 31, he confides that his experience in San Francisco left such a sour taste in his mouth that it affected his desire to continue playing, even elsewhere.

Jackie Brandt, Joe Shipley, Dom Zanni, Bob Speake, Ray Crone, Don Johnson, Jim King, Don Taussig, Jim Constable and Nick Testa all played minor roles with the '58 Giants, and all were delighted to sit down and talk about their careers. When I first introduced myself to Taussig, I feared I was, in fact, talking to his son, by the same name. He has kept himself in tremendous physical shape over the years playing *and* teaching squash. Ramon Monzant, from Caracas, Venezuela, treasures his one and only full season in the major leagues, with the '58 Giants, so much so that he dreams openly of receiving a Giants jersey with his uniform number 41 on the back. Herman Franks and Wes Westrum, from the '58 Giants coaching staff, were most willing to share their lifetimes of baseball experience.

Lon Simmons, a rookie play-by-play voice with the Giants in '58, and Bob Stevens, Giants beat writer in '58 for the *San Francisco Chronicle*, were happy to sit down and share their recollections. And so were Mike Murphy and Roy McKercher, batboys in '58. Mike has never missed working a San Francisco Giants home game (*more than 3000 straight*), first as a batboy, then a visiting clubhouse attendant and now the Giants equipment manager.

Finally, there was no better spokesman for the '58 Giants or for the game of baseball in general than Bill Rigney, who passed away in February 2001 at the age of 83, after 63 years in professional ball. Bill never tired of talking about the game he loved so dearly, and there were few, if any, better treats in baseball than sitting down for a few minutes or, better yet, a few hours with Bill Rigney. I consider myself so fortunate to have done so.

More than anything else, this book is a tribute to these gentleman who brought big-league ball to San Francisco. A way of saying thanks. Sure, if these guys hadn't done it, some others would have. But these *are* the men who did it. Their stories are rich and varied. Hopefully, this book will help preserve their memories of the game, our memories of them and their contributions to baseball in San Francisco.

PART O N E

THE MOVE TO SAN FRANCISCO, SEALS STADIUM AND THE 1958 PENNANT RACE

THE MOVE

SO WHY ON EARTH did the New York Giants move to San Francisco? This question seems a logical place to start. After all, doesn't New York have the biggest fan base in all of professional sports? Yes, it does. Have the Yankees, the football Giants or Jets, the Knicks or Nets, the Rangers or Islanders ever moved out of the New York area? No, they haven't. But the Giants and Dodgers did, after the 1957 season. Of course, it is no coincidence that they moved west together. After all, prior to 1958, the entire major leagues were centered east of the Mississippi River. Traveling to *St. Louis* was considered a western road trip. It would have been impossible, therefore, for either the Giants or Dodgers to move to California without the other. Simple economics dictated that, not to mention the survival of the rivalry, unprecedented in terms of sheer emotion.

The Dodgers' move to Los Angeles has been described over the years as the most controversial move of a franchise in sports history, although the Raiders' move to Los Angeles may be argued with equal passion. The Dodgers were a central part of the social fabric and psyche of Brooklyn, and they made money, with big crowds, year after year after year. The same can

be said for the Raiders in Oakland. The same cannot be said, however, for the Giants in New York.

The Giants' history in New York dates back to 1883 when they were known as the Gothams. Manager Jim Mutrie is said to have been the first to term his club "my Giants," and by 1888, the nickname became official. The Giants' first game in the Polo Grounds took place July 8, 1889, their first game at the Coogan's Bluff site of the Polo Grounds was in 1891, and their first game at the actual concrete Polo Grounds that eventually housed the expansion Mets occurred June 28, 1911. *That* Polo Grounds served as the Giants' home ballpark for more than 46 years.

The New York Giants won 15 National League Pennants after 1900 (two before) and five World Series Championships. They first broke the one million mark in home attendance in 1945, following the end of World War II. By then, the Dodgers had already broken the million mark three times. From 1945 through '57, the Giants broke the million mark eight times. The Dodgers broke it *all 13 years.* The Giants topped the million mark at the Polo Grounds seven straight years beginning in '45. But from '52 through '57, they topped it only once, and that was in '54, when they finished 97-57, won the pennant by five games over the Dodgers, and then swept the heavily favored Cleveland Indians in four games to win the World Series. But while the Dodgers' attendance at Ebbets Field stayed consistently between one million and 1.2 million, the Giants' home attendance took a noticeable swan dive. Then again, so did their performance on the field. Falling to a distant third-place finish in '55 with an 80-74 record, the Giants drew only 824,000. Falling further to sixth place, with 67 and 69 wins respectively, in '56 and '57, the Giants drew well under 700,000 both years. The Dodgers continued drawing well, but they also continued winning, taking the pennant in both '55 and '56, and finishing a respectable third in '57.

The point is this: Giants owner Horace Stoneham said in 1957 that to keep his team in New York would be stupid, that he was losing money, with declining attendance. Giants fans, of course, upset with the pending move, complained that to expect bigger crowds to watch a mediocre team was asking too much. Stoneham countered by saying his Giants had fallen to dead last in the National League in attendance in '56 and '57, and in all of baseball during those two years, only the woeful Washington Senators drew fewer fans. And this was in New York, of all places, with more fans to tap from than any other market in the country.

New York was huge, all right, but there were *three* major league teams essentially sharing the same market, and the Giants were clearly losing out to the Dodgers and the Yankees. From 1945 through '57, the Giants outdrew the Dodgers only twice, in '48 and '54. They outdrew the Yankees only once, in '45. Averaged out over the 13-year period, the Giants drew roughly 1.05 million fans a season, the Dodgers 1.29 million, and the Yankees 1.78 million. Narrowing the time frame, from '52 through '57, the Giants' average attendance fell to 842,000 per season. During that same six-year period, the Dodgers averaged 1.09 million, and the Yankees 1.52 million.

Did the three teams' fortunes on the field parallel their ability to draw fans in the stands during those time periods? Let's take a look: From 1945 through '57, the Giants averaged 79 wins a season, the Dodgers 93 wins and the Yankees 95. The Giants won two pennants in those 13 years, the Dodgers won six flags and the Yankees won nine. Enough of the statistical analysis. It's clear to say that in the 13-year post-war period, the Yankees and Dodgers dominated the hearts and minds of New York baseball fans, while the Giants suffered both at the gate and on the field, by comparison.

Meanwhile, more than 3,000 miles to the west, the San Francisco Seals were enjoying the post-war boom in attendance like no other team in minor league baseball. In 1946 the triple-A Seals drew a minor league record 670,000 fans to Seals Stadium to watch Pacific Coast League ball. That was even more than two American League teams, the Philadelphia Athletics and the St. Louis Browns, drew in '46. It was nearly as many as two more clubs in the National League drew, the Cincinnati Reds and the Pittsburgh Pirates. The Seals drew more than 600,000 each of the next two years, and then began a gradual decline in attendance figures until the Boston Red Sox took over the franchise in '56. Then the numbers began climbing back up, peaking with their best numbers of the decade in '57, at 343,000—still excellent by minor league standards.

Giants owner Horace Stoneham (SF Giants)

But four years prior to that, in 1953, the first step toward bringing big league ball to San Francisco was undertaken by supervisor Francis McCarty, who offered a resolution to the board, asking for $5,000 to start a campaign to bring a major league club to the city. The measure passed, the money was appropriated and a committee of leading citizens was appointed to do just that, with McCarty himself serving as chairman. San Francisco and Los Angeles both had made noise over the previous 10 to 20 years about bringing a major league club to California, but never with any success. Remember, there had not been a single franchise shift in the majors in some 50 years, prior to the Boston Braves' move to Milwaukee in 1953. Now, suddenly, with the Braves in Milwaukee, a big league team coming to the West Coast didn't seem so far fetched.

In November of '54 San Francisco voters took a *Giant* step in the same direction by approving a $5 million general obligation bond issue to provide for the construction of a new stadium. A two-thirds majority vote was needed for the passage of any general obligation bond issue in the city and county, and this was no exception. If there was any significant public sentiment against bringing big league ball to San Francisco, this bond issue would have exposed it. Instead, flying in the face of what would later become a very popular trend in the city, the voters this time overwhelmingly supported the measure, along with all four daily newspapers (The *San Francisco Chronicle* and *Examiner* were both morning papers; the *San Francisco News* and *Call-Bulletin* were both afternoon papers) and the entire business community. The people of San Francisco wanted a major league baseball team, and the committee appointed by the board of supervisors went into action immediately. The committee conducted a series of preliminary meetings with owners of struggling clubs, probably not yet including the Giants, given the fact that they had just won the World Series and drawn 1.55 million fans. Supervisor George Christopher, who would be elected mayor the following November, said later that the effort at that point was not concentrated on any particular franchise. Rather, he told reporters, the committee was simply content to "play the field."

At the risk of returning to attendance figures, a simple glance suggests that team owners who might have had at least a passing interest in looking at San Francisco prior to the '55 season included the Cincinnati Reds, Pittsburgh Pirates and Washington Senators. Three other clubs, struggling badly at the gate, may have had informal talks with San Francisco in the past, but had just moved elsewhere, or were about to. The Boston Braves, after drawing a pathetic 281,000 in 1952, and just 487,000 in '51, moved to the much greener pastures of Milwaukee. The St. Louis Browns, after drawing fewer than 300,000 fans four of the previous five years, moved to Baltimore in '54, where they have flourished as the Orioles ever since. And the Philadelphia A's, after drawing fewer than 400,000 fans three of the previous five years, moved to Kansas City in '55 where they enjoyed great success at the gate, at least until a decline in the sixties forced them to Oakland.

It's clear that the Giants conducted at least exploratory talks in 1955 about moving out of New York—manager Leo Durocher actually told Willie Mays late in the '55 season that he was being replaced as manager, in part, because Stoneham wanted a new direction for his team prior to its move out of New York. The Dodgers, though, had given no indications whatsoever that they might eventually leave their beloved Brooklyn. But that began to change in '55, at least to those astute in their observations, when owner Walter O'Malley sold Ebbets Field for $3 million *and* sold minor league parks in Ft. Worth and Montreal for $1 million each. He said at the time that the $5 million would go towards building a new ballpark for the Dodgers in Brooklyn. He said he was prepared to sell a bond issue to help finance the construction, and said he was negotiating with Skiatron, Incorporated, to broadcast games on pay television. The technology, O'Malley told reporters, would involve a coin box on TV sets, with a slot for two quarters, that would enable fans to unscramble the broadcast signals. Those receipts would also help finance the new stadium. O'Malley said his intention— and he said this over and over—was to build his own park with his own money (which he would eventually do in Los Angeles), own the team, and run it *and* the stadium his own way. He said the Dodgers would purchase the land for a new ballpark but would need help from the city of New York to acquire the land at a reasonable price. He also said the Dodgers hoped to leave Ebbets Field by 1958.

In fact, the Dodgers would no longer play all their home games at Ebbets Field, beginning in

'56. O'Malley announced the Dodgers would play seven home games at Roosevelt Stadium in Jersey City instead. It marked the first time the Dodgers broke their exclusive association with Brooklyn, dating back to their minor league debut as champions of the Inter-State League in 1883.

O'Malley's intention to build his own stadium with his own money was in sharp contrast to the trend of publicly financed ballparks. But the help he needed from other boroughs was not forthcoming. As an independent city, Brooklyn probably would have done anything to keep the Dodgers. But Brooklyn hadn't been an independent city since 1896. As a borough, it needed cooperation from the other four boroughs, through the New York City Board of Estimate, with equal political representation conferred on each borough, regardless of size. Brooklyn's interests, therefore, could be frustrated by smaller rival communities.

Meantime, on September 28, former Giant great Bill Terry told writers he wanted to buy the Giants and have them play at Yankee Stadium. Stoneham had a simple reply: The Giants were not for sale, although he was open to the idea of the Giants moving from the Polo Grounds to Yankee Stadium. More and more, Stoneham felt, the Polo Grounds was becoming an obsolete stadium in an undesirable part of New York City. As poor as the Giants attendance was in the fifties, it was also far too heavily dependent on the club's rivalry with the Dodgers. Of the 629,000 fans who turned out at the Polo Grounds in '56 to watch the Giants play 77 home games, more than 210,000 (one-third of the overall total) came out to see the Dodgers. Moreover, the Giants owned the Polo Grounds and rented it to the New York Giants football team, as well as to local college teams, but by '57 all of them, including the football Giants, had abandoned the Polo Grounds for other sites, including Yankee Stadium.

For historical perspective, although most fans nowadays think Yankee Stadium has been around forever, or at least since the turn of the century, that is not the case. Yankee Stadium opened its doors for the very first time to the Yankees on April 18, 1923. It was in better shape than the Polo Grounds, it was a better stadium for baseball and it was in a better neighborhood.

In January 1956, George Christopher took office as mayor of San Francisco. One of his top priorities, he told reporters, was bringing major league baseball to San Francisco. Three days

later, Christopher spoke by phone with Los Angeles Mayor Norris Poulson, who told him that he had indications the Dodgers might be considering a move to LA. He asked Christopher if LA could count on San Francisco's support. Christopher knew that one major league club wasn't going to move to California without the other, so of course, he pledged full support. He, in fact, wanted Poulson and Los Angeles to lead the way. He knew that the first team to move to the West Coast would help bring a second one in its shadow. Poulson told Christopher that he and a delegation from LA would visit O'Malley in Florida, during spring training in March.

O'Malley made his first fact-finding trip to Los Angeles in October of '56, meeting with city officials during a Dodger stopover en route to Japan for an exhibition series. O'Malley met with supervisor Kenneth Hahn to discuss specifics of a possible Dodger move to LA. Hahn told Neil Sullivan in *The Dodgers Move West* that he had just returned from New York himself, where he attended the Dodgers-Yankees World Series, and where he pursued the possibility of the Washington Senators moving to LA. By the time O'Malley left, he and Hahn had shaken hands on an understanding in principle that would eventually lead to the Dodgers moving to LA, not the Senators.

In January 1957, Stoneham and O'Malley talked, agreeing that it would make far more sense for both teams to move west at the same time, if at all possible. And the big trade the two clubs had pulled off in December, sending Jackie Robinson to the Giants, was voided when Robinson decided he'd rather retire at age 38 than wear a Giants uniform. Even though Robinson's skills were in decline, many felt he would have played another year or two if he had remained a Dodger. The thought of becoming a Giant was probably too much to bear. The rivalry in those days was *that* intense.

On February 21 O'Malley continued clearing a Dodger path to Los Angeles when he purchased the Los Angeles Angels of the Pacific Coast League from the Chicago Cubs. O'Malley now owned territorial rights to LA. This was a front-page headline story in the *Los Angeles Times*. It didn't get the headlines in the *New York Times,* but it did make the front page, the story calling O'Malley's purchase a "bombshell," and saying the Dodgers were "a little closer to becoming the Los Angeles Dodgers."

In March, while LA city and county officials met to discuss the Chavez Ravine property that interested O'Malley, the Dodgers owner invited LA baseball writers to visit their spring camp in Vero Beach, Florida. Mayor Poulson, meantime, continued his discussions with O'Malley, but now Christopher was part of the talks as well, in a series of face-to-face meetings.

On April 18 the head of the New York Board of Estimate proposed a $10- to 12-million stadium at Flushing Meadow, on the site of the 1939 World's Fair, to house the Dodgers. O'Malley wasn't interested. He wanted the land instead so he could build his own ballpark in Brooklyn.

On May 3 O'Malley told Christopher that he would begin talks with Stoneham immediately, suggesting the Giants join the Dodgers in moving to the West Coast. Sure enough, O'Malley called Christopher three days later, inviting him to New York to join in the talks. Christopher flew east the night of May 9, to meet with Stoneham on the 10th, to begin the task of selling Stoneham on the idea of moving the Giants to San Francisco. Christopher wrote in *The American Weekly* in September 1957, that in order to effectively sell Stoneham, he had to clear three major hurdles: (1) convince him that San Francisco's climate and love of competition would nourish major league baseball; (2) convince him the city could build a $10 million stadium with the $5 million it had available from the bond issue; (3) convince him the potential was greater in San Francisco than in Minneapolis, where the Giants already had a triple-A club, and where a new stadium was already in place.

Christopher said he never let up on Stoneham. He flew back to San Francisco that night, opened his *Chronicle* the next morning and saw the front-page headline: NY GIANTS 'SURE' FOR S.F. IN 1958. He then called Stoneham day after day after day, just to reinforce the notion that San Francisco was the ideal future home for the Giants. They agreed to negotiate almost exclusively by phone, just to maintain a sense of privacy, newspaper headlines notwithstanding.

On May 28 National League owners voted unanimously to allow the Giants and Dodgers to move to San Francisco and Los Angeles, respectively, if they wished, as long as they did it together. If only *one* team wanted to move, it would have to seek permission from the owners all over again. Poulson left LA immediately for New York. Christopher talked with O'Malley by phone, while waiting for Stoneham to visit San Francisco the following week. Meanwhile, Stoneham asked Giants announcer Russ Hodges if he'd like to move to San Francisco, telling Hodges that Christopher came to New York personally to invite the Giants, and to discuss preliminary lease terms. All the while, the Seals were in first place, chasing a Coast League pennant, with team president Jerry Donovan saying there was nothing he or the team could do about the possibility of being supplanted for major league ball. All they could do, Donovan said, was keep trying to win the PCL pennant.

New York mayor Robert Wagner convened a meeting of city, Giants and Dodgers officials June 4, to discuss ways of keeping both clubs in New York, including the possible sharing of Yankee Stadium. On June 20 George McLaughlin, the former head of the Brooklyn Trust Company, said Stoneham rejected his offer to purchase the Giants and keep them in New York, at Flushing Meadow. Giants general manager Chub Feeney later said the Flushing Meadow package was never presented to Stoneham.

Stoneham made front-page headlines in both New York and San Francisco on July 17 when, testifying before a congressional subcommittee investigating professional sports, he said the Giants would leave New York at the end of the '57 season. Stoneham said New York couldn't support three teams, that the Giants were suffering the most as a result, that the Giants board of directors had, in fact, discussed a move out of New York the last four or five *years*. Stoneham said it was impossible for the Giants to make money if they stayed in New York.

Besieged by reporters, Stoneham held a news conference the following day and garnered front-page headlines once again. He said he would recommend to the team's board of directors a move of the franchise, unless one of two things happened: Either a new city-owned stadium for the Giants would have to be constructed near the Bronx-Whitestone Bridge, in the Baychester area; or satisfactory terms would have to be arranged for the Giants to share Yankee Stadium with the Yankees. Yanks' co-owner Daniel Topping told the *Times* that he hadn't discussed the possibility with Stoneham, and that he could not say whether the Yankees would even be receptive to the idea. (Ironically, the Giants shared the Polo Grounds with the Yankees from 1913 through 1922, and the first time the Yankees

Young baseball fans react with joy outside Seals Stadium to headlines announcing the Giants' move to San Francisco. (SF Giants)

plied, "I feel bad about the kids, but I haven't seen many of their fathers lately." Stoneham said the Giants' move to San Francisco was not tied directly to a possible Dodgers move to Los Angeles. He insisted that he was planning to move the Giants out of New York even before he knew O'Malley wanted to move the Dodgers out of Brooklyn. He said he had been unhappy with the Polo Grounds for years, and that it was nearly impossible to finance the building of a new ballpark in the area. Stoneham said he planned initially to move the Giants to *Minneapolis*. Not only did the Giants have a triple-A club there, with a new stadium in place,

topped the one million mark in home attendance was in 1920, in the Giants' ballpark. The Giants didn't top the million mark themselves for the first time for another 25 years.) The Giants

Horace Stoneham also said a deal with Skiatron was set for pay TV for the Giants in '58 (which never got off the ground). Stoneham said it would be stupid for the Giants to stay in New York with continuing financial losses, and said even though the Giants' lease on the Polo Grounds land ran to 1962, he had a friendly agreement with the Coogan estate [the landlord] and didn't anticipate any difficulty working out a compromise deal.

On August 9 Stoneham got a letter from Christopher detailing what San Francisco would do for the Giants. It included an agreement to build a 40,000 to 50,000-seat stadium, with parking for 12,000 cars. Christopher predicted annual profits of $200,000 to 300,000 for the Giants. Nine days later the Giants Board of Directors voted 8-1 to approve the transfer of the club. Stoneham, asked by a reporter how he felt about taking the Giants from the kids of New York, re-

Minneapolis also was relatively close to two other National League cities, Milwaukee and Chicago. Feeney confirmed as well that the Giants were planning to leave New York before he ever

Owner Horace Stoneham, flanked by club secretary Ed Brannick, tells New York reporters that the Giants are moving to San Francisco, August 19, 1957. (NY Herald Tribune)

learned of O'Malley's interest in vacating Brooklyn.

Obviously, Christopher was elated. He predicted the Giants would add 25 to 40 million dollars a year to the San Francisco economy. He predicted the Giants would draw 1.25 million fans to Seals Stadium in 1958. Recent history suggested he had done his homework. The Milwaukee Braves drew 150,000 fans their final minor league season, before drawing 1.83 million in the National League in '53. The Baltimore Orioles drew 207,000 their final minor league season, in '53, then drew 1.06 million in the American League in '54. And the minor league Kansas City Blues drew 141,000 in '54, after which the Kansas City Athletics drew 1.39 million in '55. Christopher was confident the Giants would have been able to draw more than *two* million fans in '58, except for the fact that Seals Stadium's increased capacity for big league ball was going to be limited to 23,000, standing room only. (Christopher wasn't far off in his prediction: The Giants drew 1.27 million fans in '58, despite the limited capacity at Seals, ranking fourth in the league in attendance, ahead of St. Louis, Chicago, Philadelphia and Cincinnati, all of which played in much bigger parks.)

The San Francisco mayor wasn't right on everything, however. Writing in *The American Weekly,* Christopher said, "I think Mr. Stoneham has 'bought' the city I was proudly selling—fog and all. I would be foolish to deny we have fog. But it is troublesome only in certain sections, and **not** at the site of the proposed new stadium."

On August 23 Arthur Daley wrote in the *Times* that with the Giants irrevocably gone, the Dodgers would have the National League segment of the rich New York territory all to themselves, if they wanted it. Yankees manager Casey Stengel was elated the Giants were leaving town, gloating, "We chased them out of town." He only hoped the Dodgers would soon follow.

On September 15 a crowd of 15,484 at Seals Stadium saw the final game in San Francisco Seals history, ending the 55-year history of the club. The Seals lost to Sacramento, 14-7, but won the Pacific Coast League pennant with a 101-67 record.

One week later, on the 22nd, a crowd of 2,600 turned out at the Polo Grounds to see the Giants play the Cubs. Later that same week, 2,300 came to see the Giants play the Reds. On the 28th, 2,700 showed up for the next to last Giants

game, against the Pirates. And on the 29th 11,606 saw the finale, a 9-1 Pirates victory, as Bob Friend tossed a six-hitter. The historic game was preceded by a poignant home-plate ceremony, featuring former Giant greats Carl Hubbell, Rube Marquard and Larry Doyle. Mrs. John McGraw and Bill Rigney also took part, among others. Bill Terry and Mel Ott were among those remembered. The Giants players were largely apathetic. After all, most didn't live in New York anyway. Giants fans of the nineties will recall a similar apathy that permeated the Giants in '92, when it appeared the team would be sold and moved to Tampa Bay at the end of the season. Dave Righetti, a San Jose native, was openly upset about the proposed sale and move, but he had little if any company. Most of his teammates were simply anxious to put all the off-field news surrounding the team behind them. And many were looking forward to playing before bigger crowds, even on a carpet under a roof. A similar situation characterized the Giants of '57. Even Rigney, with emotional ties to the Polo Grounds as a player and manager, was eagerly anticipating the move—he was a Bay Area native, born and raised in Alameda.

Rigney, in tribute to the Giants World Series championship team of 1954, started as many players from that '54 lineup as possible, in the Polo Grounds finale. He had Mays, Mueller and Rhodes in the outfield, Lockman at first, Thomson at third, Westrum behind the plate and Antonelli on the mound. The only starters missing from the '54 club were the departed Davey

San Francisco mayor, George Christopher, with Willie Mays outside San Francisco City Hall. (San Francisco Chronicle).

Williams at second and Alvin Dark at short, re-placed by Danny O'Connell and Daryl Spencer.

The crowd had several banners, one of which read, STAY, TEAM, STAY. It saved its loud-est cheers for Mays, who had two of the Giants' six hits. The fans surged toward the field as the game ended, in something of a wild assault on any souvenirs they could get their hands on. They walked away later with home plate, the bases, pitching rubber, bullpen canopies, green foam rubber covering the outfield fences, signs, telephones, dirt, grass and even the bronze plaque from the Eddie Grant memorial monu-ment in deep center field (in honor of the late Gi-ant infielder, killed during World War I). They chased Giants players across the field, toward the clubhouse in deep center. They chanted, "We want Willie." But Mays, along with the rest of the team, under instructions from Rigney, refrained from stepping outside the clubhouse doors. The fans sang two songs, one for Stoneham:

> We want Stoneham,
> We want Stoneham,
> We want Stoneham,
> With a rope around his neck.

And they sang another song for the team, to the tune of *The Farmer in the Dell:*

> We hate to see you go,
> We hate to see you go,
> We hope to hell you never come back,
> We hate to see you go.

The New York Giants were history. The ban-ner headline in the *New York Daily News* the fol-lowing morning read, 11,606 ATTEND GIANTS WAKE. The Brooklyn Dodgers would soon follow. On October 8, four days after the Los Angeles City Council approved the Chavez Ravine agree-ment, transferring 183 acres of city-owned prop-erty to the Dodgers, in exchange for the Wrigley Field property (where the PCL's Angels played), pending voter approval (which came the follow-ing June), the Dodgers announced during a New York-Milwaukee World Series game that they were, indeed, moving to Los Angeles. For the first time since 1883 the National League would not be represented in New York. Many fans in Brook-lyn would never forgive O'Malley. Unlike the Braves, A's and Browns, who moved earlier in the decade, and unlike the Giants as well, the Dodg-

ers were *making* money. The Dodgers were more financially prosperous than any other team in the National League in the fifties, they had won six pennants in the last 11 years, and they were just two years removed from capturing the World Se-ries championship over the Yankees that had eluded them for so long. And now they were skipping town.

However, the wheeling and dealing of fran-chises was not over. On October 15 the Giants traded their triple-A Minneapolis Millers farm club to the Boston Red Sox, in exchange for Boston's San Francisco Seals farm club. The deal involved the transfer of franchises, but not play-ers. Six days later the Giants purchased the class-C Phoenix farm club and took immediate steps to have the Pacific Coast League accept the Phoenix Giants as a replacement for the Seals. The accep-tance was considered routine.

The following day Rigney signed a two-year contract to manage the Giants in '58 and '59, at about $30,000 per year. He told writers that any Giant could be traded with the exception of Mays. More than a month later, on November 25, Stoneham confirmed a report in the *St. Louis Globe-Democrat* that said he turned down a $1 million offer from the Cardinals in June that would have sent Mays to St. Louis, in exchange for $750,000 cash and several players. The story said the Giants seriously considered the deal at one time because of poor attendance and the steady loss of revenue, but didn't pull the trigger on the offer because of the pending transfer of the club to San Francisco. Chub Feeney report-edly told Cardinals general manager Frank Lane that if he traded Mays *and* the Giants moved to San Francisco, the people of the Bay Area would throw him into the San Francisco Bay. Lane told the *Globe-Democrat* that he made four separate of-fers for Mays, all with the approval of Cardinals owner Augie Busch. Cards executive Vice-Presi-dent Dick Meyer was quoted as saying, "We were really anxious to get Mays. He's the kind of excit-ing ballplayer that any club would want."

The Giants, *with* Willie Mays, were coming west. Fifty years of franchise stability in the ma-jor leagues came to an end when the Boston Braves moved to Milwaukee following the 1952 season. The St. Louis Browns moved to Baltimore a year later. The Philadelphia Athletics moved to Kansas City a year after that. And now, two of the game's marquee franchises were vacating New York City, and expanding the major leagues west of the Mississippi River, all the way to the California coast. The majors would never be the same again.

SEALS STADIUM

 SEALS STADIUM, like a fine bottle of Cabernet, keeps getting better with age. In part because it was such a beautiful and intimate minor league ballpark to begin with, in a wonderful location, and in part because it was replaced by a disaster in Candlestick Park, in 1960, it has been easy to wax nostalgic about Seals Stadium over the years.

Built between 1930 and '31 at a cost of more than $600,000 by a trio of Seals owners, Seals Stadium was home to the San Francisco Seals from 1931 through '57, and home to the San Francisco Missions, also of the Pacific Coast League, from '31 through '37, after which the Missions moved to Southern California and became the Hollywood Stars. Seals Stadium replaced Recreation Park which, at two different locations, had been home of the Seals from 1903 through '30 (although the Seals played one season at Ewing Field, at Geary and Masonic, in 1914). The original Recreation Park, located at eighth and Harrison Streets, was destroyed by the 1906 earthquake. The new Recreation Park opened in 1907 at 15th and Valencia Streets.

A single-deck, completely open-air ballpark, Seals Stadium was located in the Northeast section of the Mission District of San Francisco, at the corner of 16th and Bryant Streets. The first base line ran parallel to Bryant Street, the right field seats ran along 16th Street, the left field line was somewhat parallel to Portrero Avenue, and the third base line was parallel to Alameda Street. This particular plot of land was chosen because it was located in one of the warmest belts of the city, relatively free of fog during the summer, and just a five-minute drive or 20- to 30-minute walk from downtown.

The original capacity at Seals Stadium was over 18,500, although that grew to about 20,000 before the Giants moved west. There were 16 rows of lower box seats and 26 rows of grandstand seats, divided by a wide aisle that ran parallel with the field. All 42 rows were filled with comfortable wood seats. The stands curved around home plate and extended down both lines. Home plate was 56 feet from the first row of box seats behind the plate. Box seats down both lines were closer to the field as they stretched along the outfield. The right field bleachers had 15 rows of backless benches. A 30-foot-high scoreboard was in center field. Just beyond the left field wall was a small parking lot.

The original dimensions were tailored toward low-scoring games. It was 385 feet to right field, 365 feet to left, 404 feet to a small corner in left-center, and 424 feet to a small corner just to the right of center. The outfield wall was 20 feet high all around, from left to right. The one big bonus for hitters was the prevailing breeze that blew from right to left field. It was something that right-handed hitters grew to love.

The first game played at Seals Stadium took place March 13, 1931, with the Seals beating the Detroit Tigers and future Hall of Famer Waite Hoyt, 5-2. Sam Gibson, a six-time 20-game winner for the Seals, got the win, future Yankee Frank Crosetti had three hits, and 14,235 fans turned out for the first of 11 straight exhibitions featuring big league clubs. The first Pacific Coast League game took place April 17, with the Seals blanking the Portland Beavers, again behind Gibson, 8-0. The first PCL home run hit in Seals Stadium history was hit by the Seals' Jerry Donovan, who would later become Seals president, and then Giants business manager.

The first night game took place April 23, 1931. Once again, Gibson pitched the Seals past Sacramento 5-1. Seals Stadium had six light towers, 125 feet above the field—four behind the grandstand and two behind the outfield.

In the 1930s the Seals sent 13 players to the major leagues, including Crosetti and "The Yankee Clipper" himself, Joe DiMaggio. DiMaggio, in fact, had three wonderful years at Seals Stadium, setting a Coast League record in 1933 that still stands today, when he hit safely in 61 consecutive games, hitting .340 for the season, with 28 home runs and 169 RBIs. Two years later, in '35, he led the Seals to the pennant, hitting .398 (finishing second in the league to the .399 hit by the Missions' Oscar Eckhardt, who hit .414 in '33 with 315 hits), with 34 home runs, 154 RBIs and 173 runs. In '36, "Joltin' Joe" was an All-Star center fielder for the New York Yankees, which he continued to be throughout his 13-year major league career.

Crosetti and DiMaggio were two of the hundreds of San Francisco area natives who went on to star in the major leagues, many of whom polished their skills in the Coast League at 16th and Bryant Streets, at Seals Stadium. That list includes Ernie Broglio, Dick Stuart, Jackie Jensen, Billy Martin, Dolph Camilli, Lefty Gomez, Harry Heilmann, Tony Lazzeri, Ernie Lombardi and, of course, Lefty O'Doul.

O'Doul, who ended his 11-year major league career in 1934 with a lifetime average of .349, returned to San Francisco in '35 to manage the Seals for the next 17 years, winning two pennants. O'Doul was a legend at Seals Stadium from his days as a player, hitting .338 for the Seals in 136 at-bats *and* winning 25 games on the mound, in 1921. He also hit .378 for the Seals in '27, with 33 homers and 158 RBIs. O'Doul was so popular in San Francisco that late in the '51 season, with the Seals mired in last place, when it became clear that he would not be brought back to manage in '52, outraged fans organized a "D-Day for O'Doul" rally at Seals Stadium. They returned to pack the ballpark April 15, 1952, when O'Doul returned as manager of the San Diego Padres. Fans held signs and placards welcoming Lefty back home. Big cheers rang out whenever he came out of the dugout, and he responded in kind, blowing kisses to the fans. Today, just a long fly ball from where home plate will be when the Giants' new PacBell Park opens in the year 2000, is the Lefty O'Doul Bridge. In 1992 the Bay Area chapter of the Society for American Baseball Research voted overwhelmingly to rename its group "The Lefty O'Doul Chapter." And the most popular sports bar in San Francisco throughout the sixties, seventies and into the eighties was *Lefty O'Doul's,* opened in '58 by Lefty himself, across the street from the St. Francis Hotel.

Seals Stadium underwent a major face-lift in 1946, when millionaire industrialist Paul Fagan became part owner of the ball club. Fagan wasn't content with Seals Stadium being one of the finest minor league parks in the country. He wanted it to be one of the most beautiful ballparks in the nation of *any* kind, the major leagues be damned. He had the fading white facade repainted mint and forest green, which effectively changed the nickname of the park from "The Queen of Cement" to "The Queen in Green." He replaced the outfield wall advertisements with solid green paint, giving up some $20,000 a season in revenue in exchange for aesthetics. Flower boxes

adorned the windowsills of the front office, where Fagan added a lovely ladies lounge, stocked daily with fresh flowers. He hired a turf expert from Scotland to help ensure that the Seals would have the finest playing field possible. He became the first baseball team owner to hire uniformed usherettes, had the ladies rooms at the ballpark enlarged and painted, and hired a band to perform between innings.

Fagan replaced the wire screen or mesh on the backstop with Plexiglas, to remove the distraction for box seat holders behind home plate. The screen returned, though, because of complaints over glare, the glass fogging up and deafening noise from foul balls hitting the glass. He took care of his players, too. He added a workout room with whirlpool baths, a soda fountain, beer taps, a barber chair and shoeshine stand to the Seals' clubhouse. He upgraded the players' travel arrangements, having them stay in the best hotels and eat in the finest restaurants, and travel regularly by air, something no other minor league club did. He took the Seals to lovely Hana, on the island of Maui, for spring training in '46 and '47, building a training facility and diamond there, which still stand today. And he paid every one of his players at least the major league minimum salary of $5,000. He even had a flower garden built beyond the left field grandstand.

Fagan's attention to both aesthetic detail and luxury paid immediate dividends. The Seals won the 1946 pennant, with a 115-68 record, and set an all-time minor league attendance record, which stood for nearly 40 years, until the St. Louis Cardinals' triple-A farm club in Louisville broke it. But as the Coast League began to fall on hard economic times in the 1950s, with stiff competition for top talent from both the majors and other minor leagues, Fagan sold the Seals to the Coast League itself in '53, which eventually turned it over to the Boston Red Sox in '56. Fagan held onto Seals Stadium but said he planned to tear it down and replace it with retail businesses, once his lease commitment to the Seals expired at the end of the '59 season.

Seals Stadium, though, went out with a bang. The Seals, strengthened with talent supplied by the Red Sox, drew 14,401 fans for Opening Day in '56, a 6-3 win over Vancouver. Albie Pearson and Marty Keough played the outfield, Ken Aspromonte was at second, Frank Malzone at third and Joe Gordon was managing. Oakland native Pumpsie Green joined the infield in '57.

They even *looked* like the Red Sox, with new uniforms, trimmed in black and red, with "SEALS" written across the shirt fronts in the traditional Red Sox style. Attendance climbed 24,000 above 1955 numbers, and climbed another 100,000 in '57 to a league-best 344,641 (the LA Angels were third, with 265,968), when the Seals won the pennant again. They were led by reliever Leo Kiely, who finished 21-6 with a 2.20 ERA, in 59 games, finishing second in league MVP voting to Steve

Seals Stadium (San Francisco History Center, San Francisco Public Library)

Bilko (Kiely followed that up by going 5-2 with 12 saves and a 3.00 ERA with the Red Sox in '58), and by Aspromonte, whose .334 led the league in hitting.

As the '57 season played itself out, it became more and more apparent that it would be the Seals' final one in San Francisco, with the Giants replacing them in '58. In June, Mayor Christopher accepted a proposal for a new stadium from construction magnate Charles Harney, who owned some 70 acres at Candlestick Point. Harney was willing to sell the property to the city for $2.7 million *and* insisted the park could be built in eight months.

The Seals ended their 55-year history September 15 with a doubleheader against Sacramento, before 15,484. The public address announcer said to the crowd, "This may be a day to remember—a day of nostalgic sadness." It was a bittersweet afternoon, filled with tears from fans having to say good-bye to a team they had loved for so many years, but also filled with joy and anticipation from others looking forward to the arrival of the Giants. Typically, the more poignant and pointed comments came from the more melancholy side. Seventy-three-year-old retired fire lieutenant William Peterson told the *Chronicle,* "It's a sad day. I've seen the Seals from the first, and now the last, and, well, I'd liked to have gone on seeing them till I die." Another said, "The Giants are no good back there, so we're bringing 'em out here. What is this, a dumping ground?"

A carnival atmosphere permeated the nightcap, as Pearson pitched the first four innings of a 14-7 loss, then proceeded to play first, second, third and short. (Pearson, traded to Washington for Pete Runnels after the season, hit .275 for the Senators in '58, winning American League Rookie of the Year honors.) Manager Gordon himself played second, going two-for-three, and even pitched. When umpire Chris Pelekoudas called one of his deliveries a ball, Gordon stormed the plate in protest. Pelekoudas suggested *he* could do a better job of pitching, so the two traded places, with Pelekoudas on the mound and Gordon wearing the umpire's gear behind the plate. After one very off-speed delivery by Pelekoudas, the two switched back. At game's conclusion players embraced and saluted the fans. Nobody from the Seals roster showed up with the Giants in '58 but Jerry Donovan went from Seals president to Giants business manager and Walter Mails moved from Seals promotions man to the head of the Giants speakers bureau.

SEALS STADIUM UNDERWENT a $75,000 upgrade before the Giants' '58 opener. It was repainted dark green and the seating capacity was increased to about 23,000, with the addition of 2,600 bleacher seats in left field. The 20-foot-high wall in the outfield was shortened to 15 feet in left field and 16 feet in right, and the walls were brought in as well, from 424 feet to 415 feet in center, and from 385 feet to 355 feet in right.

Fans line up for more than one city block outside Seals Stadium, April 9, 1958, to buy tickets for opening day, six days later. (San Francisco History Center, San Francisco Public Library)

able to the city by the Hamm's Brewery, across Bryant Street, behind home plate.

Giants announcer Russ Hodges visited San Francisco in January of '58 and saw Seals Stadium for the very first time. That's when "I first saw the beautiful little watch-charm ballpark, all green and cozy, and freshly painted," Hodges wrote in *My Giants*, adding he watched workmen dismantle the huge purple sign over the clock in center field which read, "Daphne Funerals— Eventually," replacing it with a more appropriate "Longine Watches." Hodges also saw the radio broadcast booth halfway up the grandstand behind home plate. He liked the intimacy of it but recoiled at the fact that it was protected by shatterproof glass. At his urging, the glass was removed before the season opener, Hodges explaining, "I've had enough peace and quiet at the Polo Grounds."

In February, Mayor Christopher predicted if the Giants won the National League pennant in '58 the World Series would probably be played in the new stadium at Candlestick Point. Architect John Bolles was a little more cautious, saying the new stadium would certainly be ready for Open-

Names of Coast League players who hit record-distance home runs remained on the wall, including the name of Jerry Casale, who won 19 games for the Seals in '56 *and* who cleared the center field wall with his bat. A new row of 10 lights was added to each of the six light towers, with the total wattage available boosted from 300,000 to 540,000. A new auxiliary press box was added, up a ladder from the smaller existing press box. A new photographer's stand was built, as well as a new press room in the clubhouse. One thousand curb parking spaces were added, along with 700 spaces in areas beneath the Central Freeway, and 300 off-street spaces elsewhere (offsetting the loss of some 300 spaces by the addition of the left field bleachers). Before Opening Day 2,000 more parking spaces were added, on land made avail-

Giants arrive at S.F. Airport April 13, 1958, from Omaha, Nebraska; 400 fans greet late night flight. (SF Chronicle) Manager Bill Rigney (with glasses & light-color overcoat) stands to left, alongside a smiling mayor George Christopher; waving hand, is Orlando Cepeda; Ramon Monzant and Ruben Gomez are to Cepeda's left; Andre Rodgers, with V-neck sweater and dark jacket, stands to right.

ing Day in '59. Neither, of course, would turn out to be correct. But those were far from the only faulty predictions surrounding that new stadium. On the other hand, supervisor Clarisa McMahon said she was disappointed there would be no dome on the new stadium. She advised, "It's a windy area." Few listened but she stuck to her guns and suggested a radiant heating system for the stadium, in return for her vote. The *Chronicle's* Herb Caen wrote on March 16, "Anybody care to bet that the Giants won't play their '59 season in Seals Stadium, too? That's what I thought. No takers."

On March 22 a citizen's group announced it would file suit to block the construction of the new stadium, saying it was a bad financial deal for the city. Nevertheless, supervisors approved the $15 million stadium plan two days later. But just when supervisors and the mayor thought there would be clear sailing on building their stadium, a group of downtown businessmen decided to promote the construction of a new ballpark south of Market Street. In a front-page story in the *Chronicle* April 3, the group said its proposal would be much better for downtown businesses. Supervisor Leo Halley expressed support for the idea, while others cried foul. Supervisor McCarty said the downtown area was not financially feasible. Christopher called the plan "ridiculous." McCarty said a downtown stadium would cost more than $40 million, including $25 million for underground parking garages for 10,000 cars. Why a downtown stadium would need 10,000 parking spaces was anybody's guess. Halley said he'd introduce a resolution in support of the downtown ballpark plan April 7.

Sure enough, Halley produced preliminary plans and backers for the downtown stadium plan on the 7th, saying a ballpark at Third and Mission Streets, between Fourth and Howard, could be built for just $14.5 million. Halley's cost estimate came from contractor James Cahill, who said the ballpark itself could be built for $4.5 million, adequate parking facilities for $6.4 million and land acquisition for $3.6 million.

Downtown parade welcomes Giants to S.F., down Montgomery Street, April 14, 1958.(SF Chronicle)

Halley said a downtown stadium would be within walking distance of 70,000 people. His initial blueprint was drawn up by architect John Warnecke. Supervisor McCarty angrily called for a hearing on the plan for the 10th. Unfortunately for Halley and the downtown businessmen's group, the downtown ballpark idea was shot down on the 10th, after four hours of testimony.

Valmy Thomas and Willie Kirkland in first car, followed by parade queen Shirley Temple Black in second, during downtown motorcade welcoming Giants to SF, April 14, 1958 (SF Chronicle)

Halley got only one other supervisor to support his plan, William C. Blake.

Meanwhile, as the Giants were slugging their way to the Cactus League title in spring training, fans were told that box seats to see the Giants would cost $3.50, reserved seats $2.50, left field pavilion seats $1.50 and the right field bleachers 90 cents. Those same prices remained in effect into the 1970s, at Candlestick Park. Fans coming to Seals Stadium from the Peninsula (more than from the North Bay and

"Play Ball" Lunch welcoming Giants to S.F., at Sheraton-Palace Hotel, S.F., April 14, 1958. (SF Chronicle)

East Bay put together) were advised to take the Vermont Street off-ramp from the Central Freeway, turn left on 16th Street and take 16th to the ballpark at Bryant Street. Those coming from downtown would pass billboards along city streets saying, "Welcome SF Giants. Swat Them Bums." Opening Day against the Dodgers was less than a week away.

The city was getting ready. The Giants were headline stories in all the local newspapers, radio and TV stations. *Joseph Magnin* clothing store downtown handed out booklets to women explaining the game of baseball and advising the correct apparel to be worn to the ballpark on any given day or night, depending on the weather. *Macy's* dressed its mannequins in Giants uniforms.

San Francisco threw a downtown ticker-tape parade for the Giants, upon their return from spring training, on the 14th. The players doubled up in the motorcade down Montgomery Street, riding in sparkling new convertibles, with their names on both the driver and passenger doors, so that when they waved to the crowd the fans were sure to know just who they were. Willie Mays and Hank Sauer rode together, two of the more notable returnees from the New York club. Mayor Christopher rode in his own car, as did Horace Stoneham, although the two doors on the Giants' owner's car were marked, "Stoneman." Shirley

Temple Black rode as the parade queen and then collected autographs afterward at a big luncheon for the team at the Sheraton-Palace Hotel, where the only standing ovation among the crowd of nearly 1000 patrons, at $5 per plate, was reserved for Mrs. John McGraw. Bill Rigney was given a key to the city. Police later estimated the crowd lining Montgomery Street, side streets and watching from overhead office buildings in the hundreds of thousands.

A standing-room sun-bathed crowd of 23,449 was on hand at Seals Stadium April 15 on a warm, breezy afternoon to witness the first major league game in West Coast history. Several dozen more watched on the hill from Franklin Square, across 16th Street, beyond the right field bleachers. Scalpers were getting as much as $15 per ticket. The freshly painted ballpark was draped

Shirley Temple Black gets Johnny Antonelli's autograph at "Play Ball" luncheon. (SF Chronicle)

with red, white and blue bunting all around the diamond, from one foul pole around home plate to the other. Appropriately, the game matched the first two West Coast teams, the Giants and Dodgers. Also appropriately, San Francisco native Gino Cimoli was the first hitter to step into the batter's box, to face the Giants' Ruben Gomez, who threw the first pitch at 1:34 p.m. and who struck out Cimoli a couple of

Opening Day, Seals Stadium, April 15, 1958; Bryant street on left; downtown SF in background. (SF Chronicle)

minutes later, en route to a six-hit 8-0 win. Cimoli, a North Beach resident and graduate of Galileo High, said later that he felt proud riding in his car by Seals Stadium the night before, calling it "my city."

Mayor Christopher actually took the mound before Gomez, throwing four ceremonial "first pitches" to his LA counterpart. Two of the four went behind Mayor Poulson, one bounced on the plate and the fourth was hit on the ground by Poulson, who promptly ran toward *third base.* During the introductions of the players, Mays got the biggest ovation but the Dodgers' Reese, Snider and Hodges got cheers that nearly matched Mays'. Hall of Famer Ty Cobb was in attendance, saying 75,000 would have shown up if there had been enough seating. Despite being an American Leaguer his entire playing career, Cobb, a Bay Area resident, said the Giants had rekindled his long-dormant interest in watching games.

It was the most heavily covered regular-season game in big league history, with some 110 credentialed journalists on hand. Dick Young of the *New York Daily News* wrote, "The general consensus of visiting newsmen is that the new Giant fans have big-league maturity. They have a restrained enthusiasm. They are not the wild, fanatically partisan fans of the Milwaukee breed. They seem hep about baseball: Cheer when a play rates it, and not over a routine catch of a

foul pop. And they are fair." Joe King of the *New York World Telegram* wrote, "It is sad for most of the old Giant fans to see their team depart, but the wrench is eased to know that it has a new home in the city which keeps alive the spirit of old New York in which the great Giants prospered."

When Gomez struck out Reese to end the game, the overflow crowd filed out into the streets, some heading for their cars, others for buses and trolleys, and still more to the three neighborhood saloons—the *Double Play Bar,* on 16th Street, (which still stands today, under the name *Double Play Bar & Grill), Third-Base* and *Lou's,* all within a short walk from the ballpark. By 4:45, traffic was running smoothly in the neighborhood. An afternoon paper boy outside Lefty's restaurant on Geary Street called out, "New York Giants win opener." That made Russ Hodges feel better since he frequently called the Giants the New York Giants during his first month or so of the season on the air. Also outside Lefty's was the score of each Giants game, updated daily, but *only* if they won. If they lost, someone wrote, "No game today—rain."

In the opener's fifth inning, with the Giants ahead 6-0, court was prematurely and mistakenly adjourned in San Rafael. It seems that when a reporter held up six fingers in Judge Charles Brusatori's courtroom, he meant to convey the score. However, the judge, a big baseball fan, mis-interpreted the sign, given that he was expecting the birth of a sixth grandchild any day, and promptly announced to the court that he was a grandfather for the sixth time. And court was adjourned.

The Bay Area was going wild over the Giants, particularly when they got out of the gate fast, sharing first place during the first half of the season with the defending World Series champion Milwaukee Braves. Despite playing in the smallest ballpark in the majors, the Giants would draw 1.27 million fans to Seals Stadium in '58, the second-best attendance total in franchise history, and double what they drew in New York in '57, in a ballpark twice as big as Seals. The '58 Giants broke the '57 Polo Grounds attendance total in *July.* Four-fifths of all Sunday games and three-fourths of all Saturday games were sold out before Opening Day. Stoneham said this confirmed what he had said when he moved the franchise, that San Francisco was one of the most substantial baseball cities in the country. He also predicted that over the long haul, the Giants would equal the Dodgers in home attendance in spite of the disparity in population (and smaller stadium). Unfortunately, for Stoneham, the Giants *never* outdrew the Dodgers on the West Coast during his ownership of the club. In fact, the San Francisco Giants did not outdraw the Los Angeles Dodgers at the gate until the 2000 season, their first at Pacific Bell Park, when they drew a franchise-record 3,315,330 fans, third most in the majors, and more than four million ahead of the ninth-place Dodgers.

Regardless, the Giants were a hit. Seals Stadium was a hit. Bob Stevens of the *Chronicle* wrote, "The Giants, in victory or in defeat, have captured San Francisco and San Francisco has captured the Giants. The Giants already have learned to like it here in the big league city that didn't need big league ball to be big league." And yet, the later in the season that the Giants were in first place (as late as July 30), the more baseball officials around the majors were concerned about the possibility of World Series games being played at Seals Stadium, because with the top four finishers in both leagues getting a share of Series money, the limited capacity at Seals Stadium would offer the least. *Chronicle* columnist Art Rosenbaum went so far as to suggest that if the Giants won the pennant, the first game of the World Series should be played at the 92,000-seat LA Coliseum, just to boost the financial take. Dick Young of the *New York Daily News* agreed, saying it was a well-known fact that LA's geographic limits ran right into San Francisco anyway. It turned out to be a moot point but the Giants, as well as visiting ballplayers, grew to love playing at Seals Stadium. The only discordant point of view was expressed by left-handed power hitters who realized how difficult it was to hit a ball out of the ballpark to right field, and by an occasional left-handed pitcher, upset about the prevailing winds blowing out toward left field that worked to the advantage of right-handed hitters. Otherwise, few if any players around the league enjoyed a road trip to another locale as much as they did San Francisco. Of course, the city itself had a lot to do with that.

One ballplayer, in particular, wrote about his affection for Seals Stadium, not to mention his disdain for Candlestick Park, in a pair of books. Relief pitcher Jim Brosnan, who spent nine years in the majors, played at Seals Stadium in 1955 with the Los Angeles Angels in the Coast League, and then in '58 and '59 with Chicago, St. Louis and Cincinnati. His feel for Seals Stadium was vividly expressed in *The Long Season:*

"One of the more pleasant aspects of Seals Stadium is the smell. Walking fromthe hotel to the ballpark, you pass by a bakery, which dispenses the scent of sugary rolls and freshly brown-crusted bread as though from a huge atomizer.

"The visiting team clubhouse overlooks this bakery. The windows cannot be opened in the clubhouse without causing immediate hunger pangs to twitch athletic stomachs. Especially in the morning, before a day game. San Francisco is a nighttime wonderland. There's too much to do and see after a night game that breakfast time usually comes too soon to be properly attended. (In fact, baseball games interfere seriously with the visiting ballplayer's social life in San Francisco.)

"However, the clubhouse man in Frisco does keep a pot of coffee hot, and somehow you can manage to get through the meeting and dash down the steps, through the runway and into the fresh air. Only there isn't any. The brewery behind the park advertises its product by wafting vast clouds of freshly brewed beer fumes over the left field grandstand into the visitor's bullpen. There's nothing quite like the smell of new beer in the morning after a night on Frisco town."

Brosnan later pitched at Candlestick Park from 1960 through '62 with Cincinnati. His feel for "the Stick" came through in *Pennant Race:*

"Candlestick Park is the grossest error in the history of major league baseball. Designed at a corner table in Lefty O'Doul's, a Frisco saloon, by two politicians and an itinerant ditchdigger, the ballpark slants toward the bay—in fact, it *slides* toward the bay and before long will be under water, which is the best place for it.

"One architectural expert, writing for *Harper's* Magazine, called the park a "monstrosity," but he was obviously a baseball fan, a Giant rooter, and genteel."

On May 22, Herb Caen quoted Lefty O'Doul as saying why not just double-deck Seals Stadium? What a crime, O'Doul felt, to tear down the most beautiful ballpark in the country. Unfortunately, Caen and O'Doul were in the minority, perhaps even within the *Chronicle.* Sports editor/columnist Bill Leiser wrote on May 25 that there were several good reasons against double-decking Seals Stadium. He said it would cost $10 million to do it, compared with $15 million to build a new stadium, so why not spend the extra $5 million and have a brand new park? Leiser also claimed the weather at the new site, at Candlestick Point, was better than at Seals Stadium, "which I will prove at a later date after accumulating direct evidence." Readers are still waiting.

General manager Feeney never insisted the weather was better at the new stadium site but did say on June 4, in response to growing inquiries, that double-decking Seals Stadium was out of

the question. Parking was the major problem, he said, underscoring the fact that Stoneham insisted on a new stadium with at least 10,000 parking spaces when he was negotiating terms of the Giants move with Mayor Christopher. Feeney also suggested that no more than 10,000 additional seats could be added to Seals Stadium, which would have left the capacity just over 33,000—not enough to survive financially. City engineers earlier developed a plan for increasing the capacity at Seals Stadium to 37,000. Still not enough, insisted Feeney. Maybe not, but if Seals Stadium could have seated 37,000 fans, it would have been the fourth largest park in the National League, bigger than Busch Stadium in St. Louis (32,900), Forbes Field in Pittsburgh (33,700), Connie Mack Stadium in Philadelphia (33,000) and Crosley Field in Cincinnati (30,000). Even today, two of the most successful draws in baseball are the Cubs at Wrigley Field (39,100) and the Red Sox at Fenway Park (35,200). Lending further support to the argument that Seals Stadium should have been enlarged, consider this: In 1959 the Giants drew 1.42 million fans to Seals Stadium, for 77 home games. That figure topped the Giants' attendance figures at Candlestick Park for 18 of their first 28 years there, even though Candlestick was nearly twice as big *and* even though there were 81 home games a season beginning in '62, compared with 77 previously.

Another lonely voice expressing concern about the Candlestick Point site was *Chronicle* outdoors columnist Bud Boyd, on June 24. "The area stinks," he wrote, "literally." He called it a

Giants general manager Chub Feeney. (SF Giants)

major pollution source. It didn't matter. Proponents of the Candlestick site were determined to bulldoze it through whatever opposition may have come up. The voters approved a $5 million bond for the building of a new stadium, Stoneham moved the Giants to San Francisco with the understanding that he was going to get a new stadium *with* 10,000 parking spaces, and even if the stadium was going to cost a hell of a lot more than $5 million, the damn thing was going to be built.

Supervisors gave final approval to the new stadium plans in July, with groundbreaking scheduled to begin in August. Architect Bolles pointed to two distinct features that he felt were revolutionary in stadium design: One, a radiant heating system, whereby the temperature surrounding 20,000 reserved seats could be raised some 20 degrees [that never worked; attorney Melvin Belli filed suit and won a $1597 judgement, covering the cost of his six 1962 season tickets]; and two, a rounded shield to be built at the top of the upper deck, which would act as a wind baffle (that never worked either, with some actually believing it helped to *foster* the swirling winds). In defense of contractor Harney, architect Bolles, Mayor Christopher, Supervisor McCarty and others who actively supported the Candlestick project, this was going to be the first stadium built in America since the Depression. There were no other new ballparks to study, no new standards by which to compare. The fact that the Dodgers would unveil their new stadium two years after the opening of Candlestick simply rubbed salt into the wound. Dodger Stadium was a masterpiece and *still is,* nearly 40 years after it opened.

Still, something smelled rotten, and it was more than simply what the *Chronicle's* Bud Boyd was referring to. To arrange additional financing for the new stadium, the city approved the formation of a nonprofit corporation, Stadium, Inc., with Harney and two of his employees as directors. The three were eventually replaced after a public outcry. The San Francisco Grand Jury in September ordered a probe of the stadium financing, particularly of the city's payment for Harney's land. It eventually concluded that while there were no legal improprieties in the transaction, San Francisco "did not get a good deal." It noted the overall stadium project cost was now close to $20 million, far beyond what the voters had approved four years prior.

Two months after the first shovel went into the ground at the new stadium site, the first batch of cement was poured into the foundation. It was October 28. Supervisor McCarty said, "This is one of the greatest days in the history of San Francisco." Once the stadium opened in April, 1960, few would agree. In June, 1960, the monthly magazine *The Californian* had a big story titled, "The Giants Ball Park: A $15 Million Swindle," in which it ripped the new stadium because of gale-force winds, the prevalent odor of sewage, and the deaths already of six fans from heart attacks climbing what became known as "Cardiac Hill" to get from their cars to their seats (the hill remains today, although fans now have the escalator option). After being elected mayor of San Francisco in '67, Joseph Alioto asked, "Why perpetuate a mediocrity?" His committee recommended the construction of a new downtown stadium, the first of many such suggestions over the years that got shot down, until the ballot box success of PacBell Park in '96. On September 1, 1964, in the *Philadelphia Inquirer,* Paul Avery had a by-line story titled, "Candlestick: How **Not** to Build a Park." As part of a multi-series "Special Report" on the fate of new ballparks, with Philadelphia considering building one of its own, Avery wrote, "In contemplating constructing a new home for the probable National League pennant winners [sic], the City Fathers of Philadelphia would be wise to dispatch a delegation of assorted experts to San Francisco to find out how *not* to build a baseball stadium."

Meanwhile, as great as the Giants attendance was at Seals Stadium in 1958, the numbers were even better in '59, as the Giants spent much of the season in first place. The fervor was such that in September Mark Harris wrote a piece for *Sports Illustrated* titled "Love Affair in San Francisco," in which the entire article centered on the September 2 game at Seals Stadium between the Giants and the Cubs, which the Giants won in the ninth inning on a Jackie Brandt home run. What made the article unique, though, was that author Harris did not watch the game from the comfort of the Seals Stadium press box. Rather, he wandered around the city, accompanied by an artist/ illustrator, and everywhere he went he found every day city folks glued to their radios, listening to the game on KSFO. From the airport to Coit Tower, Fisherman's Wharf and the stadium construction site at Candlestick Point; from Chinatown to Union Square, North Beach and

Nob Hill; from the cable car stop at the foot of Powell Street to Twin Peaks and Lefty O'Doul's bar—everywhere they went they found Giants fans, clinging to hope that their heroes would pull this particular game out, not to mention the pennant itself, but invariably fearing the worst. It was a magical time to be a baseball fan in San Francisco. Aside from the sheer novelty of being able to see big league baseball in person, in a charming little ballpark, absolutely *none* of the Giants' 154 games were televised locally. It meant that the only way to see the Giants was to see them *in person.* That added to the magic of going to Seals Stadium, in ways that young fans nowadays will never be able to experience. It also added to the magic of listening to the game on the radio because, if you weren't at the game, the radio was your *only* vehicle for seeing the action, through Russ Hodges' and Lon Simmons' descriptions and your own *imagination.* The lack of locally televised games made going to the ballpark far more special than it could ever be again.

Sure enough, despite fading the final week of the season to finish third, 1.42 million fans came out to that charming little bandbox known as Seals Stadium to watch the Giants. On September 20, another sellout crowd of 22,923 turned out on a sunny Sunday afternoon to watch a ballgame that was far more bitter than sweet. The Dodgers completed a three-game sweep of the Giants with an 8-2 win to take over first place by one game with five remaining, all on the road. It was the final game in Seals Stadium history.

Demolition began at 16th and Bryant Streets in October, taking several months to complete. The vacant lot was filled eventually with a succession of retail shops. Today, the San Francisco Autocenter (the headquarters for several new car dealerships), and an adjacent Safeway supermarket reside where Seals Stadium once did. The landmark Hamm's Brewery left several years later. Today, the only remnant from the days of watching minor and major league baseball games at Seals Stadium is the *Double Play Bar & Grill* at 2401 16th Street. Should you stop by for lunch on a pretty afternoon, ask for a table on the patio outside. You'll be surrounded by a miniature replica of old Seals Stadium.

Giants announcer Russ Hodges (SF Giants)

THE '58 PENNANT RACE

The Pre-Season Picks

 **HEADING INTO** the 1958 season, virtually nobody picked the Giants to win the pennant, not even Bob Stevens of the *Chronicle,* who had a penchant for picking the Giants in later years, if he thought it at all conceivable they could contend. Stevens picked the Giants to finish fourth, at the bottom of the first division. He was one of the optimists. *The Sporting News* tabbed the Giants for fifth, Dick Young from the *New York Daily News* pegged them to finish sixth, right where they finished the previous two years. Arthur Daley of the *New York Times* had them in fourth, Joe King from the *New York World Telegram* slotted them in fifth, and the Baseball Writers Association of America picked them to finish fifth; 209 writers from the BBWAA picked the Milwaukee Braves to win their third straight pennant, 21 picked St. Louis, six went with the Dodgers, three had Cincinnati and only one picked the Giants. The Santa Anita Sports Club in Las Vegas listed Milwaukee the favorite at 3-5, then the Dodgers at 3-1. The Giants were sixth, at 50-1.

The predictions and the longshot odds were no surprise. Not only had the Giants finished a distant sixth in both '56 and '57, but management did some major house-cleaning before the '58 opener. Gone from the team that finished the '57 season were, among others, outfielders Bobby Thomson, Don Mueller and Dusty Rhodes, first baseman Gail Harris, utilityman Ozzie Virgil and catcher Wes Westrum. Moreover, the only hold-overs from the Giants World Series championship team of '54 were Mays, Lockman, Antonelli, Gomez and Grissom (besides Worthington and Giel, who combined to throw just 22 innings in '54). Instead, the Giants opened the '58 season with six rookies, three in the Opening Day lineup. And, before the All-Star break, they would call up two more rookies from triple-A Phoenix, with both playing major roles on the team immediately. The typical pre-season prognostication on the Giants said something like, "Look for them to endure a long, grueling season, unless their banner rookie crop comes up big." Well, it did.

The Dodgers, on the other hand, went with an older, veteran team, led by Snider, Hodges, Furillo, Reese, Podres and Newcombe, and why not? Unlike the Giants, who had struggled badly in '56 and '57, the Dodgers won the pennants in both '55 and '56, and finished a strong third in '57. As the old saying goes, "If it ain't broke, don't fix it." O'Malley didn't.

Team-By-Team Previews

MILWAUKEE: The Braves, coming off a 95-59 record, the pennant and the World Series title in '57, had no significant weaknesses. They had great hitters, with power, adequate speed and defense, and superb pitching. Southpaw Cy Young winner **Warren Spahn** (21-11), **Bob Buhl** (18-7) and **Lew Burdette** (17-9) looked to provide a virtually unbeatable one-two-three punch in the starting rotation, with the fourth spot up for grabs between **Bob Rush** (6-16 with the Cubs), **Gene Conley** (9-9), **Juan Pizarro** (5-6), and rookies **Carlton Willey** (21-6 at triple-A Wichita) and **Joey Jay** (17-10 at Wichita). No matter who got that fourth spot, the rest figured to give the staff tremendous depth. **Ernie Johnson** (7-3, 4 saves) and **Don McMahon** (2-3, 9 saves) anchored the bullpen.

The lineup was basically set: **Del Crandall** (.253-15HR) was behind the plate, with **Joe Adcock** (.287-12HR), health permitting, at first, coming off a season in which he missed nearly 90 games with a broken leg, after hitting 38 home runs with 103 RBIs in '56. **Red Schoendienst** (.309) was at second, **Eddie Mathews** (.292-32HR-94RBI-109R) at third and **Johnny Logan** (.273) at short. MVP **Henry Aaron** (.322-44HR-132RBI-118R), **Wes Covington** (.284-21HR-65RBI) and **Bill Bruton** (.278) were in the outfield. Ready to come off the bench were **Frank Torre** (.272), **Andy Pafko** (.277), **"Hurricane" Bob Hazle** (.403) and **Felix Mantilla** (.236)

The Braves led the league in '57 in most runs, home runs (199), complete games (60) and fewest home runs allowed (124). Their .269 team batting average was second, as was their 3.47 ERA. If **Fred Haney's** troops stayed reasonably healthy in '58, they were clearly the team to beat.

ST. LOUIS: The Cardinals were coming off a fine season (87-67), yet still finished a distant second, eight games behind Milwaukee. A nice blend of youth and experience in the every day lineup, plus a talented pitching staff, gave the Cards as good a chance as any to upset Milwaukee.

The starting rotation was led by **Larry Jackson** (15-9), **Lindy McDaniel** (15-9) and **Sam Jones** (12-9), with **Wilmer "Vinegar Bend" Mizell** (8-10) or **Herm Wehmeier** (10-7) holding the fourth spot, and **Billy Muffett** (3-2, 8 saves) in the bullpen.

Hal Smith (.279) and **Hobie Landrith** (.243) figured to share the catching, with the incomparable 37-year-old **Stan Musial** (.351-29HR-102RBI) manning first base, **Don Blasingame** (.271-21SB-108R) at second, **Alvin Dark** (.290) at third and **Eddie Kasko** (.273) at short. The starting outfield featured **Wally Moon** (.295-24HR-73RBI), **Ken Boyer** (.265-19HR-62RBI) and **Del Ennis** (.286-24HR-105RBI), but rookie **Curt Flood** (.299-14HR-82RBI at class-A Savannah) was about ready to bust into the lineup, either in the outfield or at third. **Joe Cunningham** (.318-9HR-52RBI) was manager **Fred Hutchinson's** dream coming off the bench and spot-starting, at first and in the outfield.

The Cardinals led the league in hitting in '57 at .274, were third in pitching with a 3.78 ERA and second in shutouts (11). If their pitching stayed strong, and Milwaukee faltered, the Cards seemed poised to take advantage.

LOS ANGELES: The Dodgers, coming off a third-place finish (84-70), after winning two straight pennants, were hoping to combine a talented youth-sparked pitching staff with an aging yet talented lineup *and* new surroundings in LA to offset the loss of starting catcher, sparkplug and team leader **Roy Campanella,** paralyzed in a January car accident. If the pitching could come through, the Dodgers could contend.

Veterans **Don Newcombe** (11-12) and southpaw **Johnny Podres** (12-9), along with youngsters **Don Drysdale** (17-9) and lefty **Sandy Koufax** (5-4) had a shot at providing the Dodgers with an excellent starting rotation, with veteran **Carl Erskine** (5-3), sophomore **Danny McDevitt** (7-4) and rookie **Stan Williams** (19-7, 3.04 at triple-A St. Paul) ready in reserve. The bullpen was anchored by **Clem Labine** (5-7, league-leading 17 saves) and **Ed Roebuck** (8-2, 8 saves). The Dodger staff was coming off a season in which it led the league with a 3.35 ERA and 18 shutouts.

Manager **Walter Alston** was hoping that one of two rookies, **Joe Pignatano** (.299 at triple-A Montreal) or **John Roseboro** (.273 at Montreal) would take over the every day catching duties, with veteran **Rube Walker** (.181) available to back up. **Gil Hodges** (.299-27HR-98RBI) would be at first, **Charlie Neal** (.270) at second, **Jim Gilliam** (.250-26SB) or rookie **Dick Gray** (.297-16HR at St. Paul) at third, and **Pee Wee Reese** (.224) or **Don Zimmer** at short (.219). Gilliam also figured to play some second. **Duke Snider** (.274-40HR-92RBI) anchored an outfield that also would include **Gino Cimoli** (.293-10HR-57RBI) and one of two rookies, **Norm Larker** (.323-12HR-68RBI at St. Paul) or **Don Demeter** (.309-28HR-86RBI at St. Paul).

On paper, the Dodgers looked like a legitimate contender. However, there were some serious questions. How would the Dodger pitchers react to working in a new home with a left field fence *just 250 feet from home plate,* with someone *other* than Campanella as their number one batterymate (for the first time since '47)? And how would Snider, coming off five straight 40-home run seasons, react to hitting at that same new home—the LA Coliseum—hardly a mecca to power-hitting *left*-handed hitters? The answers to these questions would go a long way toward telling how seriously the Dodgers would threaten Milwaukee in '58.

CINCINNATI: The Redlegs nearly won the pennant in 1956 (91-63), falling just two games short, but fell off in '57 (80-74), finishing a distant fourth. It's easy to see why. Their team ERA shot up from a respectable 3.85 in '56 to a league-worst 4.62 in '57. With power—the Reds were second in the league in both runs scored and home runs (187) —speed and defense no problem, this team would return to contention only if the pitching returned to respectability.

Brooks Lawrence (16-13) was the only starting pitcher in '57 with a winning record, but the rest of the rotation was certainly capable of getting back into the black. **Hal Jeffcoat** (12-13) and **Joe Nuxhall** (10-10) figured in the mix, but newcomers **Bob Purkey** (11-14 with Pittsburgh) and Harvey Haddix (10-13 with Philadelphia) certainly did as well. **John Klippstein** (8-11) was a capable spot-starter. **Willard Schmidt** (10-3 with St. Louis), **Tom Acker** (10-5, 4 saves) and **Hersh Freeman** (7-2, 8 saves) were in the bullpen.

Ed Bailey (.261-20HR) and **Smokey Burgess** (.283-14HR) gave the Reds the most potent one-two backstop combo in the league. **George Crowe** (.271-31HR-92RBI) was at first, **Johnny Temple** (.284) at second, **Don Hoak** (.293-19HR-89RBI) at third and **Roy McMillan** (.272) at short. The outfield would be **Frank Robinson** (.322-29HR-75RBI) and **Gus Bell** (.292-13HR-61RBI), with **Jerry Lynch** (.258) or rookie **Vada Pinson** (.367-20HR-97RBI at class-A Visalia) of Oakland being counted upon to replace **Wally Post** (96HR the previous three years), traded to Philly for Haddix. The Redlegs had good power off the bench, with **Bob Thurman** (.247-16HR), **Pete Whisenant** (.211) and **Steve Bilko** (.300-56HR-140RBI at triple-A Los Angeles).Manager **Birdie Tebbetts** would enter the '58 season with his fingers crossed, hoping his pitching staff could rediscover its good form. If so, he might have a contender.

PHILADELPHIA: Coming off a so-so fifth-place finish (77-77), during which they finished next to last in runs scored and next to last in home runs (117), the Phillies only hope in '58 figured to be its talented pitching staff, to offset an aging lineup lacking in power.

Jack Sanford was hoping to avoid the sophomore jinx after a 19-8 Rookie of the Year campaign. Joining him in the rotation were veterans **Robin Roberts** (10-22) and southpaw **Curt Simmons** (12-11), with the fourth spot a battle between veterans **Jim Hearn** (5-1) and **Warren Hacker** (7-6), sophomore **Don Cardwell** (4-8) and rookie sleeper **Ray Semproch** (12-4, league-leading 2.64ERA at triple-A Miami). Another sophomore, **Dick Farrell** (10-2, 10 saves), anchored the bullpen for manager **Mayo Smith.**

Veteran **Stan Lopata** would return behind the plate (.237-18HR-67RBI), **Ed Bouchee** at first (.293-17HR-76RBI), **Ted Kazanski** (.265) or veteran **Solly Hemus** (.185) at second, **Willie Jones** at third (.247) and **Chico Fernandez** at short (.262). **Richie Ashburn** (.297), newcomer **Wally Post** (.244-20HR-74RBI with Cincinnati), sophomore **Harry Anderson** (.268-17HR-61RBI) and **Rip Repulski** (.260-20HR-68RBI) all were expected to get plenty of duty in the outfield. Rookie first baseman **Frank Herrera** (.306-17HR-93RBI at triple-A Miami) could help off the bench.

If Sanford could repeat his rookie success and if Roberts could return to the form that saw him win 20 six straight years, and then 19 the next (prior to '57), the Phillies had the capability to surprise.

SAN FRANCISCO: *Sports Illustrated,* in its 1958 baseball preview issue, said if their rookie parlay came through, "an outlandish long shot but a possibility, the Giants could be the most exciting team in the league." That seemed to be the consensus around the league, that the Giants were rolling the dice—betting the wad, in a sense—on a bunch of untested kids, and banking on a trifecta-payoff in return. *Sports Illustrated* went even further, suggesting the Giants were weak in fielding, hitting and pitching (what's left?)—specifically, weak at first, second, third, left, right, catching and pitching depth. Put another way, the magazine obviously liked Mays, apparently liked Spencer, may have liked Antonelli and Gomez, but that was about it. Yes, but those rookies ....

Ruben Gomez (15-13) and lefty **John Antonelli** (12-18) would anchor the starting rotation, with the other two spots to be decided among **Curt Barclay** (9-9), **Ray Crone** (7-9), spot-starters **Stu Miller** (7-9), **Al Worthington** (8-11), **Mike McCormick** (3-1) and **Ramon Monzant** (3-2), and rookie **Pete Burnside** (10-5, 2.47ERA at triple-A Minneapolis). Forty-year-old **Marv Grissom** (4-4 with 14 saves) would be asked to close games yet one more time.

With **Wes Westrum** retired (and coaching the Giants) and **Ray Katt** dealt to St. Louis, the catching duties would rest with **Valmy Thomas** (.249) and rookie **Bob Schmidt** (.262-17HR-61RBI at Minneapolis). Twenty-year-old **Orlando Cepeda** (.309-25HR-108RBI at Minneapolis) was going to get every opportunity to win the first base job, **Danny O'Connell** (.256) would start at second, **Daryl Spencer** (.249-11HR-50RBI) at short and veteran **Ray Jablonski** (.289-9HR-57RBI) or rookie **Jim Davenport** (.291-10HR-53RBI at Minneapolis) at third. Talented but unproven **Andre Rodgers** (.244) would also be given a close look at short, with the possibility of Spencer moving to second.

The incredible **Willie Mays** (.333-35HR-97RBI-112R-38SB), 39-year-old **Hank Sauer** (.259-26HR-76RBI) and rookie **Willie Kirkland** (.293-37HR-120RBI at Minneapolis in '56, w/military service in '57) were the likely starting outfield, although two other rookies, **Leon Wagner** (.330-51HR-166RBI at class-B Danville in '56, w/military service in '57) and **Felipe Alou** (.306-12HR-71RBI at class-A Springfield) were certain to be watched closely at triple-A Phoenix, should Sauer or Kirkland falter. Providing backup off the bench were veteran **Whitey Lockman** (.248), **Ed Bressoud** (.268), **Jim King** (.268-20HR-73RBI at triple-A Omaha) and **Bob Speake** (.232-16HR-50RBI with the Cubs), acquired in the spring for 1951 hero **Bobby Thomson.**

It's easy to see why the Giants were picked so low in the standings, albeit with the excitement surrounding their promising corps of rookies. They would enter the season with just two proven starting pitchers, assuming that Antonelli would return to the form that made him a 20-game winner in '54 and '56, and more rookies than proven vets in their every day lineup. Manager **Bill Rigney** said he had never seen so many new faces in spring training in his entire career, that there were nearly a dozen who had never even seen a major league camp before. That was the challenge for Rigney's Giants. And the anticipation.

PITTSBURGH: The Pirates tied for last in the league in '57 at 62-92, and were also last in runs scored and home runs (92). The offense would have to put many more runs up on the board in '58 to take the pressure of an otherwise capable pitching staff.

Bob Friend (14-8) headed the mound corps, followed by **Vernon Law** (10-8), **Ronnie Kline** (9-16) and **Don Gross** (7-9), over from Cincinnati for Purkey. Rookies **Bennie Daniels** (17-8, 2.95ERA at triple-A Hollywood) and **George Witt** (18-7, 2.24 at Hollywood) appeared ready to start in the bigs, putting the pressure on Kline and Gross. One of the bright emerging relievers in the game, **Elroy Face** (4-6 with 10 saves) gave the Bucs strength in the bullpen.

Hank Foiles (.270-9HR) would return behind the plate, **Frank Thomas** (.290-23HR-89RBI) to first, **Bill Mazeroski** (.283) to second, **Gene Freese** (.283) to third and **Dick Groat** (.315) to short. The mix could change early, though, if newly-acquired **Ted Kluszewski** (.268-6HR-21RBI part-time with Cincinnati) returned to form, or if rookie **Dick Stuart** (.251-45HR-122RBI at class-A Lincoln, double-A Atlanta and triple-A Hollywood) showed he was ready. Stuart's 66 home runs at Lincoln in '56 made him a legend-in-the-making. If either Kluszewski or Stuart could take over first, Thomas could move over to third, giving the Pirates tremendous pop from the corners.

The outfield looked to be set, with **Bob Skinner** (.305-13HR) in left, slick-fielding **Bill Virdon** (.251) in center and rising star **Roberto Clemente** (.253) in right. Lending depth off the bench figured to be **Roman Mejias** (.275), **Gene Baker** (.264), **Johnny O'Brien** (.305) and rookie **R.C. Stevens** (.256-19HR-68RBI at triple-A Hollywood and Columbus).

If Daniels and/or Witt could have sensational rookie seasons, and if Kluszewski or Stuart could emerge at first base, moving Thomas to third, the Pirates had a decent shot at moving from the bottom of the second division to somewhere in the first.

CHICAGO: The Cubs, after sharing last place with Pittsburgh at 62-92, looked to **Ernie Banks,** some decent power behind him in the lineup and a pair of impressive young starting pitchers to move up in the standings. They figured to need more to make a big dent, though, because they were coming off a season in which they were last in the league in hitting at .244, and next to last in pitching with a 4.13 ERA.

Second-year starters **Dick Drott** (15-11) and **Moe Drabowsky** (13-15), just 43 years old between them, would anchor a rotation backed by several possibilities, including spot-starters **Dave Hillman** (6-11) and **Jim Brosnan** (5-5), south-paw **Taylor Phillips** (3-2 with Milwaukee) and rookie **Glen Hobbie** (15-15 at double-A Memphis). The bullpen appeared in good hands with **Don Elston** (6-7 with 8 saves) and **Turk Lown** (5-7 with 12 saves).

Cal Neeman (.258-10HR) would do the bulk of the catching, unless beaten out by rookie **Sam Taylor** (.257-12HR-87RBI at double-A Atlanta). **Dale Long** (.298-21HR-67RBI) was at first, light-hitting **Jerry Kindall** (.160) at second, rookie **Tony Taylor** (.217 at double-A Dallas) at third and the amazing Banks (.285-43HR-102RBI) at short. **Walt Moryn** (.289-19HR-88RBI), Lee Walls (.237) and **Bobby Thomson** (.240-12HR-61RBI with the Giants) were expected to man the outfield. If Kindall failed to hit better, though, Taylor might move over to second, with Thomson taking over third. **Jim Bolger** (.275) or **Chuck Tanner** (.279) could then move into the outfield.

Manager **Bob Scheffing's** Cubs hoped to ride the coattails of superstar Banks, and young studs Drott and Drabowsky, to see how far they could rise in the standings.

AMERICAN LEAGUE: Yankees, Yankees and more Yankees. The Yankees had won eight of the previous nine American League pennants, including the last three in succession (98-56 in '57). The question heading into the '58 season was not whether the Yankees would win another flag, good health permitting, but whether this Yankee team was comparable to the vintage Yankee clubs of the past. A pennant for the Yankees was a virtual certainty in the fifties. The one year they didn't win, in '54, they did win 103 games. It's just that Cleveland won 111.

With a rotation made up of southpaw **Whitey Ford** (11-5), **Bob Turley** (13-6) and **Tom Sturdivant** (16-6), and either **Don Larsen** (10-4), **Art Ditmar** (8-3) or **Johnny Kucks** (8-10), and with **Bob Grim** (12-8 with 19 saves) heading the bullpen, the Yankees league-best ERA of 3.00 was no accident. It figured to be just as strong in '58.

The Yankees also led the league in hitting at .268 and in runs scored. With a lineup of **Yogi Berra** (.251-24HR-82RBI) or **Elston Howard** (.253) catching, **Moose Skowron** (.304-17HR-88RBI) at first, **Bobby Richardson** (.256) at second, **Jerry Lumpe** (.340) or **Andy Carey** (.255) at third, **Gil McDougald** (.289-13HR-62RBI) at short, and an outfield of **Mickey Mantle** (.365-34HR-94RBI-121R), **Hank Bauer** (.259-18HR-65RBI) and Rookie of the Year **Tony Kubek**

Spring Training camp opens for Giants, Phoenix, Arizona; manager Bill Rigney stands to left alongside coach Wes Westum; Felipe Alou, Pete Burnside, Al Worthington & Marv Grissom run onto field; coach Salty Parker stands to right. (SF Giants)

Spring Training

THE GIANTS LAUNCHED the early portion of their spring camp, known as "Operation Great Wash," at Buckhorn Mineral Wells outside Mesa, Arizona, February 14. This 10-day pre-camp was for older players who might need a little extra therapy to get their bodies ready for the season, as well as for younger players who might simply need a little more time to get aching muscles in shape or rid themselves of excess pounds. Keep in mind, 1958 was long before the days when players had strict, daily off-season workouts to keep their bodies in tip-top shape, as most have now. No, these were the days when players had to maintain off-season jobs simply to make ends meet financially. It wasn't unusual for players to arrive at spring training in late February needing the entire six weeks or so to get in shape to start the season. Nowadays most players complain, with justification, that spring training is far too long. They simply don't need all that time to get ready physically or get their timing down at the plate, in the field or on the mound.

The earliest arrivals at the Buckhorn Baths were vets Hank Sauer, Bobby Thomson, Dusty Rhodes and Ray Jablonski. They'd sweat off unwanted winter weight in the morning, in the

(.297), plus rookie **Norm Siebern** (.349-24HR-118RBI at triple-A Denver) ready if Kubek moved to the infield, the Yankees appeared a sure thing to get on top of the standings early, and stay on top. Berra and Howard both could play the outfield, when the other was catching, depending on Siebern's progress. Either way, **Casey Stengel's** troops wouldn't lose, at least not often.

The best of the rest would probably be Chicago or Boston. The White Sox, after a second-place finish in '57 (90-64), could boast 20-game winner **Billy Pierce,** 16-game winner **Dick Donovan** and 14-game winner **Early Wynn.** They led the league in complete games (59) and shutouts (16), and had great team speed but did not have enough power to match the Yankees. The Red Sox, third in '57 (82-72), could boast one of the majors' best outfields, with 39-year-old **Ted Williams** (.388-38HR-87RBI), **Jackie Jensen** (.281-23HR-103RBI) and **Jimmy Piersall** (.261-19HR-63RBI-103R), and a solid third baseman in **Frank Malzone** (.292-15HR-103RBI). But the rest of the Sox lineup was relatively weak, although there was hope for rookie second baseman **Ken Aspromonte** (.334-7HR-73RBI at triple-A San Francisco), and the pitching couldn't compare with the Yankees or White Sox. The rest of the American League? Forget it.

Manager Bill Rigney and owner Horace Stoneham watch Giants during Spring Training. (SF Giants)

baths and from exercising, undergo body massages, all within the confines of a low-fat diet, and then have the afternoons free to play golf or lounge by the pool. Coaches Herman Franks and Wes Westrum were on hand as well, and manager Bill Rigney was already spilling over with optimism, saying the spirit at the baths was tremendous, that if these players could carry that enthusiasm into Opening Day, it could infect the rest of the team and, well, who knows? Rigney said pennants had been won before on desire like that. Hope springs eternal every February and March, for every manager, for every club.

By the 17th, several more players arrived at the Buckhorn spa, including pitchers Curt Barclay and Marv Grissom, rookie catcher Bob Schmidt, and infielders Danny O'Connell, Andre Rodgers, Foster Castleman and Jim Finigan, who hit .270 in a backup role with Detroit in '57. Meanwhile, Willie Mays was continuing his hectic hot-stove banquet schedule. He attended a "Welcome Willie" dinner, with wife Marghuerite, at the Merchandise Mart on Market Street in San Francisco, at $10 per plate, with the proceeds benefiting the interracial program of the Urban League of the Bay Area. He then flew to Los Angeles to rehearse a taping of the Bob Hope Show, and returned to the Bay Area the next day for an appearance at the Sports and Boat Show in Richmond, benefiting the Police Widows & Orphans Fund. Later in the week he'd be at Seals Stadium to pose for a photo session for *Life* magazine. He'd be on the magazine cover in two months.

Although the mandatory date for players to report to the Giants spring camp in Phoenix was March 1, Rigney expected some 38 players to report by February 24. He was right. Mays and pitcher Ernie Broglio were the last of the 38 to arrive, on the 23rd, just an hour before President Eisenhower himself landed in Phoenix, not to see the Giants, but to play golf at the Maine Chance Resort. The only two

Giants minor leaguers relax at minor league camp in Sanford, Florida. (SF Giants)

players missing, then, were pitcher Ramon Monzant, en route from Venezuela, and catcher Valmy Thomas, who reportedly had tonsillitis in his native St. Croix, in the U.S. Virgin Islands.

Rigney held a press conference at the Giants' Adams Hotel headquarters, saying the most impressive-looking Giant he'd seen thus far was rookie first baseman Orlando Cepeda. "He looks like a bronze statue standing at dress parade," Rigney cooed. "It's up to him and (fellow rookie Willie) Kirkland. If they hit, we're going to move for sure out of sixth place." Rigney also suggested that Ruben Gomez (traditionally a late arrival) getting to camp on time and in shape was a good omen for the club. "There's something about playing in San Francisco, and the change from the

Willie Mays poses for photographers at spring training. (SF Giants)

East, that has the kids pretty well souped up," Rigney said. "It's a new life for us all."

There would be a strict midnight curfew instituted on the 24th, with no alcohol permitted until the start of exhibition games, and then only a beer or two per day. Initially, the players would be on the field by 10 a.m., and work out for two to two and a half hours a day.

Bob Stevens of the *Chronicle,* longtime Seals beat-writer, said the only difference he could see from dozens of minor league camps he'd covered was that the Giants were bigger, better and wealthier than their Pacific Coast League counterparts. Mays led the batting practice home run parade at Municipal Stadium with a 450-foot shot, while the most impressive on the mound were Gomez and Paul Giel, the All-America halfback from the University of Minnesota, fresh out of the Army. Gomez, asked if he missed New York, replied, "I'm a gypsy at heart. The only place I miss is Puerto Rico."

Back in San Francisco, ticket sales were brisk. Three-thousand season tickets already had been sold ($262.50 per box, $187.50 per reserved), whereas the Giants seldom reached the 2,800 mark in New York. Ticket manager Peter Hoffman predicted the Giants would sell 3,500-4,000 season tickets before Opening Day.

The Giants signed catcher Tom Haller on the 26th, out of the University of Illinois, where he played quarterback for the Fighting Illini, and lettered in basketball as well. Meantime, Johnny Antonelli blasted Dodgers vice president Buzzy Bavasi, after having earlier criticized the Dodgers' decision to play baseball in a football stadium, after which Bavasi said Antonelli wouldn't last three innings there anyway. Hence, Antonelli's rip. On the diamond, Rigney called Broglio the best-looking rookie pitcher in camp. The Berkeley native was 17-6 for double-A Dallas in '57.

Rigney endeared himself to longtime Seals fans on the 28th by naming San Francisco native Lefty O'Doul special hitting instructor. The 60-year-old O'Doul had a lifetime major league average of .349, including .398 for the Athletics in 1929, in 638 at-bats. He also played several years for the Seals, and later managed them for 17 straight seasons.

At least a half-dozen New York writers were reporting regularly on the Giants, and would continue to do so, at least through the opening series in both San Francisco and Los Angeles. The two groups of writers typically kept to themselves, with the New York writers no doubt looking askance at their San Francisco counterparts, as new to the majors as they were. What they may not have understood, though, was that San Francisco newspapers for many years carried as much in the way of major league stories and box scores as any Eastern newspaper, in part because so much major league talent either came from the sandlots of the Bay Area or from the Pacific Coast League, or both. Of course, local beatwriters, columnists and photographers would have to adjust to some decided differences from covering Coast League games: Major-league regulations stipulated that the press had to leave the field a half hour before gametime; photographers could not take on-field close-up shots of close plays at home and first, as they could in the minors; managers could take only two trips to the mound per inning before having to remove their pitcher (three trips in the PCL). Strategy was sometimes different than it was in the minors as well. For example, the *Chronicle*'s Bill Leiser explained to readers early in the season the thinking behind the double-switch, noting that managers never employed the tactic in the PCL.

More than a half-dozen Bay Area papers had a writer assigned to the daily Giants beat, including four dailies in San Francisco alone. The *Oakland Tribune* would characterize itself, editorially, by refusing to print the name, "San Francisco," in any of its stories, datelines or standings, *all season,* obviously a reaction to losing its beloved Oakland Oaks of the Coast League, an obvious byproduct of the fervent effort to bring big-league ball to San Francisco.

The Giants won their Cactus League opener March 8, beating Cleveland 5-1 in Tucson. Only 3,668 turned out on a sunny, but cold and windy afternoon. Mike McCormick, just 19 years old, threw three scoreless innings to get the win, while the 20-year-old Cepeda singled, doubled, homered and drove in three runs. The following day the Giants beat the Cubs in Phoenix 5-1, with Al Worthington and rookie Joe Shipley throwing three scoreless innings apiece. Giants owner Horace Stoneham called Shipley the kid with the most stuff on the club, but then remembered watching him hit six batters in a row a few years back in the minors.

Gomez made his spring debut on the 11th, with three shutout innings in a 4-2 loss to the Cubs. Spencer hit a pair of homers on the 13th against the Cubs, then rookie catcher Roger

McCardell homered twice against Cleveland on the 14th, in the first major- league exhibition played in the Southern California desert town of El Centro, with an overflow crowd of 4,000 showing up. McCardell would hit well as high as triple-A Phoenix, yet his major league career would be limited to four at-bats with the Giants in '59.

Gomez threw five more scoreless innings against Cleveland on the 19th. Overall, the pitching was impressive, the hitting was consistent and the record was several games over .500. Of concern was the fact that '54 World Series hero Dusty Rhodes was hospitalized with migraine headaches, later diagnosed as an "inflamed artery of the scalp." Meanwhile, the Giants entered into the bidding for USC outfielder Ron Fairly. Remember, this was long before the advent of the June free-agent draft. High school and college kids were up for grabs, often depending on which organization had the best scouting.

The Giants sold the contract of outfielder Don Mueller to the White Sox on the 22nd. That left Mays, Antonelli, Lockman, Grissom, Thomson, Rhodes and Katt as the only key cogs from the '54 World Series title club still with the Giants. Thomson and Katt would go shortly, and Rhodes would spend the season in Phoenix. On the field that day, the Giants outlasted the Cubs 18-12 in Phoenix, with Cepeda and Sauer hitting a pair of home runs each, Mays hitting one, and the three combining for 11 RBIs. Two days later the Giants sold the contract of utilityman Foster Castleman to the Orioles.

Bob Speake, Willie McCovey, Ray Jablonski, Bill White, Ed Bressoud, Jim Davenport, Daryl Spencer, Danny O'Connell, Andre Rodgers, Orlando Cepeda (left-to-right) at Spring Training. (SF Giants)

Mays and Cepeda continued their onslaught with two homers each in a 7-5 win over the Orioles on the 26th. A day later the Giants hammered the Birds 10-0 as Ramon Monzant threw six shutout innings, and Andre Rodgers homered twice and drove in five runs. Rodgers, the cricket player from the Bahamas, was a personal favorite of Stoneham, who saw Ernie Banks potential in the six-foot-three, 190-pound Rodgers.

The Giants (14-7) clinched the Cactus League crown with a 4-1 win over the Orioles April 1, as Worthington became the first pitcher to throw seven innings. The next day the Giants sent 31-year-old catcher Ray Katt to St. Louis for 25-year-old outfielder Jim King, a left-handed hitter, then took the field and beat the Orioles again 9-8 on Rodgers' inside-the-park two-run homer in the ninth. The Giants left Phoenix the next day on what was then a very common practice, employed by other clubs as well—barnstorming through minor league cities, typically by train, leading right up to Opening Day. In '58, the Giants' tour took them through Texas, Oklahoma, Iowa and Nebraska, before they would fly to San Francisco on the 13th. Their total attendance for 10 home games in Phoenix was 25,452. Before leaving, though, they made another deal, sending 34-year-old Bobby Thomson to the Cubs for 27-year-old left-handed hitting first baseman/outfielder Bob Speake. Shipley was sent back to Phoenix,

Manager Bill Rigney (second from left), with coaches Herman Franks, Salty Parker and Wes Westrum (left-to-right) at spring training. (SF Giants)

leaving the club just one over the Opening Day limit of 28, which did not count recently released servicemen Kirkland and Giel. Rigney later acknowledged that he had been hoping to get the Cubs' Walt Moryn, or the Reds' Smokey Burgess for Thomson. He liked Burgess in particular because he was not only a left-handed hitter, like Moryn, but a catcher as well, and Rigney would have preferred more punch from that position in the lineup than he figured to get with either Thomas or Schmidt.

Seals Stadium, San Francisco, April 14, 1958 (SF Giants)

The crowds to see the Giants play the Indians on their tour through the Bible Belt were impressive. There was an SRO crowd of 4,500 in El Paso to see Gomez throw eight innings of seven-hit ball in a 5-4 Giants win; 6,700 in San Antonio to see Monzant hurl seven innings of four-hit ball in a 9-7 win; 3,182 in Austin to see Antonelli duplicate Monzant's effort in a 7-0 win; two crowds of 5,100 each turned out in Corpus Christi, once to see McCormick throw seven innings of six-hit ball. Rigney, meantime, nixed a St. Louis offer of Wally Moon for either Willie McCovey or Bill White. McCovey, coming off a good year at double-A Dallas (.281-11HR-65RBI) would be the starting first baseman at Phoenix in '58. White, who hit 22 homers as a rookie first baseman for the Giants in '56, was expected to complete his two years of military service by August.

The emergence of White in '56, Cepeda, Kirkland, Wagner, Alou and Davenport in '58, and McCovey in '59 served as a good illustration for the brilliance of the Giants scouting department in the fifties, and you could actually include Stoneham himself in that category, in part because the Giants owner was very wired into the Caribbean baseball scene, before much of the rest of the baseball world caught on. But this was true also because Stoneham was willing to pour big money into the farm system. Former Giant pitching great Carl Hubbell, as farm director, governed the seeding, signing and cultivating process.

Cepeda, for example, was recommended to the Giants by a man outside the organization, Pedro Zorilla, when Orlando was just 17. Zorilla recommended three others with Cepeda, in '55, including shortstop Jose Pagan, who became a Giants regular in '61. Alou also was recommended by a man outside the organization, Horacio Martinez, who advised Giants scout Alex Pompez about Alou in '56, when Felipe was 20. Martinez had once played ball for Pompez in the Dominican Republic. And Rodgers was recommended by yet another man outside the organization, a gentleman named Harry Joynes, who played softball with Rodgers in the Bahamas, who also knew of Rodgers' prowess as a cricket player, and who called the Giants to suggest they take a look at this 18-year-old kid at their next spring camp, in '54. They did, and signed him. Andre excited

Giants opening day lineup poses at Seals Stadium, April 14, one day before opener–(left-to-right)–Jim Davenport, Danny O'Connell, Willie Mays, Willie Kirkland, Orlando Cepeda, Hank Sauer, Daryl Spencer, Valmy Thomas, Ruben Gomez. (SF Chronicle) (note: manager Bill Rigney substituted Jim King for Hank Sauer the next morning, because of an unusual wind blowing out to right field.)

Stoneham by tearing up the class-C Northern League in '55, and would tear up the Pacific Coast League in '58, causing Baltimore general manager Paul Richards to offer $100,000 for his services. The Giants, understandably, expecting great things from Rodgers, declined.

The barnstorming tour continued as 3,000 fans turned out in Houston April 10 to see the Giants lose a wild one, 15-14 in 10 innings. Mays and Kirkland combined for two homers and seven RBIs. Gomez continued his excellent spring with five innings of one-hit, shutout ball on the 11th, in a 2-1 win before 5,800 in Tulsa. After the game, Rigney announced Gomez would be his Opening Day starter on the 15th. The next day 7,165 saw the Giants win again, 12-11, in Des Moines, as Cepeda boosted his spring average to .370 by going four-for-four, with a homer and three RBIs. Finally, the biggest crowd of the spring, 14,070, turned out on a sunny Sunday afternoon in Omaha on the 13th to see Cleveland win 8-5. The Giants finished the spring with a 21-11 record, two and a half games ahead of the Cubs. In Florida, Milwaukee finished 16-12, and the Dodgers went 15-16. The Giants' leading spring hitters: Spencer (.413-7HR-13RBI), Cepeda (.370-9HR-27RBI), Mays (.322-9HR-21RBI) and Kirkland (.260-9HR-25RBI). Leading pitchers: Gomez (1-0, 1.80), Monzant (4-0, 1.95) and Antonelli (2-1, 1.81).

The Giants were met by about 400 fans at the airport in San Francisco that night, after which all the players, except Mays, were taken to a downtown hotel. Mays went to the home he purchased in November, in the exclusive St. Francis Wood neighborhood of San Francisco. The Dodgers had arrived two hours earlier, on a flight from Las Vegas. Both teams would work out the next day at Seals Stadium, first the Giants, who would then be toasted in a downtown parade, after which they'd feast in a big luncheon at the Sheraton-Palace. Hundreds of thousands were at the parade, and about 1,000 at the luncheon.

The Season

APRIL: The front-page banner-headline in the *Chronicle* said it all, after the historic opener on the 15th: WE

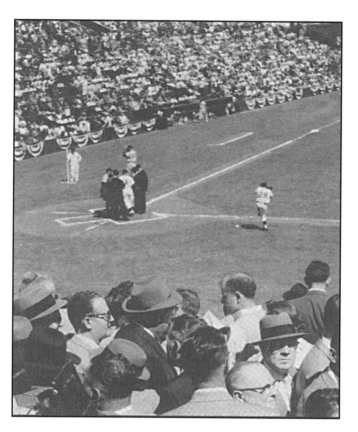

Starting pitchers Don Drysdale of the Dodgers and Ruben Gomez of the Giants warm up alongside home plate, before firstpitch, Opening Day, April 15, 1958, at Seals Stadium; managers Bill Rigney and Walt Alston exchange lineups with umpires at home plate. (SF Chronicle)

Giants lined up along first-base line, Dodgers along third-base line, Opening Day, April 15, 1958, at Seals Stadium. (SF Chronicle)

Ruben Gomez throws first pitch, Opening Day, April 15, 1958, at Seals Stadium, to Gino Cimoli of Dodgers; Valmy Thomas is catching, Jocko Conlan is the umpire. (Dick Dobbins)

MURDER THE BUMS. Ruben Gomez outdueled young Don Drysdale, spinning a nifty six-hit shutout, as the Giants beat the Dodgers 8-0. Daryl Spencer hit the first home run in San Francisco Giants history, earning himself a place in the record books, as well as six pairs of shoes from a San Francisco shoe store. Orlando Cepeda also homered, Willie Mays had two hits and two RBIs, and even Gomez had two hits, scored one run and drove in another. Bill Rigney received a wire at the ballpark before the game, from his former manager Leo Durocher. It said, "Get off on the right foot buddy. Win the first one and let the rest take care of themselves. Will be pulling for you and the boys. Good Luck. Leo"

Pee Wee Reese also got a wire at the ballpark before the game, also from Durocher. It read, "Good luck, buddy. Let's make this the best year ever, and especially for one of the great guys of all time, Roy Campanella. Leo"

The SRO crowd of 23,448 could have been tens of thousands more, if only Seals Stadium were bigger. One year earlier, the Giants drew 8,585 fans for their home opener at the Polo Grounds.

Other National League openers found Pittsburgh winning at Milwaukee, 4-3 in 14 innings, on R.C. Stevens' RBI

single, as Eddie Mathews homered twice, in front of 43,339 fans at County Stadium; Chicago beat the Cardinals at Busch Stadium 4-0 behind Jim Brosnan, before 26,246; and Philadelphia beat the Reds in Cincinnati 5-4, with 32,849 fans at Crosley Field.

The *Chronicle* headline on the 17th said it all, after the first major league *night* game in West Coast history, on the 16th: BUMS MURDER US. They did. Johnny Podres pitched the Dodgers to a 13-1 win over Ramon Monzant and the Giants, before 22,735. But the Giants came back to win the rubber-game of the series 7-4, as Jim Davenport had four hits and two RBIs, Bob Schmidt hit his first major league home run and Curt Barclay picked up the win in relief of John Antonelli, who was knocked out early. Antonelli said later he couldn't get loose on the mound, that he had pitched in colder (57 degrees) weather before, but that the wind affected his curve and change-up. Back in Milwaukee, Mathews homered twice *again*, in the Braves' 6-1 win over the Bucs.

Fittingly, following the Giants-Dodgers three-game series at Seals Stadium to christen big league ball on the West Coast, the two teams traveled south to play three more times and christen baseball at the LA Coliseum. On a sunny Friday afternoon, in front of a major league record crowd of 78,672, the Dodgers edged the Giants 6-5, despite a pair of home runs by Hank Sauer. The old major league attendance record had been 78,382, set in Cleveland in August of '48, when

Opening Day, Seals Stadium, April 15, 1958 (SF Chronicle)

the Tribe hosted the White Sox. The old National League record had been set in May of '37 when the Giants hosted the Dodgers at the Polo Grounds before 60,747. It's also worth noting that the Dodgers drew just 11,202 to their home opener in '57, in Brooklyn, despite the fact that the Dodgers had won the pennant in both '55 and '56.

The Giants came right back, though, and won twice in succession on the Dodgers' home field to take the series. They won 11-4 Saturday on Gomez' seven-hitter (Ruben also had two more hits, scored twice and drove in a run), as Sauer and Cepeda homered and drove in three runs each. And they won 12-2 Sunday on Monzant's eight-hitter, as Danny O'Connell hit a pair of homers. They had 15 hits for the second straight day. Spencer went three-for-three with a homer and three RBIs, and Mays had three more hits, going eight-for-14 in the series. Because of the smog, though, Spencer was relieved to be getting out of LA, saying if there had been a doubleheader Sunday, he couldn't have played the second game because he was coughing so heavily. Fifteen hundred fans

Willie Mays singles off reliever Don Bessent, driving in Ruben Gomez and Jim Davenport, in fourth inning, Opening Day, April 15, 1958, at Seals Stadium; Herman Franks is the third-base coach. Jim King is the base runner at first. (San Francisco History Center, San Francisco Public Library)

greeted the Giants when they arrived back in San Francisco, having taken four of six from the Dodgers. They were just a half game behind the Cubs, who had taken four of five from St. Louis. Milwaukee was a half game back of the Giants, having taken three of five from Pittsburgh, with Warren Spahn throwing a five-hit shutout on Saturday.

For the record, the Dodgers drew 167,207 fans for the three-game series, during which those fans spent an average of $1 apiece on concessions, including 240,000 sodas, 160,000 hot dogs, 140,000 ice creams and 125,000 bags of peanuts.

Back home at Seals Stadium, the Giants drew 22,786 on a Tuesday night but lost to the Cardinals 7-5, as Antonelli took the defeat and Kirkland hit his first big league home run. But the Giants came back again, with a pair of heart-stopping ninth-inning rallies to beat the Cards 8-7 Wednesday, and 6-5 Thursday, to win their third straight series. Spencer's two-run homer capped a four-run ninth in the first victory, and his RBI single capped a two-run ninth in the second. Sauer hit two more home runs, and the *Chronicle* responded in kind with two more front-page headlines: MIRACLE WIN BY GIANTS on Thursday morning, and ANOTHER MIRACLE WIN on Friday. Cards manager Fred Hutchinson professed to be unimpressed, saying, "Those guys will be down where they belong by July." Still, the Giants were 6-3 after nine games, a half game

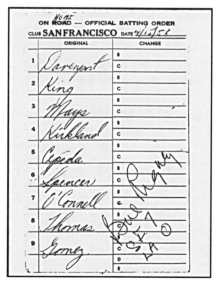

Giants official lineup card, opening day, April 15, 1958, signed by manager Bill Rigney, who also wrote the wrong score; Giants actually won 8-0 (fortunately for Rigney, this wasn't a golf scorecard). (National Baseball Hall of Fame Library, Cooperstown, N.Y.)

ahead of Milwaukee, which beat Cincinnati 6-2 Thursday on a Spahn seven-hitter and two homers by Aaron.

But the Cubs were the surprise leaders out of the gate at 6-2, after a 15-2 win at LA, as Lee Walls hit *three* home runs and drove in eight. Yes, the same Lee Walls who hit all of six home runs during the entire '57 season. Walls' explosion underscored the controversy already exploding over the short home run porch in left field at the Coliseum, just 250 feet away (as Antonelli remarked, it was just a football stadium), although there was a 40-foot high fence you had to hit it over to get it out. Adding to the controversy was the fact that it was just 320 feet to left center, yet 440 feet to right center and 390 feet to right. Drysdale already was depressed. He called the screen a joke, and said it was enough to make him cut his throat. He said it was impossible to set up a hitter. He said he had a two-and-one count on O'Connell, in his second start, and threw him a pitch high and inside. What happened? O'Connell popped it up over the fence. "To win here," Drysdale complained, "you're going to have to be awfully good or awfully lucky."

Most of the right-handed power hitters loved hitting at the Coliseum. Sauer took one look at

Carl Erskine pitches first inning in Dodgers' home opener, against Giants, April 18, 1958. (Dick Dobbins)

Willie Mays hits Carl Erskine pitch back toward mound, first inning, at LA Coliseum, of Dodgers' home opener, April 18, 1958; umpire is Tony Venzon, catcher is John Roseboro, and baserunner at second is Jim Davenport. (Dick Dobbins)

the short left field porch and said, "Whaddya know, *Disneyland*." Then he hit three home runs in his first three games there. There was already concern around baseball that somebody would break Babe Ruth's single-season home run record of 60, with many suggesting that if a Dodger did it, there would have to be an asterisk in the record books. But Sauer dismissed those thoughts. As much as he liked hitting there, he predicted no Dodger would come close because the short distance to the seats in left would make too many hitters *try* for home runs and, as a result, pop the ball up.

Even Lee Walls himself put a damper on the home run record theory, suggesting that in the long run a hitter would be hurt by the short porch, that he'd start thinking too much about how close the seats were, and that he'd find himself trying to pull every pitch over it. Walls also noted that the 40-foot fence in left would stop many a home run ball. He noted that during the Cubs-Dodgers series, Banks hit a line drive to left that hit high on that fence and bounced back on the field, and that Thomson hit the fence with line drives twice. All three shots, Walls said, would have been home runs at Wrigley Field.

Pittsburgh batting coach George Sisler predicted there would not be the overflow of home runs in LA that most others seemed to expect. Sisler said a hitter should not change his batting style to fit one park out of eight.

Still, the writers had a field day writing about baseball being played in a football stadium. Shirley Povich of the *Washington Post & Times Herald:* "Major-league baseball was meant to be played in Los Angeles but not in the Coliseum, which was designed for things like lion feeding or chariot racing. Home run records should be suspended for the life of the Coliseum as the home of the Dodgers. The left field screen is a horror."

Red Smith of the *New York Herald-Tribune:* "It's a magnificent park—for football."

Charlie Park of the *Los Angeles Mirror-News:* "It's a good thing the Coliseum will be only the temporary home of the Dodgers. Otherwise, Duke Snider, Rube Walker, John Roseboro and the rest of the left-handed hitters would either have to learn to hit from the other side or cut their throats. There simply can't be another ballpark in the world which is so extreme—favoring the right-handed hitter so much, and penalizing the left-handed hitter so severely." Echoing that sentiment, left-handed-hitting Harry Anderson of Philadelphia said only, "I'm sick." And Babe Herman, former Dodger slugger and then Philly scout, said, "If I were Duke Snider, I'd start hitting right-handed, and I'm not kidding."

Dick Young of the *New York Daily News:* It is deplorable that Walter O'Malley was forced to play in a stadium which makes a mockery of big league baseball. I'm sure he is crying all the way to the bank."

Art Rosenbaum of the *San Francisco Chronicle:* "In his graying state, Hank Sauer has suddenly become a million-dollar ballplayer—in Los Angeles."

The owner of the Cubs, Phil Wrigley, said the Dodgers made a mistake moving to the Coliseum, that they should instead have moved to LA's Wrigley Field (the former home of the PCL's Angels, and future one-year home of the American League's expansion LA Angels). But Dodger VP Bavasi countered by saying that he didn't regard Wrigley Field as a big league ballpark either, that a ton of home runs would have been hit at Wrigley, with short fences there all around. Bavasi also pointed to the capacity of just 20,000 at Wrigley, saying the Dodgers would have lost money to boot. For the sake of argument, while 193 home runs were hit at the Coliseum in 1958 (26 shy of the National League record), there

were a major league *record* 248 home runs hit at Wrigley Field in LA in 1961. In addition, the '58 Dodgers would finish with a total of 172 home runs, second in the National League to the Giants, while the '61 Angels hit 189 home runs, second in the American League.

Meanwhile, the Giants welcomed the Cubs to Seals Stadium for a three-game weekend series beginning Friday night the 25th, Monzant putting them in first place with a four-hit 2-0 win. Antonelli tossed a six-hitter Saturday in a 3-1 victory, with Mays hitting his first home run. But the Cubs avoided the sweep by taking Sunday's finale 5-4 before another sellout crowd of 22,696. Still, the Giants (8-4) had taken their first four series, and led the league by a half game over the Braves (7-3).

The Phillies invaded Seals Stadium Monday the 29th to kick off a five-game series, winning 7-4 in the opener, before the Giants finished the month with a 10-1 win on Antonelli's six-hitter. Davenport homered twice, including his first big league poke, and Spencer, Cepeda and Schmidt homered once each. The joy surrounding the Giants clubhouse was missing, though, with the news that Eleanor Bressoud, the 25-year-old wife of Giants infielder Ed Bressoud, had died of a brain tumor in Los Angeles, leaving behind two small children.

Through April, the standings looked like this:

San Francisco	9-5	.642	—
Milwaukee	8-5	.571	1/2
Chicago	8-5	.571	1/2

The Giants led the league in hitting (.305), in home runs (23) and in runs (86). Mays was fourth in hitting at .397 (well behind Musial's .528), Sauer was fifth at .389, Spencer was 10th at .340. Sauer was second in home runs with seven, one behind Walls (left field bleacher fans at Seals Stadium named their section, "Sauerbraten Gardens"). Spencer was second in RBIs with 14, two behind Walls. Cepeda and Sauer were tied for third with 13.

All Giants home games thus far had been reconstructed for Eastern fans over the Major League Network, Inc. WINS Radio in New York was the first station to sign up, with WINS sports director Les Keiter doing the play-by-play from teletype reports. *Look* magazine was the sponsor.

Thus far, Dodgers games were not being similarly reconstructed, although Armed Forces Radio occasionally would tape LA home games for rebroadcast at 11pm New York time via shortwave.

Of course, all the Giants games, home and away, could be heard throughout all of central and Northern California, through the club's flagship station, KSFO. Network stations broadcast the games as far south as Fresno, as far east as Reno and as far north as Crescent City, near the Oregon border.

The Giants, meantime, rejected a KPIX Television (San Francisco) offer to televise Giants road games on a nonprofit basis. The Giants, instead, were holding out for pay-TV through Skiatron, Inc., which they already had a contract with, but which thus far had failed to materialize in any telecasts.

MAY: The Giants had one more roster cut to make before the May 1 deadline, and Barclay was the casualty, sent to Phoenix. The Giants went on to lose their first series of the season, as the Phillies took three-of-five, the Giants (10-7) falling a half game behind the Cubs and staying a half game ahead of the Braves.

Pittsburgh came to Seals Stadium to begin a five-game series on Sunday the 4th, kicking it off with a doubleheader, before another sellout crowd of 22,721. Roman Mejias, who had two home runs in 58 games in '57, and who had failed to go deep in a three-game series at the LA Coliseum, slammed *three* home runs to beat Antonelli and the Giants in the opener 6-2. But the Giants came back to win the nightcap in dramatic style, 4-3 in 10 innings, on an RBI single by Bressoud, in his first game back with the club since the tragic death of his wife less than a week before.

In LA, the Dodgers took a doubleheader from the Phillies, 8-7 and 15-2, before nearly 40,000, moving over the half-million mark in home attendance after just 15 dates.

Monday afternoon the 5th drew just 5,506 fans, the Giants' smallest home crowd of the season. But what those fans saw—at least the fans who stuck around for the finish, and Russ Hodges swore on KSFO that most of the 5,506 were still in their seats—was a game they would *never* forget. Forty years later, it is still the greatest ninth-inning comeback in San Francisco Giants history. The Pirates carried an 11-1 lead into the bottom of the ninth, with Vernon Law working on a four-hitter. This is what happened next:

Jablonski and Cepeda singled. Sauer was safe on an error by Frank Thomas. The bases were loaded with nobody out. Kirkland popped up. Pinch-hitter Jim King roped a two-run double. Antonelli, also pinch hitting, laced another two-run double. It was 11-5. Pinch hitter Bob Speake ripped an RBI double. Curt Raydon relieved Law. Mays walked. Spencer was safe on a force play at second. Jablonski hit a three-run homer. It was 11-9. Ronnie Blackburn relieved Raydon. Cepeda homered. It was 11-10. Sauer walked. Don Gross relieved Blackburn. Schmidt walked. Pinch hitter Jim Finigan (batting for pinch hitter King) was safe on Dick Groat's error. The bases were loaded with two out.

Pinch hitter Don Taussig (batting for pinch hitter Antonelli) popped up to short center field. Mazeroski and Groat went out, Mejias came in, but Mazeroski caught the ball. The Giants, despite a nine-run ninth, lost 11-10.

The Giants, though, came back to take the series. McCormick shut out the Bucs on three hits, 7-0, then Worthington got the win in the rubber game, 8-6. Before welcoming the Dodgers back to Seals Stadium for a three-game weekend series, the Giants spent Thursday afternoon up in Portland, beating the triple-A Beavers in an exhibition game 12-5, before 26,507 at Multnomah Stadium. It was the first, but not the last, such exhibition the Giants would play before the '58 season was out.

The Giants continued their early-season dominance of the Dodgers by ripping them 11-3 on Friday night, before 20,653. Monzant went the distance, scattering 10 hits, and Mays homered twice and drove in five runs. Taussig, who ended the Giants' miracle rally against the Pirates Monday, came through Saturday with a two-out RBI single in the ninth for a 3-2 win, before 20,774. The Dodgers, 2-6 against the Giants thus far, and 1-4 in San Francisco, might have been excused if they had prayed for rain, to avoid a three-game sweep Sunday. If so, they had their prayers answered. Sunday's game was rained out. The Giants were 15-9, including 13-8 at home. It was time to hit the road.

Fortunately for the Giants, it was still time to play the Dodgers. Back at the LA Coliseum the Giants exploded Monday for a 12-3 victory, as Mays hit two more homers—five in three days—and drove in five more runs. Spencer also homered twice, and Gomez tossed a six-hitter, striking out 10. Tuesday the Giants exploded again, in a 16-9 win, ripping Dodger pitching for 26 hits—five each by Mays and Spencer, and four by Cepeda.

Mays and Spencer combined for four home runs and 10 RBIs. The Giants were now 17-9 on the season, and 8-2 against the Dodgers.

From LA, the Giants flew to St. Louis, where they split a pair with the Cardinals, after

Giants fans cross playing field to exits, after Giants–Dodgers game was postponed due to rain, Seals Stadium, May 11, 1958; tradition of fans being able to cross field to exit ballparks vanished throughout major leagues in early sixties. (San Francisco History Center, San Francisco Public Library)

which Cards manager Hutchinson was already changing his opinion of the Giants, saying this time, "They're tough. They got kids who want to play." Apparently a 17-10 record impressed Hutchinson more than a 6-3 mark did earlier, not to mention a look at the league leaders in the morning paper: Mays was second in hitting at .411, Spencer was third at .364 and Cepeda ninth at .333. Cepeda was second in home runs with nine, while Mays, Spencer and Sauer were tied for third with eight. Spencer was tops in RBIs with 27, Mays was third with 24 and Cepeda fourth with 23. Hutchinson admitted he was stunned at the numbers.

The Giants then hit Chicago for four, dropping the opener, but then winning three straight. Gomez seven-hit the Cubs Saturday, 9-4, knocking in a pair of runs in the process, and Cepeda homered twice. Then the Giants took a doubleheader Sunday before 33,224, 7-3 in the opener on Antonelli's 5-hitter, and 4-0 in the nightcap in Stu Miller's three-hitter. The Giants were 10 games over the .500 mark, at 21-11, one game

ahead of the Braves, who lost Sunday to Cincinnati 4-1, as Bob Purkey masterfully scattered 13 hits. In St. Louis, the Cards nipped the Dodgers 6-5, as Drysdale fell to 1-7 on the season. His only win came in relief.

Monday the 19th may have looked like an off day on the schedule but, just like the 8th, it wasn't. The Giants flew to Minneapolis and beat the White Sox in an exhibition game 10-1, before 12,659, on a bittersweet afternoon for the locals, who couldn't help but wonder how it might have been if Minneapolis had gotten the Giants, and not San Francisco. If Walter O'Malley had gotten the land to build the stadium he wanted in Brooklyn, it's highly unlikely the Giants would have moved to San Francisco. Instead, they probably would have moved to Minneapolis.

The Giants road trip then took them to Crosley Field where they took two straight from Cincinnati, 4-2 in the first game on a McCormick five-hitter, and 5-4 in 10 innings in the second, on a game-winning home run by Mays. Milwaukee, meantime, was losing two straight to the visiting Dodgers, one on a Sandy Koufax two-hitter, so the Giants (23-11) had a two and a half game lead over the Braves (18-11).

Finally, it was time for the Giants to *really* be tested. They took their first-place standing to County Stadium, Milwaukee, for a three-game series with the defending World Series champs. The Braves won Thursday night 9-3, Burdette beating Gomez, as Frank Torre homered and knocked in five runs. The Giants came back to win in dramatic fashion Friday night 5-3 on an Antonelli three-hitter. Spahn retired the first 19 Giants, before losing his no-hitter in the seventh. Schmidt and Kirkland then tied the game with homers in

Giants fans head home via 16th Street, outside Seals Stadium, after May 11, 1958, game vs. Dodgers was rained out; note "Double Play" restaurant (left) at corner of 16th & Bryant Streets–"Double Play" remains in same location today. (SF Chronicle)

Gomez, but was tackled by Mays. Murtaugh was thrown out of the game by Dascoli for causing the dispute to get out of hand. More than 35,000 Pirate fans were irate that Gomez stayed in the game (and more irate that he beat the Bucs with a complete game). Jack Buck announced the game for New York television. The Giants (26-13) boosted their league-lead back to two and a half games over the Braves, who split two with the Cubs.

The Giants had an "off day" Monday the 26th, so how did they celebrate? They took a bus to West Point, New York, and beat the U.S. Army Cadets 17-1 in yet another exhibition, as Kirkland hit an inside-the-park home run. The Cadets fell to 0-19-1 in their long series with the Giants, their only success a 2-2 tie back in 1946 (not coincidentally, perhaps, '46 also had been the last time the Giants finished in last place, with a 61-93 record).

Connie Mack Stadium was the next venue for the Giants, who split two with the Phillies, beaten by Jack Sanford 5-1 in the first game, then winning 7-6 on Kirkland's two-run homer in the ninth. The Giants (27-14) carried a two-game lead into St. Louis, where they would wrap up their long 21-game road trip with a four-game series. The Cardinals, though, would take the first three, as Ken Boyer did the major damage with two homers and four RBIs in game two, and with a 12th inning homer to win game three, as the Giants blew an 8-1 lead. The sudden three-game skid left the Giants percentage points behind the Braves as May came to a close. The standings:

the eighth. Mays' two-run shot in the ninth won it. The Braves took the rubber game of the series 6-3 but the Giants (24-13) left Milwaukee still on top by a game and a half.

The Giants' traveling road show then took them to Forbes Field for a Sunday doubleheader with the Pirates. Once again, the Giants took both ends of a twin bill, 5-2 in the opener on Gomez' nine-hitter, and 6-1 in the nightcap on Monzant's nine-hitter. But that was hardly the story of this particular afternoon in Pittsburgh. The day was highlighted by a benches-clearing brawl in the opener, that began when Gomez hit Mazeroski with a pitch in the bottom of the fourth. The dispute, in fact, went all the way back to the previous September 3, when Gomez hit Law on the left ear with a pitch, rupturing his eardrum and putting him on the disabled list for the remainder of the season. There was more beanball-throwing when the Bucs visited Seals Stadium in early May, and now the Pirates were claiming that Gomez' pitch would have hit Mazeroski in the head if he hadn't thrown up his hand at the last minute.

Mazeroski swore at Gomez. Manager Murtaugh swore at Gomez. Naturally, when Gomez came to bat in the top of the fifth, Law's first pitch sent him down. Umpire Frank Dascoli gave Law a warning (automatic $50 fine). Murtaugh charged Gomez, who gave him an obscene gesture. Catcher Danny Kravitz tried to shield Murtaugh, who was grabbed by third base coach Herman Franks. The benches emptied. Cepeda grabbed a bat to protect his friend

Milwaukee	25-15	.625	—
San Francisco	27-17	.614	—
Pittsburgh	22-20	.524	4
Chicago	22-24	.478	6
St. Louis	19-21	.475	6
Philadelphia	18-22	.450	7
Cincinnati	16-20	.444	7
Los Angeles	16-26	.381	10

As the month of June arrived, baseball fans in Los Angeles were not happy over the fate of their Dodgers but, in fact, were even more concerned for the future of baseball in the Southland. On June 3 LA registered voters would go to the polls to decide the fate of Referendum B, which would provide for the transfer of dozens of acres at Chavez Ravine to the Dodgers, for the sole purpose of building a new baseball stadium. National League president Warren Giles said if the measure failed, it would have to be considered an expression of "a lack of enthusiasm for major league baseball." Giles also said if the measure failed, he would recommend that the league "take immediate steps to study ways and means of relocating the franchise to another city." Even mayor Poulson said the Dodgers "would have no alternative but to move," and that the city would be the "laughing stock of the United States."

JUNE: The Giants opened the month by salvaging the final game of the four-game set in St. Louis and the final game of the road trip, with a 7-2 victory on Antonelli's nine-hitter. They returned home back in first place (28-17) by one game over the Braves, having gone 13-8 on the road swing. Several hundred fans welcomed them home when their flight arrived in San Francisco.

After a badly needed off day Monday, with *no* exhibition game to play, the Giants welcomed the Braves to Seals Stadium Tuesday night to kick off a big three-game series. Aaron and Covington hit two home runs apiece to beat Gomez 7-6 before another sellout crowd of 22,934. On Wednesday the Giants fell one game back, blowing a 7-1 lead and losing 10-9 in 11 innings as Spahn, one of the game's best-hitting pitchers, delivered an RBI pinch-single to win it (Spahn hit .333 in '58, with 36 hits in 108 at-bats; he was a career .194 hitter with 35 home runs). The Giants not only blew a six-run lead, but led 7-4 entering the ninth, only to have Covington tie it with a three-run homer off the first pitch thrown by reliever Pete Burnside. The Braves went ahead with two runs in the top of the 10th, but the Giants came back to tie it on back to back pinch hit home runs by Sauer and Schmidt. It marked the first time in National League history that one team had back to back pinch hit homers, the feat having been accomplished once in the American League, by the Yankees' Bob Cerv and Elston Howard at Kansas City in 1955. But Rigney cared little about records at that point. He was fuming over the

pitching, sending Burnside to Phoenix after the game, and suggesting to reporters that he might start Antonelli the next three games in succession.

In Los Angeles, the Dodgers lost a weird one, 8-3 to the Redlegs, as 22-year-old Sandy Koufax showed why he didn't turn into a big winner until age 26. His line, in defeat: 2 2/3IP, 0H, 5R, 5ER, 6BB, 3K. But O'Malley was smiling nevertheless because Referendum B passed, just barely, with 62% of the registered voters of LA turning out—a record in a nonpresidential election. The final count was 345,000 (52%) in favor, and 321,000 (48%) against. O'Malley forces, in fact, staged an eight-hour telethon on KTTV three nights before, in an effort to swing the election, featuring Jack Benny, Dean Martin, George Burns, Debbie Reynolds, Laraine Day, Danny Thomas, Chuck Connors, Jeff Chandler (a big *Giants* fan), Jerry Lewis and Joe E. Brown. Despite taxpayer lawsuits, O'Malley would eventually get his Chavez Ravine Property, where he would build a beautiful new ballpark for the Dodgers that would open in April, 1962.

Back at Seals Stadium, the Giants (29-19) moved back into a virtual first-place tie with Milwaukee (27-17) by nipping the Braves 5-4 in 12 innings on an RBI single by Cepeda, driving in Finigan, whose double nearly won it before Mays was thrown out at the plate, trying to score from first. Grissom gave Rigney some relief, in more ways than one, with three-and-two-thirds perfect innings out of the bullpen. The cover story of *The Sporting News,* dated June 4, was titled "CAN GIANTS CAPTURE PENNANT? WHY NOT?"

The Yankees, meantime, were running away with the American League pennant—again—and on this day, New York beat Washington 2-0 in 13 innings in a classic pitchers duel, the likes of which are no longer seen in the majors. Ralph Terry went the distance for the win, with a seven-hitter. Camilo Pascual went the distance for the loss, with an eight-hitter. And yet, there was concern in some baseball circles in the late fifties that the complete game was becoming a lost art. Some critics blamed overmanaging. Some cited the so-called lively ball, or the shorter fences. There were a major league record-low 710 complete games thrown in 1957, an average of 44 per team. In comparison, there were 2,185 complete games thrown in 1904, an average of 137 per team. The Boston Red Sox threw 148 complete games that season, out of 154 games total. The

Yankees' Jack Chesbro completed a modern major league record 48 of his 51 starts in '04. Cy Young threw 749 complete games in his 22-year big league career. The downward trend in complete games has been going on the entire century. In 1991, the New York Yankees threw three complete games all season.

Back in San Francisco, with the Braves off to LA, the Giants' sudden slump got worse, as they dropped three of four to the visiting Redlegs. The series finale saw Bob Purkey boost his record to 8-1 with a six-hit shutout, as three-time Coast League MVP Steve Bilko's two-run homer was the difference in a 3-0 win. Adding insult to injury was the fact that not only did Grissom take the loss in the third game, but his eight-year-old son Bruce suffered a broken nose and black eye when struck by a foul line drive behind the Giants dugout. The Braves, though, lost three straight to the Dodgers, before 171,326 at the Coliseum. Don Zimmer's ninth-inning homer off Don McMahon won the opener, and Pee Wee Reese homered twice, in support of Koufax, to win game two. As a result, the Giants (30-22) still led the league by a half game over the Braves (27-20).

Milwaukee players were polled after their West Coast trip on which park was easier to hit in. Nineteen picked Seals Stadium. Only four picked the Coliseum. Those who preferred Seals said, of course, that it was because of the wind blowing out to left field. In the first 34 games at Seals Stadium, 81 home runs were hit, 66 by right-handed hitters. In the first 33 games at the Coliseum, 79 home runs were hit, 77 by right-handed hitters. The Giants' Spencer certainly loved hitting at Seals Stadium, although he confessed the wind could cause problems in the field. "Someday," he told reporters after one game, "I'm going to throw a ball to first base, and it will come right back to me."

The Giants would continue their first disappointing homestand by exacerbating their slump with a three-game sweep at the hands of the Pirates. In a 14-6 win in the middle game, Frank Thomas hit two home runs and drove in seven, and Mazeroski belted a three-run homer off Gomez, exacting some sweet revenge. The only bright spot for the Giants was Felipe Alou's first big-league homer. Alou made his major league debut the day before, called up from Phoenix, with Kirkland (.217) going down. Already, local papers were writing about Alou's prowess as a sharkhunter back in his native Dominican Repub-

lic. An expert diver, Alou estimated he had killed some 50 sharks by knife, and noted that the Giants had already requested that he give up that part of his athletic career.

The Giants had lost eight of 10 in the homestand, five straight overall and 12 of 16. "We've hit rock bottom," Rigney said. "There's nowhere to go but up." The Braves (29-21) had taken two of three at Chicago to move a game and a half up on the Giants (30-25), although the one Cubs win was a memorable one—Bobby Thomson hit two of a record five home runs off Spahn in a 9-6 victory. Before the last game against the Pirates, there was a picket named Wayne Nelson outside Seals Stadium with a sign saying, "Stoneham, Save Our Giants—Get Satchel Paige From Miami, Please." It was no joke. Satchel Paige, nearly 52 years old, was having a very decent season for the Phillies' triple-A farm club in the International League. He would finish 10-10 with a 3.06 ERA.

The Giants wrapped up the 13-game homestand by taking two of three from the Phillies. Antonelli five-hit them in the opener, 6-1, and Worthington eight-hit them in the finale, 3-1. Another Sunday sellout crowd of 22,462 bade farewell to the Giants, who took just four-of-13 at home, and departed (32-26) still a game and a half back of the Braves. Meanwhile, at Comiskey Park in Chicago, the Cubs edged the White Sox 1-0 in their annual exhibition, with 18-year-old bonus baby Dick Ellsworth from Fresno tossing a four-hitter. Ellsworth had just graduated from high school, signing a $50,000 bonus. He would become a regular part of the Cubs rotation early in the '59 season.

Before the Sunday, June 15, trading deadline there was a flurry of moves. The Dodgers sent Don Newcombe (0-6) to the Reds for Johnny Klippstein and Steve Bilko; The Cardinals purchased Sal Maglie from the Yankees, and traded Dick Schofield to the Pirates for Gene Freese and John O'Brien; Kansas City acquired Roger Maris and two others from Cleveland for Vic Power and Woody Held; and Detroit picked up Tito Francona from Chicago for Ray Boone and Bob Shaw.

The June 16 *Sports Illustrated* was on the newsstands with a feature on the Giants, titled "Giants: A Smash Hit In San Francisco." Author Robert Creamer wrote, "They've been the only truly exciting element in the baseball picture this spring."

Tuesday night the 17th, as the Giants were beginning a three-game series in Pittsburgh, a storybook debut was taking place at Briggs Stadium (renamed Tiger Stadium in 1960) in Detroit. Ozzie Virgil, the first black player in Tigers history, went five-for-five at the plate, with four singles and a double, in a 9-2 win over the Senators. Virgil had already played one season-plus for the Giants, but on this night was making his American League debut. In Cincinnati, Newcombe made his Reds debut in style, with a six-hit 6-1 win over the Cardinals. Bilko, meantime, would win two of his first seven starts for the Dodgers with home runs.

The Giants lost two of three in Pittsburgh, then moved on to Philadelphia, trailing Milwaukee by three games. Things only got worse. First, they had to play without Mays, who was hospitalized in New York with stomach pains. Then Gomez walked home the winning run in the ninth in the series opener. The second game was rained out, as Taussig and King were sent to Phoenix, with Kirkland and Leon Wagner getting called up. Then Kirkland won the opener of a Sunday doubleheader with a homer, and Wagner made his big league debut in the nightcap by going three for three in a game the Giants *thought* they had. They led 1-0 in the bottom of the sixth, behind Gomez, under clear skies, when the game was suddenly called because of Pennsylvania's 7pm curfew—the game would have to be completed at a later date. The Giants (34-29) were a game and a half behind the Braves (33-25), who lost to the 41-year-old Maglie 2-1, the "Barber" throwing seven innings of five-hit ball.

County Stadium and the Braves were next up. Rookie Carlton Willey tossed a six-hit shutout in his first big league start, a 7-0 win, that left Rigney impressed, saying that was the best fastball the Giants had seen all season. "He looked like Walter Johnson," Rig said. Spahn then outdueled Miller 2-1, but the Giants salvaged the series finale with a 10-2 win behind Worthington. The Giants (35-31) trailed the Braves (35-26) by two and a half games.

The Giants then split four in Cincinnati, while the Braves split four with the Dodgers, who won the first two games of the series behind Drysdale and Koufax to make it seven straight over Milwaukee, before the Braves bounced back. The Giants got a series-opening seven-hitter from Antonelli, who then came back in the series finale to save Worthington's 2-0 win over

Newcombe. That same weekend, in the American League, the second-place Kansas City Athletics hosted the first-place Yankees, hoping to cut into the Bronx Bombers' seven and a half game bulge. New York won the opener 10-3, before 31,602 at Municipal Stadium. New York won the second game 8-0 on a Whitey Ford three-hitter, before 31,395. Finally, Kansas City took the finale 12-6, before 30,606, as Maris had three singles and a home run.

In Chicago, on Friday night the 27th, the White Sox' Billy Pierce came within one out of pitching baseball's first regular-season perfect game in 36 years. But after the first 26 Washington Senator hitters were retired, pinch hitter Ed Fitzgerald doubled just one foot inside the right field foul line. Pierce had to settle for a masterful one-hit 3-0 win, before 11,300. Meantime, at the Polo Grounds, the World Championship Rodeo was just beginning a 10-day run.

The month of June ended Monday with the Braves increasing their lead over the idle Giants to three games with a 9-2 win over the Redlegs, on Spahn's three-hitter. The streaking Cardinals, meantime, won again to move a half game ahead of the Giants, into second place.

Milwaukee	38-28	.576	—
St. Louis	36-31	.537	2.5
San Francisco	37-33	.529	3
Chicago	35-36	.492	5.5
Cincinnati	32-33	.492	5.5
Pittsburgh	34-37	.479	6.5
Philadelphia	30-34	.469	7
Los Angeles	31-39	.443	9

The major league All-Star Game in Baltimore was just a week away, but the Giants' top brass was watching the Pacific Coast League All-Star Game Monday night the 30th in Vancouver, as Andre Rodgers smacked a two-run homer and Dom Zanni picked up the win in relief with two scoreless innings, in the South's 13-4 win over the North, before 8,349 fans. Rodgers, sent back to Phoenix in early May so he could be in the lineup every day, was leading the Coast League in hitting at .385, with 13 homers and 43 RBIs. Dick Stuart was leading the Coast League with 30 home runs and 76 RBIs, in just 285 at-bats, playing for the Pirates' triple-A farm club in Salt Lake City.

CBS Television had just announced its Game of the Week schedule for Saturdays and Sundays, for the balance of the season, with Dizzy Dean and Buddy Blattner at the mike. NBC Television released its Major League Baseball on Saturday schedule, with Lindsay Nelson and Leo Durocher at the mike. And Mutual Radio announced its Game of the Week schedule, with Gene Elston and Bob Feller calling the action.

JULY: The Giants began the month with five straight against the Cubs, two at Wrigley and three at Seals. They lost three of five. The highlight, surely, was in the first game of a July 4 doubleheader when the Giants scored five times in the bottom of the ninth to win 6-5. Kirkland's two-run single got them close. Mays' two-run single won it. The Giants, once 13 games above 500, were now just three over. But on Saturday the 5th and Sunday the 6th, the Giants again rallied in the ninth for dramatic wins over the Cardinals. First, they tallied two in the ninth for a 5-4 win, Kirkland walking with the bases loaded off Larry Jackson to force home the game-winner. Twenty-four hours later, in front of their third straight sellout crowd, Davenport was hit with the bases loaded, by Jackson again, to force home the winner. At the All-Star break the Giants (41-36) were back to within one game of the Braves (40-33), with the Cardinals falling back to third.

The 1958 season marked a return of the All-Star voting to the players, coaches and managers, as a result of the ballot-stuffing scandal in Cincinnati in '57 that led to seven Redlegs named to the starting lineup. Commissioner Ford Frick liked the fact that there would be no more selections based on local favorites or aging veterans with great pasts—rather, selections would much more likely be based on players' performances each given year. The fans wouldn't get the vote back until 1970, long after Frick had left office.

The National League starting lineup, as voted by the players, coaches and managers, had Musial at first (201 votes to 12 for George Crowe, and eight each for Cepeda and Harry Anderson), Mazeroski at second, Thomas at third (122 votes to 65 for Mathews), Banks at short (184 votes to 16 for Johnny Logan and 14 for Spencer), Skinner in left, Mays in center, Aaron in right and Del Crandall catching.

The American League starters were Moose Skowron at first, Nellie Fox at second (108 votes to Gil McDougald's 104), Frank Malzone at third, Luis Aparicio at short, Bob Cerv in left (104 votes to 86 for Ted Williams), Mickey Mantle in center,

Jackie Jensen in right and Gus Triandos catching.

The balance of both squads were named by managers Haney of Milwaukee and Stengel of New York. Haney named Antonelli and Schmidt from the Giants, but left off the deserving Cepeda (.310-14HR-45RBI) at first, in favor of Anderson (.292-9HR-38RBI), and left off the deserving Spencer (.303-9HR-41RBI) at short, in favor of Logan (.298-7HR-29RBI).

The 25th All-Star Game was held at Baltimore's Memorial Stadium on Tuesday, July 8, at 1pm. Imagine an All-Star Game at 1 o'clock on a Tuesday afternoon. The American League won 4-3 on a combined four-hitter by Bob Turley, Ray Narleski, Early Wynn and Billy O'Dell, before 48,829. The win gave the American League a 15 to 10 lead in the series. Mel Allen and Al Helfer called the action on NBC-TV, while Ernie Harwell and Bob Neal called it for NBC Radio.

The hot gossip scandal at the All-Star Game concerned a story in the *Los Angeles Herald-Express* on inappropriate behavior by four Braves players during a party at the home of a Hollywood television producer, during which several fully clothed guests were thrown in the pool, including at least one young woman. Frank Torre, one of the players cited, admitted he pushed the young woman in the water, as a playful prank. The producer, Warner Taub, said that contrary to what the story suggested, there was no wild party, no excessive drinking and that all the guests left his house by 11:30pm. Manager Haney was not happy with the incident, given the Braves' reputation as a team that liked to party. Jackie Robinson, in fact, in an off-season speech following the '56 season, said one reason the Dodgers overtook the Braves the final weekend to win the pennant by one game was because the Braves "left their game in the nightclubs."

Following the break, the Giants split two with the Redlegs at home while the Braves took two of three in LA, including an 8-4 win that saw Burdette go the distance and hit two home runs, one a grand slam. Burdette had hit only two home runs in his six-year-plus major league career—coincidentally, both came in the same game, in '57, against Cincinnati. Burdette's feat put him in the record book with Newcombe as the only National League pitchers to hit two home runs in a game twice.

When the Braves invaded Seals Stadium Saturday the 12th to begin a three-game series, they had a game and a half lead over the Giants. When they left, following three straight sellouts, the lead was down to a half game. The Giants won the first two, actually moving into first place by a half game for the night, when Antonelli beat Milwaukee 5-2, followed by a 6-5 win on an RBI single in the ninth by Alou.

The Giants, suddenly back with the momentum and ninth inning heroics of April and May, then swept three from the Phillies, while the Braves swept three in St. Louis. McCormick outdueled Robin Roberts 1-0, Antonelli beat Sanford 9-2, and a three-run ninth beat Dick Farrell 8-7. Before the series finale, the Giants went shopping down at triple-A, but not at Phoenix, where Andre Rodgers was tearing the cover off the ball, to the tune of a league-leading .412 average, with 22 home runs and 57RBIs. Rather, the Giants worked out a deal with independent Toronto, in the International League, sending Ernie Broglio and Jim King [on loan] in exchange for veteran right-hander Don Johnson, who won 20 games in '57 and was named MVP of the league.

Next came the Pirates, and the Giants swept three from them as well, the middle win coming on a pinch hit three-run homer by Jablonski. Two of the three were sellouts, the third nearly. The Braves (48-37) took two of three in Chicago, so the Giants (50-38) were back on top by a half game. The Giants won 12 of 16 on the homestand. That same Sunday, Detroit's Jim Bunning threw the first no-hitter of the season, 3-0 over the Red Sox at Fenway, before 29,529. Bunning (8-6) walked two and struck out 12.

On Monday the 21st, the Giants moved a game ahead when the Braves returned home and lost to the Cardinals 5-4 in 14 innings on a game-winning home run by rookie Curt Flood. Burdette went the distance in losing, giving up 10 hits. The Braves came back to win Tuesday night, while the Yankees got 23 hits in blasting the Tigers 13-3, on a seven-hitter by Bob Turley (15-3). Wednesday, while the Braves won again, the Giants lost two in Philly, in most painful fashion. The opener was the resumption of the curfew-suspended game of June 22—Gomez had a 1-0 lead in the sixth, with two on and two out, when the clock struck seven, and Pennsylvania law said everybody had to leave the ballpark. When the game resumed, Antonelli took over, gave up a three-run homer to the first batter he faced, Harry Anderson, and Gomez was charged with the toughest of hard-luck defeats. He could have been back home

in his native Puerto Rico that day and *still* would have been charged with the loss. The Yankees, meantime, blasted the Tigers again with 18 hits, 16-4.

Thursday the Giants (50-40) sold Ray Crone to Toronto and moved back to within a half game of the Braves (50-39), who were shut out by the Cards' Sam Jones 4-0. Oh yes, the Yankees ripped the Tigers again, 10-7, sweeping the three-game series with 39 runs, to move 31 games-over-500, and 13$\frac{1}{2}$ games ahead of second-place Boston.

The Giants then lost two of three in Pittsburgh, where the first game was delayed for several minutes when fans threw beer cans at Gomez, warming up in the bullpen. It was supposed to be a four-game series, but the second game of the Sunday doubleheader was suspended in the eighth inning, tied 3-3, again because of the 7 p.m. Pennsylvania curfew law. The Braves split four with the Cubs, getting a nine-hit win from 21-year-old Juan Pizarro, in his first start since getting called up from triple-A Wichita. The Braves (52-41) led the Giants (51-42) by one game. That same Sunday, in Toronto, Satchel Paige (9-6) threw a seven-hit shutout, in a 3-0 Miami win, before 3,240. Satch walked one and struck out one, saying later he was particularly happy because Toronto manager Dixie Walker had left him off the International League All-Star team two straight years. Again, the record books say Satch was 52 years old in '58, although many players believe he was several years older.

Monday the 28th, the Giants returned to Philadelphia for a makeup doubleheader, sweeping the Phillies 3-2 and 2-1. Rigney had to enjoy this one, from a pitching perspective, as McCormick scattered nine hits in the opener, and Gomez tossed a four-hitter in the nightcap. The Giants (53-42) were just .001 out of the league lead. Moving from clubhouse bulletin board to clubhouse bulletin board, on the road trip, was an article in the *New York Times,* in which Casey Stengel was quoted as saying the Giants were freaks, with no business near first place. Rigney's reply: "I'd like to take this bunch of freaks right into Yankee Stadium." The Giants then briefly moved into sole possession of first place before dropping two of three in Cincinnati, winning the opener 4-3 on a two-run homer in the ninth by Jablonski. But Purkey stopped them 5-1 for his 13th win, and then the Redlegs rallied back from a 6-0 deficit to win 10-9, offsetting a pair of Wagner home runs. The Braves took two-of-three from the Dodgers, on a six-hitter by Spahn and a four-hitter by Pizarro. Heading into a four-game showdown in Milwaukee to kick off the month of August, the Giants were just one game back.

Milwaukee	54-42	.562	—
San Francisco	54-44	.551	1
Pittsburgh	48-49	.495	6.5
Cincinnati	48-49	.495	6.5
Chicago	49-51	.490	7
Philadelphia	45-49	.479	8
St. Louis	46-51	.474	8.5
Los Angeles	44-53	.454	10.5

In Washington, the Senate antitrust and monopoly subcommittee was holding hearings on legislation granting antitrust law exemption to professional sports. Winding up the baseball phase, the committee heard from former greats Jackie Robinson and Bob Feller, both of whom said players should have a voice in the naming of a commissioner, and in determining their own destiny.

Robinson, vice-president of the Chock Full O' Nuts restaurant chain and coffee firm in New York, said he felt the commissioner was, at times, under the owner's thumb, and that players may not have all the opportunities they should have. Robinson said the average major league career was about eight years, that if a player was with a particular club four to six years, he should have the opportunity to move on, that some bench-warmers around the majors may not be getting the chance to show their true ability, that they might be good enough to start on other clubs.

The committee chair, Tennessee senator Estes Kefauver, said he had the impression that the players organization was not very strong, and asked whether it should be strengthened. Robinson said he'd like to see the players have the power to make decisions, and then carry them out.

Meanwhile, Giants ticket manager Peter Hoffman said he was getting an average of 25 requests a week in the mail for World Series tickets. In fact, Hoffman said he got a $1,000 check in the mail as a deposit on a box for eight seats, for all four home Series games. Since tickets were not yet being sold, Hoffman returned the check. The fans back home weren't the only ones noticing the fact that the Giants were one game from the top with two months remaining. Those Vegas odds, which had the Giants at 50-1 to start the season, had been revised. Milwaukee, 7-10 in

April, was still the favorite at 1-2. The Giants and St. Louis were now 4-1. The Dodgers, 3-1 in April, were downgraded to 12-1. Ten and a half games out, yet they were only 12-1.

AUGUST: The Giants went into Milwaukee hoping at least to split the four-game series, and stay just one game back. Instead, they lost all four games, and their league lead the morning of July 30 seemed a distant memory. The Braves won 4-2 Friday night, Burdette beating McCormick. They won 10-0 Saturday, Willey tossing a four-hitter. And they swept a doubleheader Sunday, 4-3 in the opener and 6-0 in the nightcap, on a Spahn four-hitter. The Braves not only swept the series, but they outscored the Giants 24-5 in the process. They (58-42) suddenly had a bulging five-game lead.

As the Giants were licking their collective wounds on a bus trip down to Chicago, their triple-A Phoenix farm club, in first place in the Coast League standings, was having its problems in the air. A brawl erupted between pitcher Joe Margoneri and outfielder Dusty Rhodes over a game of hearts during a Western Airlines flight from Portland to LA. Teammates Barclay and Rodgers pulled the two apart once but couldn't *keep* them apart. The pilot made an unscheduled stop in San Francisco, of all places—Rhodes had, after all, vowed all season that he'd be back with the Giants before the summer was over—where police met the plane, took a report, but never filed charges. Both players were heavily fined. Rhodes, with 20 home runs and a league-leading 83 RBIs (Dick Stuart was called up by the Pirates, with 82 RBIs), may have blown his big chance to rejoin the Giants with the mid-air brawl, coupled as it was with the sign the Giants were about to fade from pennant contention (Rhodes made it back up with the Giants, but not until '59, when he appeared in 54 games, all as a pinch hitter, going 9-for-48).

The Giants split two in Chicago, lost two in St. Louis and, suddenly, were a whopping seven games back of the Braves, having lost nine of 10 since enjoying that one-game lead nine days before. What they needed were the Dodgers, and that's what they got, taking two-of-three in LA, hitting five home runs in the rubber game—two by Davenport—to win 12-8. The Giants (57-52), after a 7-14 road trip, were headed back home. When they left San Francisco July 21st they were 12 over 500 and one game ahead of the Braves. When they returned they were five over 500 and six and a half games back. Nevertheless, 3,000 fans greeted them at SFO, a record crowd to meet any sports team in San Francisco history. If the Giants had returned home in first place to 3,000 well-wishers, that could have been chalked up to being on top. But to come home closer to third place than first, after a disastrous trip, and find 3,000 to greet them, *that* convinced what remained of the naysayers that the Bay Area had, indeed, taken in the Giants as its own.

Perhaps with spirits lifted by the big homecoming, the Giants took two-of-three from St. Louis, two-of-three from Chicago and three-of-five from Cincinnati. The Braves stayed hot as well, though, so the Giants could only knock a half game off the league lead, heading into the final five-game series showdown with Milwaukee, at Seals Stadium, beginning Sunday the 24th. Highlights from the hot stretch included the Cards' Sam Jones walking eight in a 7-3 loss, and then asking, "How can they ask a guy to pitch in this park?" Jones said his dislike of Seals Stadium dated back to his days with San Diego, in the Coast League in '51, when he said he'd "never pitch in that [expletive] place again." (One can only imagine Jones' reaction in March of '59 when he was traded to the Giants—Seals Stadium must have been kind to Sad Sam, though, because he led the league with 21 wins and a 2.83 ERA)

On the 19th, Antonelli 5-hit the Redlegs *and* hit a home run. And on the 20th, Bill White, back from the Army, delivered a pinch hit two-run single in a 4-3 win. Cubs manager Bob Scheffing, among others, said the Giants had the best bench in the league, that the Giants' bench was the difference between a first and second division finish. Also on the 20th, Miami's Satchel Paige two-hit Buffalo 6-1, walking none and striking out two, and going two-for-three at the plate with a pair of singles. He may have been 52 at the time, or older, but remember Satch is the one who coined the phrase, "Don't look back, because somebody might be gainin' on you."

As the Giants-Braves series was getting started in San Francisco, the 26th Negro League All-Star Game was being played at Comiskey Park, Chicago, with 40 players from the four existing Negro League clubs participating—the Birmingham Black Barons and Detroit Clowns formed the East, while the Kansas City Monarchs and Memphis Red Sox made up the West. Jackie Robinson would throw out the ceremonial first ball.

Maybe Jackie could have helped the Giants, who dropped four-of-five to the Braves, giving them a 5-15 record against Milwaukee on the season, with one game left to be played in September. More significantly, the series left the Giants (65-60) in third place, a game and a half behind the Pirates and *nine* back of the Braves. Milwaukee won the opener 8-5 in 10 innings on a three-run homer by Aaron, 6-1 in the second game on a Spahn five-hitter, and 7-3 in the third game on a Burdette six-hitter. The Giants got game four 3-2 in 12 innings, on a bases-loaded walk to Cepeda, but the Braves took game five 3-0 on a 10-hitter by Bob Rush. The only good news for the Giants was that more than 105,000 fans attended the series, even though the Braves were showing their clear superiority, and the Giants were effectively fading from the pennant race.

Giants third base coach Herman Franks, meanwhile, ripped those San Francisco fans for booing the club's baserunning mistakes. Franks said Giants fans were becoming the worst in the league, that they had no conception of the game, that it looked as though they were going to be bigger boo-birds than those in Philadelphia, "where they ride you every minute, whether it's justified or not."

Once again, just when it appeared nothing would go right for the Giants, along came the Dodgers to boost their egos. LA came to town for a six-game series, and actually won the Friday night opener 4-1 on a Drysdale five-hitter. Quite a turnaround for Drysdale (10-11), who started the season 1-7. The Giants came roaring back to finish the month, though, taking a Saturday doubleheader 3-2 and 3-1, behind Gomez and McCormick, and then winning Sunday 14-2 behind Miller, as Schmidt ripped a grand slam off Koufax. With another doubleheader set for Monday, the month was over. In New York, Bob Turley (20-6) became the majors' first 20-game winner, throwing six and two-thirds innings of four-hit ball in a 7-6 win over Washington.

Milwaukee	77-53	.592	—
San Francisco	68-61	.527	8.5
Pittsburgh	68-61	.527	8.5
Cincinnati	64-67	.488	13.5
St. Louis	61-67	.477	15
Los Angeles	61-67	.477	15
Chicago	60-71	.458	17.5
Philadelphia	57-69	.452	18

There was at least one area, though, in which the Giants and Braves were still tied as league-leaders. The two clubs were the leading trend-setters in off-field wardrobes. Both were being decked out in new sportcoats, with team insignias. Giants players wore black coats with dark gray flannel slacks. Braves players wore navy blue jackets with light gray flannel slacks. The idea by the clubs, to employ a sense of unity and style on road trips, had been used by Olympic teams for years, and by the NFL's Los Angeles Rams and New York Giants, but never before in baseball. The Braves' Crandall said the club-issued wear saved wear-and-tear on personal clothes, that players liked it. *The Sporting News,* in reporting the story, said it received 100 percent favorable comments from players on both clubs, and that rival teams were interested in following suit.

SEPTEMBER: The Giants swept another doubleheader from the Dodgers to start the month. Mays went five-for-five with two home runs in an 8-6 win in the opener, and the Giants scored twice in the bottom of the 16th to win the nightcap 6-5 on what turned out to be a tragic day for the city, as Police Chief Frank Ahern died of a heart attack in the 15th inning, while watching the game from a box seat behind home plate. Ahern, a big baseball fan, was 58 years old.

It was the longest game of the season in the majors, at four hours, 35 minutes. Lockman tied it in the 16th with a home run, and Jablonski scored the game-winner from first on a bunt single by Gomez, followed by two errors. Mays was 11-for-20 with four homers in the series. The Giants (70-61) had won 15-of-19 over the Dodgers on the season, with three games between the two rivals remaining. LA then got a little revenge at the Coliseum, taking two-of-three, but the Giants won the finale 13-3 with an eight-run first inning, behind Miller's five-hitter.

Meantime, the minor league seasons were ending, including the Pacific Coast League, where the Phoenix Giants clinched the pennant September 5 with a 10-8 win over Vancouver, earning the players $310 each for the title. Andre Rodgers, who hit a two-run homer in the clincher, won the Coast League batting title at .354 *and* was named league MVP, with 31 home runs and 88 RBIs. Spokane manager Bobby Bragan called Rodgers a *better* player than both Willie McCovey and Vada Pinson. McCovey hit .319 with 14 homers and 89 RBIs (before exploding in the PCL *and* the majors

in '59), while Pinson hit .343 with 11 homers and 77 RBIs for Seattle. Dom Zanni led Phoenix pitchers with 14 wins, while the "little Giants hit a PCL-record 205 home runs, 25 by Dusty Rhodes, who hit .269 with 100 RBIs, and 26 by 27-year-old Panamanian third baseman/outfielder Bobby Prescott, who also knocked in 96 runs and batted .309. Alas, Prescott never got a chance to showcase his talents for the Giants, in San Francisco, but did get a cup of coffee in the majors in '61 with Kansas City, to the tune of 12 at-bats and one hit.

In the International League, Toronto's Rocky Nelson was named MVP, winning the triple crown as well, hitting .326 with 43 home runs and 120 RBIs. The 33-year-old Nelson had been a most dangerous minor league hitter for years, but couldn't put it together at the major league level, in much the same manner as Steve Bilko. The Pirates would make Nelson the first pick of the winter draft in December, after which he had two productive seasons as a part-time player, before retiring in '61. While Nelson was the premiere hitter in the International league in '58, the top pitcher, as voted by the managers, was Montreal's Tom Lasorda, who spun his curveball to the tune of an 18-6 record and a 2.50 ERA.

Meanwhile, a front-page story in the September 3 issue of *The Sporting News* questioned the integrity of the Kansas City Athletics for trading 42-year-old pitcher Murry Dickson (8-3) to the Yankees for a player to be named later, and cash. Collusion had long been suspected between the two clubs, with the Athletics frequently referred to over the years as a "Yankee farm club."

Following their final series with the Dodgers, the Giants went on to lose 11 of their last 20 games to finish their inaugural season in San Francisco with an 80-74 record, an 11-game improvement over the '57 season, and good enough for third place, 12 games behind the pennant-winning Milwaukee Braves. The Dodgers would finish their first season in Los Angeles with a 71-83 mark, a 13-game downturn from '57, in seventh place, 21 games back. The highlights over the final two weeks of the season included a 19-2 win at Philadelphia on the 12th, when the Giants put eight runs on the board in the first inning for the second time in eight days. The Yankees clinched their ninth pennant in 10 years under Stengel with a 5-3 win over the Athletics on the 14th. Baltimore's Hoyt Wilhelm spun the majors' second no-hitter of the season on the 20th, beating the Yankees 2-0, before 10,941 at Memorial

Stadium. The 35-year-old knuckleballer walked two and fanned eight. Hank Bauer tried to *bunt* for a single with *two out in the ninth* but the ball rolled foul. If Wilhelm had more than a two-run cushion to work with, and if he had any zip on his fastball, he probably would have thrown his next pitch up around Bauer's eyes, simply for breaking protocol. As it was, Bauer flied out to end the game.

The Braves clinched their second straight pennant on the 21st, beating the Redlegs at Crosley Field 6-5 behind Spahn, who won his 21st. The Giants ended their first season in San Francisco on a sunny Sunday afternoon, the 28th, with a 7-2 win over St. Louis, before 19,435 at Seals Stadium. Dom Zanni got his first big league win, with four sharp innings of relief. Rigney let Mays lead off, in an effort to get him an extra at-bat and help him overtake Richie Ashburn for the batting title. Mays responded by going three-for-five with a homer, to finish at .347. But Ashburn went three-for-four in his finale, to finish at .350. *The final standings:*

NATIONAL LEAGUE

Milwaukee	92-62	.597	—
Pittsburgh	84-70	.545	8
San Francisco	80-74	.519	12
Cincinnati	76-78	.494	16
St. Louis	72-82	.468	20
Chicago	72-82	.468	20
Los Angeles	71-83	.461	21
Philadelphia	69-85	.448	23

AMERICAN LEAGUE

New York	92-62	.597	—
Chicago	82-72	.532	10
Boston	79-75	.513	13
Cleveland	77-76	.503	14.5
Detroit	77-77	.500	15
Baltimore	74-79	.484	17.5
Kansas City	73-81	.474	19
Washington	61-93	.396	31

POST-SEASON: The Giants dominated *The Sporting News* 1958 All-Rookie Team, named in early October. Four Giants were named to the starting eight—Cepeda at first, Davenport at third, Kirkland and Wagner in the outfield. The rest of the lineup included the Cubs' Tony Taylor at second, Coot Veal of Detroit at short, Albie Pearson of Washington in the outfield and the Cubs' Sammy Taylor behind the plate. The two starting pitchers cited were Milwaukee's Carlton Willey and Pitsburgh's George Witt. The reliever was the Yankees' Ryne Duren.

Cepeda (.312-25HR-96RBI) was a unanimous choice for National League Rookie of the Year. Among the many accolades, this one from teammate Ruben Gomez: "He's the greatest player to come out of Puerto Rico since Ruben Gomez." Pearson (.275) beat out Duren for American League Rookie of the Year. The Cubs' Ernie Banks (.313-47HR-129RBI) was named National League Most Valuable Player. Boston's Jackie Jensen (.286-35HR-122RBI) was named American League MVP. The Yankees' Bob Turley (21-7, 2.98) beat the Braves' Warren Spahn by one vote to win the Cy Young Award (the current practice of naming one winner from each league did not begin until 1967).

Month by month, the Giants went 9-5 in April, 18-12 in May, 10-16 in June, 17-11 in July, 14-17 in August and 12-13 in September. They manhandled the Dodgers, winning 16-of-22 against them. But they were similarly manhandled by the Braves, by the same margin. Conversely, the Dodgers managed to beat the Braves 14-of-22. Go figure.

The 193 home runs hit at the LA Coliseum was 26 shy of the National League record, set at Crosley Field in Cincinnati in 1957, and even 14 shy of the Dodgers own home park record, set at Ebbets Field in 1950. The visiting Giants led the Coliseum onslaught, with 27 home runs in 11 games. There were 173 home runs hit at Seals Stadium, and at Wrigley Field.

Philadelphia's Richie Ashburn, as mentioned, won the National League batting title, at .350, while Boston's Ted Williams won the American League crown, at .328. The home run winners were Banks with 47 and the Yankees' Mantle with 42. The RBI winners were Banks with 129 and Jensen with 122. Spahn and the Pirates' Friend led the National League in wins with 22 each, while Turley led the American League with 21.

The Braves held first place in the National League for 120 of 168 days. The Giants were next, on top for 33 days. The Yankees held first place for 165 of 168 days in the American League.

The World Series looked to be another great matchup between two great teams, and a rematch of the '57 Series, won by the Braves in seven games.

The Braves got 31 home runs from Mathews, 30 from Aaron, 24 from Covington and 19 from Adcock. Covington had a remarkable season, driving in 74 runs and hitting .330, in just 294 at-bats because of injuries. Aaron hit .326 with 95 RBIs. Spahn finished 22-11 and Burdette 20-10.

The Yankees got 42 home runs from Mantle and 22 from Berra. Mantle hit .304 with 97 RBIs. Berra knocked in 90 runs. Howard hit .314 and Siebern .300. Turley finished 21-7 with six shut-outs, Ford 14-7 with seven shutouts. Duren had 20 saves, with 87 strikeouts in 76 innings.

The World Series looked like a Milwaukee re-peat, as the Braves had a three-games-to-one lead, including Spahn's two-hit shutout in game four. But Turley tossed a five-hit shutout of his own in game five, sending the series back to Milwaukee. The Braves had two chances to close it out at home, but couldn't do it. Turley came right back on one day's rest to get a 10th-inning save in game six. Then Skowron smacked a three-run homer to key a four-run eighth, breaking a 2-2 tie, and giving the Yankees a 6-2 win in game seven. The rubber-armed Turley again came back to pitch six-plus innings of relief to get the win, giving Casey Stengel his seventh (and last) Series title, and the 18th for the Bronx Bombers.

But when *Sport* magazine came out with its December issue, the big baseball story was not on the Braves or Yankees but, rather, the Giants. Titled, "Sudden Success in San Francisco," author Arnold Hano wrote, "The Giants were the success story of '58—the team nobody wanted making good in a spectacular way while the Dodgers, the team everybody wanted, fell on their faces.

"The story of the Giants is partly the corn-ball legend of young America—a bunch of brash, swaggering youngsters going forth to challenge the world."

TOPPS PRESENTS
THE '58 SF GIANTS

felipe alou

SAN FRANCISCO GIANTS
OUTFIELD

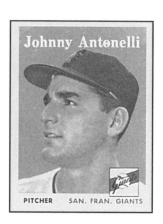

Johnny Antonelli

PITCHER   SAN. FRAN. GIANTS

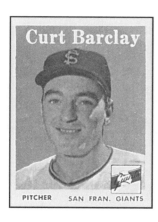

Curt Barclay

PITCHER   SAN FRAN. GIANTS

jackie brandt

SAN FRANCISCO GIANTS
OUTFIELD

Eddie Bressoud

SHORTSTOP   SAN FRAN. GIANTS

Pete Burnside

PITCHER   SAN FRAN. GIANTS

Orlando Cepeda

1st BASE   SAN FRAN. GIANTS

jimmy constable

WASHINGTON SENATORS
PITCHER

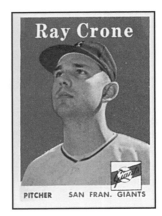

Ray Crone

PITCHER   SAN FRAN. GIANTS

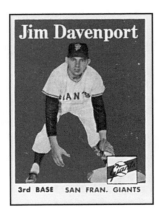

Jim Davenport

3rd BASE   SAN FRAN. GIANTS

Jim Finigan

3rd BASE   SAN. FRAN. GIANTS

HERMAN FRANKS

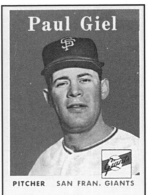

Paul Giel

PITCHER   SAN FRAN. GIANTS

Ruben Gomez

PITCHER   SAN FRAN. GIANTS

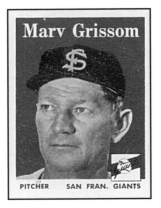

Marv Grissom

PITCHER   SAN FRAN. GIANTS

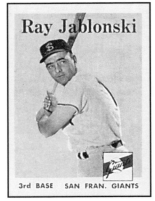

Ray Jablonski

3rd BASE   SAN FRAN. GIANTS

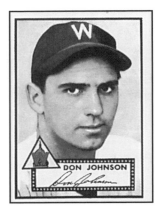

DON JOHNSON

gordon jones

SAN FRANCISCO GIANTS   PITCHER

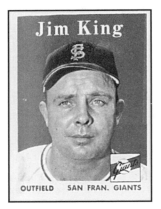

Jim King

OUTFIELD   SAN FRAN. GIANTS

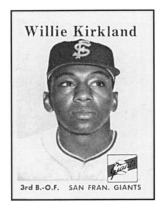

Willie Kirkland

3rd B.-O.F.   SAN FRAN. GIANTS

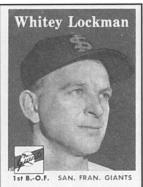

Whitey Lockman

1st B.-O.F.   SAN. FRAN. GIANTS

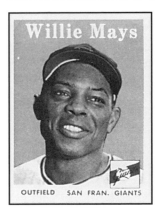

Willie Mays

OUTFIELD   SAN FRAN. GIANTS

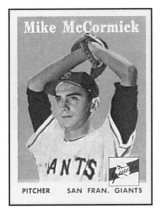

Mike McCormick

PITCHER   SAN FRAN. GIANTS

Stu Miller

PITCHER   SAN FRAN. GIANTS

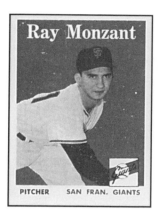

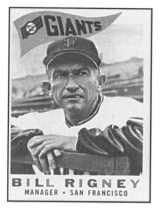

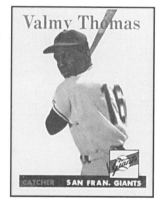

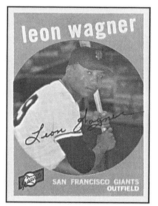

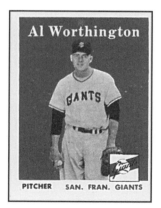

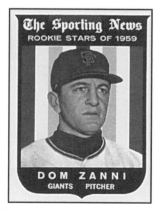

(All photos on pages 47-50 courtesy of The Topps Company, Inc..)

Because they played in only one major league game apiece, no Topps Cards were ever made for John Fitzgerald and Nick Testa.

PART TWO
THE BALLPLAYERS

BILL RIGNEY

 Following an eight-year major league career as an infielder, all with the Giants, Bill Rigney went straight into managing, for two years in the minors and then 18 in the majors, including the Giants' first season in San Francisco, in 1958. He later piloted the Angels to the best record ever for an expansion club, in '61, and then the Twins to the American League West title in '70.

A Bay Area native, Bill signed his first professional contract in 1938 with the Oakland Oaks of the Pacific Coast League. He retired as an active player with a .259 big-league average and 41 home runs. The final 19 years of his 63-year pro baseball career were spent as a front-office executive with the Oakland Athletics.

Rigney died in February 2001 at the age of 83. He left behind three children and six grandchildren.

I REALLY LOVED NEW YORK and I loved the Polo Grounds. I not only loved playing there and managing there, but I loved the fan reaction to each team, because in New York you were one of three. You weren't *two* of three, or *three* of three. You were a Giant, Dodger or Yankee fan. And the core of New Yorkers loved this club and loved that great ballpark. I knew I would miss it. On the other hand, I was coming home to the San Francisco Bay Area, and that was going to be ex-

citing, for sure. I hated to leave New York, in a sense, and never dreamed the two bulwarks of the National League would dare get up and move. Baseball tradition was built around those two clubs, as much as the Yankees.

I really loved the Polo Grounds. I think it could have withstood time like Wrigley, Fenway and Tiger Stadium. It wasn't a fair park, because

Manager Bill Rigney (Dick Dobbins)

it was only 279 feet to the scoreboard in left field, and only 258 to right. But it was the kind of park you could build a team around, much like they did with the Yankees with that short right field porch. You had an identity in the Polo Grounds, because of the configuration of it. You had to pull it or be able to hit it to the opposite field. There were lots of outs for Willie Mays to make in center field.

The last game of the '57 season, our last game at the Polo Grounds, was one of the toughest days for all of us who had been part of the New York scene. I remember Mrs. [John] McGraw came out that day and I gave her some flowers at home plate. Carl Hubbell was there. And the ground crew that had been there 30 years or more was all sitting along the third base line, waiting to say good-bye, after the game. These guys were not coming west. It was a tough day. I almost got a ticket driving home, got mad at the cop and had a terrible day. To see this place I first saw in 1946, and now they were about to tear it down. It was tough.

Blanche McGraw told me before the game that she couldn't believe what was happening, and that New York would never be the same. I had the same feeling. I said, "Mrs. McGraw, I agree. The name 'Giants,' even though it's embedded in all of us, for our lifetimes, will never be the same, because it will have a new definition, a new identity."

I started as many of the veteran Giants that day as I could, guys who had done so well over the years—Mays, Don Mueller, Dusty Rhodes, Bobby Thomson, Whitey Lockman, Wes Westrum, John Antonelli. I told them, "This is going to be our last game here, and their last look at you guys. And I'll tell you this—they're going to be mad, not at you so much, but they're going to take it out on you. So Willie, and all of you, when the game's over I want your caps and gloves left

behind. We'll get you new caps and gloves. Let's just get into the clubhouse." And boy, they dropped out of the stands. They were bitter and heartbroken. They tore up everything—the infield grass, the mound, home plate, the bases. And they stayed out there for a long time, just in front of our clubhouse, wanting [Horace] Stoneham to come out. They yelled, "Stoneham! Why? Why?" Because their lives were about to turn around.

I remember before the game Matty Schwab [head of the ground crew] and I went out to center field and cut a big piece of grass, and we said we'd take that and plant it in San Francisco. Matty had a little apartment he lived in, right inside the Polo Grounds. But he came west with us, and soon the excitement of coming back to San Francisco began to take over.

The New York writers were at a loss the following spring, because they were so used to coming out for years to cover the Giants. Most of them came to Arizona anyway, along with the new writers from San Francisco. I didn't see much of a conflict there, but I think the San Francisco writers all thought Lefty O'Doul should have been the manager, because he was a great pal of them. We finally made him a coach and brought him to Arizona, until I couldn't stand it, when he tried to make Don Blasingame a pull hitter, a home run hitter, in 1960.

We started spring training in early February with Operation Great Wash, at the Buckhorn Mineral Baths near Mesa. Horace had met this fellow out at Buckhorn Springs many years earlier, where the hot water came out of the ground. And so he'd have guys like Johnny Mize, Walker Cooper, Ernie Lombardi and Willard Marshall—all big men—come to Arizona 10 days early every spring to take the baths, to get rid of some of that winter fat. And the manager had to be there, too, so even Leo [Durocher] had to do it. Then I became the

Manager Bill Rigney works with Giants pitchers and catchers, Spring Training, Phoenix, Arizona, March 1958. (SF Giants)

manager, so I had to go, but I didn't lose any
weight. You'd get in the tub, have a steambath,
then they'd wrap you up and give you a massage.
Boy, you'd come out of there so hungry you ate
all the food they could bring, and you'd put the
weight back on. But Johnny Mize once said that it
really helped his career, and Horace never forgot
it. And Mize had a marvelous career. So we did it
every year until finally it just wore itself out. But
I'm sure it helped some of the players, and Mize
swore by it.

One of my first memories from spring training in '58 was of Orlando Cepeda. I was watching
Lockman and Cepeda doing something around
first base, so I walked closer to listen. Lockman
was showing Cepeda how to get off the bag
quickly on a close play, but not so quickly that
the umpire would call the man safe. In other
words, *cheat* a little, but just a little. I liked that.
Pretty soon it was Lockman's turn to hit, so as
he's approaching the cage I said to him, "So what
do you think [about Cepeda]?" And he said, "It's
too bad he's a year away." And I said, "A year
away from what?" And he said, "The Hall of
Fame." That's exactly what he said. Then Cepeda
singled, doubled, homered and drove in three in
his first Cactus League game.

This team had a dramatically new identity
from the '57 club. Here was Cepeda, Bob Schmidt,
Andre Rodgers, the Alous, Leon Wagner, Willie
Kirkland, Jim Davenport, Jackie Brandt. A whole
new identity and maybe rightly so. The Dodgers
thought they had to bring their whole team west,
because of the names and reputations—the
Reeses, the Furillos. They'd all reached the end of
their careers, but the Dodgers went another year
with them. We
decided the
other way, that
we'd bring the
quality guys,
but that we'd go
with as many of
the younger
players as we
could, and see
if we could es-
tablish them as
major league
players.

I loved
Seals Stadium,
from my days

*Manager Bill Rigney and wife Paula check out the Giants'
1958 schedule. (SF Giants)*

in the Coast League. It had a great infield, and I
was always a good cold weather player anyhow. I
didn't mind the cold nights there. I liked playing
there also because it brought the fans into the
game, like the lower deck in the Polo Grounds,
where the fans were right there for you. And I
thought with the new identity, the new players,
these were not going to be the New York Giants,
they were going to be the San Francisco Giants. If
we could have just kept Seals Stadium .... The
only thing about that, though, was Willie saw the
balls go up the fence or over it, and he'd say,
"Gosh darn, Skip, if I had a little more room I'd
have caught it." He had been so used to all that
room in the Polo Grounds.

The San Francisco writers
used to say to me, "When is he
going to do all the stuff you tell
us he does?" And I'd say, "I
want to tell you something.
Bucky Walters [*San Francisco
Examiner*], and all you guys,
you just wait and see, just bide
your time. You'll have so much
to write about him that there'll
be pages you can write." I felt
any time as manager, when I
saw him walk into the clubhouse, we had a chance to
win—just when he took his
shirt off. To me, there was noth-

*Bill Rigney, at manager's desk, Seals Stadium home clubhouse.
(SF Giants)*

ing he couldn't do. And as ferociously as Jackie [Robinson] played it, Willie played it with a happiness of doing the thing he loved to do best, especially in those formative years. Of course, he loved Leo, and Leo did a lot for him. I remember saying to Willie, "I can't be Leo, because only Leo's Leo. I'm going to be the best I can, because you're the best player I've ever seen."

The writers asked me about my relationship with Mays, and I said, "Gee, Willie Mays is the last thing I have to worry about because I've got 24 other guys I have to be more concerned with." Well, Willie took what I said the wrong way. He thought I didn't care about him. Well, I *did* care about him. I just worded it poorly, that's all. I think that Willie felt that Leo wouldn't have said that, that Leo would have said, "Hey, he's my man." But I had a great respect for him, because I knew that every time we played we had a chance to win, with him in the lineup. If I had it to do over again, I think I would have been a little bit more active in his life. But I don't think anybody was going to have the kind of relationship with him that he had with Leo. They were that close, that's all.

April 15th, 1958, was one of the greatest days of my baseball life—the first major league game ever played on the West Coast. But I did a terrible thing that day, the worst thing I've ever done in baseball. The morning of the opener, the *San Francisco Chronicle* put a photograph of the starting lineup right across the front page: Willie hitting third, Hank Sauer fourth, Valmy Thomas catching, Daryl Spencer at short, Ruben Gomez pitching, and so on and so on. I parked my car about nine a.m. beyond left field, and I knew Drysdale was pitching for the Dodgers. And as I was walking from left field to the first base dugout, to go up to the clubhouse, I got to the pitcher's mound, and the wind was blowing out to right field. I mean, it was *blowing.* And I'm thinking, Drysdale, sidearm, . . .

Chub [Feeney, general manager] had just got me Jim King, a fastball-hitting, left-handed-hitting outfielder. I got up to my office, and I kept thinking about Jim King and Hank Sauer [laughs]. I thought Sauer would be overmatched, and I thought I had to go with what my gut was telling me. So I scratched Sauer and put King in the lineup. Well, Sauer didn't speak to me for two weeks. He said I embarrassed him with his family in the stands. I told him I had to do it, that if I backed off for personal reasons then I wouldn't

be a good manager. King had two doubles and two RBIs, so it looked like I made a smart move. But Sauer was heartbroken because it was Opening Day.

And, of course, Ruben pitched a marvelous game. I personally liked Ruben Gomez, and I liked his ability. Ruben was not just a marvelous pitcher, but a marvelous *athlete.* He could have played left field, center, he could have played anywhere. He was emotional. But he had quality, quality ability. I think he'd have been great out of the pen because he had a rubber arm. He never had a sore arm in his life. But he didn't like relieving. He just didn't like relieving. He wanted to be a starting pitcher. I had to respect that, and he was a good one. He was the only man I ever saw . . . when Richie Ashburn came to home plate and the third baseman would come in on the grass to take away the bunt, Ruben would turn toward the third baseman and tell him to get back, and then he'd turn toward Ashburn and say, "You want to bunt? I'll take care of you. Come on." That's asking for a *lot.* But then he *would* take care of him. He was a cat out there. He could have played anywhere. Even today he's a marvelous golfer. I liked him. I think he could've been better, with that ability, because he had a marvelous screwball.

But Sauer . . . Then I compounded it because I took him out for a pinch hitter once, and he had never been taken out in his life for a pinch hitter. It was a game against the Phillies. We were ahead by a run in the eighth inning, and Mays doubled leading off. Well, leading Robin Roberts, 2-1, I wanted to get that third run. So Hank's the next hitter, he's walking up to home plate and I yelled at him. He turned around, knowing that I *couldn't* have been yelling at *him.* And I said, "Hey!" and motioned him to come back. He looked at me again as if to say, "Are you out of your mind?" Finally, he came back and said, "What?" I told Lockman to get a bat, that he was hitting for Sauer. I just wanted a better bunter to get Mays over to third. So now the big fellow's feelings are hurt, his heart is broken. For two weeks *again* he didn't speak to me. He said, "Well, I'm not a bad bunter." And I said, "Not as good as the guy I sent up there." Lockman got the man over, but two more weeks went by before he spoke to me again.

John Antonelli supposedly had all sorts of problem with the weather in San Francisco but I don't think he had as many problems with it as the writers wrote about. Curley Grieve [*Examiner*] and I really went at it hammer-and-tong, because we had a chance to win it all in '59, and I told him, "You're destroying this guy."

Hey, the wind was blowing out one day and Charlie Neal, the skinny little second baseman for the Dodgers, hit a nice flyball. And it was either Kirkland or Wagner who went back, and it just sailed right over the fence. And beat him. So John came in and said, "This [expletive] ballpark," or something to that effect. And the San Francisco writers reacted with indignation, like it was *their* park, and they really rode him on it. I finally went to Curley Grieve and said, "Curley, that's the second article you've written about this; we're trying to win a pennant here and we've got a chance. Now get off his case or I'm going to keep you out of the clubhouse." He said I couldn't do that. I told him, maybe not, but that I'd sure try if he didn't let up on this guy. He could've carried us down the stretch. He won 19 games but I don't think he won a game in Sep-

Rigney works with Andre Rodgers on sliding technique, Spring Training, Phoenix, Arizona, March 1958. (SF Giants)

tember. [author's note: *Antonelli lost his last three decisions in September to finish 19-10.*] I think it affected him. He was a wonderful competitor, a real decent guy and a good pitcher. But that bothered him. The only other park in the league where wind was a factor was Wrigley.

Even in '58 we made a good run. We were so young. But as Milwaukee grounded it out you could see that they had a little better team than we did, that's all. We finished third but the club we saw coming was exciting, and we didn't need to add a lot of things to it. When you built the outfield around Mays, with Felipe Alou or Jackie Brandt, both of whom could run and throw, and the infield had Jimmy Davenport coming along at third with the Baby Bull [Cepeda] at first, how could you get better than that? We weren't sure up the middle. Andre Rodgers never quite did the things we hoped he could do. Maybe we didn't give him enough time, I don't know. Horace and I always had a big dispute about who should be the shortstop. I argued for Eddie Bressoud, he argued for Rodgers. Then we had Danny O'Connell at second base and Spencer, who was a good hitter, [also] at short.

But Rodgers was there. Horace had seen him play in the minors—a big, tall, handsome cricket player from Nassau [Bahamas], with great power.

Stoneham favorite Andre Rodgers (SF Giants)

And Horace kept thinking about having a shortstop like Ernie Banks who could hit 30, 40 home runs. But he never did, not only for us, but not for the clubs he went to later on. He had a great arm and could run. Sometimes you look back and say to yourself, did I go long enough with him? Did I give him enough of a chance? Maybe he could have done a little more if I had left him alone a little longer. But when you get the chance to win, the price is never too big to pay, and I thought our chances were better with Bressoud or Spencer, than with Andre.

The city of San Francisco, for the most part, really embraced us when we arrived from New York. I think for the society people who loved to be part of the social scene, this was the thing to do, so they embraced us. And for the fans who had never seen major league ball before, this became their own, and I think their enthusiasm was different from the laid-back fans we had in New York who knew every move we made, what we did at night and what we had for dinner. I think the move gave the people of San Francisco not only a new identity with a major league team here, but also a new group of players for them to follow—Davenport, Cepeda and Alou—who they could really latch onto. These were not *New York* Giants. Mays was a *New York* Giant. And I think there was always that little bit of a difference in the way they felt about Cepeda than how they felt about Willie.

I loved Cepeda but I fined him $50 in September for playing dumb baseball. I told him he was too good a player to keep making bonehead plays, that running through coaches' signs cost us several times. He had a bad habit when he was on first base of always trying for third on a single to left, with nobody out. Finally, after he was thrown out several times, running through signs, I told him, "Orlando, that cost you $50." He had a terrible time dealing with that. The next day he was taking batting practice and I could see him sulking. So I stopped BP, right in front of everybody, and I said, "I'll tell you what. If you sulk today, it's going to cost you a hundred." Then he came to life a little. I told him I loved his hustle, but that play's right in front of him, and he'd messed it up two or three times, and taken us out of innings.

But when you have a player like that you'll go to any end to see that he becomes a player that you think he can be. And I thought he needed something, a wake-up call, because you

can't just run amok out there. If you're going to be a Hall of Famer you better be able to do everything—not just hit, but catch it and throw it, too, because he could steal a base. He could run, bad feet and all. And he had no fear.

We won 16 of 22 from the Dodgers that first year in San Francisco, but the rivalry definitely changed. Sure, I thought it did. It was the newness of both of us being on the West Coast that kept it going, but there was a special element lacking here because we were in the same city in New York, where you had to listen, hear, watch and see *everything* about each other. But 400 miles away you could cross them out of your mind once in a while.

What stood out about that '58 team was the ability of the Latin players—the Cepedas, the Alous. If I had to do it again I'd have learned Spanish a long time ago, because I know it would have helped me like it helps Tony LaRussa today. For us in those days it was just a question of how well we pitched, and so Chub went and got us Sam Jones and Jack Sanford. That's what I'll always say about Chub Feeney: He wasn't afraid to pull the trigger. But as great as it was to deal for Sanford [from Philadelphia, after the '58 season], it was hard to trade Ruben and Valmy. They didn't do very well with Philadelphia and I remember their general manager calling me and asking just what it was that I'd sent him. I said, "I sent you two darned good players. You're probably not handling them very well." But Sanford later pitched great for Alvin [Dark] in '62. He came to me one day and said, "I'll tell you one thing. I may not be the smartest guy, but I can sure as hell throw it." And he did. He had a great arm, and I later got him with the Angels toward the tail end of his career.

One of the big highlights of the '59 season was Willie McCovey's debut in July against Robin Roberts—four-for-four, two triples and two singles. I never saw anything like it. [*author's note: Nor did anyone else—the last player to make his major league debut with four hits was Casey Stengel with the Dodgers in 1912.*] Every time he swung he hit it right off the sweet spot. He was amazing but that became a dilemma for me because I couldn't convince Cepeda to play left field. If I had been able to talk Cepeda into playing left field, which I think he could have done well, I think we'd have won the pennant. But he kept saying he was the first baseman. I said I knew but that Willie also was a first baseman.

McCovey said he'd play left field but he couldn't play it very well, because he couldn't run like Cepeda. I couldn't sell Orlando on the idea. I tried him at third base but I could see that wasn't going to work. So it became a dilemma, which the front office finally had to resolve by trading one of them.

We led the Dodgers by two games with eight to go, but we just couldn't hold on. I might have overworked Sam Jones a little bit because I used him out of the bullpen to save a game once in a while. If I had managed as well in '59 for the Giants as I did in '62 for the Angels, we'd have won it. We had a tough game up here with the Dodgers—Antonelli against Drysdale. We loaded the bases in the first inning with nobody out. Drysdale walked those first three hitters. Walter [Alston] already had the bullpen going. Danny McDevitt was warming up. Cepeda, hitting fourth, got to three-and-one. What do you do if you're the manager? The guy's walked three in a row but he's your cleanup hitter. I let him hit. He swung at ball four, then swung at ball five and struck out. Then Willie Kirkland swung at ball six and struck out, and Spencer flew out and we didn't score. And it seemed like that just sank us a little bit. They finally beat us, 5-3, and went on to sweep the series. [*author's note: Roger Craig, who would later manage San Francisco, 6-hit the Giants in one of those Dodger wins.*] And I think Horace wanted to fire me right then. I think he thought it was my fault, and it could have been.

As good as that '59 club was, we should have been better in '60. Chub went out and got Billy O'Dell, but also got Don Blasingame—a terrible blow. He was the best player the Cardinals had but didn't play worth a hoot out here. [Eddie] Stanky was scouting for the Cardinals in those days—he didn't know whether he wanted Wagner, Kirkland or Bill White. Turns out he got two of the three—White for Sam Jones [before the '59 season], and Wagner and Spencer for Blasingame [before '60]. Horace didn't like White because he was too *smart.* He was a very intelligent guy so why would you like him? *Really* [shakes his head in disbelief]. Because White could have played anywhere. He was a great athlete, as we all found out, but Horace didn't like him. He was too smart. OK. Horace, again, liked the home run hitter. White didn't look like one at the time but turned out to be one anyhow.

But that was probably my toughest season and the biggest blow of my baseball career, when I got fired [on June 18, with a 33-25 record, after a three-game sweep of Philadelphia]. Horace had been told by everybody that if the Russians didn't attack, we should win the pennant by 20 games. Well, Milwaukee, the Dodgers and Pittsburgh were still pretty good. But even though we were only two and a half games behind, Horace got it into his head that we should have been ahead by eight or 10 games. That was our first season in Candlestick, too. I never liked the place. I never wore a jacket there, though, because I didn't want the players to think I was cold, because then *they'd* think it was cold. I remember saying to Davenport and Cepeda that when Junior Gilliam walks onto the field, go tell him how bad this place his, that it is so cold he's going to hate it [laughs].

Two more things happened in '60: Detroit manager Charlie Dressen died, and it was down to Bob Scheffing or me to succeed him. I knew their GM Jim Campbell wanted me, so they flew me in and I met with the new owner, John Fetzer, as did Scheffing. Two days later they named Scheffing, who did pretty well—he won 101 games in '61. The Yankees just won 109. Then the American League expanded and Gene Autry got the Angels. He hired Fred Haney as GM and Bob Reynolds, the head of Golden West Broadcasters, as president and Gene's right-hand man. So Chub called Reynolds and recommended me [as manager]. I flew down and met with Haney, who didn't really want me. I knew that and could sense that. He wanted Bob Elliott. But I think Chub had a lot of influence with Reynolds, and they hired me.

Years later I found out from Jim Campbell why I didn't get the Detroit job. He said that Fetzer thought I was too nervous. Well, he was right. I *was* nervous. I was out of a job, had a wife and three kids, and had never been out of a job before.

So we went to the draft, and Chub was a great help because I didn't know anything about the American League. I was named manager on a Saturday in LA, and flew back to San Francisco Sunday morning, where Chub met me. He took me up to his office at Candlestick and opened up all his scouting reports on players who would be available in the draft. I took notes, and he gave me a great bit of advice. He said, "You're sharing the same town with the Dodgers. Haney's gonna want to take a lot of veteran name players. You've got to manage next year and hopefully for years to come. Take some prospects, too. You don't have a farm system."

So, we got Jim Fregosi. Pretty good. Bob Rodgers. Dean Chance. It was through those Charlie Fox scouting reports that I took those three guys. And when I was named manager I told Haney the one player I *really* wanted, a player I already knew a lot about, was Leon Wagner. I saw that Wrigley Field in LA and I said, "That park was made for Daddy Wags. *Made* for him." Haney asked about his fielding. I said he wasn't that bad, and he wasn't. He had good hands. But we got him out there and he just loved it. He had two great years, with over 100 RBIs each.

I loved that little ballpark. The Yankees won everything in '61, Maris hit 61 homers and they set a new team home run record with him and Mantle [240]. But they never won a series from us at Wrigley. We won two of three every time they came to town. I think Hollywood had a little to do with it, too.

The next year was probably my most enjoyable year managing of all. We made some great trades, sending Bob Cerv back to the Yankees for Ryne Duren and Lee Thomas. We got George Thomas on waivers from Detroit. Our PR people said, "Hey, we got TNT—Thomas 'n' Thomas." One played first base, one played right field. Albie Pearson played center and scored 115 runs. Daddy Wags played left, hit 37 home runs and drove in 107. We won 86 games. We won 70 our first year. They said we wouldn't win 50. We won 70. We won 86 the next year, and on the fourth of July we were leading the league. On Labor Day we were two and a half games behind the Yankees, and had just split a four-game series in New York. Then we went to Baltimore and swept the Orioles, went to Minnesota and swept the Twins, while the Yankees were also sweeping. Then we came home and the balloon kind of busted on us.

I never had a club that responded by getting men in from third base with less than two out as well as that club—the best I ever saw. Felix Torres, Joe Koppe, Jim Fregosi, Billy Moran—all these guys came out of the minor leagues, one out of the Mexican League. Buck Rodgers caught 155 games. Albie played 160. So did Lee Thomas, Wagner and Moran. Never took them out of the lineup. That year we won *nine doubleheaders.* That'll never happen again. Of course, we don't play them anymore. Nine doubleheaders. That's 18 games over .500. I mean, if you win one, espe-

cially with an expansion team ... we won *nine* doubleheaders.

We had five starters and five relievers. McBride, Bowsfield, Chance, Belinsky and Lee were the starters—every time I walked to the mound they knew exactly who I was going to bring in, and who would be next. Jack Spring would come in and get a left-handed hitter out. Art Fowler would come in and strike out the next two. We had such a good bullpen. Tom Morgan, Art Fowler, Ryne Duren, Jack Spring, Julio Navarro—they never threw a ball. Strike one, strike two, strike eight.

Dean Chance wasn't one of the greatest pitchers but he had one of the greatest arms I ever saw. He should've been better. He should've lasted longer. He loved the night life. Hollywood. He and Bo Belinsky. *What is this?* All these lights, *come on.* And Chance was the worst hitter of all time. If he'd have had to hit against himself, he'd have quit. Mickey Mantle told me he was the toughest right-handed pitcher he ever faced. In '64 he pitched against the Yankees four times and gave them one run [20-9 for the season, a 1.65ERA]. *One run.* We got a run off the Yankees in the first inning one of those games, and he walked down the bench and said to everybody, "That'll be enough. I won't need anymore." And he beat 'em, 1-0.

Belinsky had talent but had stars in his eyes, too. I think if Bo had had his way he'd have pitched on Sunday, then taken Monday through Thursday off, and then come back to the park and pitched on Friday. But he had some ability. He had a good screwball, and that no-hitter in '61 was a solid no-hitter. It really was. Of course, that opened a whole can of worms with the Hollywood starlets. He and Mamie Van Doren had a thing going. He just loved the limelight, and wasn't willing to pay the price.

It really was frustrating that I couldn't get more out of Belinsky and Chance. Because I cared about both of them, not only because they were good for our club. But every night on the Sunset strip, there was Bo's red Cadillac convertible parked in front of some club at 2 a.m. He knew I didn't like it. I told him why, that his personal life ought to be a little more personal. People knew where he was all the time. I wanted him to think more of baseball first, and the night life second.

The next spring in Palm Springs he asked to see me. He knew I never liked that red Cadillac convertible, so he told me he got rid of it. I said, "Hey! All right, good move!" And as he's walking out, I said, "By the way, what'd you get?" He said, "I got another Cadillac convertible. Gold." Oh, swell.

I stayed with the Angels for nine years and then managed the Twins in 1970. We finished first with 98 wins. It was a wonderful team. Billy Martin had just won 97 there the year before but Calvin Griffith [Twins owner] and Billy got into something, so Calvin fired him, even though he won. So I took the job, for more money than I'd ever made before. And, of course, I had managed there before with the Millers in triple-A. So I knew I was under the gun because all the fans liked Billy. I took Buck Rodgers there with me, his first year as a coach. And Frank Crosetti—I got him out of retirement. I got Marv Grissom as my pitching coach and away we went. And I kept one of their coaches, Vern Morgan. And Morgan said he hoped we'd win one more game than we did the year before. We did. We won 98. That was a good team. We clinched it right here in Oakland.

When I went up there for the banquet in January, to be introduced as manager, Calvin had already been booed. And I was sitting there, not knowing what to say to those people, because I was replacing Billy Martin. He was their favorite. So the speeches went on and on, and finally it was time for the manager. And when I got to the mike 1,800 people stood up and gave me the darnedest ovation I ever got in my life. I could see Calvin, who had been sweating bullets. And I said, in finishing, "Oh, by the way. When I got off the plane last night I didn't realize how many of you remembered I had managed the Millers here, because I saw all these bumper stickers: *Bring Billy Back.* Hey, you got him."

It really was disappointing that we didn't beat Baltimore in the playoffs. Baltimore's pitching was just so good for a short three-out-of-five, with Palmer, Cuellar and McNally. They were loaded and, in a short series, they got the best of us.

My last stint managing, after three years in Minneapolis, came in '76 back here with the Giants, as a favor to Bob Lurie. Bob and I were friends, and he asked me to come back and manage for a year so he wouldn't have to worry about finding a manager [after Lurie bought the club from Stoneham, averting a last-minute franchise sale and move to Toronto]. I didn't really want to.

I could see the game was changing. Players were getting more demanding, the free agent thing was around, and Walter Alston and I had discussed it. He said he thought he'd had enough. He said he was just staying on because he didn't want that *other* guy [Tommy Lasorda] to get it yet. But I did it for Bob, and then I told him if there was anything else I could do for him in the organization that I'd be happy to. But there was nothing there.

Managing wasn't fun anymore. I used to say, with free agency upon us, "The players are the tail wagging the dog." I had a good coaching staff, with Bobby Winkles, and Buck back. But I could tell I had worried about babysitting and changing pitchers long enough. But for Bob I said I'd be happy to do it, and I did it. But I knew that my time was up, that I had had enough. I wasn't burned out. I still loved the game. And Darrell Evans and four or five other guys came in to me and said, "Look, you found out how bad we really can be. Why don't you give us a chance, and come back one more year?" I told them I'd be watching, but that I'd had enough. We won 74 and lost 88.

Evans was great, but [John] Montefusco was not. He was a very selfish kind of guy. He had good ability but I remember taking him out of a game once, and he told the press I had waited too long to take him out, and blamed me for all the problems he was having. I remember once Derrel Thomas made an error behind him at second base and it cost him the game. He, of course, was great with the press. The press loved all the b.s. he could give them. So he said he'd never pitch another game with Derrel Thomas on second base.

A week later it was John's turn to pitch, and I penciled Derrel Thomas in at second. So I was sitting in my office when there was a knock on the door, and it was Montefusco. He said he told the press he'd never pitch another game if Derrel Thomas were on second. I said, "Oh, yeah, I remember you said that. Wait right here." I told Buck Rodgers to come in the office and I said, "Montefusco can't pitch with Derrel Thomas playing second base. Who else have you got to pitch?" Buck said he had so-and-so. I said to tell so-and-so he was pitching. Montefusco said, "Wait a minute." He thought I was going to take Derrel Thomas out of the lineup. I said, "No." He was not among my favorite players.

I also had [Bobby] Murcer, [Gary] Matthews and [Willie] Montanez. I thought it was a pretty good team. I liked Matthews the best. But they were all thinking free agency. It was on all their minds.

I managed 18 years in the big leagues, for four different clubs, including my last year back with the Giants. Quite different from my playing career—eight years, all with one club, the Giants.

I WAS BORN IN ALAMEDA [California] and raised in Oakland. My parents were born in San Francisco and lived through the big fire and earthquake, so we're real solid natives of San Francisco.

I didn't make the baseball team at Oakland High until my senior year. The coach and I never saw eye to eye. I always thought I was a little better than he thought. It doesn't happen very often that a guy makes it for the first time as a senior. They'll keep a junior around but not a senior. So that was fun.

After graduating I played a lot of semi-pro ball, and they had a four-team league that played its games in Emeryville in the Oakland Oaks ballpark, on Sundays. I played with the St. Francis club and one day I went five-for-five. I'll never forget it. Two triples, two doubles and a single. And as we were walking out of the clubhouse in center field, my pal said, "I'll bet some scout's going to grab you before you get to our car." Sure enough, scouts from the Giants, the Yankees and Cincinnati all started making inquiries, and we met with all of them. The Yankees wanted to sign me and send me to El Paso, but a friend of mine in the Giants organization said if I signed with the Yankees I'd be a Yankee forever, whereas if I signed with a local club, like the Oaks, I'd have 16 [big league] clubs with a crack at me, if I were any good. I took his advice and signed with Oakland in 1938—my first contract.

My first dream was to make it in the Coast League. But there was no doubt what my ultimate dream was. And oddly enough my favorite major league team as a kid had been the Giants. Mel Ott was my idol—the 16-year-old kid who came up to the Giants in the 20s and never left. [*author's note: Ott arrived at the Giants' spring training camp in 1926 at the age of 16, made the club and played 22 consecutive seasons there before retiring in 1947, with 511 home runs and a .304 career average.*]

In 1940 I was optioned to Topeka, Kansas, and I still remember eating a vanilla ice cream cone on the team bus my first road trip. The manager glared at me and said, "What is *that*?" I told him it was an ice cream cone. He said, "Let me tell you something, kid. See that barrel? Go toss that ice cream cone in the barrel, and then go to the back of the bus and grab a beer. You won't hit on ice cream but you *might* hit on beer." Well, maybe he knew something. I had a good year [.276], and he told me if I could play there I could play anywhere. It was a hot, tough league—the Western Association.

I came back to the Coast League and played two years here, and then I knew that I had a chance to go to the majors. I had a great arm, was a shortstop and finally learned to get a hit or two. And I thought that, then, maybe this thing wasn't out of reach. Yeah [laughs], I had a great arm but I also cleared out the section behind first base quite a few times [165 errors in three years]. I had a very strong arm and was a little erratic. But that got better.

My first full year in the Coast League I played in 173 games and hit .208. I turned to the right [toward the dugout] an awful lot of times, on my way to first base. But the next year I hit .288, and that's when I felt I caught somebody's interest. And then I went into the service [1943, '44 and '45].

I was in the Navy pre-flight, stationed at St. Mary's College in Moraga, which was a break for me because they had a big athletic program. They were all pilots there. We had 2,500 cadets, 110 officers and 80 enlisted men. I was one of the enlisted men. And all these pilots to be had to get in shape. We also had a baseball team, which was fortunate for me, too. I lived at home then. Only the cadets lived on the base. The enlisted men lived at home. And I came home one day in 1944 just before Christmas, and as I walked into the house my father said I got a little early Christmas present, that the Giants just bought my contract from the Oaks, that I was to report to the Giants when I got out of the Navy. That was about as big a thrill as I could ever have, right there.

With pre-flight we knew eventually the turnover would come, so I told a pal that if we eventually had to go we should go together. So we did something we were not supposed to do. We volunteered, to a carrier aircraft service unit, in the Mariana Islands. So they shipped me out of pre-flight to the Naval Air Station in Alameda. We were standing at inspection one day, and I knew the time was coming that we were going to go. We were all packed and ready. It was condition red, with 30-to-40,000 men a month coming in and going out. So one of the lieutenants came over to me and said the commodore wanted to see me. I had no idea why, but the commodore told me we were going to have a baseball team at the air station because the sailors coming back would need some entertainment. And he wanted me to stay and be part of it. He rescinded the orders to go to the Marianas. I said OK and started to leave, but then wondered about my buddy. So I went back to the commodore and told him I volunteered to go to the Marianas with a buddy. He asked if my buddy were a ballplayer. Right away I told the truth and said no. He said there was nothing he could do. So there I was, saying goodbye to my buddy. Thank God he came back from the war.

So I stayed, we played 110 games and beat everybody. We had a great team. Joe Hatten, Si Johnson, Cookie Lavagetto and Lincoln Blakely joined us. We had a marvelous team. And the commodore was great. He flew us all over the state, playing Navy and Army teams. We beat everybody, entertained our troops and even built a ballpark. Everybody in the athletic department built that ballpark—the fences, everything. So the commodore came out to see it and told us what a great job we did. I asked him if he ever played ball. He said, "Oh, yeah." Then I said we had a problem. The transportation building was in center field, it was grey and the pitcher threw right out of it. So he stood at home plate, I got out on the mound and threw a couple of pitches. He understood and painted the transportation building green. It was the only green building on the whole base. And I remember, after we won everything, we had a party at Jack London Square and he got up on the table and recited *Casey At The Bat*. He was so proud of our team and almost fell off the table. And years later, when I was with the Giants, I saw him again. He was then an admiral. And he told me to come back, that he could get me a good rank, that we could have some fun. I told him he had me for two years and that was enough.

I went straight from the service to the Giants' spring camp in Miami in '46. I remember that Dick Bartell was still playing, and we had been friends for a long time, and I knew that if I made the club he wouldn't. The Giants had brought every player that was in the service to camp. We had 94 players in spring training. We had two workouts, one in the morning and one in the afternoon. And you never knew the afternoon group because you never saw them. We

stayed at different hotels. And, you know, Bartell helped me all spring, showing me the little things about playing shortstop, because he was a shortstop. I made the team, and they made him a coach. I never forgot that.

Making the major league club was the culmination of a dream. Absolutely. When the squad was cut and we were heading north, playing exhibitions all the way up the coast with Cleveland, and I was named the Opening Day shortstop, that was a dream that, as far away as it had once been, was now a reality. And now it was just up to me to prove that I belonged.

I can tell you *everything* about my first big league game. It was at the Polo Grounds. John McGraw had started this tradition with West Point that if the Giants opened at home, the day before they would play the cadets at West Point. So when we finished our road trip we all went to West Point, played the cadets and stayed for dinner. And I remember driving back on the bus, and coming to the Polo Grounds. I had never seen a major league *city* before, let alone a major league park. As a matter of fact, the very first major league game I ever saw I *played* in. So we got our bags and walked into this magnificent clubhouse. It was three stories high. And I walked down to the lower deck where all the lockers were, found my locker next to Johnny Mize's, put my stuff in there, looked around and said to myself, "This is where Babe Ruth, Lou Gehrig, Christy Mathewson, Stoney [Travis] Jackson, Carl Hubbell and Mel Ott all dressed. And now it's my turn."

The clubhouse was in center field, I walked down the steps, the night lights of the golden horseshoe were on and it was breathtaking. It was so big it sent a chill. I remember it so well. I thought, Well, here you go, pal. Tomorrow there'll be 50,000 people here rooting for you, or against you. We were playing the Phillies. This is where it all began.

I struck out my first time at bat. My friend George Will [the columnist] once asked, "How do you remember that?" And I said, "Well, his name was Oscar Judd, I was leading off, he threw me a three-and-two screwball and I thought, 'Good God, if this is the major leagues, this is gonna be tough.'" But I got two hits that day, drove in a couple of runs and we won, 8-2. I remember the first play of the game, when I ran out to shortstop, and their shortstop Skeeter Newsome was leading off. I said, "If there's a Lord in heaven, let him hit the first ball to me and let's get it over with." He hit a ball through the box, I went over and sucked it up, threw him out and said, "Hey, this might not be so hard after all."

My second year we set a major league home run record, and I hit 17 of my own. We had a club built for the Polo Grounds. We had Mize, Willard Marshall and Walker Cooper—all power men. And Horace Stoneham loved the home run. He didn't like the bunt, he didn't like the good pitching, we couldn't beat you, 2-1, but we could beat you, 9-8. When we started hitting home runs the writers started asking whether we'd break the major league record. We broke it by *40*. We hit 221 home runs. As a matter of fact, my roommate and I hit 69. Of course, the fact that Mize hit 51 is really not part of the story [laughs]. And the reason I say 69 is because I had one rained out. Chub would never count that. He said, "You only hit 17. I don't care what you say about the 18th." [laughs]

1947, of course, marked Jackie Robinson's debut in the big leagues. I can tell you the exact date of the first time I saw him play: It was April 18th, at the Polo Grounds. One reason I remember it so well is that Jackie hit his first major league home run that day, and the other reason I remember it is that I hit *two* home runs that day, one a grand slam. But there was no doubt to any of us that they had picked the right man to carry the cross for the black player. I never saw in all my days in the major leagues a tougher man, a tougher competitor, who played with a fury, really, every game he played. He was a marvelous competitor, maybe the best I ever saw.

Even though we had some players from the South I think we all felt it was just a matter of time before the game was integrated. These guys were too good. They were outstanding. And aside from off-the-cuff remarks from one or two guys like, "Who we lettin' in next?" or something else that was uncalled for, this man's great ability and desire quieted everything. Because sooner or later, if you were a competitor of his, an opponent or a teammate, you had to realize what he was bringing to the game. He was bringing a dedication that you thought you had the market cornered on yourself. But he was bringing it a little bit further, and beyond that. At least this is the way I felt, as well as a lot of my teammates, too, like Buddy Kerr.

I had such a great start in '47. I think I was hitting .398 after the first 25 games and Dixie

Walker was leading the league at .401. But we couldn't make a double play. I was playing third and Buddy Kerr was playing short. Buddy was a marvelous fielder but didn't know a lot about getting a hit. I could get a hit and third was perfect for me, I thought, but they asked me to move to second base, and I had never caught a groundball on that side of the diamond in my entire life. I had been a shortstop all my life but what do you say when the manager asks you to make a change? Looking back on it I probably should have said, "No," because I was never a good second baseman.

It was going to take some getting used to. We came back home to play Philadelphia, made five double plays and they thought I was the greatest second baseman since Burgess Whitehead. And I hadn't tagged the bag right once, on *any* of the five. As time went on I existed as a second baseman but Buddy was a magician at short. Then when Leo came over to manage us in '48, being an ex-infielder, he could see that I wasn't a good second baseman but that I could get a hit and knew how to play his game. Then they made the big trade for Stanky and Dark in '49, and that's when I knew that they'd either give me a good crack back at third base or that I'd be a backup infielder.

But the arrival of Hank Thompson at third precluded that, as soon as Henry came. He was a left-handed hitter with great power for a little man, and a good fielder. A good *everything*. That was in 1950. I was 32. So it was about then that I began to think about what was after baseball. I had some time to think about it because I was on the bench more.

Of course, the '51 season was everyone's dream to be a part of. We all grew up that year and aged a little, but aged for the better, in that we knew then that Yogi [Berra] was right—it's never over until it's over.

Knowing Leo, as little as I did as the opposition's manager, I knew that we were not his type of club when he joined us in '48, that he liked the speedier club, a better defensive club, with better pitching. He thought home runs were great—Bobby [Thomson] hit the biggest one in the world—but he wanted that to be *part* of a team. And I had a feeling that sooner or later his influence into the front office would lead to some changes. We traded Sid Gordon, Willard Marshall, Buddy Kerr—three regulars—along with Sam Webb and another player to the Braves for Stanky and Dark. Leo knew that was important. We had a fairly good nucleus of pitching, Sal Maglie was back from the Mexican League and you could see that if we could defend the game better, hey, we'd be a better team. And we sensed that.

Leo was a good s-of-a-b. You can take that any way you want to. But it was fun playing for him. He never gave up. If he had a weakness it was that if he had a team he didn't think he could win with, he'd lose interest. But if he had a team that he thought had a chance, boy, he'd take you to the moon. He gambled a lot but that was his style, while Ott's style had been low-key—you know, hit the home run. And Horace Stoneham liked that.

The arrival of Henry Thompson and Monte Irvin in '49 changed the team. Once we saw them we knew they were players. They weren't here just because they were black, that because the Dodgers had one we should, too. No, we knew they were a fit. And Monte Irvin was probably one of the most decent men I ever knew, not only a good player. And in those years we had him he was as tough a two-out hitter with men on base and two strikes as anybody we had. Henry was a little looser. Henry liked to have a drink. But Henry could play. I think he still holds the record for double plays from a third baseman in one year. And he could certainly hit. So we welcomed these two guys. We thought they were great, because they fit. And I think, when I look back on the players we had—the Maglies, the Jansens, the Stankys, the Darks, the Rigneys, Lockmans and Westrums, these were all guys that loved the game and simply *took* to these two guys. There was never anything said about black and white. It was just, "Hey, it says, *Giants.* Come on in, have a beer. Let's go."

Then, of course, there was the coming of Willie Mays in '51. We were playing a spring training game in St. Petersburg one day when Leo went over to see our farm club in Melbourne, because he had heard about Willie Mays. He went over there to see him play a minor league game. Well, when we saw Leo the next day he didn't talk about anybody from then on except Willie Mays. So we all had an idea that even though Leo could exaggerate quite a big at times, we also knew that he knew talent, and we couldn't wait to see this young man. He was just 19 years old. Leo said he could do everything: He could run, throw, hit and hit with power, and that if you could keep the ball in the ballpark, he'd catch it. So we realized this kid was something special,

even before we had ever seen him. When he finally did join us, we had just been waiting.

He joined us in Philadelphia. When he got in uniform on the field we had about five more minutes of batting practice left. The Phillies were on the sidelines warming up to take infield. Leo said that since Willie was going to play that night, he should get the last five minutes. So we gave it to him. He fouled one out, hit a groundball, popped one up and then, all of a sudden, he nailed one that hit the upper deck in left field. Then he hit another one in left-center. Then I looked over at the Phillies, and everybody had stopped warming up. It was so special because you got that *feeling.* Then he hit the scoreboard in right. Then he hit one *over* the scoreboard. Here was this baby-faced 19-year-old, with an enthusiasm you couldn't bottle nor buy. And right then there was no doubt in any of our minds that this kid was special.

They hated us in Brooklyn when we went over there to play the Dodgers. When we got off the subway the kids were awful to us, just *awful.* They'd yell, "Sign this!" And if we didn't they'd throw ink on us. They were terrible. And Jackie had a great thing he did in the Polo Grounds, when the Dodgers came to play us. When we were taking batting practice, the Dodgers would come onto the field from center field and all the Giant fans would start to boo. But Jackie wouldn't come then, he'd come alone about five minutes later. He'd get his own boos, deliberately. I kind of liked that. He stood up and got counted. The games against the Dodgers, then, were like going to war. Every day. You could feel it from the manager, with Leo, and with one of his ex-coaches, Charlie Dressen, managing over there. You could see the fire within those two, who was going to out-manage whom.

In Ebbets Field you'd come out of a runway and have to climb a ladder to get into the visiting dugout. But while you were in that runway fans could throw stuff at you, spit at you, whatever they wanted to do. You were a little bit under the gun but it was all part of New York Giant—Brooklyn Dodger baseball, that's all.

We were 13½ games behind the Dodgers on August 12th but I thought we were still in the race, and I'll tell you why. We were in second place so we didn't have to climb over anybody. There's a big difference. If you're in third or fourth you've got to worry about two or three clubs. They had just swept a series in Brooklyn from us on the 11th, and whether this had anything to do with it or not, I don't know, but I still remember what happened then. The two clubhouses there were back to back and there was a door, always locked, on their side. And a door, always locked, on our side. And there was, maybe, six feet of space in between. Well, they had opened their door after the sweep and we could hear Ralph Branca singing, "Roll out the barrel, the Giants are dead." I remember years later Ralph said he didn't do that, but Newk [Don Newcombe] said, "Yes, you did."

Then, Jackie took a bat and beat it against our door and called out to Leo. He didn't like Leo. He hated him. And he yelled, "Leo? How do you like it, Leo? How do you like it in there, Leo? We can smell Laraine's perfume in here." Now, that was a little personal, right? I remember Stanky, Dark, Lockman, Monte Irvin, Hank and I were all changing and listening. He was *right there.* You *had* to listen. What else could you do? Finally, when it got a little quiet, Stanky yelled back, "Stick that bat up your [expletive], you [expletive]." Oh, he said it all, right then and there. I remember Monte Irvin looked up and said, "That's good enough for me, Ed." And that was that.

So we left Brooklyn, beaten down, but not to a point where we were crushed into the ground. And a lot of people forget that we then went on to win 16 in a row to seriously close the gap. And 39-and-8 the rest of the way. People never thought we could catch the Dodgers so when we did, there was so little advance ticket sales for the playoff that even the third and final game wasn't sold out.

We won the coin toss to open the playoff and chose to play the first game in Brooklyn and the next two back in the Polo Grounds. So we went to Brooklyn and I couldn't wait. Ebbets Field was packed. We came up that ladder to the dugout and who was in the batting cage hitting, but Jackie. So Lockman, Westrum and I walked over behind the cage and I said, "Hey, Jackie. Turn around. You'll never guess who's here." He wouldn't turn around [laughs]. He wouldn't turn around. I said, "You'll never guess who's here, Jack." So I had my say, so to speak.

Then [Jim] Hearn pitched and Bobby hit a home run off Branca. Monte Irvin hit one, too, we won, 3-1, and came back to the Polo Grounds. I rode back home with Stanky—we lived in the same neighborhood in Westchester County. He was hoping Maglie would pitch the second game but that would mean Maglie on two days rest, so

Leo went with Sheldon Jones. Clem Labine was awfully good that day and they scorched us. So now we were down to one game. Here, we'd played 156 games and nothing had been decided.

I can tell you whatever you want to know about that last game because I'll always remember it all. We were down, 4-1, entering the last of the ninth but we never despaired. Stanky came back to the dugout in about the sixth inning after hitting and said the big guy [Newcombe] was losing it, that if we could hold him there we could beat him. And it was just 2-1 then. So they got two more runs and I was leading off the eighth, batting for Westrum. I took a strike, with Stanky on deck, and the pitch looked no bigger than an aspirin. And I backed out and said, "Yeah, Ed, he's sure lost a lot. He really has." He struck me out, struck Stanky out and struck Thompson out.

Later, we heard that on the Dodger bench Newcombe said, "Hey, I've had it." And Jackie kept saying, "No, you *haven't* had it. We've got one more inning to go. *Come on.*" Of course we were thrilled to see Newcombe taken out. Of all the games we played against Newk, with that hard-quick slider, that was the best I ever saw. He was up for this game, no doubt, yet he was coming back on short rest, too. And I think that weighed on him a little bit. Then here came Branca out of the bullpen.

I was on the bench, having struck out to open the eighth. And this was typical Durocher: At the start of the ninth he got up to walk down to the end of the bench, then turned around and said, "Well, you [expletive], you've come this far, let's give 'em a finish."

Dark gets a line drive base hit, and then one mistake I think was made that would live in infamy was that Gil [Hodges] held Dark on first, with Don Mueller the next hitter. That left the hole open a little bit between first and second, and Mueller hit a rocket that Gil dove for, and it just ticked off his glove. If he were behind Alvin, it might have been an easy three-six-three double play. So we had first-and-third, no out. Then Monte popped up the first pitch, right down the middle. He was so stricken. I told him later in the clubhouse, "Hey, you could have hit into a double play, too, you know. Come on. It wasn't that bad."

Then Whitey doubled off the left field wall. Alvin scored but Mueller broke a bone in his foot sliding into third base. Guess who carried him into the clubhouse? Bill Rigney, because I was out of the game. We carried him out to the clubhouse in center field. So then, I was in the club-house, looking through the windows in center, watching the game. That's where I saw the home run. I saw it hit that kid right there in the belly. The foul pole was right there, and it hit the kid in the first seat. And the wall was right there. How it got under the scoreboard and over the wall and into that kid's belly, only the good Lord above knows.

Horace had already come into the clubhouse and said he had decided that we weren't going to win. He was a pessimist. He was not an optimist. That was just his nature. I don't mean that as a putdown of the owner of the Giants. But he said another thing, too, that he'd have a drink with the entire group of players when they came off the field, because this had been the darnedest season he'd ever been a part of. And then to have Branca enter the game for Newcombe, and on an oh-one pitch, Thomson hits the line drive. I've still got the record, at home, of Russ Hodges' call. And I still get the goose pimples every time I hear it.

Even then, you just *knew* that this home run would go down in history as one of the greatest ever. Absolutely. To look where we'd been, how the whole season went, with Willie Mays and all the changes—Leo took two outfielders and made one a third baseman [Thomson] and the other a first baseman [Lockman]. And Lockman must have saved Thomson 20 years over there because he was a magician. All that, just to get Mays in the lineup. I remember the writers came in the clubhouse and said, "How are we going to write this? They write this kind of stuff in Hollywood."

And I remember something else that showed a lot of character about the Brooklyn club, when it was over. All the press, and the radio and TV, were in the Dodger clubhouse. Then suddenly, they had to move everything outside this little catwalk into our clubhouse. I remember Herman Franks [coach] was drinking scotch out of a keg, crying. I asked, "What are you crying about?" He said, "I'll be darned if I know." I think all the nerves and tension of the whole season just came out for everybody. *Whew.* But four Dodgers came in: The Preacher [Roe], Pee Wee [Reese], Duke [Snider] and Jackie. The Preacher came in and said, "You've got to be kidding me. You've got to be kidding me. You guys are too much." And he left. Pee Wee said, "Hey, do good in the Series. You had a hell of a year." Duke was in tears. I don't think he even remembers that he

was there. Then Jackie came in, tapped me on the shoulder and said, "I want you to know one thing. We didn't lose it. You won it." And he turned around and walked out. A classy guy.

We had enough left for the Series but the Yankees were just better. We won the first game there, 5-1, but then Lopat beat us, 3-1. I missed a home run by an *inch.* I backed [Hank] Bauer right up to the right field seats. Yup, still burns me. And Lopat said to me the next day, in a teasing tone, "You just didn't *wait* long enough, did you? You really got to wait on my stuff. It doesn't get up there very fast."

We lost the Series in six games but I don't think in all the years I've been in this business, and it's been my whole life, that there was another season in which I could tell you everything about it, like that one. George Will asked, "How do you remember everything?" I said, "George, our lives were on the line every day." Jansen and Maglie won 46 games between them, 23 apiece. And I was on the bench, keeping a book on certain pitchers, and certain catchers' signs, so as soon as we got a man on second base, by the time we saw three pitches we knew what was coming next. And when you told Monte Irvin what was coming, you had to buy a ticket to find it. Let me put it this way: Leo never let us stop playing or believing that we had a chance.

By then I was already preparing myself to eventually manage. What I didn't know was that Carl Hubbell and Chub Feeney were already hoping that I'd go into managing. I didn't know that. But I'd just moved my family east in '53 when Chub asked me midway through the season to take over the Minneapolis club, in the American Association. I really wanted to do it. I had watched Leo, Mel, Walter Alston, Ralph Houk, Stengel and Al Lopez. But I told Chub that I'd rather start fresh with *my* team, *my* way, and see if I were capable. Chub said I might not get the chance if I waited until '54. I said I'd have to take the chance. So I stayed with the Giants through '53. Leo asked me to stay on as a coach. I said, "No." He asked why not and I said, "Because I want your job." And I did. I meant it. I felt that if you managed the New York Giants, you had reached the top of the line.

I didn't enjoy managing Minneapolis the first month. The team lived in barracks at spring training in Melbourne and I didn't even have a bathroom. I had a cot and a wash basin. And I'm lying there the first night thinking, "Why have I done this?" But I learned a lot from the other managers in the minor leagues who had managed for years and years. And with the major league team in Arizona I didn't know what kind of team I was going to have because, at the triple-A level, I'd get the best of what Leo didn't want. So I had to play myself. I'd work out the guys we had, let them go, then I'd get the trainer to hit me ground balls for an hour, then I'd run 25 laps in the outfield to get myself in shape as well as the team.

We finished third in Minneapolis that year [78-73], then won the pennant in '55 [92-62]. And we won the playoffs in eight straight—no team had ever done that. Then we won the Little World Series over Rochester in seven games [triple-A series between champions of American Association and International League]. I was named manager of the Giants after that. 1955 just kept getting better and better.

In a way it was tough not being a part of the Giants in '54 when they went all the way. I got to go to the World Series and see them beat Cleveland four straight, and I realized I could have still been a part of it. But then I also realized I was so caught up in managing, and I knew that I liked it. And I had an inkling Horace would ask me to manage the Giants.

We finished sixth in both '56 [67-87] and '57 [69-85]. After '56 Chub said, "Do me a favor and not finish sixth again in '57." I said I'd do my best but we finished sixth anyway. We still had some quality players but little by little the faces were changing, and I was hearing about what was happening in the minor leagues, with names like Cepeda, Kirkland, Wagner, Davenport, Bressoud and the Alous. I didn't know if they were satisfied with what I had tried to accomplish as manager in New York, or if I would be renewed. And I didn't know it until they decided to move to San Francisco, and Horace asked me if I'd like to manage a couple of more years.

AFTER 51 YEARS IN THE GAME I finally got a World Series title in '89 with the Oakland A's. They hired me as an adviser in 1982 and I've been with them ever since. Winning the Series was a thrill that ranked on top of all my others. Oh, sure. To be part of a World Series championship—that doesn't happen very often. It happened a lot if you were a Yankee 35 years ago. But to see this Oakland A's team come from zero and become the best team in baseball for maybe four or five years, and then culminate it with a World Series ring, that's pretty tough to beat.

Bill Rigney, now a front office executive with the Oakland Athletics. (Oakland A's)

This was a team you had to like because you had to like the manager, Tony LaRussa, the way he handled everything and everybody. The *Bash Brothers* [Canseco and McGwire] and everything else was such a positive. Even though we had some disappointments when the Dodgers beat us [in '88] and Cincinnati beat us [in '90], we were there every year, with a chance to be the World Champions. That's all you can ask for.

I still love this game as much as ever, as much as when I played semi-pro ball at Oaks park in Emeryville, as much as when I played my first big league game, at the Polo Grounds. *Of course.* I never get tired of talking about it, and I certainly never get tired of watching it or reading about it.

Oakland, California

FELIPE ALOU

The National League Manager of the Year with the Montreal Expos in 1994, Felipe Alou began his major league career 36 years earlier as one of several talented rookies for the 1958 Giants, hitting .253 in 182 at-bats, after tearing up the Pacific Coast League in Phoenix over

the first half of the season, hitting .319 with 13 home runs and 42 RBIs, in 216 at-bats.

Felipe's best year with San Francisco came in its National League championship season of 1962 when he hit .316 with 25 home runs and 98 RBIs, and scored the winning run in the ninth inning of the third and final playoff game against the Dodgers.

Felipe became part of major league history in '63 when he joined Matty and Jesus as the first trio of brothers ever to start a game together in the out-field for the same team. But Felipe was traded after that season to the Braves, for whom he enjoyed his finest season, in '66, hitting .327 with 31 home runs, 74 RBIs, 122 runs and 218 hits.

A three-time All-Star, the right-handed-hitting Alou retired after 17 seasons as one of only 31 big leaguers with 2000-plus hits and 200-plus homers, with a lifetime average of .286. He later became the first native of the Dominican Republic to manage in the major league.

Felipe is married, with four children and two grandchildren. He spends his off-sea-sons both in the Dominican Republic, and in Boynton Beach, Florida.

I GREW UP IN HAINA, a sub-urb of the capital city of Santo Domingo. Now it's just another one of the many neighborhoods of Santo Domingo, with stoplights and big av-enues. Haina is also one of the big-gest ports—maybe *the* biggest port—in the Caribbean. When I was grow-ing up, there was not a port there. It was a lot of fun in those days. We had a lot of trees, a lot of fish and a lot of beautiful blue and green wa-ters in the ocean, with no pollution whatsoever. Now we have pollution. It's changed so much. Now we don't see the trees we used to have. I can see maybe a dozen trees I remem-ber from when I was a kid. That's about all that's left.

The quality of life has changed because you can find things now in Haina that can kill you, that we didn't have during our childhood. Red meat, for example. In fact, we were told that we weren't eating *enough* red meat. We were eating chicken and a lot of fish, and veg-

etables and a lot of fruits. I can see now why we were so healthy, because we didn't eat all that red meat [laughs]. We had red meat maybe once or twice a month at the most. But the good chicken, the good birds—my father would go hunting sometimes for ducks, and a bird they called *guinea*. They still have guinea but you have to go way up into the central mountains to find them. They used to almost come right to your backyard. And you didn't hear all the loud music you hear now.

I still live in the same area where I grew up. I built a home there in 1974. But it's changed so much. There are a lot of cars, a lot of pollution, a lot of noise—the normal life of a developing country—and a lot of crime. It used to be a safe place, under General Trujillo's dictatorship. But nobody wanted to live under a dictatorship. Ev-erybody wants to be free. The problem is, free-dom from what? We freed ourselves from the dic-tator. The dictator was killed. And then we were

Felipe Alou (SF Giants)

free to do more sin than we were allowed under the dictatorship. I'm not defending the dictator, because he was wicked and he had to go, but after that the rest of hell broke loose on our island, until this day. Until this day.

I know that ever since I was born I've known the dictator for 32 years, and the man who's the president now for 30 more. There's always been something terribly wrong with our government.

I WENT TO HIGH SCHOOL in Santo Domingo and joined the Dominican track team, because I could run fast and had a strong arm. I also played a little baseball. Of course, when I went to college I became a full-time baseball player. But before that I went to Mexico for the Pan American Games, in track and baseball. And the only reason I played ball was because we had a shot at winning a gold medal.

When I entered the university the coach I played ball for was Horacio Martinez, who later became a scout for the Giants. He didn't have to go too far to pick his first player. He said, "Well, you're gonna be the man," and went to talk to my parents. He passed away in 1993, a tremendous man. And I have to attribute part of my success in life in general to him, and to the kind of man he was.

It was a big day when I signed with the Giants but it was not the kind of day like it is today. A guy gets a big bonus now, and all sorts of celebration. When I signed there was a little division in our home because my mother wasn't all for it. My father really wasn't all for it either but it was a situation that we needed somebody to start contributing some earnings to the house, and it was like, hey, I *had* to go. I had to leave my brothers and parents and go into an adventure in the United States. That's the way it was. For $200. That's not a very good way to break in but I knew one thing, and so did my dad—that a man was leaving. It was not a boy or a kid. A *man* was leaving the house, and I was going to prevail. There was no question about that, in spite of some of the hardships I faced.

In fact, Matty Alou left he was 17 and he was another *man* who left. And Jay Alou was only 15 and he was a 15-year-old *man* who left. So we left to stay in the game and we are *still* in the game, all three of us. But in that home where we grew up we had all the necessary ingredients to develop men. My dad didn't know he was develop-

ing a player, or three players, but he knew that he was developing three men. In fact, it was four men because my older brother's an architect. And my two sisters are also professionals.

The way baseball is now, there are a lot of ballplayers being developed in homes, but not men. What we're doing now, especially in the Latin countries, is developing players, and not men. But that's the trend now, in life in general. People are preparing to make as much money as possible and neglecting some of the other very important things. And this game has no time to build character. This game is only about baseball. If a guy like Dwight Gooden or Darryl Strawberry has a drug problem he's sent to rehab, but only after the problem is evident. But there is no development of character. In fact, you bring your own character from home.

We did, the three Alous. And we've kept it to this day. This game teaches people how to throw a slider, a fastball, how to pitch and how to swing—I know, I was in development for 20 years. But we don't have time to have seminars on how to develop men. We have baserunning instructors, hitting and pitching coaches. This game is rude. Its purpose is to make millions and to win pennants.

But I'm proud to have worked with kids in the minors who have been successful in the majors. Some of those kids like Henry Rodriguez, Ramon Martinez, Raul Mondesi and Rafael Bournigal all looked up to me, like a father. There were times when those kids would hit two home runs against me, and the next day I would go and talk with them about various things and congratulate them on their development. The respect they have for me is great. And I remember what it was like to play in the minors, although it's much better today, especially for minorities. Much better.

I started my professional career at Lake Charles, Louisiana, in 1956. But I was sent to Cocoa in the Florida State League after only nine at-bats because of a law in Louisiana that said Negroes couldn't play on the same field with whites. Because of my Spanish roots, in not being used to the racial situation in the States, not being part of it until I got here, and not being afraid of it, I really never did bend to it. It's not that I was fighting anything, but I never did bend to it.

But I was so sad at Lake Charles because I didn't know any English, and it was my first city in the U.S. Maybe God put me there to understand right away what His call was and what to be prepared for. And I got prepared. But it didn't change my way of life. I had to go to a certain part of town, like behind the railroad tracks. It was something I had to learn, that in the U.S., the black area was on the other side of the railroad tracks. And I had to go to the black barber.

But I went fishing right away in Florida. I always loved fishing and diving. I went fishing where everybody else went fishing, and I didn't see many blacks. Sometimes I was the only one there at the pier in Cocoa.

I actually thought about quitting, riding the bus to Cocoa from Louisiana. I had a deep feeling that I could probably continue on to Miami because I had enough money to go home. I had been paid my first paycheck already. But any time that thought came into my mind I thought about this scout who signed me. I didn't want to fail him. I was a college student. I knew I was his first choice, his first player, and I didn't want him to get off to such a bad start. I wanted to make sure his first player was going to be a man. And I got off that bus in Cocoa with no place to go. I didn't know anybody, and there was nobody waiting for me.

I had to wait until daybreak to start making a move, with a suitcase in my hand, hoping to run into somebody, or maybe the ballpark itself, to find my way. That was a really good situation for anybody to just quit and go home. But Florida turned out to be a much better situation than Louisiana [a league-leading .380, 21HR, 99RBI].

When I got to Minneapolis in 1957 I couldn't believe how cold the weather was. Both Florida and Louisiana were very warm, like home. This was the first time in my life that I had to wear a sweater and I didn't even have a good one. I was hitting just over .200 when I was sent out. They could have kept me there and waited for warmer weather. I knew I could hold my own but they sent me to Springfield, where I finished second in the Eastern League in hitting [.306, 12HR, 71RBI,

Felipe Alou playing left field before another full house at Seals Stadium, 1958, with Potrero Hill in background. (Dick Dobbins)

359AB], a very tough league at that time. I think only two or three guys hit .300 that year and I was one of them. It was still too cold and I had to get used to that. But it was a lot better than in the North, in Minneapolis.

The Giants brought me to spring training with them in 1958, in Phoenix. Usually they wouldn't bring a guy to the big league camp who played only class-D and class-A ball, and that's what I did. Cocoa was class-D and Springfield was class-A. But I hit .380 in one of the toughest class-D leagues and came in second in another tough class-A league, so they wanted to know who I was. More than half the people with the Giants didn't know me so they brought me to spring training, and I did very well. I filled in for Willie Mays, got a few hits and they told me I was being sent out for more seasoning.

I went to triple-A and tore that league apart. I had 42 RBIs in less than two months, with 13 homers, a .319 average and a 35-game hitting streak. And I was going to do some serious damage if they kept me there. So they brought me up. The problem is that when they brought me up I didn't play a lot. See, that was the problem. I didn't play very much for the next three years. But because I played winter ball after every summer, I was getting readier for the big leagues.

The day I joined the Giants in San Francisco was one of the most important days of my life. That was the day my new teammate Al Worthington introduced me to Jesus Christ. And I don't believe in accidents. I believe that was a man who was there waiting for me. Yes, he was a tremendous man of God, a tremendous teammate and a tremendous friend and example to other players. Later on I got to know another tremendous man of God who played for the Giants, Lindy McDaniel. I had heard about his Christian life when he was with the Cardinals, and then we were teammates with the Yankees. He baptized me into the new faith. That was a tremendous experience that polished me into the Christian way of life. But 1958 marked the beginning, and since then I have continued to grow to believe more, to stand more and to be more outspoken, even now at the major league level.

Of course, all of this did not bring me closer to my family back home. It has been like that for 2,000 years. The gospel is not here to bring families together. It is the other way around. But yes, we are close. It's a close family. And when I say it doesn't bring people close I'm talking about the spiritual part of it. There's a tremendous disparity in the spirituality because of all the denominational situations, and all of the names of all the beliefs. That separates people spiritually and sometimes physically. But our family, physically, is very tight. We call each other, we see each other—the three brothers—almost daily in the off-season. My mother is a very strong Catholic. My father was always in the middle of the line, a non-practicing Catholic, and to me that was always a shame. I hate for him or for anyone to go down without having the hope that I have now.

I WAS FORTUNATE to have played with people like Mays, McCovey, Cepeda and Marichal in San Francisco. And after I was traded to the Braves, just think about the people I played with in Atlanta—Aaron, Mathews, Torre, Carty, Spahn, Burdette—that was *incredible*. You name the Hall of Fame people that I had the luck to play with,

just on those two teams. That is enough of an experience to carry you the rest of your life. And I've said many times that these people were not only Hall of Famers in uniform, they were Hall of Famers *off* the field. All of those guys are still serving the game in some capacity, with a lot of pride in their communities. I'm very thankful that I grew up in professional baseball with all of those guys.

Even the Phoenix club I played with in '58 was loaded with guys like that—McCovey at first, Leon Wagner in left, Tom Haller catching, Andre Rodgers at short. We had a guy named Jack Dittmer at second base who was a tremendous triple-A player, Jose Valdivielso [also] at short and we had Ernie Broglio pitching. We had some good people.

At that time the Giants were a very special team because of their understanding of, and acceptance of, Latin ballplayers. We had six Latin players on the Giants in '58. But unfortunately, it didn't last very long. For some reason, like many good things that don't last, the Giants lost the grip that they had. More organizations started to sign Latin players, and the Giants lost the power in the Caribbean they once had. I believe the Giants got very careless along those lines.

They also got careless with their ballpark. Seals Stadium was like a Pacific Coast League ballpark. In fact it *was*, the year before we moved west. Of course, I wasn't here for Opening Day—I didn't make the club. I only got here after a month and a half in Phoenix. So to me it was another triple-A field but I liked it. It was fun, because it wasn't cold, and it wasn't that windy. And the fans were right there. It was very intimate and it was downtown. It was great. We all felt the Giants should have stayed there. They could have made Seals bigger and we could have stayed.

I am a fisherman, you know, and after I got to San Francisco I got in touch with people and wound up fishing with a lot of Japanese guys, and other Asians, right in the area where Candlestick Park is now. When I was told that this was going to be where we were going to play baseball, I couldn't believe it because it was almost impossible to fish there. There were days after a ballgame at Seals when I would go fish and the wind wasn't blowing at all. But in the next five minutes you got the hell out of there and went back home because the wind would be so strong, the temperature so cold and the water so choppy.

I couldn't believe the difference between those two places, Seals and Candlestick.

I remember my first major league game, against Brooks Lawrence of Cincinnati. I hit a line drive base hit off a slider. First pitch. I remember my second hit, against the same pitcher. I remember my first home run, against a guy named Dave Hillman of the Cubs. Those are big, big memories.

Orlando [Cepeda] was my closest friend on the team that year. We knew each other from spring training and we had played against each other in the Dominican, when he was 16 and I was 18. He came with a Puerto Rican club to play a couple of games and I could see a good hitter right away when I saw Orlando.

I don't really stay in touch with all those guys anymore, from my days with the Giants and Braves. I imagine that's the way it is with the majority of Latin players because we go home after each season. And I'd have to say one reason you don't see more Latins managing or coaching is because we all go home after we finish playing.

I used to see Hank Aaron a lot because the Braves and Expos both trained in West Palm Beach, at the same complex [the Braves now train in Orlando]. But that's about it. When I come to San Francisco, Cepeda always comes over to say hello, and so does Willie Mays. I see Willie McCovey every once in a while, too.

My first year with the Giants I lived in Daly City with Ruben Gomez and Orlando. In '59 I got married and moved to an apartment in North Beach, in San Francisco. When we'd come back home late from an Eastern road trip, or even

from LA, the neighborhood was packed with people. It was fun to see. Like, at three o'clock in the morning everyone was on Columbus Street, and around there. I really enjoyed living there, very much, except that when I came back in '60 there was nothing available in the area so we had to move to Third Street, not far from Candlestick.

In '59 they tried to send me back to triple-A but I refused to go. I always believe in respecting the other person. I don't care what their race is,

Felipe Alou, after hitting a two-run home run to help Mike McCormick beat Chicago Cubs 5-4, September 9, 1962, as the Giants battled the Dodgers for the National League pennant. (SF Giants)

their language, their accent, their color, or their nationality. My wife, the mother of Moises Alou, who played for me in Montreal, was pregnant with our first baby, the boy who died in a swimming pool accident. The day I was sent out I had permission to take her to a doctor. She was only 18, pregnant and didn't know any English. Nowadays, teams have ways to help players in situations like that, with hired people who speak Spanish. But during that time, when the blacks had to sit in one corner of the clubhouse, and the Latins were told not to speak Spanish or be fined, the teams didn't have help for us in situations like that as they do now.

So I asked for permission to go with her to the doctor, and show up at 12 o'clock for a 1:05 game. It was granted. I had played the last two games and had gone two-for-four and two-for-four. I was playing regularly and I thought I was doing well. But when I arrived at 12:30 as expected I didn't have a locker. My locker had Jose Pagan's name on it, and I saw Andy Rodgers out of uniform. I asked what happened, and the clubhouse guy came and told me the manager [Bill Rigney] wanted to see me in his office. That's when I realized something was wrong. I went to the manager's office, and the manager said he had decided to send me to Phoenix with Andre Rodgers, and that Pagan and McCovey had been brought up. He said they'd bring me back at the end of the triple-A season. And right away I said, "No." I didn't even think about it. I thought *no* was the right word. And I explained to him the best way I could that my wife was pregnant and that I had to go with her to the doctor. "And you're gonna tell me that I'm gonna go to Phoenix? To 140 degree weather with my wife? And then come back here?" I said, "Listen, I'm going home. If you want me in Phoenix, I'll be very glad to go there in 1960, from day one." He said I'd have to tell Chub Feeney [general manager] the same thing. I said, "Fine."

I told Chub I was going to go home and then I went to the apartment, and my wife was so surprised to see me. I said, "We're going home," and she was very happy about it. We paid the landlord, picked up our things and we were ready to go on American Airlines, at 10:40 p.m. to New York, and then to Santo Domingo.

The clubhouse guy came over, saw that we were packed and ready to go, went back to Seals, told them, then came back and said, "Hey, you're staying with us." I didn't even have a telephone in my apartment. They had to commute back and forth between Seals and my apartment. It turned out they made Hank Sauer a coach. I remember Hank saying, "Hey, you retired me, because you didn't want to go to triple-A." He became a hitting coach, I returned our plane tickets and the landlady gave us back our apartment. But I knew I was done with Rigney. I never played the rest of the season. Then, I had a really good spring in 1960 and made the club, but I wasn't used until Rigney got fired during the All-Star break. The next year Alvin Dark took over.

At the end of that season, though, in 1960, the Giants went to Japan to play a series of games. It is a pleasant memory. I got to visit a lot of churches and talk to the Japanese people who came to see me and hear me. The thing about the major league is that people really come to see you. A lot of times what you say is not important to them, but people just want to see you. They want to say, "Hey, I saw Orlando Cepeda," or "I saw Felipe Alou." They want to have their picture taken with you but don't really want to hear what you have to say. People want to have that picture taken so they can show it around. So we used that opportunity in Japan to talk to people about Christianity and about Jesus Christ, and about baseball also. It was a tremendous experience to play against the Japanese teams and get to know Japan. Even in 1960 they were so far ahead of everybody in technology.

I didn't have any idea then that [Sadaharu] Oh would turn out to be such a great home run hitter. But you had to believe what the people told us. All the Japanese players, coaches and managers said this guy was a phenom. Of course, when he played against us he was facing Jack Sanford and Juan Marichal. And he hit a couple of home runs, but you could see this kid, even at 19, was special. We kept track of him over the years because he kept hitting more and more homers. And guys would say, "Hey, I wish I had *my* picture taken with him." This goes back to what I just said. People want to have their picture taken with you so they can say, "Hey look, this is Oh with me." And I did. I had my picture taken with him. You could see that he was a tremendous athlete, really focused and dedicated. And a fine man.

The biggest year of my baseball life was 1962, winning the pennant and playing the Yankees in the World Series. It was not only that, but *everything* that happened that year. It was my first .300 year in the *big* leagues, my first big year [.316, 25HR, 98RBI], my first pennant and one of the richest spiritual years of my life, with all the friends that God sent my way. It was like a miracle. But I've got to say the '62 season was one of the most revealing and educational seasons baseball-wise and life-wise as well, because I know as a team we had given up. We were ready to pack it in. The players were ready but not the manager, Alvin Dark. He surprised us in St. Louis with a meeting, saying we had a shot at winning the pennant. We flew from Chicago to St. Louis, having just been defeated. But in St. Louis the manager said we were going to have a workout in the morning, that we were better than we were showing, that we had time to catch the Dodgers. I didn't really believe it. I've got to be honest. And

I know Orlando, my best friend and roommate, didn't believe it either.

We worked out that morning and won that night. And worked out the next day, and won that night. We caught fire. On our last night in St. Louis, the Dodgers came in after a day game in Chicago. Both teams were staying at the Chase Hotel. And some of the Dodger players said, "Hey, see you next year." They weren't being rude or playing jokes, but they had a big lead, maybe six or seven games with just a dozen left. We had some good friends on that team. There was some animosity, yes, but there were some people like Ron Perranoski and Sandy Koufax whom we considered to be good guys.

Of course, we caught the Dodgers the final day of the season and then beat them in a play-off. So I always use that, that you've got to let the players know, as a manager, that you think you can win it, even under the most adverse circumstances. If you have a shot you've got to go for it. You see, I was one of the good players on that team. I hit .300, drove in 98 runs and played good defense. And I was ready to pack it in until the manager told us we were good enough to win.

In that final playoff game in LA, trailing 4-2 after eight innings, I went into the clubhouse and it was one of the few times in my life that I asked God to give us a win. Even now I don't do that but I did it then. I went in and out in one minute. I said I couldn't believe we'd come that far to get beat, then I went back out. And as soon as Matty Alou got on base leading off I knew we'd win. You could feel there was something there that was on our side, whatever you want to call it. They [the Dodgers] couldn't do anything right that inning. They couldn't throw a strike. Ed Roebuck, the best fielding pitcher in baseball, dropped a soft line drive hit at him by Willie Mays, then dropped it again.

But I felt sorry for the Dodgers when that game was over. They came so far, only to lose. That is a bad taste, to go such a long way just to get beat. It's not a good taste. You don't want your worst enemy to suffer through that. Of course, it happened to us in the World Series, partly because I failed in the ninth inning of the seventh game. Matty led off with a bunt single, we were down, 1-0, and I struck out, after being asked to bunt. I was asked to bunt Matty over. I was never asked to bunt before. We were not a bunting team. I hit 25 home runs, 30-some doubles. I was a power hitter that year and was used as a power

hitter. But I was asked to bunt, and I bunted poorly and the ball went foul. Then, with the infield charging for the bunt, I swung at a bad pitch and fouled it off for strike two. Then I struck out. Ralph Terry made a good pitch inside and I swung right through it. It wasn't the manager's fault. I should have bunted fair because I had a good runner, my brother, on first. But I hadn't been practicing bunting.

What I do now is have my players practice a lot of bunting. *All* of them. Our club last year led the league in sacrifice hits. This year we are right there again. We are capable of moving people over. We get people out on the field early at home to practice bunting because if we're in the World Series one day, and I'm going to have to ask a guy to bunt, I want to make sure the guy has been practicing it during the season.

That was the lowest point of my career. This is something I'm going to die with because I failed in that situation. And I know that even though I wasn't asked to bunt much before or made to practice before, I should have done it because I was a good athlete. That ball was fair for a while, until they let it roll foul.

After Chuck Hiller struck out, Matty got to third on Willie Mays' double to right. He had no chance to score. He would have been out without a slide. The field was very slow because of the rains. The only reason he couldn't score was because the ball didn't roll to the fence. Roger Maris was a tremendous defensive right fielder but Willie Mays was a *pull* hitter. Willie hit the ball, a line drive, close to the right field line. So Maris had to go a long way to pick up that ball. But when he picked it up it was almost dead. If that ball makes it to the fence Matty scores standing up and Willie goes to third base. But it was so wet that when the ball hit the grass it died right away. And with Willie McCovey coming up that was the right decision. Bobby Richardson was one of the best second basemen of that time, and the throw he made to the plate was perfect. But it was not a hard throw. It was like a warning, like, "Hey, what you doing? Stop."

I've been with Ralph Houk since then, when he was asked why he didn't walk McCovey intentionally with first base open to pitch to Orlando. He knew if the line drive by McCovey went through he would be crucified. But he was the kind of manager who didn't like to load the bases and put his pitcher in the position of having to throw strikes.

Cepeda was struggling then, but he drove in 140 runs that year. And he was starting to come out of it. He was starting to hit the ball to right-center, where he was so good. And I imagine Ralph decided to let Terry pitch to McCovey carefully. Then, if he walked him, he'd go after Cepeda. But Cepeda was the kind of man that, if you walked somebody to pitch to him, you were in trouble. They knew all of that stuff. And it worked for them, in the form of a rocket hit right at Richardson. I know Terry was trying to get the ball up and in to McCovey, but he made a bad pitch. He left it out over the plate and Willie ripped it. Right at Richardson.

I had another great experience in 1963, playing in the same outfield with my two brothers, Matty and Jay, although, at the time, it was the most normal thing to us, because we played together in the winter-league for years. All three of us dominated, with our club winning the pennant three or four years in a row. But with the more time that passes by, playing together in the same major league outfield becomes to us a bigger accomplishment.

We've never seen it in the majors since '63, and like I keep saying, I don't see how it's ever going to happen again. Because people don't want to have children anymore. People now want to have two, and that's it. They're planning families. Even some of the Latin countries are starting to plan families. They have been taught how *not* to have children. So now the trick is to come up with a family that has at least *three* children, but they have to be *boys*. Not only that, they have to be *baseball* players, have to be in the *big leagues* and have to be on the same *team*.

I was traded to the Braves after the '63 season but I knew I was going to go. I was one of the voices raising certain issues relating to Latin players and to my Christian stand. And there was a feeling in the Giants front office that I really was not that interested in baseball, and also a fear that I was going to get out of the game because of my commitment to my religion, which wasn't really true. The only truth there was that I was really committed to what I believed. But I wasn't ready to leave the game.

But I knew after meeting with Alvin at the end of the season that I would be traded. He met with every one of us in his office. It took him about 10 days to do it and I believe I was the only one called in more than once. I told him everything. And the first day of the winter meetings I

was gone to the Braves [with Ed Bailey, Billy Hoeft and Ernie Bowman, in exchange for Bob Shaw, Bob Hendley and Del Crandall]. I was surprised because there is always an element of surprise when a player gets traded for the first time. You know it's coming, you know the possibility is there, but you're still surprised when it happens.

I played two years in Milwaukee before the Braves moved to Atlanta. I always liked Milwaukee—great fans. There was something special about the fans in Milwaukee. I don't know what it was. I wound up going back to Milwaukee in my last season, in 1974, and it was the same warm relationship between players and fans.

But Atlanta was something incredible, too, when we moved. There was some fear with the black players about the reception we would have there but it was incredible. It was great, all positive. A lot of people came to see us. Every banquet was jam-packed, sold out. The street people recognized us after one or two weeks there—they knew all of us. What a situation it was. I was surprised there were no racial problems there back then. There were some instances, like Rico Carty getting clubbed by the cops, but that was not in '66. It was later than that. Atlanta had tremendous racial balance in those days. I don't know if it's still that way but the blacks and whites created a tremendous balance of respect there. They respected each other a lot and treated each other well. And we arrived there at the right time.

On July third of '66 Moises Alou was born, and I hit a home run that day. Maybe that's why my kid is hitting all these home runs now. But while I hit one that day, nobody remembers because our pitcher hit two [Tony Cloninger hit two *grand slams* in a 17-3 win over the Giants at Candlestick]. I remember hitting one in Milwaukee in 1961 the day Willie Mays hit four. Nobody remembers that I hit one that day, either [laughs].

I never presented myself as a home run hitter or as a guy who got 2,000 hits, or as a guy who played 17 years. But in this world of materialism it is good sometimes to do so because my message and my feelings are spiritual. I want to be respected not because of the 2,000 hits or the 200 home runs, or all the years, or the managing. I want people to love people, and recognize me and respect me because of my stance about life in general, and because of the spiritual part of me, and my hope for eternal life. I love to tell people that, but the baseball numbers help, because they attract people who then listen to me.

Felipe Alou, manager, Montréal Expos (Montréal Expos)

Once I got nine consecutive hits with the Giants, in 1962, one short of the league record. That brought a lot of people my way and I got a lot of mail. You know how people are. They're front runners. When I was hot, everything was Felipe, Felipe, Felipe. When Matty Alou was hot, everything was Matty, Matty, Matty. And then when Jay Alou was hot, I got a lot of mail addressed to Jay Alou, Milwaukee Braves. *Jay Alou? Milwaukee Braves?* That's the way people are. So you use the good days to attract people and let them know about some of your beliefs, because to me the most important part of my life is not just to have been a baseball player but that the people know there is more to me than that, regarding society and spiritual life.

The word that we Christians preach and tell people hasn't changed over the years but society has. So we have to adjust it to the times, in the way we present it to the people. The way it was when I was a player was the way it was in society. When people started to grow mustaches, beards and long hair in the street, baseball tried to keep players from doing that. But baseball didn't prevail. Ballplayers wore long hair and beards. And then came society's drug problem. Players come from society, not the other way

around. People saw Dwight Gooden fail a drug test. Hey, Dwight Gooden is a young man of this time so he's subject to the same evils as anybody. The world is more materialistic now and teams are making more money. Therefore players are going to make more money. Basketball players make more money. That's just the way it is now, and as a Christian that's the way I have to understand it and approach it. But I have no regrets. In a way I'm glad that I played during that time when we didn't make that much money.

When I came to San Francisco to interview for manager of the Giants in 1985, I was told [by general manager Tom Haller] that anybody could write a lineup and make a pitching change, that they wanted a manager who could relate to all their millionaire ballplayers. I said, "No." I looked at the interview as something just so that they could say they interviewed a minority. I came over all the way from the Dominican for the interview but at least I managed to have the opportunity to say no. Not everybody's capable of controlling a game, writing a lineup and getting the most out of his players. I believe that to relate to the players making the big money you're going to have to have a track record, a known track record, and you've got to prepare yourself so that you know yourself, so that you're good enough to relate [to], to command and to control the players. It's not just writing the lineup and taking the pitcher out. It's a lot different than that, in many ways. So right away I knew I was not going to be the Giants manager. And I thought I'd never be anybody's major league manager because of what they told me. If they were looking only for somebody who could deal with these millionaires then they'd never have a good manager, because the game is the same as it ever was, dating back 125 years. Everything else takes care of itself.

When I took the job with Montreal I was asked about the clubhouse. What about it, I asked. I said I very seldom go to the clubhouse. I go from the manager's office to the field to the manager's office to home, and very seldom go to the clubhouse. Well, they said, if you don't have a good clubhouse then you might have problems on the field. But that's not the way I look at it. I said you have to have a good situation on the field, *first*. To me the problems come from the field to the clubhouse, not the other way around. If you're not winning games, if you're losing games in the late innings, if you bring in the wrong reliever or send up the wrong pinch hitter, you don't have the right club. All of these are field problems that, sooner or later, will be reflected in the clubhouse. You've got to have a good situation between the lines and be able to control it. And then you'll always have a hell of a good clubhouse. That's what I told the people in Montreal. I knew the front office and the front office knew me because I had been managing 20 years for them in the minor leagues, and winning. But it's been a saying with the press that the first thing you have to do with a team is control the clubhouse, and then you're going to go on and win games. That's not the way it works. It works the other way around. There's no question about it. I don't have any doubts about that.

You win your games. You go all out with everything you have and everything you know, and win the game. And then you don't worry. You don't have to go the clubhouse. The clubhouse belongs to the players. It belongs to them. I can't control it. That's their domain.

I don't know how much longer I'll keep managing but it won't be very long. I've always signed one-year contracts. I've always felt comfortable and confident to work with a one-year term because I've always felt if I'm not doing the job, they should have the freedom to fire me. And if I don't like the way things are I should also have the freedom to get the hell out when the season is over. We've been very successful developing players, just the way I expected it to be, but I just don't want to make any long-term commitments. On the other hand, as a Christian, I don't have any doubts that this is where God wants me now and I go out every night trying to control the game, use my players to the best of their ability and win games.

I still enjoy the game. Oh, yeah. I feel like I'm playing. I feel like I'm one of the players. My will to go home is not because I don't enjoy the game. It is that I miss being home with my family, in the summertime, with all the fresh fruits, and the good fish and chicken.

I have two young children in Montreal, and another son, Felipe Jr., who's 19. We think he is going to be a hell of a player. He's got the same body as Moises. He can run, he plays center field, he can throw and he's a switch hitter [he plays for Cañada Junior College in Redwood City, south of San Francisco]. He could play, even at 15. And he's already been seen by some organizations. Some people already know who he is and where he is, including my brother Jay, who's working

for the Marlins. Matty's working for the Giants but Jay knows him better, because Jay and I are closer than Matty and I are. We fish a lot together and are next-door neighbors. So ever since Felipe Jr. started to throw in the yard there, Jay Alou has been saying, "Look at the *arm* he's got. Look at the *moves* of this kid. Look at the *feet* he's got." But I haven't even told you that he's also a hell of a good student. I should have told you that also.

Moises began playing for me in '92 — my son, who fished with me and played catch with me when he was a kid, and used to come to the winter games and be in the outfield just like my Felipe Jr. is doing now. So I know my son, the man. And now I know my son, the player. He is a hell of a player. He's independent. Independence comes to a player when he's a good player. If you are not a good player you're in the hands of the manager. He can take you out of the lineup, bench you, pinch hit for you. But if you are good there's nothing the manager can do with you. He cannot platoon you. We are very close. But once he's in uniform I have to disassociate myself from that.

THE DAYS WHEN I needed to speak out against Latin players being unfairly criticized are gone. They're not gone *totally* but I don't believe there's a need to speak out anymore. It wasn't always that way. I was once fined $10 repeatedly by Warren Giles [National League president] for speaking Spanish to Orlando Peña of the Reds, on the field before a game. But I never paid the fines. Never. I was always reluctant to pay fines I didn't feel were just. Like when I was fined for playing against a Cuban team that came to the Dominican to play us. I didn't pay that fine, either. To this day it's an unpaid fine. Orlando Peña was from Cuba and was probably just looking for someone to speak Spanish with. Alvin Dark once told us in spring training not to speak Spanish while in uniform. We had 11 Spanish-speaking players on the *team*. That order didn't go anywhere. When you have people like Orlando Cepeda, Juan Marichal, Felipe Alou, Jose Pagan and Manny Mota, trying to get a law like that through isn't going to go anywhere. The people running the Giants did not have a very good vision or knowledge of the people they were dealing with.

I was once stuck one night in Hamilton, Bermuda, on a flight from Santo Domingo to New York to Phoenix for spring training. They had a snowstorm in New York City and had to close the airport, so we had to land in Bermuda and spend the night there before proceeding the next day. At the airport in Bermuda I ran into a man from Spain who kept looking at me over and over, until he finally came over to talk to me. He asked if I was one of the Alou boys. I said, "Yeah." He said, "Felipe, right?" He said he was good friends with Horace Stoneham, and said, "Horace really likes you guys, you Latins, because you guys don't have to be given a big bonus. You guys don't make problems with salaries. And you guys are damn good ballplayers." And to this day I say that was a wake-up call to me, and I told the other Latins about this conversation.

This has *always* been nothing but business. Nothing but business. They don't do you any favors in this business. If you're good you have a job. If you're failing you get fired. And that goes with managing a team now. It's the same thing. If there is anything that still needs to be done, it needs to be done by baseball itself in terms of bringing more minorities into the front offices. All of us minority managers have been more or less successful, so there'd be no question.

I have three minority coaches on the Expos and a fourth I consider a minority—he's French-Canadian. So I have four. I don't know how the other black managers feel but I take tremendous pride every day when I come to the ballpark and go about my work. I want to be on top of everything. I want to be in control of the game. I want to show that I know the game, not only to my players but to anybody who's concerned, that I'm going to make the right move, even if it doesn't work, and that it's my win or loss. This is *my* game, because I *know* what I represent. Right now I'm the only Latin manager in the big leagues and one of, what, four minority managers. And the way I see the other black managers go about their work and how they present themselves, I believe they have the same feeling I have. The Tony Perez thing was a disgrace. I don't really know how all that came about, how he got the job [Cincinnati manager] and how he lost it. That was a setback. But I'm glad we're holding our own in Montreal so there will be no more saying that we lack the *necessities* to be in charge.

San Francisco, California

HANK SAUER

The National League Most Valuable Player with the Cubs in 1952, when he hit 37 home runs with 121 RBIs, Hank Sauer was a 41-year-old part-time outfielder by the time the Giants moved west in 1958, finally retiring in '59 after 15 big league seasons, 288 homers and a .266 average.

A native of Pittsburgh, Hank didn't reach the majors to stay until 1948, at the age of 31, when he hit 35 homers and drove in 97 runs for the Redlegs. He hit a career-high 41 homers with the Cubs in '54, and won National League Comeback Player of the Year honors in '57 with the Giants, with 26 homers, 76 RBIs and a .289 average. Sauer added a dozen homers for the Giants in '58.

Hank became the first player to twice hit three homers in a game off the same pitcher, against the Phillies' Curt Simmons. The right-handed-hitting Sauer also hit the first home run ever at the Los Angeles Coliseum, against the Dodgers, in '58.

After 57 years in baseball as a player, coach and scout, Hank retired in '93. He lives with his wife in Millbrae, California, and has three children and four grandchildren.

I HAD BEEN in San Francisco only once before, to play an exhibition game when I was with the Cubs, before the Giants moved west in 1958. But I was happy about the move because I was near the end of my career anyway—I was 41 years old—and because I had lived in Los Angeles during the off-season for the previous 25 years. And I had heard nothing but good things about San Francisco. So I was pretty happy about it. The change was going to be good. Even though I was born and raised in Pittsburgh, my brother coaxed me into moving to California a long time ago. He said I'd never go back if I came west and he was right. I never did move back and I've been here ever since.

I liked Seals Stadium as well. Actually, if they would have thought about it, and if the brewery had moved out a little sooner, I think they might have double-decked Seals and kept the Giants right there. I thought it was in a terrific part of San Francisco. It was a nice neighborhood to move into, with nice people. I lived at the

Hank Sauer (SF Giants)

I remember spring training in '58 started at the mineral baths [Operation Great Wash], outside Mesa, for eight to 10 days. We'd work out in the early morning, then go into the hot tubs and get massaged and we'd never get stiff or sore. I really enjoyed that, especially at my age [laughs]. It was mostly for the older players like me, Dusty Rhodes, Ray Jablonski and Bobby Thomson.

When Cepeda arrived in camp he pointed at me and asked, "Who's the gray-haired guy? Is that Mr. Stoneham?" [laughs] It was a kick in the pants with all the young players we had. They called me *Dad* and I guess I was old enough to be the father of some of them. But it was fun.

Bill Rigney's right when he says I didn't talk to him for two weeks after our first game at Seals Stadium against the Dodgers. I didn't say a word to him for two weeks. In fact I tore up several of his lineup cards throughout the summer because he kept me out [of the lineup]. Of course, I didn't think I was through, see, and they all knew I was hanging by a thread at 41. I loved playing for Rigney, actually. We played against one another for years. And then when I was a player and he was the manager, we went at it pretty good but we always stayed friends. And we always will be friends. He's one of the nicest guys in the world.

In fact, in the summer of '59 they wanted to send Felipe Alou back to the minors but I went up to Bill and said, "Make me a coach, and let him play. He's more valuable to this ball club now than I am." Well, it didn't take Rigney more than two minutes to run up to Stoneham, who OK'd it. So I stayed on as a coach the rest of the year, and Felipe Alou stayed in the big leagues from then on. Felipe is one of the nicest guys in the world and I'm so happy for him now because he deserves to be a big league manager, and a successful one. He's a very intelligent guy, and a strong guy, too. One time he was in the shower alongside Cepeda and Orlando kept hounding him. Alou said, "I'm gonna give you one more chance—you keep your mouth shut or I'm coming after you." Cepeda never said another word. You want to see a real body on a person, Felipe had it, and still does. And he's a great guy to boot.

Westin Hotel, about a mile away. I thought it was the best town to eat in in the world. *Paoli's* was great for crabs. There were tremendous restaurants everywhere.

Seals was a great place to play because there was such little space from the foul lines to the seats. It felt like the fans were right on top of us, and that's the way it should be. It's the same in Chicago, at Wrigley Field. It was tough to play in a ballpark like Atlanta [Fulton-County Stadium], especially after striking out, because it's about a 100-yard walk from home plate to the dugout. And it's tough to hit .300 in a ballpark like that because of all the foul territory—the fielders can run all day and catch those foul pop flies. Same with Candlestick, although they recently closed it up a little bit, but not enough. They should have rebuilt Seals Stadium and kept the Giants right there. The wind wasn't as bad as it is at Candlestick, either.

But when I found out Rigney substituted Jim King for me on Opening Day at Seals it was kind of strange. He told me I'd be playing left field that day, with Mays in center and Kirkland in right. And then when I got to the park he said to me, "Hank, I need to get some left-handers in that lineup." I said, "We've got enough left-handers. We don't need anymore left-handers. I can hit right-handers as well as I can hit left-handers. Better, in fact." But I really didn't talk to him at all after that for two weeks. He's right [laughs]. I tore up many a lineup card that season. One time Rigney said, "The next guy I catch tearing up a lineup card gets fined $200." He knew who it was, too [laughs].

Fortunately, I got to start Opening Day in LA, at the Coliseum. I hit two home runs off Podres that day. That ballpark was what I called *Disneyland*. Jeez, if you hit the ball in the air to left it was a home run. And yet, some balls that would have been home runs in any other park hit the top of that screen that was sixty feet high, and came back. But I always hit fly balls. And it was only 250 feet to left. In fact, the Dodgers tried to make a deal for me that year so I could play every day in that ballpark. But Stoneham wouldn't let me go because he had already promised me a job when the season was over. Then, in '59, he said to me, "You'd better quit pretty soon or we're going to trade you away from here anyway." So I had no choice [laughs].

But even before I retired as a player I was already doing some coaching, unoffically. Some of the young guys needed a pat on the back. When Rigney would cuss out one of them it was my job to go over, pat him on the back and say, "Hey, he's giving you the business, so don't worry about it. He hasn't given up on you. Just keep playing hard and you'll be OK." Same with Herman Franks [coach]. He'd say, "Hank, when I give someone hell I want you to go over there afterward and clean it up for me."

I got off to a great start in '58. I was hitting .310 and tied for the league lead in homers with Cepeda in late May. It felt good but as the season rolled on, age caught up with me and I went down a bit. Then, in '59, I knew I was through when I was facing a left-hander in Cincinnati. I saw the pitch coming in and I said, "That ball's gone." That's how quick I was *thinking*. But I hit it off my fists and then I said, "No, *I'm* gone [laughs]." My last big league at-bat came in Philadelphia, with two guys on. I just barely missed

hitting it into the left field bleachers. The guy caught it to end the game. I really hit it good but said, "That's it, I *know* I'm through now."

My closest friend on that Giants club was probably Mays. And Davenport, too. I call him my son now. When they make a nicer guy than Davenport I want to know who he is. Jim really is like a son to me. If he or any of the young kids on the club had a bad day, I'd say, "C'mon, let's go have a beer or go have something to eat." And they'd enjoy that. They'd think, here's a guy who's played this game for 15 years and he's taking us out to lunch.

We had a good ball club in '59, especially. I think we'd have won the pennant if Chicago hadn't cheated on us. They had guys in that scoreboard at Wrigley stealing our signs. I'm the one who spotted it. They put two feet up for a curveball, one for a fastball and none for a change. Rigney asked me to get dressed and go up into the scoreboard to stop it. I tried but the door was locked. They wouldn't let me in. They were hitting Sam Jones like he was going out of style. They wore him out. Nobody ever hit him that good unless they knew what was coming. We led the Dodgers by two games with eight left but collapsed during that final road trip in Chicago and St. Louis.

We had some great characters on the Giants those first two years in San Francisco. Gomez was a dandy. He'd start the fights but he was never around to finish them [laughs]. Like in Milwaukee, when Adcock chased him around the outfield and he ran into the dugout and came out with an icepick. Then Adcock took off. Gomez was a good pitcher and a nice guy, but he had that Latin blood and it roused up in a hurry.

I thought Kirkland was going to be a tremendous player but he didn't last that long. After we traded him he went down the tubes. Why, I don't know. [*author's note: In fact, Kirkland hit 27 homers and had 95 RBIs with Cleveland in '61, his first year away from the Giants, and his best of nine big league seasons.*] Some guys, when they come up, can't stand that pressure. That last step from triple-A to the big leagues is like it used to be from class-D all the way to triple-A. That's how big it is. I've known quite a few guys who could hit 40 or 50 home runs in the minor leagues, and then when they get to the big leagues they just can't cut the mustard. Steve Bilko was one of them, Howie Moss was another. They had tremendous minor league stats but when they got to the big leagues they just couldn't do it. Our short-stop, Andre Rodgers, was another great hitter in triple-A but didn't do nearly as well in the big leagues as he should have.

Cepeda was a wonderful player, though, right from the start. And a lot of people never knew this, but he could run. He could fly. We had a race in Arizona between Cepeda and Bobby Thomson. Cepeda told me, "I can outrun him." I didn't believe it. Nobody else did, either. We all bet on Thomson. Cepeda beat Thomson the first time, and even *Thomson* couldn't believe it. So they ran a second time and Cepeda beat him again. Thomson said, "I *know* I'm going downhill now, it's time for me to retire." Cepeda could really fly then but now he's lucky he can walk. He had great speed before his knees started to go.

But I could never understand why he didn't want to play left field so McCovey could play first base. We all talked to Cepeda about it—he not only could run, he had a pretty good arm. He could've done fine in left. But he was just hard-headed enough. He said, "I will not go out there and play left. Put McCovey out there." Well, McCovey couldn't play left field nearly as well. It was frustrating for Rigney and for *all* of us. We eventually had to trade him.

Once I retired I became the Giants' batting coach, for about 20 years. I'd coach the big league club when it was home. And when they went on the road I'd go through our minor league system, coaching there. I really enjoyed it. That was the job I always wanted and I loved it. McCovey said I was the best batting instructor who ever lived. I knew Mac so well I could usually spot what he was doing wrong immediately. Same with Cepeda and Mays. I couldn't teach these guys to hit but I could usually spot whatever they were doing wrong if they were in a slump. Same with Daven-port, although he kept saying, "Hell, why didn't you make *me* a .300 hitter like Mays, McCovey and Cepeda?" And I'd say, "You didn't listen, that's why." [laughs]

After coaching I went into cross-checking [reviewing scouting reports nationwide] for about 10 years, then major league scouting, for trades. Eventually I just scouted American League players in Oakland and National Leaguers here in San Francisco. The guys I'd really want the Giants to trade for they couldn't get anyway. So I'd check out the borderliners, the guys who might im-prove, as an extra pitcher, pinch hitter or backup infielder. I'd write them up and let the front of-fice make the eventual decisions. That job ended after the '93 season. Then I was out of baseball for the first time in 57 years. The Giants said, "Well Hank, we need the money." I said, "The money I'm making isn't even as much as the players' meal money."

Unfortunately, it wasn't handled properly. The least the Giants could have done is handle it properly. They had Bob Hartsfield [scouting di-rector] tell me by phone that they weren't going to renew my contract. And I said, "You mean to tell me that *you're* the one telling me I'm done with the organization, when I was your boss for 20 years? Why couldn't Bob Quinn [general man-ager] have done this?" So I hung up on him, called Quinn and said, "This is the worst treat-ment I've received in 50-plus years in baseball. The least you could have done is tell me yourself, but to let a shoeshine boy like Hartsfield fire me .... It would have taken only 15 minutes to call me and tell me you were not going to renew my contract. The least you could have done was that. If this is how I have to get out of baseball, then forget it." And I wasn't through. I then told Quinn, "Your father was a tremendous person, and your grandfather a better one yet. And now it's come all the way down to *you*." And that's the way it ended [laughs].

But I did tell Hartsfield, "What a shame to be fired by a shoeshine boy." [laughs]

SINCE I WAS EIGHT YEARS OLD I always knew I was going to play in the big leagues. As a boy growing up in Pittsburgh anytime my mother wanted to find me she knew exactly where to look—out in the field, playing ball. If I had to go out there by myself and throw the ball up against the backstop I'd do it. I'd sneak over to Forbes Field and just watch the big league players come out of the locker room gate, to go to their cars. And I said to myself, "I'm going to be walking out that gate one of these days, too." But I never went to see a game because I couldn't afford it. We were lucky if we were eating good. But my par-ents didn't want my brother and me playing ball at all. They said, "We didn't raise you kids to play, we raised you to make a few bucks for the house." Well, we did that, too, but I still snuck around and played my baseball.

I was playing semi-pro ball in Pittsburgh one day in 1937 when a Yankee scout offered me a contract to play in the pros. I said, "Sure," but went home and asked my mother whether she wanted me to play baseball or stay at home and keep my job. She said, "This is a decision you have to make." I said, "I'm going to go play baseball." And that's when it started, in class-D, in Butler, Pennsylvania, in 1937.

I led the Penn State League in hitting in '38, then played class-C in Akron, Ohio, in '39, hitting over .300 there. Then Cincinnati drafted me when the Yankees made a mistake by leaving me unprotected. Four or five guys were fired for letting me get away. They didn't realize the six weeks I played in '37 counted for a half year. After two and a half years you were eligible to be drafted. Cincinnati sent me to Birmingham, in the Southern League. That was A-ball.

I made my big league debut in Cincinnati late in the '41 season. I homered in my first big league game, at Crosley Field. Butterflies? You must be kidding. When I swung at the first pitch it felt like I

Hank Sauer hit 198 home runs as a Chicago Cub from 1949 through '55, and won National League MVP honors in '52. (Steve Bitker)

was on a washboard. I was so scared, my first two at-bats. Then I calmed down, hit a home run later and we won 1-0, with Paul Derringer pitching for us.

But I was back in the minors, at Syracuse [triple-A] most of '42 and '43, before going into the military in '44. I enlisted because I knew I'd be drafted if I didn't. They told me to go in the Coast Guard, then I wouldn't have to worry about going overseas. Well, that didn't last long. I was on an ammunition ship, out in the Pacific. We put ammunition on the battleships, then we'd run like hell [laughs]. Because, if they ever hit us, we're gone.

I came back to Cincinnati in September of '45 and hit nearly .300 that final month, with five home runs and a bunch of RBIs. And I thought

that would keep me with the Reds the next year but I never had a chance. Three weeks into spring training in '46 I was back in Syracuse. Finally, I put up some numbers there in '47 [.336, 50HR, 141RBI, 130R] that got me in the big leagues for good.

I played against Jackie Robinson in '47 when he was with Montreal. We all knew he'd be a great ballplayer. Same with Campanella. There were so many tremendous black players then. Josh Gibson was another great one. I played against him when I was in the military and he was with the Homestead Grays. You talk about a guy who could hit a ball—he could hit it a *ton*. And he was a great catcher, too. Then there was Satchel Paige and Ernie Banks. I was fortunate enough to have played with Ernie in Chicago.

There was no doubt in my mind he'd become one of the all-time greats. He was so quick with the bat, with such great wrist-action. And he's one of the all-time great guys who ever played the game. He just loved baseball. Even if it was like ice outside he'd come into the clubhouse and say, "It's a *great* day for two." Even now, if I see him on the golf course, he'll say, "Hey Hank, this would be a great day for two, wouldn't it?"

I played every day in left field for Cincinnati in '48 and had a pretty good year. I broke the club record for home runs with 35, but the next year our manager Bucky Walters wanted me to hit the ball to right field. I said, "I thought you guys wanted a power hitter. Now you've got a power hitter and you're trying to make a punch-and-judy hitter out of me." Well, I got off to a terrible start. I was hitting .334 but had only two home runs in June, and was traded to Chicago. I finished that season with 31 homers.

I loved Wrigley Field but people don't realize how tough it was to see the ball coming out of the pitcher's hand there in those days. Because for my first five years in Chicago they had fans with white shirts sitting in the center field bleachers, before they put that green canvas backdrop in. It wasn't easy.

I made the All-Star team in 1950 but the year that stood out was '52, when I not only made the All-Star team but won the MVP award as well [.270, 37HR, 121RBI]. It was a two-way battle between me and Robin Roberts for the MVP that year and I beat him two or three times with home runs. Even though I hit more homers in '54 [41], my best year was '52. I hit so many homers in '54, they cut my salary. They sent me a contract calling for a $1,500 cut in pay, despite over 100 RBIs. I said, "Are you sure you sent this to the right guy?" They said, "Yeah, we could've ended up in fifth place without your 41 home runs." I said, "Yeah, but you wouldn't have drawn a million people without me."

I think Chicago has the best fans in the game. They're great to the players. They very rarely boo the player unless he loafs. In '54 they had a special day for me at Wrigley. I got five bushel baskets full of tobacco. That lasted me and the entire club about five years. I was a real chewer but only when I put the uniform on. As soon as I did that the tastebuds said, "Let's go." Every day I chewed. I'd say at least 75 percent of the players in those days chewed, many to keep from drinking a lot of water and getting water-

Hank Sauer (Steve Bitker)

logged. The fans threw so much tobacco to me in left field that I'd stuff it in the ivy, and then I'd tell our clubhouse man Yosh Kawana to go out and bring it in for all of us, including Yosh, who chewed as much as I did. My nickname was "The Mayor of Wrigley Field." Great fans.

I got to room with Stan Musial when I was traded to St. Louis before the '56 season. He was one of the nicest guys I've ever met. If he dies I want to go where he goes because he was such a tremendous person, and still is. You get to know a fellow when you room with him and he was one of the nicest guys in the world. He was also the second-best hitter I ever saw, behind Ted Williams. I never saw Williams hit the ball off the fists or off the end of the bat. Only on the sweet spot. And I played against him every spring.

Best pitcher I ever saw was Ewell Blackwell, my teammate in Cincinnati. Everybody hated to face him. Drysdale was the toughest I ever faced because he'd knock you down if you hit one ball halfway decent, although Koufax had the best stuff I ever had to face, once he mastered the curve and change-up to go with the great fastball.

I hit .298 with the Cardinals in '56 but come September the general manager, Frank Lane, told me he was going to have to let me go. I said, "Why? I thought I had a pretty good year." He said, "You did but your roommate had a lousy year. He hit only .315." I said, "What's wrong with

.315?" He said, "Stan Musial is no .315 hitter. You're on your way to New York." [laughs]

So the Giants signed me right away and I had a pretty good year in '57, even at age 40. I had 26 home runs, 80 RBIs and won National League Comeback Player of the Year. The Polo Grounds was a funny park to hit in, though, and I never did like it because most of my power was to left-center, and a 425-foot flyball to left-center there was just a long out.

I'm glad I played the game when I did. I think the forties and fifties marked the greatest era in baseball. In the forties they could tell you from the mound they were going to knock you down and nobody said a word about it. And we wore only those felt hats. Then in the late forties the league tried to put a stop to it. We'd tell the pitchers they couldn't do that anymore, so they stopped threatening us and telling us they were throwing at us. But they'd throw at us anyway. Then, in '58, they started fining pitchers $50 for intentionally throwing at hitters.

Nowadays, if they throw two inches inside the hitter falls down and looks at the pitcher like he wants to go out and kill him. I can't believe what we're seeing. Baseball was better served when the brushback pitch was a key part of the game. It's so easy for the hitters today it's not even funny. If a pitcher knocks down one guy he gets warned, so the hitter immediately digs in and swings from the butt. Back in my day if you swung hard at a ball the pitcher would say, "Hey, you're swinging too hard. Let's see you swing at *this* one." A guy like Marv Grissom would think nothing of throwing it right at you. Sal Maglie would throw *curveballs* at you, and he could do it.

I'd love to see baseball go back to eight teams in each league. Then we'd have major league ballplayers. I'd say about half the players in the big leagues today belong there and half don't. In my day the Yankees had 21 minor league clubs. You had to walk over all those bodies just to get to the big leagues. Cincinnati had 18. When you got to the big leagues in those days you belonged there. I'd say more than 80 percent of the big league players then had at least five years experience in the minor leagues. Now, kids get rushed to the majors so fast they often don't know how to cope, and they make too many mistakes.

I still follow baseball. It's still in my blood. Sometimes it irritates my wife because regardless of where we go, somebody always seems to recognize me. We even went to Switzerland on vacation and were up in the mountains in the snow, and people recognized me there. She says, "Can't we go anyplace without someone knowing you?" [laughs] It's like when I was with St. Louis. Stan Musial and I would walk down Broadway in New York and everybody would say, "Hi, Hank. Hi, Hank." And I'd say, "See Stan, everybody knows me, nobody knows you." And he'd say, "How could anyone forget that face of yours?" [laughs]

Millbrae, California

Hank Sauer (Steve Bitker)

JIM DAVENPORT

The smooth-fielding Jim Davenport was one of three rookies to crack the Giants' 1958 Opening Day lineup, going on to hit .256 with 12 home runs and 41 RBIs, and joining three teammates on The Sporting News *All-Rookie Team. His manager Bill Rigney later called him the greatest third baseman he ever saw.*

Jim had his best season in '62 for the Giants' National League champions, hitting .297 with 14 home runs and 58 RBIs, earning an invitation to the All-Star Game in Washington, D.C. The right-handed-hitting Davenport retired after 13 seasons with a .258 average, 77 home runs and one Gold Glove.

Davvy later managed the Giants, in '85, coached and managed in the Giants' minor league system, returned to the parent club as first base coach in '96, then was named manager of their triple-A farm club in Fresno, in November of '97.

Jim and his wife live in San Carlos, California. They have five children and 10 grandchildren.

I LIKED SEALS STADIUM. The fans were a lot closer to you, and everything was new and exciting because it was my first year in the big leagues. And the fans were a lot more friendly, too. The ballpark was in a good location in San Francisco, and it didn't seem to me that it was anywhere near as windy there, or as cold as it was at Candlestick. If they could have had better parking there, and double-decked it, I see no reason why Seals Stadium couldn't have been a fine major league ballpark. It had a super playing field.

When I arrived at the Giants spring training camp in Phoenix, in 1958, Ray Jablonski was the starting third baseman. He was a very good hitter. I was fortunate in that I could catch the ball but I couldn't hit with Ray at that time. We got to be very good friends after a while, before he was traded at the end of that season. I was fortunate because we had so many good hitters around me, so that I didn't have to be a home run hitter to make the ball club. Being able to catch the ball as well as I did helped me make the club in '58. No knock on Ray but he was not a real good fielder.

I had never been to a lot of big towns, coming from a little town in Alabama, so April marked my first trip ever to San Francisco. Of course, *any* town would have been big to me at that time because I was so excited about making the club coming out of spring training. To tell you the truth, I didn't think I'd make it because I had only a triple-A contract. Of course, [Orlando] Cepeda did, too. But I had a good spring and I showed [Bill] Rigney enough, that I could catch the ball and do the little things you had to do to play in the big leagues.

It's amazing, because as a kid in Alabama I never dreamed I'd play major league baseball. I actually went to Mississippi Southern on a football scholarship in 1952 and played quarterback there for three seasons, before signing with the Giants in '55. I wasn't a good enough football player to play in the NFL but I was good enough to get a free college education, and get into the university's Hall of Fame. I should have made it into the Hall in baseball instead of football, but didn't.

We played the Dodgers our first ballgame in San Francisco, and I knew a lot of their guys from following them in high school, the Pee Wee Reeses, the Gil Hodges, those types of players. It was exciting, to say the least, to open against the Dodgers. I was the leadoff hitter that day. My first major league at-bat, Don Drysdale struck me out. I got a base hit my second time up against him but he struck me out on three or four pitches my first time up. Ruben Gomez threw a shutout for us that day. He was a good pitcher. We got to be good friends and played a lot of golf together. He was a great competitor and a great athlete.

I was pleased with the way my first season in the big leagues went and the way I played, because I played defense fairly well. But I didn't

Jim Davenport (SF Giants)

know what to expect from my hitting, and I never was a really high average hitter. I remember hitting the Dodgers well, though. I probably led the league against Dodger pitching. I hit around .450 or .460 against LA that year, which was satisfying. I also got to be very good friends with Hank Sauer that year. He took me under his wing, and we're still very close. He's like a father to me now. But back in '58 he'd say, "Hey rook, let's go grab a beer." Jablonski helped me a lot at third also, and Mays, too. I was tickled to death to be around those types of players.

I married Betty when I was a junior in high school, and we've been married for 43 years. We've got four boys and a girl, and 10 grandchildren. One of my youngest boys went over to Italy to play ball, but the others all live here in California. We bought a house in San Mateo Village, next to the Bay Meadows race track, in '58. I think I paid $14,000 for it. No telling what it's worth now. I had four kids at the time. Then in '63 we moved to the house we're in now, in San Carlos.

Back in '58 and '59 we had six or seven guys on the team from Alabama, like Mays, McCovey, [Al] Worthington, [Dusty] Rhodes and myself. I got along great with everybody. I can't ever remember having a racial problem with the team. But when we went to St. Louis back then, the blacks on our team had to stay in one hotel, and the rest of us in another. You'd feel sorry for them, looking back, but it was no problem.

I thought Rigney was an outstanding manager. Rigney and Alvin Dark stand out in my mind as outstanding managers that I played for. They valued my defense. A lot of guys may take more pride in their hitting but I took more pride in my fielding. I knew I had to be able to catch the ball, and do all the other necessary things like bunt the runner over, to stay in the big leagues, because I wasn't going to hit a lot of home runs. And I knew I wasn't going to be a .300 hitter.

No question about it, my best season came in 1962. I played in the All-Star Game, the World Series and nearly hit .300. I think I was hitting about .315 when Drysdale broke my hand in mid-August. *Everybody* in that middle infield in '62 had best years—myself, Chuck Hiller, Jose Pagan. We won 101 games that year and beat the Dodgers in a playoff. We beat them, 8-0, in the first game here, then went down there and had them beat before blowing a big lead that second ballgame. Then they had us beat, 4-2, in the ninth inning of the third game, but we had the type of

club that year where we felt like we were always going to catch up. I don't care how many runs we were behind, we had the type of club that could put some quick numbers on the board, with McCovey, Cepeda, Mays, the Alous. We just felt going into the ninth inning that we were not beat. Luckily, Stan Williams walked me on a three-one pitch to bring home the winning run. We got to be good friends after that, and now when I see Stan he says, "I should be wearing that World Series ring."

Juan Marichal was with us then. He was, by far, the best pitcher I ever saw. And he was just great to play behind because you were always on your toes, because he always threw strikes. He wasn't the type of pitcher who had to change the ball all the time or walk around the mound. He was very, very serious when he got on that mound. He was an outstanding pitcher and an outstanding individual. Game in and game out he was the best I ever saw.

As my career began winding down I wanted to be a manager. I felt I could have played another year or two, but I was 37 when the opportunity came to manage triple-A ball in Phoenix. So I jumped at the chance and managed there in '71, '72 and '73. Then John McNamera hired me to coach San Diego in '74 and '75. Then I came back with the Giants in '76 to coach, until I got a chance to manage here in '85.

I'm glad I had a chance to manage in the big leagues, although I wish the opportunity had come a few years after that. But you never know if you'll get another chance to manage. I felt we'd have a much better ball club than it turned out. [*author's note: The Giants fired Davenport in September with a 56-88 record, en route to a franchise-record 100 losses.*] I thought we'd hit a lot, and I knew our pitching wasn't that good, but I thought our club on the field was going to be a lot better. We had Jeff Leonard, Chili Davis and Dan Gladden in the outfield. Of course, we made a trade for David Green at first base, who did not do *anything* [.248, 5HR, 20RBI]. We had Manny Trillo at second, Jose Uribe at short, Chris Brown at third and Bob Brenly catching.

I thought Chris Brown, in particular, would be an outstanding ballplayer. Sparky Anderson said the same thing when he had him in Detroit. But it looked like he just did not like to play. He was always looking for reasons to get out of the lineup. He did not like to play with any kind of little injury.

I'm sure I made some mistakes, like the players did, but we just could not hit the ball. We lost so many 2-1 and 3-2 games. The year before we almost led the league in hitting. We kept the same hitting instructor, Tom McCraw, but we did not hit the ball. And Greg Minton could not do anything out of the bullpen. I'm glad I had a chance to manage but wouldn't want to do it again. But I'm glad the Giants gave me the chance.

Jeff Leonard and I had our ups and downs that year. I started the season by naming him captain, which maybe was a mistake, but I thought it would make him a better person around the media and around his teammates in the clubhouse. But it just didn't seem to work out that way. Jeff played hard on the field but just had a different personality than some people. He did not have a good year hitting but nobody else on the team did, either. He led us in RBIs with 62. That's it. These guys today have 61 RBIs the first two months of the season.

When I started managing I said I would treat people like I'd like to be treated, and I don't think I mistreated anybody on that ball club. But I never heard one of the players admit he had a bad year, or maybe it was his fault—it was always the manager's or the coach's fault. No question about it, we were losing the respect of the players as the season went along. Maybe, looking back, I should have put my foot down a little more. But when players are making the kind of money they make in the big leagues I don't think I need to bed-check them at 1 a.m. You should be able to take care of yourself because you've got a job to do, and you're paid good money to do it. We started losing that season and everybody was pointing fingers. But sometimes you've got to look at yourself in the mirror and say, "Hey, what am I doing?" And I don't think any of our players did that, to tell you the truth.

That's how it is nowadays, too. That's how the game has changed. Players don't like to blame themselves. They're always looking elsewhere for reasons why they're having bad years or reasons why things aren't going well. There aren't too many ballplayers nowadays who say, "Hey, maybe some of this is my fault." You don't hear that too much. It's always the manager who should've done this or the front office that should've done that, or the coaches. You never heard the Mayses pointing fingers, the Hall of Famers. But, of course, they always had good years.

The game is as great as it ever was but I don't think players really get after it like they used to. I think the money, the big salaries, has had an effect. The players don't seem like they're as close. I remember we used to sit around for an hour after games and talk baseball in the clubhouse. I don't think you see much of that anymore. The long-term contracts have changed a lot of players. There are still some good ones who will play hard every day, even if they've got 20-year contracts. But I think the money and the long-term contracts have taken away some of the excitement of what the fans should be getting to see from some of the ballplayers.

When Bob Lurie replaced me as manager in September it was hard, but it was also a relief. I could not sleep at night, worrying about what I could do to make the club better. I hated the situation, and hated to lose at the end, but mentally it was a relief. Not that I was ready to get out, but I felt bad because it was my first year and it went so badly. I lost the desire to manage anymore after that, especially without enough say-so with the general manager [Tom Haller], in terms of who we should get rid of or what we needed to win. I didn't have that. I should have had a little more say-so in terms of what players we should have moved or kept. But it didn't happen that way.

I went to Philly in '86 to coach for two years, to Cleveland for two years and then to Detroit for three. Then I came back with the Giants in '93 to coach A-ball in San Jose. It was great to have [Giants President] Peter Magowan invite me back with the Giants. I jumped at the chance because I've always had a soft spot in my heart for the Giants because I've been with them for more than 25 years.

I've really enjoyed working with the young kids. They work hard. And I enjoy seeing the improvement from one month to the next. These kids are fun to work with. They know what they've got to do to try to get to the big leagues. We've got five or six kids in the system now who are great prospects with a chance to be good big league ballplayers in a couple of years. It's going to be interesting to see this group in a couple of years and see what they look like.

It's refreshing to coach these kids. I've always got my arm around them, talking to them. I couldn't do that much with the Giants. These kids haven't played but a half year or a year, and haven't been away from home much, so they've got a lot to learn about life and baseball. And that's our job, to stay with these kids and spend as much time with them as we can. And I really enjoy it. I went fishing with a couple of them on off days, and a couple of others have come to spend the night at my house and go fishing the next day. So I've really enjoyed this.

I got to be very close with Salty Parker, my first manager in the Giants system, at El Dorado in 1955. He was like a father to me. He taught me a lot about life and baseball. And I feel like coaches in the minor leagues should pass these lessons along and be close with the kids, and work with them.

I still enjoy the game as much as ever. I don't enjoy losing but I don't think you ever get used to that. But you've got to take the bitter with the sweet. I get to the ballpark early every day. It's fun. I'm 64 years old now, and I've got my pension. I don't need this job to live. But as long as it's fun and I enjoy it, and as long as I feel like I can help and pass along something to these kids in the minor leagues, I'm going to stay with it.

San Carlos, California

MIKE McCORMICK

A nationally recognized southpaw from Southern California, Mike Mc- Cormick made his major league de- but with the Giants at the age of 17, in 1956, after winning 49 of 53 American Legion games, including four no-hitters and one 26-strikeout performance.

Armed with a great fastball, McCormick be- came the youngest National League pitcher to win three games, in 1957. He won 11 games for the '58 Giants, then won 15 in '60 when he captured the league's earned-run-average title, at 2.70. Mike led the league with 22 wins in '67, when he won both the Cy Young and Comeback Player of the Year awards. By then, he had lost his great fastball be- cause of arm injuries, but had replaced it with one of the league's best breaking pitches and screwballs. He retired several years later after 16 seasons, 134 wins, 91 complete games, 23 shutouts and a 3.73 ERA.

Mike currently works as a regional sales man- ager for an office machine business. He, his wife and young daughter live in Sunnyvale, California. He has four other adult children, and three grandchil- dren.

I NEVER HAD a big fantasy to pitch in the major leagues. My fantasy was the Pacific Coast League. That's what I grew up with, in Alhambra, in Southern California. There was no television. What little exposure we had to the majors was usually on recreated games on radio, and they were usually on at a time when I was playing. So I didn't get to hear them. I mean, I had heard of the Musials, the Mantles, the Williams and the Mays, but if somebody had told me to name a ros- ter I bet I couldn't have named more than three players on any major league team, other than maybe the Yankees.

As it turned out, I not only made my major league debut with the Giants at the age of 17, I also married my high school sweetheart at 17. Was I ready? Was I ready for *anything* at 17? Who knows? I was just a crazy young kid. We ran away and got married, and *then* we told our parents. All mine could see at that time was the pro baseball potential and the college potential all going down the drain. Her parents were more supportive but said they always wanted their daughters to be married in a big church wedding. So we got re- married in a church. My folks were a little ... I won't say hesitant, but they looked at it as if it were going to destroy their son. It turns out it was a good marriage for a long time. Shoot, ev- eryone always said I was more mature than my age, but was I *that* mature? Probably not. Just a crazy young kid who did something and nobody stopped it, because it really could have been stopped.

The day after I signed with the Giants I was in a Giants uniform, at the Polo Grounds, against the Dodgers. It was August of 1956. I was out on the field, shagging balls for one of the coaches hitting fungoes, when the next thing I knew I had this big hand grabbing my left arm. And the guy was saying, "So that's what they paid all that money for, huh?" I turned around and it was Gil Hodges, sizing me up [laughs]. I was a typical 17- year-old. How else could you define it? I didn't look 30. I was a young, baby-faced 17-year-old scrawny kid. I threw batting practice that night and somebody hit a line drive right back at me. I had never pitched with a screen before, and I didn't know how to flinch or duck, so I flinched back and, in my excitement, lost my footing and fell right off the back of the mound [laughs]. So you *know* everybody's watching this phenom throw, and here I am flat on my back.

In hindsight, I wish I had written a diary. There were some very interesting experiences. But the hardest thing for me—and I didn't think it was so hard at the time—was that I spent a tremendous amount of time by myself those first two years, in '56 and '57. Because, when the game would end, the married guys would go with their families, and the single guys certainly didn't want a 17-year-old around. I didn't drink anyway. I was married then, but my wife didn't come east until June of '57. So, when I left the ballpark until I went back to the ballpark the next day, I was by myself. I lived in a hotel downtown, at 57th and Columbus Circle. At the time you could walk the streets of New York safely. I just kept busy, going to movies, wandering around shopping. I went back years later and looked at the places I thought were so neat as a 17-year-old, and it was just a coffee shop or something like that. But, you know, it's all your perception. I might have had the best steak dinner of my life there but, at 17, compared to what? I never ate out as a kid. But when I went back years later, I thought my values sure had changed.

At the time I didn't feel so lonely but, looking back, I *must* have been. I felt so out of place with my teammates. I mean, these were men, some of them my *Dad's* age. I think the next youngest player on that team was 25 or 26. And then me, at 17. It was an old team: Wes Westrum, Hank Thompson, Davey Williams, Whitey Lockman, Don Mueller, Marv Grissom. Willie Mays may have been the next youngest player [at 25].

I pitched my first game within days after signing. Labor Day weekend we went to Philadel-

Mike McCormick (SF Giants)

phia and I relieved on Labor Day. I pitched one inning, to Del Ennis, Jim Greengrass and Stan Lopata. I don't remember the order but it was those three right-handed batters. And I got three ground balls to second base. My ball used to really run away [from right-handed hitters]. It happened so quickly that I wasn't even nervous, because I was in the game so quickly after the phone rang. But when the game was over, everyone was in the clubhouse talking to me, you know, "Mike, your first game, what were your thoughts?" And then Bill Rigney told me I was starting Wednesday night against Curt Simmons. That was a mistake because then I had two days to think about it. He'd have been better off letting me do whatever I was doing, and then before the game telling me I was going to pitch.

I pitched three innings and was wild all over the place. And wildness was never a problem with me in high school. But that night I was all over the place. I was just nervous. I probably didn't even sleep the night before, thinking about it. I always had had great control before, dating back to American Legion ball. Everybody else was in high school then, mostly juniors and seniors. And there I was, 14 years old, light years behind them in maturity and—quote—talent, even though I held my own [finishing with a 49-4 record, with four no-hitters]. To me, the guys were *really* old, 17 and 18.

I played football my freshman year of high school, on the line, because I was slow. It was fun knocking heads with guys but that wasn't the direction I wanted to go with my life. And my dad kept saying somebody would break my hand or break my fingers or break my arm, and I wouldn't be able to pitch. It didn't take a lot of enticing on his part. I didn't care that much about football. If I couldn't be quarterback I didn't want to play. So I played basketball. I was a very good basketball player, all-CIF [California Interscholastic Federation], junior and senior year. I had basketball scholarships to USC and Stanford, in addition to baseball.

They started recruiting me heavily in my junior year, by making campus visits. I had to take the college entrance exam, and I did extremely well in everything but English, because I was a terrible reader. Terrible in the sense that I didn't like to read, because that deprived me of time, and time to me was well spent shooting baskets or throwing balls, you know? Stanford took a look at my scores, and I was so high in math—I wanted to be an engineer—that they said the test was an aberration, that there was some problem with the test itself, that this guy couldn't score this high in everything else and so low in English. I was accepted at Stanford, but I enrolled at USC because I really wanted to go there.

I was starting to set up my curriculum at USC, when I went back to New York to pitch in the *Journal-American* game, which was a prep All-Star Game, sponsored by the Hearst newspapers. My roommate on the trip was Ron Fairly. We went back to New York for a week as teammates to play against the New York state All-Star team, sponsored by the Hearst newspapers in New York. Whereas we were representing Hearst newspapers everywhere else in the country. Two of us were selected from LA, two from San Francisco, Seattle, Chicago and so on. I was picked number one in LA, after pitching three innings in an All-Star Game and striking out all nine batters. I was supposed to go with Deron Johnson but he signed with the Yankees instead. Fairly was the alternate, so he and I went. We were in New York for a week, wined and dined, as much as 17-year-olds can be wined and dined. We were more entertained than anything. And at the end of that week, after playing intersquad games, there was a game in the Polo Grounds called the *Journal-American* game, the *Journal-American* being a big newspaper then, in New York.

There was a lot of controversy as to why the U.S. coach didn't pick me to start the game, and his rationale was that if he started me, he could pitch me only three innings, whereas if he pitched me the last three innings and the score were tied, then I could pitch more. This was the U.S. All-Star team against the New York state-New York City All-Star team. We had quite a few guys on that team who went on to play pro ball, including our shortstop from Texas, Joel Horlen.

And to make a long story short, I pitched the last three innings and struck out all nine. So here I pitched in two big All-Star Games and I struck out 18 of 18. And at that game, along with close to 40,000 people, was Horace Stoneham, with his brass, out in the center field area near the clubhouses, because Stoneham had an office out there. Stoneham asked who that left-handed kid from California was. None of his people had any idea. I was the highest-rated, most recognized and honored pitcher in the LA area [a major market for baseball players] for two years, and they had no idea who I was. I had talked previously with scouts from several major league clubs, including the Yankees, with their limos and their prestigious ways, but they wouldn't offer a bonus. Because, in those days, you had to stay in the major leagues for two years if you signed for over $6,000; they couldn't send you to the minors.

It was interesting that Fairly and I stopped en route to New York in St. Louis, and the *Herald-Examiner* guy with us who made the arrangements took us to a Cardinal game at the old Sportsman's Park. And, boy, that was obviously the first time I'd ever seen a major league game, or even been to a major league park. And there was something very special about this. I had never been in humidity before, didn't even know what it was, and just that it was my first major league game and seeing Stan Musial—that in itself was exciting. Then, in New York, they took all of us as a group to see Cleveland play the Yankees, and I saw Herb Score pitch a shutout. And, man, I'd never seen anybody pitch like that. I saw two major league games that week, then we went home, and a week later I was on a plane with my dad going back to New York to sign.

All things being equal, I would have signed with the Pirates because, as a kid growing up, they had the Hollywood Stars—that was their triple-A team. And they were gracious to me, coming out to work with me and let me pitch BP to them both my junior and senior summers. Friday nights we'd go out when they were in town, and that's when Bill Mazeroski was there, and Bobby Bragan was the manager. They were just really good to me, even though my loyalty was to the LA Angels. For whatever reason I grew up an Angels fan. They were affiliated with the Cubs. But I didn't know anything about the Cubs. I didn't even like the Cubs. My whole world was the Pacific Coast League. I didn't even know what the heck the major leagues were, you know?

An interesting sidelight is that when we got ready to sign with the Giants, we called Joe Brown [Pirates' general manager]. They made it very clear they wanted to sign me, but couldn't sign me to a *bonus* because they had the O'Brien twins and Paul Pettit. That was the bottom line with me. Without a bonus I was going to attend USC. I would not have signed without a bonus. Education was important to me then. I knew I could always go play baseball, so why pass up a free education at USC, which was another goal in my life. And pitching at SC would have been like pitching for the Yankees, in those days. They were so dominant, it would have been like being in the Yankee organization. That was before you had good college baseball as we see it today, with all those great Sun Belt teams. I mean, it was USC, and then the gap between them and whoever was next was huge.

The Giants came forward and talked with my dad, and were the first club to offer me a bonus, based on that game at the Polo Grounds, and on Horace Stoneham asking, "Who was that kid?" And I think part of it was the Giants were old at the time, and they were lousy. I mean, that New York Giants team in '56 was really not very good. Before me, they had signed Joey Amalfitano and Paul Giel to bonuses—Joey was with them for two years, then he went to the minors, and Paul was there for two years, then he went into the military.

Back in those days, it took five years to get in the baseball retirement plan, to get the *minimum*. Now, it's one day. Paul got five years without ever having to *pitch*. He got two years on the bonus, two years in the military, which counted, and then they could carry him free of charge for one year once he came out of the military. So he, in essence, got his five years minimum in the major leagues without ever having to pitch. He pitched a little, but never had to.

The Giants had been accustomed to having some kids sit on the roster for this two-year period. So I don't think there was any hesitation on their part. I got a $50,000 bonus. In those days a guy signing without a bonus would have had to settle for $350 to $400 a month, for a five-month season at most. $50,000 went a long way then. That's when houses in Hillsborough [a wealthy San Francisco suburb] were in the high thirties and low forties.

I was surprised to get the bonus from the Giants in that they had no record of me, and had really done very little scouting, even though I saw an old scouting report many years later with some information on one, but it was sketchy. It talked about my girlfriend and my thoughts about getting married, which we ultimately did, so somebody knew a little bit. But, apparently, it never got back to New York.

My Dad and I talked it over, and I told him I had this feeling for the Pirates, so he called Joe Brown. And through the years, whenever we played the Pirates, Joe Brown would make it a point to come over and talk with me. He said he'd been in baseball a long time, and nobody had ever called and said, "Just match something and you got me." And he said he'd never forget that. So, I *would* have been a Pirate. But they had three guys on bonuses already on their major league roster. Half to two-thirds of the teams in those days had guys on bonuses. The Yankees would never sign one. They took the position that they were not going to deprive a deserving player a spot on their roster. But, you know what I think they did? I think they paid guys under the table. There wasn't a system in those days to check for that type of thing. I'm convinced Deron Johnson got a lot of money under the table, because he was a big, strong talent as an outfielder and could hit with power. This guy could not have signed for just $4,000 or whatever the minimum was. I never did ask him, though. I'd still be interested to know.

Again, I was just a Coast League fan growing up. My buddy, who was not an athlete, and I used to get on the bus in Alhambra, take it to downtown LA, get off, get on the trolley and take it to Wrigley Field. The two of us were 10 to 13 years old, and my parents would never worry. They might have thought we'd get lost, but there was *never* any fear of getting hurt. Can you imagine doing something like that today? *Jeez*. Then, we'd just reverse the process going home. And in the fall, we'd take the trolley to the Coliseum to see the Rams, and come home in the dark.

If I had any baseball hero growing up, it was a lefty named Joe Hatten. I used to call him Lefty Joe Hatten. He pitched for the Angels. I always liked him. He was a journeyman who never did much in the major leagues—just had a drink [cup] of coffee—one of those guys who was up and down, up and down, but never really did a lot. But he was a good Coast League pitcher, and because he was left-handed I always kind of liked him. [*author's note: In fact, Hatten won 56 games for the Brooklyn Dodgers between 1946 and '49.*]

I PROBABLY WAS the last guy on the Giants in 1957 to hear that we were going to move west, or at least the last one who could grasp what it really meant. My only thought at the moment was, had I been a Dodger I'd be going back home to LA. I had never been to San Francisco. My family never went anywhere, other than within the greater LA area. But I was never enamored, certainly not at a young age, with New York. So, in that sense, moving to San Francisco seemed appealing.

My wife and I came up north that winter to look for a place to rent, from Bakersfield, where we were attending Bakersfield College. My first reaction seeing Seals Stadium was that it was small. Where was the upper deck [laughs]? It was a neat little park, though. I pitched pretty well there. The wind blew more out to left-center than it did to right, like it did at Candlestick. When I say it was small, it was intimate, very much like East Coast parks. Smaller, but the fan was right there. In other words, you got on the on-deck circle and you could literally have a conversation with the people in the first row. I liked that. From a pitching perspective, I hated parks where you felt you were isolated way out there in the middle of nowhere. I always liked the intimacy of the background being right behind the catcher. I don't know why. It was just a visual feel, just a more comfortable feeling.

I had to pitch well in spring training to make the team in '58 because they voided that rule—you didn't have to stay two years in the major leagues with a bonus, even somebody like myself who had three-quarters of a year left under that rule. So I could've been optioned out to the minors. It never entered my mind that I might have been, but I could've been. But, as it turned out, I pitched well that spring. [*author's note: McCormick made history by pitching three scoreless innings in a 5-1 win over Cleveland March 8, in the first San Francisco Giants spring training game.*]

I was embarrassed that spring, though, to be picked as a teenager to go to the Giants' mineral bath resort [outside Mesa, in Apache Junction], which was so far out there the wooden Indians used to wink at you. I mean, you were in the middle of nowhere. I signed at about 185 pounds but showed up at my first big league camp in '57 at 205, because it was the first year of my life that I didn't play all the school sports with all the workouts, when I was always in shape. That particular winter I did a little bit of school, a little bit

of work, and laid around to eat. It didn't really slow me down but it made me a pudgy 205. So the next spring, in '58, they put me on that list because they had no idea what I would look like. Nobody kept in touch with you in those days. You'd show up, and never know whether another guy had one leg, two legs, was way overweight, in good shape or not, because we all went to spring training to get in shape, which is different than today.

At the baths we had to get up at 5 a.m., and be done with everything before they opened it up to the public. It was a very popular place, with hot mineral baths, massages and mud baths. We had to be completely done as a group and be out of there by about 8 o'clock. So we'd be up at five and it'd be freezing, and they'd have us out in the middle of the desert by the main highway, running on these dirt roads in the dark. To me, it was a great time, but I don't think it accomplished a doggone thing. But I think Stoneham had this relationship with the guy who owned that place for years—they were drinking buddies, and he'd send a group out there each spring. And it was fun, but I never saw any conditioning benefit to us, unless you had a muscle pull or something where heat and massage would help. We'd run and exercise, then go inside and start with the baths. They'd wrap you in hot blankets on a table, and you'd lay there sweating for a half hour in a steamroom-type environment. They you'd get a 30-minute rub, which was great. Maybe even an hour. And then you'd be gone. You'd be done for the day. Guys would then spend the day golfing, hunting or just laying around.

At the end of spring training those years, we'd get on the train in Phoenix, pick up the Cleveland club at the first stop in Tucson and wind up usually around Baltimore. We'd go to El Paso, Lubbock, Houston, Mobile, Jacksonville, then up the coast to a couple of towns and finally to Baltimore, playing exhibition games all along the way. Then the Indians would go to wherever they'd be opening the season, and we'd do the same. One year I spent all my free time on the train with Roger Maris. Roger was the new young star with Cleveland, very shy. I was new, young and relatively shy with the Giants. He was a little older but we just kind of hit it off with each other. We used to meet and go to the club car or the train to eat, and just sit and talk or play cards. And we developed a nice friendship.

The train was always our hotel because every night we were on the move to the next city, and sometimes we would arrive at two in the morning. You could hear them park the train. That was our hotel. But once we got to the park, we always went as a group in the morning to a hotel. Maybe there'd be four of us to a room, to put on a uniform and to come back after the game to shower. And then eating could be either in the hotel or back on the train, depending on where our next stop was. But once we got into the Deep South, the blacks couldn't go with us. We'd get off the train and there'd be a pre-arranged vehicle waiting to pick up the black players, and we wouldn't see them until we'd get to the park. We'd have to go to different hotels, even if it was just to change. The South was still segregated then. I couldn't believe it. I mean, I grew up in California.

I didn't have exposure to many blacks growing up. There were always a couple in school, but not a lot. I just never gave segregation any thought. But I'd go to some of these ballparks, and there'd be two water fountains this far apart [spreading his arms], one saying *White Only*, the other *Colored Only*. I couldn't believe it. Man, those people followed the rules. And the bleachers in left field would say *Colored Only*. Same with the bathrooms. And I'm thinking, my God, this is the fifties, the *late* fifties. You see, California never had any of that, at least to my knowledge. I never saw any of this in the major league cities either, at the major league ballparks, just in the Deep South. Baltimore, which was probably on the cusp of the South, didn't have it. Atlanta still had it. That's probably as far north as I recall seeing it. That was a shock. They couldn't eat with us, couldn't dress with us. I never heard them complain about it, never heard them say anything. I'm sure there were some things being said, or most of them were

from the Deep South, so they just accepted it as a way of life. I think the guys that probably had a more difficult time with it were the Latin guys. The blacks may not have liked it, but it had been kind of a way of life. But I couldn't believe it.

I REMEMBER OPENING DAY in '58. It was a pretty day—windy but sunny. I remember the streamers, the opening-day banners, the full house and the *excitement* of the city. And, the day before, we had that great parade through downtown San Francisco. At that point it was always exciting, and the place to be or go then was Seals Stadium, for a ballgame. It was exciting just to be part of something new.

I remember parking was a real problem there. Fortunately, we got to park right behind the center field fence. They had it blocked off for players. I remember that fence opening up after games so fans could walk across the field to their cars. Just stay off the infield. And that would take you almost literally right into the players' lot, because that's the way we vacated the field, too. We'd come out through the dugouts and walk across the field.

I didn't have a lot of points of reference but it seemed to make sense to just double-deck Seals and keep the

Mike McCormick holds one-year-old daughter Susan Lynne.
(SF Giants)

team there. When you come from New York, where we didn't have any crowds—the only crowds we ever had was when the Dodgers and Giants played—to a place that was always full, or close to full, *that* was exciting. So why would you want to move to another location? There was talk that parking was the big issue, and there was talk of building a multilevel garage beyond the right field fence at Seals.

My best friend on that team was Johnny Antonelli. We used to go out with our wives to the city for dinner. In fact, we roomed together on the road. Antonelli was not just my best friend on the team, he was also my mentor. But he hated the wind at Seals, because it would blow out toward left field. And there was one specific game when he got beat by a wind-blown home run. But hell, I mean, over the life of a stadium or a career there's always going to be something freakish that happens. If it happened every time you played, then .... Unfortunately, he popped off, and there was a writer, Walter Judge with the *Examiner*, who jumped right on it. So, when you picked up the paper the next day, it was front-page headlines: *Antonelli Criticizes Wind*, or something like that. And John just stuck his head in the sand after that. Instead of saying, "Hey, I was mad and made an off-the-wall comment," he just went the other way and withdrew, and went from a good pitcher to a pitcher who looked like he was trying to get the season over with.

I think for a long time the Giant-Dodger rivalry still existed among the players then, but from a fan's perspective it was never as intense between LA and San Francisco as it was between Brooklyn and New York. I mean, for those people, it was like a bloodline. You either were on *this* side or *that* side, but you were not in between. But what I couldn't believe in New York was that Dodger fans or Giant fans would *not* be Yankee fans, too. I mean, it was the American League. You could be both, right? But, no way. You *liked* one of those three teams, and that was it. Remember, I was there in New York when we traded for Jackie Robinson. And he wouldn't go to the Giants. He *quit*. But that's how intense that rivalry was in those days. I guess when Durocher went from managing the Dodgers to managing the Giants it must have been just incredible. We wouldn't even talk to each other on the field before games. If we did, it was a sarcastic conversation. I was young, so I had my mouth shut most of the time. But as I got older, there was still this intense dislike for the Dodgers.

My first game in '58 was our first road game, against the Dodgers, at the LA Coliseum, a very strange place to play. There was nothing equitable about that place. It was so out of kilter. From center field to almost straightaway right you couldn't hit a home run. And yet, from left-center to the left field line *left-handers* were popping balls up for home runs. Line drives would wind up like at the green wall in Boston, but way in. Line drive home runs that right-handers would hit would be long singles off the wall.

We had a good young team in '58 but I never had a sense that we could overtake Milwaukee. I just viewed it as, what an improvement from the New York club, which was old and salty. I mean, that was a real whiskey group—hard livers, but older, too.

Actually, I thought we should have won it in '59. I pitched the most pivotal game in that big series against the Dodgers when they came up here for a three-game series in late September. We led them by two games with eight to go. They swept us and we never recovered. The only one we *should* have won was the one I pitched. We got rained out Friday night so we had to play a day-night doubleheader on Saturday. Antonelli pitched the morning game and we lost [to Roger Craig], 4-1. Then I pitched the night game. It was the seventh inning, with one out, men on first and third, and I was ahead, 1-0. And Rigney came out to talk to me because they were pinch hitting Chuck Essegian. He left me in, which showed how much control I had of that game. There was no hesitancy, even in that situation, in that important a game, because I really was pitching well. So I threw Essegian a change-up, and he hit a one-hopper to Davenport at third. And Jimmy, who never missed a ball or threw it badly, caught it and turned to throw to second. And Spencer, who's normally a shortstop, was playing second. Here came the ball, chest-high, right at the bag, but all Daryl could see and hear was Pignatano coming from first. And that was the year that Spencer put two players out with what they said were dirty slides at second base, where both had to have surgery. [Bob] Hazle, with the Braves, never recovered. So instead of catching the ball, and turning the easy double play to end the inning ahead, 1-0, the ball hit him right in the glove and he dropped it. The tying run scored, the next guy got a base hit and we lost, 5-3.

The next day I relieved. That's where part of my arm problem came from, from the way Rigney used me. I just loved to pitch so I never said no. I was mainly a starter in '59 and '60, and yet Bill would always ask me to do my midday workout in the bullpen, late in the game, in case he needed me for a batter. I'd say OK. Well, invariably, the batter would be an *inning*, and I did that a lot in my career. And that's what caught up with me and caused my sore shoulder [from '58 through '60, McCormick had 93 starts *and* 36 relief appearances]. It happened mostly with Rigney, but also a little with Dark because we never had a good left-handed reliever. Even if I didn't go in the game, by the eighth or ninth inning at night it's freezing, and I've been sitting around all evening, whereas a starter would normally get his workout in *before* the game, then shower and bundle up, and be done with it.

Bill was always a tough guy to pitch for because he'd average about four and a half pitchers per game, if you plotted his career as a manager. I saw that pattern in Rigney. But I thought he was a good manager. He possibly could have handled his pitchers a little better. He never had a pitching coach that I think he looked upon for advice. Those guys had more of a job of just keeping you in shape. I think it's a little bit different today. Bill was tough with pitchers but I think he had a pretty good baseball mind. He had an overreactionary temper. You could excite him or ignite him real quickly. And he was always chewing antacid pills, so we knew he had a big ulcer.

Jimmy Davenport had one, too. In fact, if it hadn't been for Hobie Landrith in '59, I think Jimmy would have bled to death in his room. He had a bleeding ulcer, bleeding through his mouth, and passed out in his room. Fate had it that five to ten minutes later Hobie came back to the room, found him and got the ambulance there right away to get him to the hospital. They said another 30 minutes and he probably would have bled to death.

Fifty-eight was the year they took the All-Star vote away from the fans [because of the ballot-stuffing scandal of '57 in Cincinnati], and I think they should do it again. I still don't think it's right the way the All-Star voting is today. I think if you're going to do it, have the writers do it, the players, managers and coaches do it, and *then* let the fans do it, and let each have a weighted percentage. But not 100% with the fans, because then it becomes a *popularity* contest. And you get ushers walking around the ballpark handing fans stacks of ballots. So what do you expect? Particularly when a deserving player isn't even on the ballot. And I've always said, even when I was a player, that you should be rewarded for what you're doing *this* year, because that's the whole premise of an All-Star Game, and *not* what your name represents and what you've done in the past. But it doesn't work that way.

In '59 I pitched a five-inning no-hitter, in Philadelphia. It rained like a son of a bitch. It rained the whole game. And it was one of those games where everyone just wondered if we could get five innings in. It wasn't just a thunderstorm that came and wouldn't go away. It was kind of a misty rain, and then when the sky did open you could have sailed *boats* in the dugout, there was so much water. Of course, the commissioner threw those no-hitters out a few years ago. That's stupid, because all those have an asterisk by them anyway, so it doesn't take a rocket scientist to realize that, hey, these people on this list are different than those on that list. But now no-hitters like mine aren't even officially recognized. When that game got called there was no particular sense of elation at having thrown a no-hitter. There was a lot of joking, but that's all.

I also pitched Willie McCovey's first game in the major leagues, in '59, when he went four-for-four against Robin Roberts: Two triples, two singles and I had a complete-game win.

None of us realized what we were getting into with the move to Candlestick in 1960, how bad the weather would be there, and how much worse it was on the field than at Seals Stadium. But it's funny—I think my whole career I pitched better in San Francisco than I did on the road, so I can't in fairness criticize Candlestick, or anywhere in San Francisco, even if they had put the stadium on the Golden Gate Bridge. Because I did better in San Francisco.

I still remember Vice President Nixon throwing out the first ball in the Candlestick opener. He came down to the clubhouse to talk baseball with us before the game and Billy Loes asked him, "Would you please take care of our fucking income taxes?" The whole clubhouse went stone quiet but Nixon did his best to answer the question. He sure loved baseball.

But there were big differences between Seals and Candlestick. Seals was a very comfortable park to pitch in, and being on the mound there I never had the sense of irritation I had on the mound at Candlestick, because of the wind. It was distinctly different. And I think a lot of it was you were closer to the stands at Seals, so if there was wind it was going *over* you, whereas at Candlestick you were way out there on your own. And remember Candlestick wasn't enclosed when I pitched there. You'd start the game and the wind would be in your face. In the third or fourth inning it would hit you from the third base side, and then, if you survived, later in the game it would come at you from behind. We'd all know it was the same wind, but how in the hell it would do all those kinds of crazy things I never knew.

Vice President Richard Nixon shakes hands with Orlando Cepeda before the Giants' first game at Candlestick Park, April 12, 1960; Manager Bill Rigney is to Nixon's right, with coach Bill Posedel in background. (SF Giants)

Statistically, 1960 was one of my best years [league-best 2.70ERA], even though I think the best year I had in the major leagues was when I was 13-16, in '61. I lost 13 of those 16 games by a score of 3-2 or less. But the team never made the play, or I never got the run. All kinds of things happened, but taking the whole season into account, that was the best year I ever pitched [despite a 3.20ERA, compared with 15-12, 2.70 in '60, and 22-10, 2.85 in '67].

In hindsight, the hitters at Candlestick had a bigger disadvantage than we did. They had no backdrop in those days to hit out of. They were hitting out of those Hunters Point apartment houses way back in the hills, and they were painted Navy gray, so in the daytime I knew I had the advantage. Even though the hitters could eventually pick up the ball, it wasn't like they had some big green backdrop to hit out of. The next year they planted about a dozen trees, and eventually put a big green wall out beyond the center field fence.

Plus, it was 385 feet to the left-center field alley. And I remember night games, going out there and taking your glove off and holding it against the wire fence in right field, and then letting go. And the gusts would be so strong that the glove would stay up against the fence for a couple of extra seconds. We'd be out there trying to do our running before the game, and you literally had to run with your head straight down into the wind. It was incredible. And the worst part was

when you weren't playing, because when you were playing at least you were busy, and you were caught up in the game, at least as a pitcher. I always felt sorry for Mays and those guys in the outfield out there, watching and waiting, not involved, getting cold. There was *always* dew on the grass in those days. I don't know why. So your shoes were always damp. I don't ever hear that complaint anymore. Maybe the enclosure of the stadium changed that. But there was *always* dew on the grass at night and when we'd come out first thing early in the morning. And boy, when your feet are wet and cold, your whole body's cold.

When I wasn't pitching I'd always watch the games from the dugout. It was supposed to be heated but it didn't work. We'd be all bundled up. Even in the stands there was supposed to be a heating system, but it didn't work either, so Melvin Belli sued them. Actually, it did work, but by the time they turned it on and the stadium would start to get warm, we'd be going on the road. They set the pipes so damn deep into concrete that there was no way it was going to work.

Late in the '61 season I started having arm trouble. But I was in such good shape, and still in the rotation, that I could take a little extra time to warm up and it would be OK. But then during the off-season, whatever damage I had done had a chance to calcify. Whatever it did I don't know because medicine in those days wasn't very sophisticated. When I went to spring training in '62

I had this shoulder pain, but I wasn't in shape arm-wise, and I just couldn't get through it. So then I started looking for ways to throw to compensate for the pain so the arm would be comfortable. But then you start doing everything wrong and really compound the problem.

Of course, '62 was that great year we won the pennant. But I just got kind of shunted aside. If they'd have been really hurting for pitching, maybe I'd have got more, or better, attention. But I don't know. They felt that if the trainer couldn't correct the problem, then it wasn't correctable. That was the mentality back then. The only alternative, then, was surgery, and surgery in those days meant they just opened you up, shook your hand and said good-bye. You'd probably never come back.

That '62 season was a tough, tough year for me, because I felt in '59, '60 and '61, I was the number one-or-two pitcher on that team, depending on how you wanted to look at it. And all of a sudden, to just be shunted aside was tough. That really affected my enjoyment of what for the team was a great season. I had real bitterness at not being able to participate more. I mean, I won five and lost five and, as it turned out, of the five I won, a couple were at very crucial times in the season when they needed another starter, and I pitched and I won. The bitterness came from the way I was neglected.

I think in hindsight, which is always 20-20, they could have done more for my pain, because that off-season I got traded to the Orioles as part of a six-player trade, and as soon as I went to Baltimore the first thing they did was admit me to Johns Hopkins Hospital under specialized care to find out what the problem was. And, apparently, I had developed a little bit of a bone spur on the end of the shoulder, from some hemorrhaging. I got a lot of different attention there that I didn't get from the Giants, and yet I was still young and still should have been considered a valuable asset. But the Giants never thought that way. Billy O'Dell was doing OK and so was Billy Pierce, so I just got shunted aside, and I think their opinion was that I was done. And if I wasn't done, then it wasn't a problem, and I was a throw-in on a deal.

The Orioles were able to diagnose the problem, but not correct it. It probably would have taken surgery to correct it, and that wasn't even considered as an option. But I took cortisone shots that kind of got me over a hump. Now, as I say that, it wasn't until a couple of years later that I really got my feet back on the ground, with the Senators. And then I got traded back to the Giants in '67.

Yeah, the old guard of the Giants, none of which would take credit for getting rid of me, *all* took credit for bringing me back, after the fact. I was excited to be back. I had kept my home here, the family had only been able to join me during the summer months in Baltimore and Washington because the kids were getting more and more into school, and there were more and more of them [four]. I was at a gas station on El Camino Real when somebody told me about the trade. It broke on the radio before they were able to track us down. I was traded for Cap Peterson.

I didn't throw as hard by '67 as I used to, but I still threw harder than people ever wanted to give me credit for, because I threw more breaking stuff. But I had to have it all because the breaking stuff made the fastball better, the fastball made the breaking stuff better, and the change-up obviously made them both better. And I started throwing the screwball.

Even though I won 22 games in '67, I didn't become a regular starter until *June*. On June 6th my record was 3-4. I was there to be a spot starter and a long reliever. I was an experienced journeyman left-hander. We were playing in Houston, Gaylord Perry or Bob Bolin missed a start, and Herman Franks told me I'd be pitching that Thursday. So I started, went nine innings and beat Houston in the dome, and pitched so well that it warranted another start. Then I won eight or nine in a row, and they couldn't get me out of the rotation. Otherwise, who knows what my year might have been? I was 19-6 after June 6th. It happened so fast that even though I should have been on the All-Star team, I wasn't. And Walter Alston, who picked the team that year, apologized later that I wasn't on it. And I told him, what could he do, that it happened so quickly.

I did make the All-Star team in '60 and '61, pitched in both games and pitched well. And I was in one World Series, in '62, although I didn't pitch. I was active, warmed up every game and there was a rumor that I might start the opening game, because we'd run out of our starters in the playoff with LA. But O'Dell got the nod.

When McCovey lined out to Bobby Richardson [to end the Series], I was in the bullpen, sitting on the bench out in right field. It happened so fast that you were trying to figure out where the line drive was going to go. I mean, it was a crack, and you didn't know whether to look up, or where it was. I think one of the interesting things there was—and I don't have any film to confirm this, but I swear I saw this—when that ball was hit Ralph Terry threw his glove into the air in *disgust,* because he thought the game, and the *Series,* was over. It wasn't in excitement because he did it *before* he turned and saw that Richardson had caught it. I swear I saw it. Of course, I've never seen any footage to confirm or deny it, but I could swear I saw it. Had McCovey just got under it, that probably would have been a tape-measure shot. But that's how it is. And the Giants still haven't won a Series since.

That's why Stoneham gave us these gold money clips instead of rings, on the premise that that would be incentive for us, this great team, to win it the next year. You see, if you win the World Series you get a ring. If you don't, at least in those days, it was at the discretion of your owner as to whether he wanted to buy you rings. Stoneham opted not to. He had a jeweler in the city make these for us. So we all got gold money clips. Then, seven years ago, Bob Lurie [former Giants owner] asked why the '62 Giants didn't get rings. So we got diamond rings, finally, for 1962, from Lurie. They were able to track down all of us who played on that team, but only 18 opted because there was a $1000 investment on our part, with the Lurie group picking up the balance. I've got this ring, and another one the Giants made for me after I won the Cy Young award in '67—it's a gorgeous ring. So each of my two sons will have a ring of some description.

No question, winning that Cy Young was a great honor, because the longer I'm retired the only recognition I have anymore is that. People don't remember the tough times. They just remember, "He's the Cy Young award winner." And as I said then, as I say now, it was not the best year I pitched. It may have only been the third-or-fourth-best year, but when I needed someone to make a play they did, and when I needed a sac fly I got it. If a guy had to relieve me and get the out he did it. I had terrible luck early in my career with relievers, *terrible* luck. And we had good relievers. But if I didn't win that game myself, or leave with a huge lead, they could never hold it for me. Gaylord Perry, very early in his career, also had the same problem with the Giants. We were both snake-bit. But, hey, it comes with the territory.

I was traded to the Yankees for John Cumberland during the All-Star break in 1970. I had back problems by then. I hurt my back, which may have been related to my arm problems, in the spring of '61. I got a spasm in my back during one of those drills when they roll the balls and the pitchers run over and pick them up. I went down and didn't come up. It set me back about 10 days, and all Dark said was, "The future of the Giants is McCormick and Marichal. They will not relieve. They are starters." So what could I do? I was scheduled to make my first start of the season on a Friday night against Philadelphia, and Dark asked me to throw in the bullpen Opening Day in case he needed me. This was the same guy who said all spring that Marichal and I were the future, and that we would not relieve. Well, as fate would have it, I came in to relieve Opening Day against the Pirates at Candlestick. First pitch, Bill Virdon hit a three-run homer against the foul pole. One pitch and we lost. We had all these festivities planned after the game, in the city, for dinner, because I wasn't going to pitch until Friday. And Christ, now I was 0-1, my ERA was near infinity, my wife and I and friends were driving out of Candlestick behind a bus, and somebody in the back of the bus recognizes me. Now, he's got to tell *everybody* in the bus who's behind him in the car, and *everybody* has to get a look, and give me a nasty one in the process.

I shutout the Phillies on three hits Friday night, and went from an ERA of about 54 to under two. But that spring my back started bothering me, and every so often I'd have a problem bending over. But in 1970 it really started to bother me with the Yankees. I was trying to find ways to be comfortable, so it affected my pitching. Then I went home in the off-season, returned to spring training with the Yankees in '71 and got released, right at the end of spring training. I came back to California, wasn't home even one day and the Kansas City Royals called. It was Easter Sunday and they were in Oakland playing the A's. So they asked if I'd like to go out and throw on the side for them. I threw, went up into the press box and they signed me. I knew my back was bothering me, but it was one of those things where you think you'll be able to just twist it and everything will pop back into place. I never thought it would be bad. But I went to KC and it got progressively worse, and I was sneaking around looking for chiropractors, and not telling the club because I knew they'd probably release me.

The only way I could be comfortable was in a catching position, so you'd see me in the outfield at BP, squatting like a catcher, because when I would squeeze down it would take the pressure off my lower back. It was a mess. So Bob Lemon [manager] came up to me one day and told me I was pitching the second game of a Sunday doubleheader against the A's. Sunday morning I got up at eight, took a pain pill, another pain pill at 10 and another at noon, because I figured the game would start around four. I took another at two, and another just before I went to warm up. Well, I knew I wasn't right, but I had no pain [laughs]. The pain pills did the job. I struggled through the first inning but got out of trouble, then settled down and pitched well until the sixth or seventh inning. I was out there warming up, got the ball back from the catcher and looked at it, and it was covered with blood. I had rubbed a blister on my finger and yet I had no sensation of pain. I didn't even know it. I had never had a blister in my life. To this day I don't know how I did that.

So I called time, and that was the last pitch I ever threw [in the majors]. I went from there to the hospital, and the Royals released me. But it was on pretty amiable terms, because they had put me in the hospital in traction, and the doctors advised them that I needed more than traction. The process looked like it was going to be slow, so they released me, so I got a severance package for the rest of the year. And they suggested finding somebody as soon as I got home. So when I got back I called the Giants' team doctor, who put me in touch with a doctor at Stanford. He injected a dye into my spine and showed me the problem, that I had a herniated disc. One option was surgery, the other was complete rest, and he said if I altered my lifestyle I could probably circumvent the surgery for the rest of my life. I asked what that meant, *altering my lifestyle.* He said I shouldn't do anymore jogging and should probably minimize my golf. I said, "Why don't you just shoot me?" So we had the surgery, and I haven't had any problems since.

I went to the Coast League after the surgery. I was invited to spring training by the Giants in the spring of '72, as a non-roster player. I was still only 33. My personal opinion? I made the team. But two things happened: One, I was a potential liability because I had had back surgery; and two, Charlie Fox was the manager. He never really liked me. I was always the player rep before,

when Charlie was a coach, and I always felt that Charlie just felt threatened by me personally. But whether it was real or imagined, it was just a feeling I had. I would not have made the team as anymore than the ninth or 10th pitcher—I wasn't going to be a starter—but I had had a good enough spring, was healthy enough and had enough savvy, that I think I should've made the team.

I never had respect for Charlie, even as a coach. Take him away from the field and he was OK. But he's one of those guys who never did a damn thing in his life. He was mediocre at best. But if you ever listened to him you'd think he was just one or two votes shy of making the Hall of Fame, and just got shortchanged. And yet, I'm far enough back of a generation that I *knew* what he did. And you may shit these 20-year-old kids today, but back when he was coaching and managing we were right with you, Charlie. We knew what the hell you did and didn't do.

So they let me go, I went home and I wasn't home even a day before Chub [Feeney, general manager] called and said he was sorry it didn't work out. I told him I thought I had done better than I evidently did, but also that I had understood the liability aspects, with no hard feelings. He asked how I'd like to pitch at Phoenix [triple-A], that I was in good shape, just to see how it worked out. I told Chub I'd go there but only with a clear understanding that I'd be going with a mission, not to pitch the entire year there, but only within a certain time frame, at Chub's discretion.

So I went to Phoenix, split my first four starts or so, and then started to win. But they said it didn't look like I'd be getting called up anytime soon. So I said, "Fine," and went home. Well, I wasn't home even a day again and I got a call from Bob Quinn, who was running the Hawaii Islanders in the Coast League. He asked if I wanted to pitch there, and bring my family along. They paid me $2,000 a month, plus all my expenses for my family and me to go back and forth to the mainland, plus another $2,500 a month in cash, that nobody even knew about. So that was $4,500 plus expenses. It was such a nice package that I figured, what the hell, I was in shape, I could take my whole family to Hawaii. I made the Coast League All-Star team, pitched in the All-Star Game, and I figured for sure in September that somebody would pick me up. The Islanders were affiliated with San Diego, but I was there as a free agent, not connected with the Padres. That's the way the Islanders survived over there. They'd pick up these over-the-hill ex-major-leaguers and pay them big bucks for a year. But San Diego eventually got more involved, they [the Islanders] moved to the new Aloha Stadium, attendance fell off and the franchise finally relocated in Colorado Springs. We had a great time there, but to my knowledge there wasn't even a feeler. That was it.

It was kind of ironic to make the All-Star team my last year in pro ball. Yeah, with my background and my savvy, and my arm certainly not an issue, I think I could have continued pitching. But suddenly my career was over. I had to accept that it was the potential liability of the back. But I think I still could have pitched. I think I got through the worst part. My arm was never going to be what it was when I was 20, but I had learned to pitch with my head, and still threw hard enough to make everything else respectable.

I had already been working in the security business as a broker, so when my baseball career ended I just continued with it full-time. Now, I'm in the office-machine business, and have been for over 20 years. I enjoy the work. It's different. I've done it so long now that I know what I'm doing, and I guess you could say I do it well. But it's not like the athletic community. When we get big deals there's still not the *high,* there's not the camaraderie. I miss that. There's a certain high there. Even with the little things I do for the Giants as a guy who's been retired for 25 years, there's a recognition factor you don't get in business.

Aside from fantasy camps, I've been invited the last few years for a week, or as long as I want, to spring training to work with young pitchers. I like to sit down with these young left-handers and talk to them about pitching, and say, "OK, what are you thinking about when you're throwing the ball?" Because I'm of the opinion that most of the kids don't know how to pitch. All they want to do is throw hard. I keep trying to get them to change speeds, unless they're Nolan Ryan. And why can't they throw two change-ups in a row? They'll tell you they can't do that, but I don't believe that at all, if you've got a good change-up.

If the right opportunity ever presents itself I might like to get back in the game. As a coach, no. I've talked with the Giants about a front-office position. That would have appeal to me. I think I have a lot more to offer than just on the field. If I

could run their minor league system that would be great. Something like that. But I'm so far removed from it now. You've got to really be on top of who's doing what, yesterday and last month, and last year. Corporate ticketing is another area. I wouldn't get back into the game just to get back, but for the right job ....

I'm sorry I didn't get more involved in broadcasting a long time ago. I see the opportunities that exist now. I looked into it right after I retired, but there wasn't much available then. There weren't the ESPNs and the Sports Channels, and *all* of the existing opportunities that there are today. That's the big change.

I always had a great relationship with the press during my career. The press treated me nicely, for some of the shit that I did [laughs]. I had a pretty fiery temper. Oh, God. I'd bounce the ball off the mound to the manager when he walked out to ask for the ball. I'd come in the clubhouse and tear it up. Not all the time, but more than occasionally. In hindsight, I did some things I don't know how I got away with. I really don't. The press was always kind and cordial to me. Once I put on the uniform I was as competitive as you could be, but I guess they treated me well because I was a good story. I'd always talk with them.

THE HIGHLIGHTS OF MY CAREER
would certainly have to include winning the Cy Young award, for the recognition factor. I'm still the winningest left-hander in San Francisco Giants history, and one of only three pitchers who have won over 100 games as a Giant, along with Marichal and Perry.

I stay in touch with some of my ex-teammates, the ones who live around here, like Davenport and Tom Haller. And Ray Sadecki is one of the few I stay in touch with elsewhere because he and I roomed together for three or four years, and he's a super guy. I remember the year I came back to the Giants, in '67, and Herman Franks or somebody in the organization said, "If we can get 12 wins out of McCormick and Sadecki, we'll win the pennant." We won 34 games between us and finished a distant second.

Marichal was the greatest pitcher I ever saw in my day. No question he was the best. And Mays was the best hitter, the best all-around athlete day in and day out. For power, McCovey was certainly scary in his own right, but Mays could do so many more things. I've always said I thought Mays was the best all-around player I ever saw. The toughest hitter I ever had to face was probably someone that neither one of us ever heard of, but of the *name* players Clemente was the most difficult. There was no rhyme or reason as to what to do with him.

I don't go to the ballpark now as much as I keep telling myself I could or should. But I'm here at work during the week, and I've always been really selfish on weekends. If I play golf it's usually on Saturday, and then Sunday's always been kind of a family day. But in being selfish, sometimes I can deprive those same family members the enjoyment of going to a game with me, and talking about it and all that.

Mike McCormick (Steve Bitker)

The game has changed somewhat since I played, but not a lot. Obviously, it's an age of specialization in pitching. I have some issues with *some* of that. No question the way they use it, pitchers are probably stronger. The only issue I have is that I can't believe somebody can be expected to give only six good innings, and then can't pitch every fourth day because they're tired. *That* one I have a problem with. But the way they do it with setup men—hey, it looks like the guys that come in are fresher and stronger. But when I hear them talking about rotation and how a guy needs an extra day's rest—we pitched 250-300 innings, going every *fourth* day. Now, has the game changed that dramatically in terms of talent? I don't know. I would question that. I don't say it's any better or worse.

Otherwise, there are still only certain ways you can hold the ball, certain ways you can throw it. I think the aluminum bat and the speed gun have been bad for baseball. When you start making pitching change decisions based on a gun rather than what's really going on, I think that's wrong. And aluminum bats have taught pitchers how not to throw inside, and have taught batters that they can hit the inside pitch, whereas with a wooden bat it's shattered or broken.

I don't like the DH, although that started at the tail end of my career. I always prided myself in my hitting. That changes strategy, too, I think, from a manager's standpoint.

I don't think back on my career much anymore, but sometimes when I go to a game and get caught up emotionally when the crowd gets real excited, I think, *I've been there before.* I've been

part of that excitement. I've generated that excitement that's taken hold of the fans. That's something you don't get in the business world. You don't get that in life, I don't think. And unless you've experienced it, you can't really tell people what it is. I mean, you *have* to experience it to appreciate it. I mean, I can go to these hockey games and basketball games, and when the fans go berserk at something, all at once I'll get goosebumps because I've *been there,* and I know what that feeling is for those guys who are down there making it happen.

I fulfilled a dream that so many people have and don't even get an opportunity to do, which is something I wanted to do. I think if I could do anything over in my life, I'd love to have done the same thing, in the same period of time, but *healthy.* Because, for a long time, Lon Simmons [Giants play-by-play announcer] told me that I was the youngest player in the history of the major leagues to win 50 games. This is what Lon told me, so I can't substantiate it, that when I won my 50th game, I was the youngest player in the history of the game to do so. Because, there were a lot of comparisons back then to me being the next Warren Spahn. And then, when I hurt my shoulder, it became a matter of survival. I had a good year, a bad year, a good year, a mediocre one. But that's the only thing I'd do differently. It would be great to make the money players do today but, no, I don't have any qualms with my own era. I just would have liked to see what I could have accomplished just being healthy.

I truly loved the game when I played it. I literally would have been one of those guys who would have played for nothing. I think we all were that way. It's just that we got paid. We didn't get paid a lot, even though that's relative. I loved the competing. I'd play every day if I could, and that's probably part of the reason I hurt my arm. I'd never say no. I'd say, "Fine, give me the ball, I'll go get 'em." I loved it.

Hayward, California

ORLANDO CEPEDA

A unanimous choice for National League Rookie of the Year in 1958, at the age of 21, Orlando Cepeda took San Francisco by storm.

Adopted quickly by Giants fans as one of their own, Orlando hit .312 that maiden season, with 25 home runs and 96 RBIs. He was just getting started.

Orlando hammered 46 homers and drove in 142 runs in '61, both career highs, and then won Comeback Player of the Year honors in '66 with the Cardinals, after a knee injury sidelined him most of the '65 season, leading to one of the most controversial trades in Giants history.

Nicknamed "The Baby Bull," Cepeda won the National League Most Valuable Player award in '67 with St. Louis, and DH of the Year in '73 with the Boston. He played in nine All-Star Games, hit .300 or better nine times, hit 25 or more homeruns eight times and was inducted into the Hall of Fame in Cooperstown, July 25,1999, with a career average of .297, 379 home runs and 1365 RBIs.

Cepeda became the second member of the '58 Giants to have his number officially retired, following Willie Mays, during a pre-game ceremony at Candlestick Park, July 11, 1999.

Orlando currently works for the Giants in their Community Affairs Department. He has four sons, and lives with his wife in Suisun City, California.

MY FATHER WAS A LEGEND in Puerto Rico, and still is. I don't care how good I was as a baseball player. They say I could not compare with my father. I saw him play when I was a boy. He played with some of the greats—Josh Gibson, Satchel Paige, Cool Papa Bell. They all came to my house. Ray Dandridge, Roy Campanella. I met Campanella in 1944. Larry Doby and Monte

Irvin, too. All those people. This was in winter ball. My father didn't play in the Negro Leagues because he said it would be too hard for him to not be accepted because he was black. So he chose to play in Venezuela, the Dominican Republic, Cuba and at home in Puerto Rico instead.

I realize how special it was to meet all those great players. Very, very much so. Those baseball players were my idols. Even today, those players are special to me.

My father [called *The Babe Ruth of the Caribbean*] was a great player, a very intense player. I remember very well in 1946 when the Yankees came to Puerto Rico, and my father was playing for the Puerto Rican team. He went four-for-four against Allie Reynolds, Vic Raschi and Eddie Lopat, even though he was 44 years old. He was my idol. I remember he used to work during the week, and play on weekends. So on Sunday night he'd come home late, around midnight, because he played two games that day. I'd wait for him to come home. And still today he's my idol. He was also a great, great human being. He'd work, and

Orlando Cepeda (SF Giants)

play, and never made much money. We grew up very poor, but with a lot of dignity.

My older brother Pedro gave up baseball early on but my younger brother Jose played minor league ball in the States for Cincinnati and Detroit.

I signed with the Giants at 17, for a $500 bonus. Pedro Zorrilla signed me. He owned the Santurce team in Puerto Rico, and used to bring all those great players to Puerto Rico, like Mays, Gibson, Paige and Irvin. He was very close to Horace Stoneham and Walter O'Malley. He'd bring all the great black players to Puerto Rico. So in 1954 he went to the ballpark to watch Jose Pagan play ball. I was playing for the other team and hit a home run, a double and a single. He liked what he saw, even though I was only 16. So the following year he sent me to a spring training tryout with the Giants, in Melbourne, Florida. A month later the Giants signed me.

It was very hard at first because the Giants farm director Jack Schwarz really didn't want me. He didn't like me at all as a baseball player. He said I didn't have the tools to be a good player. Alex Pompez, a Giants scout who helped get me signed, really fought for them to keep me. So finally, the day before they were going to release me, they sent me to an independent team in Salem, Virginia, in the Appalachian League.

I remember taking a Greyhound bus from Florida to Salem. It took a couple of days. When I got there they took me to the other part of town because I was black. Right from the beginning I faced a lot of obstacles. But I didn't understand what was going on. I flew to Miami from Puerto Rico on the same plane with Roberto Clemente. He told me to be careful, to follow the rules. He was older than me and had already spent a year in the States. Felipe went through hell, too, his first year in Louisiana. Even in the big leagues, in '58, we went through hard times together.

My father died of malaria when I was in Salem. Pedro Zorrilla called me and told me my father was very ill, so I had to fly to Puerto Rico. He died while I was there, the day before I was to start my first game. When I came back, already we had played five games. So I never played. I was looking forward to playing Opening Day so much. And my father never got to see me play pro ball.

The Giants released me [after hitting .247, 1 HR, 16RBI, 93AB]. I was going to return to Puerto Rico but then the third baseman from Kokomo,

an independent team, got hurt, and they needed a 10-day replacement. So Zorrilla convinced me to go there, play 10 games, make $75 and whatever. So I went there and played for Walt Dixon, the manager. He really opened his arms for me. He told me I had tools and that I'd be a good ballplayer. He hit me eighth my first game, then cleanup my second game, because he saw the potential. His wife and son were also very nice to me. I still love the man, even today. He believed in me and I led the league in hitting [.393, 21HR, 91RBI].

The Giants re-signed me in 1956 and sent me to St. Cloud, in the class-C Northern League, where I played for Charlie Fox. I led the league in hitting again, and in homers and RBIs [.355, 26HR, 112RBI]. But even though I won the triple-crown, stole a lot of bases and played every day, I wasn't even voted the MVP for my *team*. I don't know who did the voting. Maybe Charlie did the voting. The guy who won it was a second baseman who hit .250 and didn't play every day. I was so naive. I couldn't figure out why. But I loved St. Cloud and I loved Minnesota. They loved me there, too. It was wonderful. Great folks. The whole league was wonderful.

Then I went home to Puerto Rico and hit .311 in winter ball. It used to be, and still is, a very strong caliber of play, between triple-A and the big leagues. I hit 10 home runs and told the Giants I'd like to go with them to spring training, that I thought I could play in the big leagues. They thought I was crazy and wanted to send me to A-ball. But I wanted to go to spring training. They said, "No way." I said, "What about triple-A, in Minneapolis?" They said, "No way," [that] I couldn't play triple-A either. I said, "Let me go to triple-A and see what I could do." They said, "No way, no way."

Finally, I convinced them. They told me they'd send me a class-A contract for $350 a month, that I could go to spring training with the triple-A team, but that I wouldn't make the Minneapolis club, that I'd have to go back to A-ball and that somebody else would [already] be playing first base there, and that I might [then] have to go back to C-ball. But I knew I could do the job, and when the triple-A first baseman went in the Army Reserve, they *had* to play me.

My English was still very poor in those days. It was very difficult, particularly in restaurants. I'd memorize the name of one dish, like a hamburger, or steak and eggs, and eat the same dish every day for three weeks. But at least I *could* eat in the restaurants in Minnesota, in '56 and '57. My first year of pro ball, in Virginia, I had to stay in the car so my teammates could get food for me.

Even in the big leagues, in '58, we had difficulties in St. Louis, Cincinnati, Pittsburgh and Chicago. We stayed in the same hotel but we couldn't eat in the nice restaurants. We had to eat either in our rooms or in the black section of town. I had great white teammates then, like Johnny Antonelli, Hank Sauer and Jim Davenport, but nobody ever spoke on our behalf in those restaurants.

But San Francisco was great. And I believe in all my 17 years in the big leagues, 1958 is the one I hold dearest to my heart. Because, in '58, when I came to spring training as a rookie, Willie Mays told me I'd love San Francisco, that it was a great city. Even though I had never been here before, Puerto Ricans who used to play in the Coast League always talked about how wonderful a city it was to play ball in. So I really fell in love with the city. And '58 stands out in my memory as a player. I recall my first game here at Seals Stadium. My first hit was a home run. Right from there the people showed they cared for me. Plus, I was lucky. I did well right from the beginning.

I didn't have the disadvantage Willie Mays had, in that sense. When Willie came here the press built him up so high. The fans figured that every time he came to the plate he'd hit a home run, or steal a base, and never make an error. And when he'd strike out or whatever, I was doing well. And I'd chat with the fans, and they liked that. I was in the right place at the right time.

I even remember my first spring training game against Cleveland, in Tucson. I had a single, double and a homer. It was funny because the Gi-

Orlando Cepeda (SF Giants)

ants didn't give me a big league contract. They gave me a triple-A contract. So spring training was like a tryout for me. And on the first day, Bill Rigney told us the regulars would take infield, so I stood back. But right from the beginning he told me I'd be his first baseman. That really motivated me. It was a great experience.

I remember we came north from spring training on a Sunday night, then worked out at Seals Stadium on Monday. I recall walking down to the ballpark and seeing so many Latin people. A lot of Puerto Ricans used to live in the Mission District, where Seals was. That really appealed to me. And the fans were so close. I made so many friends just walking from the dugout to home plate, people who are still my friends now. I used to say, "How ya doin'? See you tonight," because they were my friends and they were right there.

I lived with Felipe and Ruben that first year, in Daly City. I used to go every Thursday night to the *Copacabana* to hear Latin music, to the *Blackhawk* every Thursday and Sunday nights for jazz, with Mongo Santa Maria and Willie Bobo. I met John Coltrane there, also Miles Davis, Cannonball Adderly and Cal Tjader. It used to be my second home. And one morning when I left the *Copacabana* around 12:45, I took Broadway to the freeway with my girlfriend, and saw so many people outside the *Jazz Workshop.* I asked her to take me there one night, which she did but I couldn't get in because I was only 20 years old. But they let me in anyway and put me in the corner. Wes Montgomery was playing that night. After that, both the *Blackhawk* and the *Jazz Workshop* were my second homes. Felipe and I used to go out together all the time those first two years in San Francisco, before we both got married. We used to go the *Blackhawk* together to see Mongo.

There were six of us Latins on the Giants in '58. We were all very close. Ruben was the leader. Valmy was by himself more, very quiet. But Ruben was the veteran and he was the leader. He was my hero in Puerto Rico. I recall in 1954 when Ruben pitched in the World Series. That really helped motivate me to become a big league player.

Opening day in '58 was the number one day in my career. It will always stand out because it meant my dream came true. It's funny because when I hit a home run that day off Don Bessent, I passed second base and thought to myself, *I've been here before.* And I recall when Gil Hodges came to first base, he said, "Hi," to me. And Duke Snider, too. Hard to forget.

Bill Rigney played a very important part in my life. He really guided me in '58, '59 and '60. He showed me confidence. He knew me for some reason. He knew when to sit me out for one game. He knew me so well. Even when he fined me he was right. I was 20 years old and made a lot of rookie mistakes. I used to run through the signs. Many times Willie Mays would have a base stolen and I'd swing at a bad ball, and Rigney would go crazy [laughs]. I don't blame him, though. He let me know I did this, or I did that. He was great to me. He helped me a lot.

It was really an amazing year. We had a great team. We were in first place a long time [through July], and with so many rookies like myself, Jim Davenport and Willie Kirkland. Being named Rookie of the Year was a great honor. Nothing like that surprised me, though, because I had so much confidence. I knew I would do well. But '58 sure stands out in my memory.

I got off to a great start in '59 as well. I was hitting .359 in early July when Rigney said to me one morning, "Orlando, we're gonna bring McCovey up from Phoenix. He's hitting .380 or .390." And I knew what Willie could do because we grew up in the system together. So Rigney asked me if I'd mind playing third base or left field. He said it was up to me. I said to go ahead, that I'd do anything for the team.

I played four games at third base but I was too young to make that kind of switch. I was only 21 and had so many people telling me I shouldn't do it, that *I* was the first baseman. I didn't care for third base. Then I went to left field. Even that was rough. Now, I can deal with it, but then, I kept asking, "Why take me off first base?" I could have done better if I had put my mind to it. It didn't help that Ruben got traded to Philadelphia before the season. That was very, very hard for me. I loved Ruben so much. He and his wife Maria used to guide me.

We moved to Candlestick in 1960 and when I first got to the ballpark I said, "What is *this?*" We worked out that first day there, and I remember it was 397 feet to left-center, 420 to center, 397 to right-center, and *so* cold and *so* windy. I said, "Now, how are we going to play in *this* ballpark?" I never learned to like it. But I learned not to complain about it. Mays never complained. McCovey never complained. I knew it was hard to play there but I had to just go ahead and do it. But I missed Seals Stadium very much. Seals was cool, too, but not like Candlestick.

My best year as a hitter came in 1961, with Mays and McCovey hitting in front of me. To drive in that many runs [142] and hit that many home runs [46], playing in that park, I believe it would have been 65 or 70 home runs in any other ballpark. I also hit .311, and thought I should have been the league MVP, but finished second to Frank Robinson. That was very disappointing.

One of the most important at-bats in my career came in the final playoff game against the Dodgers in '62. I hit a sacrifice fly in the ninth inning to tie the game, 4-4. I loved being at the plate in such a situation, with the bases loaded and the pennant on the line. I remember the first pitch was very high and I swung at it. I said, "*Orlando.*" And I called time. I told Felipe [on second base], "I've *got* to do it." I told myself, "You've *got* to do it." So I hit a line drive to right field and Frank Howard made a great play. He reached up and caught it. Remember, he was so tall. But the tying run scored and we won the game.

I'm still surprised I didn't get a chance to hit in the World Series against the Yankees, in the ninth inning of that seventh game. I saw Ralph Houk and Ralph Terry later on, and they both told me they'd do it again the same way, that they'd pitch to McCovey with first base open [McCovey lined out to end the series, with runners at second and third]. Ralph Terry told me he knew that I'd get him because I just missed him a couple of times before. Yeah.

That winter I hurt my right knee lifting weights. I made a huge mistake by not telling anyone. I didn't say anything because they kept saying Latin ballplayers were lazy, that we faked injuries, that we didn't want to play. So I didn't tell anybody, while hoping I could get well. But that was a huge mistake. Alvin Dark, really, is the one who made those remarks. He had a poor relationship with me. He didn't like Latin people. He didn't like black people. Also, being 24 or 25, instead of going out and playing *my* game, I let that talk affect me. Many times I didn't want to go to the ballpark. I missed Rigney very much. They don't realize how we Latin ballplayers felt, how we were in a strange country with a different language, things like that. They never dialogued. They never sat down and talked with us.

I had knee surgery after the '64 season, then missed most of '65. And I was traded to the Cardinals in May of '66. I knew I was about to be traded because a friend of mine in St. Louis called me the week before we went to play there, and told me of the rumors in the newspaper that I was going to St. Louis. As a matter of fact, I wanted to go *anyplace* because Herman Franks [manager] didn't want me, and said in '65 that I didn't want to play for him. So when we got there on a Friday night the Cardinal team doctor checked my knee. But the funny thing is, I gave him the *left* knee instead, the *good* knee. Instead of giving him the bad knee, I gave him the good knee. He said, "You're in great shape, man."

I was 11-for-15 that weekend in St. Louis and hit a grand-slam. It was funny. Sunday, after the game, when I saw Herman coming to me, I figured he was going to say, "Orlando, great series." Instead, he said, "You've been traded." And just before that, Juan [Marichal] told me, "They're not going to trade you, man. No way. You're going to stay here, with the Giants."

I was devastated by the trade [for Ray Sadecki], leaving San Francisco, which I loved so much. If they trade you in the winter, when you have time to think about it, to prepare mentally, that's one thing. But when they trade you in the middle of the year it's hard, very hard. One thing about me, though, is that I forget easily. Good or bad, I just [snaps fingers]. I joined the Cardinals on Sunday night. [Tim] McCarver told me to forget my sadness, that I would help them win the pennant, and they showed they cared for me. It was the best team I ever played for, teammate-wise. *Everybody.* McCarver, Gibson, Flood, Brock, Javier, Maris—still today we are all very close.

I could play my Latin music in the clubhouse there. Nobody bothered me. Alvin Dark wouldn't let me do that with the Giants. He wouldn't let me carry my record player with me. One day I was coming to the airport and Eddie Logan [clubhouse man] said I couldn't bring my record player. I said if I couldn't bring my record player I would just stay home. I didn't hurt anybody. I just played music.

I recall the headlines during spring training in '67, McCarver saying, "We're going to win because this year we have Orlando from the beginning." He was right. We beat the Red Sox in seven games, and I won the MVP [.325, 25HR, 111RBI].

The Cardinals traded me to Atlanta [for Joe Torre] a couple of days before the '69 season started. It was very hard, once again. I don't know why they traded me. Bing Devine [general manager] traded me, Flood, everybody. But I enjoyed the Braves very much, playing with Hank [Aaron], Felipe, [Felix] Millan, and I loved Paul Richards [general manager]. A great man. He knew the game. He believed in talent. If you had it you could play for him. And he liked Latin ballplayers. Great town, too. It's funny—I used to say, "If they trade me to Atlanta I'm going to retire." But when they traded me there I fell in love with the city. I thought I'd retire because it was the South, that I wouldn't like what was going on there. But when you play there it's different. I loved playing there. It's not such a great baseball town but I enjoyed playing there.

One of my very best years in baseball was 1973 with Boston, when I played on one leg and the Boston fans cheered me with every pitch. They really liked me there. It's funny—when they called me from Boston about DHing, I didn't know what they were talking about. Because, after Finley released me from the A's, I said the hell with baseball. So when Boston called me I didn't know the rule but I said, "Sure, I'm OK. I'm ready, yeah." It was a hell of a year [.289, 20HR,

86RBI]. Eddie Kasko was the best manager in the big leagues I played for, outside of Bill Rigney. Because, right from the beginning, he told me, "Orlando, you know how to take care of yourself." He treated me like a man. He was a fine, fine human being. He treated everybody the same. He was tough but a good person. He knew the game. I started that season 0-for-11, then hit a home run off Sparky Lyle to beat the Yankees. The Boston fans went crazy. They were like the fans at Seals Stadium—very close, really supportive.

But the next spring I got released. I don't know why. I was in great shape and worked all winter. I was in better shape than the year before. I was running much better. I did well at the plate. But Darrell Johnson [new manager] told the owner that with all the money he was paying me, Luis Aparicio and Bob Bolin, he had three younger guys in camp who could do even better, and cost less. The owner agreed.

Then I lost the desire for the game. If I stayed in Boston I would have felt differently. It was hard to leave the game, though, very hard. When you play ball forever like I did, and then stop, you start missing baseball the next time you come to spring training. It was very hard for three or four years. I couldn't cope with it. Even though I left the game with money and I was going to get into some business, leaving the game left me with an emptiness in my life. I divorced my first wife and didn't know what to do with myself. And when your mind is not occupied, other things take their place. A lot of players drink. I used to smoke a little weed but I was never a drug freak.

The hardest part of the drug arrest [a marijuana bust at San Juan Airport, in '75, for which Cepeda served 10 months in federal prison] was being treated as an outcast in my own country. Going to jail was a *relief.* At least I was at peace with myself. From 1975 to '78 it was incredible. I can see here in this country people going through things and making mistakes, like we all do. But it can't compare with what I went through in Puerto Rico. It's hard to believe that human beings can be so cruel, for no reason. It was very hard.

Now, it's changed. Very much so. It changed completely because *I* finally changed. Before, because they used to be hard on me, I used to be hard on everybody. I used to say bad things. But the only way I could show these people that they were wrong was to be an easygoing person, and also through my actions. So I did that.

I changed when I started practicing Buddhism, in 1984. I had left Puerto Rico because there was no hope for me there. Everything started to change for me when I moved to Los Angeles because I got guidance. People said, "When you change, everybody else is going to change. Don't blame everybody. Blame yourself." It was hard for me to take that. But the more I practiced Buddhism the more I could see that as the truth. Because, sometimes when things don't go our way, we blame everybody else. We have to look at ourselves first. So when I finally changed, everybody changed.

I was introduced to Buddhism by Rudy Regalado, a drummer who used to play with Herbie Hancock. It was easy for me because I didn't have an escape. I was looking for an escape, for somebody or something, so I could challenge myself. You know, at the beginning with Buddhism, you have to be educated, you have to read, go to meetings, to orientation. Through all of that I knew that this was what I was looking for.

Thirteen years later every day remains a new day. I'm getting where I want to be. Every morning I give thanks that I'm living back in San Francisco, which I love so much, and working for the Giants, who I love so much. And thanks that things are going so well for me. My four kids are doing well. So I'm very pleased with myself, with my life.

I didn't go to a big league game for so many years, until 1987. I was very defensive. I didn't want to go to the ballpark. I didn't want to face reality. I credit Lawrence Hyman [San Francisco publisher] with convincing me to move to the Bay Area from LA. He convinced me to come to the ballpark so I could see for myself how much the people care for me. He's the one who got me back up here. And he was right.

He brought me to the ballpark. They introduced me on the scoreboard, people stood and cheered, and he said, "See how much people love you here." Then he talked to the Giants about hiring me, and finally they did, in '89. I do community relations work now, which I enjoy very, very much. I can talk to the kids and tell them what I went through. People are people, and they talk and talk and talk. But they've never been through it. I've been though it.

I never wanted to go to the Hall of Fame because of sympathy, but because I deserved to go there. I always believed I'd make it. I always thought it was just a matter of time. I learned from my practice of Buddhism that things always work out the way they're supposed to. It's just a matter of time. Staying calm helped me. If you try to force the issue, nothing will happen. When the time is right, then things come true. But when I got the call from Cooperstown, I lost my mind. I broke down and cried. It's hard to explain the feeling, really. It was incredible. I had been ready for this for 17 years. I called my wife upstairs with the news. It was wonderful. A great feeling.

The trip to Cooperstown for the induction ceremony was incredible. My life, from the time I got the call all the way to now, has been incredible. It changed my life. Sure, it did. It is amazing what the name *Hall of Fame* means to people. Everywhere I go, I am introduced as a Hall of Famer. It's a great feeling. And I'm so glad it happened when it did. I didn't want to wait too long for this. I wanted to get in the Hall of Fame when I could still enjoy it, when I could still enjoy going to Cooperstown, when I could still enjoy traveling elswhere and meeting people and being introduced as a Hall of Famer. It's truly amazing.

I was one of the pioneer Latin ballplayers but I don't think a lot of young Latin players today know what we did for the game. Maybe in Puerto Rico they do. But in the Dominican Republic George Bell once told me, "I don't know who you are." In Latin countries history does not play a big role. It could be better in Puerto Rico, too. I'd like for people to remember me as one of the pioneers of Latin baseball in the big leagues, with Minnie Minoso, Roberto Clemente and others. And that I learned to be a man as a ballplayer, and after, because I've done everything. I went up. I went down. I came back up.

San Francisco, California

RUBEN GOMEZ

Known as much for a fiery temper as for possessing one of the game's best screwballs, Ruben Gomez will forever be a major part of San Francisco Giants history for shutting out Don Drysdale and the Los Angeles Dodgers, 8-0,

April 15, 1958, at Seals Stadium, in the first major league game ever played on the West Coast.

A native of Puerto Rico, Ruben was part of the first big wave of Latin players to star in the majors in the 1950s. He won 13 games as a rookie with the Giants in '53, and 17 more for the World Champion Giants in '54, in addition to beating Cleveland, 3-1, in game three of the World Series. Gomez won 15 games for the Giants in '57, and 10 more for the '58 Giants, after which he was traded along with batterymate Valmy Thomas to the Phillies for Jack Sanford.

Long after his big league days were over, Gomez continued pitching, effectively at that, in both the Mexican League and the Puerto Rican Winter League, not hanging up his glove until he was 52 years old. His final major league numbers, over 10 seasons, include 76 wins, 63 complete games and 15 shutouts.

A zero handicap on the links, Ruben currently teaches golf half the year outside San Juan, and the

Ruben Gomez (SF Giants)

other half north of Montreal, Quebec. He has four children.

I WAS AN OUTFIELDER when I entered high school. But they needed a pitcher, so I went to the mound and started pitching, and the coach told me he'd teach me how to pitch. I liked that because it was a challenge, because then they all had to wait for *me* for the game to begin—if I don't throw the ball, nobody moves. So I said, "Now I'm gonna be the king," and I had a beautiful arm. I used to lift weights, and that's one of the reasons why I never hurt my arm. And I pitched professionally for 31 years, until I was 52 years old.

Ruben Gomez shakes the hand of Orlando Cepeda, after throwing a six-hit shutout against the Dodgers opening day, April 15, 1958; other Giants pictured are shortstop Daryl Spencer (left), second baseman Danny O'Connell (right); Dodgers are Gino Cimoli (left) and first-base coach Greg Mulleavy. (SF Chronicle).

My pro career began in 1949 in Bristol, Connecticut, in what was then called class-B. My second year there I had a little problem with the manager. He used expressions like, "If you don't pitch good, I'm gonna send you back to Puerto Rico on a banana boat." He was kidding, of course, but I was raised in a very strict family. My father was an Englishman, my mother Puerto Rican. We had many friends around us from the States. And I didn't go to play ball in the States to hear expressions like that. One day I got mad and smashed the owner's desk with a bat when he wouldn't pay me. So they sent me to Canada.

I played there for two years, in St. Jean, then was sold to the Yankee organization and joined the Kansas City Blues, in triple-A. I won my first game there, got two doubles and then they didn't pitch me for a month. It was a tough time then for colored ballplayers in the States. I knew I had the ability.

So I got an offer to play for Licey in the Dominican Republic. I said, "I'll be there tomorrow." I took a plane and flew over there without permission. Then they called me from KC and told me I was suspended. For *life.* So I bought my own contract, from Licey, for $5000, became a free agent and then signed with the Giants. Signed by Tom Sheehan. They asked me how much I wanted. I said, "Fifteen-thousand, but give me a chance to pitch in the big leagues. Then don't pay me that unless I make the team."

I remember in spring training I wore number 73 on my uniform. I thought, oh my God, that's a *football* number. But I remember the first game I pitched was against Cleveland. The bases were loaded, with Larry Doby, Al Smith and Luke Easter coming to bat. And I struck out all three, after starting Doby with a three-oh count. So the next day when I came to the ballpark, I had number 28. I said, "Oh, I *made* it," and called my wife and told her, "Now we're gonna eat good, baby."

You see, I believe in Ruben Gomez. Now, I'm in golf. And one day you're gonna see me on the Senior Tour. I teach six months a year here, the other six at a club about 100 miles north of Quebec City. Ever since I retired from baseball, 18 years ago. I hit about a thousand balls a day to stay in shape. Have a zero handicap. Hit 250 to 260 yards off the tee, dead center.

I won 13 games my rookie year with the Giants, in '53, but winning in the big leagues was no different than winning in Puerto Rico. Because the competition in Puerto Rican winter ball was just as good, even better, and I'll tell you why. We had a lot of good Latin players here, and they were fast. Plus, we had the top American players come over. So every time I pitched, every four days, I threw against good hitters. But in the big leagues sometimes I faced good hitters, sometimes mediocre ones. Over here I faced the best hitters all the time. Plus, I had to pitch my best here because my people were always watching me, and I had to show them how good Ruben Gomez was.

When I first heard the Giants might move to San Francisco, in 1957, I felt sad, because I liked my neighborhood in New York, with so many good friends. Then, suddenly, I said, "Oh, my God, I have to go somewhere else and start all over again?" I felt like I was becoming a gypsy, moving and moving and moving and moving. And, I wondered, when am I going to stay still in one place? At least I was still with the ball club, but to me it was not a good move. Because there was such a great rivalry in New York between the Dodgers and Giants, and I felt you couldn't take that dream somewhere else without the same people watching who grew up with you.

But the welcome we got in San Francisco was really beautiful. It was like a dream, like the *Carnival* in Brazil. And I liked that old ballpark in San Francisco much better than the new one they built. I liked Seals because it was short down the lines, so it was easier to fool the hitters. Because when a good hitter stands at the plate and looks to the fences, he thinks, *I'll hit it out of the ballpark,* because he wants to look good. Then, because I was a fox on the mound, I thought, I'll give him a pitch to hit

Ruben Gomez throws first pitch in SF Giants/LA Dodgers history to Gino Cimoli, at Seals Stadium, 4-15-58. Catcher is Valmy Thomas; umpire is Jocko Conlan. (Note fan standing in first row behind screen, with camera. That is Dick Dobbins, whose own photo of first pitch also appears on page 30). Pitch was called strike. (Dick Dobbins)

close to where he wants it, but not quite where he can hit it out. That's why it was easy to pitch in the Polo Grounds and Seals, if you were a good pitcher, as long as you had control. You see, in every big ballpark they hit a lot of home runs. In small ballparks it's harder, because a good pitcher can make a hitter swing at a lot of bad pitches.

I shut out the Dodgers that first game on the West Coast and that made it special, but it really wasn't one of my best games. I pitched my best games against Milwaukee in those days. That was a great ball club— Aaron, Mathews, Adcock, all those guys. And Spahn and Burdette. You had to be at your best to beat that ball club.

We had a hell of a ball club in San Francisco, too, that first year. And we were close, all of us. We were taught to be close by Leo Durocher. Leo would not settle for a ballplayer who wanted to be alone. No way. Leo was a great influence, even when he wasn't there. One time with Leo in spring training, in '55, we were playing in Lubbock, Texas. And we couldn't stay together after the game. I was so mad because I had to sleep in a room so filthy that it was unbelievable. It was so filthy that I had to sleep with my wet uniform on. And I was so mad that I decided to tell Leo that I wouldn't be back for spring training the next year, that I'd fly straight to New York instead.

The next day we got up and rode on the train, but I couldn't sleep there because it was so noisy. Soon we arrived at another hotel in Texas, where we could stay together. So I stayed late in that hotel on purpose and came late to the bus. We were supposed to leave at one o'clock but I showed up at 1:15. When I got on the bus everyone started clapping sarcastically. So I said, "Wait, I want to say something. Willie, come over here. Hank, Monte, come over here [Mays, Thompson and Irvin]. This is for the *white* ballplayers only. I hope all of you guys, tomorrow morning when you get up, you're *black* and you wind up in a place like the *hole* I had to sleep in the day before yesterday, so you'll know how I feel." And when Leo heard that he called Horace Stoneham and said, "From now on we won't play anyplace where we can't stay together." Leo was a special guy. He made you believe in yourself.

THERE'S SO MUCH TALK about cold weather in San Francisco but I couldn't pitch in *New York* in April. It was so cold. They just left me in the clubhouse. I would drink coffee and look through the window, and whenever they said it was time for me to warm up, I said, "Oh, my God." I was so cold all the time. Here, I can swim in the ocean in *February,* but there I was freezing.

In San Francisco, at Candlestick, I thought I was gonna *die.* Candlestick was even colder than New York. Seals was much warmer. And at Seals, it was like you were in the same kitchen together with all the fans, eating at the same table, because it was so intimate. Everybody was so close you could look at their faces and remember them. At Candlestick everybody was so far away. It was sad they had to tear down Seals.

When I go to New York now, I stand where the Polo Grounds was and I close my eyes, and I can see the ballpark. I can see where I enter, where I pick up the train, *everything.* I'm a dreamer, man.

Last year I was playing golf at Dorado [outside San Juan], and I started talking to this guy and I said his face looked familiar. He said no, but I said, "I met you at Seals Stadium. There was a bakery across the street from the ballpark, and I met you over there." So he got on the phone and called a guy from the same family that owned the bakery and said, "Guess who I'm with right now?" He took a picture with me, and now you can go to San Francisco, to the same neighborhood where Seals was, and you can see a picture of me with that same guy in Puerto Rico, on the wall of the *Double Play Bar* on 16th Street, near where the bakery used to be.

My first daughter was born in San Francisco. I lived in a house on San Jose Avenue, with Or-

lando. It used to get so foggy over there. I'd say, "Oh, my God, it's coming *again."*

I used to go to a Mexican nightclub in the Mission, and to a jazz club with Orlando where Mongo Santa Maria would play the drums. And I used to visit Sausalito a lot, to eat. It's like Piñones, here in Puerto Rico, with great places to eat, right on the water.

I played a lot of golf, even back then. As a matter of fact, I hold a record. I'm the only ballplayer ever to be thrown out of a golf course the same day I was invited to join. The club pro threw me out because I broke a guy's rib with a club. That first day I played there he welcomed me personally, and said all the new Giants were welcome to play there, anytime. I said, "Oh, beautiful." But there was a shooting gallery close to the course. Made me nervous. I was afraid I might get struck with a bullet and wouldn't be able to pitch, and represent Puerto Rico. I had a craziness about Puerto Rico, to represent Puerto Rico, to do well for the Puerto Ricans. Like an *independista.* Like an overdose of my country, you know?

So my first day there on the course I get hit in the leg. I thought it was a bullet. But when I looked back I saw it was from a guy with a fairway wood about a hundred yards behind me. That's stupid, you know? So I picked up an iron and walked back to him and said, "How long you been playing golf?" He said, "Two years." And I whacked him right there. If he said it was his first time, I would have understood. But it was two years with this guy, so I whacked him in the chest and broke his rib. They took the guy to the hospital, and the club pro came up to me and said, "I don't want you here no more." So it's a record [laughs]. It took me about 30 minutes to go in, and 30 to come right back out.

Years later I was at a tournament, and the same club pro—I think it was Ken Venturi—was there giving tips. So I went up to him and said, "Hello," and asked how he was doing. He looked at me and said my face was familiar. I said, "Sure, I'm familiar." He kept looking at me. I said, "I've got a record with you. I met you years ago, and just like with a woman, it was a quick good-bye." And then he said, "Oh, *you're* the one. How are you doing, Ruben? My God, you've got a bad temper." [laughs]

It was true. I was shutting out Milwaukee in 1956 and had an oh-two count on Joe Adcock. I decided to brush him back, then come back with a curve. But he was guessing outside and stepped right into the pitch. So as he was walking toward first base, he called me a mother[expletive] Puerto Rican. I called him a mother[expletive] American. He said he was gonna rip my head off. I said, "You and who else?" He cursed me again, so I threw the ball at him and hit him in the ribs. He went down and the whole *dugout* came after me. I ran into our dugout and grabbed a bat but our clubhouse guy took it away, so I picked up an icepick we had sitting around because of the heat. By that time, Adcock was coming after me. I said, *"Come on,"* but he saw the ice pick and stopped.

At that point, Jocko Conlan [umpire] said, "Ruben, you're not gonna hurt me with that, are you?" I said, "No, not you. *Him.* Adcock. I'm gonna give him a second navel. He's tough, yeah, but let's see how tough he is now." So Conlan said, "Give me the icepick. If you don't give it to me you'll be suspended for life. And you have children, Ruben." And when he said that, I said OK, because I have four children and I love them dearly. So I said to Adcock, "Joe, I'm gonna give the icepick to Jocko, but I'm gonna crack your head next time I face you." We were both thrown out. The funny thing is, the next time the Braves came to the Polo Grounds I escorted Adcock from the stadium to their team bus, because our fans were all over him.

I remember a game against Pittsburgh, in '58. I was pitching against Mazeroski and had an oh-two count on him. In that situation I used to brush the guy back, then come right back with a curve. But I hung the curve, and he hit that ball so far into left field [foul]. So then I decided to brush him back again, but I came too close. The ball went behind him. You see, when you throw behind a guy it's usually meant to hurt him. But this pitch tailed away. And the umpire warned me.

I was the first hitter in our half of the inning, and Vernon Law threw at me. But the umpire didn't say a thing. I said, "Well, I guess it's because of my color again." Then the umpire called time, and Danny Murtaugh came out of the dugout and said, "We're gonna get you right here," pointing at my head. And this was the only time in the history of my career when I did something filthy. I put my hand on my head and screamed back, "You're gonna hit me here?" Then Murtaugh charged me, and I swung my bat at him. Thanks to God he ducked, and I took the hat right off his head with the swing. I would have cracked his head open. I'd have been in jail until now. So when he fell and realized I had swung the bat at him, he started running away, screaming, "This guy's *crazy.*" Then somebody else came at me, Orlando went after him with a bat, Willie tackled Orlando and then everyone cooled off.

Next time up I blooped a single to right. Then I looked over at the Pirates' dugout and made an obscene gesture at Murtaugh. Oh, my God. They were all ready to come after me again [laughs].

Actually, I used to throw at Clemente a lot. Then I would wait for him to go eat. Clemente and me, it was like a *marriage.* He would walk away from me, and I was like a man after a woman. He'd go to a restaurant, I'd go there, he'd get up and leave, and before the night was over we were eating together. He'd say, "Ruben, you're gonna hurt me someday, and then I'm gonna kill you." I'd say, "Listen, we're brothers. In a game I may try to kill you, but here we're brothers." I used to deck him a lot. But then we'd end up the night eating together. Every time I'd deck him we'd have to go through five restaurants and taxis, until we'd finish eating together. It sounds crazy but it was true.

Back in Pittsburgh the fans were all over me, yelling, throwing things. But I loved that, because by doing that they'd help me become a better pitcher, because the only way I could shut them up was by pitching.

We had a chance in '58 to win the pennant. We played hard. But baseball was written a long time ago, like the Bible. I don't care how long you play, you have to go through the same things—bunt, hit-and-run, bad streaks, hot streaks, managerial changes, good managers with losing teams, bad managers with winning teams.

I hurt my knee in '58. Tore cartilage. I didn't say anything because then guys would start bunting and hurt my leg even more. I took injections. I was a hell of a fielder before that. But then it took me about four years to learn how to come off the mound and be effective again. When they started bunting on me, I'd throw at them to make them mad, so they'd forget about bunting. Then they started calling me, *The Butcher of the Caribbean.* I had so many fights [laughs]. I said, "If you're gonna break my leg, I'm gonna break your head." Oh, yeah. I had a nasty reputation on the field, but when I came off of it I was beautiful. But on the field, that was part of who I was. I liked that. If the hitters were always aware I might hit them, I had them on their toes.

As a matter of fact, Aaron hit only one home run off me in his career. And he hit a lot of pitchers, man. But he knew Ruben Gomez, you know, so every time he was on his toes with me because he knew I would deck him. Clemente was the same way. It was the same with all the good hitters. Every time Musial faced me I had that screwball working, then I had that terrible ball coming at his head. And then when I'd come to bat they'd throw at me. They hit me 24-25 times a year but you never saw me charge a pitcher. I knew how to take it, too.

I was traded after the '58 season. They called me and told me they were going to trade me to Philadelphia, but that they'd bring me right back. They told me, "Ruben, we want you, but they want you and Valmy Thomas now for Jack Sanford, so we're gonna make the deal, then bring you right back. We're gonna try to get you back." So I went over there and started pitching, the Giants tried to get me back, but Philly said, no.

I enjoyed pitching for the Phillies because I finally got a chance to pitch against the Giants. And the first guy I decked was Willie Mays. You can ask him. Oh, yeah. He said, *"Hey!"* I said, "No, I don't want to hear anything." And I used to room with Willie Mays. The first ballplayer I hit in my life was my brother, and he was so strong he used to beat me up all the time. But I still decked him.

Pitching is so bad nowadays. I go to the ballpark and I bet beers with my friends. I say, he's gonna throw that, then he's gonna throw this, then he's so stupid the guy's gonna hit a home run. Then, boom—*home run*. Pitchers nowadays throw a fastball right down the middle on an oh-two count, and the guy hits a home run. In my day, look at my record, how many bases-on-balls I had. I used to walk eight or nine guys a game and *still* throw a shutout. It means I'd squeeze the batter. The hardest thing to do is get the first two strikes on a hitter. But nowadays, you get those first two strikes and you let him off the hook.

When I was a pitching coach here, I'd teach a guy to have control and be wild. Effectively wild, on purpose. Throw close to a hitter and he will never challenge you. Like Clemens and Guzman with Toronto, and Pedro Martinez with Boston. As a matter of fact, I helped teach

Guzman that. I have so much knowledge about pitching. I can teach a guy how to pitch and win, with nothing more than a fastball, without having to throw a curve. All he has to do is be deceptive.

I PITCHED IN THE American League with Cleveland and Minnesota in 1962, after going 8-0 at Jacksonville [triple-A]. I drove my '53 Chevy all the way to Cleveland, and when I arrived they asked me to pitch BP. I didn't mind. But then, in the seventh inning, they asked me to warm up in the bullpen. I walked from the pen to the dugout and said, "Listen, if you think I'm gonna drive all the way from Florida, pitch BP without any sleep, then pitch in the game, you're out of your mind."

Later, I was pitching against Baltimore and leading Robin Roberts, 2-0, in the seventh inning when my arm popped. I called for time, threw a couple of practice pitches and then the manager, Mel McGaha, came out and asked what happened. I told him my arm popped, but that I threw after that and felt good. He said he was going to take me out. I thought, well, he's the manager. He brought in a reliever who lost the game. That night I talked to my wife, and she said she heard McGaha claim on the radio that I asked to be taken out. So I waited until three o'clock in the morning, knocked on his door and woke him up. I told him if he didn't have enough guts to admit his own mistake when he took me out, then I wanted to be traded. So I left Cleveland because of my temper. They traded me to Minnesota.

Then with the Twins, I cheated on my wife. I went out with a girl. A *white* girl. When my wife was in Puerto Rico. I told her never to meet me at the airport, but one time she did. So I said to myself, if she is woman enough to go to bed with me, I am man enough to go out of the airport with her. But after that, I got a call from the team owner, Calvin Griffith. He said, "Ruben, Minnesota or the girl?" I said, "Well, I love baseball, but I have more fun with the girl. I'll stay with the girl." So the Twins got rid of me at the end of the season. Because I chose the girl.

I went to the Mexican League after that and pitched there until 1967, when Philadelphia called me back. I was 40 years old. Gene Mauch was still the manager. He came to see me pitch winter ball in Puerto Rico and told me he needed a relief pitcher. I told him I knew guys I could recommend. But he said no, he wanted me. I said, "Gene, I left you a long time ago, remember? I can't play for you." But he said, "No, I'm a

Ruben Gomez (Steve Bitker)

different manager now, I'm gonna let you pitch your way." I said, "All right, but I'm gonna pitch my way."

So we went to spring training and Mauch asked me to throw nothing but screwballs. I said sure, but even though I was getting guys out, I wasn't working on my fastball at all. Then the season started. We were playing in Pittsburgh, and had a clubhouse meeting on how to pitch to Clemente. They asked me and I said, "Fastball down the middle." Mauch asked if I were serious. I said yeah. So, we were in the seventh inning with the bases loaded, and Mauch brought me in to face Clemente. He said, "Let's see your fastball now." I threw only five pitches in the bullpen. Clay Dalrymple, the catcher, called for a screwball. I said no. He called again for a screwball. I said no. Again he called, and again. I said no. Then I said, "Clay come over here. You don't have any other fingers? I want to throw him a fastball."

He said, "You can't throw a fastball to Clemente with the bases full." I said, "You're God damn right I'm gonna throw it. If you sit back there and call for the screwball again, I'm gonna throw the fastball, OK?" So he called for the screwball and I threw the fastball, right on the corner—strike one. Then strike two on the corner. Then I threw another fastball at his head. Then another at his head. He went down both times. Then I struck him out on a fastball outside. When I came to the dugout Mauch said to me, "If you're gonna throw what you please, I'm gonna send you to the minors." I said, "See you later. Good-bye."

That night he told us curfew was at 11 p.m. We finished the game at 10:30. I didn't come to my room at the hotel until three o'clock, though I wasn't doing anything wrong. And he was sitting in a chair in front of my door. I said, "Hello, how you doing?" And then I took off again, honest to God. I went to a park, sat on a bench alongside guys who had been drinking all night, and we talked politics and so forth. I finally came back at eight o'clock and there was a one-way plane ticket to Buffalo glued to my door. It said, "Good-bye, Ruben," on it.

The Phillies flew to San Francisco that day so, instead of flying to Buffalo, I flew to San Francisco, too, and watched the whole three-game series against the Giants in the first row above the Philly dugout. Mauch came out and saw me and asked what I was doing there. I told him he wasn't my boss anymore. After the series, I reported to Buffalo. First game there I won in relief. Next day I won again. Two days, two wins. Then John Quinn, the Philly GM, called and asked why I didn't want to pitch. I said, "I don't want to pitch?" He said yeah, that he had just called my manager in Buffalo, who told him I hadn't pitched yet. I said, "Listen, look at the paper. Two days, two wins."

So I woke myself up at three a.m., then woke up the manager and told him I didn't want to play anymore for him, that he was a liar. He said he told Quinn the lie because he wanted me to stay on his team to help him win a championship, that he didn't want me to go back to Philly. I told him to just tell the truth. Later, Quinn called again, and said they wanted me back, but I told him no, that I was gonna stay with Buffalo. He said I *had* to come to Philly. So I left Buffalo and returned home to Puerto Rico instead. They were looking all over for me, and I was fishing right here. I didn't want to go back to Philadelphia and pitch for Gene Mauch.

So I pitched in Mexico instead, for Veracruz, and finished 17-1. And I never pitched in the majors again. But I played for 12 more seasons, year-round, in Mexico and in Puerto Rico. And even at 52, I could still pitch well enough to be in the big leagues. But I retired then, because I knew I wouldn't get another chance. I wanted to do it because I wanted to prove to people everywhere that if you take care of yourself, your body will respond, even at 52.

My last chance came with Earl Weaver, here in winter ball. I pitched well for him, 9-1 with six shutouts. We made it to the playoffs and he said he was going to pitch the younger guys instead. I said, "I'm 9-1 with six shutouts and you're not gonna use me? All right, I'm gonna stay home then. When you need me you call me, and I'll come running over and pitch." Sure enough, we lost the first two games and Weaver called. He wanted me to pitch the third game. By that time I had had about ten beers, and I told him, "I'll not only pitch against Ponce, I'll pitch a shutout." Next day I came to the ballpark early, went up to Weaver and said, "Remember yesterday I said I was gonna pitch a shutout? I said that because I was drinking beer. Now I'm sober, and I'm *still* gonna pitch a shutout." So I pitched a shutout with 21,000 fans watching. Weaver said after the game that he'd bring me north to Baltimore to pitch in relief for the Orioles.

He never called me, though. The next winter Frank Robinson came to manage the Santurce club. And when Weaver was asked by a reporter what he thought about Robinson managing, he said, "If he can manage Ruben Gomez, he can manage any ballplayer in the world." Sure enough, Weaver came to visit Robinson in Puerto Rico. When I saw him I turned my back to him. He started to say, "Hello," to me, but I turned and whacked him right on the nose. Oh, I hit him hard. And he fell. I was so mad. It was an obsession. At my age, acting that silly [laughs]. I went home and said to myself, "Ruben, you're *crazy.*" Oh, my God.

Twelve years ago I pitched in an old-timers game in the Dominican Republic. They saw me throw and asked if I'd like to pitch three innings in a regular game against Escondido. I said sure. And I struck out the side in one of those innings. Pedro Guerrero was one of the guys. I threw a couple of fastballs outside, one at his head, then a screwball right down the middle. Just like always. They couldn't believe it. They timed my fastball at 85 miles an hour. When I was 58. I used to put 50-pound weights on my knees, then lift in the clubhouse. Warm up five minutes and I was ready.

Pitchers nowadays get tired so easily because their legs are no good. They don't know how to stay in shape. No matter what you do, you have to condition yourself for the job you have. Pitchers and catchers report to spring training ahead of time, to build up their legs, because the power comes from the legs. When your legs start giving way you start going downhill. Same with fighters, tennis players, golfers. If you keep your legs in top shape, you can do what you want to do. Every time you pitch, if your knee gives just a bit, the ball will run three to four inches out of the strike zone. But if your leg is strong, your control is good. That is why pitchers are usually at their best in July, when their legs are strongest. Have you noticed that?

I'm glad I pitched when I did because the caliber of player was better then. Too many teams nowadays in the majors, not enough in the minors. But I still like to watch the game now. I like to watch a smart pitcher against a smart batter. I like to anticipate what's going to happen.

The big salaries haven't changed the game so much as they've changed the character of the players themselves. So many won't sign autographs nowadays, won't talk to the children, to the fans. And they don't know their history. I introduced one young player a few years ago to Curt Flood. He didn't even know who Curt Flood was. I said, "You don't know God?" He said, "I know God, but I don't know Curt Flood." I said, "He's *your* God. Thanks to Curt Flood, you're making millions now. And it's a damn shame you don't even know who he is."

I don't go to the ballpark very often now because every time I go, people recognize me and want to talk or get an autograph. I can't watch the game. Nowadays you'll find me on the golf course. You know why I like golf so much? Because it's like pitching. Every time I play against a good golfer I apply the same principles to the game as I did when I was pitching. For example, when I play Chi Chi Rodriguez I never use a driver. I stay behind him. He's little but hits the ball far. So who gets to the green first? I do, because I'm hitting behind him. Then, when Chi Chi gets ready to hit, he sees my ball close to the pin. The green seems smaller. Whereas when I look at the green from the fairway, it seems big to me, because I see only the flag. But when he hits, he sees my ball on the green as well. To beat me he has to put it not just on the green, but between my ball and the pin. I put the pressure on him, little by little.

My life revolves around golf and my children these days. I have an older son who's a retired army colonel in San Jose [California], working with the city government; another son with a business of his own in Puerto Rico; a daughter who's an interior decorator; and now I have an adopted 16-year-old girl from the Dominican Republic. I adopted her when she was two months old.

I want to be remembered as a good human being. When children come up to me now, as they did when I played, I stay with them as long as they like. I was a ballplayer, an athlete, but that was my job. Judge people by how they act around you.

San Juan, Puerto Rico

VALMY THOMAS

The first of a handful of Virgin Island natives to reach the major leagues, Valmy Thomas caught the first big league game ever played on the West Coast, as the Giants blanked the Dodgers, 8-0. He shared the catching duties in 1958 with rookie Bob Schmidt, hitting .259, only to be traded at the end of the season, along with Ruben Gomez, to the Phillies for Jack Sanford. Thomas retired after five big league seasons, with a .230 average and 12 home runs.

Today Valmy is one of St. Croix's most prominent citizens, having worked several years for the local government in sports & recreation, while currently hosting daily radio and weekly television sports shows, as well as owning a sporting goods store. He is married, with four children, nine grandchildren and one great-grandchild.

I PLAYED A LOT OF BALL as a kid but it was stickball and we made our own balls. Baseball was the sport here on the island, introduced by Catholic fathers and the U.S. Marines. But before me there were much better players here than I ever was—*much* better—when the door to the major leagues was not open to them. I happened to come along in a period when it was open, but before me there were a tremendous number of better ballplayers. Oh yes, no question about it. One went to the Negro Leagues—Alfonso Pinky Jarret. I was in the Navy, in the States at the time. I was asked to play in the Negro Leagues but declined. No way. I didn't want to

deal with the discrimination, the different restaurants and hotels. That was not for me. I had no intention of subjecting myself to those things.

In high school the big boys told me I was too small [5-8] to play ball. There was a clique in high school, a group of tough players who controlled everything. They wouldn't allow me to play. So I said OK and went into the service instead, and played ball there. After the service I played in Puerto Rico, where the teams had working agreements with many major league clubs. The club I played with had a working agreement with the Giants. But I started pro ball with Pittsburgh, in class-A.

I played one season in Canada and led the St. Jean club in hitting [.296]. I was making just $450 a month and yet Branch Rickey, the Pirates' general manager, cut me $50. You know, Branch Rickey was not a very loose individual with the bucks. So I decided to retire. I asked to be placed on the voluntarily retired list. That was in 1951. I decided to play in Santo Domingo instead. It was a matter of principle. I made two and a half times as much money in the Dominican Republic and played fewer games, through the summer of '54.

Horace Stoneham used to come to Puerto Rico every winter, saw me play winter ball and asked if I'd like to play for the Giants. I said sure, but in order to be reinstated I had to return to the Pittsburgh organization for one more season, before I could be drafted by the Giants. So I played one more season in St. Jean before joining the Giants' Eastern League club in Johnstown in 1956. We opened the season in Virginia Beach and it was so cold I told the manager I could be of no help to him in such cold weather. Really. I couldn't take the cold. I really intended to come back home to St. Croix. Fortunately, they found a warm place I could go, to Albuquerque, in the Western League. It was just like home.

Early that season my teammate Bill White was promoted to the Giants in New York. I had a chance to go, too, at the end of the season, but I said no. White said I was jeopardizing my chance to play in the majors. I said that if I went I'd be increasing my chance of catching pneumonia. I wanted to stay where the people and the weather had been nice to me.

Growing up in the Virgin Islands, playing in the majors was the farthest thing from my mind. There was no opportunity. I just loved to play ball. Rejecting the opportunity to go to the majors in '56 was a matter of principle. I was happy in

Albuquerque, with good people and good weather. I figured I could play in New York in '57.

In fact, the '57 season with the Giants was a wonderful experience, to play with people like Willie Mays. I roomed with Willie on the road in '58. He is a tremendous individual, once you get to know him. He'll give you the shirt off his back. And he was quite possibly the greatest player I ever played with or against. I played against Hank Aaron, Ted Williams and Mickey Mantle—each in his own way had something special. But seeing Mays play day to day, he was something else. You had to see him every day. He used to catch balls by bringing them back into the park. That great catch in the '54 World Series in the Polo Grounds? It didn't compare to a catch he made one night at Forbes Field, off Clemente. And he was another great one.

As the '57 season progressed I had no feeling at all about the possible move to San Francisco. I must tell you why. I live within a simple philosophy: *May God grant me the serenity to accept the things I cannot change, the courage to change the things that I can, and the wisdom to know the difference.* If it's raining all day I never think about the rain. I just cope with what is there. I can't do anything about it. And I'm not going to plug up my mind with things like that. Things I cannot change I don't give a second thought to.

My parents were very hard working and poor. If they didn't have something I wanted I never worried. I didn't expect anything. If there was no present at Christmas time it didn't bother me. Now, kids here want $140 Nike sneakers. Kids are spoiled. We wore Converse and Pro Keds. And even if our parents both worked we used to have somebody at home—a grandma or aunt—when we came home. It's not the case today. Kids are spending more time with peers, and it all depends on how they're influenced, what you can teach them and what they're going to succumb to. It's as simple as that.

The government here is not funding after-school programs as they should be. Sports and recreation is a primary concern of mine, and I've been trying to advocate this for a number of years. When I was in charge of recreation I opened so many centers throughout the island, so that while parents worked kids would have a structured environment after school. However, after I left, the brilliant jokers in charge closed them all down.

I reported late to spring training in 1958 because of tonsillitis. But I always reported as late as possible every spring because I wanted to stay on the island here as long as possible. You can see why. Spring training in Phoenix that year was nothing special. Just a job. I didn't give San Francisco a second thought. I just tried to make everything as simple as possible. Actually, though, I had already been to San Francisco once, while I was in the service, while stationed in San Diego. I loved the city. It was so cosmopolitan and compact, and I met some wonderful people out there.

I remember the big parade downtown, the day before the '58 season started. The atmosphere was very enthusiastic. But my own excitement came when I left home each day to go to the ballpark to play. Seals Stadium was a lot different than the Polo Grounds. I just had to adapt. The only problem for me was the cold, like when I had to go to a place like Wrigley Field. It freaked me out.

Opening day against the Dodgers was an exciting day, dueling in the sunshine

Valmy Thomas (Dick Dobbins)

Valmy Thomas (Steve Bitker)

against our big rival from New York. *The shootout at the OK Corral.* We always played 110 percent against the Dodgers, compared with 100 percent against others. It was very natural. In New York we used to say it was time to duck as soon as we reached the Brooklyn Bridge.

I have one distinct memory from that first game. A Dodger hit a popfly behind the plate, I was running back full-tilt and this lady stood up to follow the ball. They had field-level box seats, very close, you remember. I was looking at the ball, of course, and hit her in the head and knocked her down. Fortunately, she was OK, but I was very concerned.

That was Cepeda's major league debut. I knew Orlando from Puerto Rico. Whitey Lockman said it wasn't a question as to whether he was ready to play in the majors, it was only a question as to whether he was ready for the Hall of Fame. I think it's an abomination that it took Orlando so long to get in the Hall, because of what he did off the field after his career was over. These sportswriters who wouldn't vote for him have never even played marbles, much less baseball. They shouldn't be the judges. They can't judge me. We're not talking about morality off the field. We're talking about contributions on the field. Let him who has not sinned cast the first stone. I think it's rather ridiculous. You know who should vote? The players.

Ruben Gomez threw a shutout for us that day. He had a tremendous screwball and had about the best control of any pitcher I ever worked with. He always knew where the ball was

going. I think the reason he wasn't more successful in the majors was because he [eventually] gave that screwball away. He didn't know it. I didn't realize it in '58. But he changed his motion at the top when he threw the screwball. Scouts on other teams look for things like that. There might be a guy in the dugout with a pair of binoculars. Or in Chicago there'd be a lone guy in the center field stands. Sometimes his leg was crossed, sometimes not. He'd be sending signals from a two-way radio as to which pitch was coming. In Milwaukee sometimes you'd see a leg sticking out of the scoreboard, sometimes you wouldn't. So we'd have to constantly adjust signals. No question about it.

I loved to swing the bat. I loved to get my swings. But Rigney had a longball philosophy. He loved big hitters and home runs. I was hitting between .270 and .290 late in the season but he took me out of the lineup because he wanted more of the longball, more punch. But I'd always leave the game on the field. After I left the park I wouldn't be able to tell you what the score was, only whether we won or lost, unless it was such a close game that we had to keep track.

I lived in a two-bedroom apartment in '58 with Willie Kirkland. I can see the place in my mind, and I might be able to find it, but I can't remember exactly where it was. We had a fine landlady, very nice. I didn't hang out with anyone in particular on the team. I was more of a loner. I may have gone to Willie Mays' house on occasion but I usually just loved to read until one or two a.m., or listen to music.

I remember how cold it was our first night game at Seals. I told a writer, "If we had a night like this back home in the Virgin Islands, we'd all be buried by morning." And that fog—even in the day you could see it coming. You could see it rolling in. Sometimes you'd lose the ball in the fog and the hitter would wind up with a triple. If they had enlarged Seals it probably would have reduced the fog and the cold air. They had enough land there to enlarge it to the necessary capacity. And it was in the city, with easy access.

Then, there was the wind. I remember in 1961, at Candlestick, when Stu Miller was blown off the mound in the All-Star Game. He was something else. He had a great psychology to pitching. He didn't have much but he had the motion—he'd move his head but his arm never came around, and that would throw the hitter off stride.

We were in first place for a while in '58 [through July]. But when you give your all, whatever happens happens. But what I didn't like to see was players dogging it. You'd see it every year with certain players, complaining out there all the time. Even now, I can't take that kind of attitude.

At the end of the season I was traded with Gomez to the Phillies for Jack Sanford. I was surprised because that winter Stoneham was in Puerto Rico and asked me if everything was OK, and if there was anything I needed. But then he went back to the States, and Philadelphia wanted a catcher. Again, I've learned to accept certain things, because if I don't like something I can leave. But going to Philly was like going to jail. The fans came out to root for the other team. And there were four guys on that club that used to be referred to as the Dalton Gang: Seth Morehead, Turk Farrell, Jack Meyer and Jim Owens. They'd always drink on the road and fight. Owens had the most natural movement on a baseball I'd ever seen. Oh, man, if he stayed straight you couldn't have beaten him. He was a *natural*. His first pitch, the ball moved. He'd throw to first, and the ball moved. But he spent too much time drinking and fighting.

I retired after the '62 season because I wanted to be able to come home and be active, and not be in a position where I could not physically do something.

The highlight of my career probably came when I hit six home runs my rookie year, in '57, and every one of them tied or won a game. And that, when you think about it, was satisfying. But I don't think back to those days much. I don't associate them with what I do today. That's my philosophy. I am the first native of St. Croix ever to play major league ball. But that means nothing to me. In retrospect, if I could do it, *anybody* could have done it. There were many others better before me. I am very indebted to this island. I could not have succeeded without help from others. I cannot do enough for the people of St. Croix.

Right now, I'm obsessed with the sea. When I'm finished repairing my boat I'll turn my business over to my daughter, so that any day I can go deep-sea fishing. I am fascinated, I am charmed, I am *obsessed* with the sea, and I love to fish. What I catch or don't catch, it doesn't make one bit of difference. It's just being back on the sea. And I hope to be back in the water by next month.

Christiansted, St. Croix

WHITEY LOCKMAN

Whitey Lockman has been a part of professional baseball for over 50 years, signing with the Giants at the age of 16, playing 15 years in the majors, and later coaching and managing, and is currently scouting for the Florida Marlins.

Lockman homered in his first big league at bat, at age 19. In the deciding game of the Giants-Dodgers playoff series in 1951, his ninth inning double drove Don Newcombe from the game, and set the stage for Bobby Thomson's "shot heard 'round the world." In the ninth inning of the seventh game of the Giants-Yankees World Series in '62, coach Lockman held Matty Alou at third base on Willie Mays' two-out double, setting the stage for Willie McCovey's line drive to Bobby Richardson—the Yankees won the game, 1-0.

Whitey played 13 years with the Giants—his last was the Giants' first year in San Francisco, when he hit .238. In his 15-year career, he hit .279 with 114 home runs. He and his wife now live in Scottsdale, with their six children and one granddaughter all nearby in the Phoenix area.

FRANKLY, I HAD MIXED emotions about the move to San Francisco. I was a New York guy, started my big league career there [in '45] and played most of my career there. Matter of fact, *all* of my career except a half-season with the Cardinals in '56 [excluding 163 at-bats with Baltimore and Cincinnati, in '59 and '60]. So from 1945 through '57, it was *all* New York, aside from that half-season in St. Louis in '56. But, having played some spring exhibition games in San Francisco, and having trained in Phoenix from '47 on, I had developed a strong positive feeling about San Francisco. So, in one way I was a little disappointed to leave New York, but if there was some place we had to move to, San Francisco was right at the top of the list.

I liked Seals Stadium. I remember the atmosphere of Opening Day in '58. There was such excitement in the stadium that day, and in the city of San Francisco. I was just thrilled to be part of it. The only unfortunate part of it that year for us was that we couldn't find any housing closer than Palo Alto. So we had quite a hike every day. But I remember the enthusiasm of everybody involved—the fans, players and staff—was just outstanding.

Seals Stadium was a very intimate ballpark, and fairly close to downtown. And the fans were enthusiastic, though a little different than in New York, in that they were a little more sophisticated. The wind was a little different, too, than at Candlestick. It blew in from right field more at Seals, although that didn't really matter to me a lot—I wasn't a power hitter. But I do remember hitting one home run there the day the Chief of Police of San Francisco [Ahern] dropped dead in the stands. I'm not sure if he dropped dead *after* my home run—he might have.

What I remember most about spring training in '58 is an often-told story about Bill Rigney and Orlando Cepeda that is absolutely accurate. I can almost tell it verbatim. Rigney came to me in early March in Phoenix and, you know, I had been the first baseman for years. And I remember Rig coming to me one day and saying words to the effect of, "Do you think Cepeda's ready?" And I said, "Ready for what? The Hall of Fame?" He laughed, of course. I didn't [laughs]. But I could tell early in spring training that Cepeda was the real deal. No question about it. There was no question about the way he swung the bat, and he was a good first baseman, too. He was no donkey at first. And he was enthusiastic and strong. If I had been a scout in *those* days, I think I could have evaluated him, all right.

Even though the Cepedas and the Davenports and the other rookies were very good players, there was some inexperience involved in '58, and Milwaukee was just a little too strong. They won the Series in '57, they had a lot of bombers like Aaron and Adcock, and pitchers like Spahn and Burdette. They had a little more depth than we did. But I didn't play much, so Horace looked in to trading me to another team where I might get to play more. He asked me if I might like to play for Detroit, but the Tigers had a fine young first baseman named Norm Cash, so I said no, I'd just as soon stay with the Giants.

They finally sold my contract to Baltimore in '59, and I played another year and a half for

Whitey Lockman (SF Giants)

the Orioles and Cincinnati, before being released. I was 34 by then, but an *old* 34—my legs were tired. I drove with my family back home to North Carolina, and at the end of the season the Giants' new manager Alvin Dark called and asked me to be a member of his coaching staff. It wasn't an easy decision because we had six children, and we'd have to uproot them once again. But we all liked San Francisco a lot, so I took the job. I coached first base in '61, and then third in '62, 63 and 64.

I liked coaching third, although the call I'm most famous for is the one in '62 that resulted in us losing the seventh game of the World Series to the Yankees. It's the bottom of the ninth, we're down, 1-0, Matty Alou's on first with two outs, and Mays hits one toward the right field corner. You'd be *amazed* how often I still get asked about that one play.

You have to remember that the sixth game of the Series had been postponed two or three days already, so the field was very wet. As a result, Mays' ball died on the right field line instead of rolling into the corner. So Maris gets to it and makes a perfect relay throw to Richardson. At that point I *had* to hold Alou at third. McCovey was up next. And if they wanted to walk McCovey, Cepeda was after him. I would have sent Alou if Maris had made a bad throw, but he didn't.

I think a lot of fans still believe Alou would have scored because Richardson's throw home took two or three bounces to reach Elston Howard. But I still wouldn't have made the call any differently. The only thing that's changed over the years is that I've talked with both Howard and Richardson about the play, and Howard said he wished I'd have sent Alou because then the game would have ended one play sooner. And Richardson agreed.

I managed in the minors for several years, with the Cubs, after Alvin was fired in '64, and eventually got to manage the Cubs in '72. But not before I thought I had a great chance to manage the Giants in '69. It happened when I was managing Tacoma in the [Pacific] Coast League. Horace was in Phoenix, and told me after a game that he'd like to talk with me over lunch the next day, at the hotel coffee shop. Well, since Horace and I had never had lunch together anywhere before, I thought this might be important. But he never showed up. He never called. To this day I don't know whether he was thinking of me as a possible manager, but shortly thereafter he gave the job to Charlie Fox.

I got the Cubs managing job midway through the '72 season. We had a good team then. Actually, a *great* team. We had Williams, Monday and Cardenal in the outfield, Santo at third, Kessinger at short, Beckert at second, Hickman at first, Hundley catching, and then Jenkins, Hands, Pappas and Hooton starting. Why didn't we win with a team like that? Lousy managing [laughs]. Actually, we were two-over-.500 when I took over, played 13-over-.500 the rest of the way, but couldn't make up any ground on Pittsburgh [finishing second, 11 games behind]. Then '73 was a good year [77-84], but the Mets won a five-team race that included Montreal [Cubs finished five games back]. Then Wrigley began housecleaning in '74, and that was it for me [fired after 93 games, with a 41-52 record].

I got into scouting after that, with the Cubs, Expos and now with the Marlins. I travel the country scouting, in both National and American League cities. I've been in baseball 54 years and I still love it.

I GREW UP IN CHARLOTTE, during the Depression. My father died when I was eight months old. My mother worked 12 hours a day in a textile mill to make ends meet, for me and my four brothers and sisters. I started playing baseball when I was eight, and never stopped.

I signed with the Giants when I was just 16, two months shy of my 17th birthday, in May of 1943. I graduated from high school in April, and played American Legion ball the year before. And the manager of that team knew a Giants scout. He came by one day and asked if I'd work out. I did, the scout signed me and I joined a triple-A team, the Jersey City Giants, in the International League, with Gabby Hartnett the manager. I stayed with them about a week, then was sent down to double-A in Springfield, Massachusetts, in the Eastern League. I did well there for about six weeks [.325], and came back to triple-A. I played two more years at Jersey City [.317 in '45], then made my major league debut on July 5th of '45, at the age of 18, at the Polo Grounds. In fact, that was the first time I had ever been in a big league ballpark, the first time I had ever seen a major league game.

I was scared to death. I mean, *Mel Ott?* Give me a break. He was hitting fourth. And I was just a kid. And I was just really excited. I was kind of on cloud nine, but I managed to play all right. I hit a dinger my first time up. I was hitting third. Hit it off a fellow named George Dockins, a left-handed pitcher for the Cardinals. People still ask me [whom I hit the homer off] and I tell them, and nobody's ever heard of him. And I guess with my home run, nobody's heard of him since. [*author's note: Dockins pitched one full season in the majors, going 8-6 with a 3.21 ERA, in 126 innings, for St. Louis in 1945.*]

I recall, after the game, Mel Ott [player-manager] said, kind of in jest, "This game's pretty easy, huh?" But it *wasn't* that easy. When the ball left the park, I couldn't believe it—it went into the upper deck. I knew it was gone when I hit it. I remember going around the bases—it seemed like it took me about a month to get around. I know I wasn't walking, but I was going slow enough to really enjoy it. I got another hit in the game, and drove in three or four runs.

I hit .341 [in 129 at-bats] with the Giants, but was drafted into the Army five weeks later, then spent the entire '46 season in the service. I was discharged January 1, 1947, but broke a leg a week before the season started, in an exhibition game in Sheffield, Alabama.

I didn't have any strong feelings about Jackie Robinson integrating baseball that year, but I was curious just what kind of player he was. And it didn't take long to find out. I was a Southern boy, and things were segregated growing up, so I didn't have a lot of association with black people, although there were blacks involved in the textile factory that my mother worked in. So I was around them, and played some pickup sandlot baseball with them, but as far as being one of those southerners opposed to Jackie, no, I was not. In fact, I used to go watch the Negro League teams play against each other when I was 14 and 15. And the thing I remember most is the fun that they had playing and how much the fans got into it, how they yelled and screamed. They just had a good time.

The Giants integrated in '49 with Monte Irvin and Hank Thompson. I welcomed them on the team. They were good ballplayers, but not only that, they were good guys. You won't find a more likeable person than Monte Irvin. Henry Thompson was fine, too, but Monte Irvin was a little older and probably more intelligent, and just a class guy. As a matter of fact, I talked with a guy recently who was writing a book about Monte Irvin, and one of the things he told me was that Monte Irvin said he really appreciated his treatment from me when he joined the Giants, that I treated him like an equal, and like a ballplayer. Well, he *was* [laughs]. He was a heckuva ballplayer and a heckuva guy.

When Leo Durocher took over managing the Giants [in '48], I didn't enjoy it at first. There was a period of adjustment to Leo for most guys on our team, who had been used to a soft-spoken, introverted Mel Ott. Then, to have Leo come in, who was the exact opposite—gregarious, kind of loud, et cetera—there *was* a period of adjustment to his personality. But then, once we got to know how he operated and realized his ability to run the game, then we began to appreciate him.

I'd say by '49 I had kind of grown accustomed to his style, and I don't know why, but once in a while he'd have a clubhouse meeting after a tough loss, and he'd rant and rave, and then he'd say, "If all you guys would bust your ass like Lockman, for chrissake, we'd have a decent fucking team." When he first did that I almost fell off my chair. It would embarrass me, really. But then I realized later on that he would pick out an individual who was playing pretty well [Lockman hit .301 with 11HR, 65RBI & 12SB in '49], and use him as an example to the other guys who, maybe, were not playing quite as well.

It was nothing personal, but that was his style. And as our relationship developed—we were together about seven years—I realized that the guy was a heckuva manager. There might have been some things you didn't agree with him about, like his personal habits in life, but what the heck? You were a professional, and what he did on the field between the white lines was what counted.

The '51 season was, without a doubt, the highlight of my career. Not *everything* about it, mind you, because at one point we lost 11 in a row, early on. We had begun to jell in '50, after we got Dark and Stanky. And we figured we'd be contenders in '51. Well, we started out brutally. We were terrible. But as things started to jell, we won 16 straight, we had three pretty good pitchers in Jansen, Maglie and Hearn, and the big guy—Mays—showed up. And I think *that* really helped make us jell, although we did have a problem when Willie arrived. We had too many outfielders, guys who played every day. I'm talking about Irvin, Mueller, Thomson and myself, and then Mays. Not bench guys. There had to be a decision about how to rearrange us. So I went to first, Bobby Thomson to third, and Mueller, Irvin and Mays stayed in the outfield. That was a pretty good lineup, with Dark, Stanky and Westrum.

When Mays joined us in May it didn't take long to realize that he was something special. His athletic ability was the thing that impressed me initially. And, as you may recall, he didn't tear it up offensively right away. But his defensive ability—his quickness, his coordination, his reflexes, the way he played center field, the way he ran the bases—oh, my God, I had never seen anything like it. He was that outstanding. And by that time I had been around the big leagues five or six years and had seen some pretty good ballplayers.

The play that stands out for me, in our run that wiped out the Dodgers' 13½-game lead in August, was Mays against the Dodgers, in the Polo Grounds. They had the tying run on third base with one out, late in the game, and there was a shallow fly ball hit into right-center field. Mays had to go to his left to catch it. The runner on third tagged up, Mays whirled, making a complete 360, and threw a strike right at my noggin— I was the cutoff guy on the mound—and it carried all the way to Westrum at home. And in a bang-bang play, he was out at home. It was just *incredible*. But he continued to do things like that. It was just amazing. All those games down the stretch were so crucial. Once we made up some ground and got down to seven or eight games, we just *knew* we couldn't lose. We couldn't *afford* to lose, because if we did we were out of it. It was nail-biting time, and we didn't lose many, winning 37 of our last 44.

I remember everything about that final playoff game against the Dodgers. *Of course.* We trailed 4-1 entering the bottom of the ninth, at the Polo Grounds. Dark and Mueller singled, we had first and third and nobody out, and then Irvin popped up. So I was the next hitter. Newcombe was still on the mound. I realized I was the tying run, and although I didn't hit a *lot* of home runs [.282, 12HR, 73RBI in '51], I could jerk one out once in a while. So I figured this was the time, which was really not very smart thinking, as I look back on it. But, my God, if there's some way you can tie the game, you want to try to do it. So I said, well, I'm gonna try to jerk one out in right field.

First pitch he threw a smoker on the black, outside [corner], and I swung as hard as I could and hit a line drive down the left field line [an RBI double]. I know what happened. I know that *muscle memory* took over, because I was the type of hitter that hit the ball where it was pitched. I learned that early on, my first year in baseball, in double-A. So *muscle memory* took over, and I just hit the ball where it was pitched, although I was trying to hit a home run. I was *thinking* home run. And, of course, you know what happened after that. They brought in Branca. And I share the opinion of others who have suggested over the years that Newcombe was far from through. The pitch he threw to me was a smoker. It had to be 92, 93 miles an hour. He was throwing good. And so I was surprised to see Branca because Newcombe was throwing good, he had an open base, with Mays coming up [after Thomson], so he had that option. But I guess he [manager Charlie Dressen] didn't see it that way.

I was not only surprised to see Branca, I was also surprised to see him pitch to Thomson. Bobby was just fantastic down the stretch, and he had already hit a home run in the first playoff game, off *Branca.* Yes, I really was surprised he pitched to him. Because, don't forget, Willie was a rookie, and a walk sets up a double play situation.

I remember the first pitch from Branca to Thomson was a fastball as much down the middle of the plate—down Broadway, we call it—

as you'll ever see. It was right down in his wheelhouse, and he took it. I thought, God, what's he doing? Then the second pitch was Branca's pitch. He didn't want to throw the first one where he threw it, I know, and he got away with it. But the second one was thrown where he wanted it to be, which was up and in, a bad ball, a *ball,* a pitch that if a hitter swings at it, most of the time he'll pop it up. And that's the pitch that Bobby hit out of the ballpark. So there had to more adrenaline flowing through the hitter than the pitcher, I presume. And when it left the bat I knew the score was tied, at *least.* I thought it had a chance to get out of the park, but as I started to run toward third, the ball started to sink some. I was saying to myself, *stay up, stay up.* Well, it did. It got in the seats.

I ran by Durocher, got to home plate and I thought to myself, if there's ever been anybody that I've played with in any situation who deserves to be carried off the field on somebody's shoulders, it's Thomson, and *I'm gonna do it.* And when he got to home plate I shook his hand, I got down underneath him and I got him maybe a quarter of the way up. Unfortunately, however, in those days at the Polo Grounds the fans were allowed to exit the park through the center field gate, and I guess maybe a thousand people jumped on top of him and the rest of his teammates there at home plate. I went down, and Thomson went down. I sprained my neck and shoulder, and luckily didn't do worse, I guess. We got out of there and got to the clubhouse, and I played the World Series with a stiff neck.

I think Ebbets Field had something to do with the great Giant-Dodger rivalry in those days. It was such an intimate ballpark and the fans were Chicago Cub-type fans, maybe *worse.* Very rabid. Loud. Boisterous. They had the Brooklyn Symphony—the Sym-*phony*—a little orchestra that played. It kept time with you as you trotted back to the dugout after making an out. You couldn't fool them—you could slow down or speed up, and they stayed right *with* you. It was just incredible, the atmosphere in that park when the Giants played the Dodgers, but it was fun. When you went in there you knew you were in for a battle. You knew what you had to face, not only from their great team but from the fans, so you were up for it, you were geared for it. And we did pretty well against them. We beat them [for the pennant] twice, in '51 and '54.

Even though we won the World Series in '54, '51 was still the highlight of my career. The '51 thing was just so dramatic, because of what we accomplished the latter part of the season, and we even had the Yankees down two games to one in the Series, when our bubble burst. Don't misunderstand me, '54 was a big thrill, and after winning a World Series you can say to yourself, individually, hey, I'm on the best baseball team in the world. And, you know, that's *something.* Not to mention the fact that we beat a Cleveland team that won 111 games, with that great pitching staff.

I remember what an incredible year Mays had [.345, 41HR, 110RBI], and also Don Mueller [.342]. And I think Duke Snider [.341] was battling both of them for the batting title right up to the last day of the season. I remember Mays got three hits off Robin Roberts in Philadelphia the last day to clinch it, which I thought was quite a feat. Johnny Antonelli [21-7, 2.29ERA] had a fantastic year, as did Ruben Gomez [17-9, 2.88ERA]. And I think maybe the most outstanding thing about that year was that Durocher managed the team and won more games with moves that he made than any other manager I saw during my career. It was just one fantastic year. Everything, *everything* fell into place that he did, including the World Series with Dusty Rhodes [four-for-six, off the bench, with two homers and seven RBIs].

Everybody talks about the catch Mays made in the Series off Vic Wertz but it wasn't his greatest catch. He made a barehanded catch once in Pittsburgh that was astounding, off Clemente, in deep left-center. *A line drive.* He stuck up his hand. Remember the play that [Kevin] Mitchell made a few years ago? It was better than that. Mitchell's was a foul ball, a fly ball in the left field corner. But Mays' was a *shot* off Clemente's bat in left-center. I mean, it was *going,* and Mays was racing, with his back to everything, and reached up with his right hand and caught it. I thought, oh, my God, that's not *human.*

Mays was the best player I ever saw. No question. None. I can't say nobody came close. But I'm talking about five things that a position player can do—hit, hit with power, field, run and throw. I've never seen anybody do all those things as well as Mays. I've seen some guys do one of them, maybe, better. You know what I mean? I've seen better hitters than Willie. I've seen faster runners. But I've never seen anybody do all those things as well, and as consistently, as Willie.

The best pitcher I ever faced was Ewell Blackwell. He had the best stuff of any pitcher I faced in the big leagues. They called him *The Whip,* and he threw the ball side-arm—not submarine, but down, maybe a little lower than side-arm. He crossfired, which made him especially difficult for right-handed hitters. Fortunately, I was a left-handed hitter, but he was difficult for me, too. Spahn was maybe—quote, unquote—the best *pitcher* that I saw. But Blackwell had the best stuff. Maybe one of the toughest guys for me to hit personally was Curt Simmons, a left-hander with the Phillies. But I have to admit, in those days there was not the pitching depth as there was in the sixties and seventies. So I guess we got by easy.

I think the game is as well-played today as it was in my day. The major change is that there's more base stealing, more running. I think the athletes are bigger, stronger and better. Better conditioned. In our day we just ran around the park once in a while, and did nothing during the winter [except work]. A lot of players just played a little golf, basketball or whatever, but there was not a program of conditioning as we see today. The players are great today, and I enjoy watching them.

WHEN I WAS TRADED to the Cardinals [part of a nine-player deal in June, 1956], it was an emotional down. The Cardinals were a heck of an organization and I hit well in Sportsman's Park, but there were personal circumstances involved, including my wife's pregnancy. She gave birth three days after the trade. She was in New York. We had set up house in Westchester County, so for those reasons it was difficult. But it turned out to be OK.

I was really thrilled, though, when I was traded back. Not because I didn't like St. Louis or didn't like Musial and some of those people, but you remember Frank Lane, their GM? Trader Lane. God, he was too much. You like to feel at least a *little* secure in your profession, but you just didn't with him. So when he called me in during spring training in St. Petersburg, in '57, and said he'd traded me back to the Giants, I was *really* smiling underneath. Then he told me it was for Hoyt Wilhelm. Well, Wilhelm was my best buddy on the Giants. So I had some second thoughts about that. I knew Wilhelm was in Phoenix with his wife and family. And I was there in St. Petersburg with mine. So I left St. Petersburg, driving to Phoenix. And he did the same thing, driving from Phoenix to St. Petersburg.

And we *passed* each other in Dallas, and saw each other, and stopped and had a little chat, and went on our ways. Can you believe that?

Scottsdale, Arizona

LEON WAGNER

Leon Wagner (SF Giants)

Leon Wagner was named to The Sporting News *1958 Rookie All-Star team, hitting .317 with 13 home runs and 35 RBIs, in 221 at-bats. That came after he opened the '58 season at triple-A Phoenix, hitting .318 with 17 home runs and 58 RBIs. The powerfully built left-handed hitter was one of several outstanding rookies for the Giants in '58, although he enjoyed his best seasons with the Angels and Indians, hitting 173 home runs from 1961 through '66. He was named the Most Valuable Player of the '62 All-Star Game in Chicago.*

Wagner played 12 years in the big leagues, hitting 211 home runs with a .272 average. Nicknamed "Daddy Wags," the free-swinging Wagner was a crowd-pleaser, both because of his tremendous power to right field and his nature as a free spirit.

Leon was also a very successful businessman off the field, owning a clothing store as an active player, selling cars when his playing days were over, and then acting in Hollywood films. He is now retired, living in Los Angeles, and has five children and two grandchildren.

I WAS A ROOKIE with the Giants in 1958. I had just come off hitting 51 home runs [w/166 RBI and .330 average] in class-B, down in Danville, Virginia. And the Giants didn't know whether I was just a flash in the pan or a phenom in the making, like Mickey Mantle. Willie Kirkland was another rookie in '58—he was my roommate, and we grew up playing the sandlots together in Detroit. And Cepeda, another rookie, was a great hitter in Puerto Rico. So Mays suddenly found himself in a position where if he didn't really extend himself he might have been the fourth best ballplayer on the team [laughs]. So that really pushed him. Cepeda was going four-for-four and I was hitting home runs off the bench. Willie was our leader and we loved him. But he had to step up.

I remember my major league debut, at Connie Mack Stadium [in Philadelphia, June 22]. I was nervous [pinch hitting, in the ninth inning]. My legs were shaking. Thirty thousand people in the stands. I'd been playing in front of 8000 people in Phoenix. I had to hold my legs, you know [laughs]? I stepped in at the plate, thinking, *I better get out of here quickly.* Turk Farrell, I think, threw me a fastball about a hundred miles an hour, and I golfed that thing to straightaway center field. I saw Richie Ashburn take off running and running, and I was 'round second base by the time he hauled that thing in over his shoulder. People just went berserk. And I didn't care whether he caught the ball. I was just glad to get out of the spotlight and get back to the bench, and give it back to Mays [laughs].

But, man, when I came out of the tunnel that day and looked up at all those people in the stands, I said, "Good lord [laughs]. Let me back in Phoenix." It was homey down there [in Phoenix]. We were dating women down there, and dancing. Me and McCovey lived in a plush home where the ladies baked cornbread every day. It was *relaxing.* But in the major leagues, man, they throw you out in the front lines, like in a bull ring, with the Christians and the lions, and it ain't nothin' nice. I mean, they play for *money.* It's a different ballgame. You can forget about all that bullshit with them 2500 people and stuff. You had to just change your thinking, playing for money. It's a lot different.

When you play in front of 30-40-50 thousand people every day, six and seven days a week, it kind of makes you withdraw. The public doesn't understand. There's a lot of pressure. You can't make any mistakes. You got the whole United States watching you. And I was only 23 years old then, used to playing in front of 3000 people in the minor leagues, maybe sometimes 8000 at Phoenix in triple-A. Like I say, it's just like going out into a bull ring. And sometimes you don't want to go. You have to turn the crowds off like you turn off a radio in order to really play like you practice. I had to go get hypnotized in order to turn the crowds off. If you're aware of the crowds, then you can't play relaxed. And if you can't play relaxed, you can't *play*. You can't give 100 percent of your ability.

The next day [on the 23rd], I started. I felt better. I went three-for-four. I was still tight and nervous. But I was so quick then that any place the pitcher would throw the ball, I would hit it. I didn't know you're supposed to wait in the big leagues for a certain pitch. If the pitcher threw the ball a little bit outside, Mays would take it, but I'd pull the damn thing off the right field wall. They'd throw it down around my shoe top and I'd golf it out. Inside, I'd pull it out of the park. That's the way I was hitting. I didn't want to let *anything* pass. I'd pull three straight balls foul, way out of the park, four to five hundred feet, and the pitcher would say, "What kind of guy is

this? He won't let anything hit the catcher's mitt." They didn't know how to pitch to me. I was a free-swinger. First pitch. I was always like that because I felt like I could hit anything they threw. Out of the park. I was quick like a cat, with fast wrists, and anything that was *decent*—they couldn't even throw me a decent pitch in the strike zone. They tried to change speeds on me, and I'd look funny, but I'd manage to hit it with one hand.

When the team returned to San Francisco, that was my first time on the West Coast. I didn't like Seals Stadium. It was cold. It was foggy at night. We played against Milwaukee and a guy hit a fly ball to me in left field, and I looked up and couldn't even see it. Here I am playing in a major league ballgame and I can't even see the ball, and we're playing for money. This *can't* happen. This was *unreal*. But I knew Mays was out there, and he could take care of us. He bailed me out until I learned how to play there. So I didn't mind them platooning me there. I'd just go out there and hit a three-run homer, and let them send some replacement in for me in the seventh inning. You understand? The weather was always lousy there. So after playing a while there under those conditions, they started knocking my glove. But I saw other ballplayers having a bad time there in the outfield, so I kept my spirits up. When I got to play in good ballparks, man, I started making one-handed catches. It was easy when I could *see*.

Willie Kirkland and I were roommates on the road but we had our own separate apartments in San Francisco. We hung together just about ev-

Bestfriends and fellow rookies Leon Wagner and Willie Kirkland. (National Baseball Hall of Fame)

ery day, though. We were kind of inseparable. We were about the same age and we both looked like athletes. He was always trying to reform me [laughs]. I guess he was supposed to have been my conscience. He was always following me around to all the clubs, telling me I didn't need to mess around with the girls like I did.

I lived in the Fillmore District with a guy named Teddy, who used to be with the underworld. He had a silk bathrobe and a nice, big home there. Willie Kirkland lived with a woman named Sadie, who was an ex-madam, I guess. A fine, older lady. We were introduced to these people by Mays, his wife Marghuerite, and later by Sad Sam Jones. They knew these society people who had nice homes. Mays always looked out for us. Kirkland and I used to go out at night to the Washington Club and other spots. The Fillmore District at that time was jumping, with Jack's and all those other places. We were dating these little sisters from the Bank of America, in the Fillmore District.

I knew we had a special team in '58 because when we took batting practice, we'd get 10 straight fastballs and try to hit all 10 into the upper deck. Mays would hit six or seven out of 10 up there. I'd hit six out of 10. Cepeda would hit six or seven out of 10. Then we'd look at the other team up on the top step of their dugout just watching us. We won some of those games *before* they even started. I mean, we did this all the time, and we just absolutely scared teams to death taking batting practice. The Dodgers, the Phillies, all of them.

But Milwaukee was just too strong that year. Any time you've got Hank Aaron and Eddie Mathews in your lineup. Shit. And Billy Bruton—he was skinny and all but he was a hell of a player to have not been a superstar. And they had great pitching, with Lew Burdette and Warren Spahn.

Willie Kirkland was my closest friend on the team but I was good friends with all of them. Cepeda was playing bongo music all the time, smoking a little weed—it was *strong,* then. But we never smoked weed during the games. You can't play drugged up. Every now and then we'd smoke weed after the game, or in the off-season. But you could not play drugged up, with all those people in the stands, playing for money, man. That was out. And we never smoked a lot of weed then. You couldn't drink a lot of whiskey then, either, and I was never a boozer. But, as I said, it was strong stuff, then—two puffs [laughs].

I did try smoking weed, though, *one* time before playing in Boston. I took two puffs and I hadn't come down, and I'm out in left field and Yastrzemski hits a line drive to left. And I've got my hands on my knees and I watch that line drive sail over my head, with my hands *still* on my knees. I didn't feel like *moving* [laughs]. So I just trotted over real easy and retrieved it, and hummed it into second base. And then I went back to my position, hands on knees, and relaxed. Rigney [Angels manager] didn't say a word to me when I went back to the dugout. He didn't know. I was so glad to get that game over. I don't ever want to play *that* relaxed. I never did it again. That taught me a lesson. You don't have your quick reflexes.

The Giants did a job on me in '59. They didn't play me a lot. They kept me on the bench, and I felt like they were trying to trade me because I only hit .225, and that's *impossible.* They just didn't play me and I couldn't understand why, after my big rookie season [.317, 13HR, 221AB]. That's the year I should have really excelled.

But I liked playing for Rigney. He was all right. He was like my dad. The first guy he got when he managed the Angels ['61 expansion club] was me. He told me he'd let me play, not to worry about anything, to just go out there and do the job, to not worry about the pressure and everything, that he'd just leave me out there. And he did. And I excelled. He took that pressure off of me, you know?

But as bad as that '59 season was, that was the closest I came to a World Series. We should have won the pennant. And we *would* have won it if they had let me play like they did in '58. But they were getting ready to deal me to the Cardinals for Don Blasingame because they needed a second baseman. Danny O'Connell was weak. He was a good guy but a lot of people who don't play baseball don't realize that a team is only as strong as its second baseman. The second baseman is supposed to be the out-man, right? The pitchers get fined for walking them. But that's a big reason why Cleveland improved so much, because of Baerga. And that's why Cincinnati was so strong, because of Joe Morgan. And the Yankees, because of Bobby Richardson. I haven't told too many people that, but a team is only as strong as its second baseman.

But I *know* we would have won the pennant in '59 if they had played me like they should. I

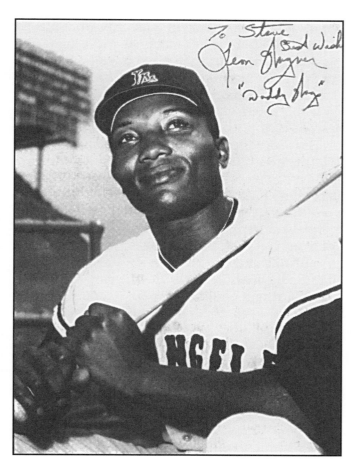

Leon Wagner hit 91 home runs as a Los Angeles Angel in 1961-62 and 63. (Steve Bitker)

was good for 15 wins. And I didn't understand it because I was young, like 24. I didn't say anything to Rigney at the time because I didn't want to make noise, and Mays told us all to be cool and keep our mouths shut. But I didn't feel like being like Mays all the time. He always believed in just not saying anything, but a lot of times I wanted to speak up, man, and tell them where to go. I was coming off 51 home runs and 166 RBIs my last year in the minors, and then 30 homers and 93 RBIs in '58, split between San Francisco and Phoenix. I knew I could hit *anywhere.* Felipe Alou and Kirkland were strong, but they weren't as strong as me with the bat. Cepeda, yeah, and Mays, but not the others. Shit, no.

I was pretty glad when I got traded to the Cardinals [with Daryl Spencer, for Blasingame—12/15/59], because they told me in St. Louis that Stan Musial was planning on retiring, so I'd get to play, and I was just happy to make more money [$12,000, versus $11,000 in '59]. Curt Flood was

over there—we played together in the Carolina League in '56. He beat me out for the batting crown [.340 to .330]. I knew he was a hell of a ballplayer then.

But Stan didn't like the idea of me taking his place in left field. He was 39 years old then. Then Joe Cunningham pulled a hamstring muscle, and couldn't open the season in right field. So Stan opened in left and I opened in right, in Cunningham's place. And I homered my first time at bat, off Sad Sam Jones, in that wind [the *first* homer in Candlestick Park history]. He threw me one of his long, hooking curveballs, the ones that broke about eight feet, and I just waited on it and hit it into the bay. Candlestick was cold and windy, too, like Seals Stadium, but I had the breeze blowing *with* me at Candlestick. I just had to get it up in the wind, and I was a pull-hitter anyway. I didn't play at Candlestick as much as I wanted to. I would have had nothing but field days at Candlestick in that wind. I hit long, towering, high fly balls anyway.

I played even less in St. Louis in 1960 than I did in '59 with the Giants. Solly Hemus was the manager. And Stan Musial wanted to play. The first two weeks of that season I had four home runs. Then Joe Cunningham got well quickly, and Stan wanted to play, so Solly Hemus sat me back down on the bench. Then they told me they didn't want me to just sit on the bench, so they sent me to Rochester, saying I was too young to sit on the bench. Well, the first thing I thought about was, *Let me sit on the bench, the hell with the age, I don't feel like going back to triple-A.*

I liked Wrigley Field in Los Angeles. Short fences. I must have hit 50 fly balls a year that went out of Wrigley Field. And it was in an all-black neighborhood. The first time I ever played there I saw 20,000 black people. It was different. It was a great hitters' park. Me, Steve Bilko and Ted Kluszewski. They were great guys. A lot of people don't realize that we were in first place at the All-Star break in '62. That's unheard of for an expansion team. That's *unheard* of. We beat the Yankees regularly. Dean Chance was pitching one time, and he was laughing and going through the Yankees like they were stepsons—he struck out 15.

I played in my first All-Star Game in '62, at Wrigley Field, Chicago, and was named MVP. I didn't even think I had a chance. I started, but when I saw Clemente out there and Mays, and McCovey and Aaron, and all those other superstars, I said, "Well, shit, I might as well pack up and go home. I'll just do my little three innings and go home." First time up, Art Mahaffey threw me a fastball inside and I said, "Uh, oh." Next pitch I put out in the street into traffic, with a man on. I also had a double, a single and a diving catch. I didn't even think about MVP. They gave me a trophy and told me to just please leave quietly [laughs]. They didn't expect me to win it, either. I didn't expect that. I was just enjoying the game.

Dean Chance and Bo Belinsky were playboys, but Bo was a bona fide nice guy who just liked to play Hollywood. He really went out there and caught the Hollywood girls. He was like a white boy who was a pimp [laughs]. From New Jersey. Yeah, I bought myself a shiny, new Cadillac in LA, and Bo went out and got himself one the same color. We were friends, though we never hung out together. He was a hustler. He could bowl and shoot pool like a hustler. I was about the only black guy on the team. Charlie Dees was there for a while and we hung together, but there weren't too many black guys to hang with. So I partied with Jim Fregosi, Bob Rodgers and Lee Thomas. We had a ball together—we were real close. And I could go work for Thomas or Rodgers or Fregosi right now, but I'm tired of those guys [laughs]. I was tired of them when I was with the Angels [laughs]. That's why you don't see me writing to Lee, "May I have a coaching job?" No, man, I'm too independent.

Even when I played I was too independent. I just didn't have the dedication that Mays and others had because I just didn't think baseball was worth going all the way out and killing myself over, and dying and not having no fun, and going to bed at nine o'clock. Because I was used to having fun. And baseball was fun to me. The superstars like Mays and Aaron made a lot of sacrifices, man. I just didn't want to dedicate myself like that. I was a better than average ballplayer, but I was raised going to dances and roller skating and stuff, and going out when I got older. I didn't stay out so late, I wasn't a late-owl bar-chaser, but I just got used to going out. I went to clubs in New York and saw Dizzy Gillespie and Cannonball Adderly. I enjoyed myself. I never had any problem catching ladies, even in high school. And I'm not a male whore. I knew how to conduct myself and I got along with everybody, and I could go anywhere in the world, whether there were white people or black people or Hispanic people or whatever. I knew how to act and stay

out of trouble. But some of those guys that played ball were boozers and troublemakers. A lot of those guys went out and stayed out all night and got drunk and went to jail. I never had that problem. I was always ready to play the next day.

I hit about 30 homers a year for six straight seasons [173] with the Angels and Cleveland, until they [the Indians] started platooning me in 1967. They started saying I was over the hill, but if they would have left me alone and let me play every day, I would have piled up hellacious numbers. But they were so afraid of my defense. Ballplayers were getting better defensively as I got older, but they weren't as strong at hitting.

I had a clothing business on the side in LA in those days, while I was playing ball. I had a 14-unit apartment building, a store and three houses. I was worth $800,000 in 1963. That was like 10 *million* now. I was trying to hit home runs, everybody was telling me I should go into this business or that, I had a clothing store here, an apartment building there and there was just a lot of pressure on me, man. I was only in my 20s. We sold Italian-style clothes, socks and silk suits. It was a good line. One of the local disc jockeys, Chuck Mann, managed my store and came up with the line, "Buy Your Rags at Daddy Wags."

In '68 I went to the Chicago White Sox and played for Eddie Stanky, so I decided to run for a while like the White Sox. I always admired that style of play. I liked running and stealing bases, and I was real slim. I only had one home run [and hit .284], then I went back to triple-A in '69 and hit about 20 home runs for the Hawaii Islanders. That was the end of my major league career. I was 35.

I lived over there [Honolulu] for a couple of years, selling cars in the off-season. I loved it. That's where I learned how to sell cars. A Chinese guy taught me. He told me the customer is always right, even if they're wrong, as long as they've got the money. That was the key, and that's what I taught my salesmen. I continued selling cars in San Francisco for about eight years. I didn't really intend to but I got into it because I found out these guys were making five, six and seven thousand dollars a month selling Hondas, man. I did four and five thousand myself.

I needed about 45 days then, to qualify for 10 years in the majors. So the Giants brought me back as a pinch hitter in '69 to help me get my 10 years in. I did a good job pinch hitting for the Giants [four-for-12 with two RBIs], then I went back to Hawaii and played a couple of more years. 1971 was my last year.

I was pretty much ready to retire. I didn't take it hard like a lot of guys. I didn't feel like trying to make a comeback. I was tired of battling back. I got so tired of having to prove myself and come off the bench. I was actually relieved to get away from all that pressure. I always knew there was life after baseball, because I had a great life while I was playing. And so I was looking forward to some fishing, roller skating, raising my son.

But if a big league manager told me then that I could have played every day for him and not be platooned, I could still have hit 30 to 35 home runs. Yeah. I could get out of bed at four o'clock in the morning *now,* and hit 30 home runs. Like *The Natural.* I was a natural hitter. I don't know why.

My own career highlights that stand out are all the grand slams I hit, including a pinch slam in the ninth off Sandy Koufax to beat the Dodgers in LA [May, 1959]—"Wagner, would you mind waking up, coming in and helping us out in this game here?" And hitting line drives off the pitchers' knees [laughs]. I hit one pitcher—he tried to jump over it but I hit it so hard it broke his ankle. Yeah, we tried to hit the ball back between the forehead. They're always throwing at *our* heads. It's a dangerous game. And when you look at it like that, it's a contest whereby you turn everything else off. And you know the pitcher's nervous when you've got people on base. And I know I've got the advantage because I don't care how hard he throws, he's scared to make a mistake because he knows the crowd's on him, the papers are waiting to write him off and I know that I can hurt him. So he's out there shaking, trying to figure out what to throw me and I know that, so I've got the advantage. That's how I beat them, because I knew they were nervous. It was whoever could stand the pressure the most. With 50,000 people watching. When you're playing for money.

You know how I learned how to hit? When I was six or seven years old, in Chattanooga, Tennessee, I didn't have anybody to play with. So I hit rocks outside. I was pitching rocks up in the air, and got so frustrated swinging up trying to hit those rocks. Until I learned to start hitting down on the rocks as they were coming down. Then I started lining 10 out of 10. As a *six*-year-old. I kept doing that when I was seven or eight, then

started hitting a baseball like that, because the baseball comes down from the pitcher's mound, and I started hitting down, like I hit those rocks. And I hit the baseball like that.

I saw Ted Williams hit like that. He was hitting bullets when I was about 14 years old, past the Detroit Tiger infielders before they could move. That woke me up, and I started hitting the ball like Ted Williams. And I started having hand movements like Ted Williams, because I never before saw a guy like Ted Williams go five-for-five, from the left side, off Herb Score, throwing 100 miles an hour. And I'm talking about *home runs,* to straightaway center field, to the upper deck. I watched him in batting practice hit 10 straight pitches out of the park. So that's what I started practicing. And I started watching Walt Dropo's stance, with his foot in the bucket. I learned to hit with all those stances, to see which one I was most comfortable with. Then I came up with my own. But Ted Williams was the greatest hitter I ever saw in my life. I *never* saw a hitter like that.

I tried to get somewhere *close* to him, and just getting close to Ted Williams is what carried me to the heights I accomplished, just trying to get *half* like that. He didn't swing at too many bad balls, but I started golfing some bad balls that Ted Williams never would have touched. I started golfing them out of the ballpark [laughs]. He would have had a heart attack [laughs]—high fastballs, low off the shoe top, a foot outside—he never said anything about my style, but I know he saw *some* of me in him. I always talked to him. He inspired me from age 14, at Tiger Stadium, watching him play.

I was born in Chattanooga, but grew up in Detroit, from the age of five on. We lived in the suburbs, about 50 miles from Detroit, in a town called Inkster, out by Dearborn and the Ford factory. In high school my grandmother was the cook at the grammar school. She was 60 when I was 12. I'm about 70 percent Cherokee. My grandma was full-blooded Indian. Everybody loved my grandma because she fed all the poor kids in the projects. She was a little Indian squaw. We called her "Big Mama." And she was my heart. She just let me be a real boy, like Huckleberry Finn. She told me, "All boys and dogs belong outdoors." [laughs] There were four ladies in the house—my grandma, my mother, sister and cousin. Then me and my brother. So my grandma let me roam the streets with my dog going fishing, hunting and roller skating. I never stayed out all night long because I didn't want to worry her, so I was always home by 11 o'clock. I did my homework on my own.

My father was friends with the chief of police—a black guy—in Inkster, along with all the black detectives, and all the men they were chasing. My dad had a poker game every Saturday night with all the numbers men, while their wives and the chief of police were all chasing them. So I grew up *not* a friend of the police. All the policemen's sons and I played basketball together. I got out of high school at two in the afternoon, and went to work at Lincoln-Mercury by four. And I was only 14. We said we were 18 to work in the factory. We got off at 12 midnight, and were back at high school at nine the next morning. J.C. Hartman, who played with the Houston Astros, worked after school at the Ford factory—he came from a family with 14 kids. I got out of high school with a C+ average, with a scholarship to Tuskegee Institute [Alabama] and a few more schools. And I didn't even get a chance to play with the high school team my freshman and sophomore years. So I played semi-pro with the older guys on weekends, guys from the Birmingham Black Barons and Kansas City Monarchs, on the sandlots. We traveled all over Michigan. Willie [Kirkland] was playing downtown, in the Detroit league sandlots. I was in the suburban league. I'd heard about Willie. We played against him once or twice.

Willie and I were the big stars of the Detroit area sandlots. Willie's family was kind of conservative. His mom had a home, with trees arched over the street. And I was in the projects, in new project homes built by the government, with lawns, a new high school built by the government, with glass backboards. We had it good out there. It was nice. I had a good life. Kids are always talking about how they had *this* kind of life, or *that* kind of life. But I had a *good* life, man, coming up. I was raised good.

Freedom. I worked—cut grass, washed cars, set up pins at the bowling alley, worked in the factory after school my freshman and sophomore years. I couldn't practice with the high school team until I was a junior. So when I got with the high school team, 50 scouts approached me. I was 14 or 15. They thought I was 18, traveling all over Michigan. The Phillies, Cleveland, everybody came up to me. I was playing American Legion ball. They'd come over to pick me up and take

me to games in the white areas. So I was hitting home runs when I was 15 years old. In high school I was hitting 500-foot home runs, and the coach couldn't believe it. And I was just having fun.

I went to a black college—Tuskegee Institute, in Tuskegee, Alabama. I played football in the fall, then made the traveling squad in basketball. Then went back home after Christmas to work in the factory to make some more money to come *back* to Tuskegee. That's where my nickname "Daddy Wags" comes from—I was down there at Tuskegee with the Detroit style, and the other brothers were right off the farm picking cotton, and I called them "country boys." And they said, "Daddy Wags." [laughs]

I was a center in football, only weighed 200 pounds, but I was fast, and good at downfield blocking, and made second team all-state. I also played linebacker, going up against schools like Dillard, Morehouse, Florida A&M, and all those black schools down south. And I liked it because I had never experienced playing against all-black teams before, because in Detroit we had integrated sports. We saw some great white ballplayers in Detroit. I got used to playing against white guys. I mean, we saw some guys play basketball that shot from the center of the court and made eight of eight. In high school. *White* guys.

When I came back to Detroit after Christmas, that's when the Giants offered to sign me a second time. They wanted to sign me right out of high school but I wouldn't. I told them I had to help my grandma. But the second time they gave her money to pay off the project house we had. So I started my pro career in Danville, Illinois, in the MOV [Missouri-Ohio Valley] League. My first game, I went five-for-five, in the rain and mud. That was in class-D, the lowest level of organized ball. They had me signed for class-A but it was a little too strong for me in spring training, so they wanted to release me. But Chick Genovese [Giants scout] told them, "This kid can hit. He doesn't play all year like those Spanish guys." We only played when it got warm. I had only been in spring training about two weeks and was striking out a lot, so they dropped me down to class-B. And that's when I hit home runs every day for about two weeks. Every day. Cepeda was there, on a different field, along with McCovey and Willie Kirkland. Then when they began making final cuts from the majors and triple-A all the way down, I ended up in class-D in Danville, and ended up hitting .332 [w/24HR & 115RBI], and being named Rookie of the Year.

In 1955 they jumped me up to class-C, at St. Cloud, Minnesota, in the Northern League. I said, "Well, I ain't moving too fast." Charlie Fox was my manager up there. He was an Irishman with red hair and a violent temper, but he was good to me and Willie Kirkland. We loved him. He talked that talk but, man, we gave Charlie Fox so many high points in his life [laughs]—he had the key to the Rolls-Royce with me and Willie Kirkland, Cepeda and McCovey. He was proud of us. I hit 29 home runs [w/127RBI & .313 average]. Twenty-five thousand people in St. Cloud and only one black man, and he passed as an Indian [laughs]. So I had to get involved in an all-white environment but, psychologically, you learn to deal with classes and stuff like that. No problem, you know? People were fine there.

I found out later on that the Giants had reasons for sending us black guys to different parts of the country, because before they brought us up to the major leagues they wanted to see how our PR was and our mentality was in dealing with the South, the North, the West, ... so they sent me to Danville, Illinois. That was right up my alley because I'm from the Midwest. Then they shot me up to St. Cloud, Minnesota. Then they shot me to Danville, Virginia, in the South. So that's how they got me ready for the big leagues, not just with hitting.

I played left field for Danville, Virginia [class-B, Carolina League], and one time we went through Charlotte, North Carolina, to play. A guy was sitting out in left field and he told me, "Nigger, if you catch the next ball that comes out here, I'm gonna shoot you, and I've got my shotgun right here." I didn't know if he was joking or not. But, man, I was *diving,* catching balls out there. I *couldn't* let that bother me. I knew I was in the South but I was focusing on trying to win. And I know, if they respect you, if you play the game all right, ... eventually they started applauding me in that stadium. I was just beating them to death with home runs. I hit 51 that year, and Dick Stuart hit 66 [at Lincoln, Nebraska, in class-A]—that was phenomenal but the Carolina League was a *pitcher's* league—that's why the Giants sent me there. McCovey played first base for the same team—he hit 20 home runs and drove in 90 runs. I was in left field, hit 51 homers and hit six more in the playoffs, and drove in 166 runs [both fig-

ures led league]. And McCovey's in the Hall of Fame. But I went into the army after that for two years, while McCovey kept playing. He was a good kid. He only weighed about 195 pounds. He was so skinny, and he thought I was Babe Ruth.

The Giants had us stay in a black lady's very nice home [in Danville]. They put us in homes in those cities, with the cornbread, the macaroni & cheese, the baked chicken. It was just like home. We stayed at a white family's home in St. Cloud, but it was still like home. Willie Kirkland stayed there the year before I came through.

I was the type of kid who really enjoyed his life coming up, and I had a lot of drive because I didn't think about failing no way, because there was nothing to go home to. My grandma was an older lady and I didn't want to go back to the projects and work in the factory. There was nothing to go back to. So I had total motivation.

I was in the Air Force ROTC at Tuskegee Institute and I was going to be a flier, because Tuskegee trained black pilots. I was a good student. Tuskegee *made* you study. I'd have been a genius if I had stayed there four years. I could always think. I had good teachers all the way through high school. Even now, I recently went through Anthony's real estate school in San Francisco. I just did it for the hell of it, to see if I could pass the test. And I started going to school to be a stock broker.

So after I hit those 51 home runs in Danville, Virginia, the Giants sent me to play winter ball in Puerto Rico, getting ready to bring me up to the major leagues. Then I went home to Detroit and got greetings from Uncle Sam—I got drafted. For 18 months. With Willie Kirkland, George Altman and Charlie Pride. We were all in Special Services together, at Fort Carson, in Colorado Springs. We played ball there. Willie Davis, the Hall of Fame football player, was there, too. We all partied together. They put us on orders to go to Korea about five times, but the General pulled us off the orders, so we could continue to play ball with the Army team. We traveled all over and we beat everybody in the Army, man.

When I got out of the service I went straight to Phoenix. I didn't even go home. I drove from Colorado Springs to Phoenix. We had a great team in Phoenix in '58. We had McCovey, Felipe Alou, Andre Rodgers, myself, Dusty Rhodes, and a center fielder named Bill Wilson—a white guy who was hitting .360 and leading the league. He was the best triple-A player in the world. He hit .350

every year in triple-A. The Giants sent Kirkland down to Phoenix in May and he couldn't make the lineup. We had McCovey at first base, Alou was in right, I was in left, Bill Wilson in center. Everybody was hitting .300 and we were leading the league by 15 games. Kirkland sat on the bench for about two weeks, then the Giants called the two of us up together, and we joined the team in Philadelphia [despite having so many of their top players called up by the Giants, Phoenix hung on to win the PCL championship with an 89-65 record, four and a half games ahead of San Diego].

I'M GLAD I PLAYED when I did because I got to play with Clemente, Mays, Elston Howard, Yogi Berra, Roger Maris, Mickey Mantle, Bobby Richardson, Tony Kubek, McCovey, Cepeda. The hitters today aren't even close to what they were when I played. The hitters were bigger then, and they were better. And you had more great *white* hitters then, in the sixties and seventies. I mean, big guys. They could *hit.* You have guys like Barry Bonds now, a big superstar, but you had 20 white guys who hit like Barry Bonds when I played. Guys like Bobby Allison and Al Kaline—these guys hit *every* game. They could beat you, man. You couldn't mess around with them. Richie Ashburn would line 10 straight balls foul—he'd wear out the pitcher with foul balls in the first inning. Maybe they took it more seriously then, but they were just better hitters. These guys now are showmen. They all play like Deion [Sanders]. They're 17 home run, 80 RBI hitters. When I played you had to hit 30 home runs just to stay out of Phoenix.

The greatest hitter I ever saw was Ted Williams. But Jimmy Ray Hart could have been as good as Rogers Hornsby if he didn't have a drinking problem. When I finished with the Giants in '69 we'd get to the ballpark to get ready for the game, and Jimmy Ray would be on the training table. They were trying to sober Jimmy Ray up. *Before* the game. I said, "Man, I ain't never seen nothing like this in my life. What are you doing on the table, Jimmy Ray?" But he was one of the greatest hitters I ever saw, just for pure strength. You could fool him and he'd still hit it out of the park. He was so strong. He wasn't a Yale man, but you could fool Jimmy Ray and he'd still hit the ball up against the center field fence on sheer strength. I mean, better than Rico Carty, better than Richie Allen, better than all those right-handed hitters. He was a hell of a hitter.

Mays was the greatest all-around player I ever saw. He'd steal second base 10 out of 10 times, and every time the second baseman or shortstop tagged him, they would tag him as he came up on the bag. I've never seen this in my entire life. Never did the ball beat him there so they could apply the tag. And I saw him do that 50 times. I never saw him get thrown out diving all around the bag like Maury Wills and all those guys trying to *evade* the tag. I never saw Mays do that. People don't realize Mays was fast. He was probably a 9.8 in the 100-yard dash. He always ran the bases with his speed, turning it on and off. And he played the outfield like it was fun, like a globetrotter. And I felt sorry for him because he was a right-handed hitter. It's tougher on a right-handed hitter because all the right-handed pitchers can throw at a right-handed hitter, and he's got to make up his mind whether he's going to bail out or stay in. That's a hell of a way to hit. I'm hitting left-handed so they've got to throw *in* to me, and that's easy. So they stick left-handers on me and I bail out a little bit, until I get ready to get serious. Then the left-hander's got a problem. You know, I'd play with them a while. Then when I'd get serious, they couldn't throw *nothing* close.

The toughest pitcher I ever faced was Jim Kaat. And Tommy John. Those are sinker-ball left-handed pitchers. They throw the ball from the knee down, to the ground, and throw hard. And the ball's like a brick, sinking. And they won't throw you any strikes down the middle. So if you hit it, you'll have to hit it off your shoetop down around your knees, and you're going to have to hit it on the ground. And they're not going to give you any home run pitch. Whitey Ford was good, but he'd hang one every now and then. And he threw spitballs, too. He struck me out with a sidearm pitch behind me, at Yankee Stadium, and the people just went crazy because he struck me out twice. Then I came up in the ninth inning and I knew he was coming back with the same pitch. And he came back with the sidearm behind me, and I hit it into the upper deck and beat him. And he told the sportswriters that was the last sidearm I'd ever see off him [laughs]. I was laughing in the clubhouse. A three-run homer. Beat him.

I'm retired now. I'm living kind of a radical lifestyle, like the hippies in San Francisco in the sixties. I've got a Lincoln, and I could get an apartment if I wanted to, with cable and every-

Leon Wagner (Steve Bitker)

Often I'll get recognized as an ex-ballplayer. I enjoy that but it can also turn you off after a while, when you're being praised and stroked over and over. Sometimes, then, you feel like they're really kicking you in the ass. I like to be greeted as a ballplayer, as long as I can say *thank you,* and get on to asking about *your* family and *your* kids—you know, give me a chance to stroke you back. Because baseball was a job [laughs]. It was a party at first, in the minors [laughs], dating them little high school girls. You didn't have any pressure. You didn't have more than 3,000 people in the stands.

I'll probably stay retired now. I really don't know what else I would want to get into because, whatever it is, it takes a lot out of you. Billy Dee Williams told me I should make acting a career. I've done several films already—*Bingo Long,* with Billy Dee and James Earl Jones; *A Woman Under the Influence* with Peter Falk and Gena Rowlands; *The Man From Uncle,* and a couple of more. Yeah, I could get back into that, but I'm just not interested. It takes a lot out of you, man, whatever you do. Selling cars took a lot out of me, just like baseball. Work on Sundays? *Me ?*

Long Beach, California

thing, but I just feel free being out—I don't know whether it's the Indian in me or what. I check into a fabulous hotel every now and then. But I always felt like I was rich, whether I had only two dollars or whatever. I was raised that way. I can always get some cash. And I ain't money hungry. I'm blessed. I get paid from baseball—$1,800 a month. *Forever.*

All my life I had $4,000 or $5,000 a month expenses, a house, two cars, one for the lady you know. And when you've been doing that since you were 23 years old and you're making $40,000 to 50,000 a year ... I just got tired of all that. I just got free for a change the last couple of years. My youngest son is up and out of the way. And I don't want to be 80 years old, finally retire and just die. You understand what I'm saying? I just feel like retiring now, and I'm 63 now. I just don't want to have all that pressure on me anymore, chasing the buck. I just don't want to have a heart attack.

I might now have but 20 bucks, but I only ask for what I need. Gene Autry, Earl Wilson and other ex-ballplayers always ask how I'm doing, and they want to send me money. But I won't take money from any of them. I was raised that way.

I've got a lifetime baseball pass—I can go to a game any time, free—but I really like football now. I like the 49ers and the Raiders. I've got 49ers season tickets with a lady I know up there. I can go see baseball but I find it boring, just sitting there. I'd rather play than watch. Yeah, you can't worry about getting bored with 40,000 people waiting to boo you [laughs]. You have to stay focused. Those people will motivate you.

WILLIE KIRKLAND

Willie Kirkland was one of several talented rookies on the Giants in '58, and one of three rookies in the Opening Day starting lineup against the Dodgers, along with Orlando Cepeda and Jim Davenport. He hit .258 that season with 14 home runs and 56 RBIs, and was named to The Sporting News *All-Rookie team. Willie hit 43 homers with 133 RBIs the next two years with the Giants, only to be traded along with Johnny Antonelli to Cleveland following the 1960 season for Harvey Kuenn. What followed was Kirkland's best season in the majors, with the Indians in '61, Willie hitting 27 homers and driving in 95 runs. Over nine big league seasons, he hit 148 home runs and batted .240.*

Kirkland spent the next six seasons with the Hanshin Tigers in Osaka, Japan, where he hit 126 home runs, including 37 in 1968. He became a folk hero in Japan, known to many as "Western Monjiro," named after a toothpick-chewing, wisecracking, television samurai star.

Willie now lives in Detroit, where he works as a security officer for General Motors.

SOMETIMES I LOOK BACK on my first year in San Francisco. And I say, "I wish I could live my life over," as far as being a ballplayer. I went to spring training in '58 and got into the batting cage. Now, if all during your life—and I'll always take my hat off to a batting coach—but if a guy's got a hitch in his swing, leave him *alone.* My first spring training with the Giants, Lefty O'Doul [Giants' spring batting coach] came up to me and showed me this picture and said, "You know who this is?" And I said, "No sir." And he said, "That's me." He changed my whole batting stance. And I don't think I ever got coordinated right after that. I don't care how many home runs I hit or how many years I played, he changed my *whole* batting stance.

I know I had a hitch. But I look at Cecil Fielder. Look at Jose Canseco. Look at some of these other guys. But for my first several years in the big leagues, really, they were trying to correct my hitch. Now, guys have a hitch—look at Tony Phillips [laughs]. He's got the worst hitch, I guess, of all. And is anybody bothering him? Does he hit the ball? But since that first day with Lefty O'Doul, starting from there, ... I was just a rookie, I had to change. I don't think I ever recovered from that. Because, how could I have had such success in the minors? I hit triple-A pitching [37 HR, 120 RBI in '56], I hit Puerto Rico winter ball, I hit everywhere. But I don't think I recovered from Lefty.

He said, "Willie, we've got to change your hitch." And I had to learn how to hit almost like all over again, because I had been hitting with that hitch all my life. I would hold the bat up high right behind my neck, behind my ear, and I guess I was dropping with the pitch. I never had a problem hitting like that but I guess in those days they didn't want you with a hitch. Everybody had to just stand there, step into the ball and swing. But I never had any problems in the minors. Eddie Stanky didn't change me. Nobody else changed me. Bill Rigney didn't change me at Min-

Willie Kirkland (SF Giants)

neapolis. Then, all of a sudden, *"You've got a hitch."* So what could I do? He changed it. But it seemed like I always felt, inside, *Uh-uh.* I could never find that hitch again. I could never find how I used to hit before.

But I think I played right field better at that time than anybody I knew. I remember reading in the paper some years ago that nobody could play right field for the Giants in those days. I never had any trouble playing right field. But I read in some article, "Willie Kirkland couldn't play right field." Not true. In spring training, Mays said we had to shade Cepeda out there [in left], and shade Leon [Wagner], too. I said I'd catch anything from right-center [field] my way, because you had to protect those guys toward left. We had two good outfielders. I know I enjoyed throwing. [*author's note: Kirkland led N.L. outfielders in double plays turned in '58, and tied for the A.L. lead in '61.*] I used to dare guys to run. I learned that from Mays. Mays was good. He had his own style. But, to me, Jim Landis and Richie Ashburn could go get a ball just as good as Mays. But Mays was *colorful.* Mays was just a *natural,* if you want to call it that.

I remember one game, Mays, McCovey and I all hit home runs. Then we went to Japan at the end of '60, and we were all talking to Horace Stoneham, asking, "Why don't you get a ballpark where we can use our power, like Wrigley Field in Chicago?" See, I didn't like Seals Stadium, and I didn't like Candlestick. I didn't like Seals because the wind blew out to left field. It wasn't friendly to a left-handed hitter like me. Then we went to Candlestick, where the wind blew to right field, but it was about a thousand miles, about 390 feet [397 to be exact, until 1970] to right-center. The fences were just so far away.

I remember I hit the first Giants' home run at Candlestick, in '60, against the Cardinals, and McCovey hit the first grand-slam, against the Braves. He hit a ball, I would say, that was headed for about halfway between the infield dirt and the right field fence. It was a mile high. Hank Aaron was playing right. The ball kept drifting and drifting [makes wind sound]. And drifting and drifting and drifting and drifting. Until it fell over the fence. It wasn't like when he hit it you knew it was gone. No, it wasn't that. It was more like he hit it straight up in the air. If there was no wind, Aaron would've caught the ball probably about halfway between the fence and the infield dirt. The first Candlestick grand-slam [laughs].

I remember one day we were talking about how to pitch to Ernie Banks, and somebody said, "Jam him." Sanford jammed him. He hit a grand-slam. The ball said, "Do I want to go? Yes, I want to go. No, I don't want to go. Yes, I want to go." And it just scraped the back wall, right down the line. I remember another game at Candlestick—Mays was on first base, somebody singled him to third, the outfielder messed around out there and Buck took off for home. Buck was going to be out. The outfielder had the ball and could've waited on him. But in the process of rushing the throw, he short-hopped it, the ball got past the catcher and we won the ballgame. Of course, Mays did that all the time.

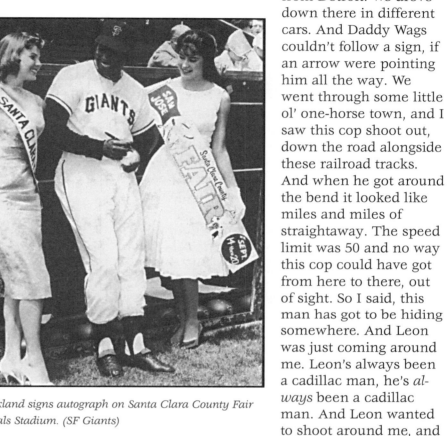

Willie Kirkland signs autograph on Santa Clara County Fair Day at Seals Stadium. (SF Giants)

But the only reason I didn't like Seals Stadium was because of the wind blowing out to left field. Otherwise I really enjoyed San Francisco. I lived down the street from Leon Wagner. I remember when we broke for spring training in '58, from Detroit. We drove down there in different cars. And Daddy Wags couldn't follow a sign, if an arrow were pointing him all the way. We went through some little ol' one-horse town, and I saw this cop shoot out, down the road alongside these railroad tracks. And when he got around the bend it looked like miles and miles of straightaway. The speed limit was 50 and no way this cop could have got from here to there, out of sight. So I said, this man has got to be hiding somewhere. And Leon was just coming around me. Leon's always been a cadillac man, he's *always* been a cadillac man. And Leon wanted to shoot around me, and I kept blocking him. And as I drove on down, I could see the glitter from the trees. This cop had backed up into the trees. If I had let Leon go around me, he was gonna floor it. He's the kind of guy—you could take Leon halfway around the world, but when he gets where he knows where he's going, he'll leave you. And if I had let Leon pass we both probably would have been in jail. Because when they stepped on you down there, you're already *guilty*.

But I really liked San Francisco. I liked the team I was on. I liked the city. I met some nice people out there. Man, I used to get in to see all the movie screenings. I knew the right people. When a film came out I was one of them guys who sat up there in that private screening room. I could sit down there and watch that movie that the writers had come to review. I just met some nice people out there. I guess the nicest guy of all was Jeff Chandler, the actor. He was a big Giants fan. He was all right. Sammy Davis, Jerry Lewis,

George Raft. We met all these guys. I liked playing on every club I was on, in fact, even Baltimore. I just didn't like [manager] Hank Bauer. Bauer and I just did not get along.

I remember going to Wrigley Field in '59, when Al Worthington was pitching. Supposedly, Chicago was stealing our signs, out of the scoreboard. And that hurt us. And supposedly, back at Seals Stadium, [coach] Herman Franks was in the scoreboard giving signs to [coach] Wes Westrum [laughs]. *Supposedly,* now. And Westrum was relaying the signs to Mays. And Al Worthington, supposedly, found out about this and said, "I'll spill everything." That's the rumor. How true that was I cannot say. But that's the rumor. Now, I'm not saying that's the reason we didn't win the pennant in '59, but having our signs stolen in Chicago that final week of the season did hurt us.

I remember in Milwaukee when Bob Schmidt hit a home run. First pitch. I'm on deck and I see Bill Rigney looking for a pinch hitter. But nobody said a word, so I step into the batter's box. First pitch I hit a home run. I circle the bases. The guys in the dugout say, "Silent treatment." Nobody says anything. And Rigney's still looking for a pinch hitter [laughs]. He's *still* looking for a pinch hitter. For *me.* And I've already hit a home run. Finally, everybody's saying, "Way to go, Willie, way to go." And Rigney says, "What happened?"

They said Rigney tried to manage like Leo. Mays could go into one of the damnedest slumps. Then we'd go to Milwaukee or wherever Leo might be, and Leo would say, "Buck [snaps fingers], get your bat, let's go." And we're in Milwaukee for three days. And Mays would go to bat 12 times with eight to nine hits easy. I don't know what Leo did to him. Leo and Hank Sauer were the only two guys Mays would listen to.

I remember one year in spring training I met Ted Williams, in Scottsdale. I couldn't believe it. I looked at this man, behind the cage. I walked up to this man. I looked at this man. I said, here I am, standing next to the greatest man who ever picked up a bat. I said, this is *Ted Williams.* It was almost like I was a three-year-old. To be next to this legend.

A kid was out on the mound pitching. He threw a ball. A strike. A ball. The kid said, "No, that was a strike." Ted said, "No, that was a ball." The kid said, "You get in the batter's box. I'll strike you out." And Ted told the kid, "One of the

Willie Kirkland (SF Giants)

three pitches you throw me I'll hit out of this ballpark," while pointing to right-center, 365 feet away, with the wind blowing right to left.

Now, he had the attention of everybody. I already had my seat. The *grand* seat. Because I was already standing *next* to the man. First pitch, about that far outside [gesturing]. Ted said, "Ball." The kid threw the man a change-up. The man just flicked his wrists. And the ball went *zzzooom.* Now, that was a change-up, not a fastball, not a curveball, not a forkball. The man just *flicked* the wrists. No stride. No gruntin'. The man just picked the wrist. And I stood there. And I said, "Yeah, you *are* the greatest."

When I got to Cleveland, Satchel Paige was pitching batting practice, for the A's. And Ed Charles said, "Get that ball over, old man." And Satchel said, "Ed, I'll throw you three. I'll strike you out, *and* I'll tell you what's coming." [laughs] And Ed said, "Ain't no way, old man." And Satchel said, "Smoker!" Strike one. And then he said, "Don't worry, I'm not gonna hit you. I'm gonna tell you what's coming. Curveball!" Strike two. He laughed. "Uncle Charlie," he said [laughs]. He struck the man out on three pitches. He said, "I'll give you three strikes, and I'll tell you what's coming, and you will not hit it." Satchel must have been a *hundred* years old then. Finally, the A's owner had him sitting in the right field bullpen with a nurse, with a blanket over him. That's how he'd sit in the bullpen.

It's amazing, really, when you sit down and listen to people talk. Charlie Pride used to tell us about the Negro League. Like right now—you could sit down here and listen to a guy talk about going deer hunting, and how cunning those deer are. It's amazing. It's really amazing when you hear people tell you about another part of life that you don't know anything about. Charlie Pride could get the whole audience in the palm of his hand talking about the Negro League. About Josh Gibson. About Satchel Paige, calling his infielders in and telling them to sit down. And you listen. And you say to yourself, "Man, this is *amazing.*"

I remember one day I got a hit off Koufax at Candlestick. My *behind* was in the dugout. I hit Koufax [laughs]. I should have asked for the ball. I swear, my behind was in the dugout. I was on one knee, and the way the wind blew there, the left fielder was probably playing center field, and I hit a stand-up double. He threw me a curveball, and I grunted and I moaned, and hit the ball with one hand through the infield for a double. Sandy Koufax died laughing. It was funny. It was really funny. The only hit I ever got off that man.

My closest friend on the Giants was probably Leon. I roomed with McCovey, though, on the road. Me and Mac. Then, when I was traded to Cleveland, I roomed with Jim Busby. That was the team I wanted to play on as a kid, because they had Luke Easter and Larry Doby. I met Luke in winter ball some years later but I never met Larry. I didn't really know anything about Doby, but they were just my idols—Luke Easter and Larry Doby. They were just ballplayers to me. I didn't even know anything about Doby being the first black to play in the American League.

The Giants scout who signed me was named George Niedson. I was 17 at the time, playing sandlot ball in Detroit. He didn't really know anything about me, but the day he came out, I hit two home runs, and for about a month or two the guy kept bugging me to sign a contract. I didn't really want to go to the Giants. I wanted to go to Cleveland, because they had Doby and Easter.

But I finally signed. I said, "Mom, what do you think? I've never been away from home." She said, "If you want to do it, do it. Try it." I was a pitcher then. I pitched a one-hitter and struck out 22 my first game. I had a fastball, curveball and a backup fastball that went *in* to the hitter—we called it an *"inshoot"* [laughs]. An inshoot [laughs]. That's what we called it. I'd throw it sidearm and hit the outside corner. The second game I pitched a two-hitter and struck out 13. The first two games I pitched I struck out 35. I also hit three guys the first game. I was wild.

That's when I first got to know Wagner. We had a hitting contest in Inkster, to see who could hit the ball farthest. He hit one out, I hit one a little bit farther. He hit another, I hit one farther [laughs]. We knew each other well in those days. Well, we knew *of* each other. He was a little scrawny kid, and so was I.

Of course, the Giants didn't want me to pitch. They wanted me to play every day, so I went with the outfielders in spring training, in 1953. They told me, "We can send you to Albany, New York, or we can send you to Maryville, Tennessee." I said, "I want to go to Albany. That's in a Northern state. I don't want to go to the South." A couple of days later they came up to me and said they had seven left-handed hitters in Albany, that I had to go to Maryville. I said, "Man, I want to go to Albany." They said, "You're going to Maryville." So they sent me to Maryville-Alcoa, in the Mountain State League [class-D], 15 miles outside of Knoxville. I went down there and it was an *experience and a half.*

When I left Detroit I got on the bus and sat in the middle of the bus all the way until I got to Georgia. I'm just sitting there, reading a book, at a rest stop. The bus driver comes down the aisle and coughs. I didn't know what he meant. Finally he said, "You have to move to the back." I said, "Why? I've been in this seat ever since I left Detroit." Then I said to myself, "Oh, my God, this is *Georgia."* I remembered that I had to ride in the back of the bus. So I said, "OK," and moved to the back of the bus. When I was in the service, I came through Birmingham. Colored. White. Airport. I didn't want any of their business. I just wanted a bathroom. Nobody said anything to me. I was not approached. I had my army uniform on. That was it. But when I played down there it was a lot different. I had heard about the KKK, but I didn't know where they were. And one night I'm staying at a friend's house, and they came marching down the street with the hoods and everything, burning a cross right there.

But once the season started, we had our own bus. We sat where we *wanted* to. One day I got on [a city bus] with no place to sit, except in the front, and the bus driver said, "Willie Kirkland?" I said, "Yes, sir." He said, "Sit right there, Willie." Now, this was a no-no, supposedly, but he told me to sit there. On the bus we just talked baseball. People didn't look at the color of my skin. They just knew me as a ballplayer, and what I was doing for the city. That's how they looked at all of us. When they went to the ballpark they weren't calling me, "Nigger," or this or that. They just called me Willie.

We had three blacks on the team. We used to eat at this lady's house. Just to show you how it was, dinner generally cost us only 65 cents because she did the cooking. And breakfast was 35 cents. The way we determined who would sit at the head of the table and get first pickings of, say, chicken or pork chops or whatever, was the guy who got the most hits the night before [laughs]. Who established that rule? We did. I stayed at one house, the other two guys stayed with her. So the guy who got the most hits or had the better night than the others would get the first two pieces of whatever he wanted.

Remember when I said before about listening to some of these stories and saying to yourself, "Man, this is amazing"? Well, get this. It was my first year of pro ball. And I saw a town—*my* town, Maryville-Alcoa—run the umpires out of town for making a bad call the night before. They just ran them out of town [laughs]. I'm *serious*. Some of these fans traveled with 30-30 handguns. I was in Morristown, Tennessee, one night and stole home. The umpire called me safe because the catcher interfered. And the fans were literally shooting holes through the clubhouse. The local cops wouldn't do anything. They had to call the highway patrol to get the umps out of town.

Another time we were in Morristown and the score was 6-5 in favor of us. I think I hit three home runs. And I was talking to this guy through the fence during the whole ballgame. He said, "Willie." I was in right field. The tying run was on third, the winning run on second. Two outs. Ninth inning. He said, "Willie." I turned around. He said, "You black nigger. If they hit the ball to you and you catch it, you're a *dead* nigger." [laughs] I said, *"What?"* He said, "You're dead, man." So I said, "If the ball's hit out here, and I

catch the ball, I'm dead?" He said, "Yeah." The ball didn't get hit out there. I would have dropped it. *Yeah,* I took him seriously. I'm laughing about it now because I can think back. But I saw two long barrels—it could have been two long pipes—but it could have been a gun, through the holes in the fence. When I turned around all I could see were two long things through the holes in the fence. So you see two little round things sticking out, how do you know what it is? He said, "If you catch the ball, you're dead." If he had hit it to me, I wouldn't have caught it. I wouldn't have.

In my first professional game I hit a home run, triple and a single. The next day in the paper some guy named Anderson writes, "Big, burly, black Willie Kirkland—six-four, 210 pounds [I was six-one, 190]—*says* he's from Detroit. But he talks and acts like Alabama sour sorghum syrup, soaked in cotton." This guy hated me for three-fourths of the season and I don't know why. I didn't even know the guy. I think it was because of a bet between me and the club. They had a center fielder they owned. He was a school-teacher, and it was a bet about who would hit the most home runs. He was the star, and then here I come, a little rookie kid, first year of pro ball. And we had a guy named Mussel Shoals. He led the Mountain State League every year [.427, 30HR, 142RBI in '53]. He had muscles like Kluszewski. He wore his shirt like Kluszewski. And he told me one day, "Willie, you're gonna be a good ballplayer. But you got to stop wearing that long-sleeve shirt." I said, "But in that sun, I don't want to get no blacker than I already am." But he said, "Just take the sweatshirt off because, what it does, it kind of impedes your swing." And I took the sweatshirt off.

The day after they ran the umpires out of town, I hit three home runs, a triple and drove in 10 runs [laughs heartily]. For the year I hit 35 home runs, 24 triples, drove in 164 runs and hit .326. I had good years all during minor league ball. In '54, I led the Northern League [class-C] at St. Cloud, hitting .360. In '55, I led the Western League [class-A] in home runs with 40, at Sioux City. That was when we went into a town in Kansas, en route to Wichita, where President Truman was born. We didn't really want to stop in the first place, but the manager had a girlfriend in this town. In Wichita the manager of the hotel had said all the ballplayers could stay at the hotel. *Everybody.* The whole team could stay *here.* The black ballplayers didn't have to stay over *there.*

Everybody could stay here and eat here. So all the guys said, "Let's wait until we get to Wichita so we can all eat together." But no, no, our manager said we had to eat in this other town.

So we stopped at the bus station, and eight of us went out to find us a restaurant, with meal money for hamburgers and hot dogs. Seventy-five cents a day, or whatever. Four guys sit here, four guys sit there. So I'm sitting on the end. The other guys, including Chico Fundora [Cuban], ate at the bus station, because we only had an hour. But the eight of us sat down, and four of them immediately get waited on. But the other four of us don't even get a menu. So finally this girl comes over. She hands out three menus. To the *four* of us. One of my teammates says, "Excuse me, miss, you didn't give him a menu." She says something and walks away. So now, these four guys there are already eating. She gets the manager and he comes out and says, "Sorry, *you* can't eat here." To me. Now, at least 20 of the 25 ballplayers on our club were from up north. All of us were from some part of the country *other* than the South. And the manager says, "You can't eat here." And we say, "Why?" And he says, "You just can't eat here." And we say, "C'mon, let's go." And my teammates cussed the manager out, poured water on the table [laughs], and all eight us left. The guys who already had been eating didn't pay. All white guys. And me.

We were just a ball team. We did everything together. So we went back to the bus terminal, got on the loud speaker, told all the Sioux City ballplayers, "Let's get out of this town," and went to the bus driver and said, "Either you drive us or we'll take the bus." And the guy said, "You're not taking my bus, so let's go." Because he didn't want to stop anyway. And we just happened to be going down this one-way street when along came the manager. We were *leaving* the manager. And we stopped. He got on and never said a word. He knew what happened. He had to have known. We were just a ball club. You can't really put it into words. The guys said, "If we lose we lose together. If we win we win together." I was leading the league in home runs at the time but I didn't hear anything like, "You're the star, you're the star, you're the star." We didn't have all that.

Anyway, I led the league with 40 home runs for Sioux City, even though I played with a broken jaw for six weeks, with teeth knocked out and my jaw wired. Oh man, you talk about an awesome bad feeling. I got down to 175 pounds,

from 205. But you know what? I hit the ball even *better* [laughs]. Don't ask me why. I was just a squirrely 175-pound kid. They said, "Willie is wired for no sound." The only thing I could eat was milkshakes, mashed potatoes, anything creamy. And I remember the day when I went to the doctor and he said, "We're gonna take the wires out." And he finally pulled all the wires out. So I went to this restaurant where if you hit a home run you could get a bunch of free food. I knew everybody there because Sioux City was a small town. I knew everybody, everybody knew me. I didn't know many *names* but they knew who I was, that I was a ballplayer. So I went into the restaurant and they had a stack of free eats waiting for me, for hitting all these home runs. When I walked in, people stopped. I mean, it was all in the papers, that I got the wires out of my jaw. I told the doctor I was going to eat. He told me, "Willie, you'll have to break yourself in." I said, "No, no, no, no. I'm going to the restaurant and I'm gonna have me a meal and a half."

So I went into the restaurant, everybody was watching me, I went up the cafeteria line and got *two* girls to carry all my food back to the table. I'm eating all this food now, even though the doctor told me to start small because my stomach couldn't take all that rich food. He said, "You know how long you been without solid foods?" I said, "I don't care, I'm gonna eat. Everything I like." Salisbury steak, mashed potatoes, peas, cake [laughs]. I had a whole table filled with food. It was phenomenal. There were at least 20 people sitting around me watching this. They said, "We're gonna see this. We're gonna watch you eat." [laughs] I was laughing, looking at all these people, saying, "Watch this, you guys." I took one bite, and something inside me said, "Ain't *no* way you gonna eat me." The *food* said, "Ain't no way." I put it down, looked around, people were laughing, saying "Go ahead, Willie, eat it. Let's see this." I said, "Give me time. Don't rush me. I'm gonna eat it." And I put some more food in my mouth and sucked on it, and they said, *"Chew, Willie, chew."* [laughs] I finally was defeated. All that food there. I finally said, "Whatever you people want. Take it."

The next year, in '56, I played triple-A, at Minneapolis, for Eddie Stanky. "The little brat," they called him. I hit 37 home runs and drove in 120 runs. In fact, in Charleston, I hit one across the river and over the tracks off Jim Bunning—Hall of Famer. But Eddie Stanky made me into a great outfielder. In spring training that year, Rosie Ryan, the Minneapolis general manager, said he didn't want me there. He said I couldn't catch the ball. But Eddie Stanky said, "I want him because he can hit." And Stanky got a pinch hitter on our ball club, Bill Taylor, and said, "Bill, Willie's yours." But if Bill Taylor said, "Willie, I'm hitting you a line drive," some way, somehow I would miss it. I mean, I could judge a fly ball. But I don't know. I just wasn't a good outfielder. But before I left spring training, I was as good as I wanted to be. And I was *good*. I'm not bragging. I'm just saying I worked, I worked, I worked, I worked, I worked. I didn't know anything about the Willie Mays catch then, but I got so good—thank you, Jesus—that I could catch a ball. I mean, I could turn it on.

Baseball today—I'm not making fun of it, but to me it's not baseball. It's not the game that we played. It's all about money. It's money, money, money, money, money. And you're making these long dollars, but you can't catch the ball in the outfield, you don't hit the cutoff man, you don't bunt. They don't do a lot of things now. But then, it's all about money.

But in '56, I went out there every day, *every* day before the game, picking up ground balls, hitting line drives, hitting the cutoff man. And I was hitting well over .300 for a while. But then I ended up hitting .293. Before I fell off, Eddie Stanky said, "Willie, now remember what they're getting you out on. They're getting you out on change-ups." Then I began to look for change-ups. And they just busted that fastball by me. And I went into what I didn't realize was a slump. See, in those days, we all didn't know about slumps. There was no such word in the minor leagues as a slump. What's a *slump?* So you don't get any hits today, you get some hits tomorrow. I think a slump is mental, really.

Then you get to the big leagues, you don't get a hit for a couple of games, you're in a slump. They *put* you in a slump. But what's a slump? Then you begin to worry about what you're doing wrong. Then you begin to *think*. In the minors, you don't think. You just work and play. If you get some hits, you get some hits. If you don't get any hits, you don't get any hits. So what [laughs]? This is the way it was *then*.

I spent 10 months in the military in '57. I got drafted. I could have got a deferment and gone back to play winter ball in the Dominican, but a guy named Charlie Pete, a St. Louis outfielder,

was killed when a plane he was riding on crashed into a mountain, in the Dominican. It killed everybody on board. And I said, "I don't want to go back to the Dominican. Not yet. I'll go into the service."

I thought I'd be stationed at Fort Minuwa, Missouri, but they said, "No, we're going to send you to Colorado Springs." OK. I went to Colorado Springs. We had a baseball team there. I was the only guy with triple-A experience. But we had Charlie Pride, who played in the Negro League. We had George Altman and Daddy Wags. All on the *same* team. We had a $38,000 bus. Now, we were in the *service*. We'd work on the ballfield for half a day—maybe practice in the morning until 12 o'clock. And we had our own special barracks. We challenged all the army and navy teams. That's how great we were. I was the captain because I had played triple-A. When we saw the major, if he was by himself, we didn't salute. But if he was with someone, that was altogether different.

One time we lost a couple of games and the post commander came aboard our $38,000 air-conditioned bus and said, "Do you guys want to continue playing ball on my post?" "Yes, sir." "Do you guys want to continue riding in this $38,000 air-conditioned bus?" "Yes, sir." We had our own barracks, ate when we wanted to [laughs], had a class-A pass to go off the post. Everybody knew us. I mean, you couldn't have asked for a better time to be in the service. We didn't pull no kind of duty. No KP. No nothing. The post commander said, "If you guys want to continue having all these nice things, don't bring me back a losing record." So we went down to Fort Knox and won the fifth army tournament in four straight games. I think the post commander in those days would say, "Well, who's available? I want this guy. And this guy. And that guy. And, sure enough, we had the best team. We had me, Leon, George Altman, J.C. Martin—all the [future] big leaguers. That was the team we had. And you *don't* beat us.

We were unbeatable. We just clobbered the opposition. From there, I think we all took about a 90-day leave of absence [laughs]. When I got back to Colorado Springs, there were guys who should've been in Korea. But their orders had been pulled. And as time went on they said, "Willie, you're up for discharge." I said, "I'm up for what?" They said, "You're up for discharge." So I stayed in the Army for 10 months, 27 days.

Charlie Pride, God knows, I can't believe this, he was playing that ... [laughs], and saying,

"One day I'm gonna be famous." He was a pitcher then. And he was singing that junk. We called it *junk.* And he kept saying, "One of these days I'm gonna be big." And we'd say, "No, man, not playing *that.*" I don't remember how well he pitched but I still remember that mess he was singing. And I'd say, "Just what are you singing?"

I HIT 27 HOME RUNS with 95 RBIs [both career highs] with Cleveland in '61, after getting traded by the Giants [with John Antonelli for Harvey Kuenn]. I remember the three home runs I hit in one game, off Calvin McLish [of the White Sox] in Cleveland [all on oh-two counts]. I think I became the 11th player in history to hit four home runs in two games. [*author's note: He also tied the major league mark with four home runs in four at-bats.*] I hit a fastball off McLish for that first homer, then a change-up for the second homer, then a curveball for the third. Then I'm coming to bat for the fourth time, in that same game. We're down a run. Man on first base. Ninth inning. I'm at the plate. *Bunt* sign [laughs]. I couldn't believe this. Jimmy Dykes was the manager. A *bunt* sign. I looked at the third base coach and said, "Wait." I go down there and he said, "Willie, you're gonna bunt." I probably wouldn't have hit a homer anyway. McLish threw me a fastball right there [gesturing letter-high], saying, "How far can you hit this one?" And I bunted it down the third base line, running half-assed to first because I was mad. Vic Power was up next. They walked him. Then the next guy hit into a double play and we lost the ballgame.

When the game ended, here came the reporters. "Why didn't you swing the bat?" "I wasn't the manager." See, in those days they'd fire you. What would have happened if I *had* swung away [sighs and laughs]? I don't know. Baseball then, you had a manager. Now, you don't worry about the manager. I had a manager. He said, "This is what you do." And that's what I did.

I remember when I got to Baltimore [in '64]. I don't know why they wanted me, I couldn't play. We had Brooks Robinson—the greatest third baseman—Boog Powell, Dave McNally, Jerry Adair, Jackie Brandt, Stu Miller with that herky-jerky change-up. We had a good team. If I went to bat there five times, it took five weeks. One time per week. I couldn't play for Hank Bauer. I don't know why. I couldn't play for him. They traded Al Smith and $50,000, I think, to Cleveland for me. I went to spring training, and Hank and I had a run-in. I don't know why. I hit a shot to the second baseman, like *bam,* a one-hopper and he catches it. And, no, I'm not going to run to first base like I'm crazy. You know, it's spring training, so you jog down to first base. It was a line drive one-hopper to the second baseman. What am I gonna do? Fly? Same game, I'm on first base on a hit-and-run. And I learned this from Mays, though a lot of guys are doing it now—you don't watch the coach. In some instances, if the guy can run, you look at where the outfielders are playing, you know what kind of arms they have, you don't *have* to look at the coach. I learned a lot from just listening to Mays, because we roomed together. This man could tell you a lot and teach you a lot. He'd say, "When you get on first base, where are the outfielders playing? What kind of arms do they have? You can *walk* to third base on some guys."

So the ball was hit to right field, on a hit-and-run, and I looked over my right shoulder. It looked like a Texas-leaguer. The guy caught the ball and doubled me up. When I got to second base I picked up speed going to third. The guy caught the ball and doubled me up. Two days later, in the clubhouse, Hank Bauer says, "Willie! Come here." He says, "I thought you could run." I say, "I think I can. What are you talking about?" He says, "The ball the other day hit to the second baseman, you didn't run at all." I say, "Hank, it was a bam-bam play. I hit the ball, bam, one-hop to the second baseman, before I got out of the batter's box. Spring training. I didn't want to run hard. I might have pulled a muscle." He says, "Well, that double play ball you messed up. What happened on that?" I say, "I was running. I looked over my right shoulder. I saw the ball. It looked like it was gonna be a Texas-leaguer." I say, "Hank, did you notice, when I got to second base, I picked up speed." I couldn't play for Hank Bauer. I'd go out to batting practice, everybody got to hit but me. Steve Barber, Boog Powell, we had a good club. Everybody wondered, "Willie, why you can't play?" I'd say, "I don't know why I can't play. You tell me why I can't play."

I go into the clubhouse one day, they said, "Willie, you're on waivers." I went in the office, came out. Boog and I were just like brothers. We had a little pre-game TV talk show. People would write in and say, "Get more of Boog and Willie." We were clowns. We were just crazy. We just enjoyed each other. We'd have 15 minutes of air time to do whatever we wanted to do. Clown around, whatever, as long as it pertained to baseball. And we would get up there, unrehearsed, and we'd just act the *fool*. But people liked it.

So I go to Washington with Gil Hodges, God rest his soul. He said, "Willie, you're gonna play every day." I said, "Gil, I'm gonna tell you right now. I'm not in shape. I'm in shape for running and throwing, but I've been to bat only five times in the last five weeks." But he said, "You're going to play." Baltimore comes to town. Steve Barber's pitching. And I did not like Steve Barber. First three times Steve struck me out. The next time up, the score was 2-2 and Steve threw me a slider that he didn't get where he wanted. But I put it where I wanted. I bet I hit that ball, with all the frustration—not from guys on the club, but from Hank Bauer—all the *frustration* and animosity I had in my heart went into that swing. I must have hit that ball 500 feet. I hit that ball into the third deck, way up yonder. That's how far that ball went. And I was hot-doggin' it [around the bases]. When I got around third base, I *stopped*. I took my hat off. And I bowed to Hank Bauer. When the game was over, they said Hank Bauer ripped his shirt off and didn't take a shower.

Now, the next day—I'm a hot dog, I admit that—I go to the ballpark, I see some of the guys on the [Baltimore] club and say, "Hey, fellas, I just want to say one thing. I hot-dogged it around third, but ..." And Steve Barber says, "Look, you hit the ball, and I threw the ball in the wrong place. I made the mistake and you hit it." I say, "Well, my hot-doggin' ..." He says, "We know, we know, you did that for Hank. We know you. We played together three-fourths of the season. We know how you think, we know how you feel. We know you did not get the chance and we all sometimes wondered why."

The rest of the season a guy named George Brunet and I had something to do with seven games in which we beat Baltimore. They lost the pennant by two games [to the Yankees, despite 97 wins]. In fact, in one of those games I could have just *killed* Robin Roberts. He fell over first base and I guess I must have jumped over him with about 20 somersaults, trying not to hurt this man. And I had him dead to rights if I had been a dirty ballplayer. When this was over Robin came up to me—he in his dugout, I in mine—and said, "Willie, thanks." I said, "For what?" We're there talking from both dugouts, during the game. Ain't a blow being thrown. We're just standing there talking. He said, "Do you know what you could've

done to me?" I said, "No, what?" He said, "If you had been a dirty ballplayer you could've just *spiked* me." I said, "But Robin, I'm not that kind of ballplayer." He said, "I know. But I tell you what, I want to shake your hand." And the ballplayers around us are saying, "Huh? Huh?" And he was right. I could have. I could have really *hurt* him, if I had been a dirty ballplayer. I said, "Robin [laughs], that's not me. I know you guys. I mean, why would I want to hurt you or anybody else?" He said, "Well, you got traded. You got mistreated." I said, "But that's baseball. There's nothing I can do about that. But you guys did nothing to me. I'm not mad at you guys." But I know that during the final fourth of that season, George and I helped beat them seven ballgames.

That's when they had Wally Bunker. That kid [19 years old] could pitch. One game he pitched a one-hitter. Next game he pitched a two or three-hitter. He won 19 games that year. And when you talk about ballplayers, look at that Brooks Robinson. And you talk about relief pitchers with that junk, [look at] Stu Miller. Boy, just to sit on the bench and watch Brooks was worth the price of admission, with that little ol' raggedy arm he had. He had no jet but he'd always just barely nip you. He'd just get it there. Just think if I had been collecting bubble-gum cards then. Just think, Topps bubble gum. All the cards right there. And I could have collected all those cards. But I didn't.

It was a different game then in a lot of ways. In those days you didn't dig no ditch at the plate. You'd come up and tiptoe to home plate. You hit a home run, you run around the bases and you go sit down. Because the next time up, man, it all depends on who's pitching. You're gonna get decked. That was baseball in those days. You hit a guy now, he wants to fight. But if you're making $20 million, then why do you want to hit a guy? If I'm making $20 million and you're making $20 million, why can't it just be either I get you or you get me? I got a five-year contract, you got a 10-year contract. My family's gonna eat, regardless if I don't win a game all year. Why should I want to knock you down? I look at these athletes today with the money they're making and wonder, why are they trying to kill each other? See, I can't understand that. You can't *make* me understand that. I could understand it if I'm trying to pitch you tight and the ball comes in on you. But why would I want to throw at you? For what?

We came in to Detroit when I was with Cleveland, and Birdie Tebbets' idea was to get the best guy in the lineup. Barry Latman and then Gary Bell pitching for us. Bell threw hard, over 90 miles an hour. First day, Bunning throws at somebody. Latman comes right back and hits Kaline on the wrist—stuck him like a line drive. The next day Frank Lary throws at somebody again—both Bunning and Lary were known for knocking guys down. So Gary Bell was ready. Kaline, you've got to *go.* And when the ball hit Kaline in the ribs, the ball just *stuck.* I know Kaline wanted to *cry* [laughs]. Because I was in right field looking at him. The ball didn't just hit him. It hit and kind of twisted. It just twisted into his ribs. That's how they got away from throwing at our guys— we got the best guys in their lineup. We played dirty then. We all didn't call it dirty. But that's how baseball was played in those days.

In Japan, when I played over there, it was just a friendly game of baseball. If a guy got hit, the pitcher would walk up to home plate, take his hat off and say, "*Gomenasai* [sorry]." And that's it. You go into second base, you don't slide. Instead, you say, "Oh, excuse me."

When I finished up with Washington in '66 I went to Hawaii and played for the [triple-A] Islanders. I hit 33 home runs in '67. And then I got a two-year contract at $45,000 a year to play in Japan [for the Hanshin Tigers, in Osaka]. And I got over there and found out it was a *whole new ballgame* there. Everything over there was different. They had their own style of baseball. I hit cleanup. Had 37 home runs my first year. It was the Americans against the Japanese. That's what they said. It took me a long time to adjust to their strike zone, and to playing over there in general. I *enjoyed* playing over there. I played with a guy named Gene Bacque, a pitcher who played triple-A for Detroit. He made a bunch of money over there, too [won 29 games in '64]. Our manager was a guy named Murayama, who was also a pitcher. It seemed like he would pitch only when the team was down, say, after they lost a couple of games. I think we won 23 of 25 in August. But then the game that broke our back came against the [Tokyo] Giants. I had two home runs and a double in the first five innings, with five or six RBIs. Then Murayama took me out of the ballgame. *Don't* ask me why. They were just *dumb.* He took me out of the ballgame and we ended up losing 11-10. I would have come up again with the bases loaded. We lost the game and we lost the pennant.

Over there, if a guy isn't hitting the ball well in batting practice, he'll say, "My condition is bad." Then he'll go take a shower, put a patch over his eye and go home. Americans want to play. I've got to play in order to produce. And yet, Murayama played with me from the first day I got there. Whenever we'd win a ballgame, I don't care what I did, I was never allowed to finish the game. Fred Valentine, who played with Washington, was there with me in 1970, and he loved it. But I don't know. When I first got there I said, "I'm not going to live Japanese-style. I left my country to come to your country. A lot of your rules I will go by. But don't ask me to sleep on the floor. I'm used to American-style hotels, and I'm used to American-style food."

In fact, they asked me to go to the minor leagues at one point. And I told Murayama, "I'm not going to the minor leagues. No. If I go to the minor leagues, that's an open door for any American to come over here. Because if I have nine years in the big leagues and you send me to the minors, then what is there to stop Blasingame or any of these other guys from winding up in the minors, too. I'm not going." It was absurd. I said, "You people are ... [laughs]. You people are *dumb.* This is not baseball. What do you call this? You all do some *stupid* things over here." I think when they asked me to go to the minors, it was all about letting me know who was the manager and how powerful he was.

Now, aside from baseball, I enjoyed Japan. I loved the sightseeing. I just enjoyed so many things over there. Their way of life. We build up, they build down. They've got a whole city underground. When it's raining you can go under the city and walk for miles almost. People there are very nice. Very friendly. And I said, "This is a nice country to come and visit." I used to go to the sumo matches. In fact, I met the American wresting champion from Hawaii, Takamiyama. He tapped me on the shoulder. I remember that one year, he went 13-2 [and won his only *basho*], and they said, "Jesse, you will never win another one." He never did. He won that one tournament.

Umpires used to call me out [on strikes] all the time. I remember one day I got on my knees and covered home plate up with about an inch of dirt. I said, "Come on, you don't need no plate. You're gonna call me out anyway." I really did. I used to do some dumb things over there. I hit a home run one Sunday off Kaneda. A shot. And I bowed. Everybody gave me a standing ovation. Whenever I hit a home run after that I bowed. That's what I would do. I didn't care where I was.

They'd be expecting it. I'd run around the bases, then along the fence, high-fiving the fans. They'd have to wait for me to get through all the fans. I did a lot of dumb things, but I did them anyway. They called me crazy [laughs]. One day I wasn't getting any hits, so I took a shower with my uniform on. They said, "What are you doing?" I said, "I'm washing the evil spirits off." I just did some dumb things. But I enjoyed myself.

One night Bacque was pitching, and he should have pitched a no-hitter. But I pulled a muscle rounding second base. Then I'm in right field, and the ball's hit down the line and I couldn't catch up with it. And the ball fell. Bacque won the ballgame 10-1, and I hit about three home runs, including a grand slam. That night they gave me a shot of cortisone. We go to the ballpark the next day, I'm trying to hit BP but I can't. Murayama's going to pitch. They're all out in right field looking at me. I can't hit so I stop. I go out in the outfield, and they all disperse. Bacque comes over laughing. I said, "Bacque, why when I walked up did everybody leave?" He said, "Murayama is saying that you played for me last night but you won't play for him today. I said, "Bacque, I can't run. I can't even swing the bat." He said, "Well, that's not the point. The point is he said you won't play for him." I said, "OK, I'll play for him."

So I'm in right field, and a guy hits a ball higher than the Empire State Building, no farther from me than that wall [pointing 10 feet away], maybe even closer than that. It fell for a double. I couldn't get to it. I couldn't hardly move, because the little bit of looseness from playing had tightened back up. I hobbled toward that ball and it fell for a double. Murayama took me out of the ballgame, just like he took me out of that ballgame against the Giants when they beat us to win the pennant. And when you hit against the Giants, *everybody* knows it because all their games are on TV throughout the country.

Sadaharu Oh [868 career HR] was the Ted Williams of Japan. Oh was good. The guy was good, and he was nice. I don't know how he could hit that way [from left side, with right foot raised], but you've got guys over here now, like Bonilla, doing the same thing. The man had a good eye. The man could hit. He choked up on that bat. The man was just awesome. They said Nagashima [Giants' third baseman] was Mr. Japan. Uh-uh. Oh was the man. But he wasn't Mr. Japan because he's only half-Japanese.

I used to love watching a TV show over there about a samurai named Monjiro. He chewed a toothpick like me. I loved watching the guy. Just like when Bruce Lee had 10 guys around him. Well, this guy had 15 guys around him, with swords. He'd holler and kill them all.

The only thing I disliked about Japan was they didn't want you talking to Japanese women. Number one. But I did meet a Japanese girl. She spoke English, and my Japanese was all right. We used to go to the movies. But basically, I met a lot of Americans over there, including one go-go girl named Goldie, from Seattle. She was white. We hooked up over there, and what was so great about it was that we went into this hotel with mostly all Americans. And they all knew me because if you played ball over there, hell, if you were at all decent, they knew who you were. And Goldie said, "Willie, what do you do over here?" And I said, "I'm on a paid vacation." She said, "Everybody knows you. Are you great?" "No, I ain't great," I said [laughs]. "I'm just an American over here on a paid vacation, having fun. You see, I own a bunch of oil wells in Texas. And I saw this young lady walkin' across the street, and said, 'Miss, how would you like to have breakfast in Paris and dinner in Japan?' And she said, 'Yes.'" Goldie was just in stitches, listening. And I said, "That's how I happen to be over here." It took her quite a while before she learned who I was.

One day we went out to eat, and this white guy came over to us and said if he were in the States he wouldn't do this but then excused himself and said, "Mr. Kirkland, I've got kids and if I tell them I saw you and didn't get your autograph, they'd probably kill me. Would you sign this?" And I said, "Yes, sir, I'd be glad to." That happened everywhere I went. And what was so great about it was this—who's looking at color? Damn, you're in a country where you've got to talk to *somebody*. Give me an American. I went up and spoke to an African one day, and he turned around and walked away. I'm *serious*. He turned around and walked away. I said, "Hey bro', what's happening, man?" And he turned right around [laughs].

Later, when I went back to Japan to play in an old-timers game, the guys said, "Willie, how many innings you gonna play?" We were playing the Giants. I said, "What you could do for me is move the fences in to about 300 feet, instead of the same fences way out yonder. Move the fences in and just let the pitchers throw the ball up there, and let Oh and the other guys hit the home runs. The game doesn't mean anything. I mean, we're all old and retired now, can't play, and so just move the fences in and play a nice, little friendly game." The guys said, "Willie, how many innings you gonna play?" I said, "Yeah, I'll play seven innings." I didn't play the ballgame hardly at all. They gave me $5000, all expenses paid, *everything*. Just to go over there. I pinch hit off Kaneda, hit a groundball to the first baseman and ran down the line. Then Kaneda and I grabbed the first baseman and beat on him, then I ran out to the outfield, came back in and Murayama said, "Thank you. That's it." I said, "Hey, you messed over me when I was playing over here, but you can't mess over me now. That's OK. That's all right. You guys invite me over here just to bat one time, go out in the outfield for a half inning and that's it. Thank you. That's fine with me."

But that's one thing about Japan. They keep up with you. Every year they send somebody to the states, and he'll call up and say, "Mr. Kirkland, what are you doing?" Last time a girl came over, and I told her some things about Murayama. I'm going to see how much of it really hits the TV over there.

I feel like I had my time in baseball. I enjoyed it. And now it's over with. A guy in Chicago called me up recently and said, "Willie, we got a bunch of guys [ex-ballplayers] coming to sign autographs at a show, and we'd like you to be a part of it." But that just doesn't seem right to me. You're going to pay me for my autograph? Uh-uh. No, no, no, no, no. Back when I played you didn't get paid for things like that. You didn't go visit a hospital because you had an agent. You just did it for the ball club, because they asked you if you'd like to go to a hospital.

This doctor I go to has this collection of autographed baseballs that's fantastic. Brooks Robinson, Willie Mays. To me, it's in here [points to his head]. I don't need a ball or a picture to remember what I did back in those days. I don't have anything in my house [from baseball days], *anywhere*. You wouldn't even know I played baseball, because I never talk about it. If two guys sit down and talk about baseball, even if they're wrong, I would never open my mouth and say, "Well, I heard Kaline say ...."

Today's era of baseball is entirely different than when we played. And I'd guess if Babe Ruth were alive today he'd say the years we played were different from when he did. Well, it is *totally*

different now. Because of money. You've got .230 and .250 hitters making $2 million a year. If we could go back, which we can't, to the Mickey Mantle days, and if they had astroturf, what would those guys be worth? If baseball was as open and spread out as it is now—I'd say if a guy could play in the big leagues back then when we had from class-D to triple-A in the minors, and just eight teams in the major leagues, I'd say he had to be *decent*. Any decent player back then could be a star now. Because when you got to 30 or 31, you had guys in the minor leagues waiting on your spot. Now, you can play until you're 100. Eddie Murray? How old is he?

But I did enjoy the game. I used to work at my game. I learned a lot from Eddie Stanky. He said, "Willie, you can be as good as you want to be." I said, "I want to be *good*. I want to be a good outfielder." He said, "Work at it. You work at it. You practice." I could never get enough practice. Every year I went to spring training it was almost like I'd never been to spring training before. I'd work at my game. And work. And work. And I learned early on that being a ballplayer opens up a lot of doors. Back in my first year of pro ball, people would invite us out for dinner. We'd go to the restaurants and, just like in the delicatessen, the waitress would say, "Aren't you Willie Kirkland?" And people would come over to our table and say, "Aren't you Willie Kirkland?" And I'd say, "Yes, I am." And the waitress or the owner would say, "Willie, whenever you're in town, feel free to stop in and have a milk shake." Then I'd get back on the bus and the driver would tell the lady sitting in the front, "Get up and move. That's Willie Kirkland's seat." Being a ballplayer opened up a *lot* of doors. For all of us, white and black. I don't care who you are. Just the name. People recognize that name. Even *now*. If people recognize my name when I go buy something, it helps. It does. And you're happy when people remember you. Sometimes they say, "Willie Kirkland? Can I have your autograph?" Kids might ask, "Can you come out and play?" And you have to say, "Yes."

We didn't make millions of dollars when we played. We didn't make a whole lot of big-time money, although I made more in Japan than I did here in the States. But you take what you get, and I'm all right now. I saw this house here [after returning from Japan] and I liked it, and I said, "You got to live somewhere." I've got a few dollars invested in General Motors. And I've still got my

Willie Kirkland (Steve Bitker)

baseball pension. So I'm not hurting. If I wanted to go buy a new house I probably could, but it's just me here. No need.

Detroit, Michigan

ED BRESSOUD

Ed Bressoud was the Giants' smooth-fielding shortstop from 1956 through '61, showing some pop with the bat as well, hitting .286 in '57, and slamming nine home runs in both '59 and '60. Ed hit .263 in '58, but went on to enjoy his best years at the plate in Boston, where he hit a career-high 20 home runs in '63, and made the American League All-Star team in '64, when he hit .293. He finished his career in style, as a backup infielder with the World Series champion St. Louis Cardinals in '67. Over 12 big league seasons, Bressoud hit .252 with 94 home runs.

Following a 12-year major league career, Ed was the head baseball coach for 17 years at DeAnza community college in Cupertino, California. He is now retired, playing golf several times a week with his wife near their home in San Ramon. He has three children and three grandchildren.

EVEN THOUGH I ENJOY wearing my World Series championship ring, I don't think of

myself particularly as a Cardinal when I look back on my career. I was just very fortunate to be traded on April Fool's day [in '67] from the ninth-place club, the New York Mets, to St. Louis [with Danny Napoleon, for Jerry Buchek and Art Mahaffey]. And that was a *great* opportunity for me. I didn't realize how significant it was at that particular time.

But really, when I look back, I still think of myself as a Giant, even though my most productive years were certainly in Boston. The Giants were the team I came up with for the first time, and my earliest memories are still vivid. My first ballgame was in Milwaukee [in '56] against Warren Spahn. We got beat 3-1 that night. Oh, I was scared to death. *Scared to death.* The first time up he threw me a curveball in the dirt and I swung at it and struck out. The fourth time up I got a base hit over third base. I went one-for-four. Interesting enough, I saw Warren about five to six weeks ago in the baseball player alumni golf series, here on the peninsula. And I talked with him and said, "You know, Warren, my first at bat in the big leagues you threw me a curveball and I struck out, and you never threw me another one." And he laughed. But that's the only curveball I remember him throwing me.

The second game I played in was against Cincinnati, and I recall getting to first base alongside [Ted] Kluszewski. He was an ominous figure, with no sleeves, and those big ol' arms were exposed, and it looked like he could wrestle any bear in captivity.

But even though Fenway was a friendly park to play in and the Red Sox treated me extremely well, my wife says the most enjoyable year we ever had was playing for the New York Mets in 1966. She said she felt that she was not a fan, that she was a participant. And I recall there was a dentist back then who used to wear a yellow poncho, and he would sit in the upper deck and run back and forth and be a cheerleader. It was *exciting.* It really was exciting. I recall we had a ballgame against Pittsburgh, and we were down seven or eight runs in the ninth inning, and we got the bases loaded, and you'd have thought we were ready to win the World Series. It was exciting playing in New York at that time. But I still think of myself as a Giant.

I grew up in the forties. The first professional game I ever saw was the Los Angeles Angels in the old Pacific Coast League, in 1942 or '43, with Charlie English, Cecil Garriott, Billy Schuster and players of that ilk. From my perspective at that point, I did not realize there *was* a major league. The PCL was it. And, in fact, there were a lot of players playing in the PCL at that time who had been to the big leagues, and who had come back down to triple-A. And they were probably making more money on the West Coast than they were in the major leagues. I know when I got to the big leagues my first year the minimum salary was $5,000. It went to $6,000, then $10,000. And, at that point, I think players in the PCL were making a similar amount *and* staying home on the West Coast, as opposed to uprooting their families and going east.

When we first started hearing news [in '57] that the Giants would move to San Francisco I was surprised. Very, very surprised. The New York Giants had been a legendary franchise, as had Brooklyn, in the New York area, and I couldn't conceive of them moving. Retrospectively, it had to be a matter of economics. But as a 24-year-old player coming in to the Big Apple, you didn't think about economics, you thought about the game. You thought about how you were going to provide for your family. But you didn't look at the entire picture like players do nowadays. We didn't have agents, we were on our own, we made decisions based on how we felt particularly, and we didn't look at the whole game from that perspective. It had survived for so many years without any changes. And that, to me, seemed to be very farfetched.

As the season progressed, I can recall seeing the fans in center field, in particular, as we would come back to the clubhouse from home plate across the field. There would be signs up there saying, "Don't go, don't go." And, at that point, they recognized it was imminent that the Giants were going to be leaving. But I think for a long period of time I just didn't believe it. Sure, I was pleased [to be moving west]. Absolutely. Yeah, I liked the idea of coming to the West Coast, being born and raised here. It was important for me to not have to travel those great lengths, and uproot my family at the time. I was still in college, going to school [in LA] in the off-season for a number of years. And if, in fact, it meant I only had to uproot my family from Los Angeles to San Francisco, that was a *lot* less significant than moving it from Los Angeles to New York.

Ed Bressoud (SF Giants)

I had seen Seals Stadium before. One time. I had come up the coast from Los Angeles, probably in the early fifties, and I had seen a ballgame at Seals Stadium at that point. *Wonderful* ballpark. And it was an interesting ballpark. It was a very intimate ballpark, somewhat reminiscent from my perspective of Fenway Park in Boston. The fans were very close. You had a feeling of relationship with the fans. And it was interesting in that we had the brewery right next to us, and you could look up and see the fog kind of surround the ballpark, but we didn't get fog *in* the ballpark. From my perspective the ballpark was significantly better to play in, from the standpoint of comfortability of the player, certainly, than it was at Candlestick. Seals Stadium probably should have been double-decked. It had the advantage of getting the people in a trolley car or a bus downtown, right to the ballpark at 1:30 or 2 in the afternoon, watching a ballgame, which at that time took two hours and 15 minutes to play. And they'd run 'em back to their office and put in another two hours, get home by 7 o'clock, and they would have worked eight hours *and* seen a ballgame. That does not exist at Candlestick, or in many other cities.

I remember the big parade through downtown San Francisco. We came down Montgomery Street and we were in open-air cars. We're riding along, I'm in the 10th, 15th or 20th car back, and all of a sudden somebody yells out my name. I turn around and it's the best man from my wedding. And I hadn't seen him in years. He was working on Montgomery Street with IBM. So we established a relationship again after a number of years of not being in touch. That's a vivid memory for me. And, of course, going down the street and seeing the ticker tape, and the people on both sides of the street, yelling and warmly receiving us. Yeah, it was a great feeling.

We had a very interesting team that year. It was surprising, in a sense, that we were in first place as late as we were [July 30], but Mays and Cepeda were great hitters, Jimmy [Davenport] had a great year at third base, Antonelli was a fine pitcher, Mike McCormick was coming into his own, Kirkland had a fine year, Wagner came along and did well, Daryl Spencer did a good job at short and I think there was an awful lot of enthusiasm on the club. Players say a lot of times that the fans are an important aspect of their performance, and I really believe that is true. When they're up, you get up. If there are very few people in the house, it's hard to get pumped up, even though you have your own pride at stake.

Willie Mays was the greatest player I ever saw. There are five areas in which you measure a player: Hit, run, throw, field, hit with power. And Willie did them all. And he was the most fantastic baserunner I've ever seen. He could goad a player into doing something with the ball he would never do, and he'd take advantage. I recall in Pittsburgh we played a ballgame and Willie was on third, and there was a pop fly into short

Ed Bressoud completes double play with throw to Orlando Cepeda; Danny O'Connell is the second baseman; John Fitzpatrick is coaching first base for Milwaukee. (SF Chronicle)

center field. *Very* short. I don't think more than 15 or 20 feet back on the grass. And Mazeroski went back to get it, caught the ball and Willie was off third. And Willie made a little bit of a fake, and Maz's arm came forward. And when his arm came forward, Willie recognized he couldn't throw it and he took off. And, of course, Maz had to return his arm to the throwing position, and by that time Willie had scored. It was fantastic. But he did that sort of thing all the time. He'd run into a base looking backwards, to find out where the ball was coming from. He was just the best player I ever saw.

I recall the time Willie Kirkland had talked Leon Wagner into having his hair processed. It was near the end of the season, with two or three days to go. And Leon came on into the clubhouse, with this processed hair, and he certainly looked different than he had prior to that. And he was very self-conscious of his appearance. And he'd take off his cap and put on his helmet almost in one motion so you couldn't see his hair. And after the game the players were saying, "Leon, what happened?" And he said, "Well, Kirkland talked me into doing this." Then we went to Kirkland and said, "Why'd you do that?" And he said, "I didn't want to go back to Detroit looking ugly." [laughs]

We used to call Ruben Gomez "Native Dancer." Native Dancer was a great race horse at that point. And Ruben ran for us, from time to time, as a pinch-runner. I think that's where he got the Native Dancer tag. He could run like the wind. Yeah, that's what we used to call him. I remember the ballgame we played in Milwaukee when he threw a pitch at Joe Adcock, and hit him. Joe responded with some gesticulation, and when Ruben got the ball back from the umpire he threw it at him again. Then Ruben ran from the mound into the dugout, and down, and Joe was chasing him. I was playing shortstop and Red Schoendienst was playing second. Red was laughing, but I was really disturbed, as a younger player. And I said, "Red, what are you laughing about?" And he said, "Looked like a hound dog chasin' a fox down a hole." [laughs]

In '59 we got swept that last home series by the Dodgers, when we were up by two games with eight to play. Drysdale was the second pitcher to face us, and we had the bases loaded with nobody out in the first inning. And we didn't score. He struck out two of the next three, and they went on to beat us. And sweep us. That really deflated us. Then we went to Chicago, and that's where they were getting our signs, from the scoreboard. Hank Sauer went out there with a bat and started banging on the lower area of the scoreboard, trying to get their attention. And the Cubs just ripped us. One game I think it was 20-10. I recall Alvin Dark hit a low, inside curveball against McCormick for a grand slam. That was an incredibly difficult pitch to hit. At that point we were trying to have the pitcher call the signs instead of the catcher. Then we went into St. Louis, where Bob Gibson beat us. By then it was over. It was *extremely* hard for us.

We moved to Candlestick in '60. I disliked it from the beginning. Oh, sure. First ballgame we played St. Louis, and Larry Jackson pitched against us. We won 3-1. Sam [Jones] pitched for us. It was a beautiful day. I think the temperature might have been in the mid-60s. But I recall in the sixth or seventh inning the public address announcer came on and indicated that "The owner of boat *such and such,* you better get back to the coast guard because your boat is adrift." It was that kind of a day. People came across in boats to see the game. The next night it turned very cold. Then Chicago came in and it was freezing. They started the heaters in the stands, supposedly, and nothing came out but smoke. I think it was probably the worst ballpark I ever played in, in terms of player comfort.

And at that time there was no left field second deck. The wind blew in. I said many times that your pants could be blowing in and your shirt could be blowing out. The wind swirled that much. I recall playing a ballgame there and Andre Rodgers was playing third, I was playing short and a pop fly went up between short and third. I was drifting on over and drifting on over, waiting for Andre to call it, and he never did. And I recall catching the ball kneeling on third base. The wind just swirled something awful. It was hard to hit in. If Mays would have played there 15 to 20 years later when the fences were brought in considerably shorter, with not so much wind blowing in from left field, his home run total would have been significantly different. I think I read some place that at night there were only 12 or 13 home run balls hit out to left field all year [in '60]. The wind blew in a gale from there. I recall our trainer, Frank Doc Bowman, would say after the ballgame was over, "Well, the cleanup crew is gonna go out there and pick up those telephone books off the fence," because *everything* blew out there. It was a very difficult ballpark to play in, particularly for a right-handed hitter. One thing that really showed it to me was when we got Don Blasingame in a trade from St. Louis [for Wagner and Spencer]. He was my roommate—we played second and short together—and Blazer was a slap-hitter. He'd hit a lot of slap balls into left field over shortstop, and it got to the point where they were playing him 200 feet away. He'd hit a line drive over shortstop, and it would be caught by the left fielder *easily.* The ball just hung up. And it took an awful lot away from his game because that's the kind of hitter he was. If you could hit the ball to right field, as Cepeda could and Mays could from time to time, it was to your advantage. But it took away an awful lot from a right-handed pull-hitter.

I lived in downtown San Francisco in '58 because my wife became seriously ill late in spring training, and died just 10 days into the season. She had a brain tumor. We didn't know anything about it. We were in Phoenix and she started to have stomach problems, so I talked to Rigney, took her on home and came back. And three days later I was told to come back to Los Angeles. She was about to have an operation for a brain tumor. And she died on the operating table.

My youngest daughter just died two years ago. So I've had two horrible experiences in my life. And until you experience those you really don't ... people say "I understand" but they don't understand. The situation then was considerably different than now. Nowadays your wife has a baby, and you go away and spend two or three days making sure that all is well. An entirely different atmosphere exists now. My wife died on a Thursday. I played Saturday. There were two reasons for that. One is there was no security in the major leagues at that point, unless you were a star. They *expected* you back. And you expected to be there. The second thing was when you have a trauma like that, the best thing to do is get away and do something else, to get your mind off of it. So it was therapeutic for me. But at the same time it was also a matter of security. I needed the security to know that if I were gone for two weeks, they weren't going to bring a player up and then send me down to the minor leagues. It was an entirely different game than it is now, from the standpoint of what's real and what's unreal.

I got married again the following year [in '59] and we lived on the peninsula for many years until I went to Boston in '62. That was an interesting thing. During the course of the '61 season Jose Pagan started playing shortstop. And I went to Alvin in August, in Cincinnati, and said, "Alvin, I don't want to sit on the bench. Would you trade me? Get rid of me." And he said, "Well, we can't do that. The expansion draft is coming up. And you'll be one of the 15 players on the 40-man roster to be put up." OK. So in November the expansion occurred, and I was the first player selected. Hobie Landrith was the second player selected. I was the very first player in National League expansion history to be selected. They had a coin flip. Houston won it. New York picked second. So Hobie and I, both from the Giants, go one and two. So I think to myself, "Well, this is great. They really want me. Two hundred players [available] and I'm the number one player for them.

That's great." Four weeks later I find out I'm traded to the Boston Red Sox. Gee, that's a strange situation. But when I get to Boston I understand what has taken place.

Mike Higgins had been the manager at Louisville when I was in the American Association, playing at Minneapolis. Well, Mike was at Louisville and he had Don Buddin with him. Don Buddin is the shortstop at Boston. Mike had seen me play and obviously wanted me to play with him, and both he and Paul Richards, the owner at Houston at the time, were the best of buddies. They were hunting buddies. And they made an arrangement: *You draft Bressoud number one, and as soon as the interleague trading period starts up, I'll give you Buddin for Bressoud. And that's what happened.*

Boston was great. The clubhouse boy and I became extremely close. In fact, we still correspond and we still see each other occasionally, after 40 years. We had a very nice neighborhood to live in. We still correspond with those people. A young girl who used to baby-sit my kids—we see her occasionally. We go back to Cape Cod to see her. In fact, my youngest daughter was blind, and when she passed away she willed her guide dog to our friend back in Boston, who had taken care of her. When she passed away we had the guide dog, Ollandra, for about two weeks and, recognizing that Jennifer wanted the dog to go east, Carol [my wife] said, "Well, we've got to get the dog east back to Cape Cod." And so she contacted the airlines, but the airlines said the dog would have to be put in the hold of the plane to fly back. And Carol said, "No, I'm not going to do that." So she said, "If I pretend to be blind I can take the dog on the plane with me, and go back to Boston and give her the dog." And, in fact, that's what she did. It was very interesting because aboard the plane there was a doctor sitting next to her, and there was Mr. Bean on the monitors—he's a British comedian who does pantomime. We've always enjoyed him and, of course, my wife is pretending to be blind but she's looking at this monitor and snickering [laughs].

Carl Yastrzemski came up with Boston in 1961, so I played with Carl for four years. An awfully good hitter, a great left fielder, played extremely hard and became a better player after I left, even though he led the league in hitting [in '63] when I was there. But then I came back with St. Louis in 1967 to play them in the World Series and, of course, Carl that year was the triple-crown winner. He just had a phenomenal season. I never thought Carl would be the home run hitter that he was, and that year he hit 44 home runs [w/121 RBI & .326 average]. But Carl was an outstanding player.

Dick Radatz, for four years I was in Boston, was probably the best, most dominant relief pitcher in the *history* of the game [100 saves, 538 IP, 608K]. In fact, a friend of mine who owns a baseball store here told me that Dick Radatz has the highest strikeout [per inning] ratio for a relief pitcher in the history of the game. Ten strikeouts per nine innings. And I don't think many people recognize it, but Radatz was an absolutely dominant figure, at six-foot-seven and 276 pounds. He was incredibly big. And saves were much harder to come by in those days. Saves today are just absolutely ridiculous—a three-run lead and you get a save. But Dick was absolutely dominant. He came on in and the players were *fighting* just to put the ball in play. But, at the same time, no one that I ever saw went from stardom to absolutely nothing in two years. In one year. And I don't know whatever happened to Dick, but I know he went to spring training with the Cubs one year three or four years later, and he was not the same pitcher.

I had 600 at-bats my first year in Boston. And that was the problem in San Francisco [career-high with Giants was 386]. There was a problem that existed, I think, between certain people in the organization. Bill Rigney wanted to do one thing, and the organization was kind of forcing him to go in a different direction. Nobody ever told me that. Bill never told me that. But that's the feeling I had all the time. I think I was a better shortstop than Andre Rodgers was, and I think Bill recognized it, that you've got to catch the ball and be able to do some other things defensively to be competitive. So I think that Bill couldn't do some things he wanted to do at the time. Andre had extremely good power—I'm sure that's what Horace [Stoneham] was counting on—he had a wonderful throwing arm and he ran quite well. Andre's failing was his inability to catch the ball. But I thought that Andre would be a good player. I really did. A better player than his career statistics show [11 years, 45HR, .249]. And then when I went over to Boston I was very, very warmly received, and they said, "Here's your job. That's it."

I hit 20 home runs in 1963—in fact, I still have my 20th home run ball, but that's only because the equipment man at Fenway recognized

that it might be important to me at a later time. Players didn't typically do that sort of thing then. There was no memorabilia concern at that time. Nowadays, the bat, the ball, the base, the fan in the stands—everybody gets some sort of a claim now, but in those days it just did not exist.

Yeah, it was a tremendous honor in '64 [to be named to the American League All-Star team]. *Tremendous.* And, frankly, I got in the back door because [Luis] Aparicio was hurt at the time. I was put on the team by Al Lopez. I frankly think I *deserved* it that year—I was hitting .315 at the All-Star break. I thought the year before I should have had a good shot at it because I was hitting well over .300 at the break. But, as you well know, the people who have fame often get the accolades even though their performances in that given year are not that great. But when you have a Luis Aparicio, who was a great player, it's hard to dislodge him. And, at that point, Jim Fregosi was just coming into his own, so they were two classy shortstops.

Ted Williams was our hitting coach for four springs. Did you read the recent *Sports Illustrated* with him on the cover? Beautiful article. True article. I was *very* fortunate to have spent four springs with him. And those springs—you're talking 40 days each, something like that. I went to dinner with Ted three or four different times when the club would go to Tucson, and some of us would stay back to take extra batting practice. *Reader's Digest* used to have an article, "The Most Unforgettable Man" or "The Most Unforgettable Character." Well, Ted Williams is possibly the most unforgettable person I've ever met. *Charismatic, vulgar, loud, opinionated, bright.* I really enjoyed being around him. And I think he made the players better offensively than they could have ever been. I'm thinking of guys like [Eddie] Brinkman in Washington. He was a .180 hitter and wound up hitting .265 and doing a very good job for Ted.

Ted exuded confidence. But if you said something—if he asked you a question and you said something back to him he didn't like—he'd tell you to go to hell and walk away from you. That's the kind of guy he was. I remember in Scottsdale, after my first year, we had dinner one evening after a batting practice session, and he says, "Eddie, you hit .277 last year but I see you struck out 106 times. Do you recognize the fact that if you'd have put the ball into play 40 more times and gotten 10 more hits you'd have hit

.300?" I said, "Yeah, I understand the mathematics." He says, "Eddie, why didn't you do it?" I said, "Well, Ted, I don't hit the curveball very well. Like most players, the curveball gives me trouble." And he says, "Why?" I said, "Well, it's breaking and ..." And he says, "Well, do you understand why a curveball breaks?" And I said, "Well, I guess rotation." He says, "You *dumb shit.*" And that's the way he would talk. And he says, "Don't you know anything about Bernoulli's Principle?" "Who in the hell is Bernoulli?" "Well, Bernoulli's a physicist. The law of equal and resistant forces. Vacuum on bottom. Turbulence on top. Rotation causes turbulence. The vacuum on the bottom makes the ball go in that direction." And he talked about it for a long period of time, and related it to airplanes, in terms of when he was a fighter pilot in World War II and Korea. And we talked and talked and talked. And I said, "Well, OK, fine, now I understand, but I still can't hit the goddamn thing." [laughs]

But that shows you the kind of approach he had to a problem. He wanted to understand everything about it. He was phenomenal from that point of view. And he'd talk about the ruler representing the difference between a fastball and a curveball. Thirty-six inches. But if you look for the curveball and forget the fastball you've got a 36-inch adjustment to make. But if you look for the slider, which is the dominant pitch, you had an 18-inch adjustment. All the time. And if it's the dominant pitch, you're going to get it 50 percent or more of the time. So, therefore, you're going to be right looking for it. And that gets to the situation of looking and guessing. He was an extremely interesting man for me.

I saw him play many times, and I played against him one time in 1960, in spring training. And I saw him take batting practice with us when he was 43 years of age. And I *have* to believe that he's the greatest pure hitter of all time. I have to believe that. There are too many people that say that, and what I saw of him in batting practice at 43, 44 years of age doing what he wanted to do with the ball, even though it was batting practice, I still believe that he was. And then, of course, his pitch selection. That was the primary thing for him—hitting a good pitch. I can still recall Ike Delock [ex-pitcher] with Boston getting so mad at Ted after Ted's retirement. He'd say, "There'd be the winning run on third base and they'd throw the ball on the outer half of the plate, miss the plate by an inch and a half, and Ted wouldn't swing at it."

I had the feeling 1967 was going to be my last year because I had my master's degree at that point and De Anza community college was opening up. I knew that. I knew I better get in on the ground floor, so I had a strong feeling that would be my last year. Also a dominant concern I had was how I felt about myself , with regard to whether I could still play at the major league level. Going to bat 67 times and playing infrequently was hard for me because I was not the kind of player that could maintain that level. Some people can, some people can't. But it was a fantastic year in that I played with some great players, and it was wonderful to be out front, as we were the majority of the year. To get a chance to play in a World Series—there are so many great players that play a lifetime, a full career, and never get that opportunity. And it's terribly disappointing. And today, just as you recognized this ring, I'll be at church or I'll be in a restaurant or someplace else, and I'll hear, "Gee, that's a pretty ring. What is that?" And it's *nice* to say, "That's a World Series ring." And then they'll say, "Oh, did you play?" "Yes, I was a player." It's a *wonderful* feeling. It truly is.

Bob Gibson probably stood out the most from that '67 Cardinal team. He was a phenomenal competitor, and in the series itself he struck out 42 guys in three games, an average of 14 per game. Cepeda at first base had a marvelous year. Lou Brock had a fantastic year. Curt Flood played great in center field. Timmy McCarver behind the plate had a very good year. Steve Carlton was just coming into his own. There were a lot of great players. [Roger] Maris in right field had a good year, a good solid year. In fact, he would do something that I think was a characteristic of a National League player, in that with a runner on third base he'd hit the ball in the middle of the diamond to score the run, as opposed to trying to pull it out of the park or something like that. I think the National League was a much more strategic game than the American League. And I think he played National League ball with runners in scoring position.

I started coaching at De Anza immediately after retiring as a player. I took one week off after the World Series, then started teaching in late October or early November, and spent 23 years there. Seventeen as baseball coach, then I became one of the deans at the college, and I was a dean for the last seven years. It was an interesting experience, to coach young people, because it keeps you competitive, and you kind of relive some of your own experiences. And I was fortunate enough to have some pretty good players. We played in a very good league, with some awfully good coaches. We didn't win it but once, but I wound up having nine players who played in the big leagues. Mike Vail was my first player—he came up with the New York Mets and wound up with the longest rookie hitting streak, at 23 games. Then I had Danny Gladden, Mike Perez, Mark Leonard—nine players in all got to the big leagues. That was nice for me to be able to say that I had some players get there. That was a great experience.

Are young players today different than when I was coming up? I think young players begin to change with the adulation they get. I think initially they're playing the game because it's fun and it's competitive, and it's an avenue for them to develop, whether it's getting a college education or getting additional moneys for their families, particularly nowadays when you talk about this young player [Matt White] with the Tampa Bay Devil Rays. What'd he get? Ten-point-three million? That sort of thing is incredible. But I think the response by the fan to the player is the thing that changes him. And I can understand that. I remember the four years I spent with Ted Williams. We'd go into a restaurant and we'd have to sit in the very back corner, maybe even right into the kitchen, so that people wouldn't pester him. *Everybody* knows the players nowadays. You watch the television. Even the average player gets his face all over the place, so it's easy to recognize the fact that they can't go anywhere with any degree of privacy. But, at the same time, it skews them. I think that many players have no idea what reality is. Somebody recently asked a player what he thought the average man in America makes today, and he said $100,000. That's unreal. I really don't think many of them have a good understanding of what it is to be a middle-income family man.

I like watching some players today, but I *don't* like the overt demonstrations that the players have. I coached for 17 years at the college level and would not allow my players ever to show up another player. If he showed up another player he was out of the game. But nowadays it almost appears to—what's the phrase they keep using all the time? *In your face.* Well, that disturbs me greatly. I just don't believe in that sort of thing. So when I see that, it irritates me. I watch

other players who I have a great deal of respect for, like Cal Ripken. Not because he broke Gehrig's record, but because the things he said that evening made me *proud* to be a baseball player. And I don't find that with a lot of other players. I don't find that with a lot of celebrities. But they're all celebrities now. They're in the entertainment field.

They talk about the golden age of baseball and, to me, honest to God, I really believe that it was. I played with Mays, and against Mantle, Clemente, Aaron, Snider, Robinson and Campanella. I faced Drysdale, Koufax, Whitey Ford and so many other very, very good ones. So many wonderful, wonderful players. And I got to play behind Marichal. Remember his major league debut [a one-hit 2-0 win over the Phillies 7/19/60]? Well, the license plate on my car reads E-6. I was at a party several years ago and had never met the hostess, but as I walked in the door she hugged me and said, "Hi, E-6." I laughed and said, "What the hell is that?" She said, "Well, you know what E-6 is." And I said, "Yeah, error on the shortstop." And she said, "Well, I was a great Giants fan, and I saw Marichal's first ballgame, and *you* made an error in the sixth inning [to end his perfect game]." I said, "Twenty-two years later, and you're still on that?" So people would call me "E-6" at the club. Now, I put it on my license plate.

I got a letter the other day from a team in Midland, Texas. They're going to auction off some autographed balls. I think I probably get more fan mail now, in the last three or four years, than I got in the previous 20 years. But nowadays there are people who are autograph hunters. And there did not used to be that kind of a population out there. So I get more of that. And also, I'm getting older, and they're saying, "Let's get him before he dies." That sort of thing happens. It really does. When I was at the baseball players Legends Golf Tournament last fall, on the peninsula, Feller and Spahn were there, along with Brooks Robinson and Harmon Killebrew. And you could still see the people want the names. Unfortunately, I think, too many times they want them for resale. And *that* bothers me. I get fan mail now and they'll have six and eight cards in there. Well, I'll sign a couple, but six and eight? What are they doing with the others?

But I absolutely love the game of baseball and care about it deeply. And I'm thrilled to have been a part of it. I spent 40 years in the game.

And it gave me important values that I have used throughout my life. Obviously, we all would like to have played when we could have provided better for our families, of course. Too many players when I played wound up having to do jobs that they hated. Just *hated*. We all worked in the off-season. We *had* to. The thinking of today's player, I think, is "How am I gonna live the rest of my life and not do something that I maybe don't want to do?" They want to make enough money so that they'll never have to work again in their lives. But for us to have played with those great players we played with was wonderful. There are some great players today but I think the players of 30 years ago had much more charisma than the players of today. To me, much of the charisma today is a negative charisma.

Ed Bressoud (Steve Bitker)

Three years ago, when we had the strike, about three weeks later, I sent a letter to Don Fehr and Bud Selig. I wrote the same letter to both of them. And at that point I indicated that I thought there were two things that needed to be done to make sure that baseball survived. One was that the players and owners had to get together and trust one another, and make some determinations based on information that's accurate. At that point the owners were saying there were eight teams making money and 18 losing money. Then, later on, they said 12, 14 and 16 teams were making money. So that was the first thing. The second thing, I said, was they had to get a commissioner who was unbiased so that everybody believed he'd make objective decisions not based on where his money was [coming from], and not where his daughter was president of a club. That sort of thing.

I didn't get a letter back from Fehr, which irritated me because I'm a member of that pension group. I did get a letter back from Selig. And he thanked me very much and indicated that he was going to refer it to the player relations committee. At that point, I indicated in my last paragraph that baseball could be in a *catastrophic* position—that's the word I used. I had no idea how prophetic that would be.

Two years ago I wrote a second letter to Bud Selig with regard to the continuing negotiations and again suggested that the players had to get more involved with where we're going in the

game, and that we had to get to a situation where we're not at each other's throat. I got a letter back from him again.

Recently, I was at this golf tournament and was talking with Brooks Robinson. There are 71 players presently who were in the big leagues before 1946. You had to be on a roster in 1946 to qualify for the pension. Freddie Fitzsimmons spent 19 years in the big leagues and never got credit for that [he retired after the 1943 season with 217 wins]. Dolph Camilli and I worked for the California Angels when I was scouting for them. And Dolph got no money after 12 magnificent seasons with Brooklyn and a couple of other clubs [Camilli retired after the '45 season with 239 home runs and a .277 average]. They got nothing. So I said, "Brooks, you're the president of the players' alumni association. Do you have any input to the present-day players or management, in terms of what can be done for these players. They're in their eighties now. They have families and they're getting nothing. Is there some way that you, as president of the alumni association, can get together with these other players to loosen up some of the money that's in the pension?" It's a huge amount. To be able to do something for these guys, even if it's only getting a life insurance policy for their surviving spouses. And his comment to me was, "Eddie, the players today really are not concerned."

I don't know if we had those feelings when I was a player or not. The dollar value wasn't there then. When I got to the big leagues I looked at the pension system and said, "Gee, if I ever get five years ..." You had to get five years in the big leagues at that time, as opposed to now, when you need just one day. " ... I can get $125 a month for the rest of my life. God, will I be sitting pretty."

San Ramon, California

STU MILLER

Stu Miller, who threw perhaps the greatest change-up in major league history, won the National League earned run average title with the 1958 Giants, at 2.47, was Fireman of the Year for the Giants in '61 with 17 saves, then American League Fireman of the Year with the Orioles in '63 with 27 saves.

Originally a starter, Stu shut out the Cubs in his major league debut as a member of the St. Louis Cardinals in 1952, and didn't become a full-time reliever until the age of 33, in 1961. During the next six years, Miller was one of the best closers in baseball, with 128 saves, in an era when saves were much harder to come by than they are today. Over 16 major league seasons, Stu won 105 games, saved 154 more, threw 24 complete games and five shutouts, with a 3.24ERA.

Despite the great numbers, Stu Miller is probably best known for having been "blown off the mound" [according to a San Francisco Chronicle headline] in the 1961 All-Star Game at Candlestick Park, a claim to fame he has tried with a relative lack of success to dispel over the years.

Miller's more legitimate claim to fame, though, was his baffling change-up. Fred Hutchinson once said facing Miller was like trying to hit an insect; Ed Bailey said Miller had control and varying speeds— all slow; Mickey Mantle said Miller faked with his head better than any pitcher he ever saw, that he would snap his head at you, and somehow you'd be watching his head instead of the ball; and Joe Garagiola said that when you faced Miller, you would say to yourself, "I'm not going to swing too soon," then you'd say, "I'm not swinging too soon," then you'd say, "Thank goodness I didn't swing too soon," then the catcher would have the ball and you'd say, "I shouldn't have swung too soon." Just a few of the many accolades for Stu Miller's change-up.

Now retired and living in Cameron Park, outside Sacramento, Stu is married with six children and three grandchildren.

GROWING UP IN Northampton, Massachusetts, I had never been west of the Mississippi, and was really looking forward to the Giants' move to San Francisco. I had heard so much about sunny California. Couldn't wait to see it.

I remember in the spring of '58, they had a lot of rain in the Bay Area. I had started out living in Marin County, and people were actually rowing boats down the streets there. It was that bad [laughs]. And I said, "So this is sunny California, huh?" [laughs] Why Marin? Well, we didn't know where the hell we were going. And [teammate] Curt Barclay's brother lived in Marin, and I guess he kind of searched around and got Curt a place, and he found a place for me, too.

It was quite warm up in Marin when I left for my first trip down to Seals Stadium for our first night game. Then I hit the slope going up toward the Golden Gate [bridge] and I see this massive white stuff hanging out there. I got the win-

Stu Miller (SF Giants)

dows down, shirt-sleeves [laughs]. God, I almost froze crossing the bridge. Got to the ballpark and they issued us football parkas, fur-lined gloves and army blankets to keep our feet warm [laughs]. So this is California, huh? Oh, man.

But I thought Seals Stadium was great. I think they should have two-tiered that son-of-a-gun and cleared out the area for parking. It was a real cozy little place. Fans were right on top of you. The weather wasn't nearly as bad as Candlestick. There was a little wind going out to left field, which Johnny Antonelli didn't like too well [laughs]. But I liked the ballpark. Oh, yeah. I never was up in the stands, but my wife and all the wives would sit there and then, after the game, they'd walk up the street together with the fans. Everybody was friendly. It's not quite like that at Candlestick, I don't believe [laughs].

Rigney was the best manager I ever played for. He was great. He'd manage 25 players. He made them all feel part of the team. And I think that's one of the biggest things a manager can do. A lot of managers pick out their four starting pitchers and eight starting players, and forget the rest of them. Starting pitchers went every four days in those days. They didn't have four days' rest and pitch every fifth day. Why they have to do that now I have no idea [laughs]. Jeez. It seemed to work pretty good back then. Anyway, Bill had the ability to make all the players feel they were part of the team.

It was surprising that we were in contention so long in '58. Our pitching was pretty thin, although Gomez had great stuff. He had a great screwball and a good fastball, too. I was split in half that year between starting and relieving—20 starts, 21 relief appearances [won ERA title at 2.47]. My best pitch has been characterized in many ways over the years—*slow, slower and slowest* being one of them [laughs]. It's really a change-up. A sportswriter in Chicago thought I threw knuckleballs. He wouldn't believe I was throwing anything other than a knuckleball. I *tried* to throw a knuckleball but I couldn't [laughs]. That's a very difficult pitch to throw. You don't throw it with your knuckles. You throw it with your fingertips.

My change-up started in 1950, in Hamilton, Ontario, in class-D ball. They had an old ex-pitcher there named Vedie Himsl. I think he finished up his career in the Cubs organization. Nice guy. And all he did was tell the pitchers that we should come up with a change of pace. He said,

"You throw it to make it look like it's a fastball." He didn't show us. He just told us that we had to make it look like a fastball. So I just started practicing. And I came up with this move that probably—I can say it now, I'm almost 70 years old—is the best change-up ever thrown in baseball. With that premise—make it look like a fastball—I came up with this move. I just snapped my arm down and it's hard to describe, but I think I pulled it down like a window shade. The thing is, for a hitter, his timing is based strictly on your arm speed. So if you can throw a fastball 90 miles an hour, and a hitter is gearing for that and sees that arm snap down, he's timing 90. However, if the pitch is thrown the same way and it's only 80, his timing is *shot*.

I threw plenty of fastballs, maybe not 90 miles an hour. But even if they looked for my change-up, they still could not time it [laughs]. They couldn't time it. I threw a straight change-up, but I also had the same good motion on a curveball. And I had a good curveball. That gave me the curve, the slow curve, the fastball and the change-up. That's four pitches. But I could throw them overhand, I could throw them sidearm. Occasionally I'd come underhand. And I could throw them over the plate. *All* of them.

I got my first call-up to the majors with the Cardinals in '52. And Eddie Stanky takes one look at me and says, "Who's the stenographer?" [laughs] He didn't know who I was. But I was very gaunt. I weighed only 149 pounds [laughs]. Harvey Haddix and I used to have a bet to see who could gain the most weight in spring training. We both started out at about 150 pounds. He used to get up to 154. I couldn't get up that high [laughs]. I'd eat like a horse but I just couldn't gain any weight. I gradually gained weight over my career. I got up as high as 175.

In my major league debut I shut out the Cubs 1-0 at Wrigley. I wasn't nervous. No. I was very confident in my ability. I'm not afraid of *any* hitter. That's one of the things a pitcher's got to have—complete knowledge that he is better than the hitter. If you're afraid of the hitters you're not going to have any success at all.

I struck out Frank Howard the first nine times I faced him. He was a monster [laughs]. But he had a flaw that hitters should not have, and it's called hitting off your front foot. In other words, he'd stride in to the pitch before the ball was actually on its way. He was already on his front foot. No way he can hit a change-up that way.

One time—I couldn't believe it and I don't think he could either—he hit a home run off me. It started off about 15 feet foul and straight up in the air. Everybody thought it was a foul ball. And that sucker—I don't know if it had some kind of spin on it or something, but it kept drifting and drifting and drifting, and came down about two seats inside the foul pole. I look back, and Frank's still standing at home plate [laughs]. He couldn't believe it either [laughs]. It wasn't the wind. We were playing at Dodger Stadium. I don't know what the hell happened to that ball [laughs].

It's funny. They've got several levels at Dodger Stadium. And one time I got on the elevator, and I'm all by myself. The elevator stops at the next level and who gets on? *The Hondo* [Frank Howard]. Oh, my God. *I hope he doesn't recognize me* [laughs]. But he's a sweet man. He's a gentleman. He wouldn't hurt a fly.

In '59, Bill [Rigney] got a little nervous down toward the end [Giants led by two games with eight to play, but finished third]. He was starting Sam Jones *and* relieving him [50 games, 35 starts]. He'd just bypass me. When he smelled that pennant he just worked Sam to death [laughs]. I don't know whether he didn't trust me, but we'd get a one-run lead going into the ninth and he'd say, "Sam." It was all right by me as long as we won the games. But I had a 2.84 ERA in '59 [second in the league to teammate Sam Jones' 2.83]. They just happened to find an unearned run, charged as an earned run, to Sam, way back in June in Cincinnati. They must've dug deep because they didn't want me to win two years in a row. I don't know who the "they" are, but I'd guess the Giants. Because Sam had a big year. He won 21 games. And they didn't want this garbage-throwing little pea-shooter [laughs] to win.

Then Bill got fired in '60. It was a *travesty.* Oh, God, it was terrible. We were eight games over .500 and two games out of first. And he got *fired.* From what I understood—hearsay—Horace tried to call Rigney in Los Angeles when we were there, and Rigney didn't respond. But they had a little battle going. Rigney did not want to play Andre Rodgers at shortstop. He wanted to play Ed Bressoud at shortstop, or Daryl Spencer. Anybody but Andre Rodgers. He didn't like him. But Stoneham *loved* him. Oh, he had great talent. But there was something missing there, somewhere. For instance, we were in Pittsburgh—this might have keyed Rigney—and this guy from the Pirates coming into second on a double play grounder

stood up. But instead of gunning him right there, Andre threw it up into the seats. He broke up the double play all right. But that is not what a shortstop does. If the guy doesn't get down, you *drill* him. Andre seemed like he could handle it [defensively], but in the clutch he *seemed* to make that little boot, or whatever.

I know when we came back home from Los Angeles Rigney said, "I might be gone today. But I'm gonna play my lineup." And, sure enough, Bressoud was at short. And Bill got fired [laughs]. I think it was the difference of opinion with Stoneham over who should play shortstop.

Stoneham hired Tom Sheehan. You remember Tom Sheehan [imitates a big, burly, mumbling guy]. A big, old ex-pitcher. He was not only Stoneham's right-hand man, he was the head scout and his best drinking buddy [laughs]. He sat up there beside Stoneham in their box and, I'm sure, proceeded to tell Stoneham, "Well, Rigney's doing everything wrong, we should be doing this," and on and on. So Stoneham fired Rigney and said to Sheehan, "You get down there and run that club." [laughs] For crying out loud, he didn't even have a uniform for four days until they made one for him. I think Omar the Tentmaker had to make it.

But Sheehan got that ball club and we *laughed* all the way down to the lowest point in the standings we could find. [*author's note: The Giants went 46-50 under Sheehan, finishing fifth.*] We just laughed at that man. He was funny [laughs]. Oh, he hated Joe Shipley. Ship could imitate him almost to a tea. I don't know if Sheehan knew that about him. But he just didn't like his pitching. Shipley could throw it through a barn door, and it was a heavy, sinking fastball. He called in Shipley one time to relieve in the old [LA] Coliseum, in a clutch situation, in a tight ballgame. And Shipley gunned two guys out in a row— *brrooooom, brroooom*—strike three, strike three. Sinker balls just booming. Then he gets two strikes on the next hitter and throws another hard sinker, and the guy breaks his bat and the ball just dunks over shortstop for a base hit, driving home a run. And Sheehan says, "How can you throw that guy a fastball?" He hadn't thrown anything *but* fastballs. And he's got two outs and two strikes, and this guy *breaks his bat.* And Clancy [Sheehan's nickname] says, "He's got to throw him a curveball." [laughs] Oh, that's just one example.

I remember one time he called for the bullpen in Milwaukee and evidently got the signals crossed, and here comes Shipley in the golfcart. And Sheehan looks over and sees him, and goes, "No-o-o-o." The cart makes a U-turn and takes Shipley back [laughs]. We used to laugh so hard at things like that. There was another time in Pittsburgh, I think, when Sanford was getting knocked around a little bit, and here comes Santa Claus. We used to call him that. He chugs along to the mound. Sanford knows he's going out of the game, and as soon as he sees Santa take that first step, he just shoots by him to the dugout. And by the time Santa gets out to the mound he looks around and says, "Where the hell is my pitcher?" Sanford was already in the dugout. He never saw him go by. *"Where's my pitcher?"* [laughs] [*author's note: Sanford was fined $200 for showing up the skipper.*]

That same year in Pittsburgh, I'm on in relief. They've got first and third, one out, we're ahead 11-10 in the ninth, and there's a pop fly to very short right. The second baseman calls for it, Kirkland calls him off, Schofield tags up at third and is going to make it do-or-die. The game's either going to be over then, or he's going to score the tying run. Kirkland throws it to *second base* [laughs]. Sure enough, it's a tie score. So Sheehan asks Kirkland, "What were you thinking of?" "Well," Kirkland says, "I didn't want the winning run to get to second base." Of course, if he just throws a nice little strike in to home plate, we're in the clubhouse and the game's over [laughs]. The very next day, almost the same situation. First and third, one out and the guy gets a base hit right to Kirkland. This time he comes up and throws the prettiest strike to home plate you've ever seen. Of course, the guy's sitting in the dugout already, by the time the ball gets to the plate [laughs]. It was a beautiful strike to home plate. So Kirkland comes into the dugout, Sheehan looks at him and says, "If I had a gun, I'd *shoot* you." [laughs]

Kirkland *should* have been a superstar. He had all the ability you'd ever want to see. He could run, he had a strong arm, he could hit, he could hit with power. Except he never seemed to hit consistently. He had the most beautiful swing I've ever seen. But he'd hit line drives to the *catcher.* When he would hit 'em, he'd hit 'em a ton.

Alvin Dark replaced Sheehan in '61 and that turned into one of my best years [14-5, 2.66, 17SV]. I enjoyed playing for him. I was totally a reliever by then. And I played in two All-Star Games. [*author's note: To raise extra money for the players' pension fund, two All-Star Games were played each year from '59 through '62.*] That was a thrill. The first one at Candlestick. No, I did *not* get blown off the mound. My God. People still bring that up today. I came on in the ninth inning with men on first and second, one out and I'm anchored into this wind, which was the worst I'd ever seen. It was my home park, but still the worst I'd seen. And, of course, the wind came from left field, swirled and came right straight back at the pitcher. So you're really bending into a stiff wind. As I came to my set position I was well aware of the wind, but then—*SHOOOSH*—an extra gust of wind came up and I just moved a little bit, maybe a couple of inches, but it was noticeable—to the American League bench, which could see me, but not to the home plate umpire. He couldn't see it. So nothing was said. And I went ahead and delivered the pitch to Rocky Colavito, and he swung and missed. *Then,* Stan Landes, the umpire, came slowly out, took his mask off and motioned to the runners to move up. And I don't think anybody knew why he was doing it, except very knowledgeable ballplayers who had seen what happened. I talked to Stan Landes and said, "You know, Stan, that wind pushed me a little bit. I didn't make any intentional balk." He said, "What can I do? Rules are rules."

I think that has changed now, so if the weather has some bearing and forces a pitcher into a balk, they won't call one. But where else are you going to find that kind of weather? It all ended well and good, though, because we won the game in the 10th inning when Clemente singled home Mays. And the next morning, screaming headlines all across the top of the paper: *MILLER BLOWN OFF MOUND.* I asked the writer, "What the hell?" And he said, "All I do is write the story. I don't make the headline." Hell, I struck out Mantle, Sievers and Howard in succession in that ballgame. [*author's note: In the two All-Star Games combined, Miller struck out nine in four and a third innings.*] But to show you what the wind can do to a ball, I threw Berra a change-up headed right for his belt, and he twisted his body to get out of the way, twisting all the way back so he was looking right at the umpire. And the umpire goes, "Strike." It broke *that* much, and went right across the middle of the plate [laughs]. And

Berra, to this day, probably does not believe that was a strike.

But that wind helped me a lot the three years I pitched at Candlestick. It would help a breaking-ball pitcher, because the ball breaks more in the wind. Knuckleballers had a problem because they didn't need the wind, or they'd be all over the place. But I liked pitching there, once I got established as a seventh, eighth and ninth inning pitcher. I wouldn't even go out there until the seventh inning. I'd be in the clubhouse.

The '62 season was my last with the Giants, and that second playoff game in Los Angeles in October had a lot to do with me getting traded. We're ahead 5-0 in the sixth inning [after having won the first playoff game in the best-of-three series, 8-0]. Sanford decides he's had enough, which Dark gave him as a prerogative, that he could take himself out. So he'd had enough. So who does Dark bring in but his ace reliever, naturally, to sew up the pennant. Well, by the time that inning was over, Billy O'Dell had come in—first pitch was a three-run triple. Then Don Larsen relieved him, and by the time the sixth inning was over they're ahead 7-5 [laughs]. I had goat horns sprouting out all over me. Oh, man. I have no idea why I didn't do the job. I felt good. I don't know. I think it's a sure thing that I finished my career as a Giant that day. The next day we score four in the ninth to win the pennant [6-4] but I still didn't feel very good. I felt good that we won it but [laughs] I did not feel good because I almost lost it. I had some champagne in the clubhouse but it didn't taste nearly as good as it should have. *Damn* [laughs].

I never asked Jack [Sanford] why [he took himself out]. I'd like to ask him why [laughs]. He was my roommate and I still didn't ask him why. Jack was a very high-strung guy. He kept everything to himself. But he was wound tighter than a string. And after a game, win or lose, Dark gave him permission to go unwind—he did not have to have curfew. And I had permission to go with him [laughs]. And he'd unwind all right. He'd unwind a few. I never saw him go out of a game like that, except in '62. He was a great competitor. Dark made a mistake and said, "All I need is five or six good ones from you." And Jack said, "Well, that's all I'm gonna give him." I don't think Dark wanted it that way. Jack won 24 games that year. And I probably saved 16 of them.

I wasn't much of a part of the World Series that followed. I was already in the doghouse. I got

into two games in the Series, games we were already losing. Then I was traded two months later [to Baltimore, with Mike McCormick and John Orsino, in exchange for Jack Fisher, Billy Hoeft and Jim Coker]. And I had a big year in '63 with Baltimore [27 saves, 2.24ERA]. I came back after that season and said to Chub Feeney [Giants general manager], "Chub, can you get me back?" Because I wanted to be a Giant. I wanted to stay with the Giants. "Any way you can get me back?" "Well," he said, "let me look in to it." But after that big year with Baltimore, they didn't want to let me go. And as I was leaving I told Chub, "You know, the best trade you ever made was when you got me [in '56 from St. Louis, for Jim Hearn], and the worst trade you ever made was letting me go." He didn't like that a bit. I left very hurriedly [laughs].

Jack Fisher, Billy Hoeft and Jim Coker. Hobie Landrith [ex-Giant] was with the Baltimore Orioles at the time. And Al Dark called Hobie Landrith and asked him who the top five pitchers were on the Orioles. Hobie told me he gave him five, and Dark says, "What about Jack Fisher?" [laughs] Then Dark told him what the proposed trade was. And Hobie says, "Don't make that trade. Do *not* make that trade." So Dark tells Chub. And Chub makes the trade [laughs]. The Giants immediately put Coker on the triple-A roster, Hoeft's arm was shot [pitched 24 innings for the Giants], and Fisher had a terrible year [6-10, 4.58ERA, after which he went on to lose 73 games the next four years with the Mets]. What a shame. I was suited for Candlestick with the stuff I threw. Maybe they said, "Well, he's done." [laughs] One bad game and I'm done [laughs].

But I enjoyed Baltimore. Nice ballpark, and a great team. When they got Frank Robinson in '66, *wow.* I did my best pitching in Baltimore. 1965 was my best season of all—a 1.89ERA, 14 wins and 24 saves. What I'm really most proud of in Baltimore is I won the Orioles MVP award *two* years. With Brooks Robinson on the team. We had four Hall of Famers on that '66 team—the two Robinsons, Luis Aparicio and Jim Palmer. We won the World Series that year against the Dodgers, who I hated, of course. And I felt better going into that Series than I did in '62 with the Giants because I felt confident I'd be used. Hell, yeah. But I didn't get in a single game. [*author's note: Orioles swept Dodgers in four, with three complete games.*] I had one chance, in the last game. McNally, a left-hander, pitched into the ninth

Stu Miller gets a pitching arm rubdown from Giants trainer Frank "Doc" Bowman. (SF Giants)

with a 1-0 lead. One out, one on, I'm warming up in the bullpen. Willie Davis, I think, was due up. The only left-handed hitter they had in the lineup. Hank Bauer [manager] told me, "Any other hitter had come up to pinch hit, you'd have been in there." But Davis stayed in the game, Bauer left McNally in, and he got him out. Then Bauer said, "The hell with it," and let him finish the game [laughs]. It wasn't disappointing, though. Why should it be? We won. A four-game sweep. Willie Davis had that miserable day in game two—three errors, and he was a damn good center fielder [laughs]. It was just one of those games. He couldn't catch it and he couldn't throw it. That game was also the last game Koufax ever pitched. He had to quit [at age 30]. The doctor told him if he didn't, if he kept pitching, he'd be crippled. He was taking shots all the time in his elbow.

I never had arm problems throughout my career. A twinge here and there, but basically

nothing. Never on the disabled list. Never. I had a rubber arm. I pitched seven straight games for Dark one time. The seventh game was the first game of a double-header in Philadelphia. And between games he says, "Get your shower, get dressed and get up in the press box, or wherever. Just get out of here. I'll use you in the second game if you stay dressed." So I got dressed. Billy Loes pitched the second game and pitched a 1-0 shutout. With a sore arm [laughs]. And I know if I had been in uniform, Dark would have put me in that game for sure.

That '66 Orioles team was the best I ever played on. By far. My goodness. Well, you could compare them with the '62 Giants. How many Hall of Famers are on that team? Mays, McCovey and Marichal. And Cepeda might eventually get in. I think he probably should, statistically. But these writers—you do something wrong and they don't like it. The Veterans Committee might vote Cepeda in, but that's not the same, I don't think.

I retired from baseball in '68. I returned to the Bay Area and opened a liquor store in San Carlos, which I owned for 17 years. Then I retired for good. Moved up to the Sacramento area about nine years ago. The same house that costs $435,000 in San Carlos goes for about $145,000 up here.

I still like to watch baseball. I follow the Giants. Sure, I enjoy watching the games on TV. I like baseball. Of course I do [laughs]. I don't like what's happened to the game. It's hard to follow a team when you don't know who the hell is going to be there from one year to the next. I'm *amazed* the Giants let Matt Williams go. My God. I guess that's why I'm not a GM [laughs].

I still get quite a few letters and cards in the mail from fans. They want me to sign cards. It's flattering to be remembered. Yeah, sure. I get these letters from kids who say, "My father told me you were a great pitcher." Hell, I get letters from kids who say, "My *grandfather* told me you were a great pitcher." [laughs] But people still recognize the name. If that hadn't happened—I didn't like it when it did happen—*MILLER BLOWN OFF MOUND*—but if it didn't happen, nobody would remember me. Everybody remembers, *BLOWN OFF MOUND* [laughs].

Stu Miller (Steve Bitker)

That wasn't one of my own personal highlights. But being a teammate of Brooks Robinson was one. He was a phenomenal player. A phenomenal guy. Maybe the greatest all-around player I've ever played with. You couldn't get a ball by him at third. A super third baseman. He couldn't throw very hard but he got rid of the ball quickly, and always got the guy at first. And he had power. He hit fourth.

But Mays probably had the best all-around ability of anybody I ever saw. He could do all five things and do them well. Mantle was a close second, though. That son of a gun was a good ballplayer. Nobody could run faster than him, and he had bad legs. He'd tape them every day. Nobody could hit them farther than he could. You had to play him deep in the outfield, and short in the infield. If it takes three hops, you ain't gonna get him [laughs].

The best starting pitcher I ever saw was Koufax, even though he had only nine years in the big leagues. You're supposed to have 10 to get in the Hall of Fame. They made an exception for Koufax because he had such a phenomenal career. When he first came up as a bonus player all he'd do is pitch batting practice because nobody would hit against him. He couldn't keep it in the batting cage. He was wilder than a fox. Then, all of a sudden, he *found* it. And once he found it .... [laughs].

I did well against all the great hitters over the years. Except Tony Oliva. No question about it. I could not fool him in the slightest. I don't know whether he knew what I was throwing, or didn't care, or didn't watch the pitcher's arm or whatever. I could throw my whole book at him, but he just had great luck against me. Not great luck—he was a great hitter. I remember one game in Baltimore with Don Larsen and me warming up in the bullpen. Oliva was due up. Bauer came out to make a pitching change, and he called for Larsen, not me [laughs], in a situation that was *mine*. So he brought Larsen in to pitch to Oliva, and Larsen got him out. He said, "Don, you're in there." "Oh, OK, who's the hitter?" "Oliva." And Larsen said, "O-li-va?" [laughs] I always figured I could get that sucker out. I just *didn't*. I could never understand how he'd hit me that well.

But the other great hitters—I did well against all of them. None of those hitters—you can talk to any hitter except Oliva—they did not want to face me. They *hated* me. They just hated me. Because I made them all look stupid [laughs].

Sacramento, California

PAUL GIEL

Paul Giel made his major league debut with the Giants' last World Series championship club, in 1954, and then pitched a career-high 92 innings for the San Francisco Giants in 1958, mostly in relief, finishing with a 4-5 record and a 4.70 ERA. He lasted six years in the major leagues, but is much better known in his native Minneapolis for being an All-America halfback at the University of Minnesota in 1952 & '53, and then the Golden Gophers' athletic director for 17 years after his baseball days were over. In addition, Paul was sports director for eight years at WCCO-AM in Minneapolis, where he did color on Golden Gopher and Viking football broadcasts.

Giel has worked since 1990 for the Minnesota Heart Institute Foundation, raising funds for heart research and education. He is married, with three children and six grandchildren, and lives in Minnetonka.

MY NUMBER-ONE SPORT growing up in Minnesota, I'd say, was baseball. Because you start playing that so much sooner. I really never got into tackle football as a child. We really only had touch ball in the streets. We didn't have anything like they do nowadays, with Little League football-type stuff. So baseball was my number-one sport growing up, from midget baseball to high school ball, Legion ball and certainly when I got to the University of Minnesota. And I had an opportunity to go into professional baseball right out of high school, with any number of teams. There was complete free agency, of course, although they didn't call it that in those days. But I idolized a number of players up at the University of Minnesota in football and I thought, gee, I'd like to see if I can make it in both sports. So that's what I did.

The day after graduation from high school I must have interviewed with six or seven professional baseball scouts, from the St. Louis Cardinals to the Brooklyn Dodgers to the Chicago Cubs, the Cleveland Indians and, yes, the New York Giants. All of them were interested in me and in those days, for example, the Dodgers scout wanted to fly me out to New York to work out in Brooklyn and have Branch Rickey look at me. I didn't want that. And, of course, in those days the Giants' top farm club was the Minneapolis Millers. I probably could have signed with some team for a couple of thousand dollars up front, and probably would have ended up in A-ball at the highest, or maybe double-A. But I'm kind of a homebody. Winona, Minnesota, is my hometown, down in the Southeast part of the state. And although some people thought I was not doing the right thing—not necessarily my parents, they let me make my own decisions—some people said, "Oh, you'll go up there and play football and get all banged up, and there goes your baseball career."

Paul Giel (SF Giants)

When I went to the University of Minnesota we didn't have professional teams in our backyard. So the Golden Gophers were everything. And while we didn't have great seasons—we didn't go to any Rose Bowls—I had some good seasons personally. So that got the lion's share of publicity. And even though I did well in baseball in college, most people associate me with Golden Gopher football. I was there for four years, but freshmen weren't eligible when I started, so I played football in '51, '52 and '53. I was all-Big-10 three years in a row, and then in '52 and '53 I was All-America, as a left halfback, in what we called the single wing in those days.

My senior year I was captain of the team, and Michigan came to town for the 50th anniversary of the Little Brown Jug, which started in 1903. Michigan was undefeated at the time and number one in the country, at 4-0. We might have been 2-2. But being captain of the team, and the 50th anniversary, and after getting kicked around a little bit my sophomore and junior years in Ann Arbor, two years in a row there, well, this game was *big*. And we beat them 22-0 at Memorial Stadium on our campus. I think I had 284 total yards running and throwing, with two touchdowns running and one passing, *and* two interceptions [playing defense]. I just had a good day. Yeah, we played on both sides of the ball in those days. I was a defensive back. We drew about 60,000 for that game. I think that was the biggest highlight from my college days.

George Halas called me after my senior year—this was before the draft—and he wanted to know what I was thinking, football or baseball. Now, this was in 1954, when bonuses were there [in baseball]. So I said, "Well, if I get a bonus," and at that time a $30,000 bonus took you straight to the major leagues for at least two years, as part of the 25-man roster. So I said to him, "If I get a bonus of $30,000 or more, I'm going to play baseball. If not, I might be thinking of the NFL. And I'm obviously flattered that you're talking to me." Because he's a legend. Or he certainly was, and still is, I guess. Other than that, I might have gone up into Winnipeg to play for the Blue Bombers, because in those days Canadian Football League teams had territorial rights. So Winnipeg, geographically, had the rights to me. And I would have gone there because they had that wide-open field, and I could run and throw, and I think it would have been more my style. If I'd gone into the NFL I'd have been a pure quarterback because I didn't really have enough speed off a T-formation. I may be putting myself down but that's the way I figured it. Plus, I would have been better off financially in the CFL from what I knew about Halas, as far as pinching pennies. Those are things I heard and read about. If I had gone to Canada, they were going to give me something like a $20,000 bonus and a three-year contract for $22,000 a year, no cut. That was pretty darn good in those days. And Bud Grant was up there, as a player-coach at the time.

Instead, the Giants came along and offered me a $45,000 bonus to play baseball. I signed my contract with the Giants at the Shrader Hotel in Milwaukee. And I remember going out on the team bus to Milwaukee County Stadium. There I am sitting with Monte Irvin. In front of me is Leo Durocher and Willie Mays. You think I wasn't awed? I didn't dress for the game that day but you get to the park, you're looking at Eddie Mathews and Del Crandall and Warren Spahn and Joe Adcock. And you say, "Wow. This is a little bit bigger than the University of Minnesota, and pitching against Michigan."

The first game I actually pitched in was an exhibition game. The Giants used to have an annual exhibition game against the Boston Red Sox. So the first time I pitched was against the Red Sox, and Ted Williams had just come back to the major leagues from an Air Force tour of Korea. Can you imagine me, standing on the mound at the Polo Grounds, with Ted Williams at the plate? I walked him the first time—not intentionally, but I was just so nervous. The second time he hit a soft fly ball to Willie Mays—it was another bad pitch but the fans wanted to see him swing the bat. So he swung at a bad ball. I remember that. I pitched about three innings that day. One guy hit a home run off me.

The guys on the Giants were pretty nice, welcoming me to the team. I didn't hear anyone say, "Gee, his fastball's not that good." [laughs] Or, "Why'd they sign that guy to that kind of money?" No, they were a bunch of good guys. Wes Westrum, a catcher in those days, was a Minnesota native. My locker was next to Willie Mays, and he was nice to me. Alvin Dark and Sal Maglie and Johnny Antonelli. Another bonus player who really helped me was Joey Amalfitano, because we were both single at the time, about the same age and we roomed together in New York, in the Bronx. And Whitey Lockman, Davey Williams, Don Mueller and Ray Katt—my roommate on the road. And of course, I wasn't doing much. I only threw four innings. I joined them in June and they were on their way to winning the pennant. All the players, regardless of their contributions, who have been there the entire year get a full share. In those days I think it was $11,000 apiece for the winners. So they voted me half a share, regardless of what I did. I threw an awful lot of batting practice and did a lot of running the outfield. But gee, they had Johnny Antonelli, Jim Hearn, Sal Maglie, Ruben Gomez, Hoyt Wilhelm and Marv Grissom. I mean, they weren't going to need me.

It was a thrill, though, just to be a small part of the Giants' four-game sweep of Cleveland in the World Series, when you think of the talent and record Cleveland had [111-43]. Just to be in the dugout. I say to people, "I saw Willie Mays make the great catch [off Vic Wertz]." But, frankly, I saw him make better ones during the regular season. I'd see him run straight across the outfield and backhand the ball about two feet from the ground, going full blast. That was tougher. He was the best all-around player I saw during my career. I was also very impressed with Hank Aaron because he could play the outfield and infield, he had a good arm and he could certainly hit for both average and power.

My major league debut was in relief. Just one inning, mopping up against the Pittsburgh Pirates at the Polo Grounds. I struck out the side. That wasn't as big a thrill, though, as pitching three innings of relief against the Cubs in 1955 and getting my first win, at Wrigley Field. That's where I saw my first major league game, as a sophomore in high school. But to get your first win—I don't care whether you pitch one inning or three innings—that's a thrill. We were trailing 3-2 when I came on in the seventh inning, got the side out, then Dusty Rhodes hit a three-run homer.

I was an ROTC graduate at the University of Minnesota. So after graduation you have a two-year hiatus before you have to fulfill your commitment. So I was there with the Giants from June on, in '54 and all of '55. Then, in November of 1955, I went to Aberdeen Proving Grounds in Maryland—officer's basic school—for about six weeks, then to Stuttgart, Germany, to finish out my two-year obligation. I played baseball overseas. Seventh Army headquarters was in a suburb just outside of Stuttgart. Shortly after I got there I really lucked out. The A&R officers rotated back to the United States, so they took me out of one unit and put me down at the gymnasium, to run the gym. And I ended up coaching baseball and football over there. I also met my wife-to-be over there. Her father was a finance officer, a colonel, a career military man. And Nancy was over there visiting. And a fellow officer told me he met a young lady that he thought I'd like. So I gave her a call at the Colonel's quarters, we started dating and in August of '57 we got married. About two months later I was rotated back home.

I probably heard about the Giants' decision to move to San Francisco while I was in Germany, through the Armed Forces Network and newspapers. But I remember thinking, San Francisco—that should be pretty nice. I had never been there before. Everything about the move was very impressive to me. The glamour of going to San Francisco, the excitement of the city, the news media and Seals Stadium. I'd heard about Seals Stadium. Didn't some great major league ballplayers come through there, like Joe DiMaggio and Lefty O'Doul? I remember the first time I went into Lefty O'Doul's restaurant downtown. Then I walked by there again just two years ago when Nancy and I, along with two other couples, vacationed in San Francisco. We made the city our headquarters, went up into the Napa Valley and down the coast to Carmel and Monterey.

I don't remember too much about Seals Stadium except that Ernie Banks hit a home run off me in left-center field that hit a Standard Oil Station about 100 yards over the fence [laughs]. But being in San Francisco for one year was a great experience for me. I remember the Giants sent me down in May. I wasn't doing very well. My total two years was up now, as far as them having to keep me because of the bonus, so they sent me

down to Phoenix. I was down there for about a month, and won three games [3-0, 2.77]. We had a tremendous team down there in the light air—Leon Wagner, Willie McCovey, Tommy Haller, Joey Amalfitano and Andre Rodgers. We'd just *outscore* everybody [winning the PCL with an 89-65 record]. Then I was in Seattle when I got the call to come back up. And I finished out the year with the Giants.

The Pirates got me on waivers in '59, although I finished the year with Columbus of the International League. Then in 1960 I went to training camp with the Pirates and had a real good camp. I made the roster, and was with the Pirates until after the All-Star Game in July. And then they called up a pitcher named George Witt, who had great potential but had some arm problems, and if he didn't get called back up he was going to quit baseball. He was more important to the Pirates than Paul Giel was so I was sent down to Salt Lake City of the Coast League. I finished up the season there and said, "That's it. I've got my five and a half years in the major leagues, and I'm going to call it a career. I'm just hanging on." I did not get a World Series ring in 1960 with the Pirates but I did get another half-share. My roommate on the road was Bob Friend, and I said when I left the team, "Hey, roomie, you take care of me. You're gonna take the pennant and I think you'll win the World Series. Make sure you take care of me and get me a half-share." [laughs] And I got a half-share. I remember when Mazeroski hit the home run [to win game seven over the Yankees]. My in-laws were finishing up their military careers at the Presidio [in San Francisco], and I'm watching the seventh and deciding game of the World Series, and Mazeroski hits the home run off Ralph Terry to win it. And I say to my father-in-law, "I just got a new set of golf clubs." [laughs]

I'll never forget I was with the Pirates when I got my five and a half years in. I knew to the date when I had it. For the pension. And this telegram's in my locker when I report to the ballpark, from Johnny Antonelli and Joey Amalfitano. They said, "Congratulations, Jangles. We never thought you'd make it." They used to call Joey Amalfitano "Jingles" because of *his* bonus, and me "Jangles." They said, "Congratulations, Jangles. We never thought you'd make it." [laughs] And at age 59½ I started collecting. And I feel so, so lucky that I did go baseball, and that even though I had such a mediocre career in baseball, I was *there,* and I had five and a half years in. There was the two years that they had to keep me, plus the two years in the service counted toward the pension—they called it the National Defense List. If you went into the service off of the major league roster, they had to count that time in the service toward the pension. So, between the two years that were mandatory and the two years in the service, and scrambling between the Giants, Pirates and Twins, I have my five and a half years.

And it's so damn *good* the pension fund the ballplayers have. The first of the month it arrives and I say, "Gee, I'm a five and a half year man and I'm getting that kind of money." So I never felt sorry for the players nor the owners when they had the strike. A friend of mine, Frank Quilici, who was on the Twins' World Series team in '65 and then managed the Twins for a while, said, "You know us alumni. We don't mind the players making that kind of money. When they think they're *worth* it, it bothers us."

So I was going to San Francisco State after the 1960 season. My wife and I and little Paul Jr. were living with my in-laws at their quarters, and I'm out on the golf course, and a reporter got me off the golf course with a long distance phone call and said, "Calvin Griffith of the Twins bought your contract from the Pirates." And I thought, "Oh, no. Do I want to try it again in my own backyard?" I talked to Calvin Griffith [Twins owner] by phone and decided I'd give it a try. So I came back with the expansion Twins and, obviously, being a hometown boy, I made the 10-man pitching roster. Then on June 1, 1961, they traded me to Kansas City [for Bill Tuttle]. I pitched one game for KC against Washington, thought I had pretty good stuff and still got hit pretty hard. At the end of the night I said, "That's it. I shouldn't have allowed the trade. I should've quit." And I did.

I took voluntary retirement, came back to my hometown of Winona to see my mom and dad, and then I got another call from Calvin Griffith. He said, "Gee, you really fouled up this deal. KC wants $20,000 in lieu of you dropping away by fouling up the trade." He was going to give me $5000 to go back, so he'd save 15 [laughs]. And I'm trying to get *out* of baseball. As a matter of fact, when I told Frank Lane, who was then the general manager of KC, that I made a mistake—"I'm sorry, I apologize, I shouldn't have accepted the trade"—he said, "Gee, you had good

stuff. Joe Pignatano, the catcher, said you had good stuff. Do you need more money?" [laughs] I said, "No, I'm trying to get *out.*" [laughs] So I didn't accept any of the offers, obviously, and I dropped out of baseball.

I went to work at the graduate school at the University of Minnesota, and the next thing I knew the Vikings were here. Their first year in the NFL, and I was offered a chance to work for them as business manager, primarily in public relations. I was with them for a year and a half. Van Brocklin was the coach. I was moonlighting in radio, doing some high school football. And evidently the people at WCCO [in Minneapolis] heard me, and asked me to become the sports director. So in April of '63 I went to WCCO and worked there for eight years. I did color on Golden Gopher football. I did color on Viking football. I did about five sports shows a day. I did color on Gopher basketball. Matter of fact, in the famous Green Bay-Dallas title game, on the frozen field in '67, I was doing color for the game with Jack Drees on CBS Radio. So I was there when Bart Starr sneaked over. And, of course, I did the color when the Vikings went to the very first Super Bowl, when they lost to Kansas City in New Orleans, at Tulane Stadium. [*author's note: Subsequently, that game became Super Bowl III, with the first two NFL-AFL title games being renamed Super Bowls I and II.*]

You don't know these games will end up being so historical at the time. Like the game at Kezar Stadium in San Francisco when Jim Marshall ran back a fumble the wrong way for a safety [laughs]. The Vikings ended up winning the game, and there's a funny story about that afterwards. Fran Tarkenton had a pretty good sense of humor, and on the flight back home he went up toward the cockpit and got the hat off the pilot—the captain's hat—and he came back, put it on Jim Marshall's head and said, "Why don't you go up and fly this thing? We may end up in Hawaii." [laughs]

Then, in '71, the president of the University of Minnesota calls. And I had no thoughts at all about ever becoming athletic director, or ever thought that anyone would call me. I had a few people hint to me that I might consider it, but I said, "Look, I don't have a business background, I have no administrative experience, I've really just been an on-air personality." But then the call came and the president said, "Would you consider becoming the athletic director at the University of Minnesota?" So I went over, visited, we got a number of things straightened out, and I was a little reluctant to take it because it would be quite a challenge, with the pros here. They were really killing the University of Minnesota. You know, the Vikings were big, so were the Twins, and the North Stars came here in 1967. So that was really hurting Gopher attendance. It really put the pressure on the college sports teams to produce, because the pros take so much of the entertainment dollar away.

But I took the job. And it was a great experience for me. That's one of the reasons I took it. I wanted to find out if Paul Giel could motivate, organize and maybe do the job. And, evidently, I did a decent one because I lasted for 17 years. The biggest highlight I think was three national championships in ice hockey. I hired Herb Brooks, who later on coached, with mostly Gophers, the 1980 gold medal U.S. Olympic team—*The Miracle on Ice,* over the Russians. I was very proud, because I hired Herb. And I remember telling Herb when he was trying to be the [Olympic] coach, "Why do you want to try that? You can't beat not only the Russians, but the Swedes and the Czechs. You want to try to beat all of those?" He said, "I just think the team hasn't been organized right."

I think the disappointment was in never going to a Rose Bowl. But Minnesota was the first team when the Big Ten allowed a second, third or fourth place team to go to another bowl. We were so frightened for years that if we went to another bowl we were going to lose that pact with the Tournament of Roses, with the Pac-8 and the Big-10. In 1977 we were 7-4 and went to the Hall of Fame Bowl in Birmingham. We lost to Maryland, 17-7 I think, but nevertheless were the first team to go. We went to two other bowls, the Liberty Bowl and the Independence Bowl, and that was fine.

But the thing I was proudest of is that when I accepted the job I inherited a $500,000 deficit. And I inherited it by saying, "Look, it may take a while before we turn this program around. I'm not going to go over there and start hacking away at some of the so-called non-resident sports." Because baseball meant a lot to me and we didn't draw a lot of fans when I played college ball. And 17 years later all those sports were still in place. And we were ranked the second-best all-around program in the Big-10, if you count how all your teams fared. But football, being so big—your pro-

gram is often judged by how your football team comes out. So we kept them all alive, and I hired most of those coaches. And I'm still welcome when I come on over to the old Bierman Building. I had a good relationship.

I remember when we recruited Tony Dungy. I'll never forget the first time I met him. He came out of Jackson, Michigan. And the minute I met him and talked to him for about five or six minutes, I got that feeling, we've *got* to get this kid. I mean, he was such a cut above. He was a good Big-10 quarterback. Not a great one, but a *good* one. But he just had the smarts, and good family background. He was like Fran Tarkenton in that sense, like a coach on the field. And you knew someday that he was going to be a head coach in college or in the NFL. And he finally got it, in Tampa Bay. And they started to play pretty well in his first season there, didn't they?

After leaving the University of Minnesota, I did a little charity work, and moonlighting work in radio again. And then the North Stars called me. Lou Nanne, the president of the North Stars, is a friend of mine. They were hurting, as far as attendance, and thought maybe I could help in sales. So I went with them for a year and a half, and then they were sold to Norm Green in Dallas. I had a half-year to go on a two-year contract, so I had a buyout. Then my cardiologist called, from the Minnesota Heart Institute Foundation, and asked me to go with the Foundation, helping them in fund-raising for heart health research and education. I've been there over seven years now. It's been a great experience. I found out there's another world out there, a worthwhile world, outside of athletics. I still pull for the Gophers. Hell, I can't even bear to watch them on TV. I *still* want them to win.

But this has been a good experience for me because I have had heart problems myself. I can sell it with a great deal of sincerity. I had bypass surgery in '83, and a couple of other complications since, but they've been taken care of. So I'm working at the right place. These cardiologists and cardiovascular surgeons are some of the best in the world.

Somebody asked me whether I miss the University, being athletic director. Well, I miss working with the coaches, trying to help them have a chance to succeed. And most of the kids who come through your total program are good kids. They *are* student athletes. And I miss competition. I miss amateur athletics. But I tell you, there are three things I don't miss. I don't miss those 11 football Saturdays that are *so* important, they just tear you apart emotionally. I don't miss being held accountable for the actions of others. And I don't miss the often-times hypocritical bureaucracy of the administration. And that's it. I'm doing my job here. They like what I've done. I've been successful in fund-raising. And I don't have to worry about somebody coming up to me and saying, "Well, look Paul, this is the big one. We've got to have this." If I ever write a book, that's what it's going to be called: *"This Is the Big One."* You know how many times you hear that? [laughs]

Minnetonka, Minnesota

AL WORTHINGTON

Al Worthington won a career-high 11 games with the '58 Giants, making 12 starts and 42 relief appearances. He was traded after the '59 season to the Boston Red Sox for first baseman Jim Marshall.

Al tied a major league record held previously by five others when he threw shutouts in his first two big league starts, for the Giants in '53, against the Phillies and Dodgers. He enjoyed his greatest success, though, as a closer for the Twins, with 85 saves from '64 through '68. Over 14 major league seasons, Worthington won 75 games, saved 110 and had a 3.39 ERA.

Following his retirement as an active player, Al was the head baseball coach at Liberty College in Virginia for 13 years. Now semi-retired, Worthington lives with his wife in Alabaster, Alabama, outside Birmingham. He has five children and nine grandchildren.

I HAD NEVER EVEN SEEN a double-deck stadium until I got called up by the Giants in 1953. The Polo Grounds was beautiful to me. I arrived in New York about 11 o'clock at night, from Minneapolis, and went to the Henry Hudson Hotel—that was the players' hotel. The next morning I was at the Giants' offices, and they told me to go next door, go downstairs and get on the train with the team. Well, we didn't have television in Alabama in those days. I had never been to New York. I'm an old country boy down here. So I thought they must be crazy. Go next door, go downstairs and get on the *train*? Well, I walked out of that building, went next door and went downstairs, and there was the train. The subway. I didn't even know they ran underground [laughs]. So I got on that train, and there were the guys. That was one of the biggest surprises of my career.

First game I pitched was against the Phillies at the Polo Grounds. I was scared, nervous and everything else. Oh, yeah. I sure was. Shut 'em out, 6-0. Second start was at Ebbets Field against the Dodgers. Shut them out, too. Also 6-0. I remember when Alvin Dark was introduced there. After the guy said, "Alvin Dark, shortstop," everybody said, "Boo-o-o-o-o." All these people get there well before the game starts, and they're right on top of you. They're not sitting way back

Al Worthington (SF Giants)

up in the stands. There's 29,000 sitting right there hollering at you. It wasn't a very nice park. Just a little, bitty place. Dug out small. And underneath, where you walk to your clubhouse, it was just dirt. It was OK, but it wasn't what you were used to in the major leagues. But it was a great place to *play.* I'll say that.

I rode to Brooklyn for the game with Jim Hearn and Sal Maglie. I didn't know much about big league ball, but I'd read about Reese and Campanella, and Jackie Robinson, Carl Furillo and Duke Snider. So that kind of scared me to think I was going to pitch against them. I nearly jumped out of the car going over there. I had been pitching well at Minneapolis, but I don't think I took anything for granted. How could I?

Two of the earliest hitters I got indoctrinated to were Jackie Robinson and Stan Musial. It was amazing. There I was, a rookie, and I'm supposed to get those guys out. That didn't make sense. They knew where I was going to throw the ball. *I* didn't even know that. They knew the speed it would be. And I didn't know that, either. So they didn't have any problems connecting off of me.

I had to get my mind in the same set theirs was in. It took me a while to do that. I wasn't prepared when I went to the big leagues. Eddie Mathews was one of the best hitters I ever faced. He didn't hit any home runs off of me but Eddie had the ability to get the bat on the ball. He blooped a lot of them off me but, my goodness, he was a tough hitter for me. It seemed like every time I came in to relieve against the Braves, Hank Aaron was at the plate. I got him out quite a bit but he did hit two home runs off of me. Wes Covington was a tough hitter for me. Yeah, Wes could hit. He could hit me. I don't know why he didn't stay [in the majors] longer. I didn't like Roger Maris, either. I didn't get to pitch against him very much, but I didn't like him to come to the plate. There was also a boy who hit .200 with Chicago that I couldn't get out—Ron Hansen, the shortstop.

I didn't do much to help the Giants in '54 [0-2, 3.50], so getting a World Series ring was kind of a token for me. I didn't feel like I belonged, really. Then, in '55, I got a Little World Series ring with Minneapolis. *That* was a thrill. It really was. I contributed [led league w/19 wins]. That was exciting. The most exciting year I had. The most memorable year.

During the 1957 season, I was looking forward to the move to San Francisco. I thought moving was a good idea. The sportswriters ran us out of New York. They were always negative. All the time. Every day. They always said we needed a new second baseman. And that we weren't winning. And they just kind of forced the Giants out.

I liked Seals Stadium. Again, the fans were very close to the action, this time for us. I didn't like the cold and I didn't like the wind. But I kind of liked that park. I started the first major league game played at the LA Coliseum. It really didn't seem like a baseball park. For one thing, they had that short left field. They had a big crowd that day, about 80,000. We lost 6-5. One of our guys [Davenport] missed third base in the ninth inning. Would have tied the game. That was exciting to pitch the first game there, though.

I liked that '58 team. Jim Davenport came up and was really an outstanding star, especially defensively. Orlando Cepeda played great at first. I used to feel sorry for the pitcher when Orlando Cepeda was at the plate. He hit the ball hard more often than anybody I've ever seen. Willie Mays? *The Greatest.* Mays was the best all-around player I ever saw. But how'd we win with that pitching staff [laughs]? That was an exciting year. I enjoyed Seals Stadium and I enjoyed that team.

My whole life, in fact, began to change for me in 1958. I got born again that year. I had always been a religious boy. And I wanted to know when I was a little bitty boy that I was going to go to heaven when I died, and I didn't know that. Nobody around here ever told me. I went to church all my life. There's an emptiness in every person, and that emptiness was in me and I didn't know why it was there. Nobody could fill it. Sports, children, wife—nothing. They didn't have any power to fill that emptiness. The good job didn't fill it. Going to San Francisco didn't fill it. Making more money didn't fill it. Having new friends out there didn't fill it.

Billy Graham came to New York for this crusade when we were there in 1957. And I went out to hear him preach. A preacher there got ahold of me and told me that Jesus died for me on the cross because I was a sinner, and I had to receive him. I knew he died for me a long time ago, but I had to receive him in my life and my faith, and I had to turn my life over to him. It was the hardest thing I ever did. So I made up my mind that I was going to give my life to Christ. I didn't know what that meant, but I went down front, and they took me into a room and gave me some literature. I filled out everything, sent it back to them, they graded it and sent it back to me.

After I made that decision, the holy spirit of God came upon me. But I knew He was there. Jesus said a man must be born again to see the kingdom of heaven. So I was born again. And that changed my life. And it's *still* changing my life, 38 years later.

That's the reason people drink too much, the reason they steal, cheat, lie and do all those things. That's why *good* people do all those things. They've got that emptiness. They can't maintain that goodness all the time. They're cynical. It breaks out somewhere, like the measles [laughs].

So God took my house and made a home of it. It made my relationship with my family *more* binding. I was a family man anyway, but it was great. I had something to share with my children. It made my home complete. Home's not complete without Christ living in it. Nobody's is, anywhere in the world. It's so simple, yet people don't know it. It made me love my wife more and my children more, my fellow man more. It just changed me. Every aspect of my life.

As a ballplayer it gave me confidence. Life wasn't over if I lost. He was my Lord and Savior—win, lose or draw. I wanted to pitch for Him, rather than myself or the team. He was first. So I didn't have to worry about hitters, as far as confidence. This is the search every man is looking for.

I wanted my teammates to be saved, too, and I didn't know how to talk to them. I think it scared a bunch of them. In fact, they didn't want to be around me. I didn't mean to scare them. I just wanted to—there's a heaven and hell, and everybody's going to one of those places. So I loved them and wanted them to be saved, but I didn't know how to talk to them. And I think it hurt my relationship with them. Except for Felipe [Alou]. He wanted to be saved. He was kind of like me. He knew that he had to be born again, but he didn't know how. A friend over in the Dominican had given him a Bible, told him he felt sorry for him, and said he had to be born again to go to heaven. So that started Felipe wanting to know. When he ran into me, he didn't have to wait long [laughs].

But my conversion definitely put a gap between me and the rest of my teammates. And I believe it carried over into '59. I didn't have any major run-ins with anybody. I didn't have any problems with anybody. But I just think what I stood for was a little different. It was different.

That was when I went to Rigney to talk about us stealing signs. Bill was my friend. We had been together a long time. And Milwaukee came into town at the end of the season. We had a two-game lead with ten games left in the season. And we called [stole] every sign from Burdette. But they beat us anyway, and we knew every pitch that was coming. When I heard about that I went in to see Bill, said that I was a Christian, and that was cheating, that it shouldn't be. Bill took it kind of good. I believe he stopped it. I just said it was cheating to call people's signs. We finished third. I had a similar run-in with the White Sox the next year. I quit the team over it.

I spent '61 with San Diego of the PCL, and then went 15-4 with Indianapolis [American Association] in '62, and pitched three shutouts in a row. And yet, I go back up in '63 with Cincinnati and suddenly I'm a bullpen man. It didn't make any sense. The two jobs are so different. I knew I'd make it back to the big leagues but I didn't know I'd be a reliever. But you don't have any choice. I couldn't relieve before. I tried it but couldn't do it. Then, all of a sudden, I did it. The Lord blessed me. I finally found success with a sidearm curveball. I had worked on that a long time, even way back in 1953. But I finally matured with it. It came together for me in '64. It helped me get right-handed hitters out. It's amazing. I was a right-handed pitcher and had a hard time getting them out.

I had a three ERA in Cincinnati [in '63]. That wasn't too bad. I don't think I had but four bad games that whole season[4-4, 2.99, 10SV]. *Four.* But they dealt me to the Twins anyway in '64. Well, Minneapolis was my home. I played there before. I always felt good up there. I started pitching up there in 1950, in semi-pro. It was like coming back home. I always felt good up there.

A lot of things stood out from my years with the Twins. Minnesota is a great place. A great state. It's my favorite state. I'd probably live there now if they didn't have so much cold and snow. These fellows on that team were super good guys. Best group of guys I ever played with. Most of them were real gentleman. Harmon Killebrew was the greatest clutch hitter I'd ever seen. Tony Oliva was one of the greatest hitters I've ever seen. Jim Kaat and Jim Perry and Bob Allison and Cesar Tovar. It was just a real pleasure to play there. Camilo Pascual—a great guy. Of course, I had matured a lot by then. We started the church service on the Twins in 1966. And it's gone on to this day. They continued it after I left.

We would have won the World Series there in '65 if not for Sandy Koufax. We sure would have. He threw too hard that day [in game seven, throwing a three-hit 2-0 shutout]. He threw hard. We waltzed walking out of the stadium. I heard one woman say, "The Twins didn't lose that game. That Sandy Koufax—he just won it." He didn't even have a curveball that day. He just threw the fastball. [author's note: Koufax also shut out the Twins on four hits in game five.]

I quit baseball in '68. But Billy Martin called me back in '69 for one more season. Then I came home and started working for a life insurance company. But every time somebody called me to go speak, like at a high school or something, I didn't have much interest in the life insurance. Rather, I tried to get folks saved. And I returned to Minneapolis in the summer of '70 and '71 to hold baseball clinics for young people. They'd last about an hour. I'd put the uniform on and go into parks and churchyards, and share with them that Christ loves them and died for them. That he paid for their sins, and they had to receive him in their lives just like I did.

Then Calvin Griffith called me back in '72 to be the Twins pitching coach. I didn't even apply for the job. So I was their pitching coach in '72 and '73. It seemed like I could talk to the pitchers, but everybody was more interested in making money than going to heaven.

Then I had the opportunity to go to Liberty University [in Virginia] as a baseball coach. And I was there 16½ years. For 13 years I was head coach. Then I became the Athletic Director, and was the pitching coach under Bobby Richardson. Sid Bream played for me at Liberty. So did Lee Guetterman and Randy Tomlin.

Now I'm back home in Alabama. I don't run into many people down here who want to talk baseball. Not too many. There's a guy from New York who has a daughter living in my neighborhood, and he came over here twice, as soon as he found out where I lived. He couldn't wait to get over here. It's amazing. People in Alabama don't understand that. I don't either. I don't understand that either. We're not big baseball fans down here. We don't have that. That's a unique thing to have. People in New York go to the beach and take their radios with them. But we're not baseball fans like those folks. We don't understand that. We're getting better, though, since Atlanta's done so well. All of a sudden, now, everybody around here is *becoming* baseball fans. Ever since Atlanta began to do well.

I still watch baseball occasionally, but I'm always there for the playoffs and the World Series. The game has changed a lot since I played, because of the money. The *money* has changed it. But you still gotta get 'em out.

Alabaster, Alabama

DARYL SPENCER

Daryl Spencer hit the first home run in San Francisco Giants history, April 15, 1958, in the first major league ballgame played on the West Coast, an 8-0 victory over the Dodgers at Seals Stadium. Spencer went on to hit 17 home runs that season, with a career-high 74 RBIs. He slammed a career-best 20 homers as a rookie with the Giants in '53 and then, in '62, as a member of the Dodgers, watched in horror as the Giants scored four runs in the ninth inning of the third and final playoff game to come from behind for a 6-4 win and the National League pennant.

After a 10-year career, during which he hit 105 home runs and batted .244, playing mostly shortstop and second base, Daryl went on to play seven more years in Japan, hitting 124 home runs his first four seasons, and helping to lead the Hankyu Braves to Pacific League pennants his last four. He finally retired from baseball at the age of 43.

Spencer and his wife live in Wichita, Kansas. He has two children and two grandchildren.

THE THING THAT I THOUGHT about most when we knew the Giants were going to move to San Francisco was that we were losing the New York-Brooklyn rivalry. Because of all the rivalries in sports—I don't care *what* sport you're talking about—there was nothing like the Giants and Dodgers back in New York. You see some brushbacks now, but we had *knockdowns*, and we had two or three in a game. I can't even remember a series when there *weren't* some knockdown, with the teams clearing the benches.

Now, when the Giants play the Dodgers, the players socialize on the field before the game. That never happened back in New York [laughs]. Are you kidding me? You *hated* those guys. The

Giants and Dodgers almost never made a trade back in those days. You never made a trade with the Dodgers because the guy would come back to haunt you. Then Jackie Robinson was traded to the Giants after the '56 season, but he retired rather than play for the Giants. Sal Maglie wound up with the Dodgers but he went to Cleveland first. The Giants would have never traded him directly to the Dodgers.

The crazy thing with me, years later, was that after I got traded by the Giants to the Cardinals, St. Louis then traded me to the Dodgers. And, man, I've told this story a thousand times, but it's still so vivid in my mind. I was with the Cardinals, and we were in LA on a Friday night for a three-game series. I played for the Cardinals that night, and there were a lot of rumors flying around that I might get traded to LA because Durocher was a coach with the Dodgers then, and he liked me when we were in New York. And, by golly, Saturday morning Bing Devine [Cards GM] called me in my hotel room and said, "You've just been traded to the Dodgers." Oh, my God, you could have knocked me over with a feather. I couldn't go play with these guys. I hated them. I mean, I hated them. Junior Gilliam? A teammate? And Snider one time came down to first, elbowed me in the face and knocked me over covering on a bunt play. And I knocked down their catcher, and we had fights.

So we had a night game Saturday. I had to go out to the ballpark early and get my things. I went out to the Cardinal locker room and picked up my gear, then walked over to the Dodger locker room. And I *couldn't* go through that door. I'm just standing out there. It must have been 15 minutes. Of course, none of the other players had started to come yet. I said, "I can't go in there. God, I hate these guys." Well, finally I walked in the clubhouse. And the clubhouse guy greeted me, and gave me my locker and my uniform. Then the players started coming in. And, my God, it was *wonderful*. They just treated me like I'd been there all the time. All the past had been forgotten. My God, now I *loved* the Dodgers. But I sure didn't love them in '58 when we moved west. I had never been to San Francisco before except for playing in a couple of exhibition games in Seals Stadium, when we trained in Phoenix. We played in the old [LA] Angels park, too, and we played a game in Oakland, if I remember correctly.

Daryl Spencer (SF Giants)

I loved Seals Stadium. The wind wasn't that big a factor to me. I had great success there. I hit like crazy in Seals Park. I won a lot of ballgames for them. I hit the first major league home run there, Opening Day, against the Dodgers, off Don Drysdale. We beat them 8-0. I hit one out in the fourth and Cepeda hit one later in the game. I hear that as a trivia question every once in a while: Who hit the first major league home run on the West Coast? It was me. Ruben Gomez was the winning pitcher. Ruben probably had some of the greatest stuff of any pitcher I'd ever seen, but he was so stubborn. He loved that screwball. I remember several games he'd pitch great against the Dodgers, but he kept going to that screwball. He'd get guys like Snider out, then maybe in the eighth or ninth inning he'd still go with it, and he'd make a mistake and Snider would hit one out and beat us. But he was a great competitor and a great fielder. Just an all-around good athlete. But his head was screwed on a little crooked [laughs]. He was in his own world sometimes.

On May 13th ['58] we went to the Coliseum to play the Dodgers. Seemed like I could never get the headlines away from Mays. Now, the day

Daryl Spencer approaches home plate after his two-run homer caps a four-run ninth inning, giving the Giants an 8-7 win over the St. Louis Cardinals, April 23, 1958; greeting Spencer are Orlando Cepeda (#30), Ed Bressoud (#16) and Salty Parker (#2); the Cards catcher is Ray Katt, and the umpire is Shag Crawford. (SF Chronicle)

before, on the 12th, Mays hit two home runs and I hit two home runs. On the next night, Mays hit two home runs and I hit two home runs. I've tried to check that out, but I don't think two players have ever hit two home runs each in back to back games. The first game, Mays went three-for-five with five RBIs and two home runs. I was two-for-four with two RBIs and two home runs. The next game Mays was five-for-five with four RBIs and two home runs. And I was four-for-six with six RBIs and two home runs. And the headline was, MAYS 5-FOR-5, and then a little lower it says, SPENCER RIPS LA [laughs]. At the time, after that game, I was hitting .359. I was third in the league. And I was second in RBIs with 21. I always hit good down in that ballpark, with that short left field fence. I could pull 'em there.

We destroyed the Dodgers in '58 [winning 16 of 22], but it still wasn't the same as it would have been back in New York. I don't know why but it just wasn't the same. It was still there [the intensity], but nothing like Brooklyn. Brooklyn was just something different. And it seemed like the Dodgers had a lot harder time adjusting to the West Coast than we did. Then, of course, the next year was the downfall of the Giants, the last eight

games of the season. We were two games up, then finished third.

I had such a great start in '58 [including the Giants' first game-winning ninth inning homer, April 23rd, a two-run shot that beat St. Louis 8-7]. Of course, Ernie Banks was the premiere shortstop in those days. You know, he was just Ernie Banks. *Mr. Shortstop.* But I was having a great year and I wanted to go to the All-Star Game. Of course, that was in the days when Milwaukee was one of the top teams. They had won the World Series [in '57] and Johnny Logan had been in the public eye. He was hitting around .290, but I was hitting around .310 with power and RBIs. And damn if Banks gets the votes for the All-Star team, but I'm still thinking they'll take me as a backup shortstop. Well, [Fred] Haney takes his boy Logan instead. And I probably went three weeks just going through the motions almost. I was really depressed because I deserved to be in the All-Star Game.

Then I went through the same thing the next year. I started off having another great year, winning games and everything, and here I don't get picked again. Those things were really disappointing to me because you'd always like to be in the All-Star Game. But missing out on the World Series in '59, and then again with the Dodgers in '62, was really tough to accept as well.

I remember that critical series [in '59] when the Dodgers came to Seals Stadium and beat us three straight. We went from being two games up, with eight left, to being one down, with five left. And we never recovered. In that second game we had the bases loaded and nobody out right off, against Drysdale. And here's one time Cepeda didn't come through. He swung at a bad pitch, when he should have walked [eventually striking out]. Then Kirkland struck out. Then I flew out. We had them on the ropes that game and *could* have changed the whole season around.

In the end, I got blamed for the second game loss. I had a fractured thumb and I shouldn't have even played. But Rigney says, "You play. I'd rather have you out there the way you are than put somebody else in." That was fine with me because I played with a broken rib before, taped up, stuff like that. So it was just one of those things that happened. We're ahead 1-0 in the seventh inning. Men on first and third, one out. Groundball to Davenport. He makes a good throw, but it hit right on my damn thumb. And if you've ever had a broken thumb and the ball hits it, you can't help it. You can't get a grip on it. And the ball came out of my glove. Then they get five runs. Man, I'd have made that play 99 times out of 100 if I hadn't had a broken thumb. And Maury Wills, that son of a buck. We didn't even spend 10 second on him in our pre-game meeting. We just said, "Wills? Don't walk him. Just get the ball over." *That* series there made Wills a major league ballplayer. He got on, stole bases, did everything [7-for-13, 4 runs]. And all of a sudden he got his confidence. Before that, he never hit *nothin'!* But I can't live down that error. I made it.

The only other error I made to lose a ballgame came against the Cubs at Wrigley Field. The first two or three innings the sun was really bad at shortstop. I had my glasses and the black stuff under my eyes. They got a runner on second and Ernie Banks hits a popup. I go back to short left field, I got my glasses down, I got my hand up over my eyes and I lost that pop fly. It hit off my glove and Banks scored. I said, "Well, hell, it's the first inning." We lose the game 1-0 [laughs]. That's the only other game I ever lost with an error.

Speaking of errors, Andre Rodgers just killed us that year. Rigney didn't want to play him, but

Stoneham kept saying, "Put him in there. I want him to play." So he'd put him in there for a week and he wouldn't hit, and he'd cost us a couple of ballgames. Then Rigney would go back to me and Bressoud. I was playing short and second at the time. But that went on for a long time. Boy, he cost us some ballgames that, as it turned out, hurt us later on. It was a bad deal.

I had a great relationship with Rigney. He was my first roommate when I went up to the Giants in '53. Then I went into the service for two years, came back and he was the manager. But we had a special relationship. I could be on deck and he could be coaching, and he could look at me, and I just *knew* he wanted me to hit-and-run. We just read each other's minds, and I really enjoyed playing for Rig. And he had a lot of confidence in me.

It was shocking, then, to be traded after the '59 season. Yeah, I grew up with the Giants, and back in those days you had a lot of loyalty. You'd talk to the owners and everybody was family. It was so much different than it is now. It was really a shock. I came up through the Giants' minor leagues, played with them in '53, and '56 through '59. Now, all of a sudden, I'm traded.

So now I'm a St. Louis Cardinal and we open the 1960 season at Candlestick Park, of all places. It was so weird. You go out and take infield practice in a short-sleeve shirt. Then you come out for the game to start and it's like somebody turned on the fans. I guess I'm lucky I didn't have to play there. I was traded [with Leon Wagner] for Don Blasingame, and we became great friends later when we were in Japan together. And he just had a nightmare trying to catch some of those pop flies [at Candlestick]. But if I was going to get traded anywhere, the Cardinals were probably the team I'd be most happy with. I had been a Cardinal fan as a kid, being from Wichita, and had always hit good in old Sportsman's Park. That's probably why they got me. I'd always hit good against the Cardinals.

It was kind of weird, though, in spring training because late in the '59 season there was a play at home plate when Larry Jackson was pitching. He threw a wild pitch and had to cover home, and I just creamed him at home plate. He dropped the ball and I scored to win the ballgame for us. So, all of a sudden [laughs], I've got to see all these guys that I've bopped around and slid into. And they said, "Well, you play hard," and they accepted me as one of their teammates. So the transition was very easy. And about the fourth or fifth game down in Florida, I hit three home runs against the Yankees. And the headline was, SPENCER 10, YANKEES 7. That helped me to blend in right away with the ball club.

Then we start off the season and I promptly go 0-for-18 [laughs]. And the last time at bat, in LA, before we come home, I got a hit. And I told all the writers, "Don't worry, I'll be hitting about .290 by the time we get out of this homestand." And, by God, in about two weeks I was hitting .339. Then, in '61, I beat Spahn Opening Day up in Milwaukee with a home run in the 10th inning. Some of these games really stick out in your mind.

The Cardinals made a mistake, though, in '61 when they traded me to the Dodgers. And they really regretted it. I think the Giants regretted trading me, too, when Blasingame had such a terrible year. They just never did get a good replacement until Pagan came along [in '61]. I heard later the reason the Giants traded me. They said we weren't making enough double plays. Well, if they had left me at short and put somebody else at second, we'd have made a *thousand* double plays. I mean, I could play short. I could play second pretty good but I wasn't a great second baseman. Then when Blasingame came out there he never hit and never made the plays at second base, so they regretted trading me.

But the Cardinals must have really been wrong on this deal [w/LA] because they got Bob Lillis—a pretty good glove man, couldn't hit nothin'—and a kid name Carl Warwick, who they thought was going to be a future superstar. He was an outfielder who never panned out. And, my God, I had so many game-winning hits for the Cardinals. I couldn't believe it. Jeez.

The Dodgers got me to play third base [with Wills now firmly entrenched at short]. I started off slowly for them. Then we went on this road trip and I got back in the groove. In the last game we were playing in Milwaukee against a pitcher named [Don] Nottebart. I used to read his pitches so I knew what was coming, and I said, "Boy, here comes a slider." And I ripped one to left-center field. And I'm going down to first and saying, "Well, that's gone." And the wind or something caught it, and it hit off the fence. So I'm around second and it looks like the relay's going to get over McMillan's head. Now I'm heading to third, and McMillan somehow gets it and throws a strike to Mathews. Here I come into third, and I

see Mathews waiting, so I tried to knock the ball out of his glove. But he put his knee out there and damn if I don't break *my* knee. So that put me on the bench for about three weeks. Then I came back and it was unbelievable. Three straight Saturday nights I hit game-winning home runs. I beat Marichal in the bottom of the ninth, then I beat the Phillies the next Saturday night in the bottom of the ninth, then the third Saturday night I hit a home run in the bottom of the sixth to win the game. And they were calling me "The Saturday Night Kid." But I had a lot of game-winning home runs. And I'm proud of that because it's kind of fun to hit a home run in the bottom of the ninth and come in, and everybody greets you and the game's over.

In '62 I was in the Opening Day lineup for the first game at Dodger Stadium. And, oh, Dodger Stadium is still probably the most beautiful park in baseball. I haven't seen the real new ones but still, as far as beauty, I think it's prettier than the new one in Cleveland, or the ones in Baltimore or Texas. They're kind of unique but Dodger Stadium is beautiful. Have you ever been in the upper deck there to watch a game? Ah, *what a view.* One time I got out of the game early and I went up there just to see what it's like. And you can just look out there and see the whole play develop, and see the guys move after the ball. That's a beautiful ballpark, with the palm trees and everything.

I don't think it ever entered my mind that it was the *Giants* we were battling for first place that year. I just wanted to win the pennant. The team that killed us, though, was Houston. Houston didn't have nothin' that year, and I think a guy named [Al] Spangler went three-for-four and beat us in a game [the final week] we had won. Then here come the Cardinals, a team we had beaten all year, and we can't score. They beat us three straight and won the last game of the season 1-0. Gene Oliver, one of my good buddies when I was with the Cardinals, beat us [with a home run] and that pissed me off. Now we're tied with the Giants and we still can't score.

Then the Giants ripped us 8-0 [game one, best-of-three playoff]. And we *still* can't score. But we come back in that memorable second game, when we come from five runs down to beat 'em. I finally got in the game to bunt [in a seven-run sixth], and I think it was one of the first games that went coast to coast on national television. Wills was on second, somebody else on first and we needed a bunt. Well, Alston could never make a decision himself. He has to get Pete Reiser and all his crew together and say, "Well, what do you think? What shall we do?" This was one of the reasons I never got along with Alston. He never had any confidence in me. Well, Durocher speaks up and says, "Spencer will get 'em over." And that's why I liked Durocher. He made his point and gave you confidence. Well, I made a shitty bunt, but with Wills on second, they made the wrong play. They could've had him at third but they threw to first, and I had the sacrifice. And we went ahead to win the game.

Now, the final game. We're ahead 4-2 in the bottom of the eighth inning, bases loaded, two out and [Ed] Roebuck due up. *Everybody* knew Alston should have sent up a pinch hitter. Roebuck had pitched his ass off for a week and a half, and he was in every game. And he had already pitched three innings that game. You could see he had a good sinker but that type of pitcher can't pitch four innings. Koufax and Drysdale both wanted to go in [for the ninth]. And we had [Larry] Sherry down there, but that asshole—they called down and he said, "No, I don't feel good," or, "My arm's tight," or something. Yes, a pinch hitter might have popped up. But it would have given us a shot at getting another run.

OK, we still have a 4-2 lead in the ninth. But here's the play that cost us the pennant, I think. Alston puts in [Larry] Burright at second for Gilliam. Good fielder. Good hands. Makes the double play. Has a little more range than Gilliam. So Alston put him in at the start of the ninth inning. [Matty] Alou's on first, nobody out and, of course, Roebuck's *still* in there. Now, Roebuck is tough to hit to right field. He's got a sinker ball that comes in on you and even with Kuenn, as great as he is, it's really gonna be tough to hit the ball to right field. Well, Alston gets up and he moves Burright about three steps toward right field. Any other pitcher, that's OK, that's a good play because Kuenn will probably go that way. But if Gilliam's playing second, he would have moved over, maybe, *two* steps. And by the time the pitch came he'd have been back where he was, cheating for the double play. So here comes the pitch. Groundball to Wills. Here comes Burright running from right field. He has to take the throw on the run. He makes a good pivot. And it's a boom-boom play at first. Kuenn could have been called out, but he's safe. Now, instead of two outs, nobody on, all hell breaks loose. And who does Alston finally bring in? *Stan Williams.*

Everybody wanted to pitch, except Sherry. Koufax wanted to go down and warm up. Drysdale wanted to go down and warm up. Stan Williams? Well, he wanted to pitch but, my God, he's the wildest man in the world [98BB in 186IP, in '62]. He walked two guys, threw a wild pitch and the first thing you know, they got four runs. I suppose the biggest disappointment of my life was then, I guess. Because we *had* it right then, 4-2. And I had to go to Japan before I won a pennant. I played in four Japan Series over there but [laughs] it wasn't the same.

It was written that I passed out in the clubhouse after that game, but I might as well have. I think I drank a fifth of VO in about 30 minutes, and I don't even drink. I remember I was on the floor and they were pushing me along. I mean, I was just like a sled [laughs], just loosy-goosy. They could have hit my head against a wall and I wouldn't have known the difference. Of course, I knew I'd get traded by next year because I was in the locker room shouting, "Who moved Burright? Christ, how can you move Burright?" And I knew I'd get the ax because Alston didn't like me anyhow. Everybody always says how popular Alston was. Well, the older guys didn't like him at all. I guess maybe some of the young guys coming up were in awe of him. But, no, I don't know any of the older guys who liked Alston. There'd be times I'd go a week and he wouldn't even say hello to me. Of course, after I'd hit a couple of game-winning home runs for him he'd speak to me for a while. Then, the first thing you know, he wouldn't even talk to you. I guess the thing I didn't like about him was as great players as he had, he was afraid to make a decision. And that's why I appreciated Durocher and Rigney.

After I got released I had a chance to go to Washington or Cincinnati. In those days, those were the two cheapest organizations in baseball. I was very fortunate to come up with the Giants, a good organization. Then I got traded to the Cardinals, maybe even a little better. Then I got traded to the Dodgers, probably the greatest organization in baseball. So I was very fortunate.

I went to Cincinnati. I joined them in St. Louis. I walked in the clubhouse, and there's Frank Robinson. I had always worn number 20. Frank Robinson greets me and says, "If you want my number, you can have it." I said, "No, I think you'd better keep it. You'll be around a little bit longer than me." But that made me feel at home right away. And that night I went four-for-five.

Ray Sadecki was pitching. I used to know everything he was throwing. I knocked in three or four runs and won the ballgame. Next night I knocked in the winning run. And the next night Maloney throws a no-hitter, and I make two great plays. So I'm really doing good with the ball club. Then here come the Dodgers.

Joey Jay was pitching, and having a terrible year. But I went over all the hitters with him, because I knew them like a book. I could have probably managed that year, at least against the Dodgers. But if a situation came up, I'd go in from third and say, "Now, Jay, keep the ball away from him," or do this or do that. So it's 0-0, bottom of the sixth and Pinson gets a double. Now, it doesn't take a genius to know that with Frank Robinson up next, they're going to walk him. And I'm hitting fifth. So they're going to pitch to me. But it was just the way Alston reacted—I'm in the on-deck circle and he walks out there, slowly looking around. I know what they're gonna do. And, boy, my adrenaline just went sky high. And Koufax is tough. I roomed with him and I know what he's gonna do, and I knew when he was gonna throw me a curve, but you couldn't hit his curve even if you *knew* it was coming. The only thing you could hit was the low fastball. Or, that's the only thing I could hit. And this was the year he went 25-5. I wasn't battling Koufax. I was battling Alston. And he threw me a low fastball, and I lined it into left, and we won the game 1-0. I'll *always* remember that game. I didn't want to beat Koufax. I just wanted to beat Alston.

My major league career ended soon after that. I went to the ballpark in Cincinnati on my birthday [July 13]. I had been with the Reds for about a month and a half. I had won about six games for them with hits and stuff. And, all of a sudden, they decide they're not going anywhere. I'm making $27,500. And they tell me they've got to release me to cut down their payroll. So they release me on my birthday. I came home. I had offers to go to Japan then but I was so sick of baseball that I didn't even want to hardly play again.

As I said, I was very fortunate to have played for the Giants, the Cardinals and the Dodgers. I played with Mays. I played with Musial. I played with so many great players with the Dodgers. And I played with Frank Robinson with the Reds. Who was the best? Boy, I don't know. I can't say Mays because the four years I played with him he wasn't that spectacular. I suppose if I'd have played with him the rest of my career, with the things he did in the sixties, I'd probably say Mays. That's really tough. Mays was very charismatic. But Cepeda—*boy*. If you've got the game on the line, let me have Cepeda up there. That's who I wanted with the winning run on bases. Of course, I liked myself, too, but between Mays and Cepeda, Cepeda was the guy I liked to have up there in those situations.

But, my God, if Cepeda would've been willing to play left field for us when McCovey came up [in '59], you don't think we'd have had a heck of a better lineup? Why didn't he play left field for us? Hell, I played second, third, short, anyplace they wanted me to play. But Cepeda just said, "I'm a first baseman. I don't want to play left."

Every once in a while somebody will write me a letter and want to know what my All-Star team would have been from the fifties and sixties. Have you ever sat down and tried to pick three outfielders? In the National League, if you go with Mays, Aaron and Musial, then you leave Frank Robinson off. And Clemente. Now, if you include the American League, you've got Kaline, Mantle and Ted Williams. Now what do you do? It really was an incredible era I played in. All those great players. And you really have to play *with* a player to know. When I was with the Giants, Ken Boyer never played good against us. I think part of it was the two years he came out to Frisco he liked to play around a little bit, and I don't think he had his heart in some of the games out there. He just never played good against the Giants, when I was with the Giants. Then I go to the Cardinals. I'm playing short, he's playing third. That guy was a fabulous ballplayer. He did it all. He stole bases when we needed, he got the RBI, he made the plays. Ken Boyer was a great ballplayer. And as great as Boyer was, Davenport was an even better fielder, as far as making all the plays. Of course, he couldn't drive in runs. But you really have to play with guys to know. And I got to play with Koufax. What a great pitcher he was for five years. Probably the greatest pitcher ever.

Sadaharu Oh was a great hitter. He had a lot of advantages in Japan. The umpires—it's kind of like Ted Williams—if he took a pitch, the guy wouldn't call it a strike. I never saw him called out on strikes. One year he had more walks than he had hits. That's the year he hit 50 home runs. He had to hit a homer about every four at-bats. He could have done well in the States. He wouldn't have hit 50 home runs, of course, because the ballparks were smaller. But what a great hitter. Great fielder, too. He definitely could have played in the States, but they would have never let him leave Japan. Because he was just an idol over there.

When I played my first few years over there the [Yomiuri] Giants, with their great team, had Oh and Nagashima. And it was so reminiscent of the Gehrig and Ruth days when the Yankees had their great teams. I'd say 95 percent of the fans in Japan were Giants fans. And if Oh and Nagashima played, they had a full house. I don't care if they played out in the sticks. Yeah, Oh was a great hitter. And when they needed a hit, the pitcher wouldn't walk him. You think they'd pitch around him. Heck no. We played the Giants in the Japan Series one time, and had a 3-1 lead in the bottom of the ninth. They had runners at first and third, and I'm trying to get our manager to walk Oh. Jeez, the guy's a *great* hitter. OK, two pitches later he homers, we're dead, we're home, we're gone, we lose. Next day, bottom of the first, runners at first and second, and *now* we walk him. You know, walk him in the first inning but not in the bottom of the ninth when he's gonna beat you. Boy, that's why I was so frustrated over in Japan. The percentage baseball they knew nothing about.

Anyway, in 1964 I had two or three teams in Japan that I had a chance to play with, and I selected the Hankyu Braves in Osaka, because there was a kid here in Wichita—a good friend named Dick Sanders—who played in the Yankee organization, and they offered him a contract. We were going to go over there as teammates. So I went with the Braves because of Sanders. About two weeks before we were supposed to leave Sanders decides he's not going. They ended up picking up another [American] player, a guy named Gordon Windhorn.

The Braves had the biggest ballpark in Japan. It's still not big but it's bigger than some of these other bandboxes. And on the team I *could* have gone with—the Nankai Hawks—was the great home run hitter of the Pacific League, [Katsuya] Nomura. My God, if I had been with the Hawks it would have been like Oh and Nagashima in the Central League. It would have been Nomura and Spencer. As it turned out, we had battles for home run titles. Then they started walking me. Did you read about me going up to the plate with my bat upside down? I *really* did it.

It pissed me off. Did you see the movie, *Mr. Baseball?* They copied me doing that. They didn't call me and ask me if they could do that. Pissed me off when I saw that, because I'm the guy that did that over there [laughs].

THE LAST GAME before the All-Star break [in '65] I hit for the cycle. First time I'd ever done it. I was hitting .347 at the All-Star break with 25 home runs. In the All-Star Game I hit a home run off one of the best pitchers in Japan, drove in another run and made a great play in the field. Soon we're in August, I've got 32 home runs and Nomura's got 26. And my interpreter sits down with my coach who says, "Have Spencer concentrate on beating Nomura out of the triple crown." Nobody had ever won the triple crown before. He was hitting .341. I was hitting about .325. I said, "Don't worry, I'll win the home run crown." He said, "No, that's already decided. You won't win the home run crown." I said, "What are you talking about?" He said, "Just believe me." I said, "Yeah, yeah, OK, OK."

So we were playing the Hawks, and they wouldn't pitch to me because they didn't want me to hit home runs, with Nomura being their teammate. They walked me three straight times. I think I still have the record in Japan for drawing eight consecutive walks. Then we went up to this little ballpark in Tokyo, where this pitcher Koyama could throw nine out of 10 strikes blindfolded. He walked me four straight times, and the fourth time was with the bases loaded to force in a run. Now, all of a sudden, I'm into this spell where they walk me eight straight times. And that's when I just quit. I said, "Well, hell, there ain't no use to play." This great pitcher who walked me four straight times—every time he faced Nomura, if the game wasn't on the line, he'd just lob one in there. Nomura must have hit six home runs off Koyama that year. In the states, it's the best against the best. Everybody remembers Reggie Jackson and Bob Welch in the ['78] Series. Wasn't that something? They'll challenge you in the States.

Now, all of a sudden, we've got about 13 games left to play. And we're playing the Hawks again, on national TV. We've got a full house. And I wasn't gonna play. The interpreter comes in and says, "Please play, Spencer. If they don't pitch to you, we won't pitch to Nomura." So I led off, they walked me three times, and the fourth time I'm up there with my bat upside down.

They throw it outside and walk me again. Then the second game is about to start. The interpreter says, "You've got to play in the second game." I said, "I don't play. I'm pissed. Jesus, what do I want to play for?" So he said, "Nomura's in a slump. The guy can't hit shit." [laughs] I've got 37 home runs now, and Nomura's got 39. So I said, "OK, I'll play."

Nomura's up the first time and, shit, we strike him out. So I come up—and the only reason I decided to play was because an American player, Joe Stanka, is pitching. I know Joe's gonna pitch to me. And he doesn't want to give me a home run because if I hit a home run off him his teammates will just give him hell. So, first time up, I hit a line shot to the shortstop. I'm out. Then I come up in the third inning with a man on, and hit one about 480 feet. Now I've got 38 and Nomura's got 39. And as I come across home plate I look over at him and say, "I'm gonna catch you, Moose." His nickname was Moose. And he could understand English. "I'm gonna get you, Moose. I'm gonna get you." Well, he went 0-for-3. Stanka left the game after I hit the home run, so they walked me after that.

Now we've got the day off, with 11 games left, and I think eight are against the three teams in the league that will pitch to me. And I told my wife, "You better come to the game tonight. I know I'm gonna hit one, and I'll probably hit two." That's just the way I felt. I said, "I'm gonna beat that Nomura because he's pissing me off." [laughs] So I get on my little Honda bike that I used to ride to the train station, for the train to the ballpark. I get just a couple of blocks from my house, and here comes this little pickup van. I saw him coming, but there was a big wall to my left. And I started to get out of his way, but the kid just kept coming and he ran me right into the wall, and knocked me off my bike. I got up and said, "Oh, Christ, my leg's hurting." Well, I had a broken leg. So I missed the last 11 games. Nomura won the triple crown. And I'm in the hospital. And would you believe the worst thing is the damn ball club fined me about $300 because I broke my leg [laughs]? I said, "Boy, this is something else." [laughs] You don't think I wanted to play?

I had 36 home runs and 94 RBIs my first year. Gordon Windhorn was hitting first—he hit about .230. The second-place hitter hit about .215. That year I left one man in scoring position the whole year. That's the kind of year I had. And I can't tell you how many times I'd be up, with a guy on first and two outs, and I'd be up there bearing down, and then all of a sudden I'd see the guy *running*. He gets thrown out, and now I'm leading off the next inning. I finally got through to the interpreter and said, "When I'm batting, please no steal. Please no steal." I finally got that through to them. It was so frustrating.

In Japan the pitch-out was high and *inside*. They'd pitch high and inside, and the guy would hit a groundball, or hit it somewhere. It took me two-thirds of the season before I finally taught the catcher to step outside, and he threw the guy out by about 10 feet. "Oh, that's a nice play." No shit. That's how long it took me to get things through to them.

I also introduced the hard slide to Japan. It was late in the year, we're in a scoreless game, bottom of the eighth and Koyama was pitching. He threw a little palm ball. I mean, I had to battle him just to go 1-for-4. He was tough. Good pitcher. He could've pitched in the States. So I'm hitting third. And this guy behind me is a notorious groundball double-play threat. I mean, just all the time. So Windhorn was on second, and they walk me. Smart play. So I yell out at Windhorn, "If he hits a groundball don't stop, because I'm gonna get the second baseman." Well, you could tell the Japanese, "This is the way you do it," over and over, but you had to show them on the field. So I no more got that out of my mouth than this guy hits a groundball to short. He flips to second. Now, in Japan the normal procedure is the guy runs toward second and then turns toward right field about the time he gets to second, and just lets the second baseman make the throw. Well, I take the second baseman out, knock him into left field, Windhorn scores, it's 1-0, they call time out and argue for 30 minutes. "Spencer can't do this. That illegal slide. He can't do this." They finally got play resumed and we won the game 1-0. The next day one of my players slid into second, broke up a double play and, from then on, everybody started changing their style at second.

That's what irritates me about the major leagues today. A lack of fundamentals. They don't hit the cutoff man. Then they steal third with two out. Oh, crap. If Barry Bonds did that when I was playing he'd have been knocked down in his next at bat. You've got to play percentages. And they knew nothing about that in Japan. That's what irritated me.

Johnny Logan came over there and had a miserable year [.189 in '64]. And Johnny Logan was a pretty good guess-hitter. He knew the pitchers in the National League and had one of the better lifetime averages for a shortstop [.268 in 13 seasons]. I told him, "Johnny, you just won't believe how they pitch over here. In a situation where you think you're gonna get a sinker, they'll throw you one right down the middle. You were always a good guesser in the States, but over here you need to guess, and then at the last second change your mind. Because then you'll be right." He never did adjust to it.

I was very fortunate to get off to a good start every spring over there, and never had a Japanese coach come up and tell me how to hit. I saw some pretty good hitters get sent to the minor leagues over there—guys who hit good in the States—because they'd go 0-for-8, and the coaches would try to change their style. They wanted them to adjust to Japanese style. They even screwed up Murakami. [*author's note: The first Japanese national to play in the major leagues, Masanori Murakami went 5-1 with the Giants in '64 and '65, with 100 strikeouts in 89 innings, and a 3.43ERA*]. He was perfect for American baseball. A left-hander. He'd get down in the count 3-and-0, and the batter would be in the hole, because he'd be just a half-inch off the plate. And he was perfect for the situation the Giants used him. He couldn't have been a starting pitcher. He wasn't that strong. But for relief, as a left-hander, I think he could've pitched here [in the majors] 10 to 15 years. But the poor guy was pressured to go back to Japan. They built him up as the first Japanese to pitch in America, then broke him back down to pitch the Japanese way. And he had some terrible years over there. I think he had one great year [18-4, 2.38ERA in '68]. But I felt sorry for the guy having to pitch under those circumstances.

I told Windhorn one day, "Watch this. I'm gonna prove a point today." So I went up there in batting practice, took half-assed swings, and about 20 minutes before the game the interpreter comes up and says, "Manager says your condition no good today. You take rest." [laughs] See, in Japan all the coaches stand around and watch batting practice very seriously. The next day I told Windhorn, "Watch this." I go up there and hit about nine of 10 out of the ballpark. And the interpreter comes up and says, "You nice condition. Number one batter tonight." That's the way they were. There were only about three or four players on the team that had regular positions in the lineup. The rest would be decided by batting practice.

One day they put the starting lineup on the big board in center field, and I was listed as the third hitter, at first base. OK. So the interpreter comes up after infield and says, "Manager is making change. You're not playing today. Your condition not good." So I walked up through our dugout and up the stairs, to take a shower. I was just gonna take a shower and go home. So I've got these sandals on, shorts and T-shirt. And I'm walking downstairs, as they're playing the national anthem. Blasingame is coaching for the Hawks, and he's standing there in the hallway when I came down. He said, "Where you going? You're playing." I said, "No. They decided I wasn't good condition. I'm not playing." He just laughed. Then I said, "Watch this."

I was still on the scoreboard in center, as the third hitter. So I knew Nishimoto [Braves manager] was planning to pinch hit for me in the first inning. Instead, I walked around to where our dugout was, underneath the stands. By that time, the leadoff hitter was up and the second-place hitter was on deck. I walked up to the bat rack. Everybody thought I was just gonna get my bats and go. They know when it's my turn to hit, they'll announce a pinch hitter. So, the first batter makes an out. The second batter goes up. I get my bat and go up to the on-deck circle. I'm standing there [laughs], swinging my bat, with my T-shirt, shorts and sandals on. The players on the bench are going crazy. The manager's screaming, *"Get back here! Get back here!"* My interpreter finally comes out to get me. And, of course, they had pictures of it in the paper the next day. I said, "Wait a minute. I'm in the lineup. They haven't made an announcement yet." That cost me about $300. It was worth it.

I played five years in Japan, retired, then they brought me back as a coach in 1971 [two seasons later]. My God, I must have weighed 270 pounds. But they put me in charge of infield, and right away I'm hitting 5,000 ground balls a day. First thing I know, the uniform they got me was hanging off me. One day I went up and took BP and hit about three out of the park, so they wanted to know if I'd be a player again. I knew what they wanted me to do. They wanted me to play and, the first thing I knew, I'd be in there playing all the time. Well, I said OK, I'd play for X dollars per game. I ended up playing about 70 ballgames. And when the season was over they had to pull out some money for me, so that made it worthwhile. Then I came back for one more year [at age 43]. I had a good year, too. I coached, and won about six ballgames pinch hitting [4HR, .260, 77AB].

It was very satisfying to help lead the Braves to the pennant [his final four years]. When I went over there they hadn't won a championship in 32 years. [author's note: The Braves, however, lost all four Japan Series to the Giants.]

I liked living in Japan. Man, that's a man's world [laughs]. Yeah, I've been back several times. In '91, '93 and '95, They have an old-timers game over there, and the Americans who did good over there get invited back. We go over there for about a week to 10 days. Boy, it's great. They pay all your expenses. And I think we'll be going back in November ['97].

My wife didn't like it that well, though. When Windhorn and I first went over there, our wives hadn't come over with the kids yet. They were still in school. So we had this maid—an older lady. And, man, what a cook. A great, great cook. She shined our shoes and did our laundry. Everything. I wish she had been about 22 years old. But she was an old lady. And now my wife comes, and she wouldn't let my wife in the kitchen. It was *her* job. My wife took it for a little while. And then she got fed up and said, "We gotta get rid of the maid." Or she was going back to the States. But that's the way it was. The women really took care of the men over there. And I loved the steambaths and the massages. I dream of them sometimes [laughs].

Wichita, Kansas

MARV GRISSOM

Marv Grissom won seven games and saved a team-high 10, in 51 relief appearances, for the '58 Giants, at the age of 40. From '54 through '58, his final five big league seasons, he saved 58 games. His best year was also the Giants' last World Series championship season, in 1954, when he went 10-7 with 19 saves and a 2.35 ERA, made the All-Star team and won the first game of the Series against the heavily favored Cleveland Indians. Over 10 big league seasons, Marv had 47 wins, 12 complete games, three shutouts, 58 saves and a 3.41ERA.

Grissom's older brother Lee pitched eight years in the majors, mostly with Cincinnati. And his nephew Jim Davis pitched four years in the majors, three with the Chicago Cubs.

Marv is retired, lives with his wife in Red Bluff, California, and has one son and three grandchildren.

MY MOST VIVID MEMORIES with the Giants are not so much from 1958, but with the '54 team in New York. That was really the highlight of my career—not just winning the World Series, but the *whole* year. I saved the game for Maglie Opening Day against the Dodgers, and then I started on Saturday against the Phillies and beat Robin Roberts 1-0. I got to finish a lot of games in relief, pitching under real pressure the whole year. And then just being in the All-Star Game and the World Series—everything happened to me in that one year, things that a lot of players hope for but never get.

The All-Star Game was about as exciting as it could get. I came in with the bases loaded and two out, in the sixth inning, and got a fly ball to get the third out. Then in the seventh I faced Nellie Fox, Rudy Regalado and Ted Williams. I struck out Fox, Regalado grounded out and I struck out Williams [Fox fanned only 12 times in 631 at-bats in '54]. They pinch hit for me in the eighth with the score tied, and Gus Bell hit a home run to put us ahead 9-8. But then Gene Conley came in and they scored three runs off him. But it was exciting to come in with the bases loaded, at Cleveland Stadium, with 70,000 people in the stands, plus national television. By the time the World Series came around we were such underdogs [against the 111-43 Indians] that we were just happy to be there. No matter what happened, it wasn't going to bother us. We were supposed to lose but won it in four straight [laughs].

When Mays made that famous over-the-shoulder catch off Vic Wertz' bat in game one, I had a great view of it. It happened just before I came into the game. I was warming up in the bullpen at the Polo Grounds, which was in right-center field. In fact, I was only about 100 feet from where Willie caught the ball, and threw it back in. And I agree with Willie, that he made a lot of *better* catches in his career than that one. I didn't see all of them, as I left the team after the '58 season. But I remember one catch he made when I was pitching in the Polo Grounds. Our clubhouse was in center field, and there was an opening in the fence there that we had to go through to get to the clubhouse. But it was still in the playing area. And this backdrop stood four or five feet beyond the fence [485 feet from home plate]. And he went after a fly ball behind that opening and caught the ball before it reached the clubhouse steps. *That* was a great catch.

The other one I remember was in old Forbes Field in Pittsburgh. They always put the batting cage in left-center field, *on* the playing field. And I saw him go to the side of the cage and make the catch on a fly ball in dead left-center field. That was a *long* ways [457 feet away]. And with the wall, the batting cage and everything right there coming into contact with each other, I thought that was a great catch.

It's hard to say whether Mays was the best I ever saw because I played against DiMaggio, [Ted] Williams and Mantle. So there were some really great, great players I saw. He would be with the top of them. There's no question about that. I think that Willie probably could do more than most individuals, because he could run, hit, hit with power, field and throw. Some of the others could do one or two of those things excellent, but Willie could do them all. In fact, I've seen him run from first to third, looking *back* to where the ball was in the outfield, faster than the average guy could run looking straight ahead. He was amazing that way. He just had that baseball instinct. He knew exactly what to do, and how far he could go.

Many people say Ted Williams was the best pure hitter they ever saw. But not off me he wasn't. Yeah, I had good success against him. I didn't have to pitch against him that much. He didn't have me analyzed yet, I guess [laughs]. He was one of the true real pretty swingers. And DiMaggio was another one although, as I recall, I only pitched against him twice. He got a base hit. A .500 average [laughs]. Stan Musial's swing wasn't as classic as theirs was, but he was the type of hitter that could hit the ball all around the park. He was a *very* good hitter.

The two toughest hitters for me to get out were Junior Gilliam with the Dodgers, and Musial. Gilliam would just spray the ball around and not try to overpower it. I had a tough time with him. Musial was a good power hitter but he

Marv Grissom (SF Giants)

would still go the opposite way. If you pitched to him one way all the time, he would adjust to it. So you had to change on him.

I WAS BORN in 1918, so I really wasn't old enough to get the full brunt of the Depression. But I did work on the ranch for 10 cents an hour, so I guess I got part of it [laughs]. I didn't play baseball in high school, but my brother Lee, of course, was already in pro ball. And being 11 years older, he actually got me started with it. I could throw hard, and he took me to spring training in Florida, and that's how I started playing.

I went to the Cincinnati Reds spring training camp in 1938 and they sent me home. I didn't make it. With my brother already being on the big club, it was through him that they took a chance on me. Warren Giles was the general manager of the Cincinnati club. And he just told Lee to bring me back for a tryout. I didn't know how to pitch. I didn't even know how to stand on the rubber. There was an old-time catcher and coach with Cincinnati at the time by the name of Hank Gowdy, and he took me aside and showed me how to stand on the rubber, pitch, wind up and everything. But I never did get a chance to pitch in a game. And they just decided to send me home.

So I played with the town team here [in Red Bluff] on Sundays. Later on I got a tryout with the Hollywood Stars [PCL] in 1940, and they sent me a contract to play in San Bernardino [California League] in 1941. I pitched one year there and then went into the service.

I was in the medical corps, on the island of Tinian, in the Pacific. We were there in late '44 and '45. There was a little activity on the island but nothing that had much danger with it. Tinian, of course, was the island where the atomic bomb came off of. We were there when it happened. We had two B-29 bases on the island, and our hospital unit was right on top of a hill overlooking the North Field. So we saw a lot of B-29 flights leave there at about five o'clock in the afternoon for their bombing missions, and then come back the next morning. We had no idea the atomic bomb was about to be dropped, but all I can say about that is we were one of the happiest bunch of guys you've ever seen when we heard about it. We didn't know the *result* of it—how many people it had killed—but we knew that the war was going to come to a close pretty quickly after that.

My major league debut came in 1946, with the Giants. I came on in relief and didn't last too long. I was a little bit wild and only pitched a couple of innings. I had just got out of the service after four years—I played ball in the service—and had started the season at Jersey City [International League]. In fact, I pitched against Jackie Robinson in Jersey City when he was with Montreal [after signing with the Dodgers]. He didn't have a very good spring training. I had left the Giants training camp and joined the Jersey City club in Florida, and we played Montreal in an exhibition game. He didn't look very impressive at the time. But he certainly changed [laughs] pretty quickly. I think we had a three-game series in Jersey City against Montreal, and they scored 75 or 76 runs off of us. Jackie had a few hits in that series. Then when I pitched against him in the major leagues, he was a great player.

Mel Ott was at the tail end of his career when I joined the Giants, but I remember he had

that slide-and-catch thing, on the tough fly balls. He would slide, sitting down, and then catch the ball. It was like Willie's basket catch, only he would be sitting on the ground catching it. Never on a routine fly, but on the hard ones.

Then, after two more seasons in the minors, I was with the Detroit Tigers the whole year in '49 but didn't pitch much [2-4, 6.41, 39IP]. Then I played with Seattle in the Coast League in '51. It was a *super* league. In fact, I would have liked to have *stayed* there and finished my career, the way things had gone for me up to that point, and the way they went that year [20-11, 3.04, 252IP]. I felt that would be great just to stay there and finish my career out. Everything was great in the Coast League—the pay, the travel, and we could stay close to home. The guys you became acquainted with, you could stay with them for four or five years. It was super. But bouncing around like I did those years was tough [10 different teams in his first nine years of pro ball]. Every year I was with a different group of guys.

Lefty O'Doul was managing the [San Francisco] Seals then. In fact, in '51 there was some talk in the newspaper about O'Doul and [Rogers] Hornsby putting on a hitting exhibition in Sicks Stadium in Seattle. Of course, we [Seattle] were drawing pretty good anyway. So the night they were going to put on this exhibition the house was packed. And even at their age [Hornsby 55, O'Doul 54], it was *amazing*. Hornsby would wind up and hit that ball against the right-center field fence with no problem. Being a right-handed hitter, he could hit the ball to right field as hard as anyone I've ever seen. And, of course, O'Doul could spray it around the ballpark, too. They both put on quite an exhibition.

In '52 I was a starter the whole year with the White Sox. I got off to a bad start but [manager] Paul Richards stayed with me, and I ended up with a pretty good year [12-10, 3.74, 166IP]. The '54 Giants were probably the best team I ever played on—it was *no doubt* the best team I played on—but I liked that White Sox team in '52 also. The results just weren't quite as good [81-73, 3rd place]. But we had some excellent players. Nellie Fox played second. Sherm Lollar was the catcher. Jim Rivera, Minnie Minoso and Eddie Robinson played the outfield. Billy Pierce, Joe Dobson and Ted Gray were the top starters. It was a very good club.

The Giants got me back on waivers, from Boston, early the next season. And that's when I started pitching almost exclusively in relief. In '54, again, everything came together for me in one season. Then I had one of my best seasons, personally, in '56 with a 1.56 ERA [81IP]. And a year later the club was making plans to move west.

I grew up here in Red Bluff so I was well pleased when I learned the Giants would be moving to San Francisco. I knew I'd be able to get home once in a while. Although I loved pitching in New York, to finish my career out here was really nice. I had pitched in Seals Stadium before, when I played two years in the Coast League [w/ Sacramento in '48 and Seattle in '51]. I never had to pitch in Candlestick Park but I went there as a pitching coach with the Cubs. And, to me, Seals Stadium was a much better location than Candlestick. Or, what do they call it now? Tri-Com Stadium? Whatever [laughs].

After I retired, I was a pitching coach with the Angels when they first started, under Bill Rigney, in '61. In fact, I was pitching coach with the Angels three different times, for nine years all together. Then I spent six more years as a pitching coach—two with the White Sox, two with the Cubs and two with Minnesota. 15 years in all.

The game has changed a lot. I see it on TV. I don't have any particular feelings about the big salaries nowadays, except that I'm just sad and sorry that I didn't get in on part of it [laughs]. I'm sure it's had a little impact on the game, but no matter how little or how much you make, you still have to have a lot of pride in your own ability. And those guys out there—I don't care if you they're making six or seven million a year—even though they're well-set for the future, they still have pride in that they don't want to do badly in front of the television audience and the people in the stands. They're trying just as hard as we did back when we *weren't* getting paid for it.

I think in the older days you played a lot more when you were hurt than they do now, because you were afraid someone would take your place and you wouldn't get back in there. I think that's a part of the game that's really changed a lot. Now, you don't play through an injury. You get well, and then you play.

I still watch baseball now, as long as it's interesting. When it gets to be 9-0, I'll turn it to something else. I follow the people in the game I know personally. That's getting less and less. But I still follow the Giants and A's. And I still follow the Cubs quite a bit. Steve Stone [current Cubs an-

nouncer] was a pitcher when I was pitching coach with the Cubs. Little things like that I still enjoy.

I've had a lot of things happen to me since I quit coaching. But I have them taken care of, as soon as they come up. I've had both knees replaced, I've had my right shoulder and elbow scoped, I've had open-heart surgery [laughs]. So I've had my troubles. But I keep it pretty well under control. And I still play golf. I managed to shoot my age about a year ago. First time I've been able to do that.

Red Bluff, California

WILLIE MAYS

Called by many the greatest player of all time, Willie Mays could hit, hit with power, run, field and throw—the five attributes scouts look for in any ballplayer—and he could do them all brilliantly.

Mays won National League Rookie of the Year honors in 1951, when he hit .274, with 20 homersand 68 RBIs, helping the Giants win the pennant. He won National League Most Valuable Player honors in '54, when he hit a league-leading .345, with 41 homers, 110 RBIs and 24 stolen bases, leading the Giants to another pennant, and their last World Series championship, a four-game sweep over the heavily favored Cleveland Indians. Mays again won MVP honors in '65, hitting .317, with a franchise-record 52 homers and 112 RBIs. He led the league in home runs four times, was a member of the National League All-Star team 20 straight years, and won 12 Gold Gloves.

Willie played baseball, basketball, and quarterback on the football team at Fairfax Industrial High in Birmingham, Alabama, before beginning his professional baseball career with the Birmingham Black Barons of the old Negro National League at the age of 17. The New York Giants purchased his contract in 1950, after which he became the first black player in the class-B Interstate League, in Trenton, New Jersey, hitting .353. He began the '51 season with triple-A Minneapolis, hitting a staggering .477, with 8 homers and 30 RBIs in 149 at-bats, before getting called up by the Giants in late May.

In San Francisco, Mays led the '58 Giants with a .347 average, 29 homers and 96 RBIs. His league-leading 49 home runs with 141 RBIs led the Giants to their first West Coast pennant, in '62, and his league-leading 112 walks, at age 40, helped lead them to the N.L. West title in '71. He ranks third, behind Hank Aaron and Babe Ruth, with 660 career home runs. His first was also his first major league hit, off Warren Spahn. He tied a big league record with four homers in a single game, in Milwaukee, April 30, 1961. His 512th, off the Dodgers' Claude Osteen, May 4, 1966, made him the National League career record-holder. Over 22 big league seasons, Mays hit .302 with 338 stolen bases, to go with his 660 home runs.

Willie was traded to the Mets on May 11, 1972, enabling him to finish his career in New York a year later, where he started it 22 years earlier. He was elected to the Hall of Fame in 1979. Mays is back with the Giants now, serving as special assistant to managing general partner Peter Magowan. He lives with his wife in Atherton, California, and has one son.

I THINK MY INITIAL REACTION to the move to San Francisco was more sadness than anything, because I had just got out of the army in '54, and now you're talking '57, and we've got to move again? I've got to move my home to San Francisco? I knew nothing about San Francisco. It was sad to leave New York because in those days New York was a very good place to be. You could go anywhere, do anything. It was just a good time, I think, in the fifties, when I was there. We had played exhibition games in San Francisco before, but I didn't know too much about the city. I didn't know where to live, what to do or anything. So I had to come out west in the wintertime and take care of that.

Writers tried to play up the difficulty I supposedly had buying a house in San Francisco, but I really didn't have a problem. Nobody ever said I couldn't buy a house there. Nobody said I couldn't live there. Nobody said I couldn't buy a house *anywhere.* I think there was a little pressure on the contractor who sold me the house, on Miraloma Drive. But he sold it to me

anyway. And it was for a nice price, around $37,000, which in those days was a lot of money [laughs]. So I didn't have any problem with that.

There was an incident with some kids, probably, throwing a rock through my living room window. Like kids in every neighborhood. And they may not have even come from my neighborhood. Because I never had a problem *in* the neighborhood, as far as kids were concerned. They knocked on my door, they came to my house. I used to give them candy all the time. So I never had a problem with the kids. And I never found out who threw the rock. There was a big splash about it. You know, in those days, when you had a team coming to a new city, the writers try to find out all the little details. And I think they played it up too big. But the whole area was very supportive. There was even a black doctor, a Doctor Coleman, who lived on the corner near me. I never had a problem with the people there. But there was always someone trying to figure out what was wrong.

Willie Mays (SF Giants)

Willie Mays and Hank Sauer ride in downtown motorcade welcoming Giants to San Francisco, April 14, 1958. (SF Giants)

I liked Seals Stadium because it was good for right-handed hitters more than left-handers. I was told at the time we moved that they were going to double-deck it, and that they were going to take the park across the street and make underground parking there and go about two or three decks. And that they would take a lot of those warehouses around the ballpark, knock them down and make that parking. They had plans for all that. At least that's what I was told. They *should* have done that. Because if you look at our lineup over the years it was dominated by right-handed hitters. I was the guy hitting the home runs. And I think they should have taken that into consideration. When I left Seals and went to Candlestick, it hurt me a lot. I think we should have stayed at Seals where I would have hit a lot more home runs.

Seals Stadium was sort of like being in Chicago, with the fans. They were so close to us. It's still like that in Chicago. If you go to Wrigley Field, you'll see they're right close to the players, all around the field. That's the way Seals Stadium was.

I remember the parade through downtown San Francisco [the day before Opening Day]. It was something unique for me because we had one in New York [after winning the '54 Series], and you never felt that anyone could top New York. Then you came out here and saw all the people. They shut down businesses, they threw out paper. It was just a wonderful experience for me, coming from New York. I needed that, because sometimes when you go to new surroundings you don't know what's going to happen. It was a good feeling.

That whole season I made up my mind that I wouldn't go for home runs. I would go for batting average. I hit .347. Richie Ashburn beat me out for the batting title the last day of the season [.350]. He went four-for-four in Pittsburgh, I think. I got three hits against the Cardinals, but it wasn't enough. I think I tried to prove something in '58 because when I first came out, the writers said, "Well, here's a kid coming from New York. We don't know what he can do." So I said OK, I'll just go for batting average this year. I hit only 29 home runs.

What I used to try and do every year was knock in a hundred runs, score a hundred runs and hit .300. That's all that was necessary to do. Once I did that, anything beyond that was like gravy to me. You look at my record and you'll see that, after '58, I didn't go way up in batting average. But I went up in home runs. The home runs we needed, to knock in runs. You look at my record, you'll see a hundred runs scored, a hundred runs batted in, maybe .310, .319—right in that area. I would stay consistently over the .300 mark. *[author's note: In the 13-year period from '54 through '66, Mays hit .300 10 times, scored 100 runs 12 times and drove in 100 runs 10 times.]*

I had read that San Francisco fans were initially cool towards me, but no one ever said anything to me to that effect. You know, you hear things and you read things in the paper. I read that they liked Cepeda more than me. *[author's note: Fans, responding to a newspaper poll, voted Cepeda the Giants' MVP in '58, over Mays.]* Nobody ever said that to me, though. I would have to say that you would need to search a little further than me to find the truth about that. I definitely felt the fans' support. Oh, yeah. I think San Francisco supported the whole club when I first came out. Again, no one said anything to me, but you could *feel* that the fans wanted their *own* ballplayer. And I guess they chose Cepeda. It didn't bother me. I never had any letdowns in baseball. I know what I did. I think I had one of my better seasons in '58 [career-high 208 hits, career-high .347 average]. It didn't bother me because I know what I did. I did very, very well that year.

Milwaukee had a very good ball club in '58 [defending World Series champs]. They had Spahn and Burdette. They had Aaron in right, Billy Bruton in center and Wes Covington in left, Mathews at third, Adcock at first and that pesky little kid at shortstop, Johnny Logan. They had a very, very good-hitting ball club, so we thought that we could come close but I don't think we thought we could beat them. They had a very veteran team. We had a rookie team. And it was lucky that we did come that close.

I remember one game in Pittsburgh when Danny Murtaugh [Bucs manager] charged Gomez, and got thrown out. Danny said Gomez was throwing at Vernon Law. After Law had knocked us down. Gomez was pretty sharp on those kinds of things. He didn't like for a teammate to get knocked down. And Murtaugh started this big fight in the middle of the field. But in the corner of my eye I saw Cepeda charge out of the dugout with a bat. And I'm saying to myself, "No, no, that can't happen." So when I saw him, I left the crowd [on the field] and tackled him. But he's so *strong* that I couldn't keep him down. I had to pin him down on the ground, and then I saw a body come over the top of me. It was Hank Sauer. Then we pinned him down together. I didn't think many people saw it because it happened so quickly. Most people were watching the crowd [on the field]. But they saw it in the paper.

Gomez was one of our top pitchers when we won the Series in '54, along with Antonelli. He won 17 games for us then, and 15 another time [in '57].

One of my saddest days in baseball was when Cepeda was traded to St. Louis [in '66]. I felt that he should have stayed with the Giants. We got Ray Sadecki for him. But I felt we had a very, very good lineup at the time, with myself, McCovey, Cepeda and Jim Ray Hart. A very good lineup. And I said many times, "Just stick Cepeda out in left field. I'll take care of him." Because I could control left, and I could control center. That means the right fielder's got to control his half of center. That means he's got to pick up the gap. Cepeda did well in left field, when he played there. We just wanted his bat [laughs], really. That's what we needed.

Willie Mays with first wife Marghuerite, and son Michael. (SF Giants)

In '58 we had Kirkland in right, and Wagner, sometimes, in left. Kirkland and Wagner [laughs]. Kirkland and Wagner were two happy-go-lucky kids [both rookies, both from Detroit]. Kirkland had a very, very good arm. He could run. He had a lot of talent. We played him in right a lot, but sometimes he would lapse out there a little bit and we'd have to talk to him in the dugout, tell him what was going on. We got the feeling sometimes that they didn't want to play every day. They just wanted to be role players. And Kirkland was so good that we *had* to play him. We didn't have anybody else better.

Wagner wanted to play but, mainly, he just wanted to *hit*. He just wanted to sit over there, then maybe two or three days later play again. Maybe pinch hit. A very, very good pinch hitter. We had this scenario one time—see, here's the line over here [gestures]. And we'd tell Wagner, "Stay on the line. You guard the line, and I'll take everything between the line and center." [laughs] I remember one day we were playing in Seals Stadium, the ball was hit to left-center and I'm waiting for Wagner to come over. And [laughs] the ball falls in for a double. We go to the dugout and he says, "Bill Rigney told me to cover the line. Anything else, you gotta catch it." [laughs] So I'm laughing and laughing. Boy, Rigney couldn't say *nothin'.* He just looked at me and walked away. It was funny, but then, it wasn't so funny at the time. I was saying, "Hey, you gotta catch those balls." He was a funny man. A real nice man. Real funny.

Then we had Bill White [rookie first baseman in '56 w/22 HR; spent '57 and most of '58 in military]. I hated to see him get traded [to St. Louis with Ray Jablonski, for Sam Jones, 3-25-59], because there was a choice between trading Wagner and Bill White. I felt that Bill White was a very intelligent player, and he was still learning how to play baseball. He was a first baseman with Cepeda, and with McCovey coming up [in '59], so management felt we probably didn't need him. But I felt we should've kept him. It was one of those trades that I felt, if you had a choice, trade Wagner. And keep Bill, because Bill's going to be a great player. Evidently that was true, because he went on to become a great player. And, of course, White could play the outfield. He *did* play the outfield in St. Louis when he went there, when Stan [Musial] played first. He played left field but ran into a couple of walls, so they had to take him out of there and put him back at first base. A very good first baseman. *Very* good.

Willie Mays goes deep against the Braves; Milwaukee manager Fred Haney watches from the dugout. (SF Chronicle)

Davenport was among the very best I saw at third. I don't remember him making more than about eight or ten errors a year. He was very, very good, and he chipped in with about 12 home runs a year. He hit second, and they wanted to pitch to him rather than us, so he would get good fastballs all the time. He wasn't a bad hitter. He hit .260, .270 sometimes. A very good role player.

Rigney and I had a problem at the beginning, when he took over for Leo in '56. Bill was the type of guy that wanted to play team ball. And I was used to Leo. Bill wanted to put me in a group, and I wasn't that type of ballplayer. I had to be let go. I couldn't wait for the manager to tell me what to do. I had to do it on my own, and I did very well. For instance, in New York, the Polo Grounds was *big,* and when I hit a tweener I'd go two or three bases easy. But I couldn't tell Bill what I wanted to do because he was the manager. Since I played with Bill in New York, I thought he would understand how I played baseball. But I don't think he did, in that first year. By '58 it was a different Bill Rigney. He and I got along very well. Actually, Bill and I became very, very good friends after that second year.

I didn't have many friends on the '58 team. There were so many rookies that I didn't know. A few guys came from New York with me, like Spencer and Sauer, Lockman, Antonelli and Gomez, Thomas. But Antonelli went back home to Rochester every off-season. And we had so many island players—Valmy Thomas, Gomez, Cepeda, Andre Rodgers. They'd all leave San Francisco at the end of the season and go back home. So, it wasn't a case where I was friends with a lot of my teammates.

As I said, we had good fans in San Francisco. But we had good fans in New York, too. Something happened in New York in '57. The fans really realized the ball club was going. And so we didn't draw well in New York the last year [654,000]. But I think that was one of the big reasons why. Before that we drew pretty well. But then they said, "Well, we're gonna show you." I think that's what happened to us. But they were still great fans. I remember when the Giants went back to the Polo Grounds to play the Mets in '62. I came out of the dugout and the fans roared. [author's note: 43,742 welcomed Giants back w/SF winning 9-6; Giants went on to sweep four-game series w/Mays hitting three HR.] That was special for me because we had moved to San Francisco, and the San Francisco people had said, "Well, we want to get a lot of our own new players here." Then I go back to New York, and the players that they [San Francisco] picked up were not as popular as I was nationwide. I think that was a little bit of the New York fans saying, "Hey, we haven't forgotten what you did in New York, and we never will forget." I think that was kind of special.

But I also think the fans in San Francisco appreciated what I did on the field. I think they came to recognize the things I did on the field, and appreciate them. The basket catch, for example, first came when I was in the army ['52 and '53]. I had a lot of spare time and said, "Well, let me do something different for the fans." And when I came out of the army I just did it. Before I went into the army, I did not do it. I caught the ball up above my head when I first got in [pro ball]. But I found out later on that I couldn't really catch a ball any other way [than the basket catch]. It was easy for me to catch it that way. When I came out of the army, I thought Leo would be the one to say, "No." But he said, "As long as you don't miss it, I don't care how you catch it." [laughs]

I missed one one year, and I missed one 10 years later, with the basket catch. I missed one in the Polo Grounds. Ernie Banks hit a high fly ball. And the next one I missed was such a funny sight [laughs]. We were in Pittsburgh, and [Donn] Clendenon hit a long fly ball to center. When I dropped the ball, I looked in [toward the infield] and saw *nobody* left on the field. Everybody was just about touching the dugout [laughs]. Nobody was on the field. And I'm saying to myself, "What's happening?" Then everybody started laughing. They had to come back out on the field [laughs]. It was funny.

Tapping the glove is something I did all my life. Tapping was something I'd do when I was sure of catching the ball. It's nothing I did consciously. It's something I just did.

I started positioning other outfielders in 1954 with Dusty Rhodes and Don Mueller, because Leo had said to me in a meeting one day—and I guess it was more embarrassing than anything—that anything that goes up, I gotta catch it. In the 1951 pennant chase against the Dodgers in New York, I threw out Billy Cox, a very fast runner, at home plate. Carl Furillo hit a ball—and you have to picture this—I'm the center fielder, and I've got to go all the way to the right field line to catch the ball. Then I make a complete turn and throw out the runner at the plate. That's a very, very difficult play to make. You would think the right fielder would catch the ball. But when Leo made the suggestion, the other two outfielders would then look at me first. And I'm saying, "No, no, Leo, that can't happen." He'd say, "I don't care. You gotta catch the ball." So that's why I caught the ball on the right field line. Whitey Lockman was the first baseman and, as I'm turning around, I picked him up. So I hit him chest-high [with the throw]. That means if I hit him chest-high, the ball will carry all the way to home plate. And that's what happened. So Charlie Dressen [Dodgers manager] said, "Well, that's a good play. But I'd like to see him do it again." [laughs]

When I started positioning the outfielders in '54, I'd do it before every batter. That's where one writer got confused, when I said I called *every* pitch. You don't call every pitch. You wait until the batter comes up, and then you call fastball, change-up, whatever. That means you want him to hit a certain pitch. You can't call every pitch. Pitchers throw too fast. They can't be throwing a pitch, then you look around to left and look around to center. You can't do that. In New York,

Leo gave me the authority to do that. In San Francisco, Herman [Franks] did. I was manager on the *field*. They managed in the dugout. They managed—don't get me wrong—but I did the field work. As for Rigney and Dark, well, I did it without them knowing what was going on [laughs].

During infield and batting practice [for the opposition], when the rest of my teammates would be in the clubhouse, I'd stay in the dugout. *All the time*. Every game. I'm a believer that there are certain things a guy will do in batting practice. Say, for instance, a guy's not hitting. He's going to try to hit to right. During the game, he's going to try it two or three times. So I would watch to see who's swinging well. Who's throwing well. I would have a batboy bring me out a change of shirts. But I'd never go in. I always stayed on the bench to watch, and see what was happening.

Same with the guys in the outfield. Let me see them throw. Sometimes a guy would throw home—I know because I did this many times—even with a sore arm, and then go in the dugout to get treatment. So you've got to be careful of that. I did that for a whole year. I hurt myself in Milwaukee one year, and I played the whole season without being able to throw to second base. But I would take infield. *Let them see I could throw*. Then I didn't have to throw [in the game] because they weren't too sure [about running on him]. They saw me throw during infield, and it hurt. Oh, it killed me. I'd go in there and Doc Bowman would give me a rubdown. And it would still hurt. But I could hit. I hit close to 50 home runs that one year.

Now, errors are part of the game. You can't avoid them completely. But I made sure to learn from my mental errors. I'll give you an example. When I was on base a couple of times, I'd have a lapse. Bobby Avila did this to me one day in a spring training game. Bases loaded, I'm on third. Ball hit to Avila at short. I looked for him to go to first but he didn't. He threw home and forced me at the plate. We didn't score. Now, that taught me you've got to run on every play. You can't be lagging around. I was just about walking home, because I was sure he was going to first.

In the outfield, I'd put myself down for five or six errors a year. Three or four of them are going to be on throws, but not from missing the ball. I might miss one or two, but they'll be hard chances. But I had a season once when I made four errors in one game, in St. Louis. I made only seven total that season, but they were all hard chances. They hit off my glove. They'll say, "Well, if it hits your glove, you gotta catch it." And I'm saying, "Wait a minute? What about the hitter? Don't you give him a hit when he hits it well like that?" They gave me a lot of errors sometimes when they could've been base hits, when I got to balls maybe other guys wouldn't get to.

Leo once said I was my own coach. I believe that when you have to depend on a coach, you don't make the extra base. For instance, a guy hits the ball to the outfield. I *know* if I can make it home. Actually, I would lag sometimes to see if the guy *would* throw home, to make sure the catcher would catch the ball as I'm arriving, to make sure the guy that hits the ball goes to second. So you have to be thinking two or three ways when you're

Willie Mays tries to beat the tag of Braves catcher Del Crandall; Orlando Cepeda, pitcher Gene Conley and third-base coach Herman Franks all watch. (SF Chronicle)

running the bases. Not just one way. Two or three. That's what I did.

Same thing going from first base on a single. If you watch an outfielder who lobs the ball in from left field, say, and you're running on a base hit—and you're *running*—you can score, because he's going to lob it in. I did it against Wes Covington. I used to watch him. He used to just lob the ball, instead of throwing it on a line. He'd lob it. And I scored two or three times from first base [on a single] that way. Not off him every time, because you can't do it but once off any particular player. But you may do it again off another player, on another team. You've got to watch them. Different teams have different players.

Now, later on, when we lost Cepeda, I began stopping at first a lot of times, rather than take second, because McCovey was up next. The reason for that was I felt that I shouldn't take the bat out of his hands. I could've had many more doubles—balls that I hit in the gap and down the line—when I just wouldn't go beyond first. I'll give you one instance. We're playing in San Diego one day, and I hit a double. I stop at first. Clyde King was the manager and he says, "Why didn't you run?" And I said, "Clyde, we only have one left-handed hitter in the lineup." So McCovey strikes out. But I said, "Clyde, this boy's gonna hit." So I walk the next time. Dick Williams was the manager in San Diego. He has his guy throw two wild pitches. I never moved. McCovey hits a home run on the next pitch. He knocks in seven runs that day, after the strikeout. So now I'm saying to Clyde, "You never came over and said, 'Hey, I'm wrong.'" No, he never came over to say that. But that was OK. I knew what McCovey could do. I knew that we had to keep him at the plate. They were going to walk him. If I stole second, they were going to walk him, because we didn't have another big bat behind McCovey. So I always made sure of that.

Here's another example of being my own coach: Matty Alou, running from first, stopped at third on my double in the ninth inning of game 7 of the '62 Series against the Yankees [Alou was held at third by coach Whitey Lockman, with two out, down 1-0, with McCovey on deck]. You can't blame Alou. He was a young kid then. He didn't want the criticism for being thrown out at home. The safe way is to stop at third. But if *I* were the runner on that play, I'm gone. They don't stop *me*. I run right through the sign. If I get thrown out, hey, I'm thrown out. It's no big deal. I can handle that. Hey, if you don't try to win a Series, you're out of the game. As a runner, if Alou had hit the same ball [I did], I'm running. But, again, you can't fault Alou on that. He's a young kid, and he's just entered the game, in the ninth inning. So why would he want to risk getting thrown out for the last out of the game? Of the *World Series.* Most players, most likely, that's what they'd do [follow the coach's sign]. Because you're going to be the one that'll be criticized if you run through the sign. *I* did it all the time. That was just me. But, yes, after I got the double, I wished many times that I had been the guy on first base running. I've said that many times, that I'd have liked to have been on first.

Actually, it wasn't even a good throw home [from Bobby Richardson]. Richardson went out [for the relay]. Roger Maris got the ball in the [right field] corner. The reason he got the ball in the corner was because the grass was wet, and it got slowed up. Otherwise, it could have been a triple, because the ball would have rolled along the fence. But Richardson went out and got the ball [from Maris] very quickly. And he got it back in. But it wasn't a good throw home. The throw was up the line a little.

But if McCovey's ball gets past Richardson [McCovey lined out to Richardson, to end the Series, with the tying and winning runs in scoring position], we win the game. That's another choice somebody had to make. Do I pitch to McCovey [with first base open], or do I pitch to Cepeda? A lot of things happened there. *I* was surprised [they pitched to McCovey], because when Houk came out I think he gave Ralph Terry the option of pitching to McCovey, or walking him. And Terry decided to pitch to him. And the ball was hit so hard, but right at Richardson. The only thing he could do was catch it. *[author's note: Alvin Dark joked after the game that if McCovey's ball got through, by the time the Yankees got the ball in to the plate, Mays would have been dressed.]*

That finish to the '62 season was probably the most exciting time I had as a San Francisco Giant. That, and the '66 season when we were right there at the end. Koufax beat Philadelphia in Philadelphia [in the last game of the season]. We were supposed to go back and play Cincinnati in a makeup game [if Koufax had lost], to tie the Dodgers for first. That was one of my disappointments, but the exciting finish was in '62, when we were still down by one game on the last day of the season. The St. Louis catcher, Gene Oliver, hit a home run to beat the Dodgers [1-0]. And I hit a home run off of Dick Farrell [to beat Houston 2-1]. Then we beat the Dodgers in a playoff. I think that was the best comeback. Sort of like New York in '51.

I always loved to be up at the plate in all critical situations. I felt that I was just as mean as the pitcher throwing the ball. He had to throw it. I had to hit it. Some way, I just wanted to be at the plate when something was going down, or something had to be done. I didn't want my teammates to be there. I wanted to be there. For instance, final playoff game against the Dodgers in '62. We're down 4-2 in the ninth, bases loaded, one out and I'm up [facing Ed Roebuck]. I didn't *know* I was going to get a hit. I just knew I was going to hit the ball somewhere. And Roebuck didn't throw that hard. So I knew I was going to put the ball in play. I hit the ball hard back through the middle. He knocked it down, but I

got on first. At that time, I was concerned about Cepeda more than I was concerned about myself. But he hit a fly ball to right that tied the game [the Giants scored twice more to win, 6-4, and clinch the pennant]. I got more satisfaction from him getting the fly ball than from my own hit, because I knew what I was going to do.

Then I caught Lee Walls' fly ball to end it, and I threw the ball in the stands. I didn't do that kind of thing too much. I usually kept the ball, and I'd give it to a kid, or something. But that was so exciting to come back, and see the guys enjoy themselves. That was really what I played baseball for. Not for me. I felt that baseball was really easy for me. It was like a walk through the park, when you can go out and all you have to do is go through the breeze, and watch the sun come out. It was just a beautiful game. And I felt there wasn't anything I could do on the ball field that would make me excited. But evidently that one game did. If I kept the ball I probably would have given it to Billy Pierce [who retired the Dodgers in order in the ninth]. But in those days we didn't think about records and things like that. If we did, I would have given it to him. But at the time, the thought never ran across my mind. Billy did very well that year [16-6, 3.49]. And he was unbeaten at Candlestick [13-0].

Maury Wills beat me out for MVP in '62. I was disappointed because I was told that a lot of the writers didn't vote. That's the only thing I was disappointed about. I was saying, "Why do they give them the authority, and then they don't vote?" I hit 49 home runs that year [w/141 RBIs, .304 average]. The only thing Wills did that year was break the stolen-base record with 104. What else did he do? [130 runs, .299 average] The Most Valuable Player has to go to someone when you win the pennant, and you do the most for your team. And I felt that I did.

I was very fortunate in that I could hit the ball out in right, left, center, *anywhere.* The ballpark wasn't a problem for me. It was the pitchers. If I found pitchers who could throw the ball where I could hit it, it made no difference what ballpark we were

Willie Mays (SF Giants)

playing in. Now, Candlestick was *different*. The other ballparks I played in didn't have wind. All you did is hit the ball. The ball would go out, to right or center or left. Candlestick had more wind. Plus, when we first moved there, the home run mark was the bleachers. Not any fence in front of the bleachers. *The bleachers*. I said, "No, this is too far." Then, when they put the fence in, they put it too far back. I said, "Wow, how's that helping me? I've got to play 81 games here. It's gonna hamper me." So I had to change my whole style of hitting at home. I would hit, I'd say, 80 to 90 percent of my home run balls to right-center. Get it up in the wind and let it blow. That's the way I used to hit there.

I remember my first day of batting practice at Candlestick [before the 1960 opener]. I don't think I hit but two balls out to left. I hit a lot of balls to the grass out there, but not out of the ballpark. I don't think, that year, there were more than 12 home runs hit to left field. The whole *year*. Too far, too far [397 feet to left-center]. Plus, we had to fight the wind. See, we didn't have the ballpark enclosed like it is now. We had it open. Everything was against the hitter. How can you build a ballpark that's going to work against the home team? That was one of my problems.

Hank Aaron got to play in Atlanta. I used to hit a lot of home runs in Atlanta. And Milwaukee was a good ballpark to hit in. But Hank is a great hitter. I think he would have hit anywhere he played. But playing in Atlanta and Milwaukee didn't hurt him. If I had had a ballpark like that instead of Candlestick, I'd have hit a few more home runs.

Milwaukee was where I had the greatest single day of my career [4-30-61]. Only 12 guys have ever hit four home runs in one game. So that has to be one of my most special days as far as hitting is concerned. And I got very sick the night before. I really didn't think I could make it the next day. So I go to the ballpark, and tell Alvin, "I don't think I can make it." Then I'm sitting on the bench, and Joey Amalfitano comes up to me and says, "Try this bat, man." I said, OK. And I go up to the cage and mess around. *Every* ball I hit, for the first six balls, goes out of the ballpark. And I said, "Joey, something's wrong here." So I go and scratch the guy's name out on the lineup sheet. I don't even know who it was—I don't recall—but I said, "I'm playing."

When I go up to bat in the game, the first ball I hit is out of the ballpark. The second goes out, too. Both off Burdette. So I think I'm through for the day. You usually don't get but two. The next one's off a guy named Seth Morehead. And the last one's off of Don McMahon. I made an out in between, somewhere along the line, off Moe Drabowsky. I hit a liner to center field. Aaron was playing center at the time. But there were a lot of home runs hit that day. A *lot* of home runs. Aaron hit two, Pagan hit two, Cepeda hit one, Alou hit one [the Giants won, 14-4]. I didn't have any particular feeling when the fourth one went out. See, I wasn't one of the guys who would hit a home run and have feelings about it. I can't explain that, except to say that my teammates in the dugout were more excited, and the fans were more excited. In those days, we were always pulling for each other. And when you pull for each other, you don't worry about yourself. You just hit the ball and run.

I do remember wanting to be the last guy at bat. When Davenport made the last out of the ninth inning [with Mays on deck], I think that was the first time I ever heard the fans boo Davenport. I'm saying, "Wait a minute. The game's out of hand here." But they said, "No, no, we wanted to see you hit one more time."

The Giants didn't come out on top again until 1971 [winning the NL West]. That was my last full season with the club. At the beginning of the '71 season, I wanted to sign a 10-year contract so that I could be with the Giants my whole career. The year before, I had signed a two-year contract, and I felt that I wanted to be a Giant all my life, even after my playing days were over. I wanted to make sure that would happen. But Mr. Stoneham wouldn't sign me [to a 10-year deal; he signed for two years instead]. I should have known at the end of the '71 season, after we lost in the playoffs to Pittsburgh, that I would be traded. But Mr. Stoneham never told me I was going to be traded, and that's what I resented more than anything. With all the years that I had talked with him, I felt that he should have told me.

In 1971, I walked 112 times [a career-high]. At the age of 40. *I led the league* in walks, at 40. *Nobody* writes about that. But they write, "At 41, he played too long." And I'm saying, "Wait a minute. You want me to leave after I hit 18 home runs? Who hit more than that [on the Giants]?" Only Bobby [Bonds], with 33 [and Dick Dietz, with 19]. I stole 23 bases [in 26 attempts]. I hit .271 and drove in 61 runs. But I had never walked over 100 times in my career until 1971.

Now, when I was traded to the Mets [for pitcher Charlie Williams], I was *asked* to come back [to New York]. If it had been any other lady, I would not have gone. But Mrs. Joan Payson [Mets owner, formerly on NY Giants board of directors] called me on the phone and said, "Willie, you come to New York. We'll take care of you. And not only take care of you while you're playing, we'll take care of you when your career is over. You play as long as you want to, when you want to." So I said OK. And when I went back, they really showed me that, "You don't have to play. Just being back here is enough for us." That's why I stayed two years.

But, again, there were a lot of things written, saying that I played too long, which I don't feel I did. I felt that the '72 season wasn't really a *season*. I didn't play that much. I was traded. It was one of those seasons where I wasn't really into baseball, because of the trade, because of the things I went through, and I don't think I should be penalized for that. But I quit in '73, in May, because I wanted to make sure that the fans didn't look at me as just another player. So I got out. And I was still criticized for playing too long. I disagree with that. But I stayed the whole season for Mrs. Payson. Actually, when I retired in May I went home, and I was packing to return to San Francisco. She called me on the phone and said, "You can't leave." I said, "Well, I don't think I can play anymore." She said, "You don't have to play. Just come. We have a very young team, and we want you to take care of the team, and the guys on the team." She said, "The guys miss you." So I said OK. I went back.

In the Series against Oakland, there was some more disappointment for me. If you remember, in the second game, the first baseman for the A's [Deron Johnson] hit a ball to center. And they said, "Well, look at the old man falling down." But anybody could have slipped. It was a wet field. *Anybody* could have slipped. That was one of my big disappointments, when writers can criticize a guy that slips, regardless of age—that makes no difference. But I *won* that second game [with an RBI single in the 10th], mind you. They didn't write about that too much, you know? That was one disappointment I had in the Series. The next disappointment I felt was tremendous. I didn't get to pinch hit in the seventh game. The game ends with a left-handed hitter [Wayne Garrett] popping up against Darold Knowles [a left-handed pitcher], and I'm saying to myself,

"Yogi's *got* to know I'm here." Even if I don't do anything, this is my *last* time to play baseball. Who knows what might have happened? It doesn't make any difference. But if I'm managing a ball club and I know this is your last game, and I know so many of your fans are in the ballpark *wanting* to see you one last time, why wouldn't I put you in? That was really one of my low points of sadness.

I don't think a guy should be criticized for playing as long as he feels he can play. A writer can write until he's 100. If he's criticized for not being able to think as clearly, no big deal. He writes his column and goes on about his business. If you want to criticize his column, you do it. You look at Nolan Ryan—he played until he was 46. That's great. That's *wonderful.* Now, here's a guy over here that *never* played ball, criticizing a guy because he's in his forties. If he does his job, it makes no difference how old he is. He may not win 15 or 20. But he wins 12. He's *still* contributing. Very much so. And that's what I did. I contributed all the way until I quit. Look at my record. When did I stop contributing? That's what you have to look at.

Look at Eckersley right now. He's 42. He just signed again. That's great. Don't you think that's great for him to be able to pitch at 42, instead of people feeling sad for him? Who says when you reach a certain age, you've got to quit? Why? You've got to leave some room for error.

There was another memorable incident in that '73 Series with Oakland, when Buddy Harrelson was safe on a close play at home [in game two], but Al Barlick called him out. I was on deck. Al was in position *not* to see the play. He was blocked out. He couldn't see in between [the runner and the catcher]. That's why the third base umpire should have come in and made the call. But he [Ray Fosse] missed the tag, clearly. So now I'm arguing, and I look into Al's face and I say to myself, "Oh, my God, what am I arguing with this man about? He's retiring at the same time I am. Why am I arguing with this man? I've known Al for many years. What am I doing?" If you watch a film, you'll see that I'm arguing there by myself for a short time, and then I leave. And I said to Yogi, "Why'd you take so long to get out here?" That's what I was thinking, that Al was retiring, I was retiring, and why was I arguing with him?

I never argued too much. So, whenever I did, I knew I was right. I was never thrown out of a ballgame. *Anywhere.* My father taught me that you cannot help a club in the clubhouse. He was right. If you're in the clubhouse, and you're supposed to be the best player, you should be on the field. That's what I learned. Never argue with the umpire. If I argued, I knew I was right, and I would talk to the guy and explain as best I could.

When I quit baseball it took me two to three years before I could get back on the field, because I was so used to going to the ballpark at four o'clock in the afternoon. And then I found myself going *somewhere* at four, just out of habit. And I'm thinking, I'm going to the *ballpark,* but I wasn't. A lot of players go through that, playing over 20 years, and not being able to do anything else but play baseball. Or basketball, football, whatever.

But to have played when I did—oh, my God. I had some wonderful players play with me. You name every club that we played. They all had some *good* players on that particular club. I don't care what club you pick. You can start with Pittsburgh—they had Clemente. You start with the Dodgers—they had Willie Davis, Tommy Davis, Maury Wills, Junior Gilliam, Koufax and Drysdale. Then you go to Philadelphia—you've got Robin Roberts and Curt Simmons. You had some great names then, with every club. Spahn and Sain, Burdette and Buhl with the Braves. The list goes on and on.

Koufax was not the toughest I ever faced. No. He got me out consistently, but he wasn't tough. I mean, I saw every pitch he threw. Every pitch Koufax used to throw, I knew what it was. I just couldn't hit it. *I couldn't hit it.* I used to get one-for-three, maybe. I think I might have, oh, maybe five home runs off of him. Maybe. But Drysdale knocked me down every day, every time at bat, and I got 18 or 19 home runs off of him. Now, what does that mean? Maybe that's the competitor coming out in me, saying, "Hey, you knock me down, I'm gonna hit you." Koufax would *never* knock you down. You just go up, you're comfortable hitting, and you find yourself [laughs] oh-for-four. Oh-for-five. And I'm saying to myself, "How can this guy get me out?" He never threw me a breaking ball. If he did, I killed it. Every time he threw me a breaking ball, I hit it somewhere.

Actually, after the Marichal-Roseboro fight [in '65], the game was tied, he threw me a breaking ball and I hit it for a home run. And I said, "Sandy, why you throw me a breaking ball, man?" And he said, "I just wanted to see what you could

do with it." And I said, "Sandy, the game is tied. Did you realize what you threw me?" And he said, "Yeah. I knew what I was doing." But he was that kind of guy. He was a very competitive pitcher. He wanted the ball. Drysdale wanted the ball. Marichal wanted the ball. We had some really good pitchers who wanted to do the things I wanted to do at the plate. They wanted the ball. I wanted to be the hitter.

I wish that I knew what made Koufax so tough to hit [laughs]. If I could have solved that [laughs], I would have hit him. I don't know. The ball would rise a lot [out of his hand]. The ball would start here [gesturing], and then when you swing at it, it's up there somewhere. I don't know. I couldn't figure him out.

Gary Nolan—I just couldn't find his ball at all. He's the *one* pitcher who struck me out four times in one game, in Cincinnati [in '67]. I'll never forget this. And to this day, I think that was another guy out there [laughs]. Nolan couldn't strike me out—*nobody* could strike me out four times in one game. Nobody. I didn't care who he was. But he did—four times—and I said to him, "I just couldn't see the ball." Every time he came over the top I couldn't find it. I was swinging away where it was *supposed* to be. Gary Nolan. He was just 18 then. Came from Fresno. *[author's note: Nolan struck out more than just Mays his rookie season, going 14-8 with a 2.58ERA, and 206 strikeouts in 227 innings.]*

MY FATHER STARTED ME with baseball. He was working on the railroad, and would come home on weekends and teach me how to play, and bring me good equipment. But I had so many people along the line that helped me with things, starting with my father. There was also a man named Piper Davis [Mays' manager with the Birmingham Black Barons]; Artie Wilson, who played with the Giants for a while; a guy named Alonzo Perry with the Black Barons. It was just amazing how they would make sure I was taken care of. For instance, when I was with the Barons, the rule was that we had seven pitchers. The pitcher that pitched the next night was my roommate, so I wouldn't get in any trouble. He was my roommate. So I had seven different roommates on the road. They really took care of me.

That was the first time I faced Satchel Paige, in 1948, in Memphis, Tennessee. Satch didn't know who I was, so he threw me a little breaking ball. *BANG.* I hit it up against the fence. So I hear

Satch say to his third baseman, "Let me know when that kid comes back up." I didn't pay any attention to that. I didn't even know who Satch was [laughs]. I had no idea. I just saw a long, lanky guy out there. I didn't know who he was. Well, when I went back up the second time, I heard the third baseman say, "There he is." And I'm saying, "What are you talking about?"

So Satch says to me, "You got three." And I still hadn't picked up on it. So Satch says again, "You got three." Then he throws me three fastballs. Now, he says to me after I'm on my way back to the dugout, "Go sit down." [laughs] That was my introduction to Satch. He could throw hard, and I don't know how old he was then [42, according to most baseball records]. I don't know how old he was. He threw me three fastballs. I swung at 'em all. Didn't come close to any of 'em.

The Giants signed me in 1950. They sent their scout Eddie Montague [the late father of NL umpire Ed Montague] to look at Alonzo Perry, who was a big, strong first baseman. I knew he was there, because Piper had told me, but he was not there to look at me. Well, I had a couple of big nights when he was there, one in Tuscaloosa and one in Birmingham. What I was told was that there were three clubs involved, interested in signing me—the Dodgers, the Braves and the Giants. At the time, Boston didn't have any blacks on the club. That's one reason, I think, I didn't go there. And I was told that Charlie Dressen said that I couldn't hit the breaking ball. So that's why I didn't go to the Dodgers. But I was only 18 then. At that time, you couldn't talk to a player unless his class had graduated from high school. So, Eddie Montague came over and talked with my father and my aunt. And I think he gave me $15,000, and he gave the Barons another $15,000. In those days, that was a lot of money.

A lot of guys came out of the Negro Leagues into the majors. Minnie Minoso with the New York Cubans, Luke Easter with the Homestead Grays, Monte Irvin and Larry Doby with the Newark Eagles. Buck Leonard didn't make it. There was another guy you probably wouldn't know of that played very good ball in that league, too—Goose Tatum, the basketball player with the Harlem Globetrotters. He played with the Indianapolis Clowns. He was a first baseman, a very, very good first baseman, but he didn't hit that well. They used to put on shows in the seventh inning of ballgames. But a lot of good players came out of that league, including Aaron and Banks. They came after me. Aaron played with Indianapolis, and Banks with the Kansas City Monarchs. And a lot of good players didn't make it. [author's note: Other major league stars who came out of the Negro Leagues include Jackie

Willie Mays, alongside Monte Irvin (L) and Henry Thompson (R), at Yankee Stadium, October, 1951; the three made up the first black starting outfield in World Series history. (Steve Bitker)

Robinson, Don Newcombe, Roy Campanella, Joe Black, Jim Gilliam, Elston Howard, Sam Jones and Sam Jethroe.]

The Giants assigned me to Trenton [New Jersey]. I didn't have any problems in Trenton, but I did have one problem, in Hagerstown, Maryland, on my first road trip. I let my guard down a little, because I felt Washington was right here [gestures] and New York was right here. Therefore, Baltimore—hey, couldn't have a problem there. But that was the problem. I couldn't stay with the team in Hagerstown. I had to go to another private hotel. But what happened on that team was special. We had a right fielder named Eric Rodin, we had a catcher named Herb Boetto, and we had another kid named Lin Matte. They dropped me off at a hotel downtown. Then, at about one or two o'clock in the morning, I hear guys coming through my window. It was those three guys. They slept on the floor. Nobody knows about this, but they slept on the floor. And at the crack of daylight, they get up, go back out the window and go back to their hotel. Then, at around three or four o'clock in the afternoon they come and pick me up, and drive me to the ballpark. Nobody says anything. So I was protected, always, through different avenues, different ways.

When I got to the majors, I had Leo, and Monte Irvin and Hank Thompson. We had a ball club that would take care of me. And the fans in New York took to me right away. In those days, New York was very, very good. I even had more rapport with the people in my block than I had with people at the ballpark, because in my block we had a lot of kids, and we played stickball. Every morning and every afternoon, I would play stickball, when we were home. I'd play stickball with the kids. You have to understand—I was very young when I first came up at 19, going on 20. The neighbors would never let me go off by myself. That's what Mr. Stoneham did for me, but they don't do that anymore. They don't bring a young kid up anymore and say, "OK, we're going to protect him wherever he goes. We're going to find a nice place for him." They don't do that anymore, but they did it for me. They made sure I had a home—an apartment—and a family to live with. That was important, I think. They found a lady by the name of Ann Goosby. And I stayed with her family for about two or three years. By that time, I learned New York. But there were always many, many people looking out for me. Even Leo's wife, Laraine Day. When I'd go to LA, I wouldn't stay in a hotel. I'd stay at their house.

My special relationship with Leo began in 1951 when I was at Minneapolis. He came down to watch me play, and I was playing left field. The first ball that was hit there was hit over the fence, when I just missed catching it. So Leo said, "Uh, oh. Wait a minute. Switch him around." A guy named Johnny Kropf was playing center field, and we switched. That was my first introduction to Leo. He said to Mr. Stoneham, "He's got to be a center fielder. He can't be anything else. He's too strong." I hit a home run in the game, about 450 feet. So Leo said to me, "You'll be up before the year is over." I didn't pay any attention to that, but by May he was calling me on the phone.

We went to a movie that night in Sioux City. And on the screen it said, "Willie Mays, please come to the office." And I'm saying, "Who knows me in Sioux City? It's my first time here." When I got to the office the man said, "You gotta call Leo." And I thought, "What would Leo want with me?" So we got on the phone and talked, and he says, "What are you hitting?" I was hitting very well. I said, ".477." He says, "Can you hit half of that for us?" I said, "I think I can." I didn't really want to come up, though, because I felt I wanted to stay with Minneapolis and break some records. But Leo said, "No, no, we need you."

When I got to the majors, Leo picked me up. He kidded with me, played pepper with me. We played for cokes, played for dollars, whatever. He had *very* good hands. And we just got to be very good friends. I don't know the drawing power that drew me to him, but it seems that he picked me, at an early age, to be one of the kids that he would look after.

And that season, 1951, was such a special time for the Giants, even more magical than '54 when we won the World Series, because in '54 we won the pennant by a wide margin [by five games over the Dodgers]. We didn't have a playoff in '54, like we did in '51. Actually, we should have won the '51 pennant without a playoff, but Jackie [Robinson] saved the Dodgers in Philadelphia [on the last day of the season]. We played in Boston that day, and beat the Braves 3-2. Then, we were on the train going back to New York when Jackie made the catch of a line drive over second [to keep the score tied in the 13th]. And then he hit a home run [in the 14th] to win the game 9-8. So we had a playoff.

When Bobby Thomson hit the big three-run home run to beat the Dodgers [5-4, in the ninth inning, of the third and final playoff game], I was on-deck at the time. I was so scared. Oh, shit [laughs]. People said that Leo wouldn't have pinch hit for me [if Thomson had walked, with first base open]. I say he would've. Knowing Leo the way I do now, I think he would've. But Leo said no. I can't contradict him but, in my mind, that's what he was about to do. I was always so conscious of what Leo was doing. When Bobby hit the home run, everybody was waiting for him at home plate. But I'm still kneeling down in the on-deck circle. That's how concerned I was, and how relieved I became when I realized what was happening. He saved me [laughs]. If Thomson had walked, Leo said I'd have hit [w/one out, bases loaded], against Ralph Branca. Erskine was warming up in the bullpen. I liked Erskine. I could hit Erskine. He threw a lot of breaking balls. But Ralph was kind of tough, I thought, because he threw hard sliders, no breaking balls. The slider didn't break that much. It was more like a fastball.

The first time I met Joe DiMaggio was in the '51 World Series against the Yankees. And that was his last season. It was special meeting him, in a sense, but you can't really show it when you're playing in a World Series. What I found out, though, is that when he hit a home run in the series [game four], I was out there in center field clapping. And, to this day, I don't know why nobody got that picture. But I felt myself out there *clapping* because that was Joe's last year.

In 1954, Monte Irvin got hurt in Denver [in spring training], and by the All-Star break I was hitting home runs at a record pace [30, w/36 in late July]. But we weren't winning consistently. So Leo came to me and said, "You don't have to hit a lot of home runs. We want you to knock in runs." So I said OK. He said, "You might win the batting championship but you won't win the home run title." He was right. I finished with 41 [tied w/Sauer for third, behind Kluszewski's 49 and Hodges' 42]. Leo said to me, "I want you to knock in runs, and we'll win games that way." And I said OK. So he moved me from third to fourth in the order, and I won the batting championship on the last day of the season. I was surprised that he would tell me to stop hitting home runs, but I think he wanted to win games more than just have individual play. That last day I got three hits, and Don Mueller two [Mays finished at .345, Mueller .342 and Snider .341]. It was a friendly competition. Duke and I had been

friends for years, and Don Mueller and I were friends. Even if I didn't win it, I was still going to get a raise.

Going into the Series, *we* thought we could beat Cleveland. Nobody else did. We thought we could beat them because we played Cleveland something like 22 times in spring training, and beat them most of the time. I knew all the pitchers. We used to barnstorm with them—we'd play them from Tucson all the way up to around West Point [leading up to the season opener]. We didn't have any problem with their pitchers. The best pitcher on their staff at the time was Bob Lemon, and I liked facing Lemon because he threw a lot of breaking balls. I used to *love* to hit breaking balls. So we didn't have any problem with their pitchers. We felt that we could beat them, but nobody ever said anything. We never boasted about what we were going to do. *Everybody* was for Cleveland. I think *I* would have been for Cleveland, winning 111 games that year. Yeah, even I would have been for them.

We won the first game 5-2 [on Dusty Rhodes' pinch hit 3-run HR in the 10th]. That was the game when I made the catch off Vic Wertz [with the score tied, runners at first and second, no out]. I was always particularly alert when any reliever came in. They wouldn't waste *any* pitch. They want to go right at the hitter, whether it's Don Liddle pitching or anybody. And when Don came in [to face Wertz], I said to myself, "I got to be alert out there." If you watch the films, I was playing very shallow. I didn't expect Wertz to hit the ball that hard, to tell you the truth. When he hit the ball I was concerned about one thing, and that was getting the ball back into the infield. When the ball was going up, I felt that I could catch it. In my mind, I felt that I could catch *any* ball in the ballpark. That's the way I played the outfield. And when I was running, there was a wall right there, and I was running right to the wall. And I said to myself, "I have to stop." Being a [former] football player, and a quarterback, I could stop very quickly. And when I caught the ball, if you watch the film, you'll see I turned around very quickly. I wasn't worried about how I was going to get the ball back to anybody [in particular] in the infield. I just wanted to get the ball back into the infield, *anywhere.* And from what I understand—I didn't see all this, now—Larry Doby had rounded third. He had to come back to second and tag up, and then go to third. Al Rosen was on first. He had a bad leg, had gone halfway to third, and had to come back to first. All this happening on one play, that *I* don't even know about. See, I couldn't see all this. So when I caught the ball and threw it back into the infield, only one guy advanced [Doby], which is very good in the Polo Grounds. Because in the Polo Grounds, if a guy's on second, he can tag very easily and score [on a long fly ball]. It's 483 feet to the wall in center. He can score from second easily.

Despite what people say about that catch, it didn't rank with me. I was used to catching balls like that every day. Like Leo used to tell me, "That was just a routine catch." I used to make a lot of catches, when guys would ask, "How did it rank?" I never worried about that. I was so happy to make the catches, and to be in the right spot at the right time, that I didn't have time to rank a catch better than another. I made a *lot* of catches that ordinarily would be base hits, or on balls going over the fence that I brought back. There was a ball that I barehanded in Trenton, but I did that in Birmingham *many* times. That's what I'm trying to tell you. The first time I remember doing that was in Birmingham. A guy hits the ball to left-center. I run over to my right, and this hand [gestures to his glove hand] wasn't going to be able to reach it, so I said, "OK, I'll just catch it in my bare hand." That was my first time catching the ball barehanded, but I did it in the majors two or three times as well.

The next year ['55] was Leo's last managing the Giants. That was one of my saddest moments when Leo told me that would be his final year. You've got to understand. It's like when your father passes on—it's one of your saddest days. I still remember the conversation in the Polo Grounds. Leo says, "Come here. I want to talk with you." So we went into the closet, and he says, "I won't be here next year." And I say, "What are you talking about?" And he says, "I'm not going to be your manager anymore. Your team is moving, and I think Mr. Stoneham wants to get another manager so he can have a little more grip on what the club does in another city." I was so surprised because nobody had told me that Leo wouldn't be coming back. That was the first time, also, that I heard we might leave New York. So I stayed in the closet for a couple of extra minutes to get myself together because I never had another manager [in the majors] besides him. That's when Rigney took over [in '56]. That was one of the saddest moments I had in my early years.

Leo was one of those who taught me early on that it was more important how I carried myself off the field than on the field. On the field it's baseball. Off the field it's, *do you want kids to look up to you?* You have to say to yourself, "How do I want to carry myself? Do I want to be the guy that kids say, 'I don't want to be like him. I want to be like someone else'?" So I, myself, felt that it was very important to be just as good off the field as on the field. I did it for the kids, for the fans.

YOU ASKED IF IT'S HARD to *be* Willie Mays—something most people would probably never imagine. But it's true. It's very hard, because I can't do the things sometimes that I want to do. For instance, I love to go to basketball games. I love to go to football games. *I can't.* Because people love you so much, at half time they want you to sign this, sign that, and how can you say no to them? And how can you be there and not have them come up to you for an autograph? It's very, very difficult for me to do anything that I want to do, outside of my own house. When I go to a restaurant I have to go to, maybe, a private room and have dinner with my wife Mae and family, or whatever. Sometimes I would like to be able to just go, and just be *me*. But in my walk of life I chose to be like I am, I guess. Some guys can go out and say, "Hey, this is my life, my private life." But you can't have a private life when you're playing baseball. Or basketball or football, or whatever. It's very difficult for me to go out into a mall and just be Joe Blow. I can't do it. I would *like* to do it. I would like to go shopping. I would like to do a lot of things that other people do. But it doesn't seem like I can do it. Don't ask me why. You'll have to ask the ordinary fan why. I've never had that privacy since I was out of baseball. And that's very unfortunate. I'm 66 now, and I've been out since I was 41. And yet, I've still got that same charisma that I had when I got through playing. That's very unusual. Most guys don't still have that type of following, so many years later. Sure, it's nice. But I pay for it.

Atherton, California

PETE BURNSIDE

Pete Burnside graduated from Dartmouth College, in Hanover, New Hampshire, in 1952. By then, he had already pitched three summers of professional baseball in the Giants' minor league system, after signing out of high school. An 18-win season for double-A Dallas in 1955 vaulted Burnside into the major leagues, where his first big league decision was a victory over perennial All-Star Robin Roberts at the Polo Grounds in September.

Pete spent most of the '58 season at triple-A Phoenix, pitching just 11 innings for the Giants, before being dealt to the Detroit Tigers in October. He pitched five more years in the majors, for Detroit, Washington and Baltimore, throwing 14 complete games and three shutouts, and then two years in Japan for the Hanshin Tigers in Osaka.

Burnside and his wife reside in Wilmette, Illinois. They have three children and one grandchild.

MIKE REMLINGER AND I may be the only Dartmouth grads to play for the Giants. Not many guys went on to play professional baseball from the Ivy League schools. In all honesty, I'd probably never get into Dartmouth now. It's become a very selective school, but when you look back at those days, in the late forties, it wasn't as hard to get into. I loved the smallness of it. I had a chance to go to Illinois and some other schools. But I didn't go to Dartmouth basically for baseball. I went more for environment, and because the alumni there talked me into it. I'm real glad they did. It's a lovely place.

I actually signed with the Giants in '49, out of high school. I came in about the same time as Mays. He went one way, of course, and I went the other. I was with the organization for 10 years. At the time I got sent out [in '58], there hadn't been many others that had been with them as long as I had.

I had my best year in the minors in Dallas in '55 [18-11, 2.47], got called up by the Giants at the end of the year, and got a chance to pitch twice. The first time I walked myself out of the game. But the second one was against Philadelphia at the Polo Grounds. Robin Roberts was going after his 24th win of the year. And I was just starting

out. Stan Lopata hit a home run off me, but I won 5-2. Later on, in '63, I was traded from Washington to Baltimore—and I was really fading out by then—and I roomed with Roberts, who was beginning to fade out himself. And we became fairly good friends. It was exciting, getting my first win against one of the top pitchers around. I thought I was going to be pretty good after that.

I know I did very little for the Giants in '58 [11 innings, no decisions], but it was still very exciting. I had been with the Giants organization for quite a while at that time, and it was probably one of the most exciting experiences of my baseball career, although I didn't play much. Going out there to San Francisco, with all the enthusiasm, was wonderful. The reason I finally got sent out was the home run [Wes] Covington hit off me. Rigney put me in to relieve about the seventh inning, and said, "Don't give him anything high, and you gotta keep the ball away from him." Before he got in the dugout, I threw one high and Covington hit it out of the park. The next day I was gone to Phoenix. It was around early June. I started the season with San Francisco, and it probably wasn't a bad move for me because I married a girl from Phoenix. We didn't date real steady at the time but that's where the association started. Also, I also started pitching a little more down there, and improved my control [11-7, 3.91]. We had a very good team in Phoenix. We had McCovey at first—what a wonderful guy. We had Wagner, [Felipe] Alou and Kirkland in the outfield for a while, Andre Rodgers at short and Tom Haller catching.

I got to know Willie Mays, and got to see him do more things on the field the winter of '54, than I ever did as his teammate with the Giants. That's when I played winter ball with him in Puerto Rico, on what might have been the best winter-league baseball team ever put together. I doubt there's been a better one [the Santurce Crabbers finished 47-25]. You had an outfield of Bob Thurman, Mays and Clemente. It was an all-black team except for about three of us—[Don] Zimmer, myself and Hal Jeffcoat. Valmy Thomas was catching. Ruben Gomez and Sad Sam Jones were *big* major league names pitching. I didn't play a hell of a lot with them, but that was a great team. We won the league, and then went over to Venezuela and won the Caribbean World Series. And Mays could do more things instinctually than anybody else I can think of.

Pete Burnside (SF Giants)

The Giants sold me to the Tigers in October [of '58], and I got to pitch a lot more in Detroit than I had with the Giants. I loved Detroit. Actually, I was sent there on a conditional deal. It's a funny story. Three of us were traded to Detroit, and all of us were there on conditional deals. Los Angeles sent a shortstop, and Cleveland sent a first baseman. Detroit had to make a decision between the three of us. They could keep only one. I had come out of winter ball and was in real good shape, and I started pitching right away. All the shortstop did was pinch-run. He was trying to become a switch-hitter. And the first baseman didn't play at all. So they kept me. They got rid of the shortstop, who was Maury Wills. And they got rid of the first baseman, who was Tito Francona. That year I won one game, and those guys went on to have big, big years. I always laugh at that story, because they kept me and got rid of the other two guys. [*author's note: Francona hit .363 with 20 HR for Cleveland; rookie Wills hit .260 for the Dodgers, but stole 578 bases the next 14 seasons, and was a five-time All-Star.*]

I started pitching a lot more in 1960 [7-7, 4.28, 114IP]. I loved pitching in Tiger Stadium. I know it's a hitters' park but I just loved pitching, no matter where I was. My best friends with Detroit were probably Dave Sisler, Eddie Yost and Rocky Bridges. Then, we were the guys who were put on the expansion list to make up the two new teams [Washington and Los Angeles] That's when I went to Washington, a team that struggled for

many, many years. Yeah [laughs]. Playing with Washington, if you could beat Kansas City a couple of times, and maybe the Yankees once every two years, you could hang on. I threw two shutouts in '61, and I think at least one of them was against Kansas City. Claude Osteen was with us then [a rookie], and so was Dick Donovan, from the White Sox [Donovan led AL with 2.40ERA]. We drew well in the beginning. Opening Day. No, not overall [597,287]. But that was an exciting town to play in. President Kennedy was there Opening Day. I remember that, because I was about to catch a ball from him. It's on film. I knew he was young, and was standing in the back [of my teammates] because I thought he might throw the ball a pretty good distance. Well, it was coming right to me, and you can see it on film. He's throwing it out, and the players are all going for it. And I think that ball was within a foot of my glove, when Jim Rivera of the White Sox broadsided me. He got the ball, and got Kennedy to sign it. I would think that he still has that ball.

My major league career ended in '63 [*author's note: A fellow Dartmouth pitcher, Art Quirk, was a Senator teammate then*], and then I spent two years in Japan with the Hanshin Tigers, in Osaka. I loved it. I played four years of winter ball in the Caribbean, and then two years in Japan, and I loved all of it. Suzette and I were just married in January [of '64], and Washington had told me that I would go to spring training with them, but maybe not stick. I might be sent down, and I knew that I was coming to that stage anyway. They were very honest. Gil Hodges [manager] was very honest. They called the day before Suzette and I were married, and George Selkirk, the general manager, asked if I would be interested in going to Japan. I asked Suzette, and she said, "Yeah, why not?" So they flew over, and we negotiated in San Francisco, where we were having our honeymoon.

We went over [to Japan] three weeks later, and lived Japanese-style. We lived in

Nishinomiya, between Kobe and Osaka. And, again, I loved every minute of it. It was a big year, too, because we won the pennant [the *only* year in a stretch of 11 that the Giants did not win the Central League flag]. And I think that was why I was over there, being left-handed. It's the only team I was the best left-handed pitcher on, because I was the *only* one. They were looking for a left-handed pitcher to pitch against the Giants. Although I didn't have a big year [5-8, 3.36], every time we played the Giants I'd pitch against them. I don't think [Sadaharu] Oh ever got a hit off me. I had real good success with him, but then it went the other way with the third baseman [Nagashima]. I don't think I ever got him out. I got Oh out well but I didn't get Nagashima. I don't think Oh had seen a lot of left-handers at that point, and I had a fairly good curveball. And I was just lucky with him. I changed speeds on him and I got him out. The way he raised his right foot—he wasn't the only guy who ever did that. Mel Ott used to do that, too. But Oh really got back on that back foot. I think he [868HR] would have done fine in the major leagues. He would have done real well. I think Nagashima [444HR] would have done real well. I think the left-handed pitcher, Kaneda [400 wins], would have done well. They were *good* ballplayers.

There were two of us over there at the time. The other American really had a big year—Gene Bacque won 29 games [29-9, 1.89]. He never played in the major leagues. He went over there young [24 years old; pitched eight years in Japan]. Our catcher spoke a little English. Most of the other guys did, too, and a lot of the baseball terms were pidgin English. And they eventually got us a translator. I was treated wonderfully. I didn't win a lot [10-22, 3.10] my two years there but, in all honesty, I bet you that all but about four of those 22 losses were against the Giants. That was who I pitched against, basically. Very seldom did I pitch against the other teams in the league.

Hanshin was the only team, I think, where the American players lived Japanese-style. In other words, we would go to Tokyo or Nagoya, and live with the ball team in the Japanese *ryokans* [inns]. The other teams didn't do that. The Americans lived in Western hotels, and joined the team at the ballpark. With Hanshin, I thought it was a great experience. And we got to know the guys better. We'd go out with them, and

we were with them all the time. It was a wonderful experience. The *ryokans* are lovely. We slept on the floor [on *futons*]. You know, the only thing [difficult] was going to the bathroom early in the morning when it was about 23 degrees inside. No, that's a joke. But we wore the *geta* [wooden clogs] and we had our *kimonos* [cotton robes]. That was the way we did it, and it was really part of the experience.

Suzette and I had an apartment in Nishinomiya the first year. We had *tatami* mats, and slept on *futons*. Then, the second year—with the team on the road a lot—we lived in Kobe, in a Western apartment. Suzette was a horseback rider and jumper, so she joined a club and did some competition there.

I remember, in '65, the 20th anniversary of the atomic bomb. They interviewed us extensively on that. And that wasn't a long period—just 20 years. Hiroshima was the one city—I pitched there only once—where our teammates told Bacque and me, "If you go out at night, go out with us." There was still some very strong feelings there, and I could understand why. We visited the museum in Hiroshima several times. It brings tears to your eyes. And from the ballpark in Hiroshima, you can see the shell just beyond the right field foul line. We did get, "Go home, Yankee," and "Damn Yankee." That was the only place we ever heard it.

Suzette was pregnant then with our daughter, who is now a physician in San Francisco. So she left Japan early, and then I came home. I had a chance to go back the next year ['66] but didn't, because our daughter was born in January. I enrolled, got my master's at Northwestern, and then was a high school teacher for 26 years. I retired in '94.

Looking back, I suppose my biggest highlight in baseball was my first big league win, at the Polo Grounds. But I remember pitching a shutout at Nashville one time, in the minors, and getting a new wristwatch for it. That was a high point. The thing I'm remembered for most *now*—every year around September I get calls from sportswriters—is that I was the left-hander who threw more home run balls to Maris in '61, the year he hit 61. I threw three, and no other left-hander did that. He hit three off me. I probably never would have realized that, without the reminders every year. But now I can picture each one of them. Otherwise, though, I would not have realized I'm in that select group. I played against Roger in the minor leagues, when he was at Indianapolis, and I knew him. He was a wonderful guy.

I was back in San Francisco recently, went to a [pre-season] ballgame between Cleveland and the Giants and noticed all the emblems on the outfield wall, of the Hall of Famers who played for the Giants. And, personally, I missed one—a guy who played in the black leagues, the Negro Leagues, and who was also a great star in [triple-A] Minneapolis. He's in the Hall of Fame but his emblem is not out there. Unfortunately, he never got one day in the big leagues but Ray Dandridge was a paramount third baseman, and one of the nicest gentlemen I played with. And, just in my own mind, I want to remember Ray Dandridge as a real Giant. *[author's note: A perennial All-Star in the Negro and Mexican Leagues, Dandridge signed with the Giants in 1949 at age 35, had three more All-Star seasons at triple-A Minneapolis, yet was never called up to the majors. He was voted into the Hall of Fame by the Veterans Committee in 1987.]*

I played [pro ball] for 17 years, and I never had a day that I didn't enjoy. I loved it. It was the competition, and it was the fact that you made your own fortune. You did it or you didn't. I was not a celebrity, of course. That was not part of it. It was the camaraderie, the spirit and a lot of wonderful, wonderful laughs. And I can't think of a better way to make a living.

Wilmette, Illinois

BOB SPEAKE

Bob Speake hit 12 home runs as a rookie with the Cubs in 1955, in just 261 at-bats, and then slammed 16 home runs with Chicago in '57, sandwiched around an All-Star campaign in the Pacific Coast League, with the Los Angeles Angels, in which he hit 25 home runs, with 111 RBIs and a .300 average.

Unfortunately for Speake, he was traded to the Giants in March of '58, for Bobby Thomson—unfortunate because Speake went being from an every day player with the Cubs to being a left-handed pinch hitter with the Giants. His career ended in '59, at the age of 29.

Bob and his wife live in Topeka, Kansas. They have three children and eight grandchildren.

I MADE THE CUBS' Opening Day roster in 1955, after having played at class-A Des Moines in '54. I had always been a first baseman, but when Hank Sauer got sick, [triple-A manager] Bob Scheffing said to me, "Have you ever played the outfield?" I said sure. And since I played one game in the outfield in the service, I wasn't lying to him. So I got [pitcher] Paul Minner's finger-mitt and went out in the outfield. And the next thing I know I'm in the lineup, in the outfield. I did have a good first part of the year [10 home runs by June]. Then Hank got well and got put back in there. So my season sort of came to a halt.

My first home run came off the Giants' Jim Hearn at the Polo Grounds. Up, over and out. But that's not a big thing. You just had to get it high enough there, because it was a football field [258 feet to right]. But, yeah, it was a thrill all right. I'll never forget that one.

With five games left in the season, I was playing left field in Busch Stadium in St. Louis, and they didn't have pads up at that time. You know, we didn't use the batting helmets, or pads on the wall—that type of thing. I went into the wall, and broke and dislocated my left wrist. That winter, my wife's parents were in a terrible car wreck, and my father-in-law owned a small grocery store. So I left therapy to run that for him, got to spring training and it [the wrist] wasn't as it should have been. So that's the reason I went to Los Angeles [PCL]. Having to give up the therapy, the wrist wasn't where I wanted it to be.

But I enjoyed the '56 season in LA, playing on a powerful ball club for that league. Steve Bilko was there, at first base. Gene Mauch was at second, George Freese [Gene's older brother] was at third, Casey Wise was at short. Jim Bolger, Gail Wade and I were in the outfield. And El Tappe was behind the plate. So we had a heck of a ball club. We had a tremendous pitching staff of youngsters. Dick Drott was there. Dave Hillman, Don Elston and Bob Anderson. Bob Scheffing was managing. Half of us went back up with the Cubs in '57 [including Scheffing, who was named Cubs manager in October of '56].

The Angels played at Wrigley Field in LA, which was a duplication of Wrigley Field in Chicago, except that it had lights at the time. We drew real well there, and we drew real well on the road because of Bilko and his home run derby. *[author's note: Speaking of which, Wrigley Field in LA was the setting for the popular TV series* Home Run Derby, *filmed in '59.]* Bilko hit 55 home runs, after hitting 56 the year before. The PCL was a great league for so many years, but it petered out, in a sense, in '58, when the LA franchise went to Tacoma [and the San Francisco franchise to Phoenix]. The expansion of baseball sort of did away with the Coast League, as we knew it, as well as the Southern Association and the International League, because with the expansion of major league baseball, and television, the minor leagues started having a rough go of it. And the colleges became more of an apprenticeship.

Then, in '58, Bobby Thomson and I traded uniforms in spring training. It was not a good deal for me. What I went from was playing every day with the Cubs, to a franchise that was looking for the next Willie Mays. You had Wagner and Kirkland and the Alous, and everybody else coming up, and they were looking for another Willie Mays. All these guys had to be looked at in game conditions. I'm not being critical. It's just the facts of life, as far as my career was concerned.

Why did the Giants even want me? Rigney told me up front. And you have to remember that we didn't have a choice. Rigney told me up front that he wanted me for left-handed pinch hitting. My career was over. I stayed there for two years, and looked for a business opportunity while I was doing that. I didn't leave baseball at 29 because of my health. You get a year older and you see this array of talent coming through. But Rigney told me in spring training, "We've got a kid that we don't think is gonna work out [at first], and Whitey Lockman is getting a little bit old. So we'll need you for left-handed pinch hitting *and* first base, because we don't think this kid's gonna work out." His name was Cepeda. So that took care of that half of the equation. So I'm sitting there on the bench with Bill White and Whitey Lockman. Jablonski played some first base. Sauer did, too. So we had a raft of guys sitting there, waiting to get in, while these kids were proving themselves at first and elsewhere, or working themselves out. It got to the point where they traded off White and Lockman, yet I was still sitting there. Of course, they had a guy named Willie McCovey coming up from Phoenix then, too.

Rigney called me into his office one day [in '59]. It was in June. And he said, "I'm sending you to Phoenix. You have to stay down there 10 days. I want you to get in shape, and when you come back you'll be in left field." So I went down, worked my head off, came back, and I'm in left field in Pittsburgh. I get a base hit, drive in a run, and I'm feeling great. The next day I'm not in the lineup. I'm wondering what in the sam hell is going on. Well, Stoneham had called Rigney and said, "Put my boy back in there." And Wagner was back in left field, and I was headed back to Phoenix. These were days when you had the reserve clause, so there wasn't anything you could do about it. So I finished the season in Phoenix, then sent my contract back marked, "voluntary retirement." You've got two types of ballplayers— one that wants to go on the road, and one that wants to get off the road. I was the type that wanted to get off the road. So I looked around for an opportunity to get out, and some guy said, "Let's go in the bowling business." I said, "Well, you put it together. I'll hang it up and run it." So that's basically how I got out of baseball. The Giants sold my contract to triple-A Tacoma [they had moved their PCL franchise from Phoenix to Tacoma].

Bob Speake (SF Giants)

The next spring Rosy Ryan [Tacoma GM] called me and said, "We want you to come to spring training." And I said, "What for?" He said, "Well, we've got three major league clubs that are interested in looking at you." I said, "Rosy, I'll go to spring training with any one of the three on a conditional contract. If I make the ball club, fine. If I don't, fine. *Their* expenses." He said, "No, they want to look at you at our place." Well, I'd been around long enough to know. That was just a smoke screen. And that was it for me. I really don't have any pleasant memories from my two years in San Francisco. It was tough being a Giant. And when Bob Scheffing came over to my hotel and told me I was getting traded to the Giants, he said, "We'll promise you one thing. If they put you on waivers, we'll pick you up." Twice in '58 they put me on waivers. Both times the Cubs claimed me. But, as you know, the third time back then—if they put you on waivers a third time—they had to let you go. They could pull you back the first two times. Well, the Giants never put me on waivers a third time. And by '59 the Cubs had already filled what I could do for them.

When you're chattel-mortgage, and you're excess baggage, it's all over. For a lot of guys. I went down to Phoenix, looked around and said OK, let's see what we've got here. There was Jim Brideweser, Bill Wilson and Benny Valenzuela. Dusty Rhodes had just left. All of them hanging on for the expansion, like Johns Hopkins hospital patients. And they weren't major league caliber anymore. So, rather than hang around like them, and like Owen Friend and El Tappe—and I'm not being disrespectful—but you've got to know when to move on. These guys wanted to be buried under the mound.

So I got in the bowling business. We had a 16-lane house in Springfield, Missouri. *Holiday Lanes.* And it didn't take very long to realize that a 16-lane house was like a corner grocery store. You had to marry it. So I attempted putting four of the houses together under common ownership. But one guy backed out on me, so I left the business after three years and went in the insurance business. Stayed in that for 31 years. Three of us came to Kansas from Missouri, with a million dollars, and started a company. Now, it's worth three *billion.* So, it wasn't too bad. I paid more taxes in the insurance business than I ever made in baseball [laughs].

But don't get me wrong. I enjoyed my time in baseball. I enjoyed being a teammate of Stu

Miller. As a matter of fact, I beat him in a ballgame when I was with the Cubs. So Al Worthington's taking me around the clubhouse and introducing me to his Giant teammates. I knew Al. And he introduces me to Stu. And Stu says, "I don't want to shake that SOB's hand." I said, "Wait a minute. What's this?" I didn't have any idea what he was talking about. Boy, a pitcher—when you beat his ball club, and the way I did it, ... I bunted with two outs in the ninth inning with Banks on third. You could bunt on him easy, because he just lobbed the ball up there. But you try to time that thing and he'd have you spinning like a top. He probably told you how he came up with that change-up, in the minors. He stumbled. His spike hooked up into the pitching rubber, and he went ahead and threw the ball. The batter spun around about three times, and Stu said, "There it is." He had a tremendous career in the big leagues. I saw Ken Boyer break his bat at home plate, after striking out against him. He was tough to time.

So when I got to know Stu, he said, "Bob, I want you to play bridge with Daryl Spencer, Jackie Brandt and me." I said, "I don't know anything about bridge." And he handed me a little book, *Bridge by Goren.* So I read that book. And he said, "All I want you to do is stay within the covers." To this day, I don't play bridge. But I could bid, according to that book. And he beat those guys like a drum, just single-handedly, by me telling him what I had. We used to laugh and laugh. That was the funniest thing you ever saw. Spencer gets all upset. And Brandt—of course, we always called him "Flaky." You could shake his head and hear it rattle in there. But Stu would beat those guys single-handedly.

I got to play with both Ernie Banks and Willie Mays. Ernie, no question about it, was not only a great ballplayer but a great individual. Willie was a lot of *fun.* Now, Willie was a natural talent, but he was a bigger *showman* than Ernie. Ernie was Mr. Cub. That was the reputation that he enjoyed, with the kids. Willie, on the other hand, knew that the place to play was New York. It hurt him when they moved out of New York because he missed the Big Apple atmosphere. So, as great a talent as he was, he was twice the showman. He got into outside social circles that Ernie never got into, especially in San Francisco. There, you've got celebrities and the Hollywood influence. So, they were two different individuals.

If you ask me who was the best center fielder I ever played with or against, I would tell you Bill Virdon. He never made a mistake. And, of course, he carried his own weight with the bat. But defensively, he was the best center fielder I ever saw. Now, Willie was good. But when I was with the Cubs, we had a green light on Willie. We could go from first to third anytime we wanted to. Willie's liable to throw you out. But that's only one out of five. The other four may be in the stands, because Willie didn't believe that two throws are better than one. He wanted that long fly to the bag. I went from first to third on Willie a lot. Now, he was a baserunner, too. No question about it, he challenged 'em. And when he made it, he was the headline. But when he got thrown out, it was just another play.

I saw Willie at an insurance convention in LA a number of years ago. He was representing a company there, signing autographs. I came up from behind him and said, "Sign one to Bob, would you?" He turned around and just laughed. We used to play pinochle together.

So the guys that were there—you enjoyed the fellowship and the camaraderie. But then you got to look at the big picture, and it wasn't there for me. In the Polo Grounds, I ate them alive, because I was a strict pull-hitter. And I guess that's what was still in the back of their mind [when the Giants traded for him]. They should *never* have acquired me as a left-handed pinch hitter, because in Seals Stadium there were only three home runs hit to right field in 1958. And one of them was by Cepeda. That was a tremendous park to hit in if you were a right-hander, because of the current coming off the ocean. Having played there against the Seals in '56, I knew I was going into a *terrible* situation. I saw right fielders go to the wall and come back, with their backs to the infield, to catch a fly ball.

But, really, the two worst days of my career have nothing to do with the Giants. One was when the Cardinals were looking for a left-handed pull-hitter. And they were dickering with the Cubs. There were two ballplayers—Jim King and me—and one of us was going to go to the Cardinals. King went to the Cardinals and I stayed with the Cubs. Wrigley Field is the friendly confines for right-handed hitters because the wind comes down the right field line, hits those stands, and goes out into left-center. So King went to the Cardinals instead of me, and you know what a great home run park the old Busch Stadium was for left-handers [310 feet to right, 354 feet to right-center].

Then there was the last series Brooklyn had at Wrigley [in '55]. Furillo was on first and said, "How would you like to be with us next year?" I said, "Man, don't talk about things like that." Ebbets Field was a little sandbox, and I hit good in sandboxes. He said, "Yeah, they're upstairs talking about it right now. Snider's the only left-hander we got, and we need more left-handed power." Man, I swelled up like a toad. Well, five days later I go into the wall in St. Louis, and the writing was on the wall. From there, it was downhill.

Now, I don't mean to leave you with a bad thought. I loved baseball. I loved my time in baseball. The friends that I made—some are lasting, some are passing. But, all in all, it was a great pastime, and I feel sorry for the fans today who don't have that type of player we had in my day—the DiMaggios, the Musials, the Bankses. The ballplayers today—and I would be the same way—really don't care what's written across their chests. It's whatever their agent can get for them. It's a different game now entirely.

Topeka, Kansas

DOM ZANNI

Dom Zanni won 15 games twice, and 20 games once, in the minor leagues, before making his major league debut with the '58 Giants, beating Sam Jones and the Cardinals in relief. Dom returned to Phoenix that year as a starter, winning 14 games, before earning a promotion back up with the Giants in '59. He was traded following the '61 season, with Eddie Fisher and Bob Farley to the Chicago White Sox for Billy Pierce and Don Larsen. Pierce, of course, helped lead the Giants to the National League pennant in '62, but Zanni quietly had his best major league season as well, going 6-5 with a 3.75 ERA, in a career-high 86 innings.

Zanni pitched almost exclusively in relief in the majors, but did come very close to a complete game in '62 with the White Sox, when he relieved an injured Joel Horlen with nobody out in the first inning and went the distance, allowing just seven hits, to beat the Athletics.

A native of the Bronx, Zanni and his wife now live in Massapequa, New York. He has three children and one grandchild.

I REMEMBER MY major league debut well, because I had just come up with the Giants from Phoenix in '58. I pitched in relief, and I beat Sad Sam Jones. I remember that also because I went up to bat, and everybody in the dugout was saying, "Watch the curveball, watch the curveball." The side-arm curveball. I don't know whether you remember that or not. But he threw one, I sat down on my rump, and everybody in the dugout was laughing. I was a pretty good hitter. At least I thought I was [.280 lifetime]. That was at Seals Stadium.

When we went to Candlestick two years later, it was a nightmare. That was the era when Stu Miller got blown off the mound in the All-Star Game [in '61]. They had the metal cyclone fences, and we used to go out there and put our gloves up against the fences, and they would *stay* up there. And it was *cold.* I mean, we lived in Hillsdale, about 10 or 15 miles away. And, my God, to go to the ballpark I had to put on a heavy jacket and keep anti-freeze in the car. That's how cold it was. It used to take us hours just to get undressed. And the ball was like glass. That's how cold it was. I imagine it's still cold there now, but with the wind-factor and stuff, everybody in the bullpen used to pray that the phone wouldn't ring for them. That wind was *terrible.*

But I spent most of the '58 season in Phoenix [14-11, 3.67]. Not to brag about it, but I think we could've beat any major league ball club going around. We were that good.

We had Wagner and Alou in the outfield, McCovey on first, Amalfitano and Rodgers in the infield, Burnside, Shipley and Margoneri on the mound. Most of us went from there to the Dominican Republic. That's when I got married, in '58. I think about seven or eight of us went to play winter baseball down there, as honeymooners. It was strange. They treated us like royalty down there, but the political atmosphere with the army and so forth was tense. But we had a good time.

My biggest thrill in the majors came with the White Sox in '62, going into Yankee Stadium for the first time as a *player,* to play the Yankees. You know, my hometown. I left about

a *million* tickets. I didn't know I had to pay for them until I got back to Chicago. It cost me $800. I mean, everybody in the world was calling me. "I was behind you in kindergarten." "Sure, why not? Two tickets." I had my high school there, my grammar school there. Everybody who thought they knew me was there. And I came in to relieve for two innings against the Yankees, and shut them out. In fact, I struck out Mantle, Maris and Howard in succession. *And* I got fined for it. Would you believe it? We had a meeting before the game, and Lopez [manager Al] said, "Don't throw Howard change-ups," because he'd hit the slow pitch. Well, I had so much confidence that when I had two strikes on him, and [Sherm] Lollar kept calling for the fastball, I threw the change-up anyway. I said, "I'll take the responsibility." I struck him out, walked into the dugout and Lopez said, "That's gonna cost you." I didn't give a crap about anything [laughs].

Then Turk Lown came in for the 10th inning, and the first pitch he threw to Dale Long was hit for a home run, and we lost. That was my biggest thrill because coming into Yankee Stadium—going out there, with DiMaggio and Ruth—you know that business. I mean, I went out to

Dom Zanni (Dick Dobbins)

center field to look back at home plate, and it was a $5 cab ride, for pete's sakes, just to get back [laughs]. It was such a long distance away. When I came into the bullpen, my God, Lopez thought I was crazy because I was so psyched up. I grabbed a ball and said, "Get out of there." I was [still] a rookie, you know. I said, "Get out of there," and Lopez looked at me and started laughing [laughs].

That game I pitched all nine innings in *relief* also came in '62, in Kansas City. Joel Horlen started for us, and he got hit with a line drive. I came in [with two on, no out] and pitched the whole nine innings, and got the win. It was not technically a complete game [because Horlen faced two batters], but I went the whole nine innings. In the seventh inning, I had the wind knocked out of me in a collision covering first base. I think Lopez wanted to take me out, but I said, "You've got to be kidding me." There was no way of getting me out of there.

I finished up with Cincinnati [traded for Jim Brosnan], and quit in '68. Then I went into the insurance business for 27 years, and just retired in '95. Now we live over on Long Island. Even though I was born and raised in the Bronx, and have always called New York home, a lot of people say I don't have much of a New York accent. I think that's because I was never home [during a 17-year baseball career]. In fact, my Bronx accent disappeared my first year of pro ball, when I went down to Jenkins, Kentucky. I didn't understand anything those people said for the first two or three months [laughs].

Massapequa, New York

Dom Zanni (Dom Zanni)

ants in '58, appearing in just 14 games, and only one as a starter. His major league career was over, at the age of 27, after five seasons, 30 wins, 17 complete games and a 3.87 ERA.

Crone remains in baseball, however, working as a major league scout for the San Diego Padres. He makes his home in Waxahachie, Texas. He and his wife have four children and five grandchildren.

RAY CRONE

Ray Crone, signed by the Boston Braves out of high school in 1949, won 21 games his first two full seasons for the Braves in Milwaukee, in '55 and '56, before being traded to the Giants midway through the '57 season, along with Bobby Thomson and Danny O'Connell, in exchange for Red Schoendienst. With the trade, Crone missed out on an opportunity to be a part of the Braves' 1957 World Series championship team.

After making 58 starts the previous three seasons, Crone never found a comfort zone with the Gi-

IT'S EASY TO REMEMBER my major league debut because it came Opening Day in Cincinnati, in 1954. I came in to face a pinch hitter, Andy Seminick. Then I got my first start in May, in Wrigley Field, went the distance and beat the Cubs 4-2. Every once in a while I'll say to some guy, "The difference with baseball 40 years ago is that I started that game, was ahead 2-0 with a man on and two outs in the ninth, Banks hits one in the seats [laughs], and yet I *stay* in the game." The thing I always talk about to younger people or other scouts is that nowadays I wouldn't have even been *in* the game, in the ninth inning. If they start a young guy today, he goes six innings, then he's out. No matter if he's doing good or not. They say, "He's thrown too many pitches. Let's get him out." And they put in two or three other guys. So, here I am in the ninth, with a man on and two out. In the first place [today], I'd never get to pitch to the first guy in the ninth. If the guy got on, I'd never stay in the game. So Banks hits one out, the score's tied, and the next inning, in the 10th, I *collect a bat* [laughs]. That *never* happens nowadays. I think Pafko gets a double, we get two runs and I finish the game. It's just so much different nowadays.

We had very good teams in Milwaukee for four or five years. Actually, they should have been a dynasty of some sort. In '56 we should have won [the pennant], but lost out to Brooklyn on the last day. We were ahead by one game going into the final weekend, with three games to go. We lost the first two in St. Louis, while the Dodgers won three straight at home over Pittsburgh. They were going on their experience, and we were fighting to overcome our own inexperience, not knowing how to finish it off. Spahn lost 2-1 in 12 innings. Then Burdette lost. Toward the end of the season I was doing a lot of relief, so I came in to get the last out on Sunday. We had to win that game just to finish in second, ahead of Cincinnati. The Dodgers won 93 games. We won 92.

In '57 we were on our way to winning the pennant rather convincingly. Again, we had a very good club. Henry Aaron, Wes Covington and Billy Bruton were in the outfield. Frank Torre was at first, Eddie Mathews at third. And Spahn, Burdette and Buhl were having All-Star seasons. Then, in June, the Braves got the second baseman they felt they needed, Red Schoendienst from the Giants [.309, 15HR, 65RBI, 200H in '57]. They traded three players for him. And I was one of them. Of course, I was disappointed by the trade. I was signed by the Braves and brought up through their organization, and I would have preferred to stay with them. But I was also realistic enough to know that trades happen. When a team acquires a player, maybe it's because he was effective against that team. Maybe I was effective against the Giants, when I was with the Braves. But when a guy joins a new team, he might not show that same effectiveness with his new team.

So I finished up '57 with the Giants, then was part of the move to San Francisco in '58. I remember it was pleasant to be part of the new experience. But it just didn't work out for me. You see, Rigney really liked me. I'm being facetious. Everybody said I left baseball after '58 because of arm problems, but that wasn't the case. I was ineffective, but not because of any arm problems. People don't understand that. People in baseball

like to tag guys. Instead of working with them, they'll just say, "He's got a sore arm." One of the big things was that had the team stayed in New York, we'd have gone to spring training, and the New York writers would have then been asking Rigney, "Why don't you use this guy?" The San Francisco writers didn't know anybody from Adam. But let's face it. All I had to do was pitch well, and I would have pitched [a lot more]. I just got to a point where I couldn't bring back what I used to have, for some reason. And I didn't know how to fix it.

I remember [GM Chub] Feeney bringing me into his office there at Seals Stadium and saying, "Well, we tried to move you, but nobody wanted you," or something like that. And I said, "You mean *nobody?*" So they put me on waivers, Pittsburgh claimed me and, eventually, I was sold to Toronto [triple-A]. In those days, you didn't have any options. I went to Toronto, but had I gone there and done well, I'm sure someone would have bought me. Jack Kent Cooke was the owner. That's what his baseball thing was—try to get guys [from the majors] and then sell them back. So, all in all, it was my own ineffectiveness, really. But it's not like it is today. If a guy like me were around today, they [a major league club]

Ray Crone (SF Giants)

would probably keep me, because there's not that much competition anymore.

After I quit playing I didn't see any opportunities in baseball, so I did a variety of other things. Then in '71 I re-entered baseball, doing a little scouting. I was with Baltimore for about 20 years. And now I'm scouring the major leagues for the Padres. I go all over. We put in reports, and sometimes they ask us about specific players. My son scouts, too, for the Red Sox. He played in college, and a couple of years of pro ball, but he didn't distinguish himself [laughs].

Waxahachie, Texas

JOE SHIPLEY

Joe Shipley, a six-foot-four right-hander, could throw hard. In fact, he was clocked in excess of 100 miles an hour. Plagued by control problems early in his career in the minors, Shipley made his major league debut with the Giants in 1958, although he spent most of the season with triple-A Phoenix, where he went 5-2, with a 2.45 ERA, in 92 innings. Joe pitched 38 innings for the Giants the next two years, before returning to the majors with the Chicago White Sox in '63.

Following a 14-year professional baseball career, Shipley worked for General Motors in St. Louis until his retirement from GM in '95. He now works in security for a casino in his hometown of St. Charles, Missouri.

THE GIANTS SIGNED ME right out of high school when I was 17 years old. I could throw hard. They first got radar guns in 1962, and I remember I had just left the Giants and gone to the Cardinals for spring training camp. Gibson could throw hard, too. But I could throw harder than he could. They clocked me at 101 once.

People say I didn't have a longer career in the major leagues because of control problems. But, actually, the year I got traded to the White Sox ['62], I was 10-1 with Tulsa and Indianapolis [triple-A]. Then, in '63, I was 17-5 with Indianapolis. Then I got called up to the White Sox. But I

never really got an opportunity to pitch. I hurt my arm in '58 when I first got called up to the Giants. I hurt my arm in Portland, Oregon, and then got called up the next day. I didn't really know it was hurt that bad but I spent a month and a half on the disabled list when I first got called up, when we played downtown in Seals Stadium. It was a pulled muscle, from my shoulder all the way down to where it pulled away from my ribcage. I had internal bleeding as well but I didn't know it at the time. I couldn't do anything for about a month. I couldn't even raise my right arm. But it went away and I came back, and I could throw as hard as ever. Then I hurt it again, and that was it, in 1966.

It was exciting, though, when I got called up. Seals Stadium was packed almost every day in '58 and '59. That's when they had a jet stream that blew from right to left-center. The ballpark was a big ballpark. But the balls used to really fly out of there [toward left]. Mays and those guys would hit them over the scoreboard in left-center field. It was a long ways [365 feet to left, 404 to left-center]. Antonelli was there then. He kind of took me under his wing. Johnny Antonelli. He was a good guy.

I pitched one inning in '58 [after coming off the DL], and I'll never forget it [laughs]. Lew Burdette was pitching for the Milwaukee Braves. There were runners on first and second, and the first pitch I threw—my fastball would sink—he turned around to bunt the ball. He missed it, and it him right in the *groin*. And down he went. And [laughs], he thought I was throwing at him on purpose. He's holding himself while going to first base. Actually, they had to take him out of the game. And he kept saying, "I'm gonna get you, Shipley. I'm gonna get you. You did it on purpose." It was really funny. But, you know, I was just a kid, and I was kind of nervous. I wasn't throwing at him. Well, I got the next guy out. Then the next guy got a base hit, and drove in a run. I got out of the inning, eventually. It was exciting.

In Cincinnati [in '59], they brought me in with the score tied. And I struck out Ed Bailey, Frank Robinson and Gus Bell. I struck out the side, and when I went inside after the game was over—we won the game although I didn't get a save—they had the towels all leading to my locker. *That* was exciting.

In '60, we were playing in Milwaukee. And myself, Bud Byerly and "Digger" O'Dell [named after character in *Life of Riley* radio program] were in the bullpen warming up. Now, at Milwaukee County Stadium, the bullpen was in center field. And Tom Sheehan [interim manager]—he never had a uniform because he was so *big*. They couldn't make one for him. All he did was wear a Giants jacket, a cap, a pair of pants and baseball shoes. So ol' Tommy says [in an exaggerated bass], "Get the big guy up from down there." So I get up, get in the golf cart, and they ride me out to the pitching mound. Well, I get there and Tom says to me [again, in a mocking tone], "Jesus Christ, what are *you* doing here. I want the other guy. I want Byerly." "Well," I said, "you said you want the big guy. I'm here." He says, "Go back and tell Bud to come in." So, I just took a ride for nothing. I get in the golf cart, they're taking me back to center field, and everybody [in the stands] starts applauding. I get up and tip my cap to them. Then, about two weeks later [laughs], I get sent down to triple-A again.

Well, after that, in '63, Eddie Fisher and Hoyt Wilhelm—both ex-Giants—are with the White Sox. Both of them throwing that knuckleball. And I get called up from Indianapo-

lis with the White Sox. So we're all sitting in the clubhouse, and Tom Sheehan—he's a scout then with the Giants—walks in. We're all sitting there talking, me and Eddie and Hoyt. And in walks big ol' Tom. He looks at Hoyt. "How're you doin', Hoyt?" He looks at Eddie. "How're you doin', Eddie?" He looks at me and says, "Jesus Christ, how in the hell did *you* get back up here?" "Hell," I said, "I'm 17-5 at Indianapolis." He says, "Well, jeez, if you're 17-5, I could be a 20-game winner." [laughs] *[author's note: The 69-year-old Sheehan hadn't pitched since 1926.]* He never did like me for some reason. I don't know why.

St. Charles, Missouri

JIM CONSTABLE

Jim Constable was signed by the Giants out of high school in 1951, made his major league debut in '56, won his first big league game in '57 and was on the '58 Giants' Opening Day roster at Seals Stadium. He finished the season with Cleveland and Washington, and wound up his major league career back with the Giants in '63.

Jim and his wife live in Jonesboro, Tennessee. They have five children and five grandchildren.

YES, I REMEMBER my major league debut quite well [laughs]. We were playing Brooklyn in the Polo Grounds, and I had been called up the day before. Ruben Gomez started the game but he got into trouble, and they called me in from the bullpen. Of course, the bullpen was a *long* way from the mound at the Polo Grounds. And as I was walking, my knees were knuckling [laughs]. I was so scared I couldn't even throw the ball hard. I got it over the plate now and then, but that was about it. I remember the final score. They beat us 14-0 [laughs]. Of course, the runs didn't *all* come off me. That's when the Dodgers had Robinson, Campanella, Snider—all of them.

I did better in '57 [1-1, 2.89], and I remember the last game we played, against Pittsburgh. We lost. There weren't a lot of people

Joe Shipley (SF Giants)

there [11,606]. But when the game was over, it was quite a sight. There were tears, and people came out of the stands. They were ripping up seats for souvenirs, and chasing the players. The clubhouse was in centefield, behind the flagpole out there. They were grabbing caps, clothes, everything they could get their hands on. It was quite an experience.

I was happy to go out to San Francisco. Things weren't too good for us in New York anymore. New York fans can be unruly at times. But '58 turned out to be quite a year for me. I started in San Francisco, but a month or two later they sold me to Cleveland on a waiver deal. I was with Cleveland for a month or two, then they sold me to Washington. I was the only left-hander they had in Washington, and I warmed up every day [laughs]. I didn't pitch much but I was always in the bullpen warming up [laughs].

Anyway, I went to play winter ball in Cuba that year, and that's when Castro took over. And I suffered a nervous breakdown down there. I was out of baseball for—well, I tried to get back, but when I left Cuba I caught the wrong plane and ended up in Mexico. A relative had to come and get me. He brought me back, and I tried to go back to spring training with Washington, but I wasn't in shape. I had to be brought home. I didn't go back until '62. My father was manic depressive. It *is* inherited. So that hit me, but it was through heavy stress I was under down in Cuba, after the whole year I had, being with three different teams. Then, going down there, and Castro taking over, and people disappearing. Things like that. I had quite a breakdown.

I came back with Toronto in triple-A in '62, and had the best year I ever had. I was 16-4, playing for Charlie Dressen, and Milwaukee bought my contract at the end of the season. My first game with the Braves was actually my first major league start. It was in Pittsburgh, and Bob Uecker was the catcher. He was an excellent catcher. In fact, Milwaukee had three catchers at the time—Del Crandall, Joe Torre and Bob Uecker. Pretty good staff [laughs]. But Uecker, I think, was probably the best receiver of them all. And he caught the game. I remember I was pitching against a guy I pitched against that year in the International League—Tommie Sisk. He was pitching a pretty good ballgame, too, and it was scoreless in the seventh inning when Mathews came up to me. He called me by my nickname and said, "Sheriff, you think one run will do it?" [laughs] I

Jim Constable (SF Giants)

said, "I don't know." [laughs] He went up and *bunted.* And for Mathews to push a bunt, that's very unusual. Aaron came up after the bunt and hit one out of the park. That was the only scoring in the game. I struck out Clemente twice. In fact, I struck him out to end the game.

Then, I pitched against the Pirates again when they came to County Stadium. That was my *other* major league start. Bob Veale pitched against me, and he had a no-hitter through six innings. I gave up a home run to Clendenon with two men on. I came out, and the game ended up something like 7-3. So, I had two pretty good starts, and thought I had turned the corner. I actually did.

I pitched winter ball again in '62. For one thing, I had to have some money [laughs]. Back then, it wasn't like it is today. The *most* I ever made was $7500. But the Braves changed managers in the off-season. Birdie Tebbetts left, and Bobbie Bragan came in. And Bragan decided to cut me in spring training. So the Giants picked me up again. Dark was managing, and I was with them just a short while. I remember one game I pitched in. He brought me in to pitch to Mathews, and I walked him on a three-two pitch. I think that's the last time I was ever used in the major leagues. I went back to Tacoma in the Coast League for two years after that, and then I retired.

After baseball, I worked with Magnavox for 15 years, and I taught for about 11 years. Then, I had to retire on disability because I had a series of heart attacks, and bypass surgery. So I'm living on retirement now.

Jonesboro, Tennessee

BILL WHITE

Bill White slammed 22 home runs as a rookie first baseman with the New York Giants in 1956, including one in his first major league at-bat, but when the '58 Giants first took the field at Seals Stadium in April, White was in his second year of military service at Fort Knox, Kentucky. By the time he rejoined the Giants in July, Orlando Cepeda was firmly entrenched at first, and White was looking forward to playing for another team.

He got his wish March 25, 1959, when he was traded with Ray Jablonski to the St. Louis Cardinals for Sad Sam Jones. Sad Sam paid immediate dividends, winning a league-high 21 games for the Giants in '59, and 18 more in '60. But while Jones won only 12 games the next four years, before retiring, White emerged as one of the best first basemen in baseball over the next eight seasons. He made the National League All-Star team five times, hit over .300 four times, hit 20 or more home runs seven times and drove in 100+ runs four times. He also was a member of the World Series-champion Cardinals in 1964. Over a 13-year big league career, Bill hit 202 homers, stole 103 bases, batted .286 and won seven Gold Gloves.

White later spent 18 years as a radio/TV play-by-play announcer for the New York Yankees. Long respected in and out of the game as a proud and articulate man, White was then named National League President by Bart Giamatti, who was about to leave the same position to be baseball's new commissioner. In his five years in office, Bill White had many accomplishments, but the one that Giants fans will be forever grateful for was his role in keeping the Giants out of Tampa Bay, and in San Francisco. For

that, all Giants fans should maintain a special place in their hearts for Bill White.

White has five children, is retired and makes his home in Upper Black Eddy, Pennsylvania.

I WAS BORN in Lakewood, Florida, three miles from the Alabama border, but moved to Ohio about the time I started to crawl. I think I was a year old when we first moved up there. We came back to Florida, but then went up permanently when I was three. That part I don't remember much about. It was not a good time in my life. It was in the South. It was in the rural South. It was red-dirt South. No paved roads. Outside toilets.

My family were sharecroppers in Florida, and wanted to do well. And so we moved to Warren, Ohio, which was a steel mill area. And, little by little, the whole family would come up. All six boys and three girls in the family. My grandmother, my mother and her two sisters, and my six uncles all settled there. The men all worked in the steel mills. There was only subtle prejudice there but we lived in an integrated neighborhood. The only two things I remember are that we could swim in the municipal public pool only on Mondays, and we had to sit upstairs in some of the movie houses. As a child you accepted those things, I suppose. You're young, and you just do it and go on. But where we lived on the West side was totally integrated. In fact, the whole city was integrated, except the East side where most of the people with money lived.

My grandmother was a great influence on me as a child. She was very religious. We would go to church maybe five to seven times a week, including maybe three times on Sunday. She didn't want us out there fighting and stealing, or whatever it was that kids did. I didn't *want* to go, but she was strong enough that I followed her, and that kept me out of trouble. And she gave me a lot of pride in being black. I always said she was the first Muslim. I remember her lecturing me on how brave and strong we were in Africa, how we were brought out of Africa and segregated, how two people from the same tribe were not allowed to be together, how we were denied an education and became susceptible to the diseases in this country, which she said were brought on by white people. She gave me a different way of looking at things.

I was a decent student in school, and I'd go to church regularly, and I was told to turn the other cheek, but this older boy would always chase me home. He was tough, and bigger than I was. Finally, one day, I had enough of it. We tussled and fought for—I don't know—it seemed to me to be *hours*. He finally beat me, but he didn't bother me anymore. He found out that it was going to take him a long time to beat me, and that he was going to hurt, too. And that made an impression on me. He could have beat me again, but it was going to take him a while. I don't think he wanted to do that. He had more fun just chasing me home. That taught me a lesson, never to be afraid to face adversity.

I played basketball, football and baseball in high school and in college, and I wasn't very good in *any* of them. I had a scholarship to play football at Western Reserve [University], which was then separate from Case. It's Case Western Reserve now. But I decided not to take it, and went to Hiram College instead. Hiram was about 30 miles from home. I was going to study medicine there. My buddy and I were both pre-med students. He finished. I didn't. I'm jealous of him, and he's jealous of me.

Bill White (Dick Dobbins)

I think it might have been that first summer, after my freshman year, playing in an 18-and-under tournament in Cincinnati—I had a fairly decent tournament—that's when I signed with the Giants. Three teams wanted to sign me—the Giants, Cleveland and the Chicago Cubs. Cleveland, obviously, offered the most money. But they had Luke Easter there, and I didn't know how old Luke was at the time. I thought he'd be around for a while [his big league career ended in '54]. He was hitting a lot of long home runs. Chicago,

for some reason, was last on my list. It seems to me, in the back of my mind, that I hadn't read positive things about Chicago and the Cubs. I'm not sure that's true, but that seems to be in the back of my mind. I also knew the Giants had no first baseman. They were using Whitey Lockman, so I figured there was an opportunity there.

Part of my bonus agreement was that the Giants would take me to spring training. But that [spring training] showed me I didn't belong there. I couldn't hit curveballs, I couldn't hit change-ups. The only pitch I could hit was a straight fastball. I couldn't pick a ball up. I couldn't field. The Giants sent me to Danville, in the [class-B] Carolina League. I was the only black player, not just on the team, but in the entire league. They [major league organizations] had no foresight about any of those things. On the other hand, when I got through that—if I got through that successfully—I could get through anything. Of course, they weren't thinking that way because, even after you got there, they made no special arrangements to help you get through a situation like that. I didn't get to stay with my teammates, even in Danville itself. Nor did I even see them in Danville. The only place I saw members of the team would be at the ballpark. I stayed with a black minister.

I had problems with fans all season, especially those fans on the road, but never had a problem with the players. And I didn't have many problems in Danville with fans yelling at me because I was on their team. When people [elsewhere] would yell things at me, I'd just look at them and see who they were. But there was no point in yelling back. I had one incident in

Burlington, North Carolina, I think, where I gave them the finger, and we had a little problem there. But, for the most part, *looking* at them shut them up. If you could find them. Most of the players simply went their own way. I probably got more verbal support directly and indirectly from many of my Southern teammates. I don't think the Northern kids wanted to be involved at all in that. A lot of it may have shocked them. Maybe it didn't. But I got more support like, "Hang in there," or "That guy's nuts," or "Don't listen to him," from Southerners. Even guys on the opposing teams. That surprised me a bit, yeah. *[author's note: White didn't forget. More than 35 years later, he returned to Burlington to campaign for former catcher Charlie Allen, who had given him support in those lonely days, and now was running for sheriff.]*

I asked the Giants to send me up north, to [class-C] St. Cloud, where Dave Garcia was managing. But they said no. And, as I said, I just got through it. And if I could get through that, I could get through anything. Plus, I was hitting the ball [.298, 20HR, 84RBI].

I spent '54 at Sioux City [.319, 30HR, 92RBI] and '55 in Dallas [.295, 22HR, 93RBI]. I knew I had three pretty good years but I still didn't know what to expect in triple-A or the major leagues. I wasn't at Minneapolis [triple-A] long in '56 [.292, 3HR, 14RBI, 72AB] before I got called up with the Giants. Then I hit a home run my first time up [May 7], but I should have been called out on a two-two pitch. I started back to the dugout, and Lee Ballanfant called it a ball. And the next pitch—I guess the guy said, "I better throw it down the middle" [laughs]—I hit up on the roof. I think it was Ben Flowers. Was it a thrill? *No.* I don't know. You're numb the first time up. And the roof in St. Louis was only about 322 feet in right-center anyway.

I knew at the end of '56 I'd have to spend two years in the Army, at Fort Knox. I got married, we bought a trailer and lived off post about 10 or 20 miles away, in West Point, Kentucky, in an integrated trailer park. I played one year of ball there, then got out in late July [of '58]. The war in Beirut had started, and my MO was supply clerk. And a guy came to me and said, "You'd better get out of here for 30 days because they need supply clerks in Beirut." So I applied for, and got, a 30-day leave. I had used up all my leave but they gave it to me, and got me out, and I joined the Giants in Pittsburgh.

Of course, by then, Cepeda's a fixture at first base. Rookie of the Year. I played a little outfield and pinch hit. I remember when I called Rigney and told him I was back, he'd forgotten about me [laughs]. It was funny. I used to kid him about it. I said, "Bill, I'm here." I said, "Bill White." He said, "Who?" [laughs]

I wanted to play every day. They tried me in the outfield [late in the '58 season, and in '58 winter ball in the Dominican Republic], but I couldn't play the outfield. Maybe I could have played there with Willie's help, if he put me over in the corner, if he covered left-center. I was *not* a good outfielder. I could run the ball down but I couldn't throw it. I couldn't throw because I hurt my arm pitching as a kid in amateur baseball. So I just felt that in order to make a decent amount of change, with one child already, it would be best to go where I could play every day. So I asked to be traded. I don't think Stoneham wanted to keep me anyway. I was uppity [laughs]. I think Stoneham and the people who ran the Giants felt that way because I would hold out. I would say, "I don't have to play baseball," and I'd go back to school. I'd hold out by staying in school. I think I left the Danville team in the playoffs, so I could get back in school. Baseball was not everything. It was there, and I played it. But I wanted to get an education. So I'd leave whenever I had to get back in school. Plus, I didn't take shit.

Even though I wanted to get traded, I was not pleased with the deal [sent to St. Louis with Ray Jablonski, in March of '59, for Sam Jones]. I didn't want to go to St. Louis because of the problems black players had had there, the problems black *people* had had. It was the Southern most city in baseball when I was there, and it was probably the most segregated. I didn't want to go there. I wasn't happy about going to St. Louis, but at least I had the chance there to get out and play. And when Bing Devine [general manager] was there, the organization treated me *super.* Super-well.

For example, I had difficulty buying a home for my family in St. Louis, in the neighborhood I wanted to live in. The Cardinals and KMOX Radio helped me [White had a weekly five-minute sports show on KMOX], and Al Fleishman helped as well [the head of Fleishman-Hilliard, which did PR for the Busch Brewery]. And I had no problems there. My family was treated well in St. Louis. They were treated well by their neighbors, out in Des Peres, where we lived. There was tension initially. Cops would come by every hour, until I walked out and said, "I don't think you have to do this." And after a couple of days, they stopped.

When I joined the Cardinals, their spring training facilities in St. Petersburg were segregated. *[author's note: White players stayed in a nice hotel with nice restaurants, while blacks stayed in a black section of town; by '62, all Cardinal players stayed in the plush Outrigger Inn, on the bay, and ate together in a private restaurant, thanks in part to the outspoken efforts of men like Bill White.]* My involvement in changing that started innocently enough with an invitation to a yacht club breakfast, which was an annual breakfast that the St. Petersburg Yacht Club gave for the Cardinals. I heard going down there the year before that a black dentist who had a yacht was denied access. He was denied dockage there, and membership. So when this invitation went up [for the players], and remembering what had happened in the past, and feeling that, jeez, black people were paying taxes while this exclusive club was renting the best piece of property on the shoreline for a dollar a year, or whatever, I just decided that I'd say something about it. And I just said, "It's unfortunate that they're having a segregated breakfast, and not inviting the total spectrum of players," knowing that they wouldn't invite blacks anyway.

That started baseball integration in spring training, because the story went all across the country. I think Joe Reichler worked with UPI then, and he was the only writer who would write it. None of the other writers had guts enough to write it. And he wrote it. It went across the country, people threatened to boycott Busch beer in St. Louis, and I think that [Cards owner Augie] Busch decided, "We don't need that." So they did something about integrating the team [facility] in St. Petersburg. And Bing Devine had a great hand in it. He just said to me, "You know, I never really realized this. I thought you guys were happy." And Al Fleishman also helped.

The thing was to make them aware of the problem. When they first got there [St. Petersburg], that's the way it was. I think Bing told me, "Bill, if you look around this stadium here, we don't have separate facilities for people." Most of the parks in Florida had colored and white [rest rooms]. I don't believe they had that in St. Petersburg.

For the most part, I got support from my teammates when I spoke out. Some of the more conservative white guys would *joke,* but they would not be serious. Somebody might say, "Hey, come on over to my house. I'll serve you breakfast." Or, "Come room with me." But there wasn't a lack of support from whites. And, obviously, some of the black guys would rather have stayed apart. You know, you get a couple of bucks extra, there's no curfew, you can sort of do whatever you want to do. I just felt I wanted a *choice.* When I was with the Cardinals, I used to drive to St. Petersburg from St. Louis, and there's a place in Chattanooga called Rose's where I stayed. It's a black hotel. And once, after they integrated the South, I went through [Chattanooga] the next year and said to a cop, "Where Rose's?" And he said, "You don't have to stay there anymore." And I said, "I choose to stay there. All I want is a *choice."* He wanted me to stay at the Holiday Inn. I said, "Well, I choose to stay at Rose's."

I had several good years in St. Louis. My first All-Star Game [in '59] was a thrill, because it was my first time. I had just been traded by the Giants. And the All-Star Game in San Francisco stands out, when we came from behind to beat the American League in the 10th. I remember Mays and Clemente drove in the tying and winning runs. If I had to pick one year that stands out, I guess it would be '64, when we won the World Series [in seven games, over the Yankees]. Winning the Series was something special. Just *playing* in it was. A lot of great ballplayers never got a chance to do that. And *winning* it was a big plus. Icing on the cake. I didn't do anything that Series [3-for-27 w/2RBI], but that was a big highlight.

You asked about Curt Flood [one of White's teammates]. First of all, he was an excellent ballplayer. And secondly, he was different from the rest of us. He was just *different.* We were jocks, sort of. We were a little more rough-honed than Flood. We're swearing, we're reading *The Sporting News,* trying to play the harmonica, painting by the numbers. And he's reading novels, he's playing the guitar, he's painting portraits. He was just different from the rest of us. We were not especially close. He and [Bob] Gibson were close. They roomed together. I mean, we were close in the sense that all black players were close back then, even on opposing teams. We helped each other.

It was a courageous fight that Curt Flood fought [challenging baseball's reserve clause], but at the time he was traded [to Philadelphia, after the '69 season], while I appreciated what he was *trying* to do, I thought for him to do it at that time might have been a mistake. Looking back, it obviously was a mistake. It *destroyed* him. I think it destroyed both his career *and* him. I think it brought him down, too. Yeah, I do. Mentally, it hurt him pretty much. He did what he had to do. I can't second-guess what he did. I supported him in what he did. But at that time, I'm just not sure I would have done the same thing.

I was traded to Philadelphia myself [in '65, with Dick Groat and Bob Uecker, for Art Mahaffey, Alex Johnson and Pat Corrales]. I didn't want to come here. I think the reason Bob Howsam [general manager] sent me here was because I didn't like him. I didn't care much for Howsam [Bing Devine's successor]. He probably sent me here to punish me. And yet, I got here, and I've lived here since then. I've made many friends here. I've worked in radio and television here. And I declined an offer to go back to St. Louis in the '70s to broadcast, to stay here.

I spent three seasons with the Phillies. Dick Allen was one of my teammates. When you got him between the lines, he was one of the toughest, husslingest players you'll be around. He tried hard and gave you a hundred percent all the time. Then I played my final season back in St. Louis in '69. Bing had come back. He brought me back [in exchange for Jerry Buchek and Jim Hutto]. And he wanted me to go manage [triple-A] Tulsa, and then possibly manage the Cardinals. But I didn't want to manage.

After baseball, I broadcast the six and 11 o'clock sports here [in Philadelphia] for a while before going up to New York in '71 to do the Yankees [radio and TV]. I did that for 18 years, with Phil Rizzuto and Frank Messer. It was fun for a while, but it gets boring. After so many years, you're saying the same thing all the time. But I was fortunate enough to do the Series [in '77, '78 & '81]. And I'm probably the only guy that ever did the Series on national radio *and* television. I put my yellow jacket on and opened for ABC [television], and then took that off and put a blue jacket on for CBS Radio. So those are goals that it's nice to meet, but after you do that a couple of years, you're saying the same thing.

From there, I spent five years as National League president. I think the league was looking for a black guy to be president. They had 10 candidates, and then it got down to two. And somehow, my understanding is that a search committee determined that one of the two had no experience in baseball at all, and they decided to call someone else. So O'Malley called me one day and asked if I'd come up and interview. I said, "You're nuts. I don't want to work every day." I was only working 60 days a year or so by then, broadcasting. But he called back, and I talked to some people, and they said, "It doesn't hurt to go interview." So I went up to the Waldorf, and was interviewed by the search committee. Then I went out to St. Louis for a banquet honoring Fleishman, and they called me and asked if I'd take the job. I said, "Yeah, I'll take it." Obviously, I had thought about it and had talked to people about the historical significance of it, and whether I could do it. And I took it, yeah. Plus, one of the reasons I took it was I had dinner with Bart Giamatti, and he just said that he thought I should do it, that he was available to me for the next three or four months until he took over as commissioner, and that it would be a good thing. He was *more* than helpful. I lived with him for three months, almost every day. He'd take a step, I'd take a step. He was a good man. And he loved the game.

What did I accomplish on the job? I think that first of all, we guided the National League into the right two cities, in Denver, with the Colorado Rockies, and in Miami, with the Florida Marlins. I think that some people in the American League had promised Tampa a team, and that's where they wanted us to go, because they had promised Tampa a team. But I didn't think that Tampa-St. Petersburg was the place to go. So, as president of the league, I chose the expansion committee, and I double-checked on everything we did. And I think I was very responsible for where we went.

Obviously, keeping the Giants in San Francisco [was another accomplishment]. Everybody was wringing their hands, trying to figure out how in the hell to do it. And I think, for the most part, I just said, "I'll do it." Of course, I called our executive council together before I did it, and told them what I planned to do, and they gave me the OK. I went out and talked to Bob Lurie. And I think we got it done without too many lawsuits.

In my opinion, Tampa-St. Pete is a place with older, retired people. I wondered whether or not they could afford to buy the tickets. Getting to Tampa-St. Petersburg is tough. You've got to go over bridges. There's not much parking in that area. And I just felt we had two better sites [for expansion], and obviously it was true. As for the Giants, Bob did not have permission to move to Tampa. He had permission [only] to go out and look at sites. Now, he had made an agreement to sell. But what I'm saying is that he was given permission only to go out—in fact, I helped him. I gave him the proposals that we had. From the 10 possible expansion sites, I think he wanted to look at Washington, Tampa-St. Pete, Orlando I believe, and he may have wanted to look at Charlotte. And maybe even Sacramento. So I made those proposals available to him to look at. But, only assuming he ever would get permission from the commissioner or the other owners, then he could make his decision [he never got that permission]. But I *stopped* it. It was that simple. [author's note: Lurie reached an agreement, in principle, to sell the Giants to a Tampa-St. Pete group, but the deal was voted down by National League owners.] I think there was a strong feeling in baseball that the Giants moving to Tampa was not good for baseball. Not just in my office.

Did I hear from the people of Tampa-St. Pete [after the deal was blocked]? Yep. Much of it was racial. I've kept the letters. I got all kinds of letters. Many letters. I would say 99 and $^{99}/_{100}$ were negative. And probably 10 to 20 percent had some racial overtones to them. I don't know if that surprised me, but I would say it didn't *bother* me.

I went down there the next year [in '93]. Hell, if I can go down there in the early 60s when we fought to integrate, and I had to go out and play, I think I can go down there in the nineties.

I also increased pensions of some of our umpires' widows as much as 300 to 350 percent while I was there. And we changed some of our attitudes toward umpires, in terms of saying, "Hey, let's get along with the players. Respect them, and I hope the players would respect you. And I don't think you ought to yell and scream at the players, then throw them out." Is it better then, now? *No.* I was moving toward that point. And I really attempted to lower the influence of crew chiefs. I think we moved that way a little bit while I was there. I just think crew chiefs have too much influence on their crews, and also on young umpires.

I have sympathy for the two young umpires who crossed the [striking umps'] picket line [and have been ostracized ever since]. I couldn't have crossed the line but, yeah, I do. First of all,

you've got to understand that it's hard for umpires to retire. Even when they're burned out, you can't fire them. At one point you could let an umpire go at 55. You can't do that anymore because of age-discrimination laws. They have a tough job. No matter what they call, someone's going to yell at them. And they're on the road all the time. It's not an easy job, but I think it can be made easier by being a lot less confrontational. I told them, "Look, you don't have to take anything from the players. Throw them out. But don't *instigate* arguments and then throw them out." I always wanted them to make a call and walk away, instead of staying in the player's face. But I never could get them to do that, for the most part. They always thought I was on the players' side. But that didn't make any difference to me. I had a job to do, and I did it as best I could.

The biggest frustration I had with the job was in the lack of progress in baseball in hiring minorities. I would never go out and say, "You've *got* to hire minorities," because I understand that you've already got your people, and they're good people, and you can't just fire people to hire people. But I felt that for the most part, minority hiring at the administrative level didn't go that well. What I'm talking about basically is scouts, telephone operators, CFOs and whatever else. I felt if I would do a good job, they would assume that someone else could do a good job. But I don't think that happened. I was happy during my tenure, though, that Dusty Baker was hired, that Don Baylor was hired, that Felipe Alou was hired, and that Bob Watson was hired. I was glad they were hired because, before they were hired, the owner would call me. Broschu [Expos owner Claude] calls and says, "I just want to let you know, I'm hiring Alou." And McMorris in Denver, and Magowan in San Francisco. I don't take credit for that but I think if I had been a poor administrator, they may have had second thoughts about doing that.

I don't watch baseball much at all anymore. I just don't think you'll find that anyone who has played a sport will watch it much. I still *care* about the game. Oh, yeah. Whatever I've gotten, baseball's been responsible for it, although I could have done something else. But, jeez, I played it since I was 14, and made a good living at it. I am concerned about the current state of the game, in terms of concern about new ownership. I don't think many of them really know, or really *love* the game. I think many of the new owners have gotten in it for, number one, to become a little better known; and, number two, to try to figure out how they can use baseball to increase the visibility of their companies. Baseball has got to a point now, from a financial point of view with the union being extremely strong, that these new owners become disillusioned quickly. I think part of the problem we had in '95 [and '94] was these new owners felt they could break the union. I told them [laughs], "You can't do that. They're a little bit too tough. Players are used to confrontations every day." And I think that attitude is brought on because you've got an influx of new owners. They've got a lot of money, and could lower it over *their* unions, maybe. But this is a different kind of union.

I'm retired now. I have five kids. Two of them are married. They're all college graduates, except one. Baseball is a way to make a living. Unfortunately, you're on the road all the time, and your wife has to really raise the children. But I'm so proud that since I didn't finish college, four of my five *have* finished, and the one that hasn't is probably the smartest. And she only needs a few hours to finish. Every time I see her I try to get her to go back.

I taught my children, first of all, that if they worked hard enough, they can do anything they want to do. And I think that was the most important thing I did [as a father], that I don't want any excuses. I don't want any racial excuses, or whatever. Just work your butt off. Outwork everybody. And then secondly, I taught them, don't take crap from anybody. I taught them to be open, but if there is hate in their path, they have to react to it extremely strong. When it happens, you have to be extremely strong in your reaction. When I took the job as league president, somebody asked my daughter about it. I had told my kids not to say anything to anybody, but someone got to her, and she said, "My dad said that you can do anything you want to do if you work hard enough." She's right.

Upper Black Eddy, Pennsylvania

JOHN ANTONELLI

One of baseball's original bonus babies, Johnny Antonelli signed with the Boston Braves for a reported $65,000 right out of high school in 1948, after striking out 278 hitters in 129 innings of American Legion ball. He pitched in four games for the Braves that summer, before becoming a spot starter in '49 at the age of 19. After two years in the Army, and following the '53 season in Milwaukee, Antonelli was traded to the Giants in a six-player deal that sent Bobby Thomson to the Braves. It was a trade that infuriated many New Yorkers, given Thomson's immense popularity, but Johnny quickly won over the critics. He won 21 games, led the league in earned run average at 2.29, in winning percentage at .750, in shutouts with six and in opposition batting at .219. He was named to the National League All-Star team, and then climaxed his dream season by winning the second game of the 1954 World Series against Cleveland, and then saving the clincher, in the Giants' four-game sweep. Not surprisingly, Antonelli was named The Sporting News' *National League Pitcher of the Year.*

Johnny won 20 games in 1956, and again represented the Giants on the National League All-Star team, throwing four scoreless innings in the NL's 7-3 win at Griffith Stadium, in Washington D.C.

When the Giants moved to San Francisco, Antonelli was a team leader both on and off the field. In addition to being the staff ace, he also was the club's player representative and one of the game's most intense competitors. Antonelli proceeded to lead the '58 Giants in wins with 16, won 19 in '59, made the National League All-Star team both years, and threw a league-high four shutouts in '59 as well. In a six year stretch, in fact, from '54 through '59, Johnny averaged 17 wins a season, and was named to five National League All-Star teams.

It was ironic that Antonelli was the Giants' best pitcher in '58 and '59, because he was also the team's most vocal critic of Seals Stadium, never a friendly ballpark to left-handed pitchers. Unfortunately, his criticism of a beloved ballpark in a proud and provincial city such as San Francisco led to a barrage of diatribes against him from the local press, and that in turn led to him being traded, with Willie Kirkland, to Cleveland in December of '60, in exchange for Harvey Kuenn. It also led to a premature retirement from baseball after Antonelli pitched just 59 innings in '61, was sold to the Mets and then chose not to report. His baseball career was over at age 31, with 126 career wins, an ERA of 3.34 and, as one of the game's better-hitting pitchers, 121 career base hits. That included a career-high 19 hits in 1958, during which he batted .226 for the Giants, and blasted the first home run hit by a big league pitcher at Seals Stadium, August 19, off the Reds' Bob Purkey.

Known as Johnny only at the ballpark, but not in his family life, John ran the very successful Antonelli Tire business in his hometown of Rochester for some 40 years, before retiring in 1994. He and his wife now split their time between two homes, one in Rochester and one in Vero Beach, Florida. They have four children and nine grandchildren.

John Antonelli (SF Giants)

I WAS NOT REALLY EXCITED

about the move to San Francisco. I don't think any of the players were really happy about it because we liked New York. And I was certainly very happy at the Polo Grounds because I had great success there. You know, once you feel comfortable at home, it's hard to make that move. But I guess it had to be, and we made the most of it. We liked San Francisco. We liked it a lot. We enjoyed the city, enjoyed the fans and the people in general. I had a few little problems out there but, other than that, I think all in all we really enjoyed making the move, *after* it happened. I think when it was first reported it was like a big shock happening to our lives, and a big void at the point we left New York. But once we got out there it was great.

Seals Stadium was not particularly friendly to left-handed pitchers, primarily because of the wind. Of course, the wind has *always* been a factor in San Francisco. Not only is it difficult to pitch in, in terms of balls flying out of the ballpark, but it's difficult staying loose. But I guess everybody playing there has the same problems, so we're all in the same boat. And, really, everything was great in San Francisco until this article came out in the newspaper after we played the Dodgers [July 20, 1959]. I think we were leading the league at the time [by 2½ games]. I was pitching against Drysdale that day

and, of course, everybody shuddered when they had to face Drysdale. So we knew we weren't going to get many runs, and we had to hold them. And in the ninth inning [of a tie game] there was a flyball that Charlie Neal hit out to short left. Daryl Spencer, our shortstop, yelled, "I got it." Jackie Brandt, our left fielder, started coming in to say, "I got it." And before you knew it, Brandt started running back and it went over the fence for a home run. And we got beat 3-2.

As we came into the clubhouse we were very upset about losing the ballgame, and the way we lost it. And a sportswriter who, I understand now, was barred from the San Francisco locker room because he did nothing but write things that caused problems, said to me as I walked in the door, "What was that pitch that Neal pummeled off you?" And I guess [laughs], after having lost a tough game [despite a four-hitter], and losing to a team that we hated to lose to, it just got to me. So I threw him out of the clubhouse. And before I knew it, he sent a cameraman in to take pictures of the "bad guy" while I was shaving. Then I asked *him* to leave. And the story got blown way out of proportion.

It was so ridiculous because the statement that I made to this writer was that they could take the ballpark and do something with it. I didn't say anything about the San Francisco weather, or San Francisco in general. I just said that they could take the ballpark and .... And then it came out in the paper that I was against San Francisco. Then, of course, the people took offense to that. And, you know, you just don't do that in San Francisco. Or *anywhere,* but certainly not in San Francisco. Consequently, I think there was a big misunderstanding. Khrushchev came into San Francisco that weekend, and I got two-inch headlines, while he got one inch. I think that was kind of ridiculous. *[author's note: San Francisco newspaper headlines read: ANTONELLI RIPS S.F. BALLPARK and ANTONELLI CRIES PARK COST GAME, and the* San Francisco Chronicle *suggested in a news editorial July 22 that the city didn't need any crybabies, that Horace Stoneham should hang a pacifier in the clubhouse, and that if Antonelli didn't like it there he could go back where he came from; the next day all 14 letters to the editor in the news section of the* Chronicle *concerned the editorial on Antonelli—half in support, half against. One, in particular, read: "It seems to me that the losing pitcher ought to be allowed to blow off steam in the locker room without being jumped on ..."]*

To top it all off, I had some friends like Russ Hodges, and he said, "I'd like to interview you. We've got to get this thing stopped." So I went on [KSFO] and apologized for anything that I may have said or did with this incident. And the next morning, I had headlines again. *Antonelli apologizing on radio is like an ant attacking an elephant.* I can almost remember verbatim what was in the paper. So the apology didn't do any good. The newspaper—the old green sheet—is that the *Chronicle?* Yup, they just wouldn't let it die. One writer came up to me and apologized and said, "Look, I have to write these articles because I've been told it's a story." And I said, "Hey, do what you have to do. Forget it." But he did come up to me and apologize for what he had to do. It was just one of those unfortunate things. *[author's note: The* San Francisco Examiner *joined in the anti-Antonelli chorus, ripping the lefty for criticizing "our lifegiving summer breeze, the sweet wind that sweeps San Francisco clean each morning, the tangy wind that puts a joyous spring in every step and soothes every fevered brow . . ."]*

Unfortunately, I think it ruined my desire to continue pitching in the Bay Area. I had 14 wins at the time [14-5], and never did win 20 [finishing 19-10]. I never pitched effectively after that. I think the whole thing knocked the wind out of my sails. And the team's, too. I think the whole situation affected everyone. I think it's very possible the whole controversy hurt the team's chances of winning the pennant that year. Because you just don't blow a lead like we had. If you go back a few weeks before the season ended, we had a seven or eight game lead. Then we led the Dodgers by two games in late September, with eight to play, but blew it. And the Dodgers beat us out for the pennant.

Other than that, though, I loved San Francisco. My wife did, too. In fact, people would ask me where we'd live if we had the choice, if I had not been in business in Rochester, and I'd say, "Well, my first choice would be San Francisco." Or the Bay Area, I should say. Maybe not San Francisco proper. We lived in San Mateo, Redwood City and then down toward Palo Alto one year. And we just felt that it was an excellent, excellent area to live in. Unfortunately, I was in business here. Or fortunately [laughs], whichever way you want to look at it. I was in business and *had* to come home. My second choice probably would have been the Boston area. My wife is from the Boston area. But, of course, we're here in Rochester and we like this, too.

But I tell you, I think that whole incident kind of soured me. I was never one for traveling. I probably, having a business to fall back on, thought I was in position to do what I did [retiring from baseball at age 31]. But I think the whole situation kind of got to me in San Francisco. Because I felt I was a winning pitcher. I had 19 wins. I had a pretty good year for the Giants. And when I went in one day to talk to Chub Feeney, our general manager, I said, "You know, Chub, we're fighting for a pennant here. But I haven't heard a word from this office, not that I have to ask. I shouldn't have to ask, but don't you think a little word of confidence or something would maybe get these guys off my back?" Because this went on for days. It wasn't just a one-day thing. And he said, "Well, if I come to your aid they may get on us." I said, "Well, in that case you better take the rest of my starts because I don't think I'm going to be pitching for this team anymore."

That was really the end of it. I guess I just lost interest in playing the game. It's amazing.

Maybe a little childish, too, but that's how it is. When you give your all to the game, and something like that happens ... maybe if I had it to do over again I wouldn't [retire]. But I didn't even want to pitch the last day of the season [a doubleheader in St. Louis], when I could have won my twentieth. When you're hurt, you're hurt. I just lost the incentive to be out there. [author's note: There were seven more letters to the editor in the news section of the Chronicle July 29 related to the Antonelli story, and all seven were in support of the Giants' lefty—one prophetic letter, in particular, read: "What can possibly be gained by undue criticism of our number one pitcher? Ultimately, the blame must rest on the city's sportswriters if this incident affects the play of Antonelli and the rest of the team."]

YES, IT'S TRUE. I was one of the original bonus babies. In 1948 I was pitching for my high school team here in Rochester, while my father was very active in spring training. He used to go down to Florida every year and watch spring training. He loved baseball. And one year he brought some scrapbooks of mine to show off his son to whoever would listen. So I guess they all heard enough from him and said, "If he's so good, why don't you arrange a game, and we'll send some scouts up." So something like 13 scouts came to Rochester and they set up a game at Red Wing Stadium, our triple-A stadium here. Thirteen of the 16 major league teams were represented in the stands, watching this game between a high school All-Star team and a local semi-pro team. I hadn't pitched for a little over three weeks, as we were into our final exams for our senior year. But they said, "Well, we have to see this kid pitch. If you think he's so good, before we give any money, we want to see if he can throw. Even if he only throws three innings."

So I started, and I pitched three innings. And they started to warm up another pitcher. And the scouts said, "Oh, no, no, no, no. Let's see if he can go five." So I went five. Then I went seven. Now, that's all we ever played in high school. I never went more than seven innings in my life. So they said, "Well, look, let's see if he can go nine." Well, I went nine innings. I struck out 17 of those semi-pro men. I threw a no-hitter [laughs], which I probably could never have done again in my lifetime, particularly under the circumstances. I was just young enough not to be overcome by it all.

The next day they all came in, one by one, and made their offers to my father. I had just

turned 18 years old, and you had to be 21 to make this kind of decision. So my dad accepted the Braves' offer, which wasn't the largest offer I received. But that's the one my father chose. Lou Perini [Braves' owner] was in the contracting business, and my father was a contractor of his own. And Perini being Italian, I would say that had something to do with it. That's how I ended up a member of the Boston Braves in 1948.

I think I threw a grand slam home run to Andy Seminick of the Phillies in my first major league game. I came in to relieve after throwing 30 minutes of batting practice because we were being slaughtered. Billy Southworth [manager] said, "Can you pitch an inning?" And I said, "Why not?" I was only 18 years old. I pitched only four innings that year after signing. You hate to throw a grand slam your first inning in the major leagues [laughs] but the point is, I had just thrown 30 minutes of batting practice and I probably was a little tired. But maybe that woke me up a little.

We like to tell a lot of trivia at our golf club here in Rochester, and one day I said, "I've got a trivia question. What was the youngest battery ever to win a major league ballgame?" So, of course, the guys all said Joe Nuxhall and whoever was his catcher. They were jumping around all over the place on that one. And I said, "No, no, no." They couldn't figure out who it was. So finally I said, "Del Crandall and John Antonelli." They looked at me and said, "You're kidding." I said, "No, that's true." In 1949. He was 19 and I was 19. He was born in March of 1930 and I was born in April. We were both just over 19 years of age, and beat the Cubs 2-0 against Dutch Leonard, who was 42 years old [laughs]. He was older than we were *combined.* I threw 89 pitches and he threw 86 pitches, in the whole ballgame [laughs]. I think the game was over in about an hour and 30 minutes. The next time I got a start was six weeks later. The next time I got in a *ballgame* was six weeks later.

Del Crandall and I were known as "The Milkshake Twins," because neither one of us drank. In fact, I didn't think an athlete would ever drink or smoke. We got that nickname in 1953 when we were both 23 years old. And we were *still* drinking milkshakes. I liked strawberry. He liked *anything.* He'd drink two quarts of milk at a dinner. He was a big milk drinker [laughs].

I didn't get to pitch a lot with the Braves in '49 and '50. Then I spent '51 and '52 in the Army, at Ft. Meyer, Virginia, and got to pitch a lot more. I brag about that only because we did so well as a team. And we played against everyone in the country, at different tournaments. We had Sam Calderone catching—a third-string catcher with the Giants. We had Danny O'Connell playing shortstop—a very good ballplayer, I think. And those were the only major-leaguers we had on our ball club. And since we won the MDW [the Military District of Washington Tournament], we were invited to Kansas City to play in the all-service *whatever.* They had the Navy, the Army, the Marines, the Air Force—everybody had a team out there. We played against all these teams. Fort Monmouth had Whitey Ford and Harvey Haddix and, my God, you look at the rosters and they all had pretty good ballplayers. But we played 29 playoff games that year in Kansas City, and in both Hawaii and Japan, and we won all 29. 29-0. I thought that was a pretty good record for a team that probably didn't have an average of maybe A-level ballplayers, among the nine that played. We probably didn't average better than a class-A ball club.

Willie Mays came in and played for Ft. Eustis, and that's the first time I faced him. And he may have been one of the reasons—I don't *know* this—that the Giants traded for me. Maybe he was [laughs] or wasn't impressed, I don't know. But the point is, I ended up going to the Giants right after the '53 season.

I never lost a game in the army [42-0 in two years], and then went to Milwaukee [in '53], straight into the starting rotation, making $5,500 a year. But first I went in to get a raise, because by now I'm married, I have a child coming, and I didn't know if I could make ends meet on $5500. So I went up and asked for a raise, and they said, "Well, what have you done the last two years? You haven't been around." I said, "Well, I was 42-and-zip in the army. Even if I worked in the WBA, I think after a couple of years like that they'd give me a few dollars raise." Well, they gave me a $500 raise [laughs], so I got to $6000. That was it. I won 12 and lost 12 that year.

I felt like I was pretty well entrenched at that point. We had a good ball club, and a good nucleus coming. And Milwaukee was a great baseball town. We had just moved there that season. So, yeah, I was a little disappointed at getting traded [to the Giants], because I thought this team was going to be a pretty good ball club for at least 10 years, and I'd like to have been a part of

it. Mathews had just come up in '52, and I didn't even know anything about Henry Aaron, or I would have felt even worse. He was playing second base in the minor leagues in '53 [in Jacksonville, in the Sally League]. But with Spahn and Chet Nichols coming out of the Army at the same time I came out, I think they felt they had a pretty good pitcher who could fill in where I was. Consequently, they made the decision to trade me, being able to get Bobby Thomson in return. I went to New York and Bobby, who became a very good friend of mine, unfortunately broke his leg in spring training and never really played much for the Braves. And within another three years or so he was back with the Giants, and we became roommates back in New York. [author's note: Nichols, also a left-hander, won 11 games as a rookie in '51, spent two years in the army, then won nine games in both '54 and '55, but won just five more games in his major league career, over the next six years.]

As it turned out, I probably did everything that first year with the Giants ['54] that a person would want to do in his career. For instance, I got to pitch in the All-Star Game in July—I thought that was great—I won 20 games, we won the pennant, and I was *The Sporting News* National League Pitcher of the Year, which was the forerunner to the Cy Young Award. The next year, the Cy Young Award started, so I never got that. I also won a World Series game [eight-hitting Cleveland, 3-1, in game two], I drove in the winning run in that game, and I saved the final game [with one and two-thirds innings of hitless relief]. All of that was in one year. I couldn't tell you what else I could have done that year but maybe win a few more games. I certainly had a chance to win 24 or 25 games. I think I won one out of my last six starts, or something like that, for a 21-7 season.

I always relate that season to Bob Feller because there's probably one of the greatest pitchers of all time, but a guy who never, never won a World Series game. That's strange, as great as he was. I played against him [in the Series] in '48 when I was with the Boston Braves, and then again in '54 with the Giants. He didn't get a chance to pitch in '54 but he certainly got a chance in '48. But we won the ballgame on a controversial play at second base. So after all the great things he did in his career, not having won a World Series game is kind of strange. [author's note: The Braves won game one, 1-0, despite a Feller *two-hitter; the run came in the bottom of the eighth after a walk, a sacrifice, an attempted pickoff and an RBI single; photographs supported Feller's contention that the runner should have been called out on the pickoff throw.]*

We were very fortunate against Cleveland [in the '54 Series], because we trained in Phoenix and they trained in Tucson. We saw a *lot* of that team every spring, and we barnstormed back east with them. So we played probably 18 games every spring against them, and we had a lot of confidence because we did very well against them. I think we won 14 of those 18 games in '54. We certainly didn't think we were going to beat them four straight but we felt enough confidence that we were going to have a good series. Of course, they won 111 games that year. They had two 20-game winners [Wynn and Lemon with 23 each] and Garcia with 19. They had great relief pitching. They just had a great ball club.

I remember the first pitch I threw in that series, to Al Smith. I figured, in a World Series, he might be taking the first pitch. You would assume that he would, anyway, to get rid of the jitters. Well, I threw the ball—a pretty good pitch—and he hit it on the roof, in the old Polo Grounds, for a home run. Of course, I couldn't disappear. I couldn't hide [laughs]. I didn't know what to do. All the wind in my sails left. But after taking a deep breath and getting back in there, we won the ballgame, 3-1. That was the only run they got. But I will admit I was in a lot of trouble that whole game. They left about 17 runners on base, or something ridiculous like that [laughs]. So that meant the bases were loaded a few times, you know?

We had a pretty good ball club in '54, though, and I think half a dozen of our players eventually became either coaches or managers in the major leagues. But we had some characters, too. We had Dusty Rhodes. I still see him quite a bit in Florida. He lives in Boca Raton. We had Bobby Hofman. Not much is said about Bobby Hofman but he was our *right*-handed pinch hitter. It's just that Dusty had such a great World Series that they kind of forgot that Hofman did the same thing from the right side of the plate as Dusty was doing all year long from the left. Consequently, we had two great pinch hitters that won games for us. In most cases we had great pitching. I think our team ERA was something ridiculous, like 3.10 [tops in the NL]. But we would win ballgames in the bottom of the ninth and the bottom of the eighth. Somebody would get a base hit, Dusty'd hit a home run or Hofman would hit a double and we'd win the ballgame 3-2 or 2-1. And that's about how the year went. We didn't have a high-scoring team, but we had guys that knew how to win. We had Hank Thompson at third, Stanky at second, then Davey Williams there when Stanky got hurt. We had Whitey Lockman at first base, Willie Mays of course in center field, Monte Irvin in left and Don Mueller in right. Wes Westrum and Ray Katt were behind the plate. Ruben Gomez, Sal Maglie and I were on the mound, with Marv Grissom and Hoyt Wilhelm in the pen.

Gomez was a great athlete. I'm sure Ruben could have played football, and I think he was a good golfer, too. I remember an unfortunate incident in Milwaukee when he hit Joe Adcock with a pitch. The ball hit him so solidly that it bounced back toward the mound. Well, Joe had the bat in his hands and he started walking toward the mound. So Ruben threw the ball again and hit him *again.* Then Joe started running after Ruben, Ruben took off and, like a broken-field runner, he ran through Adcock, Mathews, Logan and Crandall. And he got to the bench. It was a *great* broken-field run. Like I say, he probably could have been a great football player, too.

We just had great camaraderie on that team. Everybody got along very well. And, of course, we had Leo Durocher as manager and he was a character in his own right. But I enjoyed playing for him. He seemed to be able to get the best out of an individual. He knew who to kick in the fanny, he knew who *not* to kick, he knew how to praise, he knew how to talk to certain people in a certain way to get the best out of them. Players all know when to hit, when to hit-and-run, they all know when to steal a base. But if you can get them to come in every day and play at their *best,* I think that's all a manager can do. And I thought that year Leo did a great job.

Another thing to add to that year I had in 1954 that's vivid in my mind is the fact that I won 12 straight games in New York without a loss until September. I was 12-0 going into the last couple of weeks of September. So you say, "Did you want to leave New York for San Francisco?" Well, it would have been kind of hard after a year like that.

Now, if you look at my record in 1956, that was probably an even *better* year for me. We were floundering around in sixth or seventh place and

I was picked for the All-Star Game. I pitched well but we weren't winning. I was 7-11 at the All-Star break. And our pitching coach came up to me and said, "You know, you can win 20 this year." I said, "Are you kidding? We're having trouble winning *a* ballgame, let alone 20." Well, to make a long story short, from the All-Star Game on I won 13 and lost two the rest of the way, and finished 20-13 [w/a 2.86ERA]. That was amazing to me, just getting that feat done. But the point is, at the time he made that statement, I think I had about 15 starts left the rest of the season. And the amazing thing was that I got a decision in *every one* of those starts. That's not normal. Usually in 15 starts you're going to get knocked out in the beginning of a game, you're going to leave another game tied 2-2 or something. The point is, I had a decision in every one of those starts, and I won my 20th game the next to last game of the season in Philadelphia. I beat them 2-0.

Surprisingly, Chub Feeney had cut me 25 percent the year before when I won 14. So I said to him at the time, "How do I get my cut back?" And he said, "Well, you're getting paid to win 20." In those days that meant 20-some odd thousand dollars a year. That's what they gave in those days for winning 20 games. So he said, "Well, you win 20, you'll get your cut back." I finished that game in Philadelphia, looked up and he was sitting up in the press box. And before I got into the clubhouse, the check was on my bench in an envelope.

We finished a distant sixth that year [20 games under .500, and 26 games behind the Dodgers]. But if you look at it, I think that was a better year for me than '54 because we were a better team in '54.

I THINK, PERSONALLY, that your best baseball took place when the war ended, and all these great players came back out of the service. I think your greatest baseball was from '45 and '46 to the expansion era, which came about in 1961 and '62. I think, at that point, the teams began thinning out. The hitters today are excellent but I think they're excellent because the pitching, in general, is so bad. In *general*. You've got some great pitching, don't get me wrong, out there today. But I think there's an awful lot of them not quite ready, and some of these hitters get pretty fat on them. Of course, Maddux is a great pitcher, along with Glavine and that whole pitching staff, and others, but they are few and far between.

And I just feel that baseball pitching-wise has had its problems. That's why we have people with 24 or 25 home runs in early June. It just doesn't make any sense. It's not that there are so many great hitters. I just think that the pitching is too poor.

I like to tell the story about some of these great hitters who are being praised today. I say, "What would happen to some of these great hitters who are hitting all these home runs if they went to Pittsburgh and had to face Bob Friend and Vernon Law , and Elroy Face out of the bullpen? Then they go to Philadelphia and have to hit a guy like Curt Simmons, then Robin Roberts and Jim Konstanty. And then they come to Brooklyn and hit a Newcombe, a Drysdale and a Koufax. Then they come to New York and hit our pitching staff." I say, "They could go 0-for-40 if these pitchers are hot." Understand what I'm trying to say? Today, you just don't have that kind of pitching. I'm not bitter about it. I think baseball is great. I think the players are doing well with what they're making. I don't *understand* it, knowing that when I was with the Giants or even the Braves, if the payroll got to a million dollars, I mean, that was the *end*. I don't care [laughs]—we just didn't pay anymore than a million dollars for the whole team. And, of course, when Mays started making $150,000, it didn't leave much for the other 24 players.

But overall, I would say Mays was the best player I ever saw—the best at being able to do *everything*. I couldn't imagine anyone having more ability nor being a better ballplayer. I never played against Mickey Mantle but I did play against some great, great ballplayers. Willie always led by performance. He didn't get up in the clubhouse and make speeches, and get the team up that way, but I think by performance he did more for the team than anything else.

I have some great memories from baseball. It certainly gave me what I have today. I met my wife through baseball, and certainly that was the greatest thing that ever happened to me. And I made a lot of good friends, too. I had a nice business that kept me going after baseball, and because of baseball I got into business. We had that business [Antonelli Tire] from 1954 to about 1994. We sold most of the business to Firestone, which is now Bridgestone. And then what was left I sold to another tire dealer locally. All I have now are buildings we acquired through our business venture. I'm hoping to either keep them leased or do something else with them. I've been retired since '94, with a second residence in Vero Beach. I still see a couple of my old teammates there—Del Crandall, now managing in the Dodgers system, and Joe Amalfitano, who was a roommate of mine with the Giants. We spend about six to eight weeks together every off-season in Florida, and it's a lot of fun to see them again.

Occasionally, people still ask me for autographs. They do remember. Or their children write to me for their fathers, or their grandfathers, who remember. It's certainly nice to be remembered, though. I think deep down you do appreciate that. No question about it.

I have four children and nine grandchildren. I have a grandson who's at the University of Notre Dame, and a granddaughter at the University of Delaware. She's there on a scholarship for both field hockey and soccer. All of them are very, very nice children.

My son was a good football player and wrestler in college. One day he came to me and said, "You know, Dad, I don't really like playing baseball." And I said, "Son, then don't play baseball. Don't do it for me." He went on to become an excellent football player—captain of his high school team and his college team, and he made Little All-America, second team. I was very proud of him.

Oh, I want to tell you one more thing. In that '54 World Series, you know, it's amazing how we beat Cleveland four straight in the first place. But secondly, we've had four reunions over the years, and would you believe we've beaten them four straight times even in those games that mean nothing? But the point is, we still win [laughs]. It is so amazing. One year, in fact, we played them in Anaheim Stadium, and we showed up with about half a team. And Cleveland was there in all its glory and splendor. They had their whole ball club, the Early Wynns, the Bob Fellers, right down the line. We came out there, and I played left field after I pitched to a couple of guys. Sal Maglie played third base. Dusty Rhodes was sick from a bad night the night before, so he didn't play at all. But we beat them, and had no right to beat them again [laughs]. But there you go. I just think we have a hex on them, or something.

Rochester, New York

JACKIE BRANDT

Following three straight .300 seasons in the St. Louis Cardinals' minor league system, outfielder Jackie Brandt made his major league debut in April, 1956, with the Cards, only to be part of a nine-player trade to the Giants two months later. The trade also sent, among others, Red Schoendienst to the Giants, with Al Dark and Whitey Lockman going to St. Louis. Brandt immediately went from a bench player with the Cards to the starting left fielder for the Giants, hitting a career-high .298 for the season.

Jackie spent all of the 1957 season and most of '58 in the Army, rejoining the Giants at Seals Stadium in late August, and making his San Francisco debut with a base hit against Warren Spahn. He hit .250 in 52 at-bats in '58, but reclaimed his starting job in left field in '59, winning a gold glove and hitting .270 with 12 home runs and 57 runs-batted-in.

Brandt was traded to Baltimore in November of '59 for left-handers Billy O'Dell and Billy Loes, and spent the next six seasons with the Orioles, making the American League All-Star team in '61, when he hit .297 with 16 homers, 72 RBIs and 10 stolen bases.

After winding up an 11-year playing career with Philadelphia and Houston in '66 and '67, Brandt managed in the minors for seven years, before returning home to Omaha, Nebraska, where he worked for 20-plus years for United Parcel. Jackie is retired now, lives with his wife in Omaha, and has six children and 11 grandchildren.

I REMEMBER MY FIRST HIT and my first home run. In 1956. They were both kind of sweet. My first hit was a single to right field off Dick Littlefield of the Pirates, and my first home run was into the left field bleachers off Lou Sleater with Milwaukee. They were thrills but, really, it was just thrilling to be there. I never, ever thought I'd *be* there. I was just dinking around in the minor leagues, and had no idea I'd ever get that far. But that first hit was a thrill. *Wow, I got a hit here.* And then I got my first home run. *Oh, my gosh.*

I didn't get to play much with the Cardinals, so I liked getting traded to the Giants. I had asked the Cardinals a couple of days before that to send me back to triple-A so I could play. I didn't want to sit on the bench. I was 22 years old. "Send me back to triple-A. I want to play. I don't want to sit and watch." So I got traded. I hit .300 with the Giants. I don't know what I hit with the Cardinals [.286 in 42 at-bats], but I know I was only there for a month and a half or two, and didn't play much.

For a couple of months with the Giants, I hit fourth, behind Mays. Me, just a little ol' guy from Nebraska. I loved it, hitting behind him or in front of him. I just loved playing. Once I got to New York, I played every day.

When I rejoined the Giants in '58 [after a two-year Army stint], I fell in love with San Francisco. I loved the Bay Area. I lived in San Mateo, had a nice little house there, the weather was beautiful and even the winters were nice. I played golf with my buddies Daryl Spencer, Jim Davenport and Gordon Jones, and I was happy as a lark out there. Seals Stadium itself was a little cold, which it still is there, no matter where you play. It's *cold* in San Francisco. You've got to wear long-sleeved shirts, turtlenecks and gloves. I remember Seals was a good park for right-handed hitters, but I was an opposite-field hitter.

In '59 I was probably the best left fielder in the league [winning a Gold Glove], because there weren't a whole lot of good left fielders. And it was easy to cover mostly to my right because the guy on my left [Willie Mays] covered so much room. You know, they *hide* guys out there in left, the home run hitters. They hide 'em out there. But I could pick it. If I played left field my whole career I probably would have won a Gold Glove

Jackie Brandt (SF Giants)

every year. But, unfortunately, they put me in center [in Baltimore] with all those jackrabbits over there in the American League. They couldn't hit but they could catch it.

We should have won the pennant in '59. We had a two-game lead with eight to play. Then we lost three straight to the Dodgers, seven of our last eight and came in third. Before the Dodgers [came to Seals], we were beating the Reds and Braves by stealing signs [purportedly from a guy in the bleachers with binoculars]. But I didn't like it. I didn't even take them. The big boys—if they knew what was coming, they could hurt you. McCovey, Cepeda and Mays. They could do some damage. But, unfortunately, four or five years before, we were stealing signs and the guy gave me [the sign for] a curveball. But the young fella on the mound threw about a 95-mile-an-hour fastball, and stuck it in my ear. When I fell down I was, like, almost in left field. And from that point on I said, "I ain't taking [stealing] no more pitches. I'll just go up there and do my own guessing." I couldn't hear for two weeks. No more sign-stealing for me after that. If anybody else wants it, that's fine. But I never looked after that. I was severely damaged there for a couple of weeks, because we were stealing signs.

The Giants said they traded me because they were moving to Candlestick [where the wind blows to right field], they were keeping their left-handed hitters [McCovey, Kirkland and Wagner], and they needed left-handed pitchers to stop the other team's left-handed hitters. I think it was between me and Felipe Alou, as to who would be traded. And it ended up me. But I was a *right field* hitter. I probably would have killed [the ball] at Candlestick, hitting to right field

The first year or two in Baltimore I felt like a stranger, and then I really got into it. I loved Balitmore. I had my own 15-minute TV show. I was kind of controversial and colorful; I played for the fans and I made a lot of speeches around town. And it got to the point where everybody around town knew me, and liked the way I did things. You know, the people make the place anyway.

I did things off the wall, when you wouldn't expect them. I don't know where I got that nickname [Flaky], though. Somebody must have made a mistake [chuckles]. I had a lot of nicknames, and that was one of them. I don't know what it was. I'm still a good ad-libber. My mind works crazy. I don't do anything canned. No canned humor, or anything like that. Whatever comes to mind, I say or do. I'd make a speech at the ballpark to a group of people before the game, and I'd hit a foul ball into their section. They'd cheer, and I'd take my hat off and run down there and yell, "I told you I'd hit you one." I kind of played for the people. And, of course, the team. I wasn't much of an "I" man.

Even though I made the All-Star team in '61, I thought my best year was my first year. The Army kind of took a little bit out of me after that. In Baltimore, they wanted me to hit 45 home runs, and all I did was hit line drives. The darn things never got over the fence. The home run you had to hit high and deep. I hit 'em hard and low. They wanted me to hit 45 home runs, so I gave it a try one year and hit 19. But I didn't hit very well—.240 or something [.255, actually, in '62, w/19HR and 75RBI -both power marks career-highs]. I led off or hit second most of my career, and averaged 70 RBIs a year leading off. That's unheard of anymore for a leadoff hitter, in the National League anyway.

But I just really enjoyed playing. That's what it's all about. I watch these games today but I don't know any of the players now, and I don't know much about them. All I know is they make a lot of money. All the old-timers I talk to at the alumni scrambles [golf] and old-timers games say it's not quite the same game. It looks like the same game to me, just different players. But I don't think they enjoy it like we did. We enjoyed *everything.* We enjoyed the days before games, the games, after the games—10, 12 guys going out to-

gether and just having a ball. I went in the clubhouse a couple of years ago in Baltimore, it took me 15 minutes to get there from my seat, and when I got there it was *empty.* Everybody had already left. We used to sit in there for two, three hours, bullshit and talk about the game. That was our home.

It's ridiculous now. I don't know. The managers are just like peacemakers, or something. They don't do anything anymore. A manager *can't* tell anyone what to do anymore because his players are making millions and he ain't. And they *tell* him. "You want to stay around here, just be quiet and mind your own business." That's what they tell the managers. "I'm making eight million dollars a year. You want to stay here? Just do your shit and leave me alone. I'll get you fired." Because they're going to get rid of the manager before they get rid of the star. Same thing in basketball. Guys are getting fired because the players don't want to play for them. Brian Hill with the Orlando Magic. Paul Westhead got fired from the Lakers because of Magic Johnson. And Doug Collins left Chicago because of Michael Jordan. It used to be that if the manager said something, that was the law.

I managed seven years when I got through playing, and it wasn't worth a shit. I mean, the players ... You tell them to do something in the *minor* leagues—I'm teaching these guys how to play—and it's, "Why do I gotta do this? Why do I gotta do that?" "Because I'm *telling* you to do it [laughs]. You want to play, let's get after it." I'd bring a guy in who missed 10 fly balls in a row— I'd bring him out in the morning and hit him fly balls, and teach him how to catch them, and what to do in the sun field. I'm an *outfielder.* I can teach hitting, I can teach pitching, I can teach catching, I can teach fielding. I've done it all. And I can do it all. Then, when he gets done with practice, he calls the general manager of the big league club and says, "I got to go out there at 10:30 in the morning and catch fly balls for half an hour, and then I got to come back and play the game at eight o'clock." Then they call me and say, "What are you doing, pulling this guy in at 10:30?" And I say, "I'm trying to save his life. He's gonna get killed out there in the outfield. Balls are gonna be peppering him on his head." [laughs] I guess I wasn't supposed to do that. I was supposed to just show up for the game, let 'em play and let 'em go home. They weren't supposed to learn anything. I couldn't take a whole lot of that. Everybody told me to get out. Paul Richards, Bob Lillis. "Get out," they said. "It ain't worth a shit anymore."

The highlight of my baseball career wasn't managing, though. The real highlight was just getting to play. Playing with Willie and Brooks Robinson and Boog Powell and Luis Aparicio and Robin Roberts. Hall of Famers. You know, just being on the same team with them and watching them play *every* day. It's amazing when you see Willie Mays. They talk about his catch in the '54 Series. That was *routine*. I've seen him make a hundred catches harder than that one. But you only see that when you play with him. If you're in there for a three-game series and see somebody—it's like seeing Clemente—he's awfully good in a three-game series, but if you see him 162 games he's unbelievable. I'm lucky to have played when I did. Oh, brother. Williams, Mantle, Mays, Musial, Koufax, Drysdale, Roberts. Shit. All Hall of Famers.

But I'm not too gung-ho about baseball anymore. I've had enough of it. It's changed, and I don't want any part of it. I watch it on TV, though. It's the only thing I've got to do.

Omaha, Nebraska

DON JOHNSON

A sandlot legend in his native Portland, Oregon, Don Johnson went 20-1 with six no-hitters in American Legion ball at age 16. After spending one year in the minor leagues and two more in the Army, Johnson spent the entire 1947 season as a spot-starter with the World Series champion New York Yankees at age 21, going 4-3 with a 3.64 ERA in 54 innings. Johnson didn't get to pitch in the Series, but he did get his Series ring. He also got to witness one of the most memorable games in World Series history—game four, in Brooklyn, when teammate Bill Bevens no-hit the Dodgers for eight and two-thirds innings, before two walks and a two-run double by Cookie Lavagetto beat him 3-2.

Johnson won seven games for a poor Washington Senators team in '52, then went 8-7 with a 3.13 ERA with the White Sox in '54. He was a 20-game winner at triple-A Toronto in '57, taking Most Valuable Player honors in the International League.

Acquired by the Giants midway through the '58 season, Don pitched just 23 innings for San Francisco, going 0-1 with a 6.26 ERA. He retired shortly thereafter, winning 27 games in seven big league seasons, with 17 complete games, five shutouts and 12 saves.

Johnson still lives in Portland, with his wife, and has three children and one grandchild.

MORE POWER TO THESE GUYS that are making all the money in baseball now but, by God, I think the old-timers ought to get a little more pension money. That's all. Otherwise, I'm glad I played when I did. Those were the good ol' days. I played with and against the best players in the world. Yeah, Ted Williams and all those guys. Bobby Doerr lives right up the coast from me. I saw Johnny Pesky recently—of course, he's still with the Boston Red Sox organization. He's about 77. God, where did those years go? I can't believe it. I still think I'm 20-something. I'd get nervous before spring training for all those years. Then, all of a sudden, it evaporated. The years went by so fast. It's really something. Of course, I stay 65 myself. I don't go any higher.

I grew up here in Portland. I guess I was one of the best [American Legion players]. I have records here that nobody's broken. Six no-hitters [in 1943]. I was 20-1. I don't think anybody's thrown six no-hitters since then. All I could do then was throw hard. I didn't have much of a curveball. See, when I was 16 I was six-feet-two and weighed 150 pounds. As time went on I picked up a change of pace here and there, and a good slider at the end of my career.

I signed with the Yankees right out of high school. I pitched real good at [double-A] Newark. I was 6-2 there, when I was 17 years old, and we got into the playoffs. I was only a kid then. I didn't know what I was doing. We got $3 a day meal money. Isn't that something? Then, I spent '45 and '46 in the army. I started out at Fort Lewis, then went overseas [to the Pacific]. I was in the fightin' 42nd division. The Marines came through all those islands, and we came through after that. We had to clean out the Japanese. I was scared to death every day, but that was OK. I got through it.

I played ball at Fort Lewis after I came back. It took me one day to get *in* the Army, and about four weeks to get out. So I played with the Fort Lewis Reception Center for a while. We had a hell of a team there [winning 40 straight games]. Jeez, we had Danny Litwhiler, Dominic Dallessandro, Hank Camelli and Gail Bishop—a basketball player at Washington State.

I finally got out just in time for spring training with the Yankees in '47. I went to New York and met the players at the hotel. Remember the boxing announcer Don Dunphy? Well, I got to be pretty good friends with him there for a couple or three days. Then we got on the plane for San Juan, Puerto Rico, and I saw all these guys, like Tommy Henrich, who I talked to last month—God, he looks great. He's 84. We talked for a long time. I think Tommy Henrich should be in the Hall of Fame. Guys like Reggie Jackson, I know, hit home runs all over the place. But Tommy—they called him "Old Reliable."

So there was Henrich, DiMaggio, "King Kong" Keller, Phil Rizzuto and Yogi [Berra]—he just got out of the Navy, while I got out of the Army. Hell, he didn't have nothin'. He couldn't hardly read or write. But he had a suitcase full of comic books and a suitcase full of navy dungarees. He didn't have any clothes to wear, hardly.

Joe Page was there—a good reliever, from Springfield, Illinois. He passed away. In fact, I've got a photograph here of our pitching staff, and in the top row I'm the only one left. There's Joe Page, Vic Raschi, Bobo Newsom, Bill Bevens—he died in '91 of a stroke. He lived in Hubbard, Oregon, about 22 miles up from where I am. Allie Reynolds is in the bottom row—he's gone, too.

I think the '47 Yankee team was one of the greatest teams I've ever seen. I really mean it, not just because I was there. I was only a rookie but we had a *hell* of a club. We had Yogi and Sherman Lollar behind the plate, George McQuinn at first, George Stirnweiss at second, Rizzuto at short, Billy Johnson at third, Keller in left, DiMaggio in center, Henrich in right. And the pitching staff was Frank Shea, Spud Chandler, myself and the guys I just mentioned. We had a good ball club. It was something else.

It was very disappointing to me not to pitch in the Series. I tell you what happened to me. Remember Charlie Dressen? Well, he [Yankee coach in '47] tried to change my delivery. I had a 4-0 record when he said, "You're not throwing right." So I started to argue with him a little bit. And that got me in a little trouble. It's who you know in this game. He says, "Well, I'll see that you don't start or relieve much after that." Yeah, I was disappointed. That's OK, though. We won the Series [in seven games].

Imagine the World Series share we got. We got about eight grand total [as a team]. Now they get, what, $215,000 a man [laughs]? That's a sign of the times.

You mentioned Bevens in game four. I was in the bullpen warming up a couple of times, around the seventh. He walked *10*. He didn't normally have control problems. Not Bill. But that was a hell of a game. We had 'em beat 2-1 with two outs in the last of the ninth. He's got a no-hitter. And Cookie Lavagetto is up [after a pair of two-out walks]. Of course we were thinking about the no-hitter. *Everybody* was thinking about it. Then Lavagetto hits this little bloop into right field. Henrich goes back and we all think he's gonna catch it. But he turns his back and plays it off the wall. It bounces off that brick wall they had at Ebbets Field, and they all score. I think we sat in the clubhouse for an hour and a half before anybody said anything. Bevens finally said, "Well, that's the way it goes." I'd have sure liked to have seen ol' Bill get that.

Remember the Mickey Owen incident [the passed ball which cost the Dodgers game four of the 1941 World Series]? Tommy [Henrich] is *still* talking about that. He said, hell, he swung at the ball and missed. Strike three. Game's over. But the ball got by Owen. He got to first. Then the Yankees get three hits, two walks, four runs and that was about all she wrote [the Yankees won the game 7-4, and the Series in five games]. The relief

Don Johnson (Dick Dobbins)

pitcher for Brooklyn [Hugh Casey], who was in there for the entire ninth inning, shot himself to death a few years later [in 1951, at age 37].

But back to '47. I would say that Joe DiMaggio was the best ballplayer I've seen in my entire life. That includes Willie Mays. That *includes* Mays. Ted Williams was a better hitter than DiMaggio. But, overall, Joe was the best. You know with those long shots to center field? Joe would be back there standing and waiting for them. Mays would catch them and run into the fence. Joe was a hell of a player. Mays was great, too, don't get me wrong. But I'd say Joe was the best. And a lot of people say that.

Joe was a moody guy. I used to hang around with him in '47. I was just a rookie but he liked me because I was a young kid. He couldn't walk onto the street. People would mob him. True story. He couldn't go on the street. He couldn't walk out of the hotel. People would mob him. That's how famous a ballplayer he was. He'd sit up in his room and stare out the window all day long. He called me up a couple of times and said, "I want you to sit here with me for a while." But I really think he was the best.

I went to St. Louis in 1950, and then Washington in '51. I had a pretty good year with the Senators in '51 [7-11, 3.95ERA]. We had a terrible club [62-92] but the worst club I've been on was the Browns, in '50 [58-96]. I won five games there. That was pretty good for that team. I lost four or five 1-0 games there. That's tough. I pitched against Bob Feller three times and lost every one of them—1-0, 1-0 and 2-1. How do you like that? He was tough. The Browns traded me to Washington [in early '51] but I got to see Satchel Paige before I left. I can say that in my life, anyway. He had that rocking chair down in the bullpen. That was when Eddie Gaedel came to bat, the little midget that [owner Bill] Veeck put up there. Yeah, I remember that [the three-foot-seven Gaedel walked in his only big league at-bat].

But Satchel was something. He was about 65 years old when I faced him again, in the International League, in '57 [official records list his birth as 7/7/06]. I think Satchel was about 70 years old when he came up again to the big leagues [in '65 with Kansas City]. Nobody knew his real age. He still could thread a needle. I'd like to have seen the guy when he was 21 years old. I bet he could throw that ball through a town, if you know what I mean. Yeah, ol' Satchel was something else. Yup.

I had a *great* year with the White Sox in '54. A great year [8-7, 3.13ERA]. We won 94 games and finished *third* [17 games behind Cleveland, and nine behind New York]. We had a good ball club. We had Nellie Fox—God bless him. He's looking down on us now. He was my hearts partner. We'd play hearts on the train. Nellie Fox, me, Jim Rivera and Billy Pierce—now, he was a good little left-hander, wasn't he? Made $14,000. Top salary in those days. But he was a good little left-hander. A good clean liver. Never fooled around, drank, nothing like that. Nothing like some of the guys I played with [laughs].

Let me tell you. Well [laughs], I will say that with old-time ballplayers in my era, there were no milkshake drinkers. You remember Casey Stengel? Well, we got to spring training down there in San Juan—and I'm just a kid—and we got off the plane, and I got down to the hotel for a team meeting, and Casey says, "Now, look it. Got a lot of rookies on this team. And I don't want no milkshake players on this team. If you're gonna drink, drink whiskey. And don't bring any whores into the same hotel you stay at." *That* was the meeting. Old Casey. He liked his scotch. And he didn't want no ice cream hitters on his team [laughs].

I could tell a million stories, like the time Pedro Ramos with Washington was facing the Red Sox in old Griffith Park and he struck Williams out. After the game he went to Ted and said, "Mr. Williams, would you autograph this ball for me?" Well, Ted *hated* to do things like that. But Pedro Ramos said, "Will you autograph this ball for me so I can take it back home to Cuba?" Well, he signed it, and four days later Ramos is pitching again, at Fenway Park. And Williams' first time up he hits one of those Ted Williams moon shots over the center field fence. And you know how far center field is there [420 feet]. It damn near went out of the whole park. And as Williams rounds second base he says to Pedro Ramos, "You want me to sign that one, too?"

I faced Ted Williams 120 to 130 times in my career. He didn't hit any home runs but a *lot* of line drives. Oh, he was tough. You couldn't get him out by fooling him. Just throw the ball down the pike and hope for the best. He had those eyes. Well, he had four years of flying an Air Force jet in Korea. A nice man, though.

The team I liked to pitch against was Detroit. I had good success against Detroit. I loved Tiger Stadium. I know they have a short porch in left field, and those high fly balls fly out of there. But I faced Al Kaline 30 or 40 times, throwing that good slider, and he'd try to pull it and he'd hit these nice little ground balls to short every time. He was a great hitter, though.

I said before that DiMaggio was the best overall player, but Ted Williams was the best hitter. Nobody came close to him. I don't care who they were. Another guy in Boston that was pretty good was Carl Yastrzemski. But there was nobody like Williams. He'd come up to the plate, and people would just stop and stare.

I came to the Giants at the end of my career, in the summer of '58 from Toronto. But I want to ask you, who was the MVP of the International League in '57? *I* was. The MVP. You can look it up in the record books. I was 26-7, including the playoffs.

I'm not going to lie to you. I had a lot of trouble with liquor when I was playing ball. Teams would keep giving me a chance, and I'd go back and forth with it. I was 30 years old in '57, and that's when you're peaking. I could throw hard. I had a good slider. And everything fell into place. And I was making good money there because Jack Kent Cooke owned the team, and he paid us three grand a month. Back then, that was pretty good for the minor leagues. And every time I won a game I'd get money under the table. Anyway, in '58, I had pitched three straight shutouts, and this scout from the Giants came along and said, "Well, we're gonna take you or another pitcher, Bob Tiefenauer." They took me. I wish they'd have left me there [laughs], back in Toronto. I really loved that town. We played at Maple Leaf Stadium, right on the lake. After I left, they moved to Exhibition Stadium.

So I went to San Francisco, and Rigney and I got into it right away. I wanted to start and I was pressuring him. But he wanted to put me in the bullpen, and I got depressed. I came in to mop up a few games. They were a little short on pitching. That's why I couldn't figure out why Rigney wouldn't give me a shot. That pissed me off, being in the bullpen, so I started drinking Hamm's beer in there. It made me mad.

When I first joined the Giants there was an article in a San Francisco newspaper saying, "Giants buy Johnson from Toronto to drink all the Hamm's beer in San Francisco." This lawyer called me from Toronto and said, "You've got something there. You could sue that damn paper." That kind of thing makes a guy mad. I guess they

wrote that because I had kind of a nasty reputation. I had kind of a lurid past. We *all* did, including my friend Billy Martin. I used to hang around with him. He was *tough* out there.

We had a bullpen catcher named Nick Testa. He was my roommate there. He was a tough little bugger. He never played in the big leagues. But I always liked Nick. My other good friend there was Whitey Lockman. I know he's scouting with the Marlins now. I didn't have many good friends on that club, but I tell you who I did like. I liked Leon Wagner—he was a good friend of mine—and Mike McCormick. He was a wonderful man. I've got a giant photograph of me and Mike from a reunion of the '58 Giants and Dodgers [in the early eighties].

I'd have liked to have got a job in baseball like Whitey and Hank Sauer and Jim Davenport. I'm glad these guys stayed in baseball. I'd have liked to have got a chance like that because that's all I know. I don't know anything else except baseball players and baseball. And I can spot kids. I know what the hell to look for.

I tell you, when I broke into baseball there were only eight teams in the National League and eight in the American League, and it was hard to make it. Do you realize that one-tenth of one percent of all the kids on these little league teams make it to the big leagues? All these kids want to be big leaguers. Well, I want to tell you something. It's hard to get there. You've got to have the right breaks. You've got to have the ability—that's number one. If you don't have the ability, get a lunch box and a peanut butter sandwich because you're not gonna make it. I know I wasn't one of those superstars but I had a great career. I don't care [laughs]. I can walk down the street and be proud.

I went back to Toronto in '59 and had a pretty decent year, but I was getting up there by then. I was 32. I was getting old as hell, wasn't I [laughs]? So they sent me out to Portland, in the Coast League. And I didn't care. I just quit. Hell, I couldn't make it. I wasn't making any money.

I drove a cab after that. I was stupid. I didn't know anything. I wasn't trained for anything. I drove a cab for 25 years. I didn't have any education. In 1967 I got shot. Some guy held me up and shot me through the head. I survived. Still got the scar. It went in below the right ear and exited below the left ear. Yeah, that was something else. The guy held me up for 19 bucks and shot me right below the ear. They took me to emergency and thought I was gonna croak. But the doctor said I had too much whiskey [laughs] in me. That's how I survived. He said, "You got too much whiskey for blood. You're gonna survive." They caught the guy. He pleaded insanity. They gave him 25 years to life. And he got out in *six months. Insanity.* Great system, huh? His name was Dennis Grubbs. He looked like Yul Brynner with thick glasses. I remember that. I never saw him again. It's a good thing I didn't. I'd have killed him.

Then, after I got through with that, I went back to driving a cab, which I thought I'd never do. And after the first couple of days back, I got held up again. Some drunk hippie tried to cut me with a piece of cut glass. But I got him. The cops and I got him. The only other bad thing was a big Indian guy I picked up at a tavern hit me over the head with a bottle. That was about it. I survived that. Took him down to the police station. Cops said, "You want to press charges?" I said, "No. How much money has he got on him?" They said, "About $300." I took the $300. See you later.

It's terrible up here in Portland. You can't walk on the street at night. You can't do anything anymore. It's tough out there. A lot of dope. A lot of drugs.

After 25 years driving a cab I retired. I don't do much of anything. I try to walk a lot. I'm still in great shape. I look pretty good. I weighed 195 as a player [six-feet-three]. That's what I weigh right now.

My oldest boy Steve is 49. He works for a Japanese company as a jet pilot. Don works for Boeing as an inspector. And Lori works for an eye doctor as an eye technician. The good thing is that all three of my kids turned out real good, because I was divorced from my first wife for a long time. The kids all come around now to see me, since I quit drinking. I've been sober for seven years. Ain't got drunk once.

Portland, Oregon

JIM KING

Left-handed hitting outfielder Jim King had a breakthrough season at triple-A Omaha in 1954, hitting

.314 *with 25 home runs and 127 RBIs. That earned him a shot at the major leagues with the Chicago Cubs in '54, when he hit .256 with 11 homers and 45 RBIs, in 301 at-bats. King hit 15 homers with the Cubs in '56, then was traded to the St. Louis Cardinals. After spending most of '57 back at triple-A Omaha, King was traded to the Giants for catcher Ray Katt 13 days before the historic West Coast opener in 1958.*

Even though King originally was not penciled into Bill Rigney's starting lineup for that opener against the Dodgers, the Giants manager had a late change of heart because of an unusual wind blowing out to right field, rather than the usual left, at Seals Stadium. Kind suddenly found himself in the lineup, batting second, between Jim Davenport and Willie Mays, and he responded by going two-for-three with a run scored and an RBI. That, however, was one of King's few starts in '58. In late June, after hitting .214 in just 56 at-bats, King was sent to triple-A Phoenix.

King spent the next two years in the minors before resurfacing again, in '61, this time in Washington with the Senators, where he enjoyed his finest days in the majors. Jim hit .270 with 11 homers in '61, then busted loose for 24 homers and 62 RBIs, both career-highs, in '63. He finished his 11-year big league career with Cleveland in '67, after being traded by the White Sox for Rocky Colavito. King had a lifetime average of .240 and 117 home runs.

Jim still resides with his wife in his native Elkins, Arkansas. They have two children and two grandchildren.

I THOUGHT I'D HAVE a better shot at playing with San Francisco [after getting traded 4/2/58]. In St. Louis, we had all kinds of outfielders [Moon, Ennis, Boyer, Flood and Cunningham]. The Giants had some young outfielders, too, but I didn't really know much about them at the time. I think it turned out we had about 11 rookies on the team in '58.

I remember getting to start Opening Day against the Dodgers. Rigney said it was because the wind was blowing out to right instead of left, which it usually did at Seals Stadium. But I would say that Drysdale helped change his mind on that, too. I remember that game. I don't know why I do, but I do. I went two-for-three and walked once. It was exciting, but I had already opened the season with the Cubs a time or two. So it was, more or less, just another day.

I didn't get to play much with the Giants. So they sent me down to Phoenix, and then sent me to Toronto for some pitching [Don Johnson]. I enjoyed playing in Toronto. I liked Cookie [team owner Jack Kent Cooke]. We got along good. Toronto was a real nice place.

In terms of my major league career, I enjoyed my days with the Chicago Cubs and Washington Senators the most. In Chicago, day ball was number one. Mr. Wrigley always said there would be no night ball at his stadium. And there wouldn't have been if he'd still be living. He was just that type of guy. I really enjoyed playing for the Cubs. I lived over on the lake, had just been married and had a baby. We enjoyed it there. I mean, if you don't like Wrigley Field—it's not the largest in the country, but you're right down on the players. I mean, you're right close to the fans when you're on the field. Now, it wasn't really a good park for me to hit in. Wrigley Field was a right-handed hitting park. The wind always blew the ball across the field to left. The wind would come off of the lake. When I broke in with the Cubs, we had an excellent infield—Ernie Banks at short, Gene Baker at second, Dee Fondy at first and Randy Jackson at third.

Jim King (SF Giants)

In Washington I played for, I'd have to say, the greatest manager who ever lived. I thought the world of Gil Hodges. But I think the main reason I did so well in Washington was that I got to play every day. I mean, you ain't gonna hit nothin' if you ain't playin'. Let's face it. Who you've got around you makes a little difference, too. I had Chuck Hinton and Don Lock, and guys like that around me. When I played for Frisco, I always hit in front of Mays. Well, that's like a stroll in the park. Where'd you rather hit, in front of him or in back of him [laughs]? Anybody who knows anything about the game would rather hit in front of him. Then, we got big Frank [Howard] in Washington, and I always hit in front of him. They couldn't pitch around me so much. Of course, hitting in front of him [laughs]—he hit the ball so hard, he hit into a lot of double plays. Your butt's always bleedin' from sliding into second base, trying to break up two. But you'd always rather hit in front of him than behind him. He hit some long, long home runs. Oh, *mercy.* I believe he's the strongest guy I've ever seen.

My last year, in '67, I got traded twice. First, to the White Sox, and then to Cleveland. I got traded for Rocky Colavito [laughs]. Yeah, that didn't go over too good [in Cleveland]. But you know what to expect at times like that, when you're traded for someone that the whole city likes. The fans weren't really *too* tough on me. Rock was more or less at the end of his career, too [the 33-year-old Colavito hit 30HR w/72RBI in '66, but fell to 8HR w/50RBI in '67].

I faced a lot of great pitchers in my day. But I'd have to say Koufax, Whitey Ford and Carl Erskine probably stand out. It wouldn't be bad to have those three guys on your club. The best player—you take Mays now, he could do anything. He could hit, hit with power, run, throw, field, steal a base for you. There wasn't anything he couldn't do. He and Mantle would be real close. But Mantle always had the bad knees. There was always something wrong with Mick. But longball-wise, Mick was one of the best.

After baseball I worked for the telephone company until I retired about five years ago. I've got two kids, although they're not too much kids anymore. My daughter works for the state of Oklahoma. My son's a high school baseball coach. I helped them both through college, although my boy got a baseball scholarship, to John Brown University. He enjoys coaching now. He's good with kids.

Say, could you send me a copy of the Opening Day [newspaper] story? From '58? I'd *love* that. I was just thinking the other day about that game, and I want to remember the score being 5-2 [laughs]. I don't know why. You say it was 8-0? Well, I remember me, Mays and Alou played the outfield. You say Kirkland played the outfield? Well, I was wrong again [laughs], see? At least I remember my two hits. Things like *that* you don't forget.

Elkins, Arkansas

DON TAUSSIG

Outfielder Don Taussig was one of six rookies on the Giants' Opening Day roster in 1958, coming off an impressive '57 campaign at double-A Dallas, where he hit .285 with 23 home runs and 90 RBIs. Taussig had very limited duty with the Giants, hitting .200 in 50 at-bats, including his first major league homer June 6 against Cincinnati at Seals Stadium. He had two hits off Curt Simmons in his first big league start.

Taussig had just 263 at-bats in his brief big league career but most of that was in 1961, when he enjoyed considerable success with the St. Louis Cardinals, hitting .287 with two homers and 25 RBIs. He finished his career with the Houston Colt 45s in '62.

Don lives with his wife in Mamaroneck, New York. He has two daughters and two granddaughters.

FOR THE MOST PART I was a so-called *caddy* for the outfield. I was the utility outfielder, so I'd spell Hank Sauer in left field, for example, in the seventh inning if we were ahead. And if

Mays ever came down with the flu or something like that, I'd play center field. They called guys like me *caddies* [laughs]. But that was my first year in the major leagues, so 1958 was very, very exciting for me.

The biggest memory from '58 for me, though, was the loss of my major league position when I was sent down [to triple-A Phoenix] in the middle of the year. I took it very hard. I played at Phoenix the rest of the year, and it was very difficult to get started because I had played utility for three months into July for the Giants. I was completely out of shape, went to 105 degree weather and was expected to perform right away, and had a big difficulty getting back into playing shape. That was a great team we had down there, though, with guys like Dusty Rhodes, Andre Rodgers—he was a great ballplayer. I played with him in Dallas also. A very nice young man. I think Andre had the potential to become a great major league ballplayer. He was tall, he was strong, he could hit, he moved well and he had great mobility. He was brought up in the Bahamas, and his father was a doctor. And he was very sensitive to all the negative things that happened to him, with all the great expectations for him here and back home.

I spoke recently with Peter Magowan, and he reminded me of a game in May of '58 against the Pirates [when the Giants rallied for nine runs in the bottom of the ninth]. I got poison pen letters over that, from New York Giant fans, because I made the last out of the game and we lost 11-10. I remember getting a few poison pen letters from people wanting me *dead*. From New York, not from San Francisco. They were from the old New York fans, and they wanted me dead. They hated me for that. Unbelievable. The wind was taking the ball, and I was praying it would fall, but it never did. Mazeroski caught it in short center.

The Giants eventually sold me to Portland, Oregon. I had a pretty decent year with them in '60 and then the Cardinals bought my contract. And then I had a good year in the big leagues. I hit about .290 and, for a while, I came back and haunted the Giants. I hit well against them, until Mays learned where to play me [laughs]. Then the line drives wouldn't fall. He'd catch 'em [laughs]. I thought St. Louis was the best organization that I had ever played with. Stan Musial was with them, and it seemed like everybody there stuck together. They were a bunch of nice men, and everything that was good happened that year.

Don Taussig (Don Taussig)

dren, and I needed to support them. And I was interested in the stock market. So I got a job with Merrill Lynch, worked for them for 12 years, then got a job with Drexel Burnham for a few years. That's where I met my current wife, Eileen. And that's the best thing that ever happened to me in that business. But I got weary of being an account executive, selling stocks and bear markets. I didn't like it.

Then I discovered a game called squash. I heard there was a squash complex for sale, and I got into it in 1980. I own the club now, in Mamaroneck, and I also teach. I'm the pro there. The name of the club is Squash One. And right now I'm trying to sell the club because I want to retire out on the West Coast with Eileen. I'd like to retire in Portland. When I played in Portland, it was a wonderful year. The people are great. There's an awful lot of nature there, and at this stage of my life I love nature.

San Francisco, California

I had a wonderful roommate in Joe Cunningham, and he showed me some of the ropes. We all had a good camaraderie. Bill White was there—a great man—and so were Kenny Boyer and Curt Flood. Actually, Curt Flood took my place in center field. That year we had two All-Star Games and, since I was hitting pretty well, they gave me a shot at center field in between the two All-Star Games. Johnny Keane, the manager, and Harry Walker, the hitting coach, said one day after that period, "You look like you're pressing out there, so we're gonna rest you and put Curt Flood in there for a day." Curt got five hits that day and he never came out of the lineup after that [laughs].

My contract was sold to Houston the following year [in '62] and I tore my knee cartilage in spring training. It wasn't operated on until May and, by the time I recovered, it was July and my season was really shot by then. I was way behind. My career wasn't shot, but they [Houston] felt it was shot. I was 30 years old at the time and they felt, why go with me, who's uncertain, when they can get an 18-year-old prospect? So I was shifted to the wayside. That's how baseball was in those days. I played a couple of years in the minors but it was downhill, really.

After baseball I became a stockbroker in New York City. I had gotten married and had chil-

RAMON MONZANT

A native of Maracaibo, Ramon Monzant became just the second Venezuelan pitcher to reach the major leagues [after Alex Carrasquel] and just the third Venezuelan over-all, when he made his big league debut with the Giants in 1954. But his biggest year in the majors came in 1958, when he spent much of the season in the Giants starting rotation, going 8-11 with a 4.71 ERA. Monzant started the first major league night game in West Coast history, at Seals Stadium April 16. He lost that game to the Dodgers, but came back to eight-hit LA 12-2 just four days later, at the LA Coliseum. His four-hit shutout of the Cubs in his next start, on the 25th, put the Giants into first place, a position they shared with the Braves throughout the first four months of the season.

Monzant signed with the Giants after trying out at their Melbourne, Florida, minor league camp in 1952. He reached the majors two years later, after winning 39 games in his first two minor league campaigns, including a 23-6 mark with class-B Danville in '53.

Unfortunately, at the age of 25, Monzant's career was effectively over after the '58 season, because of a sore arm. He sat out the '59 season, returned to pitch one inning in '60 and retired shortly thereafter.

Ramon and his wife still live in Maracaibo. They have five children and one grandchild.

THE GIANTS CALLED ME UP [from triple-A Minneapolis] in 1954, to the Polo Grounds in New York. It was a great moment in my life. And it was so special to my country for me to be a member of the Giants.

It's hard to remember my first game in the major leagues but I think it was against the Pirates. However, I do remember starting the first major league night game in San Francisco, against the Dodgers [4/16/58]. That was one of the greatest moments in my life, and one that I treasure to this day. I've been told it was a chilly night but when you play in a game like that you don't remember the cold.

Ruben Gomez and Orlando Cepeda were very close to me on that team. They helped me out a lot. Willie Mays did, too. All my teammates were great to me, like brothers. The fans were very nice, too. My wife Rita and I enjoyed our time in San Francisco so much.

My best single memory from the '58 season was a game against Chicago, at Seals Stadium. I struck out Ernie Banks three times and beat them 2-0 [on a four-hitter, 4/25]. To me, it was the best game of my life. At the time Banks played shortstop and hit over 40 home runs [47 in '58]. That gives you an idea what kind of a hitter he was.

I didn't play at all in 1959 because of pain in my throwing arm. Then I pitched one game for the Giants in 1960 before they sent me down to triple-A Tacoma. It was really hard to go back to the minor leagues. I was a reliever at Tacoma, a short reliever. I would pitch in the last three innings. I was dreaming of a return to the major leagues. But I broke my leg sliding into second base at Tacoma. My right leg. I was in a cast three months. Then I tried to throw but hurt my arm again. At that point I had to be really honest with myself and my team. So I went back home, here, to Venezuela. I tried to pitch again here, but retired after the '62 season.

After baseball I worked at a brewery as a supervisor. The name of the beer is Polar beer—the best beer in Venezuela. It still is today.

Now, I'm retired. I cannot work anymore because I have arthritis in both knees. But people here still recognize me as a former major league player. Oh, yeah. People here all know me. I was so proud to represent my country in the major leagues. Now, we have so many more Venezuelans in the majors.

I still have two dreams today. One dream is to see my nephew in the major leagues. His name is Jose Monzant. He's a catcher, 18 years old, playing for Cleveland at their instructional school here in Venezuela. My other dream is to get a Giants jersey with my old number 41 on it.

Maracaibo, Venezuela

Ramon Monzant (SF Giants)

NICK TESTA

Nick Testa spent the '58 season as the Giants' bullpen coach, after 10 years as a catcher in their minor league system. But he got his name in The Baseball Encyclopedia *in late April of '58, when he played in the first and only game of his major league career, entering the game as a pinch runner in the bottom of the eighth inning, catching reliever Marv Grissom in the top of the ninth, and then nearly getting a historic at-bat in the bottom of the ninth, before Daryl Spencer ended the game with a two-run homer.*

Testa returned to Double-A Dallas in '59 and continued playing minor league ball well into his forties. He still lives in his native New York City and works part-time for the New York Yankees.

I was always a catcher. The tools of ignorance. I proved that saying. Defensively, I was good. My problem was hitting the ball. That was it. It plagued me my whole career. I hit it, but I didn't have any power. I was 5-8, 180. I still am.

I got paid $200 a month in the beginning [in '47"], to play on a Class D team in Seaford, Delaware. I was hitting close to .400 until July, then fell off to .292 [1 HR, 73 RBI] at the end. But I played every day. From there, I went to Class B Trenton, then to C, then back to B, like that, then A, then Double A. I gradually climbed, with a couple of down steps, but for the most part was on the way up. I thought I turned the corner [in '55] when I hit .300 [.307] at Johnstown [Class A], and I guess the Giants did, too, because that earned me a shot at Double A. I hit about .240 [.236, 50 RBI] at Dallas in '57, in the Double A Texas League, and the next year they brought me up to the Giants for spring training.

Willie McCovey played with me in Dallas. I knew he was a good hitter. And I knew he was going to be a great hitter, but I never thought he'd have a career like he did. He was very thin at the time. Even then, they called him Stretch.

When they invited me to the big-league camp in '58, I was ecstatic. I thought, what the heck? After all this time, 10 years in the minors, I was really happy. I had more or less given up the idea of playing major league ball. I was content playing in the minors and making my living

doing that. And in the off-season I was going to college, so I wasn't wasting much time. I never really thought I would make it.

I hit .200 in spring training with the Giants, made the ball club as the third-string catcher and went to San Francisco with them. Of course, I was disappointed the Giants had just moved to San Francisco. Here I am, a native New Yorker, they played in New York for a hundred years, I finally make it and they move 3,000 miles away. But they really treated us like royalty in San Francisco. They really treated us well—Mays, Antonelli, all the stars they had heard about. And the rest of us, too.

Rigney [manager] told me right off the bat what I was going to be doing, which was helping out in the bullpen. Then, if they needed me to play, I'd be there. So I was sort of running the bullpen, and about a month into the season the other two catchers were doing so well, there was no way I was going to play. So he says, "Would you consider being a bullpen coach the rest of the year?" And I says, "Oh, sure, I'd love to." I was probably the youngest bullpen coach in the major leagues, at 29.

NICK TESTA (Steve Bitker)

But I did get in one game [April 23]. They put me in to pinch-run at first base [for Ray Jablonski] in the eighth inning against the Cardinals. I never scored. Then I caught Marv Grissom in the ninth inning. And we finally won in the bottom of the ninth when Daryl Spencer hit a two-run homer [to cap a four-run rally]. And I was in the on-deck circle. I thought I was going to hit. It never occurred to me that he'd hit one out. But the next thing I knew, he hit one out, and I says, "Wow, that's great." And then I realized I'm not going to hit. And when he crosses home plate—you know, you're supposed to shake his hand—I shook his hand and then cussed him out [laughs]. He didn't know what the hell was going on. That was very funny.

I didn't know for certain, but I had an idea then that that was going to be my only major league game, because they had discussed making me a full-time coach before. Rigney was very up-front with everybody. He was a great guy. And he told me what my role would be and I said, "Great, I'll do it." I figured it would still be better to coach in the majors than go back and play in the minors, because maybe I'd get a chance somewhere down the line. Of course, it never happened, but I thought it was a remote possibility. Plus, you know, I'm in the big leagues [making $5,600]. That's where I wanted to be. And I had a nice year, except for not playing.

The Giants released me after the season, and I signed to play again for Dallas, which became Triple A. I just resumed my minor league career after that, and I played until 1970. A couple more years in the States, then I went to Japan for one season ['62] with the Tokyo Orions. I didn't get to play much there, but it was a fantastic experience. I got to speak Japanese, got to see the country, got to make some friends. It was great. Then I returned to the States, played two more years and then went to play in the Canadian Provincial League for five years. That's where a lot of [former] big-league players went to play after they were finished. By that time, I had finished graduate school [at New York University] and was working as a PE teacher in New York, so I could get the summers off and still play.

I taught and played ball in Canada, and then Europe—10 different countries in all. The U.S., Canada, Japan, Colombia, Nicaragua, Panama, Mexico, England, Holland and Italy.

I knew Dick Howser when he was managing the Yankees, and I'd run into him every once in a while, and I'd ask him if I could throw some batting practice. I kept bugging him until, finally, one day their bullpen catcher got hurt and he called me. In 1978. And I've been with the Yankees ever since. I used to throw BP for the Mets, too, but I stopped working for them two years ago because my leg was bothering me. I don't throw as much BP for the Yankees as I used to. I do other things, though—help them with their skills and their workouts. I occasionally throw now, but very little. I throw hard, but it doesn't come in fast, see [laughs]? They don't like that.

Joe Torre is the best manager I've ever seen. They treat me well. I take a lot of ribbing from the players because of my age, but it's a lot of fun. Good-natured ribbing. Especially from Mariano Rivera. He's very mischievous. When I walk into the clubhouse, I've got to keep distance between him and me. He insults me, he'll hit me on the way by, he'll play tricks on me. And he gets a big kick out of it.

The players are a little different than when I played. Contrary to public opinion, they're more focused, they work harder, they work longer, they do everything right. People say they don't work as much as the old-time ballplayers, but I disagree. They work very hard, and always with a purpose, because there's so much money at stake. I have no complaints with their work ethic. I don't know if they even know I once played the game. They never ask. But they might have an inkling because I look like I know what I'm doing.

I was there [at Yankee Stadium] when they won their previous two World Series [in '98 and '99]. I remember they came storming into the clubhouse with photographers everywhere. What a madhouse. Champagne all over the place. I got a World Series ring two years ago, which I really cherish. I'm still hoping to get one from last year, and now this—another one. But I really treasure my memories from playing more. The ring is nice—in fact, it's so nice, I don't ever wear it. I'm afraid I'll lose it. Every once in a while I'll take it out when people want to see it. It's a terrific conversation piece.

New York, New York

ANDRE RODGERS

Andre Rodgers, the first native of the Bahamas to play major league baseball, spent 11 years in the majors, despite never having played baseball as a child growing up in Nassau. Instead, Andre played cricket and, later, softball. It was in the latter sport that a teammate, Harry Joynes, wrote to the New York Giants, telling them about this six-foot-three, 19-year-old athlete who might make an excellent baseball player if a team like the Giants would only give him a shot. The Giants wrote back and said if Rodgers paid his way to their spring training camp in Melbourne, Florida, they'd take a look at him, and reimburse him for the expenses if they signed him. Rodgers paid his own way to Melbourne in March, 1954, impressed the Giants enough to sign him, got his money back, and promptly hit .286, with nine home runs and 85 RBIs, for Olean, New York, in the class-D Pony League. Not bad for a guy playing baseball for the first time in his life.

Rodgers then won the Northern League batting title at class-C St. Cloud in '55, hitting .387, with 28 home runs, 111 RBIs and a league-leading 133 runs. He hit 22 home runs with 90 RBIs for class-B Dallas, in the Texas League, in '56, before making his big league debut with the Giants in '57, hitting .244 with three home runs in 86 at-bats.

Andre began the '58 season in San Francisco, backing up Daryl Spencer and Ed Bressoud at short, before being sent down to triple-A Phoenix in May. He promptly went on a tear, winning the Pacific Coast League batting title, at .354, with 31 home runs, 88 RBIs and a league-leading 43 doubles. He was the only unanimous choice to the PCL All-Star team. He rejoined the Giants in September, hitting .206 with two homers in 63 at-bats.

Rodgers spent two more seasons with the Giants before being traded to the Braves, and then the Cubs, where he replaced Ernie Banks at shortstop [Banks moved to first base], and enjoyed his finest big league season—his first as a regular in the lineup—hitting .278 in 461 at-bats. He hit a career-high 12 homers with the Cubs in '64, then hit .287 with the Pirates in '65, before finally leaving the majors following the '67 season with 45 career homers and a .249 average. Rodgers played one more year in Japan, for the Yokohama Taiyo Whales, then retired from baseball.

Andre Rodgers (Dick Dobbins)

Still living in Nassau, in the Bahamas, Andre is retired, with four children and one grandchild. He declined several requests to be interviewed for this book.

BOB SCHMIDT

Another of the Giants' sparkling rookie corps in 1958, Bob Schmidt was named to the National League All-Star team by Braves manager Fred Haney. Schmidt hit .244 with 14 home runs and 54 RBIs, sharing the catching duties with Valmy Thomas. His first homer came April 17, in the third game of the season, at Seals Stadium against the Dodgers. He also set a National League record for catchers in '58 (since broken) with 22 putouts in a single game.

Schmidt shared the catching duties again in '59 and '60 with Hobie Landrith, before being traded to Cincinnati early in the '61 season, with Sherman

Jones, for catcher Ed Bailey. He moved on to the Washington Senators in '62, hitting .242 with 10 home runs, before winding up his career in a brief stint with the Yankees in '64. He retired with a .243 lifetime average, and 39 home runs.

Schmidt lives with his wife in St. Charles, Missouri. He declined repeated requests to be interviewed for this book.

to Uncle Sam's call. He was 10-5 at class-C St. Cloud in '54, with 149 strikeouts in 130 innings. In '55, he went 14-7 at class-B Danville, with 233 strikeouts in 185 innings. Following his one big league start, Fitzgerald struggled at double-A Corpus Christi in '59, plagued again by injuries, and never made it back up.

His last known address was Middletown, New York.

JOHN FITZGERALD

Southpaw John Fitzgerald played only one game in his major league career, but surely that is a game he'll never forget. It happened on the final day of the '58 season, at Seals Stadium, after he completed two years of service in the Army. Manager Bill Rigney named Fitzgerald his starting pitcher, against the Cardinals' Sam Jones. Fitzgerald went three innings, giving up one run and just one hit, walking one and striking out three, before leaving with a 3-1 lead, a game that teammate Dom Zanni eventually got credit for winning.

Fitzgerald battled through various injuries to rise through the Giants' minor league system, prior

Bob Schmidt (SF Giants)

HERMAN FRANKS

Herman Franks, third base coach for the '58 Giants, is best known in San Francisco baseball circles for managing the Giants to four straight second-place finishes, beginning in 1965. He also managed the Cubs from '77 through '79.

Franks was a catcher for six years in the big leagues, beginning in 1938 with the St. Louis Browns and ending in '49 with the Giants. He played in one World Series, with the Dodgers in '41, finishing his playing career with a .199 average and three home runs, in 403 at-bats.

A graduate of the University of Utah, and a very successful businessman after his playing days were over, Franks is now retired, living with his wife

John Fitzgerald (SF Giants)

in Salt Lake City. He has three children and seven grandchildren.

I FIRST COACHED the Giants under Leo Durocher in New York, and when Leo retired in '55 I retired as well. I came back home to Salt Lake City. Then, when the Giants moved to San Francisco, they called me and asked if I'd move out to the West Coast with them. And I said yes. It was an exciting time, very much so. Seals Stadium was a nice little compact stadium, and it was full just about every day.

We had a lot of young players on that '58 team with great potential. I remember Cepeda, of course, but also Willie Kirkland and Leon Wagner. It was just exciting opening the season there.

I coached just that one year in San Francisco. I told them I'd come back just for '58, because my family was very young then. My wife came out, and we lived in the Sunset District [of San Francisco] and I don't think she saw the sun but three times all year. So that's when we decided to retire again. I had some businesses in Salt Lake so I retired after the '58 season.

But I came back to San Francisco when Alvin Dark called me, after he was named manager [in '61]. What happened was when I came back to Salt Lake, they asked me if I'd manage the ball club here, in the Coast League. And I had already committed to them, so I couldn't go right back to San Francisco. But Alvin kept asking me, so I finally came back to coach in '64. Then I was named manager in '65.

I managed the Giants for four years, and I think the only year we didn't win over 90 games was the last year [in '68] when we won 88. I have great memories of those teams, but it's still hard to take that we didn't win a pennant. Almost any other year if you win over 90 games you win the pennant. Los Angeles had such great pitching. I remember coming into the last week of the season [in '65] and we're in first place. And St. Louis goes into Los Angeles to play the Dodgers in a three-game series, and the Dodgers beat them three times with four runs. That's pretty tough. Things happened to us that [made it seem] it just wasn't in the cards to win the pennant, you know what I mean? Marichal was suspended for 10 or 12 days, and loses three turns. And you know, if he doesn't miss three turns, he would have won two of them. Then, Marichal comes back, and we're playing in Milwaukee, and he takes

Herman Franks with Horace Stoneham. (SF Giants)

[Manny] Martinez out to dinner, and Martinez slams the door on Marichal's finger, and he's out again. I guess we just weren't supposed to win [the Giants finished 95-67, two games behind the Dodgers].

In '66, of course, we traded Cepeda for Sadecki. I was involved in that deal. That was a bad trade. But Cepeda would not play the outfield. He would not play the outfield. Now, Cepeda was out in '65 with a bad knee. McCovey was the first baseman, and he hit 39 home runs. Now we start spring training in '66, and I can't tell McCovey to go to the outfield, because he wants to stay at first base. So I say to Cepeda, "Go along with me for a little bit. You play the outfield, and I'll eventually get you back there [at first], more than likely, and get McCovey to go out to the outfield." But no, he insisted on playing first base. It was either play me there, or trade me. Can you imagine having McCovey, Cepeda, Mays and Hart all lined up together? Oh, it's too bad. When I look back on that, if Cepeda would have just had a little compassion, and just gone along with us for a little bit ... you know, he had the bad leg, but he still could run pretty damn good. I tell you what, he was one of the most fearless hitters I ever saw [even with the trade, the '66 Giants finished 93-68, a game and a half behind the Dodgers].

After the '68 season, I retired again and came back home to my businesses here in Salt Lake. Until '77 when the Cubs called me and asked if I'd want to go back and manage the Cubs. So I said OK, let's go. Oh, I love Chicago. Greatest fans in the world, right there. They were the greatest fans. And that was one of the most satisfying years I ever had, in '77. We were in first place in August, with a very mediocre ball club. But those guys played 120 percent, every one of them. I didn't have the Mayses, the McCoveys and the Marichals. This was a mediocre team, and we were playing like hell. We were in first place in August until I lost [Rick] Reuschel and [Mike] Krukow in the same week, to injuries. And we lost [Steve] Ontiveros and our catcher. All within 10 days. Krukow was a great guy. He and Reuschel pitched great ball for me [combining for 78 wins in Franks' three years managing the Cubs].

Just being in baseball all those years has been a big thrill for me. I loved managing. And Mays was the one player I saw who stood out head and shoulders above them all. He was just a great player, and an easily managed one, too.

You know, I was in San Francisco recently and I met a guy outside a restaurant there, a guy who went to Notre Dame. And he was telling my wife that Ara Parseghian would often use my name in speeches he gave, because I always got the most out of the players I managed. *Ara Parseghian.* Well, I never even met Ara Parseghian. But I'd like to someday. I'd like to talk with him about that. Isn't that something?

Salt Lake City, Utah

WES WESTRUM

Wes Westrum began his coaching career with the '58 Giants, following 11 seasons as a Giants catcher in New York, during which he hit .217 with 96 home runs, made two National League All-Star teams and played in two World Series. He then coached the Giants for six years before being traded to the Mets for Cookie Lavagetto in the only one-for-one swap of coaches in major league history. Wes coached the Mets under

Casey Stengel for one and a half seasons before replacing Stengel as manager. He piloted the Mets for two and a half years, leaving behind the core of a club that would go on to stun the baseball world two years later with a World Series title.

Westrum returned to San Francisco to manage the Giants midway through the 1974 season, then piloted the club to a third-place finish in '75. He scouted after that, most recently for the Atlanta Braves, before retiring in '94, after 54 years in baseball.

Wes lives in Mesa, Arizona, and has one daughter and three grandchildren nearby.

I WAS PLAYING at [triple-A] Minneapolis in 1947 when I got the call to join the [Giants] ball club in Chicago. It was September 17. Mel Ott was the manager. And what a gentleman he was. A wonderful person. In 1949 they farmed me out [to triple-A Jersey City], until they got rid of Walker Cooper. That's when I hit five grand slams [an International League record] in just 51 games. It was just one of those things. Then, just prior to my coming back up, in Cincinnati, I broke my finger. Well, I reported in Cincinnati, and Durocher was the manager. He knew about the injury and said, "Just put a piece of tape around it, and rub it in the dirt." Then he said, "You're catching Jansen." [laughs] I could hardly get the ball back to the pitcher, and I couldn't swing very well. But I wasn't too bad a hitter [over the years] if I kept my fingers well. I had eight broken fingers through my career. That didn't help my batting average [laughs].

My greatest moment in baseball came in 1951, with Bobby Thomson's home run—the shot heard 'round the world. We were 13½ games back on August 12th. I remember because that was my day. Poughkeepsie, New York, gave me a day on August 12—Duchess County, I should say. And that day was the beginning of our winning streak. We won 16 in a row. And I didn't catch the 17th. I was hurt. When Bobby hit the home run, I was on the bench. Bill Rigney had hit for me in the seventh inning, and he struck out. And I said, "Well, I could have done that." [laughs] But that definitely has to be the greatest single moment in baseball because when you come from 13½ games back and then win a three-game playoff, the World Series was an anti-climax.

In 1952 and '53 I was named to the National League All-Star teams, but never got to play. I was just getting ready to go in, in '52, when the rains came in Philadelphia. In fact, I was warming up and we had already played five innings. And that was it. In '53 I didn't get in because I hurt myself. I had a leg injury. We played the Dodgers two days prior to that All-Star Game in Cincinnati. I rode to Cincinnati with Jackie Robinson and Hoyt Wilhelm.

In '54 we beat the Cleveland Indians four in a row [to win the World Series], but that would still rank second to what we achieved in '51. We clinched the pennant a week before the season was over in '54. And, of course, we knew the Cleveland Indians like a book because we played them all spring. They were in Tucson and we were in Phoenix. We played 'em exhibition games all the way up to the Opening Day of the season. We learned a lot playing them, and knew them like a book.

Wes Westrum (SF Giants)

It was sad to leave New York in '57 because we had been there so many years. The Polo Grounds had a lot of history. But San Francisco was a good baseball town, too. Just great. As cold as it was there at times, at night, we'd still fill the stands. They were great, great people. I was living in New York, in Poughkeepsie, at the time of the move. I was washing windows outside the house [laughs], when I got a call from Bill Rigney, and he says, "I can keep you as a third-string catcher, but I'd rather have you as coach." So I say, "Well, let me think it over." I waited a week, then called him back and said, "I'd be willing to coach." I was ready to give up my playing career. And I was excited about going to San Francisco.

Oh, yeah, definitely. That's a beautiful place. I remember playing exhibition games there. Of course, Seals Stadium wasn't the best—it was a minor league ballpark—but it was a very homey park, where people were close to you, and the stands were close to the playing field. That was one of the best bunch of players we ever had, under Bill Rigney. And that was my first year of coaching. I was pitching coach. I worked out of the bullpen.

You asked about the reputation I had as a sign-stealer. Yes, I was one of the best. That started in '59 when I was the first base coach. That was my forte, and I enjoyed it because it helped win a lot of ballgames. Every pitcher's different, and they hold the ball differently. A lot of them telegraph when they're going to throw the curve—they hold it a different way than they do the fastball. Later on, when people knew I was stealing signs, they kept the ball in the glove. But if they didn't know enough to just grab the ball and then change it in the glove, well, that was their fault [laughs]. Everybody holds the ball differently with sliders, curves and fastballs.

When left-handed hitters were at the plate, I called out their first names for a fastball, and their last names for the curve. If I didn't have it [the sign], they didn't hear me. Now, with right-handers, I would bend over on the curve and stand straight up on the fastball. I'd steal signs just about every other day [laughs]. A lot of 'em telegraphed their pitches. On curveballs, some of the pitchers bring the ball in the windup up to their forehead. I had about two or three seconds before the ball was delivered to signal the hitter. Even if they hide the ball in their glove, there are still signs you can pick up. They'll tilt the glove a little bit with their wrist. They're getting their wrist ready, and tilting it to throw the curveball. They used to call that "wrapping" the curveball. I got Mays and McCovey, and quite a few others, a lot of home runs that way.

I coached the Giants through 1963, and then they traded me for Cookie Lavagetto. Cookie lived in San Francisco, and Casey Stengel wanted me, so they made a deal and I went with Casey as a coach. I coached for him in '64, and then in '65 there was an old-timers game and Casey asked me, "Wes, you want to come over with me to the old-timers game?" And I said, "Well, we've got a doubleheader tomorrow, Casey." So, I go to church that Sunday morning, come to the ballpark and they tell me, "You're the man." I say, "For what?" They say, "Didn't you hear? Casey broke his hip last night." He fell off a stool, or something [laughs]. So I became interim manager. We split the doubleheader that day. I'll never forget that. We should have won the first game but didn't.

In 1966 Tom Seaver pitched his first major league ballgame for me. Jack Fisher opened the season and Tom Seaver pitched the second game. I didn't want to put the rookie out there Opening Day. But that was the beginning of the Mets [rise]. We finished ninth. And in 1967 we had umpteen injuries—I had 15 men out 20 days and over. Otherwise we'd have finished a little higher [than 10th]. Then I resigned. I wanted a two to three year contract and they wouldn't give it to me. But I was happy to be part of a great organization. The day I resigned, September 21st, 1967, I said, "Get yourself an infielder and a center fielder," and I even told them who to trade for. And they made the deal and got some ballplayers—Tommie Agee was the center fielder, and Al Weis played shortstop, second and third. We already had Ed Charles at third, Cleon Jones in left, Bud Harrelson at short and Ron Swoboda in right.

After that I called up Mr. Stoneham and he took me back with the Giants, as a coach. Then I managed again in '74 and '75. I took Charlie Fox's place. I was scouting at the time when Tom Sheehan called me and said, "Mr. Stoneham would like to have you manage the ball club. We're firing Charlie Fox." And I said, "Well, I'll think about it." Because managing wasn't my forte. But I said, "Yes. I'll help him out," because he was in dire straits [financially] at the time. We traded Bobby Bonds for Bobby Murcer after the '74 season. I can't really tell you why Bonds was traded so many times [in his career], but there evidently had to be something wrong that I never knew about. People don't realize this, but it's often how you come across at times to different people—managers, for example. And he might have given the front office a hard time—that I don't know. But Murcer paid me the highest compliment that I've ever been paid in baseball. He came to me and said, "I've played for a lot of managers, but you're the best."

I spent 54 years in baseball. Oh, I miss it. I definitely do. But after being let go during the strike [in '94], and then no playoffs and no World Series, I kind of lost interest. I was let go [as a scout] by the Atlanta Braves because of the strike. I was a part-time worker. I had cancer 10 years ago and had a part-time job, just covering spring training. I made social security wages, and it kept the wolves away from the door. It was phenomenal. I worked for the Braves for eight more years after that, just part-time. They're a wonderful organization. Just great.

I just went to see my oncologist yesterday. He put me through the mill and said, "Wes, everything's fine." I weigh 198. I was down to 128 before [laughs]. It got my ureter. But I've survived it for 10 years. I'm a survivor [laughs]. That's just what I am.

Mesa, Arizona

IN MEMORY OF:

RAY JABLONSKI

After two sensational minor league seasons in 1951 and '52, Ray Jablonski made a big splash as a rookie third baseman with the St. Louis Cardinals in '53, hitting .268 with 21 home runs and 112 RBIs. He finished third in Rookie of the Year balloting, behind the Dodgers' Jim Gilliam and teammate Harvey Haddix. Prior to that, Jablonski led the class-B Carolina League at Winston-Salem with 200 hits, 45 doubles, 28 home runs, 127 RBIs and a .363 average. At triple-A Rochester the following year, he hit .299 with 18 homers and 103 RBIs.

In 1954, Jablonski made the National League All-Star team, hitting .296 with 12 homers and 104 RBIs. He also tied a major league record by completing a 14 inning game at third base without a single fielding chance. Jablonski never put up similar offffensive numbers again, although after being traded by the Cubs to the Giants in April of '57, he went on to hit .289 with nine home runs and 57 RBIs, in just 305 at-bats. Ray hit a dozen homers for the Giants in '58, along with 46 RBIs and a .230 average, as a backup third baseman and mentor to his successor, rookie Jim Davenport.

"Jabbo" was traded back to the Cardinals in March of '59, with Bill White, for pitchers Sam Jones and Don Choate. He retired in 1960 after eight seasons, at age 33, with a career average of .268 and 83 home runs.

Ray Jablonski died in 1985, in his native Chicago, at the age of 59.

Ray Jablonski (SF Giants)

DANNY O'CONNELL

After hitting .351 with eight home runs and 50 RBIs in a half-season at triple-A Indianapolis in 1950, Danny O'Connell had an excellent rookie half-season in the majors with the Pittsburgh Pirates, hitting .292 with 8 homers and 32 RBIs, playing both shortstop and third base. After a two-year stint in the army, O'Connell came back to hit .294 for the Pirates in '53 before being traded to the Milwaukee Braves.

O'Connell played three and a half seasons with the Braves, hitting .279 in '54, and tying a major league record with three triples in one game in June of '56. A year later he was traded to the Giants, with Ray Crone and Bobby Thomson, for Red Schoendienst. Danny was the Giants' starting second baseman Opening Day in 1958 at Seals Stadium, against the Dodgers. Five days later he homered twice off Don Drysdale at the LA Coliseum in a 12-2 win. O'Connell hit .232 for the '58 Giants, played sparingly in '59, then got a rebirth of sorts as a regular with the Washington Senators, hitting .260 with a career-high 15 stolen bases in '61, then winding up his career with a .263 average in '62, at age 35. He completed 10 years in the majors with a lifetime average of .260 with 39 home runs.

Danny O'Connell coached the Senators for two seasons, got into private business and then died tragically in an auto accident in 1969, near his home in Clifton, New Jersey, at the age of 42.

Danny O'Connell (SF Giants)

CURT BARCLAY

Six-foot-three Curt Barclay turned down a contract offer from the NBA's Boston Celtics to sign with the Giants in 1952. He made a steady rise through the Giants' minor league system, winning 19 games with class-B Danville in '54, 16 with class-A Sioux City in '55, and 15 with triple-A Minneapolis in '56. Barclay joined the Giants' starting rotation as a rookie in '57, going 9-9 with a team-best 3.44 ERA in 183 innings. Barclay began the '58 season in San Francisco, beating the Dodgers in relief, in the third game of the season at Seals Stadium. However, a shoulder injury forced the Giants to send Barclay to triple-A Phoenix two weeks later, Curt finishing the year in the Coast League, going 12-8 with a 3.91 ERA.

Unfortunately, Barclay's career was all but over. He appeared in one game with the Giants in '59, then was forced to retire shortly thereafter.

Curt Barclay died in Missoula, Montana, in 1985, at the age of 53.

GORDON JONES

Sacramento native Gordon Jones had a sensational rookie campaign after his midseason call-up by the St. Louis Cardinals in 1954. Jones made 10 starts, threw four complete games and two shutouts, and finished with a 4-4 record and a 2.00 ERA. Two years later he was part of a nine-player trade that also sent Jackie Brandt to the Giants, with Red Schoendienst the key player going to the Cards.

Jones spent most of the '57 and '58 seasons in triple-A, but did make the most of his opportunity in San Francisco, going 3-1 with a 2.40 ERA in 30 innings of relief, in '58. He went 3-2 in relief for the Giants in '59, then was traded with Brandt again, to the Baltimore Orioles for Billy O'Dell and Billy Loes. Jones finished his 11-year career with Houston in '65, totaling 15 wins, four complete games, two shuouts and 12 saves.

Gordon Jones died in Lodi, California, in 1994, at the age of 64.

Curt Barclay (SF Giants)

Gordon Jones, at Seals Stadium, on Santa Clara County Fair Day. (SF Giants)

JIM FINIGAN

Jim Finigan was named to the American League All-Star team his rookie season in 1954 with the Philadelphia Athletics, when he hit .302 with 7 home runs and 51 RBIs, as the A's starting third baseman. For that performance, Finigan finished second place, behind the Yankees' Bob Cerv, in Rookie of the Year voting. The last Philadelphia Athletic to hit over .300, Finigan made the All-Star team again in '55, as a member of the Kansas City A's, when he hit .255 with 9 homers and 68 RBIs. Traded to Detroit in '57, Jim hit .269 with the Tigers, and then was traded to the Giants in January of '58 for Ozzie Virgil and Gail Harris. Unfortunately for Finigan, he rode the bench with the Giants, going five for 25, before being sent to triple-A Phoenix for the rest of the season.

Finigan wound up his major league career with Baltimore in '59, hitting .252 in 119 at-bats. In six years in the majors, he hit .264 with 19 home runs.

Jim Finigan died in his native Quincy, Illinois, in 1981 at the age of 52.

SALTY PARKER

Francis James Parker, nicknamed Salty in his hometown of Granite City, Illinois, because of a special fondness for peanuts, spent 28 years in the minor leagues before joining the '58 Giants' coaching staff. Most of his playing career, beginning in 1930, was spent as a shortstop, but he also pitched 59 innings for Temple in the Big State League in '52. In addition, Salty managed 17 years in the minors, including the '57 season for the Giants' double-A farm club in Dallas, winning a Texas League pennant with a 102-52 record.

Parker's best season as a player came in '39, with Lubbock, Texas, in the West Texas-New Mexico League, when he hit .313 with 93 runs batted in. He also managed the Lubbock team in '39 to a pennant with a 90-48 record.

Seven years into that 28-year stint in the minors, Salty enjoyed a cup of coffee in the majors, with the Detroit Tigers, playing 11 games, and hitting .280 in 25 at-bats, with two RBIs.

Salty Parker died in Houston, Texas, in 1992, at the age of 79.

Jim Finigan (SF Giants)

Salty Parker (SF Giants)

PART THREE
BEHIND THE SCENES . . .

 *Bob Stevens covered the San Francisco Seals of the Pacific Coast League and the San Francisco Giants as a beatwriter for the* San Francisco Chronicle *for nearly 40 years. Never having lost his passion for the game, Bob stays involved as a part-time official scorer for the National League at Candlestick Park.*

IT WAS SUCH A DREAM of mine to cover major league baseball that it just didn't seem like it would ever happen. I was writing Pacific Coast League ball for 17 years and having a fine time, and I thought I learned a lot. But right up to the last moment I was very dubious about whether the Giants would come. And once they did it was just a dream come true.

The Coast League was marvelous but it's like driving in a 2000-mile race, and then getting to Indianapolis and riding in the 500—there *is* a difference, although not that prominent a difference. If they took the best All-Star team of a good Coast League season, of which there were many, and turned them loose in the National or American League they would not have embarrassed themselves, except perhaps in

Bob Stevens (Bob Stevens)

one category. Pitching in the major leagues had more depth. It was just sporadic in the Coast League, although they had some fine pitchers.

Larry Jansen was one of the finest pitchers I ever covered in my life and, I might add, one of the finest gentlemen. And Vic Raschi and Bill Werle—pitchers of that caliber—could play up in the majors.

I broke into baseball as a beatwriter for the Seals, with the *Chronicle,* in 1940. And I stayed until 1981, taking only one year off, to win the war [laughs]. Baseball has always been my first love. I played semi-pro ball but found out one of the best ways to see the country was to become a baseball writer. So I tried to become one, and I did. I love the game. It's still a fascination to me, totally.

The Coast League was marvelous. But I noticed a difference in the majors right away. I covered a couple of World Series and All-Star Games before the Giants came west, as well as the Bobby Thomson playoff game in New York. So I knew what the difference between the players was. But, again, I know that had they taken the best of the Coast League players of that time and played them against a major league club, they would have comported themselves quite well. There was such a predominance of fine Coast League players—Luke Easter was another—but what they were in those days was a group that had come down from the majors combined with a group that had played four to five years in the minors, and was now ready for the majors. So when you put them all together they knew how to play the game, which is something that is not quite as common today. They have to have four to five years in the minors to know.

Coast League players all got paid well and had the idyllic life of playing baseball for one week in one town, one week in another. The transportation was by train, by bus and by plane, with nine-and-seven inning doubleheaders on Sundays. They were well paid but they had to work in the winter, not like the kids today who don't have to. But they did it, and it was just a fine league. And every year Lefty O'Doul, who managed the Seals for over 20 years, would send somebody up to the major leagues. They didn't all stay but they were up there playing. And once in the major leagues, in my opinion, you're a major league player, no matter how short your time.

I was one of the lucky Giants beat writers who started with the opening of spring training in Phoenix. There were a lot of New York writers wanting to come out west but the *Chronicle* took a chance with me. I was cheaper, I guess [laughs]. We did have spring training in some pretty exotic places with the Seals, like Honolulu. Funny thing is, my first spring training [with the Seals] was in the Valley of the Moon, Sonoma. And my second was in the Valley of the Sun, Phoenix.

Covering the Giants in spring training was exciting, and it was a lot more work. I think I was one of the luckiest guys who ever covered baseball because when I broke in with the Seals it was just before Jackie Robinson. And then from that point on the explosion of talent that came into the major leagues will never again be equaled. It won't come close to being equaled. Run around those baseball parks and see guys like Gibson, McCovey, Mays and Cepeda, and mix them with the Warren Spahns, the Stan Musials, people like that. That was the best era. That was when there was a Van Gogh at every position, in my opinion. And it won't be equaled again, essentially, because kids just don't play baseball as much anymore as they used to. Now they're going to other sports—football's getting a lot of the bigger players, basketball is so popular now. But baseball had a priority back then—it had the first shot. Everybody played baseball. Every kid in every lot. So there was more talent then, and guys lasted a little longer.

Major leaguers were as accessible as those in the Coast League, but even some of them had that attitude that we in the West were still shooting Indians on every street corner. And the Eastern sportswriters were the same. But we were covering the same game they were. It's just the uniforms were filled with different bodies. And I think we did as well.

Hank Sauer was a dream, and he was a big star, a former MVP. Anybody we wanted to meet or talk to, Hank would see that we'd get to. Frankie Bowman, the Giants trainer, and so many others who came west with the Giants treated us damn well. Then when we went east people were a little bit cool. Seemed to me like we weren't ready for their swimming pool quite yet.

When you talk about a real class man, in every walk of this business, you can pick out Stan Musial as number one. Absolutely, unequivocally, a *total* human being. Hank Sauer fills that category as well. He was that nice a guy, taking us around, showing us things, what to do, who to talk to, and if there was any problem he'd intervene. But there were no real problems to speak of.

Lefty McCall, who I knew from the Seals, was the first Giant I met, until Mays came in and lit up the whole place with his enthusiasm. I liked Willie. I still do. Best ballplayer I think I ever saw. He would talk baseball with you but if you got out into some other areas he would be real cautious. He was accepted as a person, no question about that. But there was a little resentment with Willie that I would think Todd Benzinger and Mark Carreon later had with the Giants, being compared to Will Clark. Willie was being compared to Joe DiMaggio. It was DiMaggio's territory. It was San Francisco's territory. It was an American League town. So many American Leaguers played here at one time for the Seals: Lefty Gomez, Joe Cronin, Harry Heilmann, Bobby Brown, Jerry Coleman. It was a San Francisco team, and the fans here resented Mays because he represented the elite. Willie didn't complain. He suffered because he was always being compared to Joe DiMaggio.

Even to this day the people here will not admit how great Willie was, and I can't understand that. I just cannot understand because he's the greatest player who ever played here, with the possible exception of Joe. And I don't really think it's an exception. If they both played in the same season I'd send a cab out and bring them both to the ballpark. There can't be anything that would transcend that. And yet they just picked on Willie. They applauded Khrushchev and heckled Mays. That's what kind of town this was. So provincial. But they outgrew it, although even today there are still some who don't think he was that good. He *was* that good.

Willie just wasn't accepted as he hoped he would be. He was down about it. The first time he went back to New York, during a road trip to Philadelphia, he told a sportswriter very frankly and vividly, and from his heart, that he didn't like it out here. He didn't like the atmosphere, didn't like the way he was being treated, that the fans booed him and didn't think he could play. And he was literally in tears. When I read that I went to Willie's room and asked if he really said those things. He said he did, that it was exactly how he felt. Now, of course, it's totally turned around. He's a Bay Area guy. And although he admitted that Joe DiMaggio was even *his* idol, he said it was tough in that he heard and read more about DiMaggio in San Francisco than he heard and read about himself.

The fans here didn't want to take in Mays because they didn't want to lose DiMaggio. So they adopted Orlando as the first of *their* Giants. He was their boy. He was big, burly, funny and full of excitement and joy, and could play like hell. It was an absolute crime that it took so long for Cepeda to get in the Hall of Fame. People forget that he had a heck of a career. Look at all the numbers that he put up. And he was a fine first baseman. Matter of a fact, he was a *very* good first baseman. But look at it this way: Willie Mays was not a unanimous vote to the Hall of Fame. Neither was Hank Aaron. Now, who the hell voted against them?

The *Oakland Tribune* in 1958 only referred to the team as the Giants, never the San Francisco Giants. Provincialism of the quintessence. Both sides of the bay were like that. *That's Brooklyn over there. This is New York.* That's how *we* looked at Oakland and San Francisco. San Francisco lost the Seals but gained the Giants. Oakland lost the Oaks but gained nothing. They got a big blank until the A's moved from Kansas City [in '68].

But, talk about rivalries. I was on the team bus every time the Giants came into LA. When these two teams met in LA it was a terrible thing. You could almost reach out and grab that intense desire to play—*let's get at 'em*. They didn't like each other, on the field. In fact, Tommy Lasorda told me that in spring training, in both the major and minor league clubhouses, it was always, *"Hate the Giants, hate the Giants."* And that was brought out onto the field. Mays said when they played the Dodgers they played to win. They didn't care who got hurt or how many times, but then the two sides would go out to dinner together after the game. He and Junior Gilliam were great buddies. They'd fight like hell on the diamond, not necessarily physically, and they'd very seldom talk to each other. Very seldom. That was almost a league policy at the time, not to fraternize with the opposition. Now, the rivalry isn't as intense because it doesn't have the talent to compare. It does in the mind of Tommy Lasorda. He's that way—Dodger blue. Nothing wrong with that. Of course, he comes from those years when an enormous amount of talent was centered on those two clubs.

At the end of spring training in those days we'd go on a barnstorming tour through Texas all the way to the East Coast, playing every day. I enjoyed it because it was new. I enjoyed seeing cities I had not seen, players I had not seen. We traveled mostly with Cleveland, and when you had Wynn, Garcia and pitchers like that throwing against your club every day it was quite competitive. It was marvelous traveling by train. Ballplayers were accessible. We'd play cards and have a fine time. I don't know if the players liked it or not but I didn't give a damn. I thought they were lucky to be there, as was I.

I didn't really socialize with the players. Even in the Coast League I had a different philosophy on that. They are uncomfortable with writers as we are uncomfortable with them, from a social standpoint, like going out to parties together. I tried to stay away from that, not because I didn't want to be with them, but I was more comfortable this way, and then they would be respectful of my wishes as I of theirs. We rode together on planes, in cabs, saw them every day and night at the ballparks, but no, we didn't hang out in bars with them. I didn't want to see what they did, nor want them to see what I did.

Back then the ball clubs paid for our hotels, traveling expenses and meal money. I can only speak for myself but I don't think that affected our writing at all. Matter of fact, our managing editor said he saw nothing wrong with his writers having the tab picked up when they were on business, because with all the publicity baseball got for free the clubs *should* pay part of it. Which I thought was logical. Never once did I ever sit in front of a typewriter and say, "Oh gee, one of the owners gave me a hell of a show last night in the bar and I had a fine time, so I can't criticize the club now." It never occurred to me. Same thing happened in the Coast League. It never affected us.

I *loved* Seals Stadium. You couldn't help but like it. It was intimate. It was a pretty little park. It was an old-fashioned ballpark with wooden fences. It was architecturally very attractive. It would have been their major league park for years had it not been for the inaccessibility of traffic—no place to park. I think they could have upper-decked it. It was built to do that. I thought it was a fine park. Ballplayers didn't complain about it. When the Giants first came and saw it they thought there'd be a million home runs hit in it, but there weren't. Center-field was 415 feet away and not many of them cleared it. It was a good ballpark. The fans were right down close to the field. The weather was the same [as at Candlestick]. Don't write or don't say that it was any different.

The best part of being at Seals Stadium at that time was that they had these breweries across the street, *Burgermeister* and *Hamm's.* It was great because when they brewed, puffs of that brew would come and fall down around the field and you could get a pretty good can [buzz] on by the end of nine innings. It's *true.* It was marvelous [laughs]. And there was a bakery across the street. So you'd have the smell of freshly baked breads and pastries mixed in with the beers. And there were a couple of bars down the street. But it really wasn't like the neighborhood surrounding Wrigley Field in Chicago. It was more of an industrial area.

The thing I remember most about that first game at Seals was the awareness that baseball had really become national, from coast to coast, which it had never been before. And that was the beginning of geographical expansion. Now, of course, it's become international with Montreal and Toronto. And in time the majors will expand to Japan. But I saw the first step west, a few years after the covered wagon, according to the writers in New York. But that's when baseball, in my opinion, became the national game. And that was a thrill. It couldn't help but be a thrill. And winning 8-0 wasn't any letdown either. The Dodgers had their worst club that year, I think. Horace Stoneham came here and said that within five years he'd have a World Series for us, and by God he did in four. Of course, LA did it the next year.

Ruben Gomez [the Opening Day winning pitcher] had a pretty good personality. He was a skinny guy but he could throw like hell. Gomez and his catcher Valmy Thomas, and Orlando, the Alous, Andy Rodgers and Ray Monzant were all part of that early wave of talent from the Caribbean that came into the States when Jackie Robinson broke down the color barrier. In fact, if I were the owner of a ball club right now, I'd be one of the first to suggest that we get back to political accord with Cuba. And then I'd have about 10 scouts on the first boat over there. Then you'd see another explosion of talent such as the one we saw in the fifties and sixties.

Actually, the one guy I do vividly recall complaining about Seals Stadium was Johnny Antonelli. He hated the wind. Johnny was a spoiled little guy. Or, a spoiled big man. He could pitch like hell but he wanted to be angry about something. I don't think he ever wanted to come west. Not many of the Giants did. This was really thought of as head-hunting territory out here.

They couldn't see the civilization as it really was, and Johnny just didn't like it. He was a *big man on campus* from New York, who took on a crusade against San Francisco. But he won 19 games in '59 so he wasn't too much in the doghouse. He was sort of like Will Clark in the sense that he was so competitive and he loved to talk. So he'd go out and pitch his way right back into the affections of most people. He wasn't a bad guy at all.

WHEN I GOT OUT OF POLY HIGH in San Francisco my dad gave me an option—go to college or go to work. And I told him years later that I didn't do either one. I got to be a baseball writer and never worked a day in my life [laughs]. And I believe that. It's been fascinating to me to this day, and I'm 80 years old. And to this day I see something every day I like.

I don't think sportswriting has changed all that much over the years, but it's the fine job that television does that forces us to try to keep up with it. That adds pressure because the explosion of coverage has provoked a different side of writing. I always thought, and still do, that the game is so damn beautiful to watch, that it's sufficient unto itself to form a story every day, of something essentially good. But right now there's such a surge of publicity around the game that the paper guys have to find an angle to survive. I don't blame them for it. I just don't like some of the ways they go at it.

Lefty O'Doul once told me something I never forgot. He said, "Bob, nobody loses a baseball game. Somebody wins the game. Isn't that the better way of looking at it? It would be pollyannish to say *every* game is won. Sure, there are lots of games lost. But there's always something in that one game that is positive and worth writing about. The people in the bars read your stories. Those are the guys for whom you write." And we were in a labor man's town, too, and they were all working. So I always tried to find something good. And I think one of the most flattering things ever said about me was from Willie McCovey, who said no matter how badly the Giants played and no matter how they stank out the joint, Bob Stevens always found something nice to say about them. I think that's the way it should be.

I don't think the game itself has changed much over the years but I'll tell you what has changed enormously, in my opinion. The people who watch baseball are the bloodline. They have

learned more about how the game is played by the television commentators, like Mike Krukow, Ron Fairly, Joe Morgan, so many of them, even Jerry Coleman, as much as he murders the language once in a while. They have educated people into the nuances of this game beyond all measure of the past. Oh, the enormous number of things that go into playing baseball. It is not played by rote. It is a very, very intelligent game when it is played right. And if you're listening to these guys, and watching, there's an encyclopedia of knowledge out there that's available.

In one respect, though, the game itself has changed. Pitchers throw more at hitters now than they used to. It's hard to believe, looking back now, that guys actually went up to bat without helmets. But, in fact, the helmet provoked more throwing at the hitter. I talked to Dave Duncan, the Cardinals' coach, about that recently and he said, "Sure, that absolutely gives the pitcher more freedom," knowing that if he hits a batter he won't kill him. He said the helmet gives the pitcher a larger margin for error that he didn't used to have.

I've been an official scorer for the last 20 years, and before that for many years in the Coast League and another five in the majors. And I'm very engrossed in, and fascinated and awed by scoring, because of its nuances. And the only time in all the years I've scored that I was really tight was when Tony Gwynn and Will Clark went to the wire in '89 for the batting title. Clark was playing his final three games in San Diego, and I was scoring Will's final three home games prior to that. And, believe me, I was just praying there'd be no questionable base hits or errors. I wouldn't have wanted to call it. I would have called it the best I could but I was conscious of the magnitude of this—maybe $20,000 to $30,000 involved for the winner of the batting championship. That didn't frighten me but I'll tell you, no guy in the stands has that type of pressure when he's scoring.

When I was covering the Giants many official scorers were hometown scorers. We're all different. We don't all score this game the same. The law of infallibility is out the window when you're up here scoring a ballgame. But when Russ Hodges came out here with the Giants in 1958 he knew I had scored in the Coast League and was going to score in the majors. And he asked me, on the air, about my philosophy of scoring. I told him it made no difference who was wearing white and who was wearing gray, that they'd get the best of my ability as a scorer, that I'd call the play the right way, that I didn't give a damn if the guy was a Giant or a Dodger, I'd give him his due. Russ said he didn't understand, that a guy should always get a break in his home ballpark. I said, "Not in my book." Russ took the same interview two weeks later and ran it again. And paid me again, too [laughs]. So I figured I had to be half right anyway.

But I've seen many hometown calls. There's one play that stands out in the mind of everybody who ever saw it. It was Sam Jones pitching his no-hitter [in '59] at the LA Coliseum, and Andre Rodgers bobbling an easy groundball [with two outs in the eighth]. Stories are written that he threw the ball away, but he never got *to* the ball. He never *threw* the ball. It was just a butchered play. Yet, the scorer gave him a hit. Poor ol' Sam. He'd have killed the guy if he'd seen him that night.

In that essence of scoring, it was just as bad in the essence of umpiring when Harry Wendelstedt didn't give Dick Dietz first base when he was hit by Drysdale, with the bases loaded [in 1968, thus preserving Drysdale's record-tying fifth straight shutout]. Palpably, he tried to get away from it. Who the hell is going to stand in front of Drysdale and get hit? He had a welt as big as a basketball. Harry's a good umpire but he should not have said what he said after the game. He said he was not about to let a baseball record go down the drain because of a hit-batsman. He should not even be *aware* of the record. No umpire should be aware of what's at stake out on the field. He should simply make the right call for each individual play.

I guess this is tooting my own horn but I have no objections, no timidity, to going down to the clubhouse on a scoring decision that is questionable and talking to the players. I've done it many times and I know some respect is gained by doing that. Sometimes you get yelled at, sometimes you don't. I've never been threatened. And changes have been made by talking to the players. I've found them infinitely honest. The only difference, and it's a human difference, is the pitcher wants an error and the hitter wants a base hit.

THE GREATEST HITTER I ever saw was Willie Mays, unequivocally. The greatest pitcher was probably Juan Marichal. The greatest Coast League pitcher I ever saw was Larry Jansen, and he carried it on into the majors. But when you talk about the greatest pitchers in the big leagues, good lord. Bob Gibson, Sandy Koufax, Drysdale, Warren Spahn, who didn't win a big league game until he was 25 years old. Marichal, who never won a Cy Young because he was always up against Koufax and Gibson, and yet he was every bit as good as both of them. I hate to say Marichal was a cut above the rest, but I would say so in the respect that he had so many different pitches. He could get you out so many different ways. Spahnnie was the same way. Koufax was overpowering until he had to get the curve, and then he was better. Marichal I admired for his distinguished leg kick and his command.

Let me put it this way: If I had to make a choice between the two best ballplayers I ever saw, it'd be between DiMaggio and Mays; and between the two best pitchers it'd be Koufax and Marichal, with Gibson ready. And maybe some people would take Gibson over them. When you win a Cy Young with a 1.12 ERA [in '68], you've had a pretty good season [laughs].

San Francisco, California

LON SIMMONS

After an injury sidelined his professional pitching career, Lon Simmons reached the major leagues in 1958 via the microphone, as Russ Hodges' radio play-by-play partner with the Giants. Lon has been calling games ever since, first for the Giants and 49ers, then for the Oakland Athletics from 1981 through 1995, and then back with the Giants in 1996.

I WAS SO THRILLED and happy to get the Giants' play-by-play job in 1958. It was hard to fathom that I was going to be working with Russ Hodges, and that I had a chance to do major league baseball. And the amazing thing was that when I was growing up in Southern California I always picked favorites: Jack Dempsey was my favorite boxer, Carl Hubbell and the New York Giants were my favorite player and team. When I

Lon Simmons (SF Giants)

good fastball he'd send me back to Cleveland, and I could travel the rest of the summer with the Cleveland Indians. Well, that was like giving me 10 million dollars [laughs] because I was still only 16 years old. Unfortunately, he was going to catch me that Sunday. But Friday my American Legion manager took me to work out with the Angels. They had me pitch the entire batting practice, then throw on the sidelines for about 15 minutes. Sunday when the Cleveland scout came out I didn't have a fastball to show him. I remember I was out on the mound throwing, and in about the second inning I saw him leave the stands. Boy, you talk about your heart dropping, because that would have been something for a kid to get to travel with a major league club.

As it turned out everything worked out all right. But at the time it was very disheartening because the day I signed the contract with the Phillies I hurt my arm. They put me in to pitch that night in Terre Haute [class-B], just to get my feet wet. I pitched the first inning and, as I recall, I struck out the side, then the first pitch I threw in the second inning I did something to a muscle in my back. I tore it or something, but since they were paying me a bonus—a limited amount, but a bonus nevertheless—they wouldn't let me quit pitching. So I kept pitching, and in the process of favoring my back I hurt my shoulder, and probably the rotator cuff, although nobody knew anything about rotator cuffs back then.

I pitched for Terre Haute that year and then got released when my arm got so bad I couldn't throw. The next year I went to the Sunset League in California, with El Centro. You always think the heat will help your arm and there *was* heat there, all right, but it didn't do much for my arm. I pitched part of a season there and that was it. I just couldn't throw anymore.

It was disillusioning because from the time I started first thinking about baseball I had never given any thought to the idea that this wouldn't be my career. This was something I had planned for all my life. I was a sports fan when I was probably four or five years old. During the service I was concerned about a lot of the guys who were on the ship with me. I thought, boy, what do they have to look forward to when they go back, what are their plans, what are they going to do? I always said, "I'm gonna play major league baseball," because I felt that I was. And then, all of a

was a kid playing ball I was a right-handed pitcher. Hubbell, of course, was left-handed but every time I threw the tennis ball up against the steps and played a game I made sure that Hubbell won. *Every* time [laughs]. I didn't really cheat, but I sort of hedged it a little bit.

I actually pitched professional ball with the Philadelphia organization. I played baseball, football and ran the mile in track in high school. Then I pitched at Glendale Junior College. I had a scholarship to USC but went into the service instead. When I returned the Phillies approached me. I was going to return to school but the Phills offered me an all-expenses paid trip back east. I didn't know anything about money so I increased the offer some, and they said OK. I was stuck. I didn't really want to sign because I hadn't played ball in four years. I wanted to go back to school but that didn't happen.

Actually, in my senior year in high school the LA Angels [Pacific Coast League] wanted to take a look at me. It was an interesting thing. I was pitching semi-pro and American Legion ball, and a Cleveland scout said he wanted to come out and look at me, and that if I showed him a sudden, that was taken away and I didn't have anything else to do, except go to work. I remember I used to pray for rain so I wouldn't have to go to work, but I prayed that it wouldn't rain because I needed the money [laughs].

I didn't return to school because at that point I already had a family, and was working in construction in the off-season. So I went back to working in construction, full-time, and was not

Russ Hodges and Willie Mays (SF Giants)

very happy about it. A lot of people like construction and a lot of people do a good job at it. I wasn't that good at it and I didn't like it much. And I couldn't see spending the rest of my life doing cement work or carpentry work.

My radio career got started in 1952. I had taken journalism in school, had been the sports editor and editor of my high school paper, and that was the major I was going to pursue in college. I talked to the local paper in Burbank but the amount of money they paid was not that much to support a family on. But later I found out that if you could get a first-class engineering license you could go to work for a small radio station. I went to school and quickly found that I had no aptitude at all for that sort of thing. So I decided the best thing to do was take the big, thick question-and-answer manual and memorize that sucker. At the time I had a pretty good memory so I memorized it, went down and passed the test.

I went to work in Elko, Nevada, operating the board, doing the news and disc jockey work. The fortunate thing was that it was a daytime operation, there was only one other announcer and he didn't care whether he was on the air or not. So I just took time out for lunch and was on the air the rest of the day. I was getting a week's experience every day with the amount of time I

was on air. Then I went to work in Marysville and Yuba City, doing DJ work, but they also let me do the sports for nothing, including play-by-play for high school baseball, football and basketball, and semi-pro baseball. I did all that for nothing just to get the experience, and also did a sports show on my own time. Then that led to getting a job in Fresno, strictly doing sports, at KMJ.

I went to KSFO [in San Francisco] in July of '57. They hired me as sports director because Gene Autry had just bought the station, and they were going to get into sports real heavily. They got the rights to the 49ers, and eventually the Giants, and they wanted to have a sports show and a sports director. I did the color with Bob Fouts on the 49er games, then the next year he started doing TV so I started doing 49er play-by-play. My *first* play-by-play in San Francisco, though, was USF basketball in '57.

I sensed I might have a shot to do the Giants because I was already working at the station, but it was no cinch by any means because it depended on what the Giants decided in terms of who they'd bring with them from New York. As it turned out Russ Hodges was the only one they brought west. The Giants didn't have anybody else in mind, nor did Falstaff [the sponsor], so KSFO pushed for me and, fortunately, the Giants agreed to it. Jim Woods was working with Russ in

New York, and I believe he went directly to the Pirates from there.

But, again, I was so thrilled to get the Giants job, *and* to work with Russ Hodges. Russ and I had a very special relationship. He was so thoughtful and giving that he had no jealousies or fears. He wasn't worried about what anybody else might do to take his job so, consequently, he gave whatever he had to me as his number-two announcer, and he didn't hold back a thing. And he gave me the opportunity to do things that other announcers wouldn't have done. The other announcers would have been too jealous of the situation.

In fact, on my birthday in 1960, Juan Marichal was pitching [in his big league debut] and headed for a no-hitter. I usually did the third, fourth and seventh innings. So I was doing the seventh inning and Russ said, "Just stay on the air." I asked why. "Well," he said, "it's my birthday present to you. You've never done a no-hitter." Unfortunately, Marichal didn't get the no-hitter [he one-hit the Phillies, 2-0, with 12 strikeouts], but Russ gave me that opportunity. And you could've gone through the entire list of announcers in major league baseball, and never found anybody else who would have done that.

I have a lot of favorite stories with Russ, including some you can't put into print. But there was an interesting thing about Russ, and I think this happens to some people. Jon Miller did an article for *Sports Illustrated,* and I know he was trying to be funny when he wrote about Russ eating and drinking while he was on the air. But it wasn't true, and I told him so. I talked to him about it and said I knew he was trying to be humorous, but that I thought the picture he painted of Russ was just wrong. He ate in the booth while *I* was on the air and I probably ate in the booth while *he* was on the air, but *he* wasn't eating [while he was on the air]. And Russ never drank a drop before a game. This was a rule of his and if you did drink, you had serious trouble. He never drank a drop before. *After* a game there were no holds barred. We went out and had fun. In fact, Russ said to me, "We've got a couple of rules. One, if we win we're gonna drink after the game because we're happy. If we lose we're gonna drink after the game because we're sad. The only reason we won't drink is if we're tied."

Well, there are not many ties in baseball. But one night we're in Philadelphia and the tying run was on third, and it was the curfew inning. Hobie

Landrith threw the ball back to Mike McCormick and Mike wasn't looking, and it went over his head and the tying run scored. That meant we had a tie game and it was going to be called. Russ scribbled something, handed it over to me and it said, "We're just gonna break the rule."

I'm not only fortunate to have been able to work alongside Russ Hodges for years, and to have been working in baseball since 1958, but also to have been able to stay in the San Francisco Bay Area for that long. Very few people, and Bill King [A's broadcaster] is another—we're both fortunate that we've not had to battle for jobs or move to other towns. So I do feel that I've been blessed in my career. I worked hard in the smaller stations to advance. I put my time in, working for nothing to get experience, and doing what it took to advance. When I got to San Francisco I felt that's where I wanted to be. I had no ambitions to go network and probably couldn't if I had the ambitions, but didn't want to. So I was blessed that I was able to stay here in San Francisco, which I thought was the ultimate for me in broadcasting.

THE GIANTS FILLED that little ballpark most days and nights in 1958 and '59. They'd play the games [on radio] in the markets, and ladies would go shopping and ask for the score. Plus, transistors were very big in those days. People would have their transistors going to concerts, the opera and to school. Everyone followed the Giants—even people who had not followed baseball before were interested. There was excitement because everything that happened meant something to somebody. A win was not just a win like now, when it's June and it's good to win but it's not *that* important. In '58 and in those early days each game and each pitch was important. And probably the fact that it was at Seals made it a more intimate situation. The people felt more because it was still part of San Francisco, that it was Seals Stadium. When they moved to Candlestick Park it was sort of like the game was taken away from the fans a little bit. I don't know exactly how to explain it but it was a much bigger place. It was *not* typically San Francisco. I don't think Candlestick Park *ever* was San Francisco, to tell you the truth. Seals Stadium was San Francisco, but not Candlestick Park.

It was a good ballpark. I remember we used to sit so that we could talk to the people right in front of us. The seats would come right up to our booth, behind home plate. And there was one guy who used to bring a different gal to the game every day. We used to speculate on who he was bringing and what relationship they were to him. But the people could stand up and turn around and talk to us. We could lean over and talk to them. You were *right there.* It was like Kezar Stadium for the 49ers. You could see the expressions on the players' faces. You were right there. It was much better for a broadcaster than Candlestick because you were so close to the action.

As I said, it was a San Francisco place where there was a lot of local tradition. That was one of the reasons they didn't accept Mays right away here, that Cepeda was their hero, and McCovey, too—because San Francisco was very provincial, and I think that provincialism carried over to the fact that Seals Stadium was *their* ballpark, and had *its* memories of baseball and *its* heroes. And the Giants became part of that by playing in that stadium. When they moved to Candlestick it was different—a different atmosphere, a different outlook.

I remember getting into it once with Curley Grieve [*San Francisco Examiner* sportswriter]. Eventually we got to be friends. But we were print and radio enemies for a while because Johnny Antonelli lost a game to the Dodgers when Charlie Neal hit two home runs into left field, because of the wind, at Seals Stadium. Antonelli was really bitter after the game and was griping about the wind to a group of writers.

Well, they had *editorials* in the paper—talk about provincial—about this New Yorker knocking our Bay Area weather. Editorials, sports columns, *everything.* Antonelli was like an outcast because he had dared to blame the wind for the two home runs. So I had him on the air the next day to explain his part. And Curley Grieve came to Bill Rigney and said, "What are you letting him go on that two-bit radio show for, and talk like that?" And Rig said he didn't consider it a two-bit show, and that he had a right to say what he felt. So Curley wrote something, I wrote something back and Curley said, "It's like an ant attacking an elephant." And I said, "Well, apparently the elephants in San Francisco have thinner skin because this ant got to him." [laughs] We went back and forth and then, eventually, Curley and I got to be friends. But it was amazing to me the furor of him being upset about the wind.

It was cold, foggy and windy at Seals Stadium, just like it is at Candlestick. The weather wasn't really any better. But, probably, the wind was more consistent than it is at Candlestick, because of the hill up there above Candlestick and the water around it, making the wind go all over. With Seals Stadium it generally blew out to center field all the time, and so you knew which way it was going to blow. But it was a cold, windy stadium. I wasn't familiar enough with the area, having been here only two years, to know that the wind was going to be as bad as it turned out to be at Candlestick Park. But Chub Feeney went out there when they were building it, at about 1:30 in the afternoon, and big cardboard cartons were blowing around, and he asked one of the workers if the wind blew like that all the time. And the guy said, "No, it doesn't start until about one o'clock." [laughs]

But I think at the time, with the Dodgers about to build a new stadium, that everybody thought, well, a new stadium was going to be great. And if it had been built right and planned right it *would* have been great. But, as usual, the people who were involved in building the stadium didn't really listen to people who knew about those things. It was just like when they re-did Candlestick for the 49ers. They asked me about a broadcast booth and I drew up some plans for them. They never even came close. The first week they were going to play football there Stu Smith [radio producer] came to me and said, "Look, you can't see the field from the new press box." So I went up and, sure enough. They had to build platforms up so the press sitting there could look down and see the field. This was the same way Candlestick [itself] was built. They asked people, then they didn't pay any attention. Melvin Belli filed suit because fans were cold in the stadium. They had incorporated that radiant heating but it never worked. There were pipes, supposedly with warm water running through them, that were supposed to warm up the stands but that didn't work. And he filed suit against the city and the Giants [and got the cost of his '62 season tickets reimbursed].

LOOKING BACK, the games [over the years] tend to run together, although the biggest memory of Seals Stadium I probably have is playing the Dodgers in a doubleheader when Daryl Spencer was beaned and had to go to the hospital, and the police chief [Ahern] died in the stands the same day. I think one of the games went 16 innings. Everything that could happen did. Ray

Jablonski tried to stop at every base but scored the winning run. He tried to stop at second but they waved him on. He tried to stop at third but they waved him on again. And then he tried to stop at home, and we almost had another death at home plate [laughs]. Jabbo almost passed away. Furillo had thrown the ball and it was just dribbling toward home plate, and Jabbo wanted to stop at every base but couldn't do it.

So many guys stand out from that '58 team. Orlando certainly does. Jim Davenport has been a close friend of mine for years. Mays, of course, was a standout. Felipe Alou, Bob Schmidt, Daryl Spencer, Valmy Thomas. Ruben Gomez was probably one of the biggest characters of them all. Some of the things that happened to Gomez in his career .... He was hysterical. I had Ruben on the show after the big brawl with Danny Murtaugh and the Pirates, and the fans in Pittsburgh were really brutal. He threw a baseball up in the stands at them from the bullpen, and I said to him the next day, "Aren't you a little concerned?" And he said, "I was so mad at them I don't care if I hit a baby." [laughs]

Probably the most interesting character of them all was the manager, Bill Rigney. There are certain guys that are born to be managers. I would say Rig, and the guy who managed here in Oakland, Tony LaRussa—they're just born to be managers. That's what Rig was, a manager. He had this young group of players here, and had Horace not been antsy all the time, and fired him in 1960, he would have probably won two or three pennants with the Giants. Rigney had a great sense of humor, too. I remember he once joked that he was going to have a couple of sheds built, one just outside the right field line, the other outside the left field line. Then he was going to tell Leon Wagner in left and Willie Kirkland in right, that anytime a ball was hit to the outfield, *anywhere* in the outfield, they should run into their respective sheds, and just let Mays catch it. Wagner, especially, wasn't the greatest fielder, but the point was, Mays was that much better than both.

I still enjoy the game now but I was closer to it then because I was closer in age to the players. All of them were my friends. I played golf with them and I was more involved with them. I like the players today but I'm not as close to them. I can kid them and talk with them but, as far as spending any time with them, I don't because of the age difference. So it doesn't bring me quite as close to the game as I was then. Has the game itself changed? The athletes have probably gotten better. I think the concern, though, is that the comfort and the money has made some of the athletes complacent, where they don't reach their potential, where they aren't as good as they could be. I think that's probably a disease that has stricken a few of the players, whereas before they had to play if they were going to reach economic heights. They *had* to play their best all the time. Now, if you have a five-year contract and you're a multimillionaire, it takes away the incentive. I don't mean that they quit but it takes away the incentive to work hard. When you get to a position of affluence you forget how and why you got there, and you think more about taking things easy, rather than continuing to work hard. Some can continue their work ethic but most can't. But I don't think there's any doubt the players today are better, stronger, faster and bigger than they were.

I started calling Giants games just 11 years after baseball broke the color barrier. I was not aware of segregation in baseball in those days but I was never aware of it much of anyplace because I didn't think about it. I didn't realize until later that no blacks lived in the town I grew up in, Burbank. I didn't even *think* about it. I remember the first time I ever saw a sign of segregation was when I was playing for El Centro. I was driving to El Centro and went into a restaurant to have something to eat, and I saw a sign on the door that said something to the effect of, "No negroes allowed." I had never seen anything like it before. And I never heard players discuss it much, to tell you the truth. I never really heard Mays or McCovey or any of those guys sit down and talk about discrimination. I'm not saying they didn't think about it or that they weren't subjected to it, but it was never the main subject of conversation I had with them.

I think the first time I was really introduced to segregation was when I did USF basketball, when we traveled to Louisville, Kentucky, to play in the Bluegrass tournament. The team was all going to a movie but they wouldn't let the black players inside. So all the players said forget it. They wouldn't go to the movie unless they could *all* go. We all thought that was atrocious, and couldn't understand it. We didn't think that maybe the same thing was happening out here, in different ways maybe. Maybe it was my fault that I wasn't more aware of it but I like to think that the reason I wasn't aware of it was I didn't feel that way myself. And I didn't even *think* about it. And it disturbs me when I see it happening now, or think about it now. It disturbs me that it *is* something that's still introduced to our children, because you know kids don't start out feeling that way. They don't have prejudices to start with. It has to be taught to them.

Oakland, California

MIKE MURPHY

 Mike Murphy has an ongoing Giants record that few in major league history could come close to matching. He has witnessed and worked every home game in San Francisco Giants history—well over 3,000 games, entering the 1998 season.

As a teenager, Mike spent four seasons as bat boy for the San Francisco Seals of the Pacific Coast League. In 1958 Murphy began working as the visiting team's batboy at Seals Stadium, for Giants games. Murph then ran the visiting team's clubhouse from '62 through '79, and moved over to the home clubhouse in 1980. He's been there ever since, as the Giants' Equipment Manager.

As the Giants celebrate their 40th anniversary in San Francisco in '98, Mike Murphy celebrates his 40th anniversary with the team. He's the only employee left from the original San Francisco Giants.

I GREW UP in the outer Mission District of San Francisco, in what they call the Excelsior District. I played high school and college ball at City College and at USF. And semi-pro. I wasn't that great of a ballplayer but I was a first baseman, and I enjoyed the game. I still do.

I was a batboy for the Seals from '54 through '57. Saw a lot of great ballplayers. Albie Pearson, Bill Renna, Kenny Aspromonte, Leo Kiely, Gordy Windhorn—a lot of guys. I've seen 'em all over the years. I thought of myself as a Seal when I was a kid, so when I heard the Giants were coming I cried my eyes out that Haywood Sullivan [Seals catcher and future Red Sox executive] and so many of the other guys wouldn't come back.

We didn't know our future, whether we even had a chance of working for the Giants. Then the Giants came out and we got hired back. And I've been with the Giants ever since.

Jerry Donovan was president of the Seals. Then he became the business manager for the Giants when they first came out. And he said he'd be looking for batboys when they came back from spring training in April. So I rushed out there to the park right after school on April 1, to see if I had a job. And I did. Roy McKercher and I got there at six o'clock in the morning. When they opened the front doors we rushed up to the clubhouse looking for Eddie Logan [clubhouse manager], but couldn't find him. He didn't come in that morning until about nine or nine-thirty. We'd been there since six o'clock. Just us. Eddie hired Red, and George Patriano, who was the visiting clubhouse guy from New York, hired me. I stayed with him as the visiting team batboy until 1962.

Seals Stadium was a great little ballpark. Easy to get to from anywhere in the city. They'd drop you off right there. Like myself, living in the Excelsior. I used to take the 14 Mission all the way up to 16th Street, then take the streetcar up to Bryant. The park was well-kept. It was a lot better than Candlestick. It got a little cold and windy, but never as windy as it is at Candlestick. It was a nice ballpark. The Seals, at one time, drew better than teams in the major leagues. It was in a good neighborhood, too. They had a bar across the street. It was owned by Lee Stanfeld and his brother, who used to play for the 49ers. They called it the *Double Play. [author's note: It's still there.]* There was a little sandwich place across the street also. And the brewery, of course. First it was Rainier, then Hamm's.

Of course, I had read about the major leagues in the newspapers as a kid—the Yankees and the St. Louis Cardinals and the Pittsburgh Pirates. Then, all of a sudden, you realize these guys are all coming. Couldn't hardly believe it. Then they were here. And just seeing the Giants play for the first time—Willie Mays—I used to read about him in the papers. I remember Gino Cimoli getting the Dodgers' first hit that first game. I got to meet Pee Wee Reese, and we became the best of friends. Every time I call Louisville Sluggers, where Pee Wee works, I always leave word for him, and the lady tells me, "Oh, Pee Wee called in and said to say hello." Then Mr. O'Malley used to bring his son Peter. He was just a young lad like Bob Lurie was.

I used to drive Don Drysdale back to the hotel after games. And I stayed with him, drinking. Him and Perranoski. We'd go to the *Iron Horse,* behind the Sheraton-Palace. Next day I'd be hung over, and Walter Alston would come in and say, "What's wrong with you, Murph?" I'd say, "Well ... And he'd say, "You were out with my boys last night, weren't you?" I'd say, "Well, a little bit." [laughs] He'd say, "How they doin'?" I'd say, "I don't know [laughs]. I just know I'm sick. I'm hung over bad."

Sandy [Koufax] was a sweetheart. He loved his coffee. And he's the one who started the ice with the trainers, so many years ago. And they still use ice on the players today. Sandy started that. And we used to call Drysdale the "Snapper." He was a good man. Don was a character. I miss him. I figure he died too young. Way too young. He was one hell of a guy. Now and then I'll just stop and think, "Snapper, what a great guy." One time I was on a ship. I was a merchant seaman during the winter. One day we were down in San Pedro with the ship. So I called the Snapper at his house, and his first wife Jeannie said, "You coming up for dinner?" And I said yeah. I said, "Well, I'll meet Snapper somewhere," because I didn't know LA that great. So I met him at this one bar. He said, "Murph, you ever been to my bar?" I said no. *Don Drysdale's Corner.* We went in there and started drinking at 10 o'clock in the morning. And now it's almost 11 o'clock at night. We were supposed to have gone over to his house to eat. We finally get up there at two

Mike Murphy (SF Giants)

o'clock in the morning. Jeannie had already started throwing the food out [laughs]. And to this day, I still don't know where he lived. Somewhere in the hills of LA.

The Dodgers used to hang around late after games like teams don't do now. Like Matt Williams and Kirt Manwaring did with the Giants. They'd sit and talk over the game, what they did wrong. Now, nobody does that anymore. Matt and Kirt and Will Clark used to all sit around and talk about what happened in the game, how come they lost, how they'll better themselves for tomorrow. Even Dusty [Baker, manager] doesn't know why they don't do that anymore. They're all rushing around, and they're gone.

I enjoyed being batboy for the visiting teams. Got to meet a lot of stars. They were all great. I was 16 then [in '58]. Just a kid. I kind of idolized them. The Giants were great to me, too. Marv Grissom, Eddie Bressoud and Mike McCormick all liked me. I'm still friends with all of them. Mr. Logan used to have nicknames for some of the guys. We used to call Jim Finigan "Magoo," because he had those big glasses. Leon Wagner was "Cheekie," because of his high cheekbones. We also called him "Daddy Wags." Jim Davenport was "Goofus," and we called him "Peanuts" too, because he was so small. You had more nicknames in the majors than you did in the Coast League.

Willie Kirkland was the clown on the team, the guy who kept things alive. Leon Wagner was the follower, the guy you'd play practical jokes on. Joe Shipley was the cartoonist—a *great* artist—he used to put cartoons on guys' T-shirts. Ship's a great person. I still get together with him when we're in St. Louis. Mike McCormick was the real debonair dresser. His uniform had to be just right, his street clothes had to be just right. I always tried to copy the way Mike McCormick dressed. He'd wear those fancy sportcoats and slacks, and nice shoes.

Stan Musial was a great guy, too. I remember Stan used to get drunk with Mr. Stoneham. Mr. Stoneham loved Stan Musial. After the game, Mr. Stoneham wouldn't go home. He'd call up the visitor's clubhouse and he'd say, "Bring Stan up." Out of all the [Giants] owners, Mr. Stoneham really liked me. He just liked me for some reason. He used to call and say, "Make sure you bring Stan up after the game." And I knew what they'd be doing. Stan would have a few horns [laughs]. Then they'd go to eat right down the street from the Hilton Hotel, at a little restaurant that's not there anymore. But that's where Mr. Stoneham's hangout was. No one ever knew that Stan Musial and Mr. Stoneham would drink together after games, then go to dinner. But that's the way Mr. Stoneham was, if he liked the ballplayer. Those were the good old days. Those days you could laugh about. No one ever got hurt. They'd let you drink and raise a little hell, and that was it. Now, if you do something like that, you got Joe Public with a camera looking behind your back.

I still see Stan in St. Louis when I go back there. He'll come by and see me. He came in the clubhouse last summer, and about four guys asked me, "Who's that?" I said, "That's Stan Musial." They didn't even recognize him. But they were impressed. They knew enough about him to be impressed. All of a sudden the balls started floating out, if you know what I mean. One thing about Stan, he'll sign. He stayed there for about an hour, signing balls and taking pictures with some of our ballplayers. He'll never forget you. Not Stan.

When we were in the playoffs with St. Louis in '87, I brought my wife, we went to a cocktail party and I said to her, "There's Stan Musial." And she said, "You think you can introduce me to him?" I said, "Hell yes. Come on. I'll introduce you." So we go over there and I said, "Stan, this is my wife." And he said, "Are you Mrs. Murphy? Who's taken care of this nice gentleman? We go back a long time, Murph and I," he said. Actually, he called me "Skinner." He said, "Skins and I go

back a long way." It made me feel proud that, hey, he's a Hall of Famer. Even today, with all the ballplayers I've known, they always come around. "Murph takes care of me," they say. "If I need something, Murph takes care of me." I see a lot of ex-ballplayers coming back today. If Mike McCormick ever needs something, I'll take care of him. If Stu Miller needs something, I'll take care of him. I've stayed in close contact with all these ex-ballplayers. I'll take care of things like guys needing balls, or autographed bats, or tickets for a game. Like Gaylord Perry used to say, "Murph was here when I got here, and Murph will still be here when I'm gone."

Mr. Stoneham surrounded himself with great scouts back in those days. Alex Pompez handled Cuba. He signed Jose Cardenal and Tito Fuentes from there, Jose Pagan from Puerto Rico and Manny Mota from the Dominican. He *tried* to sign Fidel Castro. A lot of clubs were after Fidel Castro. He was a hell of a ballplayer. Then he decided to go to the university to be whatever it is that he does now. But when he was young he was a great athlete.

As a batboy, I cleaned the helmets and fixed the bats—took 'em down and made sure they were in the right order. Then, there was one time that Roy McKercher couldn't make it—he had finals in school. So I was the visitor *and* home batboy at Seals Stadium. Between innings I'd have to run over to the other side, put a uniform on, then, after the next half inning, run back and change back. I think Logan kind of liked me after that. He said, "Damn, you can work, kid." They played 12 innings that day. I was one tired bastard that night. And I had to clean a whole bunch of shoes, and hang up clothes in the visitor's side, then go back and help Logan on the home side. I didn't get home until about 10:30 that night. I was one tired kid. Logan liked me after that.

His advice to me was simple: Don't borrow money [from a player] and never talk bad about a player. I've always kept that philosophy. Now, I tell my assistants, "Never borrow money from a player. If you need money, come see me. If I haven't got it, I'll go get it for you somewhere."

I tell you, the old days were great. I wish they were still here. I thought the major league players would be stuck up [when the Giants came west], but they weren't. They were down to earth like us. Same as the guys in the Coast League.

The managers were great, too. Fred Haney of the Braves—nice guy. I used to stop on my way to the park and buy Bermuda onions for him. He'd make a sandwich out of them. He'd cut 'em up, put 'em on French bread and eat it. He'd say, "Hey, kid, you eat Bermuda onions, you'll never catch a cold." I still eat Bermuda onions, to this day. Once a month, at least. He was right. You'll never catch a cold if you eat Bermuda onions. Everybody else is sick all the time but I hardly ever catch a cold.

Bill Rigney was a great guy. Drove his big fancy cadillac to the park. He always talked to me. He was just a personable guy, and he still is. He still calls me "Kid." [laughs] Felipe Alou and I are the best of friends to this day. He still calls me "Skinner." [laughs] I got that nickname from Mays because I used to look like Bob Skinner of the Pirates. One day I was sitting on the bench when the Pirates were in town, and Mays came walking by the dugout and said, "Hey, Skinner." I said, "Mr. Mays, it's Murph." He said, "Oh, OK. You looked like Skinner," because I was wearing the Pirate helmet. That's when the Pirates always wore their helmets, even in the field.

What a sweetheart that man is. Willie was good to me then, and still is. Willie is top-notch in my book. If he loves you he'll do anything in this world for you. If you're down he'll be the first one to come and sit down and talk. You'd be surprised how many people he's helped out over the years. When I was buying my house Willie called me one day and said to my wife, "I heard you're buying a house. If you need some money I got it for you." We told him no because we had good credit and a few bucks stashed away. But he said, "If you need it don't use your money. Use my money. You don't have to pay me back right away. You can pay me back $1,000 a year if you want." He's helped a lot of guys like that. A super guy.

Danny Murtaugh was the only manager that I brought a rocking chair to. I wish I would have kept that rocking chair. He told me one day, "It's too bad I don't have a rocking chair. I like smoking my cigar and rocking myself." So next time Pittsburgh came in, the rocking chair was waiting for him. He thought that was the greatest. Even when I started traveling with the Giants in 1964, when Mr. Logan got sick, we made a trip to Pittsburgh and went right into Danny Murtaugh's office at Forbes Field. And there was a rocking chair. And I said, "Hey, you like that, huh?"

My first year in charge of the visitor's clubhouse was the year the Giants played the Yankees in the World Series. Another dream come true for me, to meet my Yankees. Yogi Berra became friends during the Series, and we've remained friends to this day. When McCovey lined out to Richardson [to end game seven] I was in the Yankees clubhouse, getting the champagne ready. I was listening on the radio. If McCovey's ball had got through we would have just taken the champagne over to the Giants side. I wished it had.

I not only work all the home games, I go on virtually all the road trips now. Since '64. I enjoy that, too, very much so. I just enjoy taking care of my buddies' luggage on the road. Matt Williams, Kirt Manwaring. I was in Mexico fishing when I heard Matt got traded. I about cried my eyes out. I've talked to him dozens of times since and I *still* end up crying on the phone. He says, "Murph, it's part of the game." I say, "You treated me so great. I'm really gonna miss you." He says, "I might come back as manager or coach someday." That made me feel good.

San Francisco

ROY MCKERCHER

Roy McKercher was the Giants' number-one home team batboy their first four years in San Francisco, two at Seals Stadium and two at Candlestick Park.

McKercher works today as a San Mateo County Sheriff's Deputy. He's worked for the department for 29 years.

MIKE MURPHY AND I sneaked into Seals Stadium through a way we knew from the days when we worked as batboys for the Seals. We snuck in about five or six o'clock in the morning, knowing that there were going to be jobs offered, but not knowing who was going to be selected. So we thought, first-come first-served. We got in the park, propped ourselves up against the home clubhouse door and waited for Mr. Eddie Logan [equipment manager] to show up, which he did about 7:30. He was kind of surprised to see Murph and me sitting there. I was 14 years old, a big baseball fan. I played in the San Francisco Red League, and I played at Polytechnic High School.

So Mr. Logan says to George Patriano, the visiting clubhouse man from New York, "Well, which one do you want to take, the skinny kid or the red-headed kid?" And George said, "Well, you're the boss, you decide." And Mr. Logan says, "Well, I'll take the red-headed kid, and you can have the skinny kid, and we'll see how it works out."

My first day of work with the Giants was the day before Opening Day. They

Roy McKercher with Willie Mays. (Roy McKercher)

came in to have batting practice and a little infield, then they broke early. The Dodgers came in to work, and the Giants went downtown for the parade. That was the first time I met these major league ballplayers. It was an awesome experience and a little intimidating. Some of my fondest memories were with Bill Rigney, who I thought was one of the greatest guys in baseball, and with Willie Mays—I just can't say enough great things about the man. He's not only the best baseball player I've ever seen, he's also one of the most gracious gentlemen I've met. He was always very kind to me. He used to sit next to me on road trips when we took airplane flights. He'd walk me through how to behave on the road and how not to behave on the road. For example, when you got to the hotel and they grabbed your bags and brought them upstairs, you would give the guy a dollar tip. When you had dinner, at the end of the meal, you'd leave a dollar or two tip. And remember, he'd say, you're always being watched. Be careful what you say because they might misconstrue that as something else. So he was like my second father, as was Eddie Logan, on the road trips because they were always keeping an eye on me. John Antonelli was another great guy that kept an eye on me. And Mike McCormick, too. He and I spent one night during a 1959 road trip watching the All-Star football game up in his

room, having banana splits and just having a great time.

Opening Day was just so overwhelming because there were so many people, so many dignitaries—being introduced to all these different people and trying to remember names, and trying not to embarrass ourselves in front of 23,000 people. The batboys rallied together and said, "OK, this is about the biggest crowd we've ever been in front of, and we have to hustle at all times, run hard and don't showboat." That was the thing—we were supposed to be unnoticed. And most of the time we adhered to those basic rules.

In the summertime, when we didn't have school, we'd get to the ballpark at 8:30 or 9 o'clock in the morning for a day game, help clean up and shine the shoes, put them away, hang fresh sanitaries, undershirts, jock straps and clean uniforms in the lockers. Then we'd go down the long tunnel out to first base and start taking the bats out of the bat box we had behind the dugout, and players would select which ones they wanted to use for batting practice and the game. Then we'd go out and shag fly balls, but not until we'd play catch with a few of the guys and try to loosen their arms up. Our hands would be stinging because we didn't have much protection at the time, and our hands were pretty tender. But players were generous and gave us gloves and shoes, so they helped us look like big leaguers. Then we'd go out and shag balls, and get razzed by the players if we missed them. They would tell us that we were a liability because we couldn't get under a fly ball, but we improved with age and our time with the organization. None of us ever got a pro contract but we were always out there hustling, chasing balls and throwing them back in. We'd get in throwing contests with different players for accuracy and, naturally, we were always losing. But we always had fun with them.

After batting practice, we'd pick up all the bats, put them back in the bat rack in the dugout, and then get ready for infield. In between we'd go inside and change our shirts if we happened to break a sweat, but in those days we were 130 to 140 pounds so there wasn't much to sweat off. Then we'd put out fresh towels and be sure the coolers were ready to go. And that would bring us up to game time.

During the game one of us would take the first three innings and kneel down by the backstop while the Giants were up at bat, and go chase foul balls that were hit. If they were hit past the dugout, the other batboy would pick them up in right field. When a player hit the ball we'd go pick up the bat, put it away and exchange it for the next guy's. If they hit home runs we'd wait for them, shake their hands and run back with them. Sometimes I'd be the first to shake, and sometimes I'd pull back, depending on the situation. If it was a real exciting moment and the players rushed up there, I knew to stay back and just get my little handshake, then run back to the dugout and put the bat away.

At the end of the game we'd take all the bats and put them in the box behind the dugout, then go upstairs and start picking up all the dirty uniforms, put them in the wash and pick up all their other stuff as they were getting ready to leave the clubhouse. Then we'd get to shower and go home. We'd kind of drag ourselves at the end, in no real rush to leave, because it was just a great atmosphere. It was a tremendous dream come true. I imagine many kids would love to have done it. I was one of the fortunate young guys that just had a great, great childhood. And I had very supportive parents, that if I started to get a little conceited, my mom would just say, "Well, you know what? You don't have to go over there today." In '58 she kept a very close watch on me,

as the ballplayers did. *All* the ballplayers. I had 25 older brothers and second fathers that were very protective, and just very instrumental in my life.

I'd set up my school courses so that I'd go in about 7:15 and be out about 10:30 in the morning. Teachers were very supportive. They let me take extra work home to keep my studies up, which I did. Even when I went on the road in '59, I had to bring my homework with me.

In '59 I was elected "Batboy of the Year" by *Coronet* magazine. My mother was very proud and wrote to *What's My Line?* and told them I was the first batboy for the San Francisco Giants. Subsequently I was asked to come back to New York with my mom and appear on *What's My Line?* That was in early July. We saw all of New York in four days, came back to San Francisco, and I guess Mr. Stoneham was impressed with my appearance and how I represented the Giants, because he asked Mr. Logan to take me along on an exhibition trip to Portland. That was my first trip [with the Giants] and I roomed with Andre Rodgers. We got our $12 a day meal money and, to me, that was just a lot of money because were getting $6 a day to be the batboy. And we all got to ride in this parade down the main street of Portland, then go out to the ballpark and play in the exhibition game. Rigney was even going to let me get up and take one at-bat, but he figured he might get in a little bit of trouble with the league so he decided not to. My first road trip was in late July or early August. It was a 21-day road trip. It was very exciting, although there were some tough times because we hit a little losing streak and the players took losses very hard. But they were always very good to me.

Ruben Gomez went out of his way to have conversations with me. He was always approachable, except when he lost. You knew to stay away from him when he lost, and a day or two later he'd be OK. But he was always trying to speak to me in English, and I apologized for not knowing Spanish.

Orlando Cepeda was a great guy, although I had a couple of words with him one time when he wanted me to get a glove. I ran up to the clubhouse to get his outfielder's glove and he said, "No, I want my first baseman's glove." Then he goes, "You're a horse-bleep batboy." And I say, "Well, you're a horse-bleep left fielder." [laughs] But we got over that real quick, and he taught me a lot about the nature of competitiveness and determination. He was always friendly and playful.

Daryl Spencer was a great guy, too, and always playful. On the road we'd take in a couple of movies together, which is a favorite thing to do when you're on a road trip back east in the summertime, to get into an air-conditioned theater, and then go out to the park about 3:30 in the afternoon. The guys were always asking me if I wanted to go to a movie and to dinner, and they would pick up the tab. They were very generous with me in those days. They were caring.

Willie Kirkland had one of the strongest throwing arms I've ever seen. We'd always play warm-ups together and turn it into burnouts, and who could throw the hardest. It was always between Kirkland and Daddy Wags—Leon Wagner. They could puff my hand up pretty well, and my arm would feel like a hose at the end of the warm-up session, because I had about half the speed that they did. Leon, like Willie, was a very friendly guy, always teasing with me, always waiting to see how much of his heater I could take. I missed a few and I got a few bruises from them, but he'd always be sure I was OK.

You could tease with the guys because they'd tease with you. You learned to take the kidding and you were always taught, "If we didn't like you we wouldn't tease you." That's something I learned in 1958. In April. Real quick. John Antontelli would sneak into my locker and steal my sandwich that my mom made for me, but he would always make it up to me in other ways.

I remember Hank Sauer used to sit around in the clubhouse after the ballgames with John Antonelli and tell baseball stories. And the Honker had some great stories. We used to call him the Honker. He was a lot of fun to listen to.

Felipe Alou was a real gentleman, one of the classiest guys I've ever known. He was a great student of the game. I could tell he was always trying to figure out what Rigney was going to do.

Marv Grissom was a great man. I think I've got some of his work ethic because he was always working hard. He was always running and I couldn't figure out why. That's what kept him in the bigs so long—his leg power. He'd always do his wind sprints on his own, and do the extra wind sprints so he could keep playing the game. He was also a very strong man. Had a grip like a vice.

The most memorable thing about Seals Stadium was the smell of the peanuts, the Langendorf bread and the Hamm's beer being brewed. And, of course, that big glass of beer above the brewery that would light up. We used to watch that glass all the time. In fact, one player watched it too much one night and wound up with a big error. He couldn't pick up the ball quickly enough because he was looking up at the glass. Mr. Rigney fined him $50, as I recall. He was a left fielder, and had quite a taste for beer.

The players used to go to the *Double Play* on the corner, which is still there. There were rumors that the players would go there sometimes during the game but I never saw that. I'm sure they went there between doubleheaders sometimes to have a quick sandwich. We'd go in to have a coke with the players once in a while after games, because they'd go over there after games and have a beer or two.

The bakery was two blocks down, on Harrison Street. They baked their bread in the early evening, and the aroma with that bread and the beer hops was just the greatest smell I could ever imagine. The only kind of smell that could ever be as vivid as that would be the smell over in Maui as you get off the plane, with the flowers so fresh. If you don't understand Seals Stadium and you haven't been to Hawaii, then you can't understand what I'm saying.

Redwood City, California

EPILOGUE

THANKS TO A PAIR of key off-season acquisitions, the Giants spent most of the 1959 season in first place, only to run out of gas the next to last weekend of the campaign. Beefing up their starting rotation with the addition of right-handers Sam Jones and Jack Sanford, the Giants moved into first place July 9 and stayed there, until the Dodgers closed the curtain on Seals Stadium by sweeping a three-game series in late September, moving into first place in the process, and eventually beating the Chicago White Sox in the World Series. Demolition began at Seals eight days after the season ended, but not before 1,422,130 fans visited the cozy little ballpark at 16th and Bryant Streets, more fans than any other National League ballpark entertained in '59, with the exception of the LA Coliseum and County Stadium, in Milwaukee.

The myriad of problems surrounding Candlestick Park has been well-documented in this book and countless other publications over the years. Suffice it to say, the 'Stick–or 3Com Park as it's now called in official circles–will live in infamy as the most colossal blunder in the history of the Giants franchise. Nevertheless, the Giants managed to play some pretty fair baseball there over the years, most notably in 1962 and again in '89, when they won the National League pennant. But the *best* baseball the Giants ever played, dating back to their origin in New York, came in '93 when they won 103 games. Alas, the Atlanta Braves won 104 games, leaving the Giants in second place in the N.L. West race.

For longtime Giants fans who waxed nostalgically about Seals Stadium and who lamented the realities of the 'Stick, the turn of the millennium promised to begin a watershed era in Giants history.

Pacific Bell Park, home of the San Francisco Giants. (SF Giants)

After 40 years at Candlestick Point, the Giants moved back to within walking distance of downtown San Francisco, to a marvelous state-of-the-art ballpark on the shores of San Francisco Bay. The Giants sold out all 81 home games in their maiden season at Pacific Bell Park, setting a franchise record with 3,315,330 fans. Not only that, the Giants were victorious in 55 of those 81 games, and won the National League West with a 97-65 record. They say the best things in life are worth waiting for. Well, the Giants and their fans waited a *long* time for this.

As for the '58 Giants, two distinct and lasting impressions stay with me from having spent time with 33 of the surviving 36 members of the ball club: They're doing just fine, and they're very nice people. They have moved successfully from baseball careers to business careers and now, in most cases, retirement. That's heartening because, keep in mind, with few exceptions these guys had no particular professions to fall back on when their playing days were over. Like players of today, they successfully pursued their dreams of playing major league baseball. Unlike players of today, they didn't become independently wealthy doing so. Theirs was an era when ballplayers worked in the off-season at odd jobs simply out of necessity. Given the reality, then, of the obscene amounts of money being handed out to ballplayers today, it's worth noting that the '58 Giants to a man are glad they played when they did. They don't necessarily begrudge the players of today, but they're glad they played during baseball's Golden Era. It may not have been the richest of times in a monetary sense, but it certainly was in a competitive sense. These men believe–and historians will back them up on this—that there were more great players in the game during the fifties and sixties than at any other time in history. These men were a part of that. And that's an experience they wouldn't trade for anything.

1958 Giants reunion at Candlestick Park, *Opening Day 1997,* includes: (L to R)
Franks, McCormick, Davenport, Spencer, Bressoud, Constable, Sauer, Gomez, Burnside, Cimoli (LA), Rigney, Mays, Worthington, Taussig, Crone, Giel, Thomas, Lockman, Cepeda. (SF Giants)

BIBLIOGRAPHY

Allison, Bob. (1959, June).One More Time For Andre. *Sport*.

Alou, Felipe, &Weiskopf, Herm. (1967). *My Life and Baseball*. Waco, Texas: World Books.

Bjarkman, Peter C. (1996).*Baseball With a Latin Beat*. Jefferson, North Carolina: McFarland and Co., Inc.

Brosnan, Jim. (1960). *The Long Season*. New York: Harper and Brothers.

Brosnan, Jim. (1962). *Pennant Race*. New York: Harper and Row.

Christopher, George. (1957, June 22). How I Won The Giants. *The American Weekly*.

Creamer, Robert. (1958, June 16). Giants: A Smash Hit In San Francisco. *Sports Illustrated*.

Dobbins, Dick, &Twichell, Jon. (1994). *Nuggets on the Diamond*. San Francisco: Woodford Press.

Einstein, Charles. (1961, December). The Stu Miller Mystery. *Sport*.

Gelman, Steve. (1964, July). Bill White: A Man Must Say What He Thinks Is Right. *Sport*.

Gershman, Michael. (1993). *Diamond: The Evolution of the Ballpark*. New York: Houghton Mifflin.

Halberstam, David. (1994). *October 1964*. New York: Ballantine Books.

Hano, Arnold. (1958, December). Sudden Success At San Francisco. *Sport*.

Harris, Mark. (1959, September 28). Love Affair In San Francisco. *Sports Illustrated*.

Hodges, Russ, &Hirshberg, Al. (1963). *My Giants*. Garden City, New York: Doubleday.

Honig, Donald. (1987). *Baseball in the 50s*. New York: Crown Publishers, Inc.

Keller, Richard. (1987). *Orlando Cepeda: The Baby Bull*. San Francisco: Woodford Publishing.

Kiersh, Edward. (1983). *Where Have You Gone, Vince DiMaggio?* New York: Bantom Books.

Leutzinger, Richard. (1997). *Lefty O'Doul: The Legend That Baseball Nearly Forgot*. Carmel, CA: Carmel Bay Publishing Group.

Los Angeles Mirror-News (1958).

Los Angeles Times (1957-58).

Mandel, Mike. (1979). *SF Giants: An Oral History*. Watsonville, CA: Watsonville Press.

Mays, Willie, & Sahadi, Lou. (1988). *Say Hey: The Autobiography of Willie Mays*. New York: Pocket Books.

New York Daily News (1957-58).

New York Herald-Tribune (1958).

New York Times (1957-58).

New York World-Telegram (1958).

Noble, John Wesley. (1958, June). What They Say In The Dugouts About The San Francisco Giants. *Sport*.

Oakland Tribune (1958).

Orr, Jack. (1959, December). Johnny Antonelli's War With San Francisco. *Sport*.

Philadelphia Inquirer (1964).

Plaut, David. (1994).*Chasing October: The Dodgers-Giants Pennant Race of 1962*. SouthBend, Indiana: Diamond Communications.

Pollard, Richard. (1958, August 11). On the Road With The Freaks. *Sports Illustrated*.

Pradt, Mary A. (1995). *You Must Remember This: 1958*. New York: Warner Books, Inc.

Ritter, Lawrence S. (1992).*Lost Ballparks: A Celebration of Baseball's Legendary Fields*. New York: Viking Penguin.

San Francisco Chronicle (1957-'58).

San Francisco Examiner (1958).

San Francisco Giants Yearbook: 1958.

San Francisco Giants Yearbook: 1959.

San Francisco Giants Yearbook: 1992.

Shatzkin, Mike. (1990). *The Ballplayers: Baseball's Ultimate Biographical Reference*. New York: William Morrow and Co., Inc.

Spander, Art. (1989). *The Art Spander Collection*. Dallas, Texas: Taylor Publishing Co.

Spink, J.G. Taylor. (Ed.). (1959). *Baseball Register: 1959 Edition.* St. Louis: The Sporting News.

Sports Illustrated: Special 1958 Baseball Issue. April 14, 1958.

St. Louis Globe-Democrat (1957).

Stein, Fred, &Peters, Nick. (1987). *Giants Diary: A Century of Giants Baseball in New York and San Francisco.* Berkeley: North Atlantic Books.

Sullivan, Neil J. (1987). *The Dodgers Move West.* New York: Oxford University Press.

Tellis, Richard. (1998). *Once Around the Bases: Bittersweet Memories of Only One Game in the Majors.* Chicago: Triumph Books.

The Sporting News (1958).

Thomson, Bobby,Heiman, Lee &Gutman, Bill. (1991). *The Giants Win the Pennant! The Giants Win the Pennant!* New York: Kensington Publishing.

Thorn, John, &Palmer, Pete. (Ed.). (1993). *Total Baseball: The Ultimate Encyclopedia of Baseball.* New York: Harper Collins.

Tygiel, Jules. (1983). *Baseball's Great Experiment: Jackie Robinson and his Legacy.* New York: Oxford University Press.

Washington Post & Times-Herald (1958).

Whiting, Robert. (1977). *The Chrysanthemum and the Bat.* Tokyo: The Permanent Press.

Wolff, Rick.(Ed.). (1990). *The Baseball Encyclopedia.* New York: Macmillan.

APPENDIX A
1958 San Francisco Giants
Day-by-Day Record

#	Date	Opp.	W/L	Score	Pitcher	Record	GB	Att.(H)
1	4/15	LA	W	8-0	**Gomez**	1-0	—	23,448
2	4/16	LA	L	1-13	Monzant	1-1	1	22,735
3	4/17	LA	W	7-4	Barclay	2-1	1	12,500
4	4/18	at LA	L	5-6	Worthington	2-2	1.5	
5	4/19	at LA	W	11-4	**Gomez**	3-2	1.5	
6	4/20	at LA	W	12-2	**Monzant**	4-2	.5	
7	4/22	STL	L	5-7	Antonelli	4-3	1	22,786
8	4/23	STL	W	8-7	Grissom	5-3	1	14,715
9	4/24	STL	W	6-5	Crone	6-3	.5	13,674
10	4/25	CHI	W	2-0	**Monzant**	7-3	—	16,870
11	4/26	CHI	W	3-1	**Antonelli**	8-3	—	19,284
12	4/27	CHI	L	4-5	Grissom	8-4	—	22,696
13	4/29	PHI	L	4-7	Monzant	8-5	.5	6,801
14	4/30	PHI	W	10-1	**Antonelli**	9-5	—	7,886
15	5/1	PHI	L	0-7	Gomez	9-6	.5	6,728
16	5/2	PHI	W	4-2	McCormick	10-6	.5	13,486
17	5/3	PHI	L	2-4	Monzant	10-7	.5	13,073
18	5/4	PIT	L(1st)	2-6	Antonelli	10-8		
19	5/4	PIT	W(2nd)	4-3(10)	Worthington	11-8	.5	22,721
20	5/5	PIT	L	10-11	Gomez	11-9	1	5,506
21	5/6	PIT	W	7-0	**McCormick**	12-9	1	10,849
22	5/7	PIT	W	8-6	Worthington	13-9	1	8,052
23	5/9	LA	W	11-3	**Monzant**	14-9	.5	20,653
24	5/10	LA	W	3-2	Grissom	15-9	.5	20,774
25	5/12	at LA	W	12-3	**Gomez**	16-9	.5	
26	5/13	at LA	W	16-9	Worthington	17-9	.5	
27	5/14	at STL	L	2-3	Antonelli	17-10	.5	
28	5/15	at STL	W	4-2	McCormick	18-10	.5	
29	5/16	at CHI	L	5-6	Crone	18-11	.5	
30	5/17	at CHI	W	9-4	**Gomez**	19-11	.5	
31	5/18	at CHI	W(1st)	7-3	**Antonelli**	20-11		
32	5/18	at CHI	W(2nd)	4-0	**Miller**	21-11	—	
33	5/20	at CIN	W	4-2	**McCormick**	22-11	—	
34	5/21	at CIN	W	5-4(10)	Grissom	23-11	—	
35	5/22	at MIL	L	3-9	Gomez	23-12	—	
36	5/23	at MIL	W	5-3	**Antonelli**	24-12	—	
37	5/24	at MIL	L	3-6	Worthington	24-13	—	
38	5/25	at PIT	W(1st)	5-2	**Gomez**	25-13	—	
39	5/25	at PIT	W(2nd)	6-1	**Monzant**	26-13	—	

40	5/27	at PHI	L	1-5	Miller	26-14	—	
41	5/28	at PHI	W	7-6	Grissom	27-14	—	
42	5/30	at STL	L(1st)	6-7(10)	Crone	27-15		
43	5/30	at STL	L(2nd)	1-8	McCormick	27-16	—	
44	5/31	at STL	L	9-10(12)	Miller	27-17	—	
45	6/1	at STL	W	7-2	**Antonelli**	28-17	—	
46	6/3	MIL	L	6-7	Gomez	28-18	—	22,934
47	6/4	MIL	L	9-10(11)	Miller	28-19	1	20,886
48	6/5	MIL	W	5-4(12)	Constable	29-19	—	19,891
49	6/6	CIN	L	4-5	Monzant	29-20	—	21,952
50	6/7	CIN	W	7-3	Worthington	30-20	—	20,297
51	6/8	CIN	L	3-6	Grissom	30-21	—	22,396
52	6/9	CIN	L	0-3	Antonelli	30-22	—	10,350
53	6/10	PIT	L	4-5	Monzant	30-23	—	16,621
54	6/11	PIT	L	6-14	Gomez	30-24	.5	7,912
55	6/12	PIT	L	1-2	Giel	30-25	1.5	9,273
56	6/13	PHI	W	6-1	**Antonelli**	31-25	1.5	18,068
57	6/14	PHI	L	2-3	Monzant	31-26	1.5	16,363
58	6/15	PHI	W	3-1	**Worthington**	32-26	1.5	22,462
59	6/17	at PIT	L	1-6	Antonelli	32-27	2.5	
60	6/18	at PIT	W	2-1(10)	Giel	33-27	2	
61	6/19	at PIT	L	5-6	Worthington	33-28	2	
62	6/20	at PHI	L	4-5	Gomez	33-29	3	
63	6/22	at PHI	W	5-4(14)	Antonelli	34-29	1.5	
64	6/23	at MIL	L	0-7	Giel	34-30	2.5	
65	6/24	at MIL	L	1-2	Miller	34-31	3.5	
66	6/25	at MIL	W	10-2	Worthingtgon	35-31	2.5	
67	6/26	at CIN	W	5-1	**Antonelli**	36-31	1.5	
68	6/27	at CIN	L	5-6	Grissom	36-32	1.5	
69	6/28	at CIN	L	2-8	Monzant	36-33	2.5	
70	6/29	at CIN	W	2-0	Worthington	37-33	2.5	
71	7/1	at CHI	L	5-9	Antonelli	37-34	4	
72	7/2	at CHI	W	5-2	Miller	38-34	3	
73	7/3	CHI	L	3-4	Giel	38-35	3	
74	7/4	CHI	W(1st)	6-5	Grissom	39-35		9,477
75	7/4	CHI	L(2nd)	1-6	Antonelli	39-36	3	22,715
76	7/5	STL	W	5-4	**McCormick**	40-36	2	22,679
77	7/6	STL	W	5-4	Worthington	41-36	1	22,736
78	7/10	CIN	L	0-4	Worthington	41-37	1.5	19,349
79	7/11	CIN	W	7-4(12)	Monzant	42-37	1.5	10,216
80	7/12	MIL	W	5-2	**Antonelli**	43-37	.5	22,806
81	7/13	MIL	W	6-5	McCormick	44-37	—	22,833
82	7/14	MIL	L	3-12	Worthington	44-38	.5	22,864
83	7/15	PHI	W	1-0	**McCormick**	45-38	.5	14,523
84	7/16	PHI	W	9-2	**Antonelli**	46-38	.5	20,250
85	7/17	PHI	W	8-7(10)	Grissom	47-38	.5	10,259
86	7/18	PIT	W	5-4	Miller	48-38	—	22,770
87	7/19	PIT	W	5-4	Monzant	49-38	—	19,685
88	7/20	PIT	W	7-3	Giel	50-38	—	22,814
89	7/23	at PHI	L(1st)	2-3	Gomez	50-39		
90	7/23	at PHI	L(2nd)	0-2	McCormick	50-40	1	
91	7/25	at PIT	L	0-10	Miller	50-41	1	
92	7/26	at PIT	W	1-0	Antonelli	51-41	—	
93	7/27	at PIT	L	1-2(14)	Monzant	51-42	1	
94	7/28	at PHI	W(1st)	3-2	**McCormick**	52-42		
95	7/28	at PHI	W(2nd)	2-1	**Gomez**	53-42	—	
96	7/29	at CIN	W	4-3	Grissom	54-42	—	
97	7/30	at CIN	L	1-5	Antonelli	54-43	—	
98	7/31	at CIN	L	9-10	Gomez	54-44	1	
99	8/1	at MIL	L	2-4	McCormick	54-45	2	
100	8/2	at MIL	L	0-10	Miller	54-46	3	

101	8/3	at MIL	L(1st)	3-4	**Antonelli**	54-47		
102	8/3	at MIL	L(2nd)	0-6	Gomez	54-48	5	
103	8/4	at CHI	W	6-4	Giel	55-48	4	
104	8/5	at CHI	L	9-10(10)	Antonelli	55-49	5	
105	8/6	at STL	L	7-8	Johnson	55-50	6	
106	8/7	at STL	L	1-12	McCormick	55-51	7	
107	8/8	at LA	L	3-6	Gomez	55-52	7	
108	8/9	at LA	W	6-3	Antonelli	56-52	6	
109	8/10	at LA	W	12-8	Jones	57-52	6.5	
110	8/12	STL	L	3-7	**McCormick**	57-53	6	22,892
111	8/13	STL	W	11-2	**Gomez**	58-53	6.5	17,346
112	8/14	STL	W	4-3	Antonelli	59-53	6.5	22,892
113	8/15	CHI	L	1-3(10)	Miller	59-54	7.5	17,036
114	8/16	CHI	W	7-4	McCormick	60-54	7.5	17,617
115	8/17	CHI	W	8-6	Worthington	61-54	8	20,892
116	8/19	CIN	W	4-3(10)	**Antonelli**	62-54	6.5	9,822
117	8/20	CIN	W	4-3	Worthington	63-54	5.5	10,212
118	8/21	CIN	L	1-8	McCormick	63-55	6.5	10,983
119	8/22	CIN	L	3-7	Grissom	63-56	7	17,786
120	8/23	CIN	W	5-2	Giel	64-56	6	17,714
121	8/24	MIL	L	5-8(10)	Worthington	64-57	7	22,913
122	8/25	MIL	L	1-6	McCormick	64-58	8	21,433
123	8/26	MIL	L	3-7	Gomez	64-59	9	20,297
124	8/27	MIL	W	3-2(12)	Worthington	65-59	8	21,389
125	8/28	MIL	L	0-3	**Antonelli**	65-60	9	19,018
126	8/29	LA	L	1-4	Giel	65-61	9	18,433
127	8/30	LA	W	3-2	Gomez	66-61	9	16,905
128	8/30	LA	W	3-1	**McCormick**	67-61	8.5	9,865*
129	8/31	LA	W	14-2	**Miller**	68-61	8.5	20,744
130	9/1	LA	W	8-6	Jones	69-61	8	14,121
131	9/1	LA	W	6-5(16)	McCormick	70-61	7.5	19,800*
132	9/2	at LA	L	0-4	Monzant	70-62	8	
133	9/3	at LA	L	3-5	Worthington	70-63	9	
134	9/4	at LA	W	13-3	**Miller**	71-63	9	
135	9/6	at CHI	L	3-6	Antonelli	71-64	8.5	
136	9/7	at CHI	L(1st)	4-6	**McCormick**	71-65		
137	9/7	at CHI	L(2nd)	1-4	Gomez	71-66	9.5	
138	9/9	at PIT	L(1st)	3-4	Giel	71-67		
139	9/9	at PIT	L(2nd)	1-2	Jones	71-68	11	
140	9/10	at PIT	L	4-6(10)	Grissom	71-69	12	
141	9/12	at PHI	W(1st)	5-2	Gomez	72-69		
142	9/12	at PHI	W(2nd)	19-2	**Antonelli**	73-69	11.5	
143	9/13	at PHI	W	6-5	Jones	74-69	11.5	
144	9/14	at CIN	L(1st)	3-4	Miller	74-70		
145	9/14	at CIN	W(2nd)	6-4	Monzant	75-70	11	
146	9/16	at MIL	L	1-4	Antonelli	75-71	12.5	
147	9/19	at STL	W	8-1	**Miller**	76-71	11.5	
148	9/20	at STL	W	5-1	**Gomez**	77-71	11.5	
149	9/21	at STL	W	7-4	Monzant	78-71	11.5	
150	9/23	CHI	L	2-3	Miller	78-72	11.5	12,713
151	9/24	CHI	L	3-10	Monzant	78-73	12	7,887
152	9/26	STL	W	4-3	Antonelli	79-73	12	21,576
153	9/27	STL	L	7-11	Monzant	79-74	13	18,753
154	9/28	STL	W	7-2	Zanni	80-74	12	19,435

Pitcher's name in bold indicates complete game
*—indicates second game of day-night doubleheader

APPENDIX B

1958 Giants Batting Statistics:

Player	G	AB	R	H	HR	RBI	SB	.AVG
Mays	152	600	121	208	29	96	31	.347
Wagner	74	221	31	70	13	35	1	.317
Cepeda	148	603	88	188	25	96	15	.312
Bressoud	66	137	19	36	0	8	0	.263
Thomas	63	143	14	37	3	16	1	.259
Kirkland	122	418	48	108	14	56	3	.258
Spencer	148	539	71	138	17	74	1	.256
Davenport	134	434	70	111	12	41	1	.256
Alou	75	182	21	46	4	16	4	.253
Sauer	88	236	27	59	12	46	0	.250
Brandt	18	52	7	13	0	3	1	.250
Schmidt	127	393	46	96	14	54	0	.244
White	26	29	5	7	1	4	1	.241
Lockman	92	122	15	29	2	7	0	.238
O'Connell	107	306	44	71	3	23	2	.232
Jablonski	86	230	28	53	12	46	2	.230
King	34	56	8	12	2	8	0	.214
Speake	66	71	9	15	3	10	0	.211
Rodgers	22	63	7	13	2	11	0	.206
Taussig	39	50	10	10	1	4	0	.200
Finigan	23	25	3	5	0	1	0	.200
Giants Totals		**5318**	**727**	**1399**	**170**	**698**	**63**	**.263**

1958 Giants Pitching Statistics:

Player	GS	CG	IP	H	BB	SO	W-L	SV	ERA
Zanni	0	0	4	7	1	3	1-0	0	2.25
Jones	1	0	30.1	33	5	8	3-1	1	2.37
Miller	20	4	182	160	49	119	6-9	0	2.47
Barclay	1	0	16	16	5	6	1-0	0	2.81
Fitzgerald	1	0	3	1	1	3	0-0	0	3.00
Antonelli	34	13	241.2	216	87	143	16-13	3	3.28
Worthington	12	1	151.1	162	57	76	11-7	6	3.63
Grissom	0	0	65.1	71	26	46	7-5	10	3.99
Gomez	30	8	207.2	204	77	112	10-12	1	4.38
McCormick	28	8	178.1	192	60	82	11-8	1	4.59
Giel	9	0	92	89	55	55	4-5	0	4.70
Monzant	16	4	150.2	160	57	93	8-11	1	4.72
Constable	0	0	8	10	3	4	1-0	1	5.63
Johnson	0	0	23	31	8	14	0-1	1	6.26
Burnside	1	0	10.2	20	5	4	0-0	0	6.75
Crone	1	0	24	35	13	7	1-2	0	6.75
Shipley	0	0	1.1	3	3	0	0-0	0	33.75
Giants Totals	**154**	**38**	**1389.1**	**1400**	**512**	**77**	**80-74**	**25**	**3.98**

APPENDIX C

The Top 10 Giants Games of 1958

SAN FRANCISCO, April 15—Ruben Gomez tossed a six-hit shutout, and Daryl Spencer and Orlando Cepeda slammed home runs to lead the Giants to an 8-0 victory over the Los Angeles Dodgers in the historic first major league game in West Coast history, before a standing-room-only crowd of 23,448 on a warm, sunny afternoon at Seals Stadium.

LOS ANGELES

	AB	R	H	RBI
Cimoli, cf	5	0	1	0
Reese, ss	3	0	0	0
Snider, lf	2	0	0	0
Hodges, 1b	4	0	0	0
Neal, 2b	4	0	2	0
Gray, 3b	4	0	2	0
Furillo, rf	3	0	0	0
Walker, c	3	0	1	0
Drysdale, p	1	0	0	0
Roseboro, ph-c	1	0	0	0
Larker, ph	1	0	0	0
Gilliam, ph	0	0	0	0
Totals	31	0	6	0

SAN FRANCISCO

	AB	R	H	RBI
Davenport, 3b	4	1	2	1
King, lf	3	1	2	1
Mays, cf	5	0	2	2
Kirkland, rf	5	0	1	1
Cepeda, 1b	5	1	1	1
Spencer, ss	4	1	1	1
O'Connell, 2b	2	1	0	0
Thomas, c	1	2	0	0
Gomez, p	4	1	2	1
Totals	33	8	11	8

```
LOS ANGELES . . . . . . . . . . . . . . . 000 000  000 – 0  6  1
SAN FRANCISCO . . . . . . . . . . . . . 002 410  01 x – 8 11  0
```

E–Hodges. LOB–Los Angeles 10, San Francisco 9. DP–Gomez, Spencer and Cepeda. HR–Spencer, Cepeda. SF–Davenport.

	IP	H	R	ER	BB	SO
Drysdale (L, 0-1)	3 2/3	5	6	6	3	1
Bessent	2 1/3	4	1	1	1	0
Negray	2	2	1	1	3	1
Gomez (W, 1-0)	9	6	0	0	6	6

Balk–Negray. PB–Walker. U–Conlan, Secory, Dixon, Venzon. T–2:29. A–23,448.

SAN FRANCISCO, April 23–Daryl Spencer's two-out, two-run home run into the left field bleachers capped a four-run bottom of the ninth inning, giving the Giants a dramatic 8-7 win over the St. Louis Cardinals.

ST. LOUIS	AB	R	H	RBI
Schofield, ss	3	1	0	1
Blasingame, 2b	5	3	3	0
Musial, 1b	2	1	1	1
Ennis, lf	4	1	2	2
Moon, rf	4	0	1	0
Noren, cf	4	0	0	1
B.G. Smith, cf	1	0	0	0
Boyer, 3b	3	1	1	1
Katt, c	4	0	2	1
Jones, p	4	0	1	0
Totals	34	7	11	7

SAN FRANCISCO	AB	R	H	RBI
Davenport, 3b	4	1	2	0
King, lf	5	0	0	0
Mays, cf	5	1	0	0
Kirkland, rf	5	1	1	1
Cepeda, 1b	5	3	3	2
Spencer, ss	5	2	4	2
O'Connell, 2b	2	0	1	1
Sauer, ph	0	0	0	0
Bressoud, pr-2b	0	0	0	0
Thomas, c	1	0	0	0
Lockman, ph	1	0	0	0
Schmidt, c	1	0	0	0
Jablonski, ph	1	0	1	2
Testa, c	0	0	0	0
Gomez, p	0	0	0	0
Finigan, ph	1	0	0	0
Taussig, ph	1	0	0	0
Speake, ph	1	0	0	0
Rodgers, ph	1	0	0	0
Totals	39	8	12	8

```
ST. LOUIS . . . . . . . . . . . . . . . . . . . .5 0 0  0 0 0  1 0 1 – 7 11 2
SAN FRANCISCO . . . . . . . . . . . . . .0 0 0  1 0 1  0 2 4 – 8 12 1
```

E–Schofield 2, Testa. DP–Schofield, Blasingame and Musial; O'Connell, Spencer and Cepeda; Spencer, O'Connell and Cepeda. LOB–St. Louis 8, San Francisco 8. 2B–Katt, Moon, Cepeda, Musial. 3B–Blasingame, Cepeda. HR–Kirkland, Spencer. SB–Blasingame.

	IP	H	R	ER	BB	SO
Jones	7 2/3	8	4	3	3	8
Paine	2/3	2	2	0	0	1
Martin	1/3	0	0	0	0	0
Clark (L, 0-1)	0	2	2	0	0	0
Gomez	2/3	3	5	5	2	0
Miller	2 1/3	3	0	0	1	0
Constable	2	1	0	0	1	0
Barclay	2	3	1	1	1	2
Crone	1	0	0	0	0	0
Grissom (W, 1-0)	1	1	1	1	2	0

HBP–By Barclay (Boyer). U–Crawford, Smith, Dascoli and Donatelli. T–3:01. A–14,715.

SAN FRANCISCO, May 5–The Giants staged a remarkable nine-run rally in the bottom of the ninth inning, only to leave the bases loaded and fall a run short, losing to the Pittsburgh Pirates 11-10, before the smallest home crowd of the season, a Monday afternoon gathering of 5,506. Vernon Law carried a four-hit 11-1 lead into the ninth, but the Giants strung together two singles, back to back to back pinch hit doubles, three walks, two errors, and home runs by Ray Jablonski and Orlando Cepeda to cut the Bucs' lead to a single run. Don Taussig popped up to Bill Mazeroski in short center for the final out.

<table>
<tr><td colspan="5">PITTSBURGH</td></tr>
<tr><td></td><td>AB</td><td>R</td><td>H</td><td>RBI</td></tr>
<tr><td>Mejias, cf</td><td>3</td><td>0</td><td>1</td><td>0</td></tr>
<tr><td>Groat, ss</td><td>5</td><td>1</td><td>1</td><td>1</td></tr>
<tr><td>Skinner, lf</td><td>4</td><td>3</td><td>2</td><td>0</td></tr>
<tr><td>Stevens, 1b</td><td>5</td><td>1</td><td>1</td><td>3</td></tr>
<tr><td>Thomas, 3b</td><td>5</td><td>2</td><td>2</td><td>2</td></tr>
<tr><td>Clemente, rf</td><td>5</td><td>1</td><td>2</td><td>1</td></tr>
<tr><td>Mazeroski, 2b</td><td>4</td><td>1</td><td>2</td><td>1</td></tr>
<tr><td>Foiles, c</td><td>0</td><td>0</td><td>0</td><td>0</td></tr>
<tr><td>Kravitz, c</td><td>3</td><td>1</td><td>2</td><td>1</td></tr>
<tr><td>Law, p</td><td>3</td><td>1</td><td>1</td><td>2</td></tr>
<tr><td>Totals</td><td>37</td><td>11</td><td>14</td><td>11</td></tr>
</table>

<table>
<tr><td colspan="5">SAN FRANCISCO</td></tr>
<tr><td></td><td>AB</td><td>R</td><td>H</td><td>RBI</td></tr>
<tr><td>Bressoud, 2b</td><td>4</td><td>1</td><td>1</td><td>0</td></tr>
<tr><td>Speake, ph</td><td>1</td><td>1</td><td>1</td><td>1</td></tr>
<tr><td>Mays, cf</td><td>3</td><td>0</td><td>1</td><td>1</td></tr>
<tr><td>Spencer, ss</td><td>4</td><td>1</td><td>0</td><td>0</td></tr>
<tr><td>Jablonski, 3b</td><td>5</td><td>2</td><td>3</td><td>3</td></tr>
<tr><td>Cepeda, 1b</td><td>5</td><td>2</td><td>3</td><td>1</td></tr>
<tr><td>Sauer, lf</td><td>3</td><td>1</td><td>1</td><td>0</td></tr>
<tr><td>Kirkland, rf</td><td>4</td><td>0</td><td>0</td><td>0</td></tr>
<tr><td>Schmidt, ph</td><td>0</td><td>0</td><td>0</td><td>0</td></tr>
<tr><td>Thomas, c</td><td>3</td><td>0</td><td>0</td><td>0</td></tr>
<tr><td>King, ph</td><td>1</td><td>1</td><td>1</td><td>2</td></tr>
<tr><td>Finigan, ph</td><td>1</td><td>0</td><td>0</td><td>0</td></tr>
<tr><td>Gomez, p</td><td>1</td><td>0</td><td>0</td><td>0</td></tr>
<tr><td>Lockman, ph</td><td>1</td><td>0</td><td>0</td><td>0</td></tr>
<tr><td>Antonelli, ph</td><td>1</td><td>1</td><td>1</td><td>2</td></tr>
<tr><td>Taussig, ph</td><td>1</td><td>0</td><td>0</td><td>0</td></tr>
<tr><td>Totals</td><td>38</td><td>10</td><td>12</td><td>10</td></tr>
</table>

PITTSBURGH . . . . 0 2 0 0 0 1 5 0 3 – 11 14 3
SAN FRANCISCO . . . . 1 0 0 0 0 0 0 0 9 – 10 12 1

E–F. Thomas 2, Sauer, Groat. DP–Groat, Mazeroski and Stevens 2; Bressoud, Spencer and Cepeda. LOB–Pittsburgh 7, San Francisco 8. 2B–Clemente, Law, Mazeroski, Kravitz, King, Antonelli, Speake. 3B–Bressoud. HR–Stevens, F. Thomas, Jablonski, Cepeda. SB–Skinner. S–Mejias, Law. SF–Mays, Law.

	IP	H	R	ER	BB	SO
Law (W, 3-1)	8 1/3	10	7	5	3	4
Raydon	1/3	1	2	0	1	0
Blackburn	0	1	1	0	1	0
Gross	1/3	0	0	0	1	0
Gomez (L, 2-2)	6 1/3	9	6	6	1	4
Giel	1 2/3	1	2	2	3	0
Burnside	1	4	3	3	0	1

HBP–By Gomez (Foiles). U–Crawford, Smith, Dascoli, Donatelli. T–3:01. A–5,506.

LOS ANGELES, May 12–Willie Mays homered twice and drove in five runs, Daryl Spencer added a pair of homers and Ruben Gomez pitched his third complete game victory of the season–all against the Dodgers–as the Giants hammered LA 12-3 in front of 29,770 at the Coliseum. The outburst gave Mays five home runs in his last three games.

SAN FRANCISCO

	AB	R	H	RBI
Davenport, 3b	4	1	2	1
Taussig, rf	5	1	1	1
Mays, cf	5	2	3	5
Sauer, lf	5	0	1	0
Kirkland, rf	1	0	0	0
Cepeda, 1b	5	2	2	0
Spencer, ss	4	2	2	2
Schmidt, c	4	3	3	0
O'Connell, 2b	5	0	2	1
Gomez, p	5	1	1	1
Totals	43	12	17	11

LOS ANGELES

	AB	R	H	RBI
Gilliam, lf	4	0	0	0
Zimmer, ss	4	1	1	0
Snider, cf	3	0	1	1
Furillo, rf	4	0	0	0
Neal, 2b	4	1	1	0
Hodges, 1b	4	1	1	1
Gray, 3b	4	0	1	1
Roseboro, c	3	0	0	0
Drysdale, p	0	0	0	0
Bessent, p	1	0	0	0
Reese, ph	1	0	0	0
Larker, ph	1	0	1	0
Totals	33	3	6	3

```
SAN FRANCISCO . . . . . . . . . . . . . .  0 2 1   0 6 2   0 1 0 – 12 17 0
LOS ANGELES . . . . . . . . . . . . . . .  0 0 0   1 0 0   1 0 1 –  3  6 4
```

E–Drysdale, Zimmer, Gray 2. DP–Davenport, O'Connell and Cepeda; Bessent, Zimmer and Hodges; Gray, Hodges and Roseboro. LOB–San Francisco 10, Los Angeles 4. 2B–Schmidt, Zimmer, Snider, Gomez, Neal. 3B–Gray. HR–Spencer 2, Mays 2, Hodges.

	IP	H	R	ER	BB	SO
Gomez (W, 3-2)	9	6	3	3	1	9
Drysdale (L, 1-6)	2	6	3	3	1	1
Bessent	2 2/3	4	5	0	4	4
Roebuck	1/3	1	1	0	0	0
Craig	3	6	3	2	0	2
Labine	1	0	0	0	1	0

PB–Schmidt. U–Gorman, Burkhart, Boggess, Sudol. T–3:05. A–29,770.

LOS ANGELES, May 13– Willie Mays and Daryl Spencer hit two home runs each, for the second straight night, driving in 10 runs between them, and the Giants collected season highs with 16 runs and 26 hits, in smothering the Dodgers again, 16-9, before just 10,507 at the LA Coliseum. The win moved the Giants (17-9) back into first place by a half game over Milwaukee (15-8), while the Dodgers (9-17) dropped further into the cellar, eight games back. Mays' streak left him with 12 hits in his last 17 at-bats, with seven home runs.

SAN FRANCISCO

	AB	R	H	RBI
Davenport, 3b	5	2	2	0
Taussig, rf	7	1	1	0
Mays, cf	5	4	5	4
Sauer, lf	3	2	0	1
Kirkland, ph-lf	1	0	1	1
Cepeda, 1b	6	3	4	2
Spencer, ss	6	4	4	6
Schmidt, c	6	0	4	1
O'Connell, 2b	5	0	4	1
McCormick, p	1	0	0	0
Rodgers, ph	1	0	1	0
Worthington, p	3	0	0	0
Finigan, ph	1	0	0	0
Totals	50	16	26	16

LOS ANGELES

	AB	R	H	RBI
Gilliam, lf	4	1	0	0
Cimoli, cf	5	2	2	0
Neal, 2b	5	2	2	4
Furillo, rf	4	1	2	3
Valo, rf	1	0	1	0
Hodges, 1b	5	2	3	1
Gray, 3b	4	0	0	0
Zimmer, ss	4	0	0	0
Pignatano, c	4	0	1	0
Newcombe, p	0	1	0	0
Kipp, p	1	0	0	0
Snider, ph	1	0	0	1
Larker, ph	1	0	0	0
Roseboro, ph	1	0	0	0
Totals	40	9	11	9

```
SAN FRANCISCO . . . . . . . . . . . . . . . .5 2 0   4 2 1  1 1 0 – 16 26 2
LOS ANGELES . . . . . . . . . . . . . . . . .3 3 1   0 1 0  0 1 0 – 9 11 2
```

E–Gray 2, Davenport, Spencer. DP–Hodges, Gray and Zimmer; Neal and Hodges; Neal and Zimmer. LOB–San Francisco 13, Los Angeles 11. 2B–Spencer, Schmidt, Davenport. 3B–Spencer, Mays 2. HR–Mays 2, Spencer 2, Cepeda, Furillo, Neal 2, Hodges. SB–Mays. S–O'Connell.

	IP	H	R	ER	BB	SO
McCormick	1/3	2	3	3	1	1
Monzant	1 2/3	2	3	3	1	0
Worthington (W, 3-1)	6	6	3	3	2	2
Grissom	1	1	0	0	1	1
Newcombe	2 1/3	7	7	4	1	3
Kipp (L, 1-3)	2/3	3	3	3	1	0
Roebuck	2	7	3	3	1	1
Koufax	2	4	2	2	2	1
McDevitt	2	5	1	1	0	0

HBP–By McCormick (Cimoli), by Worthington (Pignatano). U–Burkhart, Boggess, Sudol, Gorman. T–3:15. A–10,507.

MILWAUKEE, May 23–Southpaw Johnny Antonelli spun a three-hitter and the Giants, no-hit by veteran Warren Spahn for six and a third innings, came roaring back with home runs by Bob Schmidt and Willie Kirkland to tie the game in the eighth, and a two-run shot by Willie Mays in the ninth, to beat the Braves 5-3 in front of 24,430 at County Stadium. The win boosted the Giants' [24-12] league lead to two and a half games over Milwaukee [19-12].

SAN FRANCISCO

	AB	R	H	RBI
Davenport, 3b	4	0	0	0
O'Connell, 2b	3	2	1	0
Mays, cf	4	1	2	2
Sauer, lf	4	0	0	1
Taussig, lf	0	0	0	0
Cepeda, 1b	4	0	1	0
Spencer, ss	4	0	1	0
Schmidt, c	4	1	1	1
Kirkland, rf	3	1	1	1
Antonelli, p	3	0	0	0
Totals	33	5	7	5

MILWAUKEE

	AB	R	H	RBI
Mantilla, 2b	4	0	0	0
Logan, ss	4	0	0	0
Mathews, 3b	3	1	1	1
Aaron, cf	4	0	0	0
Adcock, 1b	3	0	0	0
Torre, 1b	1	0	0	0
Pafko, rf	3	0	0	0
Covington, lf	3	1	0	0
Crandall, c	3	1	2	2
Spahn, p	2	0	0	0
Totals	30	3	3	3

```
SAN FRANCISCO . . . . . . . . . . . . . . . .000  000 122 – 5 7 1
MILWAUKEE . . . . . . . . . . . . . . . . . .100  020 000 – 3 3 0
```

E–Antonelli. LOB–San Francisco 2, Milwaukee 2. 2B–Crandall. HR–Schmidt, Kirkland, Mays, Mathews, Crandall. S–Spahn.

	IP	H	R	ER	BB	SO
Antonelli (W, 4-3)	9	3	3	1	1	5
Spahn (L, 6-1)	9	7	5	5	1	8

U–Jackowski, Landes, Delmore, Barlick. T–1:51. A–24,430.

SAN FRANCISCO, June 4– Pinch hitter Warren Spahn delivered an RBI single in the top of the 11th inning to vault the Milwaukee Braves (27-16) back into first place by one game, with a 10-9 win over the Giants (28-19) in front of 20,886 at Seals Stadium. The Giants blew a 7-1 lead, fell behind 9-7 in the 10th, but rallied to tie it on back to back pinch hit home runs by Hank Sauer and Bob Schmidt, the first time in National League history that had been accomplished.

MILWAUKEE

	AB	R	H	RBI
Mantilla, 2b	5	1	1	1
Aaron, cf	6	1	3	1
Mathews, 3b	6	0	1	2
Adcock, 1b	6	1	2	0
Covington, lf	4	1	1	3
Burton, cf	0	1	0	0
Logan, ss	5	1	1	0
Pafko, rf	6	0	2	1
Crandall, c	2	1	1	1
Rush, p	1	0	1	0
Rice, c	2	1	0	0
Roach, ph	1	0	0	0
Torre, ph	1	0	1	0
Sawatski, c	1	1	0	0
Hanebrink, ph	1	1	0	0
Spahn, ph	1	0	1	1
Totals	48	10	15	10

SAN FRANCISCO

	AB	R	H	RBI
O'Connell, 2b	4	0	1	1
Sauer, ph-lf	1	1	1	1
Speake, lf	4	1	1	1
Taussig, lf	0	0	0	0
Mays, cf	6	1	4	1
Jablonski, 3b	5	1	1	0
Cepeda, 1b	5	0	0	0
Spencer, ss	5	1	1	1
King, rf	4	1	1	1
Kirkland, rf	1	0	0	0
Thomas, c	3	1	1	1
Lockman, ph	1	0	0	0
McCormick, p	3	1	2	0
Worthington, p	1	0	0	0
Schmidt, ph-c	1	1	1	1
Antonelli, ph	1	0	0	0
Totals	45	9	14	8

```
MILWAUKEE . . . . . . . . . . . . . . . . . .  1 0 0  0 1 0  1 1 3  2 1 – 10 15 1
SAN FRANCISCO . . . . . . . . . . . . . . . 3 1 3  0 0 0  0 0 0  2 0 –  9 14 2
```

E–Crandall, Jablonski, McCormick. DP–Mathews, Mantilla and Adcock. LOB–Milwaukee 11, San Francisco 9. 2B–Mays 2, Logan, Adcock. 3B–King. HR–Mantilla, Crandall, Covington, Speake, Sauer, Schmidt. SB–Mays 2, Jablonski. S–Logan. SF–O'Connell.

	IP	H	R	ER	BB	SO
Rush	1 2/3	6	4	4	1	0
Trowbridge	2 1/3	4	3	3	1	3
Jay	2	1	0	0	2	2
Robinson	1	0	0	0	0	1
McMahon	2	0	0	0	1	2
Johnson (W, 2-0)	1	3	2	2	0	2
Conley	1	0	0	0	0	2
McCormick	6 2/3	5	3	3	3	5
Worthington	2	6	3	3	0	1
Burnside	2/3	2	3	1	1	0
Miller (L, 1-3)	1 2/3	2	1	1	0	0

HBP–By Jay (King). WP–McCormick. PB–Crandall, Thomas. U–Conlan, Secory, Delmore, Venson. T–3:35. A–20,886.

SAN FRANCISCO, July 4– Willie Kirkland and Willie Mays lined two-run singles to cap a five-run bottom of the ninth to lift the Giants to a 6-5 win over the Chicago Cubs in the first game of a doubleheader at Seals Stadium.

<table>
<tr><td colspan="5">CHICAGO</td></tr>
<tr><td></td><td>AB</td><td>R</td><td>H</td><td>RBI</td></tr>
<tr><td>T.Taylor, 2b</td><td>4</td><td>0</td><td>1</td><td>0</td></tr>
<tr><td>Dark, 3b</td><td>5</td><td>0</td><td>0</td><td>0</td></tr>
<tr><td>Walls, rf</td><td>4</td><td>1</td><td>2</td><td>1</td></tr>
<tr><td>Banks, ss</td><td>4</td><td>1</td><td>0</td><td>0</td></tr>
<tr><td>Moryn, lf</td><td>3</td><td>1</td><td>1</td><td>0</td></tr>
<tr><td>Long, 1b</td><td>4</td><td>1</td><td>1</td><td>1</td></tr>
<tr><td>S.Taylor, c</td><td>4</td><td>0</td><td>2</td><td>0</td></tr>
<tr><td>Tappe, c</td><td>0</td><td>0</td><td>0</td><td>0</td></tr>
<tr><td>Thomson, cf</td><td>4</td><td>1</td><td>1</td><td>1</td></tr>
<tr><td>Briggs, p</td><td>3</td><td>0</td><td>1</td><td>0</td></tr>
<tr><td>Elston, p</td><td>1</td><td>0</td><td>0</td><td>0</td></tr>
<tr><td>Totals</td><td>36</td><td>5</td><td>9</td><td>3</td></tr>
</table>

<table>
<tr><td colspan="5">SAN FRANCISCO</td></tr>
<tr><td></td><td>AB</td><td>R</td><td>H</td><td>RBI</td></tr>
<tr><td>Alou, rf</td><td>5</td><td>1</td><td>1</td><td>0</td></tr>
<tr><td>Spencer, ss</td><td>4</td><td>0</td><td>1</td><td>1</td></tr>
<tr><td>Mays, cf</td><td>4</td><td>0</td><td>1</td><td>2</td></tr>
<tr><td>Cepeda, 1b</td><td>4</td><td>0</td><td>1</td><td>0</td></tr>
<tr><td>Jablonski, 3b</td><td>3</td><td>0</td><td>0</td><td>0</td></tr>
<tr><td>Davenport, 3b</td><td>0</td><td>1</td><td>0</td><td>0</td></tr>
<tr><td>Wagner, lf</td><td>4</td><td>1</td><td>1</td><td>0</td></tr>
<tr><td>Schmidt, c</td><td>2</td><td>1</td><td>0</td><td>0</td></tr>
<tr><td>Bressoud, 2b</td><td>2</td><td>0</td><td>0</td><td>0</td></tr>
<tr><td>Sauer, ph</td><td>1</td><td>0</td><td>0</td><td>0</td></tr>
<tr><td>O'Connell, 2b</td><td>0</td><td>0</td><td>0</td><td>0</td></tr>
<tr><td>Speake, ph</td><td>0</td><td>0</td><td>0</td><td>1</td></tr>
<tr><td>Worthington, p</td><td>2</td><td>0</td><td>2</td><td>0</td></tr>
<tr><td>Lockman, ph</td><td>1</td><td>1</td><td>1</td><td>0</td></tr>
<tr><td>Kirkland, ph</td><td>1</td><td>1</td><td>1</td><td>2</td></tr>
<tr><td>Totals</td><td>33</td><td>6</td><td>9</td><td>6</td></tr>
</table>

```
CHICAGO . . . . . . . . . . . . . . . . . .   1 0 0   0 0 0   0 1 3 – 5 9 0
SAN FRANCISCO . . . . . . . . . . . . .   0 0 0   0 0 0   0 1 5 – 6 9 2
```

E–Davenport 2. DP–Taylor, Banks and Long. LOB–Chicago 6, San Francisco 7. 2B–Worthington. HR–Walls, Thomson. SF–Spencer.

<table>
<tr><td></td><td>IP</td><td>H</td><td>R</td><td>ER</td><td>BB</td><td>SO</td></tr>
<tr><td>Briggs</td><td>7</td><td>6</td><td>1</td><td>1</td><td>2</td><td>3</td></tr>
<tr><td>Elston</td><td>1</td><td>1</td><td>3</td><td>3</td><td>2</td><td>0</td></tr>
<tr><td>Hobbie (L, 6-6)</td><td>0</td><td>1</td><td>2</td><td>2</td><td>1</td><td>0</td></tr>
<tr><td>Drott</td><td>2/3</td><td>1</td><td>0</td><td>0</td><td>1</td><td>0</td></tr>
<tr><td>Worthington</td><td>8</td><td>5</td><td>2</td><td>2</td><td>1</td><td>4</td></tr>
<tr><td>Monzant</td><td>1/3</td><td>3</td><td>3</td><td>3</td><td>0</td><td>0</td></tr>
<tr><td>Grissom (W, 5-3)</td><td>2/3</td><td>1</td><td>0</td><td>0</td><td>1</td><td>2</td></tr>
</table>

WP–Briggs, Grissom. U–Donatelli, Crawford, Smith and Dascoli. T–3:00. A–22,715.

SAN FRANCISCO, September 1–Ray Jablonski scored from first base on a pinch hit bunt single by Ruben Gomez and two Los Angeles errors, capping a two-run 16th inning, giving the Giants a remarkable 6-5 win over the Dodgers in the second game of a day-night doubleheader, after the Giants won the afternoon game 8-6. Whitey Lockman tied the nightcap earlier in the 16th with a home run off loser Johnny Podres. The four-hour-and-35 minute game was the longest in the majors this season. The Giants' win was their 15th in 19 games against the Dodgers in 1958.

LOS ANGELES

	AB	R	H	RBI
Gilliam, 2b	6	0	1	0
Cimoli, lf	7	2	4	1
Furillo, rf	7	0	2	1
Hodges, 1b	7	1	2	1
Demeter, cf	0	0	0	0
Bilko, 1b	4	1	1	2
Snider, ph-cf	1	0	0	0
Zimmer, 3b	7	0	0	0
Lillis, ss	6	0	2	0
Roseboro, ph-c	2	0	0	0
Pignatano, c	4	0	1	0
Kipp, p	4	1	0	0
Klipstein, p	2	0	0	0
Podres, p	1	0	0	0
Totals	58	5	13	5

SAN FRANCISCO

	AB	R	H	RBI
Alou, rf	3	0	0	0
Kirkland, ph-rf	2	0	1	0
Davenport, ss	7	0	0	0
Mays, cf	4	1	1	2
Brandt, lf	7	1	1	0
Cepeda, 1b	7	0	2	0
Schmidt, c	4	1	1	2
Bressoud, 2b	5	0	1	0
Lockman, ph-2b	2	1	1	1
O'Connell, 2b	2	0	0	0
Jablonski, ph-3b	4	1	1	0
Antonelli, p	2	1	1	0
Sauer, ph	1	0	0	0
Wagner, ph	1	0	0	0
Giel, p	1	0	0	0
Thomas, ph	1	0	0	0
Gomez, ph	1	0	1	0
Totals	54	6	11	5

```
LOS ANGELES . . . . . . . . . . . . . . . . . 000 002  200 000 0001 – 5 13 2
SAN FRANCISCO . . . . . . . . . . . . . . . 000 002  002 000 0002 – 6 11 2
```

E–Antonelli, Davenport, Roseboro, Furillo. DP–Lillis, Neal and Bilko 2; Schmidt and Bressoud. LOB–Los Angeles 15, San Francisco 12. 2B–Furillo. HR–Bilko, Mays, Schmidt, Lockman. S–Gilliam, Pignatano, Demeter.

	IP	H	R	ER	BB	SO
Kipp	8 2/3	5	4	4	5	4
Klipstein	4 2/3	1	0	0	2	5
Podres (L, 12-11)	1 2/3	5	2	1	2	2
Antonelli	6 1/3	7	4	3	4	5
Grissom	1 2/3	1	0	0	0	1
Johnson	2	0	0	0	2	2
Giel	4	3	0	0	1	1
McCormick (W, 11-7)	2	2	1	1	0	2

WP–Grissom. U–Dixon, Gorman, Burkhart, Boggess. T–4:35. A–19,800.

PHILADELPHIA, September 12–The Giants exploded for their second eight-run first inning in eight days, and a season high 19 runs, in battering the Phillies 19-2 behind Johnny Antonelli's six-hitter to complete a double-header sweep at Connie Mack Stadium, after winning the opener 5-2 behind Ruben Gomez. Jim Davenport went seven for 10 in the twin-bill, scored seven runs, drove in four and homered twice.

SAN FRANCISCO

	AB	R	H	RBI
Davenport, 3b	5	4	4	3
Spencer, 2b	5	2	0	0
Mays, cf	4	4	3	2
Wagner, lf	3	3	2	2
Alou, lf	1	1	0	0
Cepeda, 1b	6	1	3	5
Kirkland, rf	5	1	1	2
Rodgers, ss	4	2	1	2
Schmidt, c	5	1	3	3
Antonelli, p	5	0	0	0
Totals	43	19	17	19

PHILADELPHIA

	AB	R	H	RBI
Ashburn, cf	3	0	2	0
Kazanski, 2b	4	0	0	0
Bouchee, 1b	4	1	1	0
Post, rf	4	0	0	0
H.Anderson, lf	4	1	1	1
Jones, 3b	2	0	0	0
Herrera, 3b	2	0	1	1
Fernandez, ss	3	0	1	0
Coker, c	3	0	0	0
Semproch, p	0	0	0	0
Mason, p	2	0	0	0
J.Anderson, p	1	0	0	0
Totals	32	2	6	2

```
SAN FRANCISCO . . . . . . . . . . . . . . . .8 2 0  0 0 5  1 0 3 – 19 17 0
PHILADELPHIA . . . . . . . . . . . . . . .0 0 0  0 0 0  1 0 1 – 2  6 1
```

E–Kazanski. DP–Spencer, Rodgers and Cepeda. LOB–San Francisco 6, Philadelphia 5. 2B–Kirkland, Ashburn, Wagner, Davenport, Cepeda, Bouchee. HR–Davenport, Anderson. SF–Kirkland, Rodgers.

	IP	H	R	ER	BB	SO
Antonelli (W, 15-12)	9	6	2	2	2	6
Semproch (L, 13-10)	1/3	3	5	4	1	0
Hearn	2/3	2	3	0	1	0
Mason	5	7	7	6	2	3
Anderson	3	5	4	4	1	3

HBP—By Mason (Spencer); by Anderson (Davenport). PB—Coker 2. U—Sudol, Venson, Secory, Conlan. T—2:39. A—16,560.

APPENDIX D

1958 Giants' Career Major League Statistics

Year	Team	G	AB	R	H	2B	3B	HR	RBI	.AVG	BB	SO	SB

FELIPE ALOU   b: 5/12/35, Haina, D.R. BR/TR, 6', 195 lbs.

Year	Team	G	AB	R	H	2B	3B	HR	RBI	.AVG	BB	SO	SB
1958	San Francisco	75	182	21	46	9	2	4	16	.253	19	34	4
1959	San Francisco	95	247	38	68	13	2	10	33	.275	17	38	5
1960	San Francisco	106	322	48	85	17	3	8	44	.264	16	42	10
1961	San Francisco	132	415	59	120	19	0	18	52	.289	26	41	11
1962	San Francisco	154	561	96	177	30	3	25	98	.316	33	66	10
1963	San Francisco	157	565	75	159	31	9	20	82	.281	27	87	11
1964	Milwaukee	121	415	60	105	26	3	9	51	.253	30	41	5
1965	Milwaukee	143	555	80	165	29	2	23	78	.297	31	63	8
1966	Atlanta	154	666	**122**	**218**	32	6	31	74	.327	24	51	5
1967	Atlanta	140	574	76	157	26	3	15	43	.274	32	50	6
1968	Atlanta	160	662	72	**210**	37	5	11	57	.317	48	56	12
1969	Atlanta	123	476	54	134	13	1	5	32	.282	23	23	4
1970	Oakland	154	575	70	156	25	3	8	55	.271	32	31	10
1971	Oak-NY(A)	133	469	52	135	21	6	8	69	.288	32	25	5
1972	New York(A)	120	324	33	90	18	1	6	37	.278	22	27	1
1973	New York(A)	93	280	25	66	12	0	4	27	.236	9	25	0
	Montreal(N)	19	48	4	10	1	0	1	4	.208	2	4	0
1974	Milwaukee	3	0	0	0	0	0	0	0	.000	0	2	0
Total	17 Years	2082	7339	985	2101	359	49	206	852	.286	423	706	107

JACKIE BRANDT   b: 4/28/34, Omaha, Neb. BR/TR, 5'11", 170 lbs.

Year	Team	G	AB	R	H	2B	3B	HR	RBI	.AVG	BB	SO	SB
1956	St. Louis-NY(N)	125	393	54	117	19	8	12	50	.298	21	36	3
1958	San Francisco	18	52	7	13	1	0	0	3	.250	6	5	1
1959	San Francisco	137	429	63	116	16	5	12	57	.270	35	69	11
1960	Baltimore	145	511	73	130	24	6	15	65	.254	47	69	5
1961	Baltimore	139	516	93	153	18	5	16	72	.297	62	51	10
1962	Baltimore	143	505	76	129	29	5	19	75	.255	55	64	9
1963	Baltimore	142	451	49	112	15	5	15	61	.248	34	85	4
1964	Baltimore	137	523	66	127	25	1	13	47	.243	45	104	1
1965	Baltimore	96	243	35	59	17	0	8	24	.243	21	40	1
1966	Philadelphia	82	164	16	41	6	1	1	15	.250	17	36	0
1967	Phila-Houston	57	108	8	23	5	1	1	16	.213	8	15	0
Total	11 Years	1221	3895	540	1020	175	37	112	485	.262	351	574	45

Year	Team	G	AB	R	H	2B	3B	HR	RBI	.AVG	BB	SO	SB

ED BRESSOUD b: 5/2/32, Los Angeles, Calif. BR/TR, 6'1", 175 lbs.

Year	Team	G	AB	R	H	2B	3B	HR	RBI	.AVG	BB	SO	SB
1956	New York(N)	49	163	15	37	4	2	0	9	.227	12	20	1
1957	New York(N)	49	127	11	34	2	2	5	10	.268	4	19	0
1958	San Francisco	66	137	19	36	5	3	0	8	.263	14	22	0
1959	San Francisco	104	315	36	79	17	2	9	26	.251	28	55	0
1960	San Francisco	116	386	37	87	19	6	9	43	.225	35	72	1
1961	San Francisco	59	114	14	24	6	0	3	11	.211	11	23	1
1962	Boston	153	599	79	166	40	9	14	68	.277	46	118	2
1963	Boston	140	497	61	129	23	6	20	60	.260	52	93	1
1964	Boston	158	566	86	166	41	3	15	55	.293	72	99	1
1965	Boston	107	296	29	67	11	1	8	25	.226	29	77	0
1966	New York(N)	133	405	48	91	15	5	10	49	.225	47	107	2
1967	St. Louis	52	67	8	9	1	1	1	1	.134	9	18	0
Total	12 Years	1186	3672	443	925	184	40	94	365	.252	359	723	9

ORLANDO CEPEDA b: 9/17/37, Ponce, P.R. BR/TR, 6'2", 210 lbs.

Year	Team	G	AB	R	H	2B	3B	HR	RBI	.AVG	BB	SO	SB
1958	San Francisco	148	603	88	188	**38**	4	25	96	.312	29	84	15
1959	San Francisco	151	605	92	192	35	4	27	105	.317	33	100	23
1960	San Francisco	151	569	81	169	36	3	24	96	.297	34	91	15
1961	San Francisco	152	585	105	182	28	4	**46**	**142**	.311	39	91	12
1962	San Francisco	162	625	105	191	26	1	35	114	.306	37	97	10
1963	San Francisco	156	579	100	183	33	4	34	97	.316	37	70	8
1964	San Francisco	142	529	75	161	27	2	31	97	.304	43	83	9
1965	San Francisco	33	34	1	6	1	0	1	5	.176	3	9	0
1966	San Fran-StL	142	501	70	151	26	0	20	73	.301	38	79	9
1967	St. Louis	151	563	91	183	37	0	25	**111**	.325	62	75	11
1968	St. Louis	157	600	71	149	26	2	16	73	.248	43	96	8
1969	Atlanta	154	573	74	147	28	2	22	88	.257	55	76	12
1970	Atlanta	148	567	87	173	33	0	34	111	.305	47	75	6
1971	Atlanta	71	250	31	69	10	1	14	44	.276	22	29	3
1972	Atlanta	28	84	6	25	3	0	4	9	.298	7	17	0
	Oakland	3	0	0	0	0	0	0	0	.000	0	0	0
1973	Boston	142	550	51	159	25	0	20	86	.289	50	81	0
1974	Kansas City	33	107	3	23	5	0	1	18	.215	9	16	1
Total	17 Years	2124	7927	1131	2351	417	27	379	1365	.297	588	1169	142

Year	Team	G	AB	R	H	2B	3B	HR	RBI	.AVG	BB	SO	SB

JIM DAVENPORT   b: 8/17/33, Siluria, Ala. BR/TR, 5'11", 175 lbs.

Year	Team	G	AB	R	H	2B	3B	HR	RBI	.AVG	BB	SO	SB
1958	San Francisco	134	434	70	111	22	3	12	41	.256	33	64	1
1959	San Francisco	123	469	65	121	16	3	6	38	.258	28	65	0
1960	San Francisco	112	363	43	91	15	3	6	38	.251	26	58	0
1961	San Francisco	137	436	64	121	28	4	12	65	.278	45	65	4
1962	San Francisco	144	485	83	144	25	5	14	58	.297	45	76	2
1963	San Francisco	147	460	40	116	19	3	4	36	.252	32	87	5
1964	San Francisco	116	297	24	70	10	6	2	26	.236	29	46	2
1965	San Francisco	106	271	29	68	14	3	4	31	.251	21	47	0
1966	San Francisco	111	305	42	76	6	2	9	30	.249	22	40	1
1967	San Francisco	124	295	42	81	10	3	5	30	.275	39	50	1
1968	San Francisco	113	272	27	61	1	1	1	17	.224	26	32	0
1969	San Francisco	112	303	20	73	10	1	2	42	.241	29	37	0
1970	San Francisco	22	37	3	9	1	0	0	4	.243	7	6	0
Total	13 Years	1501	4427	552	1142	177	37	77	456	.258	382	673	16

JIM FINIGAN   b: 8/19/28, Quincy, Ill. d: 5/16/81, Quincy, Ill. BR/TR, 5'11", 175 lbs.

Year	Team	G	AB	R	H	2B	3B	HR	RBI	.AVG	BB	SO	SB
1954	Philadelphia(A)	136	487	57	147	25	6	7	51	.302	64	66	2
1955	Kansas City	150	545	72	139	30	7	9	68	.255	61	49	1
1956	Kansas City	91	250	29	54	7	2	2	21	.216	30	28	3
1957	Detroit	64	174	20	47	4	2	0	17	.270	23	18	1
1958	San Francisco	23	25	3	5	2	0	0	1	.200	3	5	0
1959	Baltimore	48	119	14	30	6	0	1	10	.252	9	10	1
Total	6 Years	512	1600	195	422	74	17	19	168	.264	190	176	8

RAY JABLONSKI   b: 12/17/26, Chicago, Ill. d: 11/25/85, Chicago, Ill. BR/TR, 5'10", 183 lb.

Year	Team	G	AB	R	H	2B	3B	HR	RBI	.AVG	BB	SO	SB
1953	St. Louis	157	604	64	162	23	5	21	112	.268	34	61	2
1954	St. Louis	152	611	80	181	33	3	12	104	.296	49	42	9
1955	Cincinnati	74	221	28	53	9	0	9	28	.240	13	35	0
1956	Cincinnati	130	407	42	104	25	1	15	66	.256	37	57	2
1957	New York(N)	107	305	37	88	15	1	9	57	.289	31	47	0
1958	San Francisco	82	230	28	53	15	1	12	46	.230	17	50	2
1959	St. Louis	60	87	11	22	4	0	3	14	.253	8	19	1
	Kansas City	25	65	4	17	1	0	2	8	.262	3	11	0
1960	Kansas City	21	32	3	7	1	0	0	3	.219	4	8	0
Total	8 Years	808	2562	297	687	126	11	83	438	.268	196	330	16

Year	Team	G	AB	R	H	2B	3B	HR	RBI	.AVG	BB	SO	SB

JIM KING b: 8/27/32, Elkins, Ark. BL/TR, 6', 185 lbs.

Year	Team	G	AB	R	H	2B	3B	HR	RBI	.AVG	BB	SO	SB
1955	Chicago(N)	113	301	43	77	12	3	11	45	.256	24	39	2
1956	Chicago(N)	118	317	32	79	13	2	15	54	.249	30	40	1
1957	St. Louis	22	35	1	11	0	0	0	2	.314	4	2	0
1958	San Francisco	34	56	8	12	2	1	2	8	.214	10	8	0
1961	Washington	110	263	43	71	12	1	11	46	.270	38	45	4
1962	Washington	132	333	39	81	15	0	11	35	.243	55	37	4
1963	Washington	136	459	61	106	16	5	24	62	.231	45	43	3
1964	Washington	134	415	46	100	15	1	18	56	.241	55	65	3
1965	Washington	120	258	46	55	10	2	14	49	.213	44	50	1
1966	Washington	117	310	41	77	14	2	10	30	.248	38	41	4
1967	Wash/Chi(A)/Cle	89	171	14	30	3	2	1	14	.175	20	31	1
Total	11 Years	1125	2918	374	699	112	19	117	401	.240	363	401	23

WILLIE KIRKLAND b: 2/17/34, Siluria, Ala. BL/TR, 6'1", 206 lbs.

Year	Team	G	AB	R	H	2B	3B	HR	RBI	.AVG	BB	SO	SB
1958	San Francisco	122	418	48	108	25	6	14	56	.258	43	69	3
1959	San Francisco	126	463	64	126	22	3	22	68	.272	42	84	5
1960	San Francisco	146	515	59	130	21	10	21	65	.252	44	86	12
1961	Cleveland	146	525	84	136	22	5	27	95	.259	48	77	7
1962	Cleveland	137	419	56	84	9	1	21	72	.200	43	62	9
1963	Cleveland	127	427	51	98	13	2	15	47	.230	45	99	8
1964	Baltimore/Wash	98	252	22	52	11	0	8	35	.206	23	56	3
1965	Washington	123	312	38	72	9	1	14	54	.231	19	65	3
1966	Washington	124	163	21	31	2	1	6	17	.190	16	50	2
Total	9 Years	1149	3494	443	837	134	29	148	509	.240	323	648	52

WHITEY LOCKMAN b: 7/25/26, Lowell, N.C. BL/TR, 6'1", 175 lbs.

Year	Team	G	AB	R	H	2B	3B	HR	RBI	.AVG	BB	SO	SB
1945	New York(N)	32	129	16	44	9	0	3	18	.341	13	10	1
1947	New York(N)	2	2	0	1	0	0	0	1	.500	0	0	0
1948	New York(N)	146	584	117	167	24	10	18	59	.286	68	63	8
1949	New York(N)	151	617	97	186	32	7	11	65	.301	62	31	12
1950	New York(N)	129	532	72	157	28	5	6	52	.295	42	29	1
1951	New York(N)	153	614	85	173	27	7	12	73	.282	50	32	4
1952	New York(N)	154	606	99	176	17	4	13	58	.290	67	52	2
1953	New York(N)	150	607	85	179	22	4	9	61	.295	52	36	3
1954	New York(N)	148	570	73	143	17	3	16	60	.251	59	31	2
1955	New York(N)	147	576	76	157	19	0	15	49	.273	39	34	3
1956	NY(N)/St. Louis	118	362	27	94	7	3	1	20	.260	34	25	2
1957	New York(N)	133	456	51	113	9	4	7	30	.248	39	19	5
1958	San Francisco	92	122	15	29	5	0	2	7	.238	13	8	0
1959	Baltimore	38	69	7	15	1	1	0	2	.217	8	4	0
	Cincinnati	52	84	10	22	5	1	0	7	.262	4	6	0
1960	Cincinnati	21	10	6	2	0	0	1	1	.200	2	3	0
Total	15 Years	1666	5940	836	1658	222	49	114	563	.279	522	383	43

Year	Team	G	AB	R	H	2B	3B	HR	RBI	.AVG	BB	SO	SB

WILLIE MAYS   b: 5/6/31, Westfield, Ala. BR/TR, 5'11", 180 lbs.

Year	Team	G	AB	R	H	2B	3B	HR	RBI	.AVG	BB	SO	SB
1951	New York(N)	121	464	59	127	22	5	20	68	.274	57	60	7
1952	New York(N)	34	127	17	30	2	4	4	23	.236	16	17	4
1954	New York(N)	151	565	119	195	33	**13**	41	110	**.345**	66	57	8
1955	New York(N)	152	580	123	185	18	**13**	**51**	127	.319	79	60	24
1956	New York(N)	152	578	101	171	27	8	36	84	.296	68	65	40
1957	New York(N)	152	585	112	195	26	**20**	35	97	.333	76	62	38
1958	San Francisco	152	600	**121**	208	33	11	29	96	.347	78	56	31
1959	San Francisco	151	575	125	180	43	5	34	104	.313	65	58	27
1960	San Francisco	153	595	107	**190**	29	12	29	103	.319	61	70	25
1961	San Francisco	154	572	**129**	176	32	3	40	123	.308	81	77	18
1962	San Francisco	162	621	130	189	36	5	**49**	141	.304	78	85	18
1963	San Francisco	157	596	115	187	32	7	38	103	.314	66	83	8
1964	San Francisco	157	578	121	171	21	9	**47**	111	.296	82	72	19
1965	San Francisco	157	558	118	177	21	3	**52**	112	.317	76	71	9
1966	San Francisco	152	552	99	159	29	4	37	103	.288	70	81	5
1967	San Francisco	141	486	83	128	22	2	22	70	.263	51	92	6
1968	San Francisco	148	498	84	144	20	5	23	79	.289	67	81	12
1969	San Francisco	117	403	64	114	17	3	13	58	.283	49	71	6
1970	San Francisco	139	478	94	139	15	2	28	83	.291	79	90	5
1971	San Francisco	136	417	82	113	24	5	18	61	.271	**112**	123	23
1972	San Fran/NY(N)	88	244	35	61	11	1	8	22	.250	60	48	4
1973	New York(N)	66	209	24	44	10	0	6	25	.211	27	47	1
Total	22 Years	2992	10881	2062	3283	523	140	660	1903	.302	1464	1526	338

DANNY O'CONNELL   b: 1/21/27, Paterson, N.J. d: 10/2/69, Clifton, N.J. BR/TR, 6', 180 lb.

Year	Team	G	AB	R	H	2B	3B	HR	RBI	.AVG	BB	SO	SB
1950	Pittsburgh	79	315	39	92	16	1	8	32	.292	24	33	7
1953	Pittsburgh	149	588	88	173	26	8	7	55	.294	57	42	3
1954	Milwaukee	146	541	61	151	28	4	2	37	.279	38	46	2
1955	Milwaukee	124	453	47	102	15	4	6	40	.225	28	43	2
1956	Milwaukee	139	498	71	119	17	9	2	42	.239	76	42	3
1957	Milw/NY(N)	143	547	86	140	27	4	8	36	.256	52	50	9
1958	San Francisco	107	306	44	71	12	2	3	23	.232	51	35	2
1959	San Francisco	34	58	6	11	3	0	0	0	.190	5	15	0
1961	Washington	138	493	61	128	30	1	1	37	.260	77	62	15
1962	Washington	84	236	24	62	7	2	2	18	.263	23	28	5
Total	10 Years	1143	4035	527	1049	181	35	39	320	.260	431	396	48

Team	Year	G	AB	R	H	2B	3B	HR	RBI	.AVG	BB	SO	SB

ANDRE RODGERS   b: 12/2/34, Nassau, Bahamas. BR/TR, 6'3", 200 lbs.

Team	Year	G	AB	R	H	2B	3B	HR	RBI	.AVG	BB	SO	SB
1957	New York(N)	32	86	8	21	2	1	3	9	.244	9	21	0
1958	San Francisco	22	63	7	13	3	1	2	11	.206	4	14	0
1959	San Francisco	71	228	32	57	12	1	6	24	.250	32	50	2
1960	San Francisco	81	217	22	53	8	5	2	22	.244	24	44	1
1961	Chicago(N)	73	214	27	57	17	0	6	23	.266	25	54	1
1962	Chicago(N)	138	461	40	128	20	8	5	44	.278	44	93	5
1963	Chicago(N)	150	516	51	118	17	4	5	33	.229	65	90	5
1964	Chicago(N)	129	448	50	107	17	3	12	46	.239	53	88	5
1965	Pittsburgh	75	178	17	51	12	0	2	25	.287	18	28	2
1966	Pittsburgh	36	49	6	9	1	0	0	4	.184	8	7	0
1967	Pittsburgh	47	61	8	14	3	0	2	4	.230	8	18	1
Total	11 Years	854	2521	268	628	112	23	45	245	.249	290	507	22

HANK SAUER   b: 3/17/17, Pittsburgh, Pa. BR/TR, 6'4", 199lbs.

Team	Year	G	AB	R	H	2B	3B	HR	RBI	.AVG	BB	SO	SB
1941	Cincinnati	9	33	4	10	4	0	0	5	.303	1	4	0
1942	Cincinnati	7	20	4	5	0	0	2	4	.250	2	2	0
1945	Cincinnati	31	116	18	34	1	0	5	20	.293	6	16	2
1948	Cincinnati	145	530	78	138	22	1	35	97	.260	60	85	2
1949	Cin/Chi(N)	138	509	81	140	23	1	31	99	.275	55	66	0
1950	Chicago(N)	145	540	85	148	32	2	32	103	.274	60	67	1
1951	Chicago(N)	141	525	77	138	19	4	30	89	.263	45	77	2
1952	Chicago(N)	151	567	89	153	31	3	**37**	**121**	.270	77	92	1
1953	Chicago(N)	108	395	61	104	16	5	19	60	.263	50	56	0
1954	Chicago(N)	142	520	98	150	18	1	41	103	.288	70	68	2
1955	Chicago(N)	79	261	29	55	8	1	12	28	.211	26	47	0
1956	St. Louis	75	151	11	45	4	0	5	24	.298	25	31	0
1957	New York(N)	127	378	46	98	14	1	26	76	.259	49	59	1
1958	San Francisco	88	236	27	59	8	0	12	46	.250	35	37	0
1959	San Francisco	13	15	1	1	0	0	1	1	.067	0	7	0
Total	15 Years	1399	4796	709	1288	200	19	288	876	.266	561	714	11

BOB SCHMIDT   b: 4/22/33, St. Louis, Mo. BR/TR, 6'2", 205 lbs.

Team	Year	G	AB	R	H	2B	3B	HR	RBI	.AVG	BB	SO	SB
1958	San Francisco	127	393	46	96	20	2	14	54	.244	33	59	0
1959	San Francisco	71	181	17	44	7	1	5	20	.243	13	24	0
1960	San Francisco	110	344	31	92	12	1	8	37	.267	26	51	0
1961	San Fran/Cin	29	76	4	10	0	0	1	5	.132	8	15	0
1962	Washington	88	256	28	62	14	0	10	31	.242	14	37	0
1963	Washington	9	15	3	3	1	0	0	0	.200	3	5	0
1965	New York(A)	20	40	4	10	1	0	1	3	.250	3	8	0
Total	7 Years	454	1305	133	317	55	4	39	150	.243	100	199	0

Year	Team	G	AB	R	H	2B	3B	HR	RBI	.AVG	BB	SO	SB

BOB SPEAKE   b: 8/22/30, Springfield, Mo. BL/TL, 6'1", 178lbs.

Year	Team	G	AB	R	H	2B	3B	HR	RBI	.AVG	BB	SO	SB
1955	Chicago(N)	95	261	36	57	9	5	12	43	.218	28	71	3
1956	Chicago(N)	129	418	65	97	14	5	16	50	.232	38	68	5
1958	San Francisco	66	71	9	15	3	0	3	10	.211	13	15	0
1959	San Francisco	15	11	0	1	0	0	0	1	.091	1	4	0
Total	4 Years	305	761	110	170	26	10	31	104	.223	80	158	8

DARYL SPENCER   b: 7/13/29, Wichita, Kan. BR/TR, 6'2", 190 lbs.

Year	Team	G	AB	R	H	2B	3B	HR	RBI	.AVG	BB	SO	SB
1952	New York(N)	7	17	0	5	0	1	0	3	.294	1	4	0
1953	New York(N)	118	408	55	85	18	5	20	56	.208	42	74	0
1956	New York(N)	146	489	46	108	13	2	14	42	.221	35	65	1
1957	New York(N)	148	534	65	133	31	2	11	50	.249	50	50	3
1958	San Francisco	148	539	71	138	20	5	17	74	.256	73	60	1
1959	San Francisco	152	555	59	147	20	1	12	62	.265	58	67	5
1960	St. Louis	148	507	70	131	20	3	16	58	.258	81	74	1
1961	St. Louis/LA	97	319	46	79	11	0	12	48	.248	43	52	1
1962	Los Angeles	77	157	24	37	5	1	2	12	.236	32	31	0
1963	LA/Cincinnati	57	164	21	38	7	0	1	23	.232	34	39	1
Total	10 Years	1098	3689	457	901	145	20	105	428	.244	449	516	13

DON TAUSSIG   b: 2/19/32. New York, N.Y. BR/TR, 6', 180 lbs.

Year	Team	G	AB	R	H	2B	3B	HR	RBI	.AVG	BB	SO	SB
1958	San Francisco	39	50	10	10	0	0	1	4	.200	3	8	0
1961	St. Louis	98	188	27	54	14	5	2	25	.287	16	34	2
1962	Houston	16	25	1	5	0	0	1	1	.200	2	11	0
Total	3 Years	153	263	38	69	14	5	4	30	.262	21	53	2

NICK TESTA   b: 6/29/28. New York, N.Y. BR/TR, 5'8", 180 lbs.

Year	Team	G	AB	R	H	2B	3B	HR	RBI	.AVG	BB	SO	SB
1958	San Francisco	1	0	0	0	0	0	0	0	.000	0	0	0

VALMY THOMAS   b: 10/21/28, Santurce, P.R. BR/TR, 5'9", 165 lbs.

Year	Team	G	AB	R	H	2B	3B	HR	RBI	.AVG	BB	SO	SB
1957	New York(N)	88	241	30	60	10	3	6	31	.249	16	29	0
1958	San Francisco	63	143	14	37	5	0	3	16	.259	13	24	1
1959	Philadelphia	66	140	5	28	2	0	1	7	.200	9	19	1
1960	Baltimore	8	16	0	1	0	0	0	0	.063	1	0	0
1961	Cleveland	27	86	7	18	3	0	2	6	.209	6	7	0
Total	5 Years	252	626	56	144	20	3	12	60	.230	45	79	2

Year	Team	G	AB	R	H	2B	3B	HR	RBI	.AVG	BB	SO	SB
LEON WAGNER				b: 5/13/34, Chattanooga, Tenn. BL/TL, 6'1", 195 lbs.									
1958	San Francisco	74	221	31	70	9	0	13	35	.317	18	34	1
1959	San Francisco	87	129	20	29	4	3	5	22	.225	25	24	0
1960	St. Louis	39	98	12	21	2	0	4	11	.214	17	17	0
1961	Los Angeles(A)	133	453	74	127	19	2	28	79	.280	48	65	5
1962	Los Angeles(A)	160	612	96	164	21	5	37	107	.268	50	87	7
1963	Los Angeles(A)	149	550	73	160	11	1	26	90	.291	49	73	5
1964	Cleveland	163	641	94	162	19	2	31	100	.253	56	121	14
1965	Cleveland	144	517	91	152	18	1	28	79	.294	60	52	12
1966	Cleveland	150	549	70	153	20	0	23	66	.279	46	69	5
1967	Cleveland	135	433	56	105	15	1	15	54	.242	37	76	3
1968	Cle/Chicago(A)	107	211	19	55	12	0	1	24	.261	27	37	2
1969	San Francisco	11	12	0	4	0	0	0	2	.333	2	1	0
Total	12 Years	1352	4426	636	1202	150	15	211	669	.272	435	656	54
BILL WHITE				b: 1/28/34, Lakewood, Fla. BL/TL, 6', 195 lbs.									
1956	New York(N)	138	508	63	130	23	7	22	59	.256	47	72	15
1958	San Francisco	26	29	5	7	1	0	1	4	.241	7	5	1
1959	St. Louis	138	517	77	156	33	9	12	72	.302	34	61	15
1960	St. Louis	144	554	81	157	27	10	16	79	.283	42	83	12
1961	St. Louis	153	591	89	169	28	11	20	90	.286	64	84	8
1962	St. Louis	159	614	93	199	31	3	20	102	.324	58	69	9
1963	St. Louis	162	658	106	200	26	8	27	109	.304	59	100	10
1964	St. Louis	160	631	92	191	37	4	21	102	.303	52	103	7
1965	St. Louis	148	543	82	157	26	3	24	73	.289	63	86	3
1966	Philadelphia	159	577	85	159	23	6	22	103	.276	68	109	16
1967	Philadelphia	110	308	29	77	6	2	8	33	.250	52	61	6
1968	Philadelphia	127	385	34	92	16	2	9	40	.239	39	79	0
1969	St. Louis	49	57	7	12	1	0	0	4	.211	11	15	1
Total	13 Years	1673	5972	843	1706	278	65	202	870	.286	596	927	103

Year	Team	W-L	SV	ERA	G	GS	CG	SH	IP	H	BB	SO

JOHN ANTONELLI   b: 4/12/30, Rochester, N.Y. BL/TL, 6', 190 lbs.

Year	Team	W-L	SV	ERA	G	GS	CG	SH	IP	H	BB	SO
1948	Boston(N)	0-0	1	2.25	4	0	0	0	4	2	3	0
1949	Boston(N)	3-7	0	3.56	22	10	3	1	96	99	42	48
1950	Boston(N)	2-3	0	5.93	20	6	2	1	57.2	81	22	33
1953	Milwaukee	12-12	1	3.18	31	26	11	2	175.1	167	71	131
1954	New York(N)	21-7	2	**2.30**	39	37	18	**6**	258.2	209	94	152
1955	New York(N)	14-16	1	3.33	38	34	14	2	235.1	206	82	143
1956	New York(N)	20-13	1	2.86	41	36	15	5	258.1	225	75	145
1957	New York(N)	12-18	0	3.77	40	30	8	3	212.1	228	67	114
1958	San Francisco	16-13	3	3.28	41	34	13	0	241.2	216	87	143
1959	San Francisco	19-10	1	3.10	40	38	17	**4**	282	247	76	165
1960	San Francisco	6-7	11	3.77	41	10	1	1	112.1	106	47	57
1961	Cleveland	0-4	0	6.56	11	7	0	0	48	68	18	23
	Milwaukee	1-0	0	7.59	9	0	0	0	10.2	16	3	8
Total	12 Years	126-110	21	3.34	377	268	102	25	1992.1	1870	687	1162

CURT BARCLAY   b: 8/22/31, Chicago, Ill. d: 3/25/85, Missoula, Montana. BR/TR, 6'3", 210 lb.

Year	Team	W-L	SV	ERA	G	GS	CG	SH	IP	H	BB	SO
1957	New York(N)	9-9	0	3.44	37	28	5	2	183	196	48	67
1958	San Francisco	1-0	0	2.8	16	1	0	0	16	16	5	6
1959	San Francisco	0-0	0	54.00	1	0	0	0	0.1	2	2	0
Total	3 Years	10-9	0	3.48	44	29	5	2	199.1	214	55	73

PETE BURNSIDE   b: 7/2/30, Evanston, Ill. BR/TR, 6'2", 190 lbs.

Year	Team	W-L	SV	ERA	G	GS	CG	SH	IP	H	BB	SO
1955	New York(N)	1-0	0	2.84	2	2	1	0	12.2	10	9	2
1957	New York(N)	1-4	0	8.80	10	9	1	1	30.2	47	13	18
1958	San Francisco	0-0	0	6.75	6	1	0	0	10.2	20	5	4
1959	Detroit	1-3	1	3.77	30	0	0	0	62	55	25	49
1960	Detroit	7-7	2	4.28	31	15	2	0	113.2	122	50	71
1961	Washington	4-9	2	4.53	33	16	4	2	113.1	106	51	56
1962	Washington	5-11	2	4.45	40	20	6	0	149.2	152	51	74
1963	Baltimore/Wash	0-2	0	6.03	44	1	0	0	74.2	95	26	29
Total	8 Years	19-36	7	4.81	196	64	14	3	567.1	607	230	303

JIM CONSTABLE   b: 6/14/33, Jonesboro, Tenn. BB/TL, 6'1", 185 lbs.

Year	Team	W-L	SV	ERA	G	GS	CG	SH	IP	H	BB	SO
1956	New York(N)	0-0	0	14.54	3	0	0	0	4.1	9	7	1
1957	New York(N)	1-1	0	2.86	16	0	0	0	28.1	27	7	13
1958	San Francisco	1-0	1	5.63	9	0	0	0	8	10	3	4
	Cleveland/Wash	0-2	0	6.57	21	4	0	0	37	46	19	28
1962	Milwaukee	1-1	1	2.00	3	2	1	1	18	14	4	12
1963	San Francisco	0-0	0	3.86	4	0	0	0	2.1	3	1	1
Total	5 Years	3-4	2	4.87	56	6	1	1	98	109	41	59

Year	Team	W-L	SV	ERA	G	GS	CG	SH	IP	H	BB	SO

RAY CRONE b: 8/7/31, Memphis, Tenn. BR/TR, 6;2", 185 lbs.

Year	Team	W-L	SV	ERA	G	GS	CG	SH	IP	H	BB	SO
1954	Milwaukee	1-0	1	2.02	19	2	1	0	49	44	19	33
1955	Milwaukee	10-9	0	3.46	33	15	6	1	140.1	117	41	76
1956	Milwaukee	11-10	2	3.87	35	21	6	0	169.2	173	44	73
1957	Milwaukee/NY(N)	7-9	1	4.36	36	22	4	0	163	185	55	71
1958	San Francisco	1-2	0	6.75	14	1	0	0	24	35	13	7
Total	5 Years	30-30	4	3.87	137	61	17	1	546	554	173	260

JOHN FITZGERALD b: 9/15/33, Brooklyn, N.Y. BL/TL, 6'3", 190 lbs.

Year	Team	W-L	SV	ERA	G	GS	CG	SH	IP	H	BB	SO
1958	San Francisco	0-0	0	3.00	1	1	0	0	3	1	1	3
Total	1 Year	0-0	0	3.00	1	1	0	0	3	1	1	3

PAUL GIEL b: 2/29/32, Winona, Minn. BR/TR, 5'11", 185 lbs.

Year	Team	W-L	SV	ERA	G	GS	CG	SH	IP	H	BB	SO
1954	New York(N)	0-0	0	8.31	6	0	0	0	4.1	8	2	4
1955	New York(N)	4-4	0	3.39	34	2	0	0	82.1	70	50	47
1958	San Francisco	4-5	0	4.70	29	9	0	0	92	89	55	55
1959	Pittsburgh	0-0	0	14.09	4	0	0	0	7.2	17	6	3
1960	Pittsburgh	2-0	0	5.73	16	0	0	0	33	35	15	21
1961	Minnesota/KC	1-0	0	12.00	13	0	0	0	21	30	20	15
Total	6 Years	11-9	0	5.39	102	11	0	0	240.1	249	148	145

RUBEN GOMEZ b: 7/13/27, Arroyo, P.R. BR/TR, 6', 175 lbs.

Year	Team	W-L	SV	ERA	G	GS	CG	SH	IP	H	BB	SO
1953	New York(N)	13-11	0	3.40	29	26	13	3	204	166	101	113
1954	New York(N)	17-9	0	2.88	37	32	10	4	221.2	202	109	106
1955	New York(N)	9-10	1	4.56	33	31	9	3	185.1	207	63	79
1956	New York(N)	7-17	0	4.58	40	31	4	2	196.1	191	77	76
1957	New York(N)	15-13	0	3.78	38	36	16	1	238.1	233	71	92
1958	San Francisco	10-12	1	4.38	42	30	8	1	207.2	204	77	112
1959	Philadelphia	3-8	1	6.10	20	12	2	1	72.1	90	24	37
1960	Philadelphia	0-3	1	5.33	22	1	0	0	52.1	68	9	24
1962	Cleveland/Minn	2-3	1	4.45	21	6	1	0	64.2	67	36	29
1967	Philadelphia	0-0	0	3.97	7	0	0	0	11.1	8	7	9
Total	10 Years	76-86	5	4.09	289	205	63	15	1454	1436	574	677

Year	Team	W-L	SV	ERA	G	GS	CG	SH	IP	H	BB	SO

MARV GRISSOM   b: 3/31/18, Los Molinos, Calif. BR/TR, 6'3", 195 lbs.

Year	Team	W-L	SV	ERA	G	GS	CG	SH	IP	H	BB	SO
1946	New York(N)	0-2	0	4.34	4	3	0	0	18.2	17	13	9
1949	Detroit	2-4	0	6.41	27	2	0	0	39.1	56	34	17
1952	Chicago(A)	12-10	0	3.74	28	24	7	1	166	156	79	97
1953	Boston	2-6	0	4.70	13	11	1	1	59.1	61	30	31
	New York(N)	4-2	0	3.95	21	7	3	0	84.1	83	31	46
1954	New York(N)	10-7	19	2.35	56	3	1	1	122.1	100	50	64
1955	New York(N)	5-4	8	2.92	55	0	0	0	89.1	76	41	49
1956	New York(N)	1-1	7	1.56	43	2	0	0	80.2	71	16	49
1957	New York(N)	4-4	14	2.61	55	0	0	0	82.2	74	23	51
1958	San Francisco	7-5	10	3.99	51	0	0	0	65.1	71	26	46
1959	St. Louis	0-0	0	22.50	3	0	0	0	2	6	0	0
Total	10 Years	47-45	58	3.41	356	52	12	3	810	771	343	459

DON JOHNSON   b: 11/12/26, Portland, Ore. BR/TR, 6'3", 200 lbs.

Year	Team	W-L	SV	ERA	G	GS	CG	SH	IP	H	BB	SO
1947	New York(A)	4-3	0	3.64	15	8	2	0	54.1	57	23	16
1950	NY(A)/STL(A)	6-6	1	6.71	33	1	4	1	114	161	67	40
1951	STL(A)/Wash	7-12	0	4.76	27	23	8	1	158.2	165	76	60
1952	Washington	0-5	2	4.43	29	6	0	0	69	80	33	37
1954	Chicago(A)	8-7	7	3.13	46	16	3	3	144	129	43	68
1955	Baltimore	2-4	1	5.82	31	5	0	0	68	89	35	27
1958	San Francisco	0-1	1	6.26	17	0	0	0	23	31	8	14
Total	7 Years	27-38	12	4.78	198	70	17	5	631	712	285	262

GORDON JONES   b: 4/2/30, Portland, Ore. d: 4/25/94, Lodi, Calif. BR/TR, 6', 190 lbs.

Year	Team	W-L	SV	ERA	G	GS	CG	SH	IP	H	BB	SO
1954	St. Louis(N)	4-4	0	2.00	11	10	4	2	81	78	19	48
1955	St. Louis(N)	1-4	0	5.84	15	9	0	0	57	66	28	46
1956	St. Louis(N)	0-2	0	5.56	5	1	0	0	11.1	14	5	6
1957	New York(N)	0-1	0	6.17	10	0	0	0	11.2	16	3	5
1958	San Francisco	3-1	1	2.37	11	1	0	0	30.1	33	5	8
1959	San Francisco	3-2	2	4.33	31	0	0	0	43.2	45	19	29
1960	Baltimore	1-1	2	4.42	29	0	0	0	55	59	13	30
1961	Baltimore	0-0	1	5.40	3	0	0	0	5	5	0	4
1962	Kansas City	3-2	6	6.34	21	0	0	0	32.2	31	14	28
1964	Houston	0-1	0	4.14	34	0	0	0	50	58	14	28
1965	Houston	0-0	0	0.00	1	0	0	0	1	0	0	0
Total	11 Years	15-18	12	4.16	171	21	4	2	378.2	405	120	232

Year	Team	W-L	SV	ERA	G	GS	CG	SH	IP	H	BB	SO

MIKE MCCORMICK b: 9/29/38, Pasadena, Calif. BL/TL, 6'2", 195 lbs.

Year	Team	W-L	SV	ERA	G	GS	CG	SH	IP	H	BB	SO
1956	New York(N)	0-1	0	9.45	3	2	0	0	6.2	7	10	4
1957	New York(N)	3-1	0	4.10	24	5	1	0	74.2	79	32	50
1958	San Francisco	11-8	1	4.59	42	28	8	2	178.1	192	60	82
1959	San Francisco	12-16	4	3.99	47	31	7	3	225.2	213	86	151
1960	San Francisco	15-12	3	**2.70**	40	34	15	4	253	228	65	154
1961	San Francisco	13-16	0	3.20	40	35	13	3	250	235	75	163
1962	San Francisco	5-5	0	5.38	28	15	1	0	98.2	112	45	42
1963	Baltimore	6-8	0	4.30	25	21	2	0	136	132	66	75
1964	Baltimore	0-2	0	5.19	4	2	0	0	17.1	21	8	13
1965	Washington	8-8	1	3.36	44	21	3	1	158	158	36	88
1966	Washington	11-14	0	3.46	41	32	8	3	216	193	51	101
1967	San Francisco	**22**-10	0	2.85	40	35	14	5	262.1	220	81	150
1968	San Francisco	12-14	1	3.58	38	28	9	2	198.1	196	49	121
1969	San Francisco	11-9	0	3.34	32	28	9	0	196.2	175	77	76
1970	San Francisco	3-4	2	6.20	23	11	1	0	78.1	80	36	37
	New York(A)	2-0	0	6.10	9	4	0	0	20.2	26	13	12
1971	Kansas City	0-0	0	9.31	4	1	0	0	9.2	14	5	2
Total	16 Years	134-128	12	3.73	484	333	91	23	2380.1	2281	795	1321

STU MILLER b: 12/26/27, Northampton, Mass. BR/TR, 5'11", 165 lbs.

Year	Team	W-L	SV	ERA	G	GS	CG	SH	IP	H	BB	SO
1952	St. Louis(N)	6-3	0	2.05	12	11	6	2	88	88	26	64
1953	St. Louis(N)	7-8	4	5.56	40	18	8	2	137.2	161	47	79
1954	St. Louis(N)	2-3	2	5.79	19	4	0	0	46.2	55	29	22
1956	St. L(N)/Phila	5-9	1	4.50	27	15	2	0	114	121	56	60
1957	New York(N)	7-9	1	3.63	38	13	0	0	124	110	45	60
1958	San Francisco	6-9	0	**2.47**	41	20	4	1	182	160	49	119
1959	San Francisco	8-7	8	2.84	59	9	2	0	167.2	164	57	95
1960	San Francisco	7-6	2	3.90	47	3	2	0	101.2	100	31	65
1961	San Francisco	14-5	**17**	2.66	63	0	0	0	122	95	37	89
1962	San Francisco	5-8	19	4.12	59	0	0	0	107	107	42	78
1963	Baltimore	5-8	**27**	2.24	**71**	0	0	0	112.1	93	53	114
1964	Baltimore	7-7	23	3.06	66	0	0	0	97	77	34	87
1965	Baltimore	14-7	24	1.89	67	0	0	0	119.1	87	32	104
1966	Baltimore	9-4	18	2.25	51	0	0	0	92	65	22	67
1967	Baltimore	3-10	8	2.55	42	0	0	0	81.1	63	36	60
1968	Atlanta	0-0	0	27.00	2	0	0	0	1.1	1	4	1
Total	16 Years	105-103	154	3.24	704	93	24	5	1694	1522	600	1164

Year	Team	W-L	SV	ERA	G	GS	CG	SH	IP	H	BB	SO

RAMON MONZANT b: 1/4/33, Maracaibo, Venez. BR/TR, 6', 165 lbs.

Year	Team	W-L	SV	ERA	G	GS	CG	SH	IP	H	BB	SO
1954	New York(N)	0-0	0	4.70	6	1	0	0	7.2	8	11	5
1955	New York(N)	4-8	0	3.99	28	12	3	0	94.2	98	43	54
1956	New York(N)	1-0	0	4.15	4	1	1	0	13	8	7	11
1957	New York(N)	3-2	0	3.99	24	2	0	0	49.2	55	16	37
1958	San Francisco	8-11	1	4.72	43	16	4	1	150.2	160	57	93
1960	San Francisco	0-0	0	9.00	1	0	0	0	1	1	0	1
Total	6 Years	16-21	1	4.38	106	32	8	1	316.2	330	134	201

JOE SHIPLEY   b: 5/9/35, Morristown, Tenn. BR/TR, 6'4", 210 lbs.

Year	Team	W-L	SV	ERA	G	GS	CG	SH	IP	H	BB	SO
1958	San Francisco	0-0	0	33.75	1	0	0	0	1.1	3	3	0
1959	San Francisco	0-0	0	4.50	10	1	0	0	18	16	17	11
1960	San Francisco	0-0	0	5.40	15	0	0	0	20	20	9	9
1963	Chicago(A)	0-1	0	5.79	3	0	0	0	4.2	9	6	3
Total	4 Years	0-1	0	5.93	29	1	0	0	44	48	35	23

AL WORTHINGTON b: 2/5/29, Birmingham, Ala. BR/TR, 6'2", 205 lbs.

Year	Team	W-L	SV	ERA	G	GS	CG	SH	IP	H	BB	SO
1953	New York(N)	4-8	0	3.44	20	17	5	2	102	103	54	52
1954	New York(N)	0-2	0	3.50	10	1	0	0	18	21	15	8
1956	New York(N)	7-14	0	3.97	28	24	4	0	165.2	158	74	95
1957	New York(N)	8-11	4	4.22	55	12	1	1	157.2	140	56	90
1958	San Francisco	11-7	6	3.63	54	12	1	0	151.1	152	57	76
1959	San Francisco	2-3	2	3.68	42	3	0	0	73.1	68	37	45
1960	Boston/Chi(A)	1-2	0	6.35	10	0	0	0	17	20	15	8
1963	Cincinnati	4-4	10	2.99	50	0	0	0	81.1	75	31	55
1964	Cincinnati	1-0	0	10.29	6	0	0	0	7	14	2	6
	Minnesota	5-6	14	1.37	41	0	0	0	72.1	47	28	59
1965	Minnesota	10-7	21	2.13	62	0	0	0	80.1	57	41	59
1966	Minnesota	6-3	16	2.46	65	0	0	0	91.1	66	27	93
1967	Minnesota	8-9	16	2.84	59	0	0	0	92	77	38	80
1968	Minnesota	4-5	**18**	2.71	54	0	0	0	76.1	67	32	57
1969	Minnesota	4-1	3	4.57	46	0	0	0	61	65	20	51
Total	14 Years	75-82	110	3.39	602	69	11	3	1246.2	1130	527	834

Year	Team	W-L	SV	ERA	G	GS	CG	SH	IP	H	BB	SO
DOM ZANNI	b: 3/1/32, Bronx, N.Y. BR/TR, 5'11", 180 lbs.											
1958	San Francisco	1-0	0	2.25	1	0	0	0	4	7	1	3
1959	San Francisco	0-0	0	6.55	9	0	0	0	11	12	8	11
1961	San Francisco	1-0	0	3.95	8	0	0	0	13.2	13	12	11
1962	Chicago(A)	6-5	5	3.75	44	2	0	0	86.1	67	31	66
1963	Chicago(A)	0-0	0	8.31	5	0	0	0	4.1	5	4	2
	Cincinnati	1-1	5	4.19	31	1	0	0	43	39	21	40
1965	Cincinnati	0-0	0	1.35	8	0	0	0	13.1	7	5	10
1966	Cincinnati	0-0	0	0.00	5	0	0	0	7.1	5	3	5
Total	7 Years	9-6	10	3.79	111	3	0	0	183	155	85	148

boldface type indicates league-leading total

The 1958 San Francisco Giants

Front row (seated L-R): Batboy Roy McKercher and Batboy Frank Iverlich. **Second row:** Felipe Alou, Willie Mays, Jim Davenport, Willie Kirkland, Coach Wes Westrum, Manager Bill Rigney, Coach Herman Franks, Coach Salty Parker, Ruben Gomez, Orlando Cepeda, Bill White. **Third row:** Equipment Manager Eddie Logan, Don Johnson, Paul Giel, Nick Testa, Al Worthington, Jackie Brandt, Stu Miller, Danny O'Connell, Gordon Jones, Whitey Lockman, Daryl Spencer, Trainer Frank Bowman. **Fourth row:** Ramon Monzant, Hank Sauer, Bob Schmidt, Bob Speake, Eddie Bressoud, John Antonelli, Ray Jablonski, Valmy Thomas, Mike McCormick. (SF Giants)

The Original San Francisco Giants is stunning in its originality and art. I was deeply touched, and at times had to stop and wipe away tears produced by memories that gave me—and still do—the genuine thrills to a life I've lived so gratefully and so fortunately, induced by the greatest game ever invented. Each interview has its moments of realistic drama offered by men who clearly and honestly, sometimes with ego, sometimes with wrenching anger, sometimes with almost tears of their own, candidly take their readers through their successes and failures. (Bob Stevens, *San Francisco Chronicle* baseball writer, 1940-1981)

They [the stories] bring back vivid memories of the smells emanating from a bakery and brewery adjacent to Seals Stadium at 16th and Bryant. (Nick Peters, *Sacramento Bee*)

The volume is chockful of lively and penetrating interviews with former Giants players, broadcasters, journalists and even batboys. . . . [It's a] wonderful book. (*Library Journal*)

It's a beautiful book. (Lowell Cohn, *Santa Rosa Press Democrat*)

. . . a book that will bring smiles to any Giants fan. (Chuck Dybdal, *Contra Costa Times*)

. . . a wonderful new book . . . on the team that brought major league baseball to the Bay Area. (Dwight Chapin, *San Francisco Examiner*)

Bitker's nostalgic romp around the bases includes the stories of minor and obscure players and those like Willie Kirkland and Leon "Daddy Wags" Wagner, who had dropped from sight until the author personally tracked them down. (Howard Lachtman, *Stockton Record*)

Other Great San Francisco and Baseball Titles from Sports Publishing Inc.

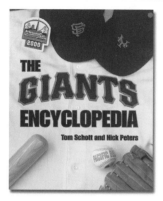

The Giants Encyclopedia ($39.95)
by Tom Schott and Nick Peters

Some of the most famous names, places, and events in baseball history can be traced to the Giants, from their storied run in New York to their 40 years of thrills in San Francisco. Now, authors Tom Schott and Nick Peters chronicle all of those seasons in detail with *The Giants Encyclopedia*. This book includes all the World Series titles, pennant winners, near misses, and disappointments that have etched their place into Giants history.

    The Giants Encyclopedia also gives fans detailed biographies of more than 100 of the greatest Giants players ever, along with prominent owners, executives, managers, and broadcasters. In addition, the authors thoroughly review every postseason game, as well as every no-hitter and other memorable and unforgettable moments. With more than 200 photographs enhancing the text, *The Giants Encyclopedia* is a must for every true Giants fan's collection, and is destined to become one of the most referenced books in any sports library.

ISBN: 1-58261-064-9
8 1/2 x 11 hardcover
600 pages, 200 + photos, eight-page color-photo insert

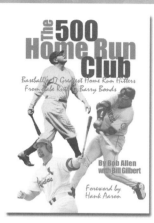

The 500 Home Run Club ($14.95)
by Bob Allen with Bill Gilbert

The 500 Home Run Club looks at the newest member of one of baseball's most exclusive clubs, Barry Bonds, along with the 16 men prior to him to join baseball's most prestigious brotherhood. It is the only book of its kind. Essentially 17 books in one, *The 500 Home Run Club* is far more than just an assortment of baseball biographies. Veteran baseball journalists Bob Allen and Bill Gilbert provide 17 different and moving human-interest stories of men who were, and are, alike in two ways: all of them rank among baseball's all-time most-feared sluggers, and each achieved his greatness while overcoming daunting odds and obstacles. As Barry Bonds pursues even greater accomplishments, *The 500 Home Run Club* stands as a significant contribution to the story of baseball and the American people.

ISBN: 1-58261-432-6
6 x 9 paperback
300 pages, 16-page B/W photo insert

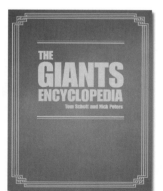

The Giants Encyclopedia
limited-edition leatherbound version ($74.95)

Limited to only 500 copies, this special edition of *The Giants Encyclopedia* is signed by Willie McCovey, Monte Irvin, Bobby Thomson, Bill Rigney, and Dave Dravecky. The many Giants' Hall of Fame signatures that can be acquired along with this book make it a valuable and rare collector's item.

ISBN: 1-58261-433-4

All books are available at local bookstores, online at
www.SportsPublishingInc.com,
or by calling toll-free
1-877-424-BOOK (2665).